VOLUME I: BEGINNINGS THROUGH THE RENAISSANCE

The Western Humanities

FOURTH EDITION

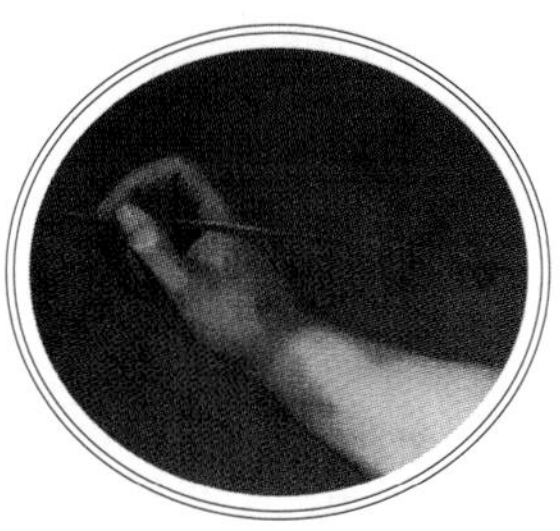

Roy T. Matthews & F. DeWitt Platt
MICHIGAN STATE UNIVERSITY

MAYFIELD PUBLISHING COMPANY
MOUNTAIN VIEW, CALIFORNIA
LONDON • TORONTO

Library of Congress Cataloging-in-Publication Data
Matthews, Roy T.
The Western humanities/Roy T. Matthews, F. DeWitt Platt.—4th ed.
p. cm.
Includes bibliographical references and index.
ISBN 1-7674-1594-9
1. Civilization, Western—History. I. Platt, F. DeWitt.
II. Title.
CB245.M375 2000 99-086580
909′.09821—dc21 CIP

International Standard Book Number information:

The Western Humanities, Fourth Edition . . . . ISBN 0-7674-1592-2
The Western Humanities, Fourth Edition, Volume I . . . . ISBN 0-7674-1594-9
The Western Humanities, Fourth Edition, Volume II. . . . . ISBN 0-7674-1595-7
Readings in the Western Humanities, Fourth Edition, Volume I. . . . . ISBN 0-7674-1596-5
Readings in the Western Humanities, Fourth Edition, Volume II . . . . ISBN 0-7674-1597-3

Shrink-wrap titles for significant savings to your students! Additional packages also available: for more information, please call us at (800) 433-1279.
Complete edition with *The Mayfield Quick View Guide to the Internet for Students of the Humanities,* Version 2.0 . . . . ISBN 0-7674-2100-0
Complete edition with both readers . . . . ISBN 0-7674-2101-9
Complete edition with the electronic study guide . . . . ISBN 0-7674-2109-4
Complete edition with *Music in the Western Tradition* . . . . ISBN 0-7674-2115-9
Complete edition with reader volume I . . . . ISBN 0-7674-2105-1
Complete edition with reader volume II . . . . ISBN 0-7674-2107-8

The Western Humanities, Volume I, with reader volume I . . . . ISBN 0-7674-2126-4
The Western Humanities, Volume II, with reader volume II . . . . ISBN 0-7674-2133-7

Please call Mayfield Publishing Company at (800) 433-1279 to inquire about additional packaging options.

Manufactured in the United States of America
10 9 8 7 6 5 4 3 2 1

Mayfield Publishing Company
1280 Villa Street
Mountain View, CA 94041

Sponsoring editor, Holly J. Allen; developmental editors, Barbara Armentrout and Kathleen Engelberg; production editor, Julianna Scott Fein; manuscript editor, Joan Pendleton; design manager, Jean Mailander; text designer, Anna George; cover designer, Linda Robertson; cover art, *Etruscan Funeral Dance.* From a tomb at Ruvo. Ca. 350 B.C. Fresco. Museo Archeologico Nazionale, Naples, Italy. © Alinari/Art Resource, NY; art manager, Robin Mouat; illustrators, Robin Mouat, Judith Ogus, and Parrott Graphics; photo researcher, Brian Pecko; manufacturing manager, Randy Hurst. The text was set in 9.5/12 Palatino by GTS Graphics, Inc., and printed on acid-free 60# Sterling Web Gloss, by R. R. Donnelley & Sons Company.

Acknowledgments and copyrights continue at the back of the book on pages C-1–C-2, which constitute an extension of the copyright page.

To Lee Ann and Dixie

There is nothing nobler or more admirable than when two people who see eye to eye keep house as man and wife, confounding their enemies and delighting their friends, as they themselves know better than anyone.

—HOMER, *Odyssey*

PREFACE

We offer this new edition of *The Western Humanities* with a great sense of satisfaction. From the start of this project we wrote from a particular perspective on the arts and humanities, and we wondered how many others shared our point of view. Today, we are gratified to know that our textbook has helped many students develop an understanding and, we hope, an enthusiasm for the arts and humanities. And now, with this fourth edition, we continue in the same spirit with which we first approached the arts and humanities. In the first edition, we placed Western cultural achievements within their historical context. In the second and especially the third editions, we expanded coverage of the contributions of women and other artists outside the traditional canon. And, in this edition, we are adding a multicultural dimension, with the expectation that students will gain a greater appreciation of world cultures beyond the Western traditions. It is our hope that the fourth edition of *The Western Humanities* will continue to assist instructors in meeting today's teaching challenges as well as help the next generation of students understand and claim their cultural heritage.

AIMS OF *THE WESTERN HUMANITIES*

When we sat down to write the first edition of *The Western Humanities,* we feared that the world of the late twentieth century was in danger of being engulfed by present-minded thinking. Now, we believe this fear is even more real. As historians, we know that history has always had its naysayers, but it seems to us that an ahistorical view is even more prevalent today. For many people, the past is viewed as either a burden to be overcome or simply irrelevant—and thus safely ignored. Students merely mirror the wider society when they show little knowledge of or even concern about the great artistic and literary monuments and movements of the Western tradition or about the political, economic, and social milestones of Western history. What intensifies present-minded thinking among today's students is their close involvement in popular culture, with its obsessive faddishness, and the Internet, which provides information and voluminous data but not knowledge.

In *The Western Humanities,* we address the problem of present-mindedness by discussing not only the works that were produced in successive periods but also the prevailing historical and material conditions that so powerfully influenced their form and content. Our intention is to demystify the cultural record by showing that literature and the arts do not spring forth spontaneously and independently of each other but reflect a set of specific historical circumstances. By providing this substantial context, out of which both ideas and artifacts emerge, we hope to give students a deeper understanding of the meaning of cultural works and a broader basis for appreciating the humanities.

At the same time that we point out the linkages between cultural expression and historical conditions, we also emphasize the universal aspects of creativity and expression. People everywhere have the impulse to seek answers to the mysteries of human existence; to discover or invent order in the universe; to respond creatively to nature, both inner and outer; to delight the senses and the mind with beauty and truth; to communicate their thoughts and share their visions with others. Thus, another of our intentions is to demonstrate that the desire to express oneself and to create lasting monuments has been a compelling drive in human beings since before the dawn of civilized life. We believe that this emphasis will help students see that they, along with their ideas, questions, and aspirations, are not isolated from the past but belong to a tradition that began thousands of years ago.

Our third aim is to help students prepare themselves for the uncertainties of the future. When they examine the past and learn how earlier generations confronted and overcame crises—and managed to leave enduring legacies—students will discover that the human spirit is irrepressible. In the humanities—in philosophy, religion, art, music, literature—human beings have found answers to their deepest needs and most perplexing questions. We hope that students will be encouraged by this record as they begin to shape the world of the twenty-first century.

In its origin *The Western Humanities* was an outgrowth of our careers as university teachers. Instructing thousands of undergraduate students throughout the years had left us dissatisfied with available textbooks. In our eyes, the existing books failed in one of two ways: They either ignored material developments and focused exclusively on cultural artifacts without context or perspective, or they stressed political, social, and economic history with too little or too disjointed a discussion of literature and the arts. Our goal in writing this book was to balance and integrate these two elements—that is, to provide an analysis and an appreciation of cultural expression and artifacts within an interpretive historical framework.

ORGANIZATION AND CONTENT

The Western Humanities is organized chronologically, in twenty-one chapters, around successive historical periods, from prehistory to the present. In our introduction for students we distinguish three sweeping historical periods—ancient, medieval, and modern—although we do not formally divide our study into parts. We explain that the first of these periods extends from about 3000 B.C. to A.D. 500 and includes the civilizations of Mesopotamia, Egypt, Greece, and Rome (covered in Chapters 1–7). The second period extends from about 500 to 1500, when Western civilization became centered in Europe and was largely dominated by the Christian church (Chapters 8–10). The third period, beginning in about 1400 and extending to the present, witnessed the gradual birth of the modern world (Chapters 11–21). Timelines are provided in the introduction to support these distinctions and to give students a basic framework for the study of the humanities.

In the body of the book, the first part of every chapter covers the material conditions of the era—the historical, political, economic, and social developments. From the mass of available historical information we have distilled what we consider the crucial points, always aiming to capture the essence of complex periods and to fashion a coherent narrative framework for the story of Western culture. In this discussion many of the major themes, issues, and problems of the period come into view.

The remaining part of each chapter is devoted to cultural expression, both in the realm of attitude and idea—philosophy, history, religion, science—and in the realm of cultural artifact—art, music, drama, literature, and film. In this part we describe and analyze the significant cultural achievements of the age, focusing on pervasive themes, choices, and elements of style. We examine how intellectuals, artists, writers, and other creative individuals responded to the challenges presented to them by their society and how they chose values and forms by which to live. Included among these individuals are those whom the Western tradition has often neglected or discounted, namely, women and members of racial and ethnic minorities. Their experiences, roles, and rich contributions are given their rightful place alongside those of the more conventionally favored artists, thinkers, and writers.

The Western Humanities strives to balance the historical background with cultural and artistic achievements. We believe that the clearest and most effective way to present this closely woven web of experience and expression is to untangle the various realms and discuss them separately. Thus, our treatment of cultural achievements is broken down into sections on art, architecture, music, literature, and so on. These sections vary in length, order, and focus from chapter to chapter, just as preferred or more developed forms of expression vary from one period to another. This approach gives students an unobstructed view of each form and reveals the continuities—as well as the strains and disruptions—in that form from one period to the next.

At the same time, we work from a unified perspective and stress the integrated nature of the humanities. We emphasize that the creative works of a particular period represent a coherent response to the unique character and deepest urges of that period. By pointing out linkages and reverberations, we show that the various areas of expression are tied together by shared stylistic elements and by the themes and issues that inform and shape the era. Rather than weave our own synthesis so tightly into this discussion that instructors would have to spend their class time sorting out our point of view from the true subject of the book, we prefer to present the material in as direct a way as possible. We believe this approach gives instructors the flexibility to teach from their own strengths and perspectives, and we invite them to do so. We have paid special attention to sorting out and explaining complex ideas and sequences of events carefully and clearly, to make the study of the humanities accessible to a broad range of students.

Each chapter ends with a brief section describing the cultural legacy of that era. Here we show what achievements proved to be of lasting value and endured into succeeding periods, even to the present day. Students will find that some ideas, movements, or artistic methods with which they are familiar have a very long history indeed. They will also discover that the meaning and ascribed value of cultural objects and texts can change from one time and place to another. Our goal here is not only to help students establish a context for their culture but to show that the humanities have developed as a dynamic series of choices made by individuals in one era and transformed by individuals in other eras. We hope to convey both the richness and the energy of the Western tradition, to which so many have contributed and from which so many have drawn.

SPECIAL FEATURES

In addition to the overall distinctive features of *The Western Humanities*—its interpretive context for the humanities, its balanced treatment of history and culture, its focus on the cultural legacy of each period—the book has some special features that we believe contribute to its usefulness and appeal. Chapter 8 includes an extended discussion and analysis of Islamic history and culture, broadening the horizons of the Western tradition to cover this important area. Chapter 15 presents a concise discussion of the seventeenth-century revolutions in science and political philosophy that laid the foundations for what we consider modern thinking. Chapter 21 extends the narrative of Western history and culture to the present day and includes expanded coverage of the global style known as Post-Modernism. Throughout the book, we consider not just art, literature, and music but also less commonly covered topics such as history, theology, and technology.

CHANGES TO THE FOURTH EDITION

The major change to this fourth edition of *The Western Humanities* is the "Windows on the World" feature—timelines that outline the most important events in Africa, the Americas, and Asia. These two-page entries, through text and art illustration, summarize historical developments and highlight cultural contributions of selected societies. Limited by reasons of space, we have focused on regional cultures in Africa; Andean, Mesoamerican, and North American cultures in the Americas; and China, India, and Japan in Asia. This new feature helps to expand students' cultural horizons by giving them the opportunity to see how other societies were developing and to note their contributions to the arts and humanities. The twelve "Windows on the World" timelines complement the major time periods covered in *The Western Humanities.*

Another innovation is "A Humanities Primer: How to Understand the Arts," which has been added to the Introduction. In order to make the West's achievements more familiar to students, this new feature includes a set of general terms and concepts used across the arts and humanities plus some basic terms that apply to the arts, architecture, literature, music, theater, history, philosophy, and religion. We have also outlined the major analytical methods used for understanding cultural works.

We have revised the art program for this edition. More than 50 new artworks are included, either replacing works previously illustrated or adding to the overall art program. Each new artwork is discussed in both a detailed caption and the text. The revised art program includes four new sections: the rise of printmaking in late medieval times; the origin of the Venetian School of Renaissance painting; and, in the Post-Modern period, video art and installation art. The new illustrations come from sculpture, painting, architecture, photography, and other media, including the *Torso of Miletus*, the Dura Europas Synagogue, *Leisure Time at the Bath* from the *Medieval Housebook,* Hans Memling's *Madonna and Child with Angels,* Giovanni Bellini's *St. Francis in Ecstasy,* Rachel Whiteread's *Untitled (Yellow Tub),* and Nam June Paik's *My Faust—Channel 5—Nationalism.*

We made specific changes to the text to address reviewers' suggestions. In Chapter 13, we rearranged the chronology of the main topics: northern humanism, the religious reformations, the Northern Renaissance, and Late Mannerism. We also expanded it to include the Golden Age of Spanish literature and shifted Hieronymus Bosch from Chapter 10 to Chapter 13. We then added Hans Memling to Chapter 10. We extended Chapter 21 to include developments in the late 1990s.

Finally, we continued with our goal of expanding our discussion of women writers and artists as well as artists from cultures beyond the Western traditions. Some of these new additions include Toni Morrison, Ann Hamilton, Nam June Paik, Rachel Whiteread, Emily Dickinson, and Frederick Douglass. We replaced nine "Personal Perspectives" (a feature added in the last edition to bring history to life for the reader) with new eyewitness accounts from such historical figures as Amenemope, Solon, Henry Knighton, Samuel Pepys, and Charlotte Brontë.

TEACHING RESOURCES

As instructors, we are keenly aware of the problems encountered in teaching the humanities, especially to large, diverse classes. We have therefore created an Instructor's Manual, as well as a comprehensive package of ancillary resource materials, designed to help solve those problems.

The fourth edition of the Instructor's Manual has been revised and expanded. For each chapter this manual includes teaching strategies and suggestions, test items, learning objectives, key cultural terms, film and reading suggestions, and a detailed outline revised to accompany the fourth edition of *The Western Humanities.* Additionally, there is background on the "Personal Perspective" boxes found throughout the book and, new to this edition, there is "Windows on the World Background," which provides additional information on the cultures and artworks described in each Windows feature. Also new to this edition of the manual are suggested Web sites that instructors will find useful for lecture preparation and additional images.

In addition to chapter-by-chapter materials, you'll find the following features in the Instructor's Manual:

- Five basic teaching strategies
- Seven lecture models
- Timeline of developments in non-Western cultures
- Music listening guides
- Comparative questions covering material from more than one chapter (designed to test students on broader patterns and comparisons)

The Mayfield Quick View Guide to the Internet for Students of the Humanities has been thoroughly revised and updated by Jeffrey Hodges of Michigan State University. This guide provides step-by-step instructions on accessing the Internet and finding and using information on the humanities. It also helps students evaluate the credibility of online information sources, use listserves and newsgroups, and even create a Web page. The guide is available to students at no additional cost.

Music in the Western Tradition offers expanded coverage of music concepts and history. This supplemental text is available to students at a minimal cost.

Electronic Ancillaries and Presentation Aids

New to this edition is an interactive Web site, which can be accessed at www.mayfieldpub.com/mp. Instructor's resources on the site include PowerPoint slides, a custom syllabus generator, and links to recommended Western and global humanities Internet sites. Resources for students include interactive quizzes for each chapter, a tutorial for doing research using the Internet, and links.

The *Electronic Study Guide,* developed by Julius J. Jackson, Jr., San Bernardino Valley College, has been thoroughly revised and updated. This CD-ROM offers students several ways to review and expand their knowledge, with study aids for each chapter that include guided tours to highlight important concepts; pronunciation guides for key terms; flash cards; true-false, multiple-choice, and fill-in-the-blank questions; and mini-lectures that provide an in-depth study of selected concepts. The study guide can be used with either Windows- or Macintosh-based computers.

For use in presentations, particularly in large lecture settings, there are two slide sets available. The art slides present 100 artworks reflecting the range of art and architecture covered in *The Western Humanities.* The 25 map slides reproduce the maps found in the text.

The complete test bank is available in both Windows and Macintosh formats. The MicroTest III testing program allows you to design tests using the questions included with *The Western Humanities,* to edit those questions, and to incorporate your own questions.

Finally, additional multimedia resources, including videotapes and CD-ROMs, are available to qualified adopters.

ACKNOWLEDGMENTS

Preparing the fourth edition of this text has been a rewarding experience for us. The task has been made more enjoyable by the participation and support of many people. We acknowledge and express gratitude for the help of former students over the years. Their questions and insights have affected the way we address certain issues and frame particular arguments.

Beyond the confines of Michigan State University we are grateful for the many comments and suggestions provided to us by the following reviewers: Judith Chambers, Hillsborough Community College; Robert Eisner, San Diego State University; Connie Frankel, Pasco Hernando Community College; Robin Hardee, Brevard Community College; Grant Hardy, University of North Carolina, Asheville; Sara Hollis, Southern University at New Orleans; Kimberley Jones, Seminole Community College; Seth R. Katz, Bradley University; Sandi S. Landis, St. John's River Community College; Michael Phillips, Brigham Young University; Robert Prescott, Bradley University; William Stockton, Johnson County Community College.

We have also benefited from the staff at Mayfield Publishing Company. First and foremost, we wish to thank Holly Allen, the sponsoring editor, who remains patient and supportive all the way. Thanks also to Barbara Armentrout and Kate Engelberg, the developmental editors who helped us especially with the new features in this edition. Susan Shook, developmental editor, helped us pull together all the teaching supplements. Joan Pendleton, the copyeditor, has done an outstanding job, checking our grammar, spelling, and punctuation. She has made it easier for all of us with her fine sense of humor. We also wish to thank the Mayfield production team. Once again, senior production editor Julianna Scott Fein has shepherded the manuscript through the production process with care and grace. Brian Pecko, photo researcher, has done an excellent job ensuring that the art reproductions are of the highest quality. Credit for the beautiful cover goes to the cover designer, Linda Robertson; for the elegant interior design to the designer, Anna George, and to the design manager, Jean Mailander; and for the handsome timelines and maps to the art manager, Robin Mouat. Manufacturing manager Randy Hurst is responsible for the printing and paper that make *The Western Humanities* so attractive. The efforts of Marty Granahan, permissions editor, ensured the integrity of the work. To all we express our thanks.

CONTENTS

PREFACE *iii*

INTRODUCTION
Why Study Cultural History? *xvii*

A HUMANITIES PRIMER
How to Understand the Arts *xxii*

1 PREHISTORY AND NEAR EASTERN CIVILIZATIONS *1*

PREHISTORY AND EARLY CULTURES *2*

THE CIVILIZATIONS OF THE TIGRIS AND EUPHRATES RIVER VALLEY: MESOPOTAMIA *5*

The Sumerian, Akkadian, and Babylonian Kingdoms *5*

The Cradle of Civilization *7*

Writing 7 • *Religion 8*

■ PERSONAL PERSPECTIVE "A Sumerian Father Lectures His Son" *9*

Literature 8 • *Law 10* • *Art and Architecture 11*

THE CIVILIZATION OF THE NILE RIVER VALLEY: EGYPT *13*

Continuity and Change over Three Thousand Years *14*

A Quest for Eternal Cultural Values *16*

Religion 16 • *Writing and Literature 17* • *Architecture 17*

■ PERSONAL PERSPECTIVE "Egypt: The Instruction of Amenemope" *19*

Sculpture, Painting, and Minor Arts 19

HEIRS TO THE MESOPOTAMIAN AND EGYPTIAN EMPIRES *25*

THE LEGACY OF EARLY NEAR EASTERN CIVILIZATIONS *27*

KEY CULTURAL TERMS *27*

SUGGESTIONS FOR FURTHER READING *27*

■ ***Windows on the World: 5000–500 B.C. 28***

2 AEGEAN CIVILIZATIONS
The Minoans, the Mycenaeans, and the Greeks of the Archaic Age *31*

PRELUDE: MINOAN CIVILIZATION, 3000–1300 B.C. *32*

BEGINNINGS: MYCENAEAN CIVILIZATION, 1900–1100 B.C. *35*

INTERLUDE: THE DARK AGES, 1100–800 B.C. *38*

THE ARCHAIC AGE, 800–479 B.C. *38*

Political, Economic, and Social Structures *38*

The Greek Polis: Sparta and Athens *39*

The Persian Wars *40*

THE EMERGENCE OF GREEK GENIUS: THE MASTERY OF FORM *41*

Religion *41*

Epic Poetry *43*

Lyric Poetry *44*

■ PERSONAL PERSPECTIVE Solon, "Political Verses: The Ten Ages of Man"; Sappho, "He Seems to Be a God" *45*

Natural Philosophy *45*

Architecture *46*

Sculpture *49*

THE LEGACY OF ARCHAIC GREEK CIVILIZATION *53*

KEY CULTURAL TERMS *53*

SUGGESTIONS FOR FURTHER READING *53*

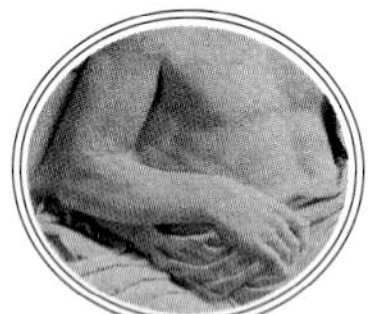

3
CLASSICAL GREEK CIVILIZATION
The Hellenic Age *55*

GENERAL CHARACTERISTICS OF HELLENIC CIVILIZATION *55*

DOMESTIC AND FOREIGN AFFAIRS: WAR, PEACE, AND THE TRIUMPH OF MACEDONIA *58*

THE PERFECTION OF THE TRADITION: THE GLORY OF HELLENIC GREECE *60*
Theater: Tragedy *61*
Features of the Tragic Theater 61 • Tragic Drama 62 • Aeschylus 63 • Sophocles 63 • Euripides 64
Theater: Comedy *65*
Music *65*
History *66*
Natural Philosophy *67*
The Pre-Socratics 67 • The Sophists 68 • The Socratic Revolution 68 • Plato 69 • Aristotle 70
Architecture *70*

PERSONAL PERSPECTIVE Xenophon, "Secrets of a Successful Marriage" *71*

Sanctuaries 71 • The Temple: The Perfection of the Form 71
Sculpture *75*

THE LEGACY OF HELLENIC CIVILIZATION *82*

KEY CULTURAL TERMS *83*

SUGGESTIONS FOR FURTHER READING *83*

***Windows on the World: 500–300 B.C.* 84**

4
CLASSICAL GREEK CIVILIZATION
The Hellenistic Age *87*

THE STAGES OF HELLENISTIC HISTORY *89*
The End of the Empire and the Rise of the States *89*
The Arrival and Triumph of Rome *89*

THE CITIES OF HELLENISTIC CIVILIZATION *90*
Pergamum *90*
Alexandria in Egypt *90*

PERSONAL PERSPECTIVE Theocritus, "A Street Scene in Alexandria" *92*

THE ELABORATION OF THE GREEK TRADITION: THE SPREAD OF CLASSICISM TO THE HELLENISTIC WORLD *93*
Drama and Literature *94*
Philosophy and Religion *94*
Cynicism 95 • Skepticism 95 • Epicureanism 96 • Stoicism 97 • Fate and the Mystery Cults 98
Architecture *99*
The Corinthian Temple 99 • The Altar 100
Sculpture *101*
Rhodes: Late Hellenistic Style *104*

THE LEGACY OF THE HELLENISTIC WORLD *107*

KEY CULTURAL TERMS *107*

SUGGESTIONS FOR FURTHER READING *107*

5
ROMAN CIVILIZATION
The Pre-Christian Centuries
109

THE COLOSSUS OF THE MEDITERRANEAN WORLD *109*
General Characteristics of Roman Civilization *111*
The Etruscan and Greek Connections *111*
Rome in the Age of Kings, 753–509 B.C. *115*
The Roman Republic, 509–31 B.C. *115*
The Early Republic, 509–264 B.C. 116 • The Middle Republic, 264–133 B.C. 116 • The Late Republic, 133–31 B.C. 116
Growing Autocracy: Imperial Rome, 31 B.C.–A.D. 284 *117*
Pax Romana, 31 B.C.–A.D. 193 117 • Civil Wars, A.D. 193–284 117

THE STYLE OF PRE-CHRISTIAN ROME: FROM GREEK IMITATION TO ROMAN GRANDEUR *117*
Roman Religion *118*
Language, Literature, and Drama *120*
The First Literary Period, 250–31 B.C. 120

PERSONAL PERSPECTIVE Marcus, Son of Cicero, "Letter to Tiro, Secretary to Cicero Senior" *121*

The Second Literary Period: The Golden Age, 31 B.C.–A.D. 14 122 • The Third Literary Period: The Silver Age, A.D. 14–200 123
Philosophy *123*
Stoicism 123 • Neo-Platonism 124
Law *124*

The Visual Arts 126
Architecture 126 • Sculpture 131 • Painting and Mosaics 136
Music 140
THE LEGACY OF PRE-CHRISTIAN ROME 141
KEY CULTURAL TERMS 141
SUGGESTIONS FOR FURTHER READING 141
***Windows on the World: 300 B.C.–A.D. 500* 142**

6 JUDAISM AND THE RISE OF CHRISTIANITY *145*

JUDAISM 145
The People and Their Religion 145
Egypt, Exodus, and Moses 146 • The Kingdom of Israel 147 • The Babylonian Captivity and the Postexilic Period 149 • The Hellenistic and Roman Periods 150
PERSONAL PERSPECTIVE Flavius Josephus, "The Destruction of the Temple at Jerusalem" 151
Societal and Family Relationships 151
The Bible 152
Early Jewish Art and Architecture 154
CHRISTIANITY 157
The Life of Jesus Christ and the New Testament 157
Christians and Jews 160
Christianity and Greco-Roman Religions and Philosophies 161
Christians in the Roman Empire 161
PERSONAL PERSPECTIVE Vibia Perpetua, "Account of Her Last Days Before Martyrdom" 162
Early Christian Literature 162
Early Christian Art 163
THE LEGACY OF BIBLICAL JUDAISM AND EARLY CHRISTIANITY 166
KEY CULTURAL TERMS 167
SUGGESTIONS FOR FURTHER READING 167

7 LATE ROMAN CIVILIZATION *169*

THE LAST DAYS OF THE ROMAN EMPIRE 169
Diocletian's Reforms and the Triumph of Christianity, 284–395 170
The Great Persecution and Christian Toleration 172 • Early Christian Controversies 173
Christian Rome and the End of the Western Empire, 395–476 173
PERSONAL PERSPECTIVE Paulina, "Epitaph for Agorius Praetextatus" 174
THE TRANSITION FROM CLASSICAL HUMANISM TO CHRISTIAN CIVILIZATION 174
Literature, Theology, and History 174
The Fathers of the Church 175
PERSONAL PERSPECTIVE St. Jerome, "Secular Education; The Fall of Rome" 177
Church History 177
The Visual Arts 177
Architecture 178 • Sculpture 181 • Painting and Mosaics 184
Music 186
WHY DID ROME FALL? 186
THE LEGACY OF LATE ROMAN CIVILIZATION 187
KEY CULTURAL TERMS 187
SUGGESTIONS FOR FURTHER READING 187

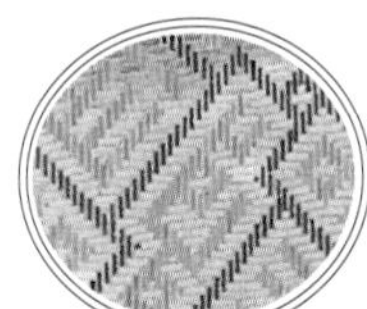

8 THE SUCCESSORS OF ROME Byzantium, Islam, and the Early Medieval West *189*

THE EASTERN ROMAN EMPIRE AND BYZANTINE CIVILIZATION, 476–1453 190
History of the Byzantine Empire 191
Byzantine Culture: Christianity and Classicism 193
The Orthodox Religion 193 • Law and History 193 • Architecture and Mosaics 194
THE ISLAMIC WORLD, 600–1517 198
History of Islam 198
Islamic Religious and Cultural Developments 199
Islamic Religion 200 • History 200 • Science 201 • Art and Architecture 201
THE EARLY MEDIEVAL WEST 204
The Early Middle Ages: A Romano-Germanic Christianized World 205
Religion and Culture in the Early Middle Ages 207
Christianity: Leadership and Organization 207
PERSONAL PERSPECTIVE Anna Comenena, "The Arrival of the First Crusade in Constantinople"; Usamah, "The Curious Medicine of the Franks"; Liudprand of Cremona, "A Mission to the Byzantine Court" 208

Literature, History, and Learning 209 • *Music* 211 • *Architecture* 211 • *Painting: Illuminated Manuscripts* 211

THE LEGACY OF BYZANTIUM, ISLAM, AND THE EARLY MEDIEVAL WEST 215

KEY CULTURAL TERMS 215

SUGGESTIONS FOR FURTHER READING 215

***Windows on the World: 500–1000* 216**

9 THE HIGH MIDDLE AGES The Christian Centuries 219

FEUDALISM 220
The Feudal System and the Feudal Society 220
Peasant Life 221
The Rise of Towns 221
The Feudal Monarchy 223
The French Monarchy 223 • *The English Monarchy* 223 • *The Holy Roman Empire* 223 • *The Papal Monarchy* 225

MEDIEVAL CHRISTIANITY AND THE CHURCH 225
Christian Beliefs and Practices 226
Religious Orders and Lay Piety 227

PERSONAL PERSPECTIVE Hildegard of Bingen, "Scivias" 229

THE AGE OF SYNTHESIS: EQUILIBRIUM BETWEEN THE SPIRITUAL AND THE SECULAR 229
Learning and Theology 230
Cathedral Schools and the Development of Scholasticism 230 • *Peter Abelard* 230 • *The Rise of the Universities* 231 • *Intellectual Controversy and Thomas Aquinas* 231
Literature 232
Monastic and Feudal Writing 232 • *Vernacular and Courtly Writing* 233 • *Dante* 234
Architecture and Art 235
Romanesque Churches and Related Arts 236 • *Gothic Churches and Related Arts* 239
Music 248

THE LEGACY OF THE CHRISTIAN CENTURIES 249

KEY CULTURAL TERMS 249

SUGGESTIONS FOR FURTHER READING 249

***Windows on the World: 1000–1300* 250**

10 THE LATE MIDDLE AGES 1300–1500 253

HARD TIMES COME TO EUROPE 253
Ordeal by Plague, Famine, and War 255
Depopulation, Rebellion, and Industrialization 255
The Secular Monarchies 256
The Papal Monarchy 257

THE CULTURAL FLOWERING OF THE LATE MIDDLE AGES 258
Religion 259

PERSONAL PERSPECTIVE Henry Knighton, "Chronicle" 260

Theology, Philosophy, and Science 260
The Via Antiqua *Versus the* Via Moderna 261 • *Duns Scotus and William of Ockham* 261 • *Developments in Science* 261
Literature 262
Northern Italian Literature: Petrarch and Boccaccio 262 • *English Literature: Geoffrey Chaucer* 263 • *French Literature: Christine de Pizan* 264
Art and Architecture 265
Late Gothic Architecture 265 • *Late Gothic Sculpture* 267 • *Late Gothic Painting and the Rise of New Trends* 271

THE LEGACY OF THE LATE MIDDLE AGES 284

KEY CULTURAL TERMS 285

SUGGESTIONS FOR FURTHER READING 285

***Windows on the World: 1330–1500* 286**

11 THE EARLY RENAISSANCE Return to Classical Roots 1400–1494 289

THE RENAISSANCE: SCHOOLS OF INTERPRETATION 289

EARLY RENAISSANCE HISTORY AND INSTITUTIONS 290
Italian City-States During the Early Renaissance 290
Florence, the Center of the Renaissance 292
The Resurgent Papacy, 1450–1500 294

THE SPIRIT AND STYLE OF THE EARLY RENAISSANCE 294
Humanism, Scholarship, and Schooling 295

PERSONAL PERSPECTIVE Laura Cereta, "Defense of the Liberal Instruction of Women" *296*

Thought and Philosophy *296*
Architecture, Sculpture, and Painting *298*
Artistic Ideals and Innovations 298 • Architecture 299 • Sculpture 303 • Painting 306
Music *312*

THE LEGACY OF THE EARLY RENAISSANCE *313*

KEY CULTURAL TERMS *313*

SUGGESTIONS FOR FURTHER READING *313*

SUGGESTIONS FOR LISTENING *313*

12
THE HIGH RENAISSANCE AND EARLY MANNERISM 1494–1564 ***315***

THE RISE OF THE MODERN SOVEREIGN STATE *316*
The Struggle for Italy, 1494–1529 *317*
Charles V and the Hapsburg Empire *317*

ECONOMIC EXPANSION AND SOCIAL DEVELOPMENTS *319*

FROM HIGH RENAISSANCE TO EARLY MANNERISM *320*

Literature *321*
Gaspara Stampa 322 • Castiglione 322 • Machiavelli 323
Painting *324*
Leonardo da Vinci 325 • Michelangelo 325 • Raphael 327 • The Venetian School: Giorgione and Titian 333 • The School of Parma: Parmigianino 335
Sculpture *335*

PERSONAL PERSPECTIVE Giorgio Vasari, "Lives of the Most Eminent Painters, Sculptors, and Architects" *337*

Architecture *339*
Music *342*

THE LEGACY OF THE HIGH RENAISSANCE AND EARLY MANNERISM *343*

KEY CULTURAL TERMS *343*

SUGGESTIONS FOR FURTHER READING *343*

SUGGESTIONS FOR LISTENING *343*

APPENDIX

Writing for the Humanities: Research Papers and Essay Examinations ***A-1***

GLOSSARY ***G-1***

CREDITS ***C-1***

INDEX ***I-1***

INTRODUCTION
Why Study Cultural History?

To be ignorant of what occurred before you were born is to remain always a child.

—CICERO, FIRST CENTURY B.C.

Anyone who cannot give an account to oneself of the past three thousand years remains in darkness, without experience, living from day to day.

—GOETHE, NINETEENTH CENTURY A.D.

The underlying premise of this book is that some basic knowledge of the Western cultural heritage is necessary for those who want to become educated human beings in charge of their own destinies. If people are not educated into their place in human history—five thousand years of relatively uninterrupted though sometimes topsy-turvy developments—then they are rendered powerless, subject to passing fads and outlandish beliefs. They become vulnerable to the flattery of demagogues who promise heaven on earth, or they fall prey to the misconception that present-day events are unique, without precedent in history, or superior to everything that has gone before.

Perhaps the worst that can happen is to exist in a limbo of ignorance—in Goethe's words, "living from day to day." Without knowledge of the past and the perspective it brings, people may come to believe that their contemporary world will last forever, when in reality much of it is doomed to be forgotten. In contrast to the instant obsolescence of popular culture, the study of Western culture offers an alternative that has passed the unforgiving test of time. Long after today's heroes and celebrities have fallen into oblivion, the achievements of our artistic and literary ancestors—those who have forged the Western tradition—will remain. Their works echo down the ages and seem fresh in every period. The ancient Roman writer Seneca put it well when he wrote, in the first century A.D., "Life is short but art is long."

When people realize that the rich legacy of Western culture is their own, their view of themselves and the times they live in can expand beyond the present moment. They find that they need not be confined by the limits of today but can draw on the creative insights of people who lived hundreds and even thousands of years ago. They discover that their own culture has a history and a context that give it meaning and shape. Studying and experiencing their cultural legacy can help them understand their place in today's world.

THE BOUNDARIES OF THE WEST

The subject of this text is Western culture, but what exactly do we mean, first, by "culture" and, second, by the "West"? *Culture* is a term with several meanings, but we use it here to mean the artistic and intellectual expressions of a people, their creative achievements. By the *West* we mean that part of the globe that lies west of Asia and Asia Minor and north of Africa, especially Europe—the geographical framework for much of this study.

The Western tradition is not confined exclusively to Europe as defined today, however. The contributions of peoples who lived beyond the boundaries of present-day Europe are also included in Western culture, either because they were forerunners of the West, such as those who created the first civilizations in Mesopotamia and Egypt, or because they were part of the West for periods of time, such as those who lived in the North African and Near Eastern lands bordering the Mediterranean Sea during the Roman and early

Christian eras. Regardless of geography, Western culture draws deeply from ideals forged in these lands.

When areas that had been part of the Western tradition at one time were absorbed into other cultural traditions, as happened in Mesopotamia, Egypt, and North Africa in the seventh century when the people embraced the Muslim faith, then they are generally no longer included in Western cultural history. Because of the enormous influence of Islamic civilization on Western civilization, however, we do include in this volume both an account of Islamic history and a description and appreciation of Islamic culture. Different in many ways from our own, the rich tradition of Islam has an important place in today's world.

After about 1500, with voyages and explorations reaching the farthest parts of the globe, the European focus of Western culture that had held for centuries began to dissolve. Starting from this time, the almost exclusive European mold was broken and Western values and ideals began to be exported throughout the world, largely through the efforts of missionaries, soldiers, colonists, and merchants. Coinciding with this development and further complicating the pattern of change were the actions of those who imported and enslaved countless numbers of black Africans to work on plantations in North and South America. The interplay of Western culture with many previously isolated cultures, whether desired or not, forever changed all who were touched by the process.

The Westernization of the globe that has been going on ever since 1500 is perhaps the dominant theme of the twentieth century. What human greed, missionary zeal, and dreams of empire failed to accomplish before 1900 has been achieved in this century by modern technology, the media, and popular culture. The world today is a global village, much of it dominated by Western values and styles of life. In our time, Westernization has become a two-way interchange. When artists and writers from other cultures adopt Western forms or ideas, they are not only Westernizing their own traditions but also injecting fresh sensibilities and habits of thought into the Western tradition. The globalization of culture means that a South American novel or a Japanese film can be as accessible to Western audiences as a European painting and yet carry with it an intriguingly new vocabulary of cultural symbols and meanings.

HISTORICAL PERIODS AND CULTURAL STYLES

In cultural history the past is often divided into historical periods and cultural styles. A historical period is an interval of time that has a certain unity because it is characterized by the prevalence of a unique culture, ideology, or technology or because it is bounded by defining historical events, such as the death of a military leader like Alexander the Great or a political upheaval like the fall of Rome. A cultural style is a combination of features of artistic or literary expression, execution, or performance that define a particular school or era. A historical period may have the identical time frame as a cultural style, or it may embrace more than one style simultaneously or two styles successively. Each chapter of this survey focuses on a historical period and includes significant aspects of culture—usually the arts, architecture, literature, religion, music, and philosophy—organized around a discussion of the relevant style or styles appropriate to that time.

The survey begins with prehistory, the era before writing was invented, setting forth the emergence of human beings from an obscure past. After the appearance of writing in about 3000 B.C., the Western cultural heritage is divided into three sweeping historical periods: ancient, medieval, and modern.

The ancient period dates from 3000 B.C. to A.D. 500 (Timeline 1). During these thirty-five hundred years the light of Western civilization begins to shine in Mesopotamia and Egypt, shines more brightly still in eighth-century-B.C. Greece and Rome, loses some of its luster when Greece succumbs to Rome in 146 B.C., and finally is snuffed out when the Roman empire collapses in the fifth century A.D. Coinciding with these historical periods are the cultural styles of Mesopotamia; Egypt; Greece, including Archaic, Classical (or Hellenic), and Hellenistic styles; and Rome, including Republican and Imperial styles.

The medieval period, or the Middle Ages, covers events between A.D. 500 and 1500, a one-thousand-year span that is further divided into three subperiods (Timeline 2). The Early Middle Ages (500–1000) is typified by frequent barbarian invasions and political chaos so that civilization itself is threatened and barely survives. No single international style characterizes this turbulent period, though several regional styles flourish. The High Middle Ages (1000–1300) is a period of stability and the zenith of medieval culture. Two successive styles appear, the Romanesque and the Gothic, with the latter dominating culture for the rest of the medieval period. The Late Middle Ages (1300–1500) is a transitional period in which the medieval age is dying and the modern age is struggling to be born.

The modern period begins in about 1400 (there is often overlap between historical periods) and continues today (Timeline 3). With the advent of the modern period a new way of defining historical changes starts to make more sense—the division of history into

Timeline 1 THE ANCIENT WORLD

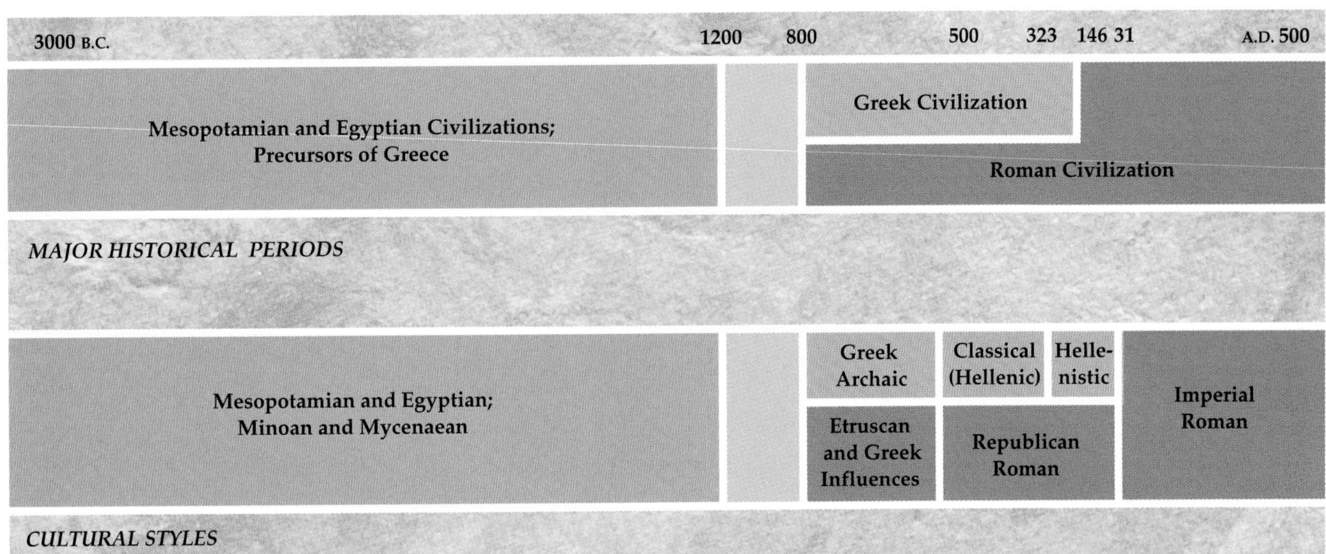

movements, the activities of large groups of people united to achieve a common goal. The modern period consists of waves of movements that aim to change the world in some specific way.

The first modern movement is the Renaissance (1400–1600), or "rebirth," which attempts to revive the cultural values of ancient Greece and Rome. It is accompanied by two successive styles, Renaissance style and Mannerism. The next significant movement is the Reformation (1500–1600), which is dedicated to restoring Christianity to the ideals of the early church set forth in the Bible. Although it does not spawn a specific style, this religious upheaval does have a profound impact on the subjects of the arts and literature and the way they are expressed, especially in the Mannerist style.

The Reformation is followed by the Scientific Revolution (1600–1700), a movement that results in the abandonment of ancient science and the birth of modern science. Radical in its conclusions, the Scientific Revolution is somewhat out of touch with the style of its age, which is known as the Baroque. This magnificent style is devoted to overwhelming the senses through theatrical and sensuous effects and is associated with the attempts of the Roman Catholic Church to reassert its authority in the world.

The Scientific Revolution gives impetus to the Enlightenment (1700–1800), a movement that pledges to reform politics and society according to the principles of the new science. In stylistic terms the eighteenth century is schizophrenic, dominated first by the Rococo, an extravagant and fanciful style that represents the last phase of the Baroque, and then by the Neoclassical, a style inspired by the works of ancient Greece and Rome and reflective of the principles of the Scientific Revolution. Before the eighteenth century is over, the Enlightenment calls forth its antithesis, Romanticism (1770–1870), a movement centered on feeling, fantasy, and everything that cannot be proven scientifically. The Romantic style, marked by a

Timeline 2 THE MEDIEVAL WORLD

500 1000 1150 1300 1500

Early Middle Ages | High Middle Ages | Late Middle Ages

MAJOR HISTORICAL PERIODS

Regional Styles | Romanesque | Gothic

CULTURAL STYLES

Timeline 3 THE MODERN WORLD

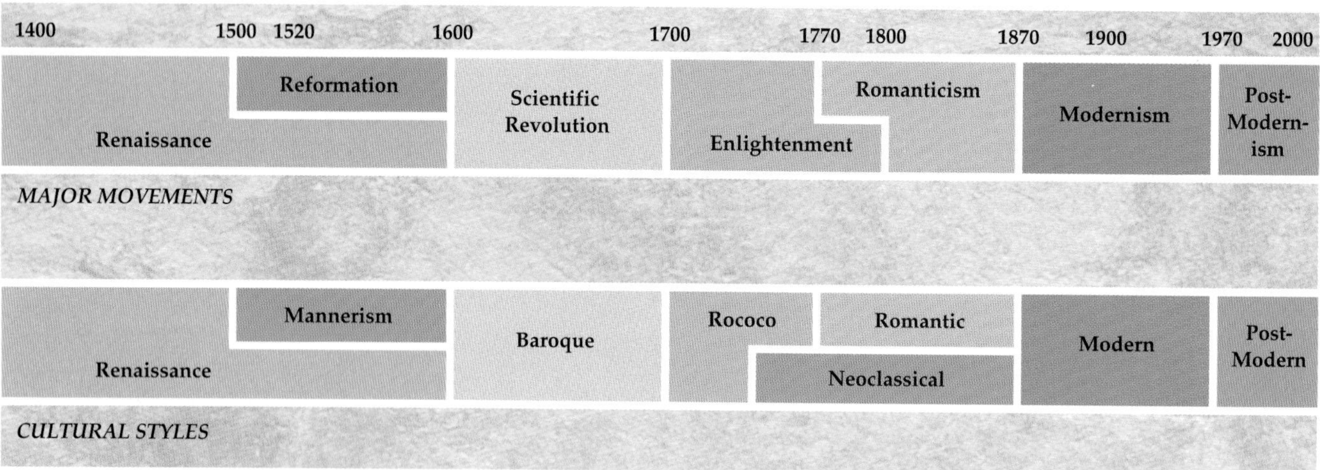

revived taste for the Gothic and a love of nature, is the perfect accompaniment to this movement.

Toward the end of the nineteenth century Modernism (1870–1970) arises, bent on destroying every vestige of both the Greco-Roman tradition and the Christian faith and on fashioning new ways of understanding that are independent of the past. Since 1970 Post-Modernism has emerged, a movement that tries to make peace with the past by embracing old forms of expression while at the same time adopting a global and multivoiced perspective.

Although every cultural period is marked by innovation and creativity, our treatment of them in this book varies somewhat, with more space and greater weight given to the achievements of certain times. We make these adjustments because some periods or styles are more significant than others, especially in the defining influence that their achievements have had on our own era. For example, some styles seem to tower over the rest, such as Classicism in fifth-century-B.C. Greece, the High Renaissance of sixteenth-century Italy, and Modernism in the mid–twentieth century, as compared with other styles, such as that of the Early Middle Ages or the seventeenth-century Baroque.

AN INTEGRATED APPROACH TO CULTURAL HISTORY

Our approach to the Western heritage in this book is to root cultural achievements in their historical settings, showing how the material conditions—the political, social, and economic events of each period—influenced their creation. About one-third of each chapter is devoted to an interpretive discussion of material history, and the remaining two-thirds are devoted to the arts, architecture, philosophy, religion, literature, and music of the period. These two aspects of history do not occur separately, of course, and one of our aims is to show how they are intertwined.

As just one example of this integrated approach, consider the Gothic cathedral, that lofty, light-filled house of worship marked by pointed arches, towering spires, and radiant stained-glass windows. Gothic cathedrals were erected during the High Middle Ages, following a bleak period when urban life had virtually ceased. Although religion was still the dominant force in European life, trade was starting to flourish once again, town life was reviving, and urban dwellers were beginning to prosper. In part as testimonials to their new wealth, cities and towns commissioned architects and hired workers to erect these soaring churches, which dominated the landscape for miles around and proclaimed the economic well-being of their makers.

We adopt an integrated approach to Western culture not just in considering how the arts are related to material conditions but also in looking for the common themes, aspirations, and ideas that permeate the artistic and literary expressions of every individual era. The creative accomplishments of an age tend to reflect a shared perspective, even when that perspective is not explicitly recognized at the time. Thus, each period possesses a unique outlook that can be analyzed in the cultural record. A good example of this phenomenon is Classical Greece in the fifth century B.C., when the ideal of moderation, or balance in all things, played a major role in sculpture, architecture, philosophy, religion, and tragic drama. The cultural record in other periods is not always as clear as that in ancient Greece, but shared qualities can often be uncovered that distinguish the varied aspects of culture in an era to form a unifying thread.

A corollary of this idea is that creative individuals and their works are very much influenced by the times in which they live. This is not to say that incomparable geniuses—such as Shakespeare in Renaissance England—do not appear and rise above their own ages, speaking directly to the human mind and heart in every age that follows. Yet even Shakespeare reflected the political attitudes and social patterns of his time. Though a man for the ages, he still regarded monarchy as the correct form of government and women as the inferiors of men.

THE SELECTION OF CULTURAL WORKS

The Western cultural heritage is vast, and any selection of works for a survey text reflects choices made by the authors. All the works we chose to include have had a significant impact on Western culture, but for different reasons. We chose some because they blazed a new trail, such as Picasso's *Demoiselles d'Avignon* (see Figure 19.21), which marked the advent of Cubism in painting, or Fielding's *Tom Jones*, one of the earliest novels. Other works were included because they seemed to embody a style to perfection, such as the regal statue called *Poseidon* (or *Zeus*) (see Figure 3.21), executed in the Classical style of fifth-century-B.C. Athens, or Dante's *Divine Comedy*, which epitomized the ideals of the High Middle Ages. On occasion, we chose works on a particular topic, such as the biblical story of David and Goliath, and demonstrated how different sculptors interpreted it, as in sculptures by Donatello (see Figure 11.11), Verrocchio (see Figure 11.12), and Michelangelo (see Figure 12.19). Still other works caught our attention because they served as links between successive styles, as is the case with Giotto's frescoes (see Figure 10.19), or because they represented the end of an age or an artistic style, as in the haunting sculpture called *The Last Pagan* (see Figure 7.15). Finally, we included some works, especially paintings, simply because of their great beauty, such as Ingres's *Madame Jacques Louis Leblanc* (see Figure 17.7).

Through all the ages of Western cultural history, through all the shifting styles and tastes embodied in painting, sculpture, architecture, poetry, and song, there glows a creative spark that can be found in human beings in every period. This diversity is a hallmark of the Western experience, and we celebrate it in this book.

A CHALLENGE TO THE READER

The purpose of all education is and should be self-knowledge. This goal was first established by the ancient Greeks in their injunction to "Know thyself," the inscription carved above the entrance to Apollo's temple at Delphi. Self-knowledge means awareness of oneself and one's place in society and the world. Reaching this goal is not easy, because becoming an educated human being is a lifelong process, requiring time, energy, and commitment. But all journeys begin with a single step, and we intend this volume as a first step toward understanding and defining oneself in terms of one's historical and cultural heritage. Our challenge to the reader is to use this book to begin the long journey to self-knowledge.

A HUMANITIES PRIMER
How to Understand the Arts

INTRODUCTION

We can all appreciate the arts. We can find pleasure or interest in paintings, music, poems, novels, films, and many other art forms, both contemporary and historical. We don't need to know very much about art to know what we like, because we bring ourselves to the work: What we like has as much to do with who we are as with the art itself.

Many of us, for example, will respond positively to a painting like Leonardo da Vinci's *The Virgin of the Rocks*. The faces of the Madonna and angel are lovely; we may have seen images like these on Christmas cards or in other commercial reproductions. We respond with what English poet William Wordsworth calls the "first careless rapture," which activates our imaginations and establishes a connection between us and the work of art. However, if this is all we see, if we never move from a subjective reaction, we can only appreciate the surface, the immediate form, and then, perhaps subconsciously, accept without question the values it implies. We appreciate, but we do not understand.

Sometimes we cannot appreciate because we do not understand. We may reject Picasso's *Les Demoiselles d'Avignon*, for it presents us with images of women that we may not be able to recognize. These women may make us uncomfortable, and the values they imply may frighten us rather than please or reassure us. Rather than rapture, we may experience disgust; but when we realize that this painting is considered a groundbreaking work, we may wonder what we're missing and be willing to look deeper. (*The Virgin of the Rocks* and *Les Demoiselles d'Avignon* are discussed in the text on pages 310–311 and pages 530, 532–533, respectively.)

LEONARDO DA VINCI. *The Virgin of the Rocks.*

To understand a work of art (a building, a poem, a song, a symphony), we need to keep our "rapture" (our emotional response and connection) but make it less "careless," less superficial and subjective, less restricted to that which we recognize. We need to enrich our appreciation by searching for a meaning that goes beyond ourselves. This involves understanding the intent or goal of the artist, the elements of form present in the work, the ways in which those elements contribute to the artist's goal, the context within which the artwork evolved, and the connections of the work to other works. Understanding an artwork requires intellectual involvement as well as an emotional connection. The purpose of this primer is to provide you with some of the tools you will need to understand—as well as appreciate—literature, art, and music.

Pablo Picasso. *Les Desmoiselles d'Avignon.*

APPROACHES TO THE ANALYSIS OF LITERATURE, ART, AND MUSIC

When we analyze a work of art, we ask two questions: What is the artist trying to do, and how well is it done? We want to identify the intent of the work, and we want to evaluate its execution. To answer these questions, we can examine the formal elements of the work—an approach known as formalism—and we can explore its context—known as contextualism.

Formalism

A formal analysis is concerned with the aesthetic (artistic) elements of a work separate from context. This type of analysis focuses on medium and technique. The context of the work—where, when, and by whom a work was created—may be interesting but is considered unnecessary to formalist interpretation and understanding. A formal analysis of a painting, sculpture, or architectural structure examines its line, shape, color, texture, and composition, as well as the artist's technical ability within the medium used; it is not concerned with anything extraneous to the work itself. A formal analysis of a literary work, such as a short story or novel, would explore the relationships among theme, plot, characters, and setting, as well as how well the resources of language—word choice, tone, imagery, symbol, and so on—are used to support the other elements. A formal analysis of a film would also explore theme, plot, characters (as developed both verbally and nonverbally), and setting, as well as how the resources of cinematography—camera techniques, lighting, sound, editing, and so on—support the other elements.

A formal analysis of *The Virgin of the Rocks* would examine the artist's use of perspective, the arrangement of figures as they relate to each other and to the grotto that surrounds them, the technical use of color and line, the dramatic interplay of light and shadow (known as *chiaroscuro*). The same technical considerations would be explored in a formal analysis of *Les Demoiselles d'Avignon.* The fact that the two paintings were completed in 1483 and 1907, respectively, would be important only in terms of the technology and mediums available to the artists. In a formal analysis, time and place exist only within the work.

Contextualism

In contrast, a contextual analysis focuses on factors outside the work: why it was created, in response to what artistic, social, cultural, historical, and political forces, events, and trends; who the artist is, and what his or her intent and motives were in creating the work; how the work fits in with other works of the same genre of the same or different eras; and how the work fits in with the rest of the artist's body of work. Time and place are very important.

A contextual analysis of the da Vinci and Picasso paintings would include information about where and when each painting was completed; the conditions from which it arose; the prevailing artistic styles of the times; the life circumstances of the artists; and so on. The paintings alone do not provide enough information for contextual inquiry. Similarly, contextual analysis of a novel by Dostoevsky would consider both his personal circumstances and the conditions in Russia and Europe when he wrote. A contextual analysis of a chorale and fugue by Bach would include information on Bach's life, his religious beliefs, and the political climate of Germany in the eighteenth century.

An Integrated Approach

In a strictly contextual analysis of an artwork, the work itself can sometimes be lost in the exploration of context. In a strictly formal analysis, important knowledge that can contribute to understanding may remain unknown. The most effective analyses, therefore, combine and integrate the two approaches, examining the formal elements of the work and exploring the context within which it was created. Such an approach is more effective and, in a sense, more honest than either the formal or the contextual approach alone. A work of art, whether a poem or a painting, a cathedral or a cantata, is a complex entity, as are the relationships it fosters between the artist and the art and between the art and its audience. The integrative approach recognizes these relationships and their complexity. This is the approach to artistic and cultural analysis most frequently used in *The Western Humanities.*

A Variety of Perspectives

Many students and critics of culture, while taking an integrative approach, are also especially interested in looking at things from a particular perspective, a set of interests or a way of thinking that informs and influences their investigations and interpretations. Common perspectives are the psychological, the feminist, the religious, the economic, and the historical.

People working from a psychological perspective look for meaning in the psychological features of the work, such as sexual and symbolic associations; they do a kind of retroactive psychological analysis of the artist. They might look for meaning in the facial expressions, gestures, and body positions of Mary and the angel in *The Virgin of the Rocks.* They might be interested in da Vinci's attitudes toward women and his relationships with them, and they might compare this painting with the *Mona Lisa* in a search for clues about who he was.

Someone working from a feminist perspective would examine the art itself and the context in which it arose from a woman's point of view. To take a feminist perspective is to ask how the work depicts women, what it says about women and their relationships in general, and how it may or may not reflect a patriarchal society. Many people have discussed the apparent hatred of women that seems to come through in Picasso's *Les Demoiselles d'Avignon.* At the same time, the work, in its size (8 feet by 7 feet 8 inches) and in the unblinking attitude of its subjects, suggests that these women have a kind of raw power. Feminist critics focus on such considerations.

Analysis from a religious perspective is often appropriate when a work of art originated in a religious context. The soaring spires and cruciform floor plans of medieval cathedrals reveal religious meaning, for example, as do Renaissance paintings depicting biblical characters. Many contemporary works of art and literature also have religious content. Religious analyses look to the use of symbolism, the representation of theological doctrines and beliefs, and intercultural connections and influences for meaning.

Someone approaching a work of art from an economic perspective focuses on its economic content—the roles and relationships associated with wealth. Often drawing upon Marx's contention that class is the defining consideration in all human relationships and endeavors, an economic analysis would examine both purpose and content: Was the work created as a display of power by the rich? How does it depict people of different classes? What is the artist saying about the distribution of wealth?

The historical perspective is perhaps the most encompassing of all perspectives, because it can include explorations of psychological, religious, and economic issues, as well as questions about class and gender in various times and places. Historical analysis requires an understanding of the significant events of the time and how they affect the individual and shape the culture. *The Western Humanities* most often takes a historical perspective in its views of art and culture.

The Vocabulary of Analysis

Certain terms and concepts are fundamental to the analysis of any artwork. We review several such general concepts and terms here, before moving on to a consideration of more specific art forms.

Any artwork requires a relationship between itself and its audience. **Audience** is the group for whom a work of art, architecture, literature, drama, film, or music is intended. The audience may be a single person, such as the Medici ruler to whom Machiavelli dedicated his political treatise *The Prince.* The audience can be a small group of people with access to the work, such as the monks who dined in the room where Leonardo da Vinci painted *The Last Supper* on the wall. The audience can also be a special group of people with common interests or education; for example, films like *I Know What You Did Last Summer* and *Scream* are intended for a youthful audience. Sometimes the audience is limited by its own understanding of the art; we often feel excluded from what we don't understand. Consequently, some art requires an educated audience.

Composition is the arrangement of constituent elements in an individual work. In music, composition also refers to the process of creating the work.

Content is the subject matter of the work; content can be based on mythology, religion, history, current events, personal history, or almost any idea or feeling deemed appropriate by the artist.

Context is the setting in which the art arose, its own time and place. Context includes the political, economic, social, and cultural conditions of the time; it can also include the personal conditions and circumstances that shape the artist's vision.

A **convention** is an agreed-upon practice, device, technique, or form. A sonnet, for example, is a fourteen-line poem with certain specified rhyme schemes. A poem is not a sonnet unless it follows this formal convention. A convention of the theater is the "willing suspension of disbelief": We know that the events taking place before our eyes are not real, but we agree to believe in them for the duration of the play. Often, conventions in the arts are established as much by political powerbrokers as by artists. The Medicis and the Renaissance popes, for example, wanted portraits and paintings that glorified their reigns, and conventions in Renaissance art reflect these demands. Today, museum directors, wealthy individuals, and government funding agencies play a role in influencing the direction of contemporary art by supporting and showing the work of artists whose conventions they agree with or think are important.

Genre is the type or class to which a work of art, literature, drama, or music belongs, depending on its style, form, or content. In literature, for example, the novel is a genre in itself; the short story is another genre. In music, symphonies, operas, and tone poems are all different genres. Beginning in the Renaissance, genres were carefully distinguished from one another, and a definite set of conventions was expected whenever a new work in a particular genre was created.

The **medium** is the material from which an art object is made—marble or bronze, for example, in sculpture, or water colors or oils in painting. (The plural of *medium* in this sense is often *mediums;* when *medium* is used to refer to a means of mass communication, such as radio or television, the plural is *media.*)

Style is the combination of distinctive elements of creative execution and expression, in terms of both form and content. Artists, artistic schools, movements, and periods can be characterized by their style. Styles often evolve out of existing styles, as when High Renaissance style evolved into Mannerism in the sixteenth century, or in reaction to styles that are perceived as worn out or excessive, as when Impressionism arose to challenge Realism in the nineteenth century.

When we talk about **technique,** we are referring to the systematic procedure whereby a particular creative task is performed. If we were discussing a dancer's technique, we might be referring to the way he executes leaps and turns; a painter's technique might be the way she applies paint to a canvas with broad, swirling brushstrokes.

The dominant idea of a work, the message or emotion the artist intends to convey, is known as the **theme.** The theme, then, is the embodiment of the artist's intent. In a novel, for example, the theme is the abstract concept that is made concrete by character, plot, setting, and other linguistic and structural elements of the work. We often evaluate the theme of a work in terms of how well it speaks to the human condition, how accurate its truth is, how valuable its message or observation is. We usually make these judgments by exploring the extent to which the theme confirms or denies our own experience.

In addition to these general concepts and terms, each art form has its own vocabulary. These more specific terms will be introduced in the sections that follow on literary, artistic, and musical analysis, along with brief illustrative analyses in each area. These informal illustrations are meant not as definitive analyses but as examples of the kinds of productive questions you can ask as you approach a creative work. The analyses differ in their depth and level of detail.

LITERARY ANALYSIS

Literary analysis begins with a consideration of various literary genres and forms. A work of literature is written either in **prose,** the ordinary language used in speaking and writing, or in **poetry,** a more imaginative and concentrated form of expression usually marked by meter, rhythm, or rhyme. Part of poetry's effect comes from the sound of words; it can often best be appreciated when spoken or read aloud. Prose is often divided into nonfiction (essays, biography, autobiography) and fiction (short stories, novels).

In literature, *genre* refers both to form—essay, short story, novel, poem, play, film script, television script—and to specific type within a form—tragedy, comedy, epic, lyric, and so on. According to Aristotle, a **tragedy** must have a tragic hero—a person of high stature who is brought down by his own excessive pride *(hubris);* he doesn't necessarily die at the end, but whatever his greatness was based upon is lost. A **comedy** is a story with a complicated and amusing plot; it usually ends with a happy and peaceful resolution of any conflicts. An **epic** poem, novel, or film is a relatively long recounting of the life of a hero or the glorious history of a people. A **lyric** poem is a short, subjective poem usually expressing an intense personal emotion. In a general sense, an epic tells a story and a lyric expresses an idea or feeling. Lyric poetry includes ballads (dramatic verse meant to be sung or recited, often by more than one singer or speaker), elegies (short, serious meditations, usually on death or other significant themes), odes (short lyric poems dealing with a single theme), and sonnets (formal fourteen-line poems identified by the arrangement of lines as either Italian [Petrarchan] or English [Shakespearean]).

In literature, the author's intent—the message or emotion the author wishes to convey—is usually discussed as the theme of the work. In an essay, the theme is articulated as the thesis: the idea or conclusion that the essay will prove or support. In a novel, story, or play, we infer the theme from the content and the development of ideas and imagery.

In fiction, the action of the story, what Aristotle calls "the arrangement of incidents," is the **plot.** There may be a primary plot that becomes the vehicle by which the theme is expressed, with subplots related to secondary (or even tertiary) themes. Plot can be evaluated by how well it supports the theme. Plot can also be evaluated according to criteria established by Aristotle in his *Poetics.* According to these criteria, the action expressed should be whole, with a beginning that does not follow or depend on anything else, a middle that logically follows what went before, and an end, or logical culmination of all prior action. The plot should be unified, so that every action is necessary and interrelated with all other actions. Few works of fiction adhere to these criteria completely; nevertheless, the criteria do provide a way of beginning to think about how a plot works.

Characters are also important both for themselves and for their effect on the plot and support of the theme. **Characters** provide the human focus, the embodiment, of the theme; they act out and are affected by the plot. The protagonist, or primary character, of the work is changed by the dramatic action of the plot and thus is a dynamic character; static characters remain unchanged throughout the story. An antagonist is a character in direct opposition to the protagonist. Some characters are stock characters, representing a type rather than an individual human being: the romantic fool, the nosy neighbor, the wise old woman, the vain beauty, the plain girl or dumb boy with a heart of gold.

Readers need to believe that characters' actions are authentic reactions to various events. The believability of a work of fiction—the writer's ability to express the truth—is called verisimilitude. Even in works of science fiction or fantasy, where events occur that could not occur in reality, readers must believe that what characters say and do makes sense under the conditions described.

The background against which the action takes place is the **setting.** It can include the geographical location, the environment (political, social, economic) in which the characters live, the historical time in which the action takes place, and the culture and customs of the time, place, and people.

The story or poem is told from the point of view of the **narrator.** The narrator is not necessarily identical with the author of the work. The narrator (or **narrative voice**) can be examined and analyzed like any other element of the work. When a narrator seems to know everything and is not limited by time or place, the work has an omniscient point of view. Such a narrator tells us what everyone is thinking, feeling, and doing. When the story is told from the perspective of a single character who can relate only what he or she knows or witnesses, the work has a first-person point of view. Such a narrator is limited in his or her understanding. Thus, we need to consider the narrator in order to judge how accurate or complete the narrative is.

Sometimes a narrator proves to be unreliable, and we have to piece together an account of the story ourselves. Other times an author uses multiple narrators to tell a story from multiple points of view. William Faulkner uses this device in his novel *The Sound and the Fury* to show that a story can be fully told only when several different characters have a chance to speak. Japanese film director Akira Kurosawa uses a similar device in *Rashomon* to show that there are many equally valid—or invalid—versions of the truth.

A literary analysis of a drama, whether a play for the stage or a film script, will consider not only the elements already mentioned—theme, plot, character, setting, language, and so on—but also the technical considerations specific to the form. In theater, these would include the work of the director, who interprets the play and directs the actors, as well as stage design, light and sound design, costumes, makeup, and so on. In film, technical considerations would include direction, editing, cinematography, musical score, special effects, and so on.

Let's turn now to a poem by Shakespeare and see how to approach it to enrich our understanding. Identifying a poem's intent and evaluating its execution is called an *explication,* from the French *explication de texte.* An explication is a detailed analysis of a poem's meaning, focusing on narrative voice, setting, rhyme, meter, words, and images. An explication begins with what is immediately evident about the poem as a whole, followed by a more careful examination of its parts.

William Shakespeare (1564–1616) was not just a great playwright; he was also a great poet. His works portray human emotions, motives, and relationships that we recognize today as well as the conditions and concerns of his time. In this sense, they are an example of aesthetic universality, the enduring connection between a work of art and its audience.

Shakespeare's sonnets are his most personal work. Scholars disagree about whether they are generic love poems or are addressed to a specific person and, if the latter, who that person might be. Formally, an English (or Shakespearean) sonnet is a 14-line poem consisting of three 4-line stanzas, or quatrains, each with its own rhyme scheme, and a concluding 2-line stanza, or couplet, that provides commentary on the preceding stanzas. The rhyme scheme in a Shakespearean sonnet is abab cdcd efef gg; that is, the first and third lines of each quatrain rhyme with each other, as do the second and fourth lines, though the rhymes are different in each quatrain. The last two lines rhyme with each other.

The meter of most Shakespearean sonnets is iambic pentameter; that is, each line has five feet, or units ("pentameter"), and each foot consists of an iamb, an unaccented syllable followed by an accented syllable (as in *alone*). An example of iambic pentameter is, "My mistress' eyes are nothing like the sun"; each foot consists of an unaccented and an accented syllable, and there are five feet. Unrhymed iambic pentameter—the verse of most of Shakespeare's plays—is known as **blank verse.**

Sonnet 130 ("My mistress' eyes are nothing like the sun") is a poem that not only illustrates sonnet form but also showcases Shakespeare's wit and his attitude toward certain conventions of his time. The poem was originally written in Elizabethan English, which looks and sounds quite different from modern English. We reproduce it in modern English, as is customary today for Shakespeare's works.

Sonnet 130

My mistress' eyes are nothing like the sun;
Coral is far more red than her lips' red;
If snow be white, why then her breasts are dun;
If hairs be wires, black wires grow on her head.

I have seen roses damask'd, red and white,
But no such roses see I in her cheeks,
And in some perfumes is there more delight
Than in the breath that from my mistress reeks.

I love to hear her speak, yet well I know
That music hath a far more pleasing sound;
I grant I never saw a goddess go,
My mistress when she walks treads on the ground.

And yet, by heaven, I think my love as rare
As any she belied with false compare.

Because the poet's intent may not be immediately evident, paraphrasing each line or stanza can point the reader to the theme or meaning intended by the poet. Let's begin, then, by paraphrasing the lines:

My mistress' eyes are nothing like the sun;
The speaker's lover's eyes are not bright.
Coral is far more red than her lips' red;
Her lips are not very red, certainly not as red as coral.
If snow be white, why then her breasts are dun;
Her breasts are mottled in color, not as white as snow.
If hairs be wires, black wires grow on her head.
Her hair is black (not blond, as was the conventional beauty standard then, when poets referred to women's hair as "golden wires").

I have seen roses damask'd, red and white,
But no such roses see I in her cheeks,
Her cheeks are not rosy.
And in some perfumes is there more delight
Than in the breath that from my mistress reeks.
Her breath doesn't smell as sweet as perfume.

I love to hear her speak, yet well I know
That music hath a far more pleasing sound;
Her voice doesn't sound as melodious as music.
I grant I never saw a goddess go,
My mistress when she walks treads on the ground.
Although the speaker has never seen a goddess walk, he knows his lover does not float above ground, as goddesses are supposed to do, but walks on the ground, a mortal woman.

And yet, by heaven, I think my love as rare
As any she belied with false compare.
His lover is as rare and valuable as any idealized woman glorified by false poetic comparisons.

Remember that to analyze a poem, we ask questions like, What is the theme of the poem, the poet's intent? How does Shakespeare support his point with specific images? From the paraphrased lines it is clear that the narrator is stating that his love is a real woman who walks upon the ground, not an unattainable ideal to be worshiped from afar. Idealized qualities are irrelevant to how he feels about her; the qualities he loves are the ones that make her human.

Closely examining each line of a poem helps to reveal the rhyme scheme (abab cdcd efef gg), the meter (iambic pentameter), and thus the form of the poem (sonnet). Explication of the formal elements of the poem would also include examining the use of language (such as word choice, imagery, comparisons, metaphors), the tone of the narrative voice, and so on.

To understand the context of the poem, we would consider the cultural climate of the time (was "courtly love" a prevalent cultural theme?); common contemporary poetic conventions (were many other poets proclaiming their eternal love for idealized women?); and the political, social, and economic conditions (what roles were open to women in Elizabethan England, and how were they changing? What influence might Queen Elizabeth have had on the poet's point of view? What comments about his society is Shakespeare making?)

Finally, we might consider how honest and accurate we find the emotional content of the poem to be, how relevant its truth. Are Shakespeare's observations germane to today, a time when the mass media present us with a nearly unattainable ideal as the epitome of female beauty?

FINE ARTS ANALYSIS

As with literature, knowledge of a particular vocabulary helps us "speak the language" of art critics. The terms introduced here are in addition to those discussed earlier, such as *medium* and *technique*. They apply to all the visual arts, including drawing and painting, sculpture—the art of shaping material (such as wood, stone, or marble) into three-dimensional works of art—and architecture—the art and science of designing, planning, and building structures, usually for human habitation. In architecture, the critic would also pay attention to the blending of artistry and functionality (how well the structure fulfills its purpose).

Generally, art is more or less representational or more or less abstract. **Representational art** is true to human perception and presents a likeness of the world much as it appears to the naked eye. An important convention of representational art is **perspective,** the appearance of depth and distance on a two-dimensional surface. **Abstract art** presents a subjective view of the world, the artist's emotions or ideas; some abstract art simply presents color, line, or shape for its own sake.

The formal elements of visual art include line, shape, texture, color, composition, and so on. **Line** is the mark made by the artist, whether with pencil, pen, or paintbrush. Lines can be straight or curved, thick or thin, light or dark, spare or plentiful. **Color** is the use in the artwork of hues found in nature; color can enhance the sense of reality presented in a visual image, or it can distort it, depending on how it is used. The primary colors are red, blue, and yellow, and the secondary colors are orange (a combination of red and yellow), green (a combination of yellow and blue), and purple (a combination of blue and red). Blue, green, and purple hues are "cool" colors that appear to recede from the eye; red, yellow, and orange are "warm" colors that appear to move forward. Color has symbolic associations within specific historical and cultural settings. For example, in Western culture, white is a symbol of purity and is worn by brides. In Eastern cultures, white is a symbol of death; Chinese brides wear red to symbolize good luck.

How the artist arranges the work is referred to as the composition. Often the artist controls how the eye moves from one part to another by means of the composition. Through the composition the artist leads us to see the artwork in a particular way. The setting of an artwork is the time and place depicted in a representational work, as defined by visual cues—the people, how they are dressed, what they are doing, and so on.

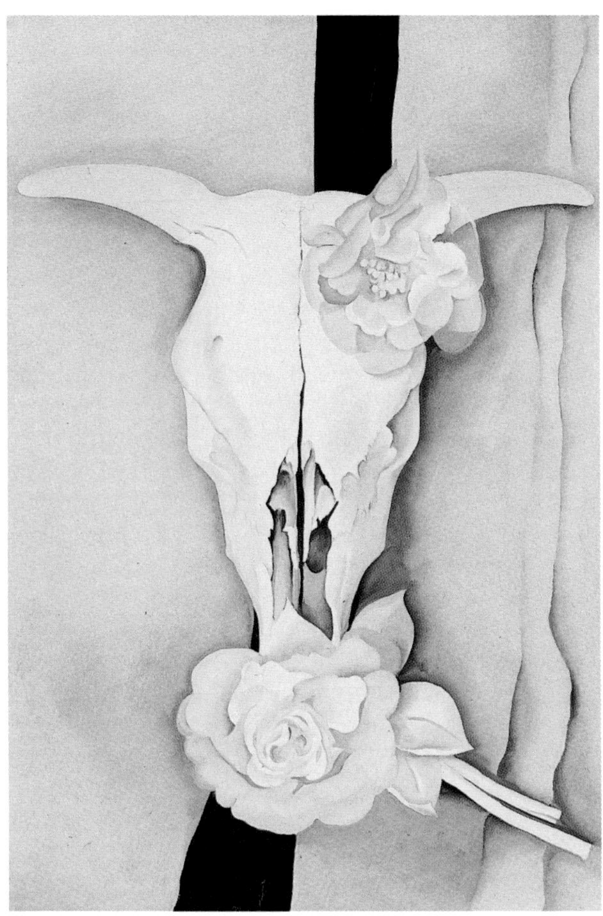

GEORGIA O'KEEFFE. *Cow's Skull with Calico Roses.*

With these terms in hand, let's consider *Cow's Skull with Calico Roses* by Georgia O'Keeffe (1887–1986), painted in 1931. What is the artist's intent? How well is that intent executed? Front and center we see the cow's skull, placed so the strong vertical line of the skull, accentuated by the skull's vertical midline crack, aligns with the center of the canvas. A broad band of black extending from the top of the canvas to the bottom behind the skull further reinforces the vertical axis, as do the wavy lines on the right. The skull's horns form a shorter, secondary horizontal line, creating a cross shape. At the bottom of the canvas, the black band seems to open; its expansion to the left is balanced by the rose stem in the lower right and the right-of-center rose at the top. The image overall is balanced and symmetrical, conveying a sense of stillness and repose rather than dynamic action.

The artist has not used broad or bold lines in her painting; rather, the lines of the skull and flowers are drawn delicately against the background; shading suggests contours and subtleties of lighting, and shadows blend softly. The surface is shallow and flat, conveying little sense of depth. The background material is ambiguous; is it cloth, paper, parchment, or some other material? The skull appears to float in front of this background. At the same time, the black band behind the skull seems to open into a mysterious space that recedes from the viewer.

The colors of the painting are muted, subtle, neutral—shades of black, gray, cream, and white. A slightly different color tone comes from the inside of the broken skull, where shades of tan and ochre are revealed. Within this world of muted tones, the white skull stands out rather starkly against the off-white background, and the flowers show up silvery gray against the white, beige, and black. The colors are quiet, almost somber, with a balance between the heavy black band and the other lighter-colored surfaces.

What are we to make of the image itself—a skull dressed up with cloth flowers? The animal almost appears to be eating or nuzzling one flower, and the other adorns its forehead. Many artists have used human skulls to remind us of our mortality, and in this painting suggestions of death and spirituality are reinforced, perhaps to the subconscious mind, by the cross shape that underlies the composition. In this context, the cow skull strikes an odd and discordant note. Cow skulls are often used to suggest the unforgiving nature of the desert, where animals and humans alike perish in a waterless, forbidding landscape. Here, the skull is transformed, first by its placement in an abstract setting and second by its adornment with artificial flowers. Is the image morbid, macabre? Is it humorous, playful, ironic? Or are we meant simply to see the skull in a new way, as a unique and interesting object, apart from the living animal it once was? Aged in the desert, bleached by the sun, the skull, though evocative of death, has its own stark beauty. The flowers too have their beauty; at the same time, the artist makes it clear that they are calico, not real. They are artificial, created by human hands to resemble living flowers

Although the skull and flowers are painted realistically, the ambiguous background suggests that the artist is moving toward abstraction, toward an expression of feeling and mood rather than pure representation. The overall feeling evoked by the painting is one of contemplation, meditation. Faced with the juxtaposition of these incongruous objects, we are reminded of the intimate relationships between life and death, beauty and ugliness, art and nature.

How can we augment our appreciation and understanding of this painting with contextual knowledge? Georgia O'Keeffe grew up on a farm in Wisconsin, where she reveled in every detail of nature, bringing to it an attention and appreciation that would later be reflected in her paintings. She knew from an early age that she wanted to be an artist, and she studied art in Chicago and New York, developing a highly refined technique that quickly became recognized as uniquely her own. Among important early influences were the paintings and theories of Russian abstract artist Wassily Kandinsky, who believed that art and especially color had powerful spiritual effects. In 1929 O'Keeffe visited Taos, New Mexico, for the first time, where she became enraptured by the desert, the light, the colors of the landscape, the expanse of the sky. She was especially intrigued by bones—their form, shape, color, texture—and she shipped boxes of them back to her studio in New York to paint. Eventually she spent more and more time in the Southwest, developing a style that blends realism and abstraction. Her trademark was the selection and abstraction of an object or a view in nature, which she then transformed in accordance with her inner vision. She became known for her particular way of seeing and for her ability to enable others to see the same way.

When she painted *Cow's Skull with Calico Roses,* O'Keeffe was at a difficult time in her personal life. Perhaps depression led her to paint in subdued colors (rather than the brilliant colors of earlier and later paintings) and to focus on bones and other images of death (rather than the images of flowers for which she was already famous). Some have suggested that the seemingly suspended nature of the skull in this painting was suggestive of her own unsettled frame of mind. Whether or not personal details like these help us appreciate and understand the work, what is clear is that when we contemplate *Cow's Skull with Calico Roses,* we see not just the beauty of natural forms but also the power of nature to transform objects and the power of the artist to transform them once again.

MUSICAL ANALYSIS

Like literature and art, music has its own vocabulary, and we need to be familiar with it in order to analyze a composition. A basic distinction we can apply to music is the one between religious music, or **sacred music**—such as Gregorian chants, Masses, requiems, and hymns—and **secular music**—such as symphonies, songs, and dances. Another distinction we can make is between vocal or choral music, which is sung and generally has lyrics (words), and instrumental music, which is written for and performed on instruments.

In music, composers choose among many different **forms,** or particular structures or arrangements of elements. Symphonies, songs, concertos, string quartets, sonatas, Masses, and operas are some of the many different forms in which composers may write their music. As in literature and the visual arts, various musical forms have been more or less popular according to the styles and fashions of the time. The madrigal, for example, was a popular vocal form of the Renaissance period; the church cantata was a common form in the Baroque period; and the symphony became the most important orchestral form beginning in the eighteenth century.

Music itself is a combination of tone, tempo, and texture. **Tone** is a musical sound of definite pitch (pitch is determined by the frequency of the air waves producing the sound). A set pattern of tones (or notes) arranged from low to high (or high to low) is known as a **scale.** The modern Western scale is the familiar do, re, mi, fa, sol, la, ti, do, with half-steps in between the tones. In other cultures, more or fewer tones may be distinguished in a scale. The term *tone* can also refer to the quality of a sound. **Tempo** is the rate of speed of a musical passage, usually set or suggested by the composer. **Texture** describes the number and the nature of the voices or instruments employed and how the parts are combined. In music a theme is a characteristic musical idea upon which a composition is built or developed.

Melody is a succession of musical tones, usually having a distinctive musical shape, or line, and a definite rhythm (the recurrent alternation of accented and unaccented beats). **Harmony** is the simultaneous combination of two or more tones, producing a chord. More generally, harmony refers to the chordal characteristics of a work and the way in which chords interact with one another.

Music differs from literature and the visual arts in some important ways. First, unlike visual art, which does not change after the artist finishes it, music begins when the composition is complete. Like drama, music is lifeless until it is interpreted and performed. The written music represents the composer's intent, but the actual execution of the work is up to conductors and musicians.

A second difference is the fleeting, temporal nature of music. When we listen to live music, we hear it once and it's gone. We cannot study it like a painting or reread a passage as we can in a novel. Of course, recording devices and musical notation enable us to revisit music again and again, but by its very nature, music exists in time in a way that literature and the visual arts do not. For this reason, it is often particularly difficult to appreciate or understand a piece of music on first hearing; instead, we have to listen to it repeatedly.

Music is also more difficult to describe in words than literature or the visual arts. At best, words can only approximate, suggest, and refer to sounds. Sometimes it's helpful to use imagery from other sense modalities to describe a piece of music. What visual images does the work evoke? What colors? What textures? If you were to choreograph the work, how would the dancers move?

Finally, when we analyze a painting, we can reproduce it for our audience, and when we analyze a poem, we can reprint it. When we analyze music, we often have to hope that members of our audience know the work and can "hear" it in their heads. Alternatively, we can hope to generate enough interest in the work that they will want to make a point of hearing it themselves.

With these few basics in mind, let's consider a well-known musical work, *Rhapsody in Blue,* by George Gershwin (1898–1937). Even if you don't know this piece by name, it's very likely that you've heard it. It's been used in ads and in the sound tracks of numerous movies, including *Fantasia 2000;* it is also a standard accompaniment to images of New York City.

Imagine that you're seated in a concert hall and hearing this piece performed by a symphony orchestra (probably a "pops" orchestra, one that performs more popular classical music). When listening to a new piece of music or one you're not terribly familiar with, it's a good idea to simply try to get a sense of its general mood and character—again, focusing on the creator's intent. What emotions or ideas is the composer trying to convey? What musical elements does the composer use to execute that intent?

You'll notice, first of all, that the work is written for a small orchestra and a solo piano, the same instrumental configuration you would expect for a classical piano concerto (a concerto is a work for one or a few instruments and an orchestra, with much of its interest coming from the contrasts between the solo voice and the ensemble voice). But the opening notes of *Rhapsody in Blue* reveal something other than classical intentions: a solo clarinet begins low and sweeps up the scale in a seemingly endless "smear" of sound, finally reaching a high note, briefly holding it, and then plunging into the playful, zigzag melody that becomes one of the major themes of the work. Within moments, the orchestra enters and repeats the theme in the strings and brass, to be followed by the entry of the solo piano. Throughout the work, piano and orchestra alternate and combine to sing out beautiful melodies and create a varied and colorful texture. Variety also comes from different instrumentation of the themes and tunes, played first by a slinky muted trumpet, then by a sweet solo violin, later by a whole lush string section or a brash horn section.

You'll notice too the constant changes in tempo, now slower, now faster, almost as if the work is being improvised. Complex, syncopated, off-the-beat rhythms give the piece a jazzy feeling, and the combination of tones evokes the blues, a style of music in which certain notes are "bent," or lowered slightly in pitch, creating a particular sound and mood. The general feeling of the piece is upbeat, exciting, energetic, suggestive of a bustling city busy with people on the go. It may also make you think of Fred Astaire and Ginger Rogers movies you've seen on late-night TV—sophisticated, playful, casually elegant—and in fact, Gershwin wrote the music for some of their films.

What can we learn about this work from its title? Musical works often reveal their form in their title ("Fifth Symphony," "Violin Concerto in D," and so on). A rhapsody is a composition of irregular form with an improvisatory character. Although you may have heard themes, repetitions, and echoes in *Rhapsody in Blue,* you probably were not able to discern a regular form such as might be apparent in a classical sonata or symphony. The word *rhapsody* also suggests rapture, elation, bliss, ecstasy—perhaps the feelings conveyed by that soaring first phrase on the clarinet. *Blue,* on the other hand, suggests the melancholy of the blues. The dissonance created by the combination of the two terms—like the combinations and contrasts in the music—creates an energetic tension that arouses our curiosity and heightens our interest.

In making these observations about *Rhapsody in Blue,* we've been noticing many of the formal elements of a musical work and answering questions that can be asked about any composition: What is the form of the work? What kind of instrumentation has the composer chosen? What is the primary melodic theme of the work? What tempos are used? How do the instruments or voices work together to create the texture? What is the overall mood of the piece—joyful, sad, calm, wild, a combination?

Now, at your imaginary concert, there may be notes in the program that will provide you with some context for the work. You'll find that George Gershwin was a gifted and classically trained pianist who quit school at 15 and went to work in Tin Pan Alley, a district in New York City where popular songs were written and published. His goal in writing *Rhapsody in Blue* (1924) was to blend classical and popular music, to put the energy and style of jazz into a symphonic format. Many listeners "see" and "hear" New York City in this piece. Gershwin created his own unique idiom, a fast-paced blend of rhythm, melody, and harmony that followed certain rules of composition but gave the impression of improvisation. He went on to write musicals, more serious compositions like the opera *Porgy and Bess,* and music for Hollywood films, all in his distinctive style. Information like this can help you begin to compare *Rhapsody in Blue* both with other works of the time and with other works by Gershwin. As in any analysis, integrating the formal and the contextual rounds out your interpretation and understanding of the work.

CONCLUSION

These three brief analyses should give you some ideas about how literature, art, and music can be approached in productive ways. By taking the time to look more closely, we gain access to the great works of our culture. This statement leads us to another issue: What makes a work "great"? Why do some works of art have relevance long beyond their time, while others are forgotten soon after their designated "fifteen minutes of fame"? These questions have been debated throughout history. One answer is that great art reflects some truth of human experience that speaks to us across the centuries. The voice of Shakespeare, the paintings of Georgia O'Keeffe, the music of George Gershwin have a universal quality that doesn't depend on the styles of the time. Great art also enriches us and makes us feel that we share a little more of the human experience than we did before.

As both a student of the humanities and an audience member, you have the opportunity to appreciate and understand the arts. Despite the formal nature of academic inquiry, an aesthetic analysis is a personal endeavor. In looking closely at a creative work, seeking the creator's intent and evaluating its execution, you enrich your appreciation of the work with understanding; you bring the emotional reaction you first experienced to its intellectual completion. As twentieth-century composer Arnold Schoenberg once wrote, "You get from a work about as much as you are able to give to it yourself." This primer has been intended to help you learn how to bring more of yourself to works of art, to couple your subjective appreciation with intellectual understanding. With these tools in hand, you won't have to say you don't know much about art but you know what you like; you'll be able to say you know *about* what you like.

1 PREHISTORY AND NEAR EASTERN CIVILIZATIONS

A Western man or woman born early in the twentieth century has seen more change in a lifetime than previous generations experienced over hundreds of years. Despite this rapid change in modern times, Western civilization stands firmly on a foundation that is almost five thousand years old, and people in the West often return to that foundation to discover their heritage and to reexamine their values. As further changes occur, the past becomes increasingly important as a guide to the future.

Before we begin to explore this heritage and what it means today, we need to discuss two important terms—*culture* and *civilization.* **Culture** usually refers to the sum of human endeavors: methods and practices for survival; political, economic, and social institutions; and values, beliefs, and the arts. **Civilization,** on the other hand, refers to the way people live in a complex political, economic, and social structure, usually in an urban setting; usually after making certain technological and artistic advances and sharing a refinement of thought, manners, and taste. Culture is passed from one generation to another by human behavior, speech, and artifacts; civilization is transmitted primarily by writing (Figure 1.1). The term *culture* can also be used to refer to the creative, artistic, and intellectual expressions of a civilization. We will use the term in both these senses. In the words of Matthew Arnold, the nineteenth-century English poet and critic, culture is "the best that has been thought and said." To this we would add, "and done."

◀ **Detail** Opening of the Mouth Scene, Funerary Papyrus of Hunefer. Ca. 1305–1195 B.C. British Museum.

Figure 1.1 Rosetta Stone. Ca. 197–196 B.C. British Museum. *Although scholars knew that Egypt had a writing system, they were unable to solve the mystery of hieroglyphics until the nineteenth century. The key was provided by the Rosetta Stone, discovered by members of Napoleon's expedition when he invaded Egypt in 1799. On the stone the same event is described in hieroglyphics, in Egyptian cursive script, and in Greek. By comparing the Greek text with the other two, scholars were able to decipher both Egyptian scripts. This discovery marks the origin of modern Egyptology.*

PREHISTORY AND EARLY CULTURES

Where and when does the story of human culture begin? The latest evidence from paleoanthropology, the study of early human life, indicates that human beings originated in the distant past in lands far from western Europe. Human development thus begins during prehistory, long before our predecessors compiled—or could compile—written records of their cultures. The first ancestors of human beings probably appeared four to five million years ago. In comparison, lifeforms appeared on earth an estimated two to three billion years ago, and the planet itself is believed to have formed some four to six billion years ago.

The periods of time involved in these processes are so vast that only metaphors can make them comprehensible. If we take the seven-day week, made familiar by the biblical account of creation, and combine it with recent scientific estimates about when the earth and life began, then the following analogy may be made. The earth was created just after midnight on the first day, the first life appeared about noon on the fourth day, and the early ancestors of human beings didn't show up until about 11 P.M. on the seventh day. To complete the analogy, the birth of civilization occurred almost an hour later, in the last tenth of a second before midnight on the last day of the week.

Although the record of human evolution is obscure, sufficient evidence exists to show that hominids, the earliest primate ancestors of modern humans, probably originated in eastern Africa. From among them, about two million years ago, in the Pliocene epoch, the genus *Homo* evolved, a form marked by a larger brain and the ability to adapt somewhat to the environment. Hominids of the *Homo* genus made and used tools and developed rudimentary cultures. Anthropologists designate this earliest cultural period as the **Paleolithic,** or Old Stone Age. It corresponds to the geological period known as the Pleistocene epoch, or Ice Age, the time of extensive climate changes caused by the advance and retreat of massive glaciers (Timeline 1.1).

Stone Age culture spread widely over a vast area, but remains of hominid life are scarce. Evidence indicates that hominids lived in packs, followed herds of wandering animals, and ate wild seasonal fruits and vegetables. Anthropologists believe that duties and work divided along sex lines as all-male teams hunted game for meat and fur while females and children gathered plant foods, prepared meals, and tended the young. During the night, all sought shelter together in

Timeline 1.1 GEOLOGICAL TIME AND PREHISTORIC CULTURAL PERIODS **All dates approximate and B.C.**

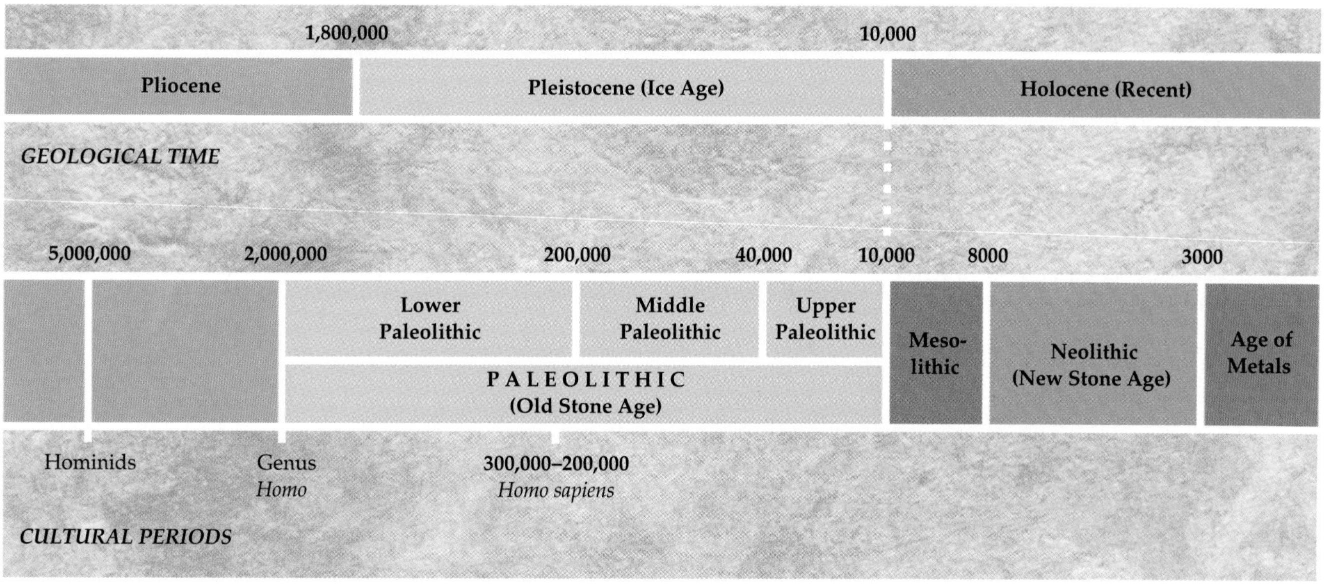

1,800,000 10,000

Pliocene | Pleistocene (Ice Age) | Holocene (Recent)

GEOLOGICAL TIME

5,000,000 2,000,000 200,000 40,000 10,000 8000 3000

Lower Paleolithic | Middle Paleolithic | Upper Paleolithic | Meso-lithic | Neolithic (New Stone Age) | Age of Metals

PALEOLITHIC (Old Stone Age)

Hominids | Genus *Homo* | 300,000–200,000 *Homo sapiens*

CULTURAL PERIODS

caves for safety and refuge against the elements. This way of life hinged on cooperation and food sharing among small social groups.

In the early Old Stone Age, or Lower Paleolithic, hominids invented crude stone tools, used fire, and probably developed speech—a major breakthrough that allowed them to communicate in ways denied other animals. Their first tools were simple choppers and, somewhat later, hand axes. In the Middle Paleolithic, more advanced hominids developed pointed tools and scrapers, which they chiseled with precision and care. In the Upper Paleolithic, double-faced blades became common.

By about 200,000 B.C., the species *Homo sapiens* had evolved from earlier hominids. More fully developed physically and mentally, they slowly spread throughout the Eastern Hemisphere and eventually migrated into the Western Hemisphere over the land bridge between Siberia and Alaska. Their more sophisticated tools included bows and arrows, fishhooks, and needles. They lived together cooperatively, buried their dead with rituals, and began to paint and sculpt. Especially through their cave paintings and carved figurines, our ancestors made a breakthrough to symbolic thought.

Ice Age cave paintings of reindeer, bison, rhinoceroses, lions, and horses in Altamira, Spain, and in Lascaux and the Ardèche region of France date from the Upper Paleolithic and are the earliest examples of human art (Figure 1.2). The purposes of the paintings in the recently discovered Chauvet caves in the Ardèche region remain a mystery, but those at Altamira and Lascaux were probably used as part of ceremonies and rituals before hunting. By painting numerous wild animals pierced with arrows, the artists were attempting to ensure a successful hunt.

Another type of Upper Paleolithic art was the carved female figurine found at Willendorf, Austria (Figure 1.3). Made of limestone, the statue is faceless and rotund. The distended stomach and full breasts suggest that the figure may have been used as a fertility symbol and an image of a mother goddess, representing the creative power of nature. As a mythological figure, the mother goddess appeared in many ancient cultures, beginning in Paleolithic times; about thirty thousand miniature sculptures in clay, marble, bone, copper, and gold have been uncovered at about three thousand sites in southeastern Europe alone. The supremacy of the mother goddess was expressed in the earliest myths of creation, which told of the life-giving and nurturing powers of the female. This figurine from Willendorf, with its emphasized breasts, navel, and vulva, symbolic of creativity, may have been used in religious ceremonies to ensure the propagation of the tribe or to guarantee a bountiful supply of food. The statue also reveals the aesthetic interests of the sculptor, who took care to depict the goddess's hands resting on her breasts and her hair in tightly knit rows.

As the last glaciers retreated from Europe, during the Holocene (Recent) epoch of geological time, human beings were forced to adapt to new living conditions. Their stone tools became more advanced and included knives and hammers. Following the Mesolithic transitional period (about 10,000–8000 B.C.), a transformation occurred that has been called the most important event in human history: Hunters and gatherers became

Figure 1.2 Herd of Rhinoceroses. Ca. 32,000–30,000 B.C. Chauvet Cave, Ardèche region, France. *This naturalistic detail of a panel painting includes lions, bison, and a young mammoth (not visible here) moving across a vast expanse of the cave wall. The repeated black lines of the rhinoceroses' horns and backs create a sense of depth and give energy to the work.*

farmers and herders. Thus began the **Neolithic** period, or New Stone Age (about 8000 B.C.). In Southeast Asia, Central America, parts of South America, and the Near East, human beings ceased their nomadic existence and learned to domesticate wild animals. They learned to plow the earth and sow seeds, providing themselves with a much more reliable food supply, which in turn encouraged the development of permanent settlements and eventually the rise of urban centers. This agrarian pattern of life dominated the West until about two hundred years ago.

Precisely why and how the agrarian revolution came at this time is a hotly debated topic among anthropologists. Nonetheless, most agree that with the retreat of the last glaciers from Europe, methods of food gathering changed dramatically, causing either surpluses or shortages. In some areas, grain surpluses allowed populations to grow, which led to forced migrations as the number of humans outstripped the available food. In less productive lands, the people began to experiment with domesticating animals and planting grains. These innovations in marginal lands caused food production to rise, soon matching that found in more fertile areas, so that eventually a uniform agricultural economy spread to many parts of the globe. Thus, economic causes accounted for the transformation from food-gathering to food-producing cultures.

The agricultural revolution expanded across the Near East and probably into Europe and Africa. Between 6000 and 3000 B.C., human beings also learned to mine and use copper, signifying the end of the Neolithic period and ushering in the Age of Metals.

Figure 1.3 Figurine from Willendorf. Ca. 25,000 B.C. Ht. 4⅜″. Museum Naturhistorisches, Vienna. *Discovered in around A.D. 1908, this female statuette measures just under 5 inches high. Carved from limestone, it still shows evidence of having been painted red. Many other statues like it have been discovered, but this one remains the most famous because of the unusual balance it strikes between symbolism and realism.*

In about 3000 B.C., artisans combined copper and tin to produce bronze, a strong alloy, which they used in their tools, weapons, and jewelry.

The Bronze Age, which extended from about 3000 to about 1200 B.C., gave rise to two major civilizations in the Near East. The earlier developed in Mesopotamia, the land between the Tigris and Euphrates Rivers (in present-day Iraq), and the other, probably emerging just slightly later, originated along the Nile River in Egypt. Mesopotamian and Egyptian civilizations shared certain characteristics: Both were ruled by kings who were in turn supported by a priestly caste; the rulers' power was shared by small, educated elites; their economies were slave-based; their societies were stratified, with class privileges at the upper end; and palaces and religious edifices were built for ceremonial and governmental purposes. These early civilizations made deep and lasting impressions on their neighbors and successors that helped shape life in the Western world.

THE CIVILIZATIONS OF THE TIGRIS AND EUPHRATES RIVER VALLEY: MESOPOTAMIA

The Tigris-Euphrates river valley forms part of what is known as the Fertile Crescent, which starts at the Persian Gulf, runs slightly northwestward through the Tigris-Euphrates valley, and then turns westerly to the Mediterranean Sea and curves south along the shoreline toward Egypt (Map 1.1). This arc of land contained some of the most arable soil in the Near East, many of the heavily traveled trade routes, and most of the early centers of civilization.

Mesopotamia is a Greek word meaning "land between the two rivers." The hill country and Zagros Mountains rise to the east of the Tigris-Euphrates valley, and the vast Arabian desert stretches to the west. The twin rivers course down to the Persian Gulf, draining an area approximately 600 miles long and 250 miles wide. Near the mouth of the gulf, on the river delta, human wanderers settled in about 6000 B.C., founding villages and tilling the land. Despite heat, marshes, unpredictable and violent floods, and invaders who came from both the mountains and the desert, some of these communities prospered and grew.

The Sumerian, Akkadian, and Babylonian Kingdoms

Three successive civilizations—Sumerian, Akkadian, and Babylonian—flourished in Mesopotamia for nearly fifteen hundred years (Timeline 1.2). Indeed, as historian Samuel Kramer asserts, "history began at Sumer."

The rulers of Sumer created an exalted image of a just and stable society with a rich cultural life. Sumer's most inspirational king, Gilgamesh [GILL-guh-mesh], ruled during the first dynasty (about 2700 B.C.) of Ur, a state centered between the rivers. His heroic adventures and exploits were later immortalized in the poem *The Epic of Gilgamesh.* A later ruler, Urukagina, is known for reforming law codes and revitalizing the economy near the end of the Sumerian period (2350 B.C.). But Urukagina's successors were unable to maintain Sumer's power, and the cities became easy prey for the Akkadians of northern Mesopotamia.

The Akkadian dynasties, lasting from about 2350 to about 2000 B.C., incorporated Sumerian culture into their own society and carried this hybrid civilization

Map 1.1 MESOPOTAMIA AND ANCIENT EGYPT: THE FERTILE CRESCENT

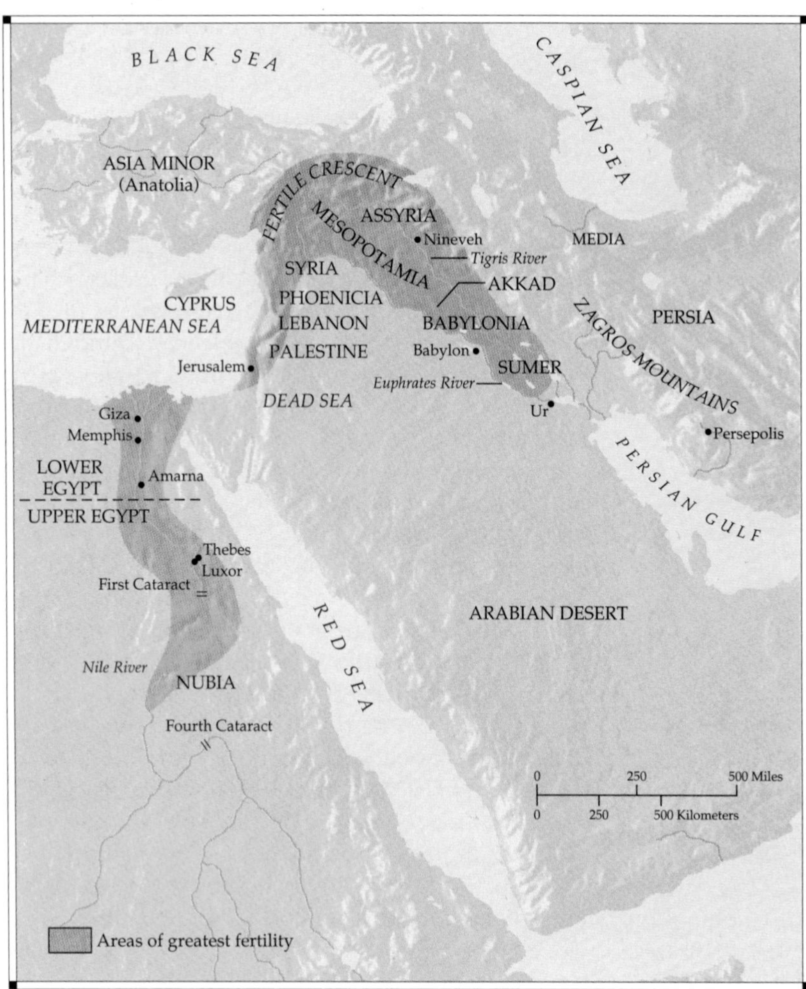

far beyond the Tigris-Euphrates valley. According to legends—which are similar to the later story of the Hebrew leader Moses—Sargon, the first and greatest Akkadian ruler, was born of lowly origins and abandoned at birth in the reed marshes; yet Sargon survived and rose to prominence at the Sumerian court. Excavated inscriptions reveal that Sargon conquered the Sumerians and founded a far-flung empire to the east and northeast. At its height, Sargon's power was felt from Egypt to India, but his successors, lacking his intelligence and skill, could not maintain the Akkadian empire. The incursions of the Guti tribes from the Zagros Mountains brought about the final collapse of the weakened Akkadian empire and the division of southern Mesopotamia into petty kingdoms.

Babylonia was the third civilization in Mesopotamia. From northern Mesopotamia, their power base, the Babylonians governed the entire valley from about 2000 to 1600 B.C. Under their most successful military leader and renowned lawgiver, Hammurabi [ham-uh-RAHB-e] (1792–1750 B.C.), the Babylonians reached their political and cultural ascendancy. However, the Hittites, centered in Asia Minor, invaded Babylon in about 1600 B.C. and toppled the dynasty of Hammurabi.

Agriculture dominated the economy of Mesopotamia. Harsh living conditions and unpredictable floods forced the inhabitants to learn to control the rivers through irrigation systems and cooperative tilling of the soil. Farmers eventually dug a complex canal system to irrigate their cultivated plots, which might have been some distance from the river. As production increased, prosperity allowed larger populations to thrive. Villages soon grew into small cities—with populations ranging from 10,000 to 50,000—surrounded by hamlets and tilled fields. Trade developed with nearby areas, and wheeled vehicles—perfected by the Sumerians—and sailboats carried goods up and down Mesopotamia and eventually throughout the Fertile Crescent.

Timeline 1.2 MESOPOTAMIAN CIVILIZATIONS **All dates approximate and B.C.**

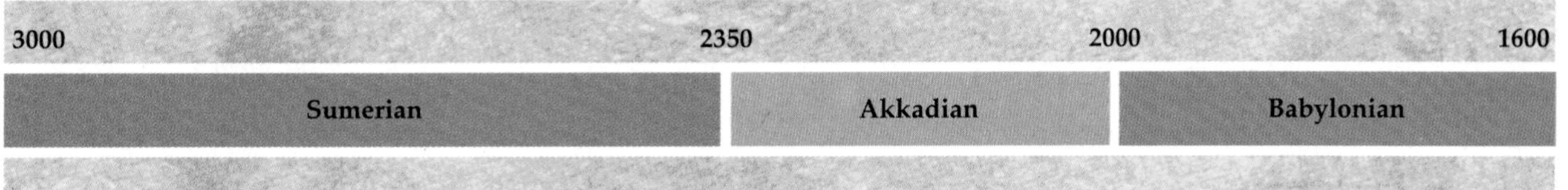

By the beginning of the Bronze Age, the family had replaced the tribe or clan as the basic unit in society. Families now owned their lands outright, and, under the general direction of the religious and secular authorities, they worked their fields and maintained the irrigation ditches. Marriages were arranged by parents, with economics an essential consideration. According to the law codes, women possessed some rights, such as holding property; however, a wife was clearly under her husband's power. Divorce was easier for men than for women, and women were punished more severely than men for breaking moral and marital laws. Recent scholarship has suggested that women's status and roles became more limited as Mesopotamian society became more complex. In sum, Mesopotamian women were originally able to participate actively in economic, religious, and political life as long as their dependence on and obligation to male kin and husbands were observed, but they progressively lost their relative independence because rulers extended the concept of patriarchy (rule by the fathers) from family practice into public law.

The political structure reflected the order and functions of the social system. At the top stood the ruler, who was supported by an army, a bureaucracy, a judicial system, and a priesthood. The ruler usually obtained advice from prominent leaders, meeting in council, who constituted the next layer of the social order: rich landowners, wealthy merchants, priests, and military chiefs. The next group consisted of artisans, craftspeople, and petty businesspeople and traders. Below them were small landowners and tenant farmers. At the bottom of the social scale were serfs and slaves, who either had been captured in war or had fallen into debt.

The Cradle of Civilization

The three Mesopotamian civilizations responded to the same geography, climate, and natural resources, and their cultures reflected that shared background. The Sumerians were probably the most influential: From Sumer came writing, the lunar calendar, a mathematical computation system, medical and scientific discoveries, and architectural innovations. However, each civilization, through its religion, literature, law, and art, deeply affected other Near Eastern people.

Writing Thousands of clay tablets inscribed with the wedge-shaped symbols of Sumerian script have been uncovered in Mesopotamia, indicating that the Sumerians had developed a form of writing by 3000 B.C. With the invention of writing, people no longer had to rely on memory, speech, and person-to-person interactions to communicate and transmit information. Instead, they could accumulate a permanent body of knowledge and pass it on from one generation to the next. With writing came the possibility of civilization.

At first, the Sumerians needed a simple way to record agricultural and business information and the deeds and sayings of their rulers. Their earliest symbols are **pictograms,** or pictures, carefully drawn to represent particular objects. To these they added **ideograms,** pictures drawn to represent ideas or concepts. A simple drawing of a bowl, for example, could be used to mean "food." As these pictures became more stylized, meaning began to be transferred from the represented object to the sign itself; that is, the sign began to stand for a word rather than an object.

Later, Sumerian scribes and writers identified the syllabic sounds of spoken words and created **phonograms,** symbols for separate speech sounds, borrowing from and building on the earlier pictograms and ideograms. These simplified and standardized symbols eventually resulted in a phonetic writing system of syllable-based sounds that, when combined, produced words (Figure 1.4). (It was left to later civilizations to separate vowel sounds from syllables and thus create a true alphabet, based on individual speech sounds.)

The Sumerians could now express complex, abstract concepts, and their system could extend to other languages. The Akkadians and the Babylonians adopted and modified the Sumerian script to keep records and preserve their literature, including *The Epic of Gilgamesh* and the Code of Hammurabi. By the end of the Bronze Age (about 1200 B.C.), other written languages existed, but Akkadian-Sumerian was the language of diplomacy and trade in the Near East.

The Sumerian writing system has been labeled **cuneiform,** a term derived from the Latin word *cuneus,*

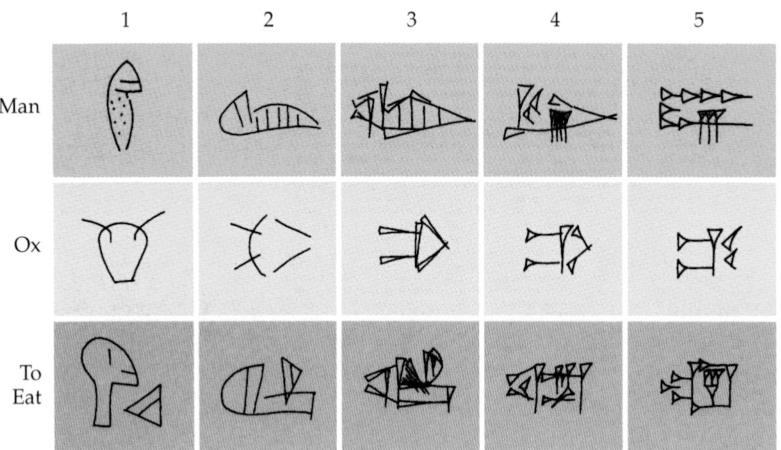

Figure 1.4 Sumerian Cuneiform Writing. Ca. 3000–1000 B.C. *The columns illustrate the evolution of Sumerian writing from pictograms to script. Column 1 shows the pictogram: a man, an ox, and the verb "to eat" (represented by the mouth and a bowl). In column 2, the pictographic symbols have been turned 90 degrees, as the Sumerians did in their first writing. Columns 3 and 4 show how the script changed between 2500 and 1800* B.C. *Column 5 is an Assyrian adaptation of the Sumerian cuneiform script.*

which means "wedge." Using wedge-shaped reeds or styluses, scribes pressed the symbols into wet clay tablets, and artists and craftspeople, wielding metal tools, incised the script into stone monuments or cylindrical pillars. Preserved for thousands of years in hardened clay and stone, cuneiform writing has provided invaluable insight into ancient Mesopotamian culture.

Religion Sumerian, Akkadian, and Babylonian religions, despite individual differences, shared many basic attitudes and concepts that became the foundation for other Near Eastern belief systems. The underlying beliefs of Mesopotamian religion were that the gods had created human beings to serve them, that the gods were in complete control, and that powerless mortals had no choice but to obey and worship these deities. The hostile climate and unpredictable rivers made life precarious, and the gods appeared capricious. The Mesopotamians held a vague notion of a shadowy netherworld where the dead rested, but they did not believe in an afterlife as such or any rewards or punishments upon death. Happiness seldom was an earthly goal; pessimism ran as a constant theme throughout their religion and literature.

Mesopotamian religion had three important characteristics. It was **polytheistic**—many gods and goddesses existed and often competed with one another; it was **anthropomorphic**—the deities possessed human form and had their own personalities and unique traits; and it was **pantheistic**—hundreds of divinities were found everywhere, in nature and the universe. Since Mesopotamians thought of their gods in human form with all the strengths and weaknesses of mortals, they believed their deities lived in the same way as people, and they were pragmatic in approaching the supernatural powers. For example, they believed that their deities held council, made decisions, and ordered the forces of nature to wreak havoc or to bestow plenty on mortals.

Mesopotamians divided the deities into the sky gods and the earth gods. In these two categories were the four major deities: Anu, the heaven god; Enlil, the air god; Enki, the water god; and Ninhursag, the mother goddess. Enlil emerged as the most powerful god for the Sumerians. He gave mortals the plough and the pickax, and he brought forth for humanity all the productive forces of the universe, such as trees, grains, and "whatever was needful."

Rituals, ceremonies, and the priesthood were absolutely essential to Mesopotamian religion. Although the average Mesopotamian might participate in worship services, the priests played the central role in all religious functions. They also controlled and administered large parcels of land, which enhanced their power in economic and political matters. Priests carefully formulated and consciously followed the procedures for rites and rituals, which were written down and stored in their temples. This cultic literature not only told the Mesopotamians how to worship but also informed them about their deities' origins, characteristics, and deeds. Religious myths and instructions constituted a major part of Mesopotamian literature and made writing an essential part of the culture.

Literature Of the surviving epics, tales, and legends that offer glimpses into the Mesopotamian mind, the most famous is *The Epic of Gilgamesh.* King Gilgamesh, whose reign in about 2700 B.C. is well documented, became a larger-than-life hero in Sumerian folk tales (Figure 1.5). In all probability, the Gilgamesh epic began as an oral poem and was not written on clay tablets for hundreds of years. The most complete surviving version, from 600 B.C., was based on a Babylonian copy written in Akkadian and dating from about

PERSONAL PERSPECTIVE

A Sumerian Father Lectures His Son

In this Sumerian text, a father rebukes his son for leading a wayward life and admonishes him to reform. The essay was inscribed on clay tablets dating from about 1700 B.C.

"Where did you go?"

"I did not go anywhere."

"If you did not go anywhere, why do you idle about? Go to school, stand before your 'school-father,' recite your assignment, open your schoolbag, write your tablet, let your 'big brother' write your new tablet for you. After you have finished your assignment and reported to your monitor, come to me, and do not wander about in the street. . . .

"You who wander about in the public square, would you achieve success? Then seek out the first generations. Go to school, it will be of benefit to you. My son, seek out the first generations, inquire of them.

"Perverse one over whom I stand watch—I would not be a man did I not stand watch over my son—I spoke to my kin, compared its men, but found none like you among them. . . .

"I, never in all my life did I make you carry reeds to the canebrake. The reed rushes which the young and the little carry, you, never in your life did you carry them. I never said to you 'Follow my caravans.' I never sent you to work, to plow my field. I never sent you to work to dig up my field. I never sent you to work as a laborer. 'Go, work and support me,' I never in my life said to you.

"Others like you support their parents by working. . . .

"I, night and day am I tortured because of you. Night and day you waste in pleasures. You have accumulated much wealth, have expanded far and wide, have become fat, big, broad, powerful, and puffed. But your kin waits expectantly for your misfortune, and will rejoice at it because you looked not to your humanity."

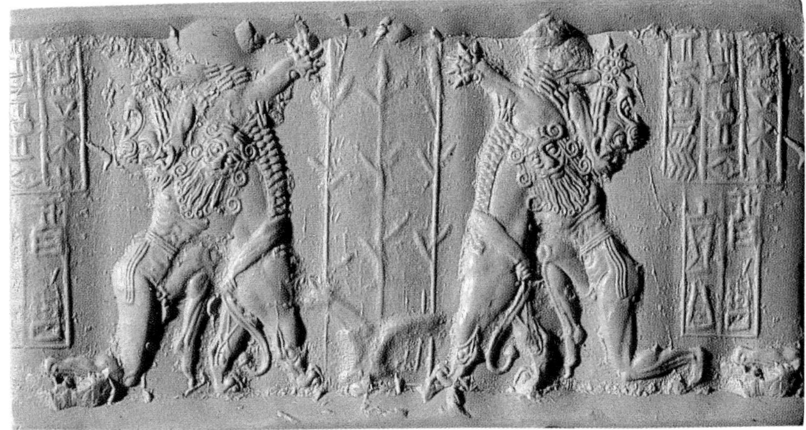

Figure 1.5 Gilgamesh Fighting a Lion. Ca. 2500–2000 B.C. Cylinder seal (left) and modern impression of a cylinder seal (right). British Museum. *The separate scenes, rolled out on this impression from the seal, which is about 1 inch high, depict the Sumerian hero in one of his many battles against beasts. The artist heightens the intensity of the physical struggle by placing Gilgamesh, with his legs bent and arms locked around the lion, at a sharp angle under the animal to muster his brute strength against his foe.*

1600 B.C. Although this poem influenced other Near Eastern writings with its characters, plot, and themes, *The Epic of Gilgamesh* stands on its own as a poetic utterance worthy of being favorably compared with later Greek and Roman epics.

Through its royal hero, *The Epic of Gilgamesh* focuses on fundamental themes that concern warriors in an aristocratic society: the need to be brave in the face of danger, the choice of death before dishonor, the conflict between companionship and sexual pleasure, the power of the gods over weak mortals, and the finality of death. Above all, it deals with human beings' vain quest for immortality. As the tale begins, the extravagant and despotic policies of Gilgamesh have led his subjects to pray for relief. In response, a goddess creates from clay a "wild man" of tremendous physical strength and sends him to kill Gilgamesh. But Enkidu, as he is called, is instead tamed by a woman's love, loses his innocence, wrestles Gilgamesh to a draw, and becomes his boon companion.

As the epic unfolds, Gilgamesh chooses friendship with Enkidu rather than the love offered by the goddess Ishtar. Gilgamesh is punished for this choice by being made to watch helplessly as Enkidu dies from an illness sent by the gods. Forced to confront the fate awaiting all mortals, a grieving Gilgamesh begins a search for immortality.

The next section of the epic, which details Gilgamesh's search, includes the Sumerian tale of the great flood, which parallels the later Hebrew story of Noah and the ark. Although the Sumerian account of the flood was probably a later addition to the original story of Gilgamesh, the episode does fit into the narrative and reinforces one of the epic's major themes: the inescapable mortality of human beings. Gilgamesh hears the story of the flood from its sole survivor, Utnapishtim. Utnapishtim tells Gilgamesh how he built an ark and loaded it with animals and his family, how the waters rose, and how he released birds from the ark to discover if the waters were receding. The old man then explains how the gods, feeling sorry for the last remaining human, granted him immortality. Utnapishtim refuses to divulge the secret of eternal life to Gilgamesh, but the old man's wife blurts out where a plant may be found that will renew youth but not give immortality. Although Gilgamesh locates the plant, he loses it on his journey home. Gilgamesh, seeing the city of Uruk that he had built, realizes that the deeds humans do on earth are the measure of their immortality and that death is inevitable.

The Epic of Gilgamesh is essentially a secular morality tale. Gilgamesh's triumphs and failures mirror the lives of all mortals, and the Sumerians saw themselves in Gilgamesh's change from an overly confident and powerful hero to a doubting and fearful human being. Those who, like Gilgamesh, ignore the power of the deities have to pay a heavy price for their pride.

Mesopotamia also gave the world the first known literary figure, Enheduanna (fl. 2330 B.C.), an Akkadian poet who wrote in the Sumerian language. Made priestess of temples in the Sumerian cities of Ur (see Figure 1.9) and Uruk by her father, King Sargon, she used her priestly offices and literary gifts to further his political goal of uniting the Sumerians and the Akkadians. In these posts, she composed hymns to both Sumerian and Akkadian deities, and these hymns—some of which have been identified—became models for later poets. Enheduanna was especially devoted to Inanna, the Sumerian goddess of love, and she made this deity the subject of her best-known literary work, *The Exaltation of Inanna.* In this work, Enheduanna exalted, or raised, Inanna to supremacy in the Sumerian pantheon, her tribute for what she believed was Inanna's role in Sargon's triumph over a general uprising at the end of his reign.

Law The Mesopotamians produced the fairest law codes prior to that of the Hebrews. The central theme of Sumerian law, whose first existing records date from about 2050 B.C., was justice. From the earliest times, the Sumerian kings understood justice to mean "the straight thing"—that is, dealing fairly with all their subjects and prohibiting the exploitation of the weak by the strong. This concept of equity applied especially to economic matters, such as debts, contracts, and titles to land.

The most important set of laws from Mesopotamian civilization is that of the Babylonian king Hammurabi. Dating from about 1700 B.C., the Code of Hammurabi was found preserved on a seven-foot-high black stone

Figure 1.6 Code of Hammurabi. Ca. 1790–1750 B.C. Basalt, ht. approx. 3′. Louvre. *Hammurabi stands on the right, his hand raised before his mouth in the traditional Mesopotamian gesture of devotion, and Shamash, the sun god and protector of truth and justice, sits on the left. The cult of Shamash (in Sumeria, Utu) emerged from the earliest times, and this god's representation—flames shooting from the shoulders and hands holding symbols of power—was established in the Sumerian period. The relief, with its incised folds of cloth and ceremonial chair, is carved deep enough into the hard stone stele (7′ 4″) to suggest a three-dimensional sculpture.*

stele, or pillar. At the top, Hammurabi is depicted standing in front of Shamash, the Babylonian and Sumerian god of justice. Like other ancient lawgivers (Moses, for example), Hammurabi received the legal code from a deity. Below the two figures are carved the prologue, the collection of laws, and an epilogue (Figure 1.6). The prologue lists Hammurabi's accomplishments and sings his praises, while making it clear that the gods were the source of his power to establish "law and justice." The epilogue warns future rulers to carry out these laws or else be subject to defeat and ruin.

The laws concerning punishment for crimes are based on the judicial principle of *lex talionis,* or retaliation, which demands an "eye for an eye," although Hammurabi's code often substitutes payments in kind for damages done. Every major area of civil and criminal law was covered in the code, including property rights, sales, contracts, inheritance, adoption, prices and wages, sexual relations (much more severely restricted for women than for men), and personal rights for women, children, and slaves. Hammurabi's code, like other Mesopotamian laws, was only one part of a complex judicial system that encompassed judges, courts, trials, legal proceedings, and contracts.

Art and Architecture The art of Mesopotamia, like the rest of its culture, evolved from Sumerian styles to the Akkadian and Babylonian schools. Artisans worked in many forms—small seals, pottery, jewelry, vases, reliefs, and statues—and in many media—clay, stone, precious gems, gold, silver, leather, and ivory. Artifacts and crafted works from all three civilizations recorded the changing techniques of the producers as well as the shifting tastes of the consumers, whether they were rich individuals decorating their homes or officials issuing commissions for statues to adorn their temples. The temples, usually the center of the city and set on high mounds above the other structures, were often splendidly ornamented and housed exquisitely carved statues of gods and goddesses.

A fine example of Sumerian artistry is a bull's head carved on the sound box of a lyre (Figure 1.7). Working in gold leaf and semiprecious gems, the unknown artist has captured the vigor and power of the animal in a bold and simple style. Such elegant musical

Figure 1.7 Restored Sumerian Lyre, from Ur. Ca. 2600 B.C. Wood with gold leaf and inlays, ht. of bull's head, approx. 12". British Museum. *The lyre's sound box, on which the bull's head is carved, is a hollow chamber that increases the resonance of the sound. Music played an important role in Mesopotamian life, and patrons often commissioned the construction of elegant instruments. Thus, even at this early stage of civilization, those with wealth influenced the arts.*

Figure 1.8 *Gudea.* Ca. 2150 B.C. Diorite, ht. 17¾″. Louvre. *Little is known of Gudea, but more than thirty small statues of this Guti ruler have been found. The body and the head of this statuette were discovered separately and later joined together.*

instruments were played in homes and in palaces to accompany the poets and storytellers as they sang of the heroes' adventures and the deities' powers.

Mesopotamian artists carved thousands of figures, many on the walls of temples and palaces and others as free-standing statues. A notable early type of free-standing statue that became standard in Akkadian temples depicts a figure in a contemplative, worshiping pose, his hands folded and clasped in front of him. Many of these are likenesses of Gudea, a ruler who flourished about 2150 B.C. (Figure 1.8).

In contrast to the finely crafted sculpture, Mesopotamian architecture often seems uninspired, particularly the domestic architecture. Most Mesopotamian houses were square or rectangular. Even though the Mesopotamians knew about the arch, the vault, and the column, they did not employ them widely; they used primarily the basic **post-and-lintel construction** of two vertical posts capped by a horizontal lintel, or beam, for entranceways. The clay bricks used in construction limited the builders in styles and decorations, notably on the exterior. If private homes of clay bricks looked drab from the street, however, they were often attractive inside, built around an open courtyard with decorated rooms. The exteriors of temples and palaces were sometimes adorned with colored glazed bricks, mosaics, and painted cones arranged in patterns or, more rarely, with imported stone and marble.

Archeologists have not yet determined exactly how Mesopotamian cities were laid out. Urban centers were protected by walls, whose imposing and elaborately decorated gates proclaimed the city's wealth and power. The most prominent structure in each Sumerian city was the **ziggurat,** a terraced brick and mud-brick pyramid that served as the center of worship. The ziggurat resembled a hill or a stairway to the sky from which the deities could descend; or perhaps the structure was conceived as the gods' cosmic mountain. A temple of welcome for the gods stood on the top of the ziggurat, approached by sets of steps. Shrines, storehouses, and administrative offices were constructed around the base or on the several levels of the massive hill. In the low plain of the Tigris-Euphrates valley, the ziggurat literally and figuratively dominated the landscape. The Tower of Babel, described in the Jewish scriptures as reaching to the sky, may have been suggested by the Sumerian ziggurats, some of which had towers.

Of the numerous ziggurats and temples that have survived, the best preserved is at Ur, in southern Mesopotamia, dedicated to the moon god, Nanna (Figure 1.9). Built about 2100 B.C., this ziggurat was laid out to the four points of the compass. A central stairway led up to the highest platform, on which the major temple rested. Other cities constructed similar

Figure 1.9 Ziggurat of Ur. Ca. 2100 B.C. Ur (Muqaiyir, Iraq). *A temple to Nanna, the moon god, stood on the top of the ziggurat, which was terraced on three levels. On the first level was an entranceway approached by two sets of steps on each side and one in the front. The base, or lowest stage, which is all that remains of this "Hill of Heaven," measures 200 by 150 feet and stands 70 feet high. In comparison, Chartres cathedral in France is 157 feet wide, with each tower over 240 feet high.*

massive podiums in the hopes that they would please the gods and goddesses, that the rivers would be kind to them, and that life would continue. Thus, the central themes of Mesopotamian civilization manifested themselves in the ziggurats.

THE CIVILIZATION OF THE NILE RIVER VALLEY: EGYPT

Another great river, the Nile, provided the setting for Egyptian civilization. Unlike the culture of the Mesopotamian valley, however, Nilotic culture evolved continuously, responding mainly to internal changes rather than to external influences. It thus achieved a unified character that lasted for about three thousand years. Isolated by deserts on either side, Egypt developed an introspective attitude that was little influenced by neighboring cultures (such as Nubia, also called Kush, which flourished between the first and fourth cataracts, or waterfalls, of the Nile River) and that led to a sense of cultural superiority. Subjected to the annual floodings of the Nile and aware of the revolutions of the sun, Egypt saw itself as part of a cyclical pattern in a timeless world.

The periodic overflowings of the Nile made civilized life possible in Egypt. Red sandy deserts stretched east and west of the waterway. Beside the Nile's banks, however, the black alluvial soil of the narrow floodplain offered rich land for planting, although the river's gifts of water and arable land were limited. Irrigation canals and ditches plus patient, backbreaking labor were required to bring the life-giving liquid into the desert.

Because the survival and prosperity of the people depended on the Nile, the river dominated and shaped the Egyptian experience. About 95 percent of the people lived on the less than 5 percent of Egyptian land that was arable and that was located along the Nile. The resulting concentration of people led to the emergence of the agricultural village, the fundamental unit of Egyptian civilization. The reward for farm labor tended to be subsistence living, yet the perennial hope that next year's flood would bring a more bountiful harvest created an optimistic outlook that contrasted with the darker Mesopotamian view.

The Nile linked the "Two Lands," Upper and Lower Egypt, two regions whose differing geography made for two distinct ways of life. Since the Nile flows northward, Lower Egypt referred to the northern lands fed by the river's spreading delta, a region made wealthy by its fertile soil. In contrast, the harsh topography and poor farming conditions of the southern lands made Upper Egypt an area of near subsistence living. In addition, Lower Egypt, because of its proximity to both Mediterranean and Near Eastern cultures, tended to be more cosmopolitan than the provincial, isolated lands of Upper Egypt.

Timeline 1.3 EGYPTIAN CIVILIZATION **All dates approximate and B.C.**

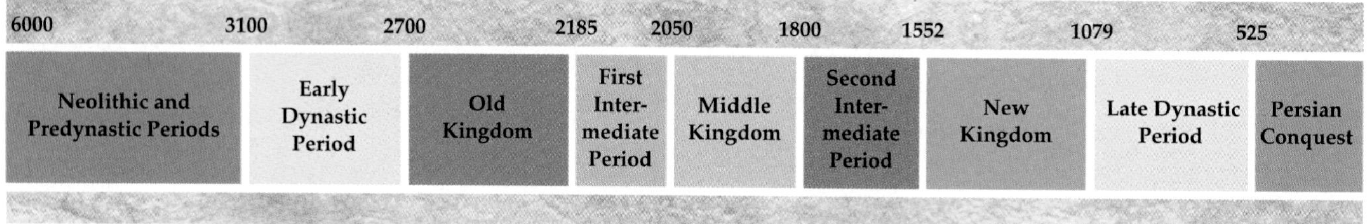

The earliest Neolithic settlers in the Nile valley probably arrived about 6000 B.C. These earliest Egyptians took up an agricultural life, wresting control of the surrounding lands, taming the river, and domesticating animals. In the rich alluvial soil, they cultivated barley, wheat, and vegetables for themselves and fodder for their animals. They hunted with bows and arrows and fished with nets, thereby supplementing their simple fare. They also planted flax from which thread was woven into linen on primitive looms. Most tools and weapons were made of stone or flint, but copper, which had to be imported, became more important after 3500 B.C. The early Egyptians lived in simply furnished, flat-topped houses built of sun-dried bricks. These basic patterns characterized peasant life throughout much of Egypt's history.

Continuity and Change over Three Thousand Years

Egypt stepped from the shadows of its illiterate past about 3100 B.C., when Menes [MEE-neez] proclaimed himself king and united the upper and lower lands. His power reached from the Mediterranean to the first cataract of the Nile, making Egypt a state to be reckoned with in the Near East. Egypt's lengthy, complex history is conventionally divided into twenty-six dynasties, which are in turn classified into groups. The three major groups of dynasties are known as the Old Kingdom, the Middle Kingdom, and the New Kingdom. They are preceded and followed, respectively, by two dynastic groups known as the Early Dynastic Period and the Late Dynastic Period. In addition, two intermediate dynastic groupings (the First and the Second) precede and follow the Middle Kingdom (Timeline 1.3).

In the Early Dynastic Period (about 3100–2700 B.C.), the kings brought prosperity through their control of the economy and fostered political harmony through diplomacy and dynastic marriages. These rulers, claiming to be gods on earth, adopted the trappings of divinity and built royal tombs to ensure their immortality.

With the Old Kingdom (about 2700–2185 B.C.), Egypt entered a five-hundred-year period of peace and prosperity, as its political institutions matured and its language was adapted to literary uses. The most enduring accomplishment of the Old Kingdom became the pyramid—the royal tomb devised by the Fourth Dynasty kings (Figure 1.10). As the visible symbol of the kings' power, the massive pyramids served to link the rulers with the gods and the cosmos. Yet, although the kings could impress their people with divine claims, they could neither subdue the forces of nature nor make their power last forever. For reasons not fully understood, these rulers loosened their control over the state and thus ushered in an age of political fragmentation called the First Intermediate Period.

In the First Intermediate Period (about 2185–2050 B.C.), civil war raged sporadically and starvation wiped out much of the populace. Eventually, a family from Thebes, in Upper Egypt, reunited the state and initiated the Middle Kingdom (about 2050–1800 B.C.). The new dynasty, the twelfth, fortified the southern frontier with Nubia and helped bring about a cultural renaissance, especially in literature, but unity was short-lived.

The Second Intermediate Period (about 1800–1552 B.C.) was an age of chaos provoked both by repeated failures of the Nile to flood and by a resurgence of local warlords. A weakened Lower Egypt succumbed to the Hyksos, Semitic-speaking invaders from Palestine. Backed by warriors in horse-drawn chariots, the Hyksos with their bronze weapons easily defeated the copper-armed Egyptians. The Hyksos era was crucial in Egypt's history because it ended the isolation that had fed a sense of cultural superiority. Egyptian nobility now joined aristocracies everywhere in employing the horse for war and sport, and Egyptian artisans fully entered the Bronze Age.

Ahmose I [AH-mos], a Theban king, drove out the Hyksos and inaugurated the New Kingdom (1552–1079 B.C.), the most cosmopolitan era in Egyptian history. Pursuing the Hyksos into Palestine, Ahmose conquered the foreign peoples along the way, creating the first Egyptian empire. To the northeast, Egypt's

Figure 1.10 The Pyramids at Giza. Ground view from the south. Pyramid of Menkure (foreground), ca. 2525 B.C.; Pyramid of Khafre (center), ca. 2590 B.C.; Pyramid of Khufu (rear), ca. 2560 B.C. *The Fourth Dynasty was the Age of Pyramids, when this characteristic shape was standardized and became a symbol of Egyptian civilization. The Great Pyramid, in the center, was the first structure at Giza; it originally stood 480 feet high but today is only 450 feet high.*

kings, now called pharaohs, pursued imperial ambitions against the cities in Palestine, Phoenicia, and Syria, a move that provoked deadly warfare with the Hittites of Anatolia. Egypt finally secured its possessions by peacefully dividing up the Near East with the Hittites and the Assyrians. To the south, the pharaohs pushed Egypt's frontiers to the Nile's fourth cataract, conquering the Nubians long in residence there. As the empire grew, Egypt's society underwent the greatest changes of its entire history, including religious innovation by a ruling family, widespread material affluence, extravagant temple building, and artistic and literary experimentation.

But imperial success declined after 1200 B.C., signaled by the pharaoh's growing dependence on unreliable foreign troops. Bands of nomads, called Sea Peoples by the Egyptians, began to disrupt trade and normal social life. Over the course of a century, the invaders forced Egypt to withdraw behind its historic borders and thus ended the empire. The success of the Sea People's challenge, despite their small numbers, lay in their new weapons, for these destructive migrants were the leading edge of the Age of Iron. Egypt's lack of iron ore probably contributed fatally to its military decline.

Egypt maintained continuity of tradition into the Late Dynastic Period (about 1079–525 B.C.). However, its independence came to an end with its successive incorporations into Nubian, Assyrian, and Persian empires.

Just as the pharaoh dominated the state, so the rulers controlled the predominantly agrarian economy, although departments of government or the priesthood of a temple often exploited the land and the king's serfs. Upper Egypt provided the bulk of farm produce that Lower Egypt exported to Mediterranean neighbors. In prosperous years, the pharaohs claimed up to half of the farm crops to support their building programs, especially funerary monuments. But in years of famine, dynasties fell and the state splintered into separate units.

Foreign trade was also a royal monopoly. The government obtained cedar from Lebanon, olive oil from Palestine, and myrrh from Punt, probably on the Somali coast. Since Egypt never developed a coinage, the pharaohs bartered for these imports with papyrus rolls (for writing), linen, weapons, and furniture. The pharaohs also exported gold from the eastern desert and copper from the Sinai peninsula. In addition, Egypt served as the carrier of tropical African goods—ebony, ivory, and animal skins—to the eastern Mediterranean.

Egyptian society was hierarchical, and at the top stood the pharaoh—the king and god incarnate. Because divine blood coursed through the ruler's veins, he could marry only within his own family. Tradition decreed that the Chief Queen, who was identified with the goddess Hathor, the mother of the god Horus, would produce the royal heir. If she failed to produce offspring, the successor pharaoh was selected from sons of the ruler's other wives or royal cousins. On rare occasions, when there was no suitable heir, the Chief Queen became the pharaoh, as did Hatshepsut [hat-SHEP-soot] in the New Kingdom.

Because there was no provision for a female king in Egyptian culture, the appearance of a female ruler is thought by scholars to signal a political crisis. Only four times in Egypt's three-thousand-year history was the king female; in contrast, there were more than two hundred male kings. Of the four female rulers, three appeared at the end of dynasties: Nitiqret in the Sixth Dynasty, Nefrusobk in the Twelfth, and Tausret in the Nineteenth. Hatshepsut's assumption of power was unique in that it occurred in the midst of a flourishing dynasty, though during the infancy of Thutmose III [thoot-MOH-suh], the heir apparent. Acting at first as regent to the young heir, she soon claimed the kingship in her own right and reigned for about ten years. After her death, Thutmose III obliterated her name and image from her monuments, though the reason for their removal is unclear. He may have been expressing hatred of her, or he may have wanted to erase the memory of a woman who had seized power contrary to *maat*, the natural order of things.

Ranked below the ruling family were the royal officials, nobles, large landowners, and priests, all generally hereditary offices. The pharaoh's word was law, but these groups were delegated powers for executing his will. On a lower level, artists and artisans worked for the pharaonic court and the nobility. Peasants and a small number of slaves formed the bulk of Egypt's population. Personal liberty took second place to the general welfare, and peasants were pressed into forced labor during natural disasters, such as floods, and at harvest time.

A Quest for Eternal Cultural Values

Until the invasion of the Hyksos, Egypt, in its splendid isolation, forged a civilization whose serene values and timeless forms deeply mirrored the religious beliefs of the rulers and the stability of the state. But as contact with other cultures and civilizations grew, Egyptian culture changed to reflect new influences. Writers borrowed words from other languages, for example, and sculptors displayed the human figure in more natural settings and poses. Still, Egyptian culture retained its distinctive qualities, and innovations continued to express traditional ideals.

Religion Egypt was a **theocracy,** or a state ruled by a god. Believing that the deities had planned their country's future from the beginning, the Egyptians thought of their society as sacred. From the time that Menes first united Egypt, religious dogma taught that the king, as god on earth, embodied the state. Egyptian rulers also identified themselves with the deities. For example, Menes claimed to be the "two ladies," the goddesses who stood for Upper and Lower Egypt. Other rulers identified themselves with Ra, the sun god, and with Ra's son, Horus, the sky god, who was always depicted as having the head of a falcon. Because of the king's divinity, the resources of the state were concentrated on giving the ruler proper homage, as in the Old Kingdom's massive tombs, designed on a superhuman scale to ensure his safe passage to the next life.

Egyptian subjects worshiped the pharaoh, but the pharaoh could venerate any deity he pleased. Hence, the shifting fortunes of Egypt's many cults depended on the ruler's preference. For example, Ptah (who, like the Hebrew God in Genesis, created through speech) became the god of Memphis, which was the capital of the Old Kingdom. The kings of the Fifth Dynasty, on the other hand, called themselves sons of Ra, the sun god, and they honored this celestial deity by building him temples more impressive than their own royal tombs. Later, the Twelfth Dynasty replaced Ptah with Amen (a word meaning "hidden one"), and a series of rulers adopted his name, as in Amenemhat [AH-men-EM-het]. Royal favor to a god generally increased the wealth and influence of the god's cult and priests. Consequently, by the time of the New Kingdom, society had become top-heavy with priests and their privileged religious properties.

Egypt came close to having a national deity during the New Kingdom when Akhenaton [ahk-NAHT-uhn] (r. about 1369–1353 B.C.) reshaped the royal religion at his capital, Amarna. Elevating Aten, the god of the sun's disk, to supremacy above the other gods, Akhenaten systematically disavowed the older divinities —a heretical view in tolerant, polytheistic Egypt. This innovation aroused the opposition of conservative nobles who supported the powerful priests of the Theban god, Amen. Akhenaten ultimately failed, and later pharaohs tried to erase his name and memory from history. The Amarna revolution, however, like the religious choices of the pharaohs generally, had little effect on the ordinary Egyptian, who continued to believe that the pharaoh could intervene with the other gods for the benefit of all.

The foremost distinguishing mark of Egyptian religion was its promise of immortality—a belief that generated a more optimistic attitude toward human existence than that found in Mesopotamia. At first, in the Old Kingdom, only the kings were accorded this reward. Eventually, nobles and royal officials were buried in the vicinity of the rulers' tombs, thereby ensuring their immortality as assistants to the risen god

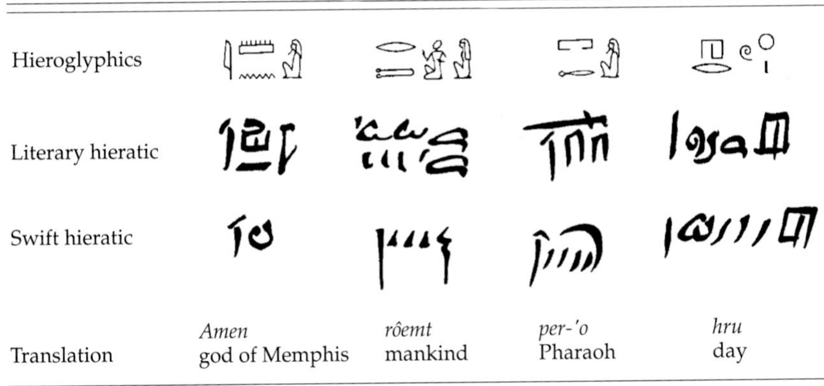

Figure 1.11 Egyptian Writing. *From the Old Kingdom onward, the hieroglyphs (in the top line) constituted the style of formal writing that appeared on tomb walls and in monuments. Religious and governmental scribes soon devised two distinct types of cursive script, a careful manuscript hand (in the middle line) and a more rapid hand (in the bottom line) for administrative documents and letters.*

in the afterlife. By the First Intermediate Period, the nobles had claimed their own right to immortality by erecting tombs on which the royal funerary texts were copied. Later, immortality apparently was opened to all Egyptians, although only the wealthy minority could afford the cost of a proper burial.

Writing and Literature Late predynastic Egypt learned the idea of writing, but not foreign words, from Mesopotamia. The Egyptians initially drew pictographs, called **hieroglyphs,** for such words as *hoe, arrowhead,* and *plow.* This early hieroglyphic script could also depict abstract words for which no adequate picture was available, but because such picture writing was time-consuming and clumsy to execute, the scribes soon made the pictographs function as signs, or clusters of consonants, for other words (Figure 1.11).

Egyptian literature produced no single great work that rivals *Gilgamesh,* but the Egyptian experience was rich in its variety of literary **genres,** or types of literature. For example, pyramid texts, the writings inscribed in burial chambers, formed the chief literary genre in the Old Kingdom. As this era gave way to the First Intermediate Period, new prose genres, such as prophecies and pessimistic writings, arose that addressed the prevalent political disintegration and social upheaval. Such was the tenor of the times that writers expressed views contradicting Egypt's otherwise optimistic attitudes to death and life. *The Dispute of a Man with His Soul* describes a desperate mortal finally choosing the emptiness of death rather than life in a materialistic and violent world.

The prophecies, **hymns** (songs of praise to the gods), and prose narratives of the Middle Kingdom constitute the classical period of Egyptian letters. The most famous work of the Middle Kingdom, as well as of all Egyptian literature, is the *Story of Sinuhe,* a prose tale that celebrates the ruler Senusert I and his subject, the hero named in the title. Fleeing Egypt, Sinuhe earns fame and fortune in Lebanon yet yearns for his beloved homeland. Sinuhe's exploits smack of the folk tale, for in one episode he subdues a taunting giant of a man, much as David defeats Goliath in the Old Testament story. Eventually, a gracious Senusert writes Sinuhe, forgiving his wandering subject's unnamed crime and inviting him to return home. The travel yarn concludes with a homecoming scene in which a joyful Sinuhe is reintegrated into Egyptian court society.

The richest period in Egyptian letters occurred during the New Kingdom. In addition to songs praising the pharaoh, poets now composed lyrics telling of the pain of parted lovers, and new genres included model letters, wisdom literature, and fairy tales. Akhenaten's revolution led to unique forms of literary expression, as in the *Hymn to Aten,* which praised this universal god. Although the hymn has similarities to Psalm 104 of the Old Testament, Akhenaten's text, unlike the Jewish scriptures, was not a declaration of **monotheism,** the belief that there is only one god. Instead, the *Hymn to Aten* recognized a special link between Akhenaten and his family and the god of the solar disk while still acknowledging the worship of other deities.

Architecture The classic Egyptian building was the pyramid, whose shape seemed to embody a constant and eternal order. During the Old Kingdom, the pyramid became the only building deemed suitable for a ruler-god's resting place preparatory to the afterlife. A modified version of the pyramid appeared first in about 2680 B.C. in the step pyramid of King Djoser [ZHO-ser] at Sakkareh, opposite Memphis (Figure 1.12). Later Egyptian rulers preferred the true pyramid form, and this design did not develop further.

The true pyramid appeared in the Old Kingdom when the Fourth Dynasty ruler Khufu [KOO-foo] erected the Great Pyramid at Giza, across the Nile from Cairo (see Figure 1.10). The anonymous architect executed this largest stone building in the world—6.25 million tons—with mathematical precision. Many of the tomb's two million stones were quarried on the site, although most were obtained farther upstream

Figure 1.12 IMHOTEP. Step Pyramid of King Djoser. Ca. 2680 B.C. Sakkareh, Egypt. *Though isolated from its neighbors until about 1730 B.C., Egypt was influenced by surrounding cultures, as the design for the step pyramid at Sakkareh shows. Resting on a rectangular base and rising in six progressively smaller stages, this pyramid was modeled on Mesopotamia's ziggurat. But unlike the ziggurats, which were made of dried clay bricks, it was built of cut stone, the first building to be so constructed in the world. The step pyramid has six levels on a 411- by 358-foot base and stands 204 feet high.*

Figure 1.13 SENMUT. Hatshepsut's Temple. Ca. 1490 B.C. Deir el Bahri, across from Luxor, Egypt. *Hatshepsut's temple was planned for the same purpose as the pyramids—to serve as a shrine for the royal remains. In actuality an ascending series of three colonnaded courtyards, this temple provided a spectacular approach to a hidden sanctuary carved in the steep cliffs.*

PERSONAL PERSPECTIVE

Egypt: The Instruction of Amenemope

Egypt's wisdom literature—aphorisms about the best way to live—culminated in The Instruction of Amenemope, *written in the late New Kingdom. In this work, the author stresses the ethical life rather than the amassing of personal wealth.*

Beginning of the teaching for life,
The instructions for well-being.

. . . .

If you make your life with these [words] in your heart,
You will find it a success;
You will find my words a storehouse for life,
Your being will prosper upon earth.

. . . .

Do not move the markers on the borders of fields,
Nor shift the position of the measuring-cord.
Do not be greedy for a cubit of land,
Nor encroach on the boundaries of a widow.

. . . .

Do not set your heart on wealth,
There is no ignoring Fate and Destiny;

. . . .

Do not strain to seek increase,
What you have, let it suffice you.

. . . .

Do not cheat a man (through) pen on scroll,
The god abhors it;
Do not bear witness with false words,
So as to brush aside a man by your tongue.

. . . .

Do not laugh at a blind man,
Nor tease a dwarf,
Nor cause hardship for the lame.

. . . .

Do not sit down in the beer-house
In order to join one greater than you,
Be he a youth great through his office,
Or be he an elder through birth.
Befriend a man of your own measure.

. . . .

Do not revile one older than you,
He has seen Re [the Sun God] before you;
Let (him) not report you to the Aten [the god of the sun's disk] at his rising,
Saying: "A youth has reviled an old man."

and ferried to Giza during the flooding of the Nile. The infinitesimally small deviation between the two sets of opposing base sides of the pyramid showed the scientific spirit already at work in this early stage of Egypt's history. Later, two of Khufu's successors, Khafre [KAF-ray] and Menkure [men-KOO-ray], added their pyramids to make the complex at Giza the symbol of the Old Kingdom and one of the wonders of the ancient world.

The pyramids eventually gave way to funerary temples when the New Kingdom pharaohs began to construct splendid monuments for themselves that reflected Egypt's new imperial status. The temple of Queen Hatshepsut is perhaps the most beautiful example of this architectural development (Figure 1.13). Designed by the royal architect Senmut, the temple of Hatshepsut was carved into the face of the mountain at Deir el Bahri, across the Nile from Luxor. Senmut, adopting the post-and-lintel style of construction, gave the queen's temple two levels of pillared colonnades, each accessible by long sloping ramps. The most arresting features of Hatshepsut's temple are its round columns, which are used alongside rectangular pillars in the **porticoes,** or covered entrances. These columns—with their plain tops and grooved surfaces—suggest the graceful columns of later Greek architecture, although some scholars dismiss this similarity as coincidental. Be that as it may, this Egyptian monument, like the later Greek temples, shows a harmonious sense of proportion throughout its impressive colonnades.

Rulers in both Egypt and Mesopotamia created zoos and botanical gardens, the first in the world, though the earliest evidence of these developments comes from Egypt. Built for pleasure and prestige and to satisfy scientific curiosity, the menageries and gardens originated before 2000 B.C.

Sculpture, Painting, and Minor Arts The Egyptians did not understand art as it is defined today. Indeed, they had no word for art. Rather than being art for art's sake, Egyptian painting and sculpture served as a means to a religious end, specifically to house the *ka*, or spirit of a person or deity. Art was more than mere representation; images embodied all of the subjects' qualities.

In the royal graveyard at Giza, artisans of the Old Kingdom carved from the living rock a mythical creature that stirred the imagination of most peoples in the ancient world—a sphinx, half lion and half man (Figure 1.14). Although this creature often inspired feelings of dread, in actuality there was little mystery to the sphinx, since its original purpose was to guard the royal tombs, perhaps to frighten away grave robbers. Indeed, this first sphinx's face was that of Khafre, the Fourth Dynasty king whose pyramid stood nearby. Today, this crumbling relic stands as a reminder of the claims to immortality of the Old Kingdom rulers.

The sheer size and mythical character of the Great Sphinx set it apart from Old Kingdom sculptures in the round, which favored human-scaled figures and realistic images. The life-size statue of King Menkure and his Chief Queen, found beneath the ruler's pyramid at Giza, show this art's brilliant realism (Figure 1.15). The sculpture embodies the characteristics of what became the standard, or classical, Egyptian style: their left legs forward, the king's clenched fists, their headdresses (sacred regalia for him and wig for her), their rigid poses, their serene countenances, and the figures' angularity. Although sculpted in the round, the couple was intended to be viewed from the front, so the work has a two-dimensional quality.

Figure 1.14 The Great Sphinx. Ca. 2560 B.C. Sandstone, 65′ high × 240′ long. Giza, Egypt. *Sphinxes, creatures part lion and part human, were often depicted in Egyptian art. The most famous sphinx is the one at Giza, carved from the rock on the site. The sphinx's colossal size prevented the anonymous sculptor from rendering it with any subtle facial expressions. More significant as a monument than as a great work of art, the Great Sphinx had a practical purpose—to guard the nearby pyramid tombs.*

Figure 1.15 *King Menkure and His Chief Queen.* Ca. 2525 B.C. Ht. 54½″. Museum expedition. Courtesy Museum of Fine Arts, Boston. *This life-size slate sculpture of Menkure, a Fourth Dynasty ruler, and his Chief Queen was removed from its resting place beneath the king's pyramid at Giza (see Figure 1.10). In this sculpture, the figures are represented as being of comparable size, unlike the usual depiction of husbands as much larger than their wives, indicating their greater importance. The sizes here probably reflect the royal status of the Chief Queen. The queen's subordination to the king is subtly shown in her position on his left side, thought to be inferior to the right, and her arm around his waist, an indication that her role was to encourage and support.*

Figure 1.16 *Hatshepsut*. Ca. 1460 B.C. Marble, ht. 6′ 5″. Courtesy Metropolitan Museum of Art. Rogers Fund and contribution from Edward S. Harkness, 1929. (29.3.2). *This sculpture is one of more than two hundred statues of Hatshepsut intended to adorn her massive and elegant funeral temple at Deir el Bahri in the western hills of Thebes. The authoritative pose and regalia convey her pharaonic status, and she is only subtly represented as a woman.*

In contrast to practices in the Old Kingdom, the wives of rulers in the New Kingdom acquired claims to divinity in their own right. A statue of Hatshepsut represents her in the clothing and with the sacred pose of pharaoh (Figure 1.16). Having first been Chief Queen to Thutmose II in the New Kingdom, after his death she seized leadership, probably with the cooperation of the powerful Theban priesthood of Amen. Although more than a thousand years separated this sculpture from that of Menkure (see Figure 1.15), in its expression of dignity and authority the statue of Hatshepsut bears a strong resemblance to the earlier work, thus demonstrating the continuity of the Egyptian style.

A major challenge to Egypt's traditional, austere forms occurred in Akhenaten's revolutionary reign. A low-relief sculpture of the royal family exemplifies the naturalism and fluid lines that this artistic rebellion favored (Figure 1.17). Akhenaten nuzzles one of his daughters in an intimate pose while his wife dandles another daughter on her knees and allows a third to stand on her right arm. The domesticity of this scene is quite unlike the sacred gestures of traditional Egyptian sculpture, but the religious subject of this relief remains true to that tradition, as the rays streaming from the disk of Aten onto the royal family indicate.

The most extraordinary artistic achievement of the Amarna period is the carved portrait head of Queen Nefertiti (Figure 1.18), a life-size sculpture discovered in 1912 by a team of German archeologists in the desert sands near the long-lost city founded by Akhenaten for the god Aten. This statue-head with its unfinished left eye, deliberate or accidental, is one of the most arresting images of world art. Painted in flesh tones and natural colors and imbued with the naturalism of the Amarna style, the queen has a fascinating vitality that is unsurpassed. A modern critic has called her the eternal female, ceaselessly watching.

Nefertiti's unusual headdress signifies her status as a potent force in this culture. Rising straight up from her forehead, this crown is decorated with the *uraeus*, the image of a cobra ready to strike. By custom, this powerful and protective symbol was part of the kingly **regalia** (tokens of royal authority) and could be worn only by rulers and their Great (principal) Queens. Modern scholars have proved that Nefertiti was the only Great, or Chief, Queen in Egypt's long history to actually share power with her husband. (Queen Hatshepsut actually ruled alone as pharaoh.) The prevalence of images of Nefertiti in so much of the art that remains from Amarna confirms this queen's importance on the political level and thus underscores her central role in the Amarna revolution.

Just as Egypt's sculpture in the round developed a rigid **canon,** or set of rules, so did two-dimensional

Figure 1.17 *Family Scene: Pharaoh Akhenaten, Queen Nefertiti, and Their Three Daughters.* Ca. 1350 B.C. Limestone, 13″ high × 15 5/12″ wide. Ägyptisches Museum, Berlin. *The religious ideas associated with Akhenaten's reforms are expressed in the lines streaming from the sun's disk above the royal couple. Each ray of the sun ends in a tiny hand that offers a blessing to the royal family.*

Figure 1.18 *Nefertiti.* Ca. 1350 B.C. Limestone, ht. 20″. Ägyptisches Museum, Berlin. *This portrait head of Nefertiti is characterized by sleekness and charm, a look achieved through the sculptor's fusing of the fluid Amarna style with the formality of Egypt's traditional art. To create the image of sleekness, the sculptor has pushed Nefertiti's face forward like the prow of a ship cutting through the wind. The figure's charm emerges from the tension between the queen's dreamy, deeply hooded eyes and her lively, arched eyebrows. The artist has succeeded in representing Nefertiti as both a woman and a goddess.*

Figure 1.19 Opening of the Mouth Scene, Funerary Papyrus of Hunefer. Ca. 1305–1195 B.C. British Museum. *Egyptian painters and sculptors always depicted human subjects from the side, with the feet in profile, as in this painting on a papyrus manuscript deposited in a New Kingdom tomb. This painting's treatment of flesh tones of the human figures also typifies the Egyptian style. Egyptian men, represented here by the officiating priests, were consistently shown with red-brown, tanned skins at least partially reflective of their outdoor lives. Egyptian women, such as the mourners directly before the mummy, were usually painted with lighter complexions of yellow or pink or white skin. The Opening of the Mouth was a burial ritual, preparing the deceased to speak in the afterlife.*

representations acquire a fixed formula, whether in relief sculptures or in wall paintings. The Egyptians never discovered the principles of perspective. On a flat surface, the human figures were depicted in profile, with both feet pointing sideways, as in the painting from a New Kingdom funerary papyrus shown in Figure 1.19. However, the artistic canon required that the eye and the shoulders be shown frontally, and both arms had to be visible along with all the fingers. The artist determined the human proportions exactly, by the use of a grid. Throughout most Egyptian art history, the human figure was conceived as being 18 squares high standing and 14 squares high seated, with each unit equivalent to the width of one "fist"; anatomical parts were made accordingly proportional. The canon of proportions was established by the time of the Old Kingdom, and its continued use, with slight variations, helped Egyptian art retain its

Figure 1.20 Banqueting Scene. Ca. 1567–1320 B.C. Fresco, 23 × 27¼″. British Museum. *In a small space, the Egyptian painter has created a delightful banqueting scene, a favorite subject in tomb decoration in the New Kingdom. No one eats at this ritual meal, for the purpose is to set the stage for the tomb owner's rebirth. The female figures, especially the young seminaked girls dancing (below) and serving (above), represent the female generative principle. The naked-girl motif in tomb paintings, which appeared at this time, was probably meant to ensure the tomb owner's fertility while living and the continuity of the family while the deceased was in the tomb awaiting rebirth. The lotus flowers on the heads of the female guests and musicians reflect the rebirth theme, since the lotus was used to symbolize the promise of immortality for the dead. The frontal pose of two of the lower figures is an artistic innovation. Faces were almost always shown in profile in Egyptian art (see Figures 1.17 and 1.19).*

Figure 1.21 *Selket.* Ca. 1325 B.C. Wood, overlaid with gesso and gilded, ht. 53⅝″. Cairo Museum, Egypt. *This life-size statue of the goddess Selket is one of the memorable artistic treasures discovered in Tutankhamen's tomb in 1923, one of the great archeological finds of this century. The sculpture's style, with its naturalism and fluid lines, reflects the art of Amarna, the revolutionary style that flourished briefly in the fourteenth century B.C., before being abandoned and replaced by Egypt's traditional formal style.*

Figure 1.22 Fugitives Swimming with Water-Skins. Ninth century B.C. Limestone, ht. 39″. British Museum. *Assyrian artists were masters of relief sculpture, as in this detail of a battle scene, created for the palace of King Ashurasirpal II at Nimrud. Archers pursue swimming fugitives, two of whom keep afloat with inflated animal skins (lower foreground). Despite the lack of depth and unconcern for relative dimensions, the relief vividly evokes Assyria's warrior culture.*

unmistakable style. Wall paintings, in contrast to relief sculptures, permitted a greater sense of space to be created, but the rules regarding the human figure still had to be observed (Figure 1.20). Given those stringent conventions, the Egyptian artists who worked in two dimensions were amazingly successful in creating the image of a carefree society bubbling with life.

Royal tombs have yielded incomparable examples of Egyptian sculpture, as in the burial chamber of the New Kingdom pharaoh Tutankhamen [too-tahn-KAHM-en]. Of the thirty-four excavated royal tombs, only that of King Tut—as he is popularly known—escaped relatively free from violation by thieves in ancient times. A freestanding, life-size sculpture of the funerary goddess Selket was one of four goddess figures placed outside the gilded shrine that contained the king's internal organs (Figure 1.21). Her arms are outstretched in a protective fashion around her royal charge's shrine. A unique feature is the turn of Selket's head, a violation of the cardinal rule of three-dimensional Egyptian art that figures face frontward (see Figures 1.15 and 1.16). Selket's pose suggests that she was looking for intruders.

HEIRS TO THE MESOPOTAMIAN AND EGYPTIAN EMPIRES

With the decline of Mesopotamian and Egyptian empires after 1000 B.C., successor kingdoms arose in the eastern Mediterranean, notably those of the Hittites, the Assyrians (Figure 1.22), the Medes, and the Persians. If the length of their rule and the richness of their achievements failed to measure up to those of Mesopotamian and Egyptian civilizations, they nevertheless brought law and order to numerous peoples over vast territories and offered a convincing model of civilized life.

The Hittites and the Assyrians were rival empires whose fortunes ebbed and flowed (Timeline 1.4). In 612 B.C., Nineveh, the Assyrian capital city, was sacked by the Medes, an Indo-European people from the southwest Iranian plateau, and the Assyrian empire passed under their control. Medean rule, however, was shortly supplanted when their empire fell to the Persians, another nomadic Indo-European tribe, in about 550 B.C. With masterful skill, successive Persian rulers forged the strongest and largest empire that the eastern Mediterranean had seen until this time. At its height, Persian rule extended from Egypt in the south to central Russia in the north, and from Cyprus in the west to the Indus River in the east. Only Greece eluded Persia's grasp. In 327 B.C., Alexander the Great defeated the last Persian king, thus allowing the Greeks to assimilate the Persian lands.

Persian culture followed in the footsteps of Assyrian culture, but Persian art lacked the savagery associated with the Assyrian style. Instead, Persian art emphasized contemplative themes with less action (Figure 1.23). Persian culture's most original and enduring contribution was the religion of Zoroaster [ZOHR-uh-was-ter], or Zarathustra [zah-ra-THUSH-trah], a prophet who lived in about 600 B.C. Rejecting polytheism, Zoroaster taught a dualistic religion in which the god of light, Ahuramazda, engaged in a universal struggle with the god of darkness, Ahriman. According to Zoroaster, those who lead puritanical lives not only gain favorable treatment in the afterlife but also ensure the triumph of the forces of good. Key ideas of Zoroastrianism influenced other religions: Zoroaster's martyrdom, the prophet's life filled with miracles, the evil spirit as the Prince of Darkness, and the notion of a Last Judgment.

Timeline 1.4 HEIRS TO THE MESOPOTAMIAN AND EGYPTIAN CULTURES **All dates approximate and B.C.**

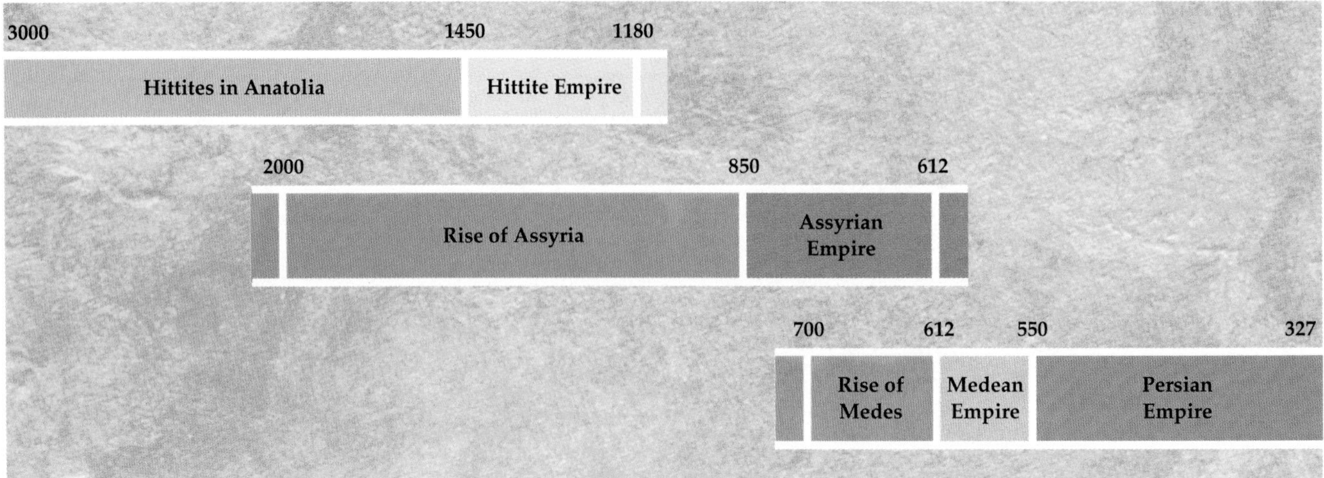

Figure 1.23 Darius Giving Audience Before Two Fire Altars. Found in the Treasury, Persepolis. Ca. 512–494 B.C. Limestone, length 20′. Archeological Museum, Teheran. *This relief sculpture, carved on the walls of the Treasury at Persepolis, shows King Darius (seated center) before two fire altars. In front of him is the master of ceremonies, with his hand raised to his lips in a gesture of devotion. Behind Darius is his son, Xerxes, with two attendants, one of whom is armed with a sword. Two bodyguards, holding spears, stand on each end of the scene. The Persian sculptural style is shown by the stylized hair and beards, precise folds in the clothing, and the formal poses of the figures.*

The Legacy of Early Near Eastern Civilizations

Mesopotamia and Egypt provided the earliest models of civilization in the West. In both, large numbers of people were organized into societies characterized by class stratification; a division of labor; complex political, economic, and religious forms; technological advances (pottery and glass-making, the extraction and working of metals, textiles, woodworking, and building techniques); and cultural achievements. They weren't the only ancient civilizations—others developed in China, India, South America, and elsewhere—but they are the ones to which Westerners most directly trace their cultural roots.

Mesopotamia's gifts to Western civilization are impressive. In addition to writing, these societies established urbanism as a way of life in contrast to agrarian or village existence. In more practical matters, they created a mathematical system based on 60 that gave the world the 60-minute hour and the 360-degree circle. They also divided the seasons and devised a lunar calendar to mark off periods of days to aid them in their planting. Trade and commerce forced them to develop methods of counting, measuring, and weighing that became the standard procedures for other Near Eastern peoples for centuries. Mesopotamian myths, legends, and epics found their way into the folk tales and literature of other cultures.

Egypt made equally impressive contributions to the West. Egyptian bureaucrats, who wanted to predict the correct date for the rising of the Nile's waters, originated a solar calendar that is the basis of the Western calendar. The Egyptian model, which divided the year into twelve months of thirty days, each with five days of holiday at the end, was conveyed to Western culture by the Romans. In architecture, Egyptian builders devised the column with a decorated capital, which later Greek architects probably adopted. The Greek builders also borrowed the Egyptian tradition of sound engineering principles rooted in mathematics. Similarly, Greek sculptors owed a debt to Egyptian forms and poses. Indeed, the Egyptian idea of an aesthetic canon influenced both sculptors and artists in Greece.

In literature, the Egyptians explored a variety of genres—such as wisdom writing—and folk tales that influenced the Hebrews and the Greeks. In science, Egyptian physicians became renowned throughout the Near East for their medical learning and knowledge of drugs. Finally, with its priceless treasures, its mysterious pyramids, and its cult of the dead, Egypt inspired curiosity and excitement in foreigners from ancient times onward. One of the first Western tourists to visit Egypt was the Greek historian Herodotus, whose writings in the fifth century B.C. helped to create the Egyptian mystique. The world's fascination with the culture of ancient Egypt has not abated today.

KEY CULTURAL TERMS

culture
civilization
Paleolithic
Neolithic
pictogram
ideogram
phonogram
cuneiform
polytheism
anthropomorphism
pantheism
stele
post-and-lintel construction
ziggurat
theocracy
hieroglyphs
genre
hymn
monotheism
portico
regalia
canon

SUGGESTIONS FOR FURTHER READING

PRIMARY SOURCES

KASTER, J., ed. and trans. *The Literature and Mythology of Ancient Egypt*. London: Allen Lane, 1970. An anthology that includes creation myths, rituals, stories, songs, proverbs, and prayers.

KRAMER, S. N. *History Begins at Sumer.* Philadelphia: University of Pennsylvania Press, 1981. A standard collection of original Sumerian sources by one of the most renowned modern Sumerian scholars.

PRITCHARD, J. B. *Ancient Near Eastern Texts Relating to the Old Testament.* Princeton: Princeton University Press, 1969. For the serious student, a collection of the most important nonbiblical texts, including myths, histories, prayers, and other types of writing.

SANDARS, N. K., ed. *The Epic of Gilgamesh.* New York: Penguin, 1972. The editor's informative introduction sets the tone for this famous ancient epic.

WINDOWS ON THE WORLD: 5000–500 B.C.

HISTORY

AFRICA

Neolithic period, ca. 3000–1000 B.C. Pastoral culture (which had begun ca. 8000 B.C.) in the Sahara disappeared as savannas dried up. Hunters and gatherers prevailed elsewhere, though farming slowly spread southward. Three racial groups: Caucasoid peoples in the north and northeast, Khoisan peoples in the open areas from the Sahara south to the Cape, and Negroid peoples in the central forests and the west. *Nubian, or Kushan, culture.* Rule by strong chieftains (ca. 3100–2600 B.C. in Lower Nubia; ca. 2050–1550 B.C. in Upper Nubia) alternated with conquest and occupation by the Egyptians. First Nubian kingdom, Kush, established 1100 B.C.: the first known African kingdom outside Egypt. Noted for art, learning, and trade. One of the first African centers of iron making, ca. 1000 B.C. Kush's kings conquered and ruled Egypt (ca. 750–666 B.C.). Capital shifted from Napata to Meroë (592 B.C.)

AMERICAS

Ca. 25,000 B.C. Humans may have first entered Western Hemisphere from Asia over Bering Strait land bridge. Had migrated throughout hemisphere by ca. 12,000 B.C.

Mesoamerica Maize introduced ca. 5000 B.C. *Olmec culture, began 1500 B.C.* South coast of Gulf of Mexico. "Mother culture" of Mesoamerican civilizations invented ballcourt, pyramid, pantheon of gods, and perhaps invented ritual calendar and glyph writing.

Andes *Pre-Ceramic period, 3000–1800 B.C.* Tribes and clans in villages. *Initial period, 1800–800 B.C.* Farming intensified. *Chavín culture, began 1000 B.C.* Center at Chavín de Huantar; importer of luxury goods.

Native North America *Clovis culture, from ca. 9500 B.C.* Southwest U.S., earliest well-documented archeological remains in North America. *Mississippian culture.* Earthworks at Poverty Point, Louisiana (after 1300 B.C.).

ART

AFRICA

Neolithic period. Rock carvings and paintings of animals and people in various regions, with the majority (over 30,000) in the Sahara.

Giraffes. Ca. 5000 B.C. Rock engraving, ht. 6–7". Libya.

AMERICAS

Mesoamerica *Olmec culture.* Altars and massive sculptures of heads, probably of rulers, in religious centers.

Andes Fine textiles from ca. 10,000 B.C. *Pre-Ceramic period.* Animal-figured textiles, mosaics, mirrors, earrings, featherwork, female figurines. *Initial period.* Fired clay pottery for cooking, ca. 1800 B.C. Giant stone sculptures, painted reliefs, and wall murals in public plazas. *Chavín culture.* First unifying Andean artistic style; images of jaguars, snakes, and composites of animals and humans.

ARCHITECTURE

AFRICA

Nubian culture. Kerma, capital of Upper Nubia, was the first settlement in Africa south of Egypt that can be called a city. Kerma in its classical period (ca. 1750–1580 B.C.) reflected Nubian traditions in wood and mudbrick palaces, temples, governmental buildings, and city walls and gates. In the Kushan kingdom, Nubian culture was fully Egyptianized, especially in building styles and city planning.

AMERICAS

Mesoamerica *Olmec culture.* Elaborate religious and ceremonial centers at San Lorenzo, La Venta, and Trés Zapotes, inhabited by the elite, with temple mounds, huge sculptures and altars, and a complex system of drains and lagoons.

Andes *Pre-Ceramic period.* Monumental public architecture, the oldest in the Americas, with traditional features, such as artificial mounds, plazas, and courtyards.

RELIGION, PHILOSOPHY, LITERATURE

AFRICA

Nubian culture. Kings, especially in the Kushan period, adopted the Egyptian practice of divine rulers supported by hierarchical administrations.

AMERICAS

Mesoamerica *Olmec culture.* A pantheon of gods identified with tropical rain-forest fauna, especially the jaguar. The key religious belief was that a shaman, or spiritual leader, could undergo a mystical transformation into a sacred creature or plant.

Andes *Chavín culture.* The capital, Chavín, was a pilgrimage center for Andean people.

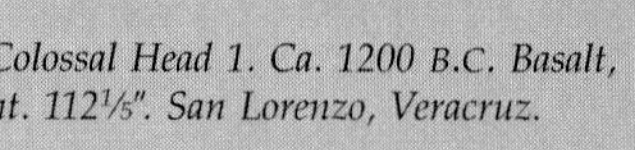

Colossal Head 1. Ca. 1200 B.C. Basalt, ht. 112⅕". San Lorenzo, Veracruz.

ASIA

China

Neolithic period, ca. 5000–1766 B.C. Tribes and clans living in villages in the Yellow River valley in the north, along the Chang (Yangtze) River to the south, and at remote sites in far northeastern China. Hunting, fishing, and farming; diet based on millet. *Shang Dynasty, 1766–1122* B.C. Rise of Bronze Age culture. Kings controlled much of China with support of warrior landlords. Capital cities Ao and Anyang founded. Rulers buried in pits with equipment and regalia for afterlife. *Chou Dynasty, 1122–481* B.C. Loose grouping of feudal vassal states; divided into Eastern and Western Chou (771).

India

Indus, or Harappan, culture, ca. 2600–1900 B.C. Urban civilization dominated by the cities of Harappa and Mohenjo-daro in Indus River valley and extending over modern Pakistan and western India. Trading society; no centralized ruler or military elite. Mixed technology of stone and bronze. First literate state east of Mesopotamia. *Aryan culture, 1500–500* B.C. Aryan peoples from Persia infiltrated and eventually conquered northern India and its resident peoples, setting up an agrarian society arranged into the Vedic caste system, with cattle as the major form of wealth. Iron introduced ca. 1000 B.C.

Japan

Jōmon culture. Beginning (ca. 2500 B.C.) of last phase of village culture, born ca. 11,000 B.C. Hunting, gathering, and fishing. By end of period, cultivation of yams and taro, imported from Asian mainland.

Neolithic period. Much traditional Chinese culture dates from this period, such as the use of jade, wood, silk, ceremonial clay vessels, and perhaps chopsticks. *Shang Dynasty.* Unique type of gray bronze used for ritual objects for royal court. *Chou Dynasty.* Bronzes, with inscriptions and animal motifs. Exaggerated details.

Four-Legged Vessel. Ca. 1523–1028 B.C. *Bronze, ht. 15¼". People's Republic of China.*

Harappan culture. Seals carved with animal and human forms, pottery, toys, and figurines of important personages.

Bust of a Priest-King or Deity from Mohenjo-daro. Ca. 2000–1750 B.C. *Steatite, ht. 6⅞". National Museum of Pakistan, Karachi.*

Jōmon culture. Jōmon, or "rope pattern," hand-thrown pottery. Also bracelets and earrings in ivory and bone.

Shang Dynasty. Timber houses with rammed earth floors, wattle and daub walls, and thatched roofs; rammed earth walls to encircle cities and to separate urban nobility from craftspeople and merchants.

Harappan culture. Brick-walled cities, laid out in grids and served by wells, bathhouses, and a system of wastewater drains. *Aryan culture.* No ruins survive.

Jōmon culture. Basic house was either a circular or rectangular hut with a pit floor.

Shang Dynasty. Writing in characters appeared soon after 1700 B.C. on inscribed bones consulted as oracles about great decisions of state. This pictographic language is the basis of Chinese writing today.

Harappan culture. The writing has not been deciphered. *Aryan culture.* Brought Indo-European languages and Vedism, the Vedic religion centered on sacrifices to deities and presided over by priests, or brahmans, who (between the 15th and 5th centuries B.C.) composed a body of religious texts, known as the Vedic corpus or simply the Vedas. These texts were written in Sanskrit, a language derived from the ancient Indo-European, ancestor of many of today's European languages. Vedism was the starting point for the later Hindu religion.

Jōmon culture. Simple burial rites in small pits dug near dwellings. Aspects of the burial (knees drawn up or stone clasped to chest) suggest either magical or religious practices. Perhaps a belief in fertility goddesses, as indicated by large numbers of female figurines made of clay.

2 AEGEAN CIVILIZATIONS
The Minoans, the Mycenaeans, and the Greeks of the Archaic Age

Although Mesopotamia and Egypt offer successful models of civilization, the tradition of Greece is often the first in which Westerners feel they can recognize themselves. What ties most moderns to ancient Greece is the Greeks' vision of humanity, for they were the first to place human beings at the center of the universe. The Near Eastern cultures focused on deities and godlike rulers, paying little heed to the strivings of humanity. The Greeks, on the other hand, no longer saw mortals as the inconsequential objects of divine whim. Men and women assumed some importance in the scheme of things; they were seen as having some control over their destinies and some moral responsibility for their actions. By the fifth century B.C., the Greek philosopher Protagoras could proclaim, "Man is the measure of all things."

With their new way of thinking, the Greeks surged forward in all areas of creativity, ultimately reaching heights that some think have never been equaled. Because of their grandeur and noble appeal, Greek poetry, sculpture, and architecture became the standard against which later works were frequently judged. From the Greeks the Western tradition has inherited many of its political forms and practices, its views on human behavior, its insistence on philosophical rigor, and its approach to scientific inquiry. In essence, through their human-centered consciousness and their cultural achievements, the Greeks laid the foundation of Western civilization.

Greek culture developed in the basin of the Aegean Sea (Map 2.1). On rocky coasts and rugged islands and peninsulas, the people coaxed a subsistence living from the thin, stony soil and turned to the sea for trade, conquest, and

◀ Acropolis, Athens. *View from the west.*

Map 2.1 THE AEGEAN WORLD

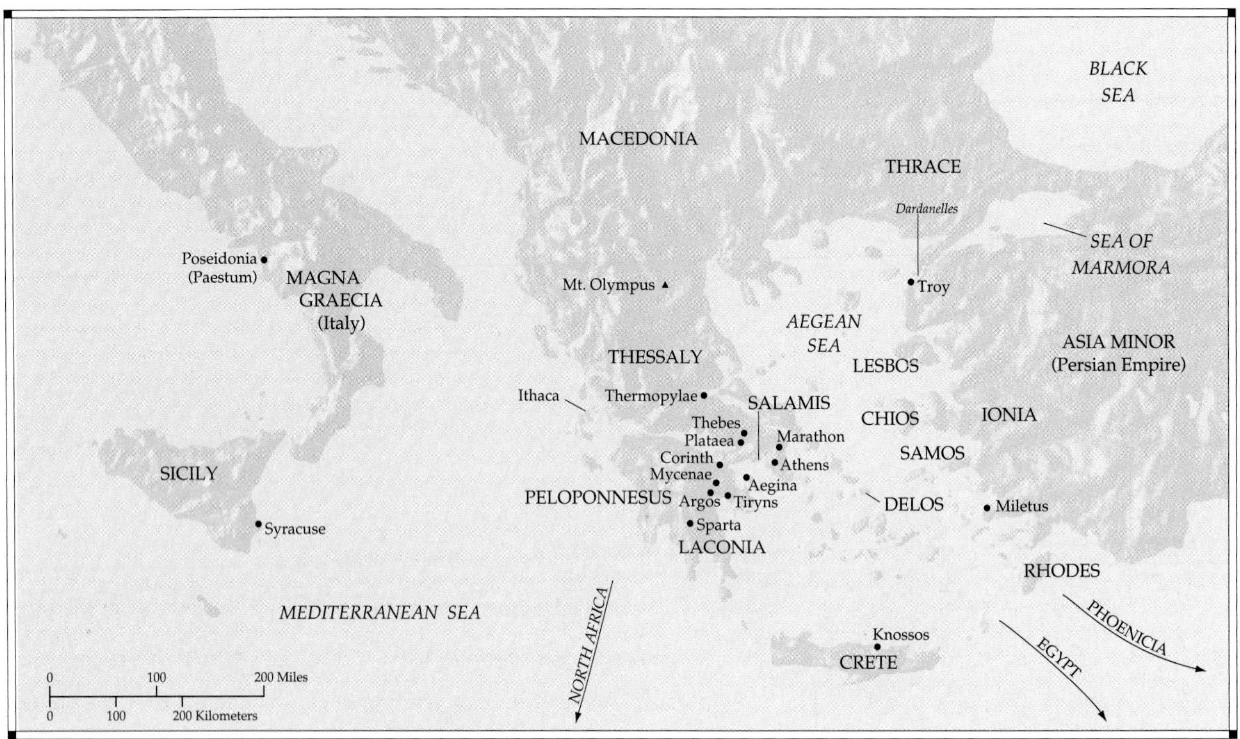

expansion. During the Bronze Age, the inhabitants of the island of Crete and the Greek peninsula traded with the Egyptians and the Hittites of Anatolia. The early Greeks borrowed and adapted a writing system from the Phoenicians. They were indebted to the Egyptians for sculptural techniques and to other Near Eastern civilizations for techniques in working with metal and clay, for music and mathematics, and for elements of their religious system.

The people we refer to as the Greeks were not the first to thrive in the Aegean basin. Two other distinctive civilizations—the Minoan and the Mycenaean—established centers of culture in the area and left their mark on the Greeks of the Archaic Age (which dates from about 800 B.C.) who followed (Timeline 2.1).

PRELUDE: MINOAN CIVILIZATION, 3000–1300 B.C.

While civilizations were flourishing in Egypt and Mesopotamia, another culture was developing among the Neolithic settlements on the island of Crete. By about 2000 B.C., a prosperous and stable mercantile civilization had emerged, and between 1700 and 1400 B.C., it reached its high point in wealth, power, and sophistication. This society, labeled Minoan after King Minos, a legendary Cretan ruler, apparently was organized into a complex class system that included nobles, merchants, artisans, bureaucrats, and laborers. Noble life was based in palaces, and twentieth-century archeological excavations of several palace sites indicate that communities were linked in a loose political federation, with the major center at Knossos on the north coast. Remarkably, no fortified walls protected the Minoan palaces, suggesting that the cities remained at peace with one another and that the island itself afforded adequate protection against invading sea raiders. Crete's tranquil image is further supported by the absence of weapons in excavated remains.

The palace at Knossos has revealed more about Cretan life than has any other cultural artifact. The ruins, though no longer paved or walled, still provide a sense of the grandeur and expanse of this once-magnificent site (Figure 2.1). It included an impressive plumbing and drainage system and a complex layout of rooms and passageways on several levels. Below ground, a storage area contained huge earthenware pots that held grains, oils, and wines, probably collected as taxes from the populace and serving as the basis of trade and wealth. Beautiful **friezes** (bands of designs and figures) decorated the walls of rooms and hallways. **Frescoes**—paint applied directly on wet plaster—of dolphins, octopuses, and other ocean creatures enlivened the palace walls.

Timeline 2.1 MINOAN AND MYCENAEAN CIVILIZATIONS **All dates approximate and B.C.**

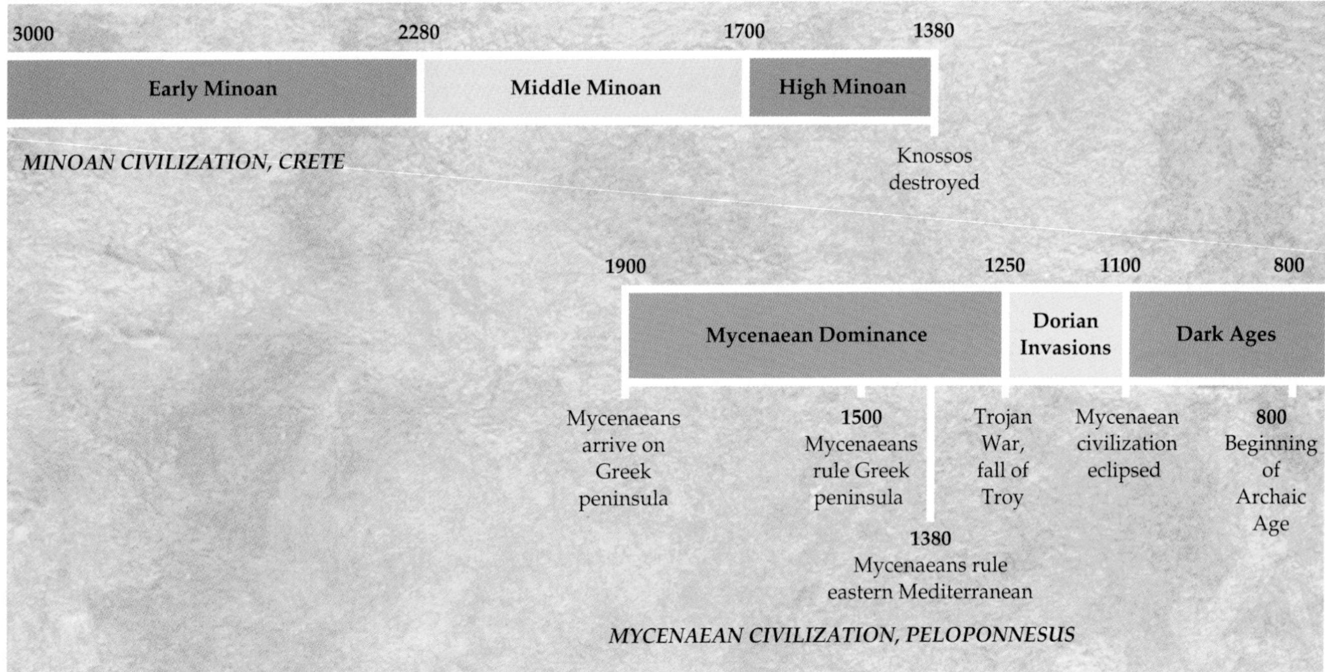

Figure 2.1 Palace at Knossos. Aerial view from the east. Ca. 1750–1650 B.C. *The palace complex, with courtyards, staircases, and living areas, now partially restored, indicates that the royal family lived in comfort and security, surrounded by works of art. When British archeologist Sir Arthur Evans uncovered these ruins in 1902, he became convinced that he had discovered the palace of the legendary King Minos and labeled the civilization Minoan—a descriptive term used interchangeably with* Cretan.

Figure 2.2 Earth Goddess with Snakes. Ca. 1600–1580 B.C. Faience, ht. 13½". Archaeological Museum, Heraklion, Crete. *This cult figure was discovered in the Treasury of the Knossos Palace. Her triangular dress, with its apron and flounced skirt, is similar to those of Cretan youths in surviving frescoes.*

Figure 2.3 *Bull-Leaping.* Ca. 1500 B.C. Archaeological Museum, Heraklion, Crete. *This fresco (approximately 32 inches high) from the east wing of the palace at Knossos is one of the largest paintings recovered from Crete. The association of young men and women with bulls in this scene brings to mind the legend of the Minotaur, in which seven youths and seven maidens were periodically sacrificed to a monster, half man and half bull, who lived in an underground labyrinth, supposedly on Crete.*

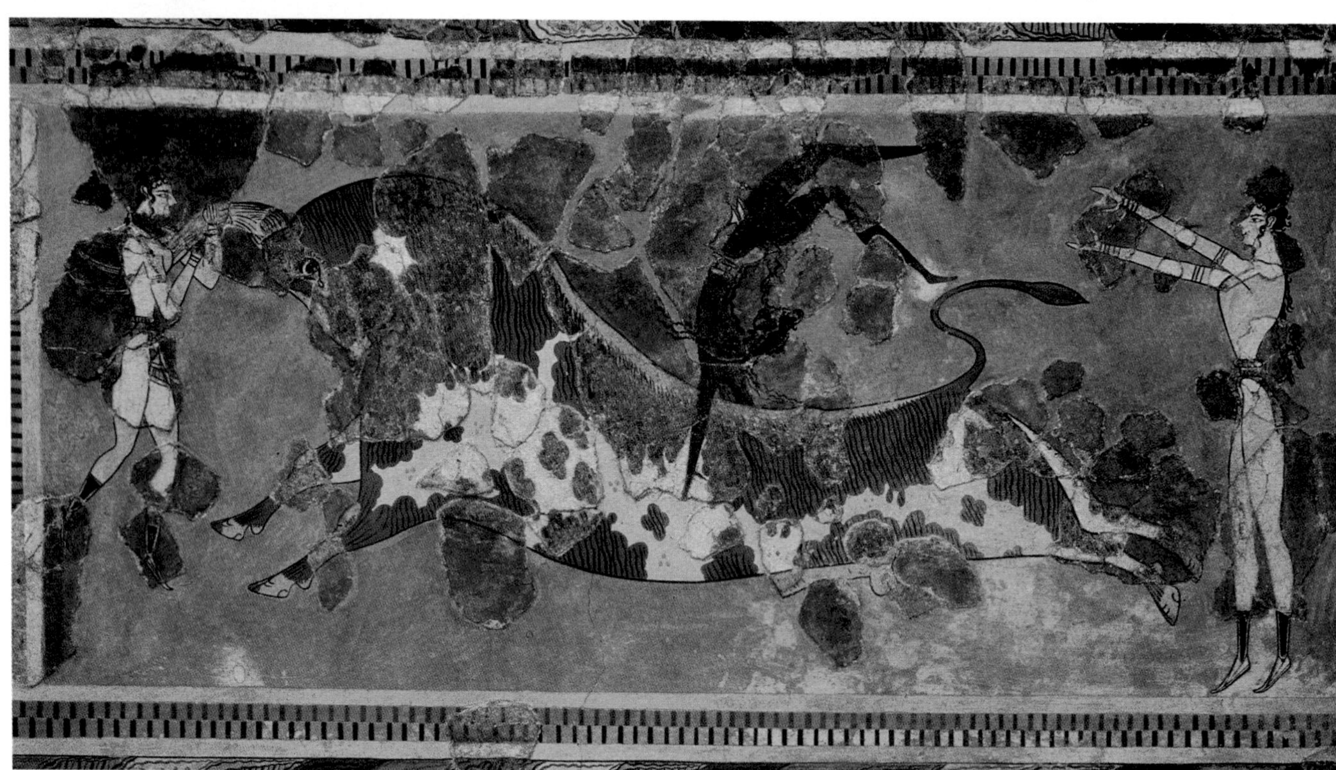

The early Minoans developed a pictorial form of writing on clay tablets that was replaced in about 1800 B.C. by a still undeciphered script known as **Linear A. Linear B,** which superseded Linear A, flourished from about 1400 to the collapse of Minoan civilization in around 1300, though it remained in use in a few scattered places on the Greek mainland for about two hundred years. When Linear B was deciphered, it proved to be an early form of Greek. The Linear B writings revealed nothing of Minoan political, social, or philosophical systems but were used to record commercial transactions.

Minoan religion appears to have been matriarchal, centering on the worship of a mother goddess, or great goddess, creator of the universe and source of all life. Statues of a bare-breasted earth goddess with snakes in her hands show how the deity was portrayed by the Minoans, but the precise purpose of these statues is unknown (Figure 2.2). Minoans also honored numerous minor household goddesses and venerated trees and stone pillars, to which they probably attributed supernatural powers. Near the end of their era, the Minoans began to bury their dead in underground tombs and chambers, but neither the reason for the new burial practice nor its ritualistic meaning has been discovered.

What has been uncovered on the palace walls is a fresco depicting bull-leaping—a sport or ritual activity that perhaps was associated with a bull cult (Figure 2.3) and that apparently had deep religious significance. Regardless of its meaning, this daring act is probably more fiction than fact: The maidens (painted white) stand at either end of the bull while a male athlete (painted red) somersaults over the beast's back, a feat that is virtually impossible to accomplish.

Minoan trade dominated the eastern Mediterranean until about 1380 B.C., when the island was devastated by a natural catastrophe—perhaps a volcanic eruption on a nearby island, an earthquake, a tidal wave, or a combination of those disasters. Weakened by Mycenaean incursions over the preceding centuries, Minoan civilization quickly fell to these raiders from the Greek mainland or to other invading seafarers. Whatever the whole story, the Minoans disappeared suddenly and mysteriously, leaving few remnants of their peaceful civilization.

The Greeks of the later Archaic Age had no direct knowledge of Minoan civilization, but the Greek attitude toward the Minoans was shaped by mythology. Myths are usually considered fiction, but buried within them are often actual folk memories or deep psychological truths.

For example, Crete is traditionally the birthplace of the god Zeus. The Minoans worshiped a Zeus who was born in a cave, grew to manhood, and died. They venerated the site of his birth and honored him as a child. The later Greeks, however, believed Zeus to be the immortal father and ruler of the Olympian deities, and they were incensed by the Minoan belief that the god died. The grain of truth in this story may be that although the Greeks eventually dominated Crete in physical terms, elements of Minoan religion found their way into later Greek beliefs; thus, in a sense, the Olympian gods *were* born in Crete. Cretan influences on Greece may also be detected in language, social organization, and economic pursuits, although the Archaic Greeks did not regard the Minoan past as part of their heritage.

BEGINNINGS: MYCENAEAN CIVILIZATION, 1900–1100 B.C.

Unlike the Minoans, the Mycenaeans continued to live for the Greeks of the Archaic Age through the *Iliad* and the *Odyssey.* The events related in these two epic poems occur during the Mycenaean Age, and the stories furnished the Greeks with many of their heroes—Achilles, the doomed warrior, for example, and Odysseus, the tough and wily wandering sailor. Eventually, the Greeks traced their tradition to Mycenae, honoring its warriors as their ancestors and as models of ideal noble behavior and values.

Mycenaean civilization, named by archeologists for Mycenae, one of its most prominent fortress cities, developed on the rugged lower Greek peninsula known as the Peloponnesus. An aggressive warrior people, perhaps from the plains of southern Russia or from the Tigris-Euphrates valley, the Mycenaeans arrived on the peninsula in about 1900 B.C., and by about 1500 B.C., they ruled the entire Peloponnesus.

A feudal order similar to that found later in medieval Europe characterized the Mycenaean political system. Family ties and marriages, tentative alliances, and uneasy truces bound the local rulers in a confederation of petty kingdoms. The kings of these fortress states and their warriors controlled the surrounding countryside. A staunch loyalty developed between the kings and their noble allies, generating a rigid class structure that exploited those who were not warriors.

A royal tax system created a need for a large bureaucracy of collectors and civil employees. At the low end of the social scale stood the merchants, traders, artisans, small landowners, peasants, and slaves—the last, like the royal servants, probably captured in wars or raids.

The ruins of the Mycenaean fortress-palaces, with their massive double walls, narrow escape passages, and wide gateways, stand as mute testimony to the

Figure 2.4 The Lion Gate at Mycenae. Ca. 1300 B.C. *The Lion Gate is a massive structure of four gigantic blocks—two posts and a beam forming the entrance and a triangular block on which are carved the two 9-foot-high lions and the central column. So impressive were the megalithic fortresses of the Mycenaeans to the later Greeks that they called them cyclopean, convinced that only a race of giants, the Cyclopes, could have built them.*

harshness of the militaristic life and the power of the local king. The best-known palace ruin, at Mycenae, contains the famous Lion Gate, constructed from four massive hewn stones, or **ashlars** (Figure 2.4). On one of these stones, two carved lions, separated by a column, face each other and stretch out their long, muscular bodies. Their heads, now missing, were made of metal, perhaps bronze or gold. Placed there to guard the fortress and to remind the populace of the ruler's power, the beasts must have intimidated all visitors who entered or left the citadel.

Within the fortresses and across the eastern Mediterranean, archeologists have found jars, containers, vessels, and terra-cotta figurines, revealing the high level of the Mycenaeans' artistic skill with clay and their wide-ranging trade and travel. The weapons and personal items crafted for the warriors show especially impressive artistic skills. A decorated sword blade of a lion hunt, inlaid in gold and silver, exemplifies the artisan's attention to delicate detail (Figure 2.5).

Mycenaean religion appears to have been a fusion of Minoan and local deities. Like the Minoans, the Mycenaeans venerated numerous household goddesses and worshiped aspects of nature in caves and natural shrines. Local deities seem to have been of two kinds: Some were predecessors of the Olympian gods and goddesses worshiped by the later Greeks and had the same names; others were nature divinities and spirits. Six **shaft graves** have been excavated at Mycenae (Figure 2.6). These graves have yielded fabulous gold treasures, such as the two carved panels from a sixteenth-century B.C. casket shown in Figure 2.7. The graves have also indicated that the Mycenaeans buried their dead with honor. Perhaps influenced by the Egyptians, they wrapped the bodies and surrounded them with precious objects and pottery. From such practices and attitudes evolved the worship of heroes, a central aspect of Greek culture.

The Mycenaean feudal system flourished for several centuries, and after 1380 B.C., when Crete fell, the Mycenaeans extended their raiding and trading activities throughout the eastern Mediterranean. In about 1250 B.C., they attacked the wealthy and strategic city of Troy, on the western coast of present-day Turkey, near the Dardanelles (see Map 2.1). Although similar expeditions had brought booty to the Mycenaeans on earlier occasions, this long, exhausting foray weakened them, leaving them open to conquest by more vigorous tribes. Ironically, this siege of the Trojan citadel probably inspired the *Iliad* and the *Odyssey*, Homer's enduring epics. Overwhelmed by the Dorians from the north, Mycenaean civilization faded, and by about 1100 B.C., the Age of the Mycenaeans had closed. A three-century hiatus in Greek history—called the Dark Ages—followed, when writing disappeared and cultural activities virtually ceased.

The Mycenaeans, as presented by Homer, gave the Greeks many of their ideals. Heir to three centuries of oral traditions about the Mycenaeans, Homer invented the Age of Heroes. He sang to the Greeks of a glittering past that both inspired and sobered them. In the *Iliad* and the *Odyssey*, the Greeks found a universe with a basic moral order and a people with a distinct ethos, or ethical code. The pursuit of excellence that Homer attributed to his Mycenaean heroes became an ideal of historical Greece. Many aristocrats even traced their ancestry back to Homer's warriors and, through them, to the gods and goddesses. So rich was Homer's world that art and literature drew on it for subjects and incentive throughout Greek history. Through him the Mycenaeans gave the Greeks their myths, their religion, their ethics, their perception of the universe, and their insight into human character.

Figure 2.5 Lion Hunt. Ca. sixteenth century B.C. Bronze inlaid with gold and electrum. National Museum, Athens. *An anonymous artisan has decorated every part of this 9-inch dagger. Whether the weapon was ever used in battle is not clear, but its fine details and realistic figures must have made it a prized possession of a Mycenaean warrior. This dagger survived because it was buried alongside its owner in a funeral mound.*

Figure 2.6 Mycenae. Aerial view of the Acropolis. Ca. 1600–1200 B.C. *Set on top of a hill, this citadel occupied a commanding position over the surrounding countryside, and the fortified wall protected its inhabitants. Hilltop citadels such as this were typical for most cities in Mycenaean culture.*

Figure 2.7 Lion Pursuing a Stag (top); Lion Pursuing a Gazelle (bottom). 1500 B.C. Two plaques from gold-plated wooden chest. Length, 3¾″ each. National Museum, Athens. *The Mycenaeans, isolated in their fortresses on the Greek mainland, learned to appreciate the beauties of Minoan art through contacts with neighbors on Crete. Mycenaean artisans adapted Cretan subjects and themes, but they ignored their fanciful and lively nature in order to cultivate static effects, as in these gold plaques with their stylized animals and lilies. These plaques, decorating a small wooden chest, were found in a grave at Mycenae, deposited there as part of the burial equipment of a dead king.*

INTERLUDE: THE DARK AGES, 1100–800 B.C.

With the fall of the Mycenaeans, a period known as the Dark Ages began, and life reverted to simpler patterns. People lived in isolated farming communities and produced only essential tools and domestic objects. Commercial and social interchange among communities, already made hazardous by the mountainous terrain, became even more dangerous, and communication with the eastern Mediterranean kingdoms nearly ceased.

Yet some fundamental changes were slowly occurring. Political power was gradually shifting from kings to the heads of powerful families, laying the foundation for a new form of government, and iron gradually replaced bronze in tools, weapons, and other crafted objects—thus ending the Bronze Age and beginning the Iron Age in Greece. Many Mycenaeans fled to the coast of Asia Minor, which later came to be called Ionia, thus paving the way for the formation of an extended Greek community around the Aegean and Mediterranean Seas.

THE ARCHAIC AGE, 800–479 B.C.

In about 800 B.C., the Greeks emerged from their long years of stagnation and moved into an era of political innovation and cultural experimentation. Although scattered and isolated, they shared a sense of identity based on their common language, their heroic stories and folk tales, their myths and religious practices, and their commercial and trading interests. They claimed a common mythical parent, Hellen, who fathered three sons—the ancestors of the three major Greek tribes, the Ionians, the Aeolians, and the Dorians—and thus they called themselves Hellenes and their land Hellas. In the next three centuries, the Greeks would reconstruct their political and social systems, develop new styles of art and architecture, invent new literary genres, and make the first formal philosophical inquiries into the nature of human behavior and the universe. By the end of this period, they would have laid the foundations for a new world.

Political, Economic, and Social Structures

By the beginning of the Archaic Age (*Archaic* is from the Greek and means "ancient" or "beginning"), the isolated farming community had evolved into the *polis* (plural, *poleis*), a small, well-defined city-state. Several hundred poleis lay scattered over the Greek mainland and abroad. Although each polis had its own separate history and unique traits, each shared certain features with all the others. An *acropolis,* or fortified hilltop, served as a citadel where the rulers usually resided (Figure 2.8). Temples and holy shrines stood on the acropolis or below in an *agora.* The agora, an open area where political leaders held forth, citizens assembled, and the populace congregated to conduct business and socialize, was the center of a polis. The pursuit of both public and private matters in an agora served to connect the citizens of a polis and to foster civic pride and loyalty. In effect, a polis, through its control of the religious, cultural, and psychological components of its relatively closed community, molded the citizenry into an organic body with a collective identity.

Simultaneously with the emergence of the polis, in about 800 B.C., the political system underwent a basic change. The kings had been deposed by the leaders of noble families who owned most of the land and possessed the weapons and horses. These wealthy warriors established **oligarchies,** or government by the few. Although the oligarchies benefited the aristocrats, they were also characterized by exemplary leadership, civic idealism, and cultural and artistic patronage. However, most oligarchies eventually failed because of unforeseen and far-reaching military and economic changes.

New military tactics now made obsolete the aristocratic warriors in their horse-drawn chariots. Foot soldiers—armed with long spears, protected by shields and personal armor, and grouped in closed ranks called phalanxes—were proving more effective in battles. These foot soldiers, or hoplites, were recruited from among independent farmers, merchants, traders, and artisans, who were also profiting from an expanding economy. As their military value became evident, these commoners soon demanded a voice in political decisions.

At the same time, a growing population, beginning to strain the limited agricultural resources, led to an era of overseas expansion and colonization. The Hellenes sent citizens to join their earlier Ionian settlements and to establish new colonies along the coasts of Spain, North Africa, southern Russia (or the Black Sea), and Sicily and southern Italy, which became known as *Magna Graecia,* or Greater Greece.

Foreign ventures and expanded trade increased the wealth of the new middle class and reinforced their desires for more economic opportunities and political influence, but the entrenched aristocracy blocked their way to power. Frustrated by the inability of reform efforts to solve deep-seated problems, in the sixth century B.C. many poleis turned to rulers whom they entrusted with extraordinary powers to make sweeping economic and political changes. Many of these tyrants,

Figure 2.8 Acropolis, Athens. View from the west. *The Acropolis dominates Athens in the twentieth century just as it did in ancient times when it was the center of Athenian ceremonial and religious life. Today it is the towering symbol of Athens's cultural heritage as well as the center of the local tourist industry. A landmark in the history of town planning, the Acropolis is the ancestor of all carefully laid-out urban environments from ancient Rome to Renaissance Florence to modern Brasilia.*

as the Greeks called them, restructured their societies to allow more citizens to benefit from the growing economy, to move up the social scale, and to participate in the political process. However, some tyrants perpetuated their rule through heirs or political alliances and governed harshly for years, thus giving the word *tyrant* its modern meaning.

Regardless of the different results of the tyrants' reigns, by about 500 B.C. life was similar in many ways in all poleis. Citizens—freeborn males who could claim the right to enter into politics by virtue of family and wealth—voiced their opinions in a widening democratic process. They sat on juries, debated in the assemblies, and defended their polis in time of war. Civic responsibility, recognized as a central element in everyday life, was now passed on by the aristocrats to this new band of citizens.

Although horizons were expanding for the male citizens, other members of this predominantly middle-class society were severely restricted in political and economic matters. Women—except for priestesses like Lysimache, who was priestess of Athena for sixty-four years in the later fifth and early fourth centuries, and a rare literary figure like Sappho—were subservient to men. In Athens, for example, women possessed no legal or economic status, for they were by law under the control of the males in the household. Families often married off their daughters for economic gain, and, once married, the daughters were expected to be hard-working, loyal, and obedient.

Foreigners, with a few exceptions, were placed in special categories that restricted their personal rights and limited their economic opportunities. Some poleis, like Sparta, simply barred most foreigners, whereas Athens was more tolerant. Slaves, on the other hand, had no rights and were treated as property, with little hope of future improvement.

The Greek Polis: Sparta and Athens

Of the hundreds of poleis that evolved during the Archaic Age, Sparta and Athens stand out for their vividly contrasting styles of life and their roles in subsequent Greek history. Sparta, the principal symbol of Dorian civilization, chose to guarantee its integrity and future through stringent and uncompromising policies. The earliest Spartans forcibly enslaved the *Helots* —the original inhabitants of the lower Peloponnesus. To prevent rebellions and to control the Helots, who

Timeline 2.2 THE ARCHAIC AGE IN GREECE **All dates B.C.**

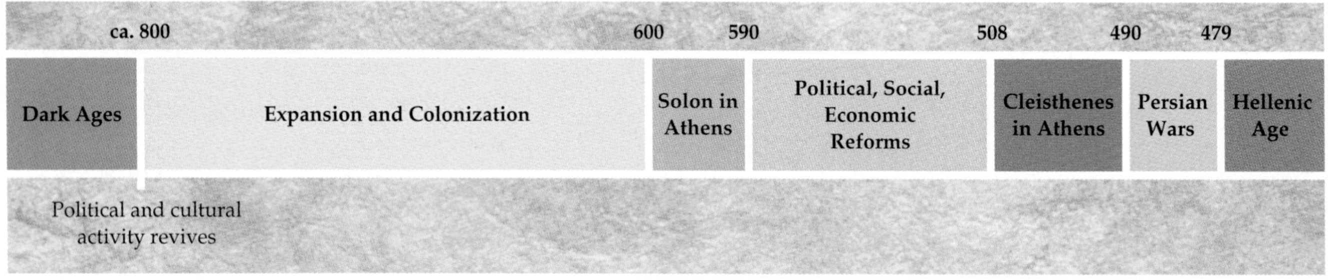

outnumbered the Spartans ten to one, a vigilant Sparta was forced to keep its military always on the alert. Thus, Sparta created a rigid hierarchical society of well-trained, tough, and athletic men, women, and children. The Spartans also established a genuine oligarchy: a constitutional government operated by five officials elected annually by a small body of citizens. The ruling class, obsessed with keeping social order, passed laws forbidding immigration, limiting material possessions, and restricting creativity. Sparta was admired for its loyal, brave soldiers and its stable social order. But Sparta contributed little to the artistic enrichment of Greece.

By contrast, Athens, the symbol of Ionian civilization, reached greater artistic, intellectual, and literary heights than did any other polis. Athens, both the city and its surrounding countryside of Attica, was a more open society than Sparta. The Attican clans shared a sense of community with the Athenians and supported them in wartime.

The history of Athens echoes the general pattern of change in the poleis during the Archaic Age (Timeline 2.2). Aristocrats initially ruled Athens through councils and assemblies. As long as farming and trading sustained an expanding population, the nobles ruled without challenge. But at the beginning of the sixth century B.C., many peasant farmers were burdened with debts and were threatened with prison or slavery. Having no voice in the government, the farmers began to protest what they perceived as unfair laws.

In about 590 B.C., the Athenians granted an aristocrat named Solon special powers to reform the economy. He abolished debts and guaranteed a free peasantry, overhauled the judicial system, and recorded the laws. Solon also restructured the Athenian constitution by giving the lower ranks of free men—those without great name or noble family but with some property or wealth—the right to participate in government.

Solon's principal successor was Cleisthenes [KLICE-thu-neez], who established democracy in Athens beginning in 508 B.C. He broadened the governmental base by opening it to all free male citizens (called the *demos*) regardless of their property or bloodlines. Cleisthenes' democratic reforms, which lasted for almost two centuries, created an atmosphere in which civic pride and artistic energy were unleashed, inaugurating the Hellenic Age (sometimes called the Golden Age) that made Athens both the pride and the envy of the other Greek city-states.

For moderns, one of the most surprising contrasts between Sparta and Athens is the difference in the roles and status of women. In general, Spartan women spent their time outside and spoke freely to men; Athenian women were kept in seclusion and rarely talked with their husbands. What made Spartan women so independent was that, above all else, they were to be strong mothers of the vigorous males needed to maintain this warrior society. To that end, Spartan women, alone among Greek women, were given public education, including choral singing and dancing, and athletics, in which they stripped just as Greek men did. Spartan women were also unique in being able to own land and to manage their own property.

In contrast, the women of Athens pursued respectability as an ideal, which meant that they were supposed to marry and stay indoors, overseeing their households and performing domestic chores. It is not clear how strictly this ideal was imposed on them in daily life. Athenian drama contains many instances of female characters complaining about their powerlessness, as when a wife is abandoned (Euripides' *Medea*) or a woman is left during wartime (Aeschylus's *Agamemnon*). These examples probably reflected reality. Athenian women, lacking public education and excluded by law from government and the military, played a subordinate role to Athenian men.

The Persian Wars

Cleisthenes' domestic reforms were one of the two major events that heralded the end of the Archaic Age and the coming of Greece's Hellenic Age. The other event, the Persian Wars, was pivotal not only for Greece but also for Western civilization. If the autocratic and imperialistic Persians had won these wars, then the democratic institutions, the humanistic values, and the cultural landmarks that the Greeks were establishing would have been lost.

By the mid–sixth century B.C., the Persians ruled a huge empire in the Near East encompassing most of the ancient world and including the Greek poleis in Ionia. When Darius [duh-RYE-us], king of the Persians in the late sixth century, demanded taxes from the Ionian Greeks, they revolted and looked to their homeland for support. A few poleis, including Athens, sent an expedition, which Darius defeated. To prevent future uprisings, Darius invaded the Greek peninsula and landed near Athens at Marathon in 490 B.C. The outnumbered Athenian army fought brilliantly, destroying many of the invader's ships and turning back the powerful Persian Empire.

However, the Persians soon found a new and determined ruler in Xerxes [ZIRK-seez], son of Darius, who overran much of northern Greece. Under Spartan leadership, the Greeks planned to trap the Persians at Thermopylae, a northern mountain pass, but they were annihilated by Xerxes' troops. Xerxes moved southward and sacked Athens, whose inhabitants escaped across the Saronic Gulf to the Island of Salamis. The Athenians drew the Persian navy into the narrows of the gulf, where the swifter Greek ships outmaneuvered the cumbersome Persian craft. After witnessing the destruction of his fleet, Xerxes returned to Persia. The remainder of the Persian army was routed at Plataea in 479 B.C., thus ending this major threat to Greece. The Greeks' final victory over the mighty Persians created a euphoric mood in Athens and set the stage for the ensuing Hellenic Age.

Table 2.1 THE NINE MUSES AND THEIR AREAS OF CREATIVITY

NAME	*ART OR SCIENCE*
Calliope	Epic poetry
Clio	History
Erato	Erotic poetry and mime
Euterpe	Lyric poetry and music
Melpomene	Tragedy
Polyhymnia	Sacred hymn
Terpsichore	Dance and song
Thalia	Comedy
Urania	Astronomy

THE EMERGENCE OF GREEK GENIUS: THE MASTERY OF FORM

During the Archaic Age, the Greeks developed a variety of literary, philosophical, and artistic forms that they used to probe the meaning of the universe and of human existence as well as to celebrate their joyous sense of life. These cultural accomplishments, like those of the older Near Eastern civilizations, were associated with the religious beliefs and practices that played a central role in Greek life and history. In fact, the Greeks believed that creativity itself was a divine gift from the **muses,** the nine goddesses of artistic inspiration (Table 2.1). Guided by their muses, they created enduring works of art, literature, and theater, each with a universal appeal.

Religion

The Greeks made religion an ongoing part of their private and public affairs. Indeed, the polis and religion could not be separated, for in the eyes of the Greeks the fate of each community depended on the civic deity. Public rituals and festivals drew together the citizens, infused them with civic pride, and reminded them of their common heritage. During the Archaic Age, Greek religion—an amalgam of deities derived from the original settlers as well as invaders and foreigners—evolved into two major categories: the Olympian and the chthonian. The **Olympian deities** dwelled in the sky or on mountaintops and were associated with the Homeric heroes and the aristocracy. The **chthonian deities** (from the Greek *chthon,* meaning "the earth") lived underground and were associated with peasant life, the seasons and cycles of nature, and fertility.

The Olympian religion shared some traits with the polytheistic cults of the ancient Near East, including the notion that the deities intervene in daily affairs, the belief that they are like humans in many respects, and the idea of a pantheon of gods and goddesses. The Greeks endowed their deities with physical bodies and individual personalities, creating a fascinating blend of charm and cruelty, beauty and childishness, love of justice and caprice. This family of unruly and willful deities quarreled with one another and played favorites with their mortal worshipers as they pleased. Faced with such favoritism among the deities, the Greeks themselves developed a strong moral sense. They came to believe that as long as they recognized the divinities' power and did not challenge them—and thus become victims of **hubris,** or pride—they would survive and often prosper.

Homer's poems lay out the complex relations and kinships in the Olympic pantheon and explain the functions and roles of the twelve principal deities, but Homer by no means invented these supernatural beings; they had been around long before his time. Indeed, their confusing traits and characters are probably the result of a fusion of numerous gods and goddesses whose origins predate the Greeks. Notwithstanding the deities' erratic characteristics, however, the Greeks never forgot that the Olympian system reflects a moral order and a sense of justice.

Zeus, a sky god and first among the immortals, reigned as king on Mount Olympus, hurling thunderbolts and presiding over the divine councils. He sired both immortals and mortals, for his sexual appetite knew no bounds. Hera, probably the great goddess of earlier cultures, was the sister and wife of Zeus. She watched over the women who appealed to her for help and kept a close eye on her wandering husband. Zeus's two brothers controlled the rest of the universe, Poseidon ruling the seas, all waters, and earthquakes, and Hades guarding the underworld. Zeus's sister Hestia protected the hearth and its sacred flame. Zeus's twin offspring, Apollo and Artemis, symbolized the sun and the moon, respectively. Apollo, Zeus's favorite son, personified the voice of reason. Artemis watched over childbirth and guarded wild creatures. Zeus's lying son Ares delighted in fierce battles, and, as the war god, he possessed a quick temper and few morals. He and Aphrodite—Zeus's daughter and the goddess of love and beauty—were adulterous lovers. Ironically, Homer has Aphrodite married to Hephaestus, the ugly and lame son of Zeus who was a master smith and the patron of craftspeople.

Two other children of Zeus rounded out the Olympic roster. Athena, the goddess of wisdom and patron goddess of Athens, was associated with warfare, the arts, and handicrafts. She was worshiped as a virgin goddess. Hermes, the god of trade and good fortune, was also the patron of thieves, although he was best known as a messenger for his fellow deities (Table 2.2).

Table 2.2 THE OLYMPIAN DEITIES AND THE AREAS THEY RULED

GOD OR GODDESS	*DUTIES AND RESPONSIBILITIES*
Zeus	Chief deity and keeper of order on Olympus
Hera	Mother goddess, protector of women
Poseidon	Ruler of waters
Hades	Keeper of the underworld
Hestia	Protector of the hearth
Apollo	God of wisdom and moderation
Artemis	Virgin goddess who aided women
Ares	Amoral god of violence and warfare
Aphrodite	Goddess of passion, love, and beauty
Hephaestus	Patron of craftspeople
Athena	Goddess of wisdom and warfare
Hermes	God of merchants and thieves; messenger for the deities

The chthonian gods and goddesses were probably derived from ancient earth and harvest deities. At first they were worshiped only by the lower orders, but as the demos grew in influence, chthonian rituals spread and were soon integrated into the civic calendar. Nevertheless, these cults were open only to initiates who were sworn to silence; hence, they were called mystery cults from the Greek word *mystos,* "keeping silent."

The chthonian practices originally invoked the powers of the earth to ensure a successful planting and a bountiful harvest. The two most important crops in Greece—grains and grapes, the sources of bread and wine, respectively—led to two major cults, those of Demeter and Dionysus. Demeter, a sister of Zeus, was a harvest goddess. She in turn had a daughter, Persephone, whom Hades abducted to his kingdom belowground. According to her cult legend, Demeter finally rescued Persephone but not before Hades had tricked Persephone into eating a fruit that made her return to the underworld for part of each year. Thus, during the winter months, the earth is bare, but when Persephone and Demeter are together, the earth is fecund and the grains grow. At Eleusis, a small village in Attica, Demeter was the focus of a mystery cult. Prospective initiates from all over Greece traveled there, apparently to receive her promise of immortal life.

Whereas Demeter's followers honored her in a dignified manner, Dionysus's worshipers, through wild dancing and wine drinking, hoped to be reinvigorated by their god and born again. Dionysus came to represent the irrational, emotional, and uncontrolled aspects of human nature to the Greeks. In contrast, the rational, conscious, controlled aspects were associated with Apollo. The two aspects—Dionysian and Apollonian—were considered opposing but complementary. Eventually, a Dionysus cult arose in Athens, where his followers annually held ceremonies honoring his power as god of the vine (Figure 2.9). Over the years these rituals became civic festivals that in turn spawned the competitive performances of tragic drama in Athens in the sixth century B.C.

Figure 2.9 EXEKIAS. *Dionysus Crossing the Sea.* Ca. 535 B.C. Clay, 12″ diameter. Staatliche Antikensammlungen, Munich. *Painted in the basin of a circular drinking bowl, Dionysus, the god of wine, is depicted sailing alone in a fish-nosed boat. This work by Exekias, one of the most admired artists of the Archaic Age, illustrates the beautiful mastery of space—the making of a convincing pictorial image on a predetermined surface, such as a pot or a tomb—that characterized the best vase painting of the time. Dionysus reclines under a billowing sail, surrounded by gamboling dolphins. Sprouting from the boat is a vine carrying bunches of grapes—the symbol of the god of wine. Exekias's simple design is typical of Archaic painting.*

Epic Poetry

The originator of the major conventions of **epic poetry** is traditionally believed to be Homer (about 800 B.C.), a **bard,** or poet who sang his verses while accompanying himself on a stringed instrument. In the *Iliad* and the *Odyssey,* Homer sang of the events before, during, and after the Trojan War, stories that had circulated among the Greeks since the fall of Mycenae. Homer entertained an aristocratic audience eager to claim kinship with the Mycenaean past. For many years, his poems were transmitted orally by other bards, and they probably did not exist in written versions until the seventh century B.C. Homer's authorship and, indeed, even his very existence are established solely by tradition; nothing is actually known about him. Nevertheless, by the end of the Archaic Age, the appeal of Homer's poetry had embraced all social levels, and his authority approached that of a modern combination of television, Shakespeare, and the Bible.

The basic appeal of the Homeric epics lies in their well-crafted plots, filled with dramatic episodes and finely drawn characters. Set against the backdrop of the Trojan War, the *Iliad* describes the battle of Ilium, another name for Troy, and the *Odyssey* recounts events after the Greeks defeat the Trojans (Figure 2.10). The earlier of the epics, the *Iliad,* focuses on Achilles, the epitome of heroic Greek manhood. In contrast to the battlefield heroics of the *Iliad,* the *Odyssey* narrates the wanderings of the Greek warrior Odysseus after the fall of Troy. Moreover, the *Odyssey* celebrates marriage, for Odysseus, despite some amorous adventures, remains fixed on thoughts of his wife Penelope, who waits for him in Ithaca.

In both poems, the deities merrily intrude into the lives of mortals, changing and postponing the fate of friend and enemy alike. So great was Homer's authority that his works made him the theologian of Greek religion. His stories of the gods and goddesses, although not completely replacing other versions of their lives, became the standard that circulated wherever Greek was spoken. Homer presented Zeus, the nominal protector of the moral order, as forever under siege by other gods seeking help for their favorite mortals. Although some later Greeks deplored Homer's inattention to moral issues, his roguish portraits of the deities remained indelibly imprinted in the minds of the general populace.

Homer's poetic expression also gave texture to the Greek language. Similes, figures of speech in which two unlike things are compared, help bring the dramatic, exotic events of the stories down to earth. For

Figure 2.10 SIGNED BY EXEKIAS. *Aias and Achilles Playing a Board Game.* Ca. 540–530 B.C. Clay, ht. of jar 2′. Vatican Museum (344). *Exekias painted this scene on an Athenian amphora, a vessel used for wine or oil. It is based on an episode from the Trojan War, Exekias's favorite source, though he, as here, often drew on traditions other than that recorded by Homer. In the scene, Achilles (left) and Aias (right), identified by inscriptions, compete over a game board; another inscription shows that Achilles has won the toss of the dice, 4 to 3. The skillful composition, arranged so as to direct the viewer's eyes to the game board, and the superb depiction of realistic details (the bareheaded Aias and the helmeted Achilles) attest to Exekias's artistic genius. This work and Figure 2.9 (also by Exekias) are in the black-figure style, characterized by silhouetted figures on a reddish clay background. Greek artists later reversed this technique, creating the red-figure style of reddish figures on a black background (see Figures 3.10 and 3.11).*

example, Homer creates a vivid image of Odysseus as a ferocious killer when he compares him to a lion "covered with blood, all his chest and his flanks on either side bloody." In a less violent simile, Homer has Achilles compare his fellow Greeks to "unwinged" baby birds and himself to their nurturing mother. Homer's images also provide a rich repertory of ready phrases and metaphors, known as **Homeric epithets,** such as "the wily Odysseus," "the swift-footed Achilles," and the "rosy-fingered dawn."

Besides shaping the language, Homer served as a guide to behavior for the Archaic Greeks. Because they became part of the Greek educational curriculum, his poems acquired an ethical function. A young man who took Achilles or Odysseus for a model would learn to maintain his well-being, to speak eloquently in company with other men, to give and receive hospitality, to shed tears in public over the death of his closest friend, to admire the beauty of women, to esteem the material wealth of other nobles, to appreciate songs of bravery, and, above all, to protect his reputation as a man and warrior. On the other hand, a young woman who imitated Penelope, the patient and faithful wife of Odysseus, would inhabit a more circumscribed world, as she learned to weave at the loom, to manage a household, to cultivate her physical beauty, and to resist the advances of other men. Although much changed, life in the United States today still pays more than lip service to these values—men, esteeming material wealth, admiring women, and protecting their masculine position; women, cultivating beauty, remaining faithful, and keeping the home.

Lyric Poetry

Verses sung to the music of the **lyre** (a stringed instrument), or **lyric poetry,** became the dominant literary expression in the late Archaic Age, and lyric verses have dominated Western poetry ever since. Lyric poetry, which originated later than the epic, expressed an author's personal, private thoughts, though the muse Euterpe was credited with the inspiration. The shift from epic to lyric poetry in the sixth century B.C. coincided with changes in the polis, where the rising democratic spirit encouraged a variety of voices to be heard.

Of the several types of lyric poetry, monody, or the solo lyric, became the most influential in Archaic Greece. Poets of monody achieved relative simplicity by using a single line of verse or by repeating a short stanza pattern. Unlike the Homeric epics, which survive relatively whole, the solo lyrics are extremely fragmented. For example, the bulk of what remains of Sappho's [SAF-oh] verses consists of random lines and references gleaned from later commentators and only one or two entire lyrics. And of the music, the whole has been lost. The ancients, however, regarded Sappho (about 600 B.C.) as the greatest of the writers of solo lyrics. The philosopher Plato hailed her as the tenth muse in a short lyric he dedicated to her. A truly original writer, Sappho apparently owed no debt to Homer or any other poet. Her work is addressed to a small circle of aristocratic women friends on her native island of Lesbos in the Aegean. She was deeply personal in her interests, writing chiefly about herself, her friends, and their feelings for one another. In her elegant but restrained verses, Sappho sang mostly about moods of

PERSONAL PERSPECTIVE

SOLON
Political Verses: The Ten Ages of Man

Solon (about 630–550 B.C.), the Athenian statesman, was also a poet of political verses and a keen observer of life. The first poem forecasts how unchecked greed may bring ruin to Athens. In the second poem, he identifies stages of human existence; he was one of the earliest writers to do so.

1

Our city will never perish by decree of Zeus or whim
of the immortals; such
is the great-hearted protector, child of thunder, who
holds her hands over us: Athena.
But by thoughtless devotion to money, the citizens are
willing to destroy our great city.
Our leaders' minds are unjust; soon they will suffer
the pangs of great arrogance.
They cannot control their greed and enjoy the cheerful
feast at hand in peace.

2

At seven, an immature boy loses the row of teeth he
grew in infancy.
When god completes another seven years, there are
signs of coming adulthood.
His limbs still grow in the third seven, and a beard
blossoms on his changing skin.
In the fourth seven, his strength is greatest, which
men consider proof of virtue.
The time to think of marriage and having children
comes in the fifth seven.
In the sixth, the mind is fit in every way; its wishes
are no longer lawless.
He reaches his best in thought and speech in the seventh and eighth, for fourteen years.
In the ninth, he is able but less inclined to strive for
greatness in speech and wisdom.
And if someone completes a tenth seven, death will
not befall him prematurely.

SAPPHO
He Seems to Be a God

In contrast to Solon's writings, Sappho's lyrical poems are vehicles for her intensely personal emotions. In this ode, she describes the pangs of jealousy and grief she feels on seeing someone she loves respond to another.

He seems to be a god, that man
Facing you, who leans to be close,
Smiles, and, alert and glad, listens
To your mellow voice

And quickens in love at your laughter
That stings my breasts, jolts my heart
If I dare the shock of a glance.
I cannot speak,

My tongue sticks to my dry mouth,
Thin fire spreads beneath my skin,
My eyes cannot see and my aching ears
Roar in their labyrinths.

Chill sweat slides down my body,
I shake, I turn greener than grass.
I am neither living nor dead and cry
From the narrow between.
But endure, even this grief of love.

romantic passion: of longing, unrequited love, absence, regret, dead feelings, jealousy, and fulfillment. Sappho's willing vulnerability and her love of truth made the solo lyric the perfect vehicle for confessional writing.

Natural Philosophy

The mental attitudes that partly accounted for the democratic challenge to established authority in the Archaic Age also brought forth thinkers who questioned the power and, ultimately, the existence of the gods. Just as the democrats constructed a human-centered state, so did the philosophers conceive of a world where natural causes and effects operated. These Greek thinkers invented what the Romans later called natural philosophy, a term that encompasses what we would call "science" and "philosophy." The close connection between science and philosophy persisted for twenty-two centuries, until the Newtonian revolution of the seventeeth century A.D. From that point on, science simply demonstrated what happened in nature without speculating about its purpose.

The origins of natural philosophy, like those of lyric poetry, are hidden in the incomplete historical record and distorted by the fragmented extant writings, but we can nevertheless say that formal Western

Table 2.3 PHILOSOPHERS OF THE ARCHAIC AGE

PHILOSOPHER	*TIME*	*ACHIEVEMENT*
Thales	About 585 B.C.	First philosopher and founder of philosophic materialism
Pythagoras	About 580–about 507 B.C.	Founder of philosophic idealism
Heraclitus	About 545–about 485 B.C.	First dialectical reasoning; belief in continual flux

philosophy began on the Ionian coast in the sixth century B.C. There, in the polis of Miletus, a set of thinkers known as the Milesian school speculated that beneath the ever-changing natural world was an unchanging matter (Table 2.3).

Thales [THAY-leez] (fl. 585 B.C.), the founder of the Milesian school, reasoned that the fundamental substance was water—an outlook that made him a materialist, because he thought that everything was made of matter. From the standpoint of modern science, Thales was wrong and so were the rest of his circle, who proposed other elements—air and "the infinite"—as the underlying essence. But more important than their conclusions regarding matter were their convictions that there is regularity in the universe and that human reason can ultimately understand the natural order. Their belief in rationality not only determined the direction of speculative thought but also initiated the steps that led to physics, chemistry, botany, and other sciences. Proposing that the universe was governed by natural laws, these first philosophers questioned divine explanations for natural events, a development deplored by those who found the key to life in a divine spirit.

When the Persians conquered Asia Minor near the end of the sixth century B.C., the center of intellectual thought shifted to Athens and to southern Italy and Sicily, where a tradition had emerged that challenged the Milesian School. Pythagoras [puh-THAG-uh-ruhs] (about 580–about 507 B.C.), the leader of the Sicilian school, rejected the concept of an underlying substance. Instead, he proclaimed, "Everything is made of numbers," by which he meant that mathematical relationships explained the basic order in nature—an outlook that made him an idealist, because he thought that an immaterial principle was the root cause of things. His musical studies probably led Pythagoras to this conclusion. He may have observed that a plucked string vibrated, making a certain sound; if the string were cut in half and plucked again, then a new note an octave higher than the first, with twice as many vibrations per second, would be heard. Hence, mathematical ratios determined musical sounds. Pythagoras then concluded that "numbers" explained everything in the "cosmos," his term for the orderly system embracing the earth and the heavens. Later, ancient astronomers building on Pythagorean beliefs claimed that the planets, in moving through their orbits, made music—the "music of the spheres."

A third philosopher, Heraclitus [her-uh-KLITE-uhs] (about 545–about 485 B.C.), appeals more to the modern age than does any other thinker in Archaic Greece. Rejecting the materialism of Thales and the idealism of Pythagoras, Heraclitus pioneered a philosophic tradition that found truth in constant change, as in his well-known idea that a person cannot step twice into the same flowing river. In addition, Heraclitus devised the earliest dialectical form of reasoning when he speculated that growth arises out of opposites, a fundamental tenet of dialectic thought. This original idea led him to argue that "strife is justice" and that struggle is necessary for progress. Heraclitus's dialectical reasoning anticipated certain nineteenth-century thinkers, and his notion of continual flux has attracted modern physicists.

Architecture

The supreme architectural achievement of the Greeks, the temple, became the fountainhead of the building components, decorative details, and aesthetic principles that together have largely shaped Western architecture down to Post-Modernism in the late twentieth century. In its origins during the Archaic Age, the temple was a sacred structure designed to house the cult statues of the civic deities. The early houses of worship were probably made of wood, which explains why no remains of these Greek temples have been discovered. However, as the Archaic Age gathered economic momentum and wealth accumulated, each polis rebuilt its wooden sanctuaries in stone.

A diagram of a typical temple illustrates how much the building has influenced Western architecture (Figure 2.11). Generic Greek architecture is called **post-beam-triangle construction** (also known as post-and-lintel construction). *Post* refers to the columns; *beam* indicates the horizontal members, or **architraves,** resting on the columns; and *triangle* denotes the triangular area, called a **pediment,** at either end of the upper building. Other common features include the **entabla-**

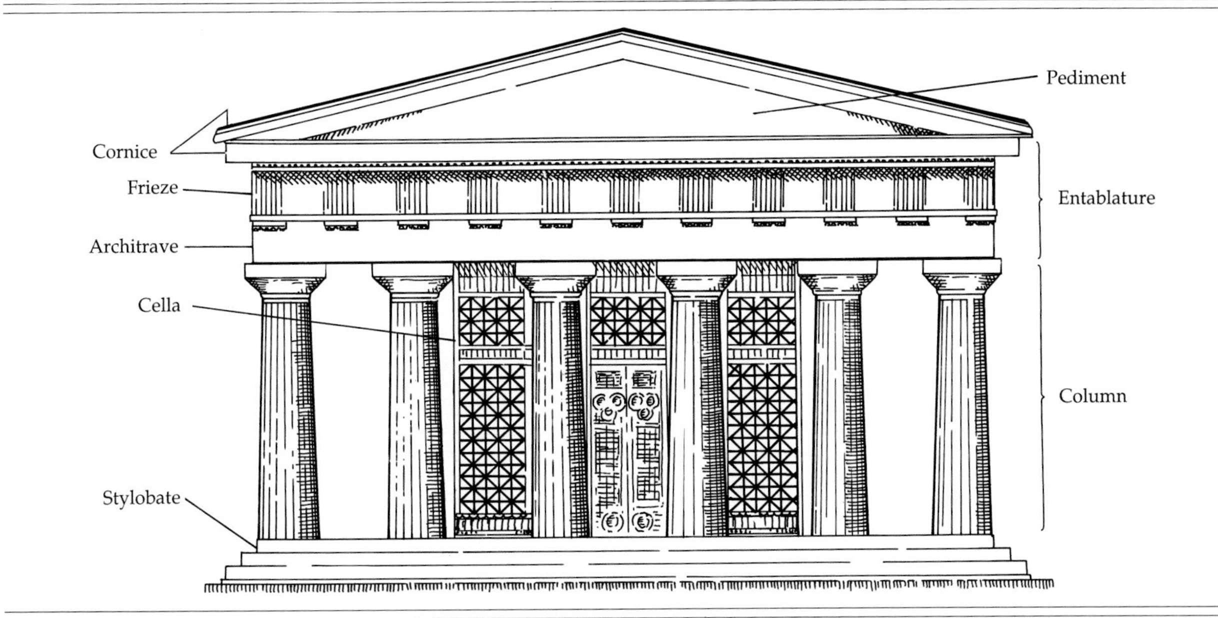

Figure 2.11 Elements of Greek Architecture

ture, which is the name for all of the building between the columns and the pediment; the **cornice,** the horizontal piece that crowns the entablature; and the **stylobate,** the upper step of the base on which the columns stand. A typical temple had columns on four sides, which in turn enclosed a walled room, called a **cella,** that housed the cult image. Each temple faced east, with the doors to the cella placed so that, when opened, they allowed the sunrise to illuminate the statue of the deity.

The earliest temple style in Greece was called **Doric,** both because it originated in the Dorian poleis and because the style's simplicity of design and scarcity of decorative detail reflected the severe Dorian taste (Figure 2.12). The Doric columns have plain tops, or **capitals,** and the columns rest directly on the stylobate without an intervening footing. On the entablature of each Doric temple is a sculptural band, called a *frieze,* which alternates three-grooved panels, called **triglyphs,** with blank panels, called **metopes,** that could be left plain or filled with **relief** sculptures. The triglyphs are reminders of the temple's origin as a wooden building when logs, faced with bronze, served as overhead beams.

An excellent example of the Doric style in the Archaic Age is the Temple of Hera in Poseidonia, now called Paestum, in southern Italy (Figure 2.13). The Temple of Hera is the oldest (about 550 B.C.) and best-preserved of three cult sanctuaries on this site. Constructed from coarse local limestone, this large temple has a somewhat ungainly appearance, due in part to the massive architrave and the small spaces between

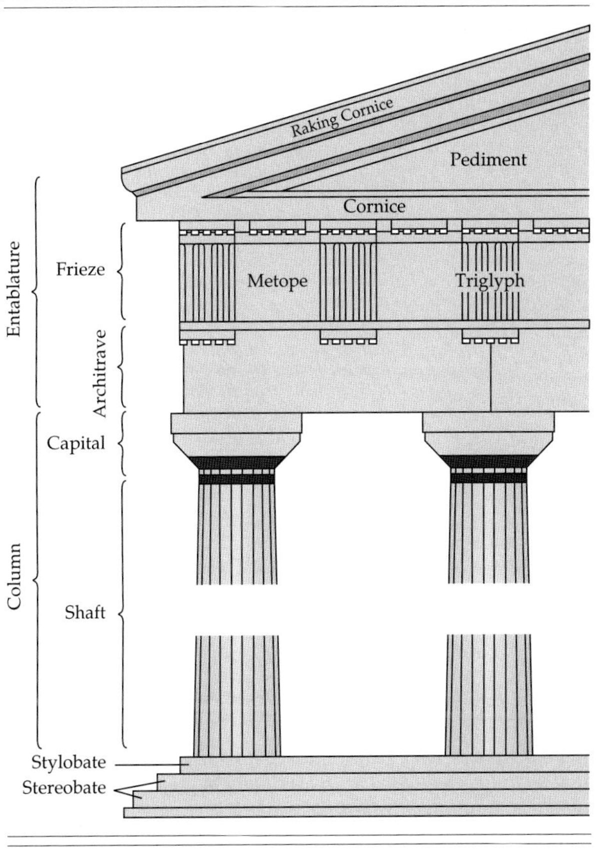

Figure 2.12 Greek Architecture of the Doric Order

Figure 2.13 Temple of Hera at Paestum. Ca. 560–550 B.C. Limestone. *This temple, with its heavy, squat columns, stands not only as a model of Archaic Greek architecture but also as a reminder of Greek wealth and expansion. Colonists from mainland Greece settled in southern Italy, the land they thought of as "Greater Greece," in the seventh and sixth centuries* B.C., *bringing with them the Olympian gods and goddesses and ideas of how to build temples in their honor.*

Figure 2.14 Temple of Aphaia, Aegina. 510 B.C. *The Temple of Aphaia in Aegina became the standard for the Doric temple style from its creation until it was superseded by the Athenian Parthenon in the 440s. Built of local limestone and covered in stucco and painted, the Temple of Aphaia gleamed like a jewel in its carefully planned site overlooking the Saronic Gulf. Constructed and decorated with strict attention to artistic refinements, such as the slender columns and the lifelike sculptures, this temple represents the climax of Archaic architecture.*

the columns. The builders attempted to remedy this defect (without total success) by introducing refinements into the temple's design. The columns were made to appear strong and solid enough to support the entablature by enlarging the middles of the shafts, a technique known as **entasis.** The artisans also carved vertical grooves, called **fluting,** along the shafts to give the columns a graceful, delicate surface and enhance their visual three-dimensionality.

Eventually, after much experimentation, Greek architects overcame the awkwardness of the early Doric style by deciding that a temple's beauty was a function of mathematical proportions. The Temple of Aphaia—erected in 510 B.C. by the citizens of Aegina, Athens's neighbor and perennial enemy—seemed to embody this principle (Figure 2.14). The architect of this temple achieved its pleasing dimensions by using the ratio 1:2, placing six columns on the ends and twelve columns on the sides. The Temple of Aphaia, with its harmonious proportions and graceful columns, became the widely imitated standard for the Doric style over the next half century.

Sculpture

Like the art of Mesopotamia and Egypt, Greek sculpture was rooted in religious practices and beliefs. The Greek sculptors fashioned images of the gods and goddesses to be used in temples either as objects of worship or as decorations for the pediments and friezes. Of greater importance for the development of Greek sculpture were the **kouros** (plural, *kourai*) and the **kore** (plural, *korai*), free-standing statues of youths and maidens, respectively. Before 600 B.C., these sculptures had evolved from images of gods, to statues of dead heroes, and finally into memorials that might not even be directly related to the dead person to whom they were dedicated.

What made the **Archaic** statues of youths and maidens so different from Egyptian and Mesopotamian art was the Greek delight in the splendor of the human body. In their representations of the human form, the Greeks rejected the sacred approach of the Egyptians and the Mesopotamians, which stressed conventional poses and formal gestures. Instead, Greek sculptors created athletic, muscular males and lively, robust maidens. For the Greeks, the health and beauty of the subjects was as important as the statues' religious purpose.

The first Archaic statues of youths owed much to the Egyptian tradition, but gradually Greek sculpture broke free of its origins. An early example of the kourai type of sculpture is the New York Kouros (Figure 2.15), named for its present location in New York City's Metropolitan Museum of Art. Artistically, this marble statue of a youth with the left foot forward, the clenched fists, the arms held rigidly at the sides, the stylized hair, and the frontality—that is, the quality of being designed for viewing from the front—shows the Egyptian influence (see Figure 1.15). The Greek sculptor has moved beyond Egyptian techniques, however, by incorporating changes that make the figure more lifelike, such as by attempting to show the correct shape of the knees and suggesting an actual person's mouth. That the result is not a realistic or an idealized human figure is less important than that the sculptor has studied the human body with fresh eyes and endeavored to represent it accurately. With such groundbreaking works as the New York Kouros, the Greeks launched a dynamic tradition that later artists continually reshaped.

A generation after the New York Kouros, new sculptors expressed their changed notion of a beautiful living male body in such works as the Ptoon Kouros (Figure 2.16). This sculpture, which was probably a dedicatory offering to a god or a goddess, still shows a powerful Egyptian influence, but it takes a giant step forward to a greater sense of life. The taut body and

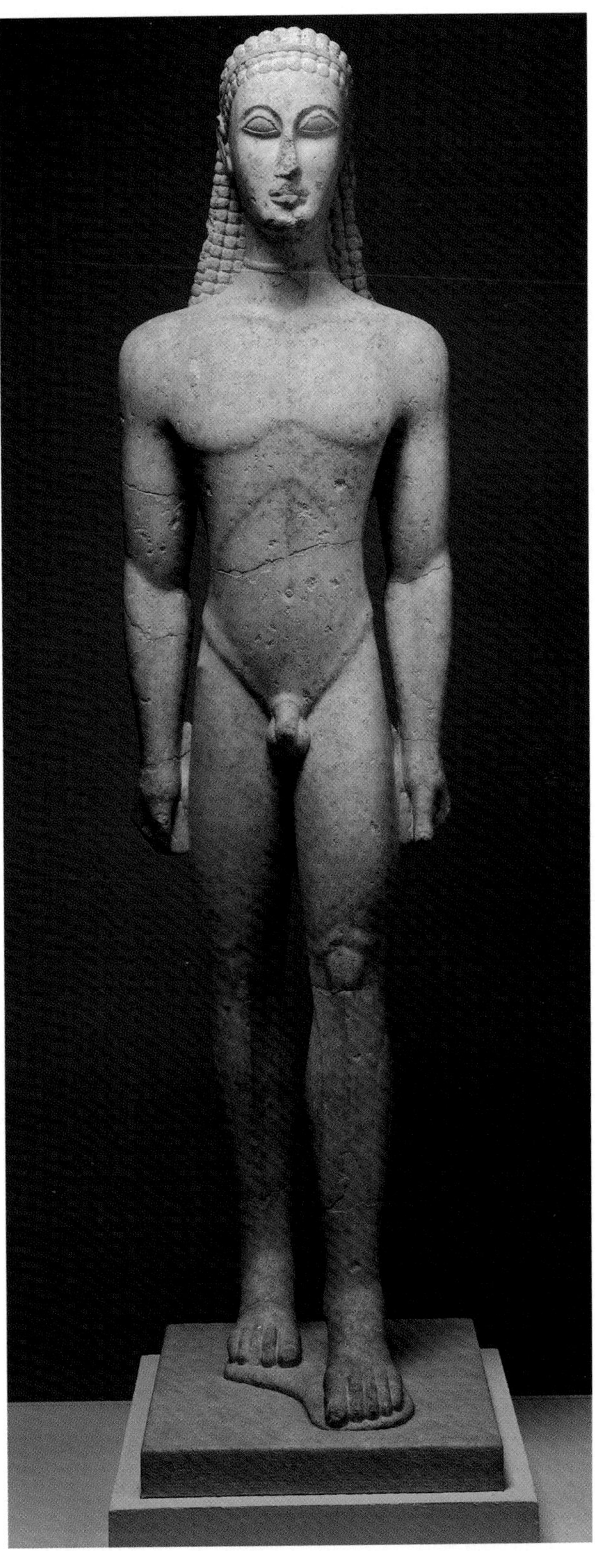

Figure 2.15 New York Kouros. Ca. 615–590 B.C. Marble, ht. 73½″. Courtesy Metropolitan Museum of Art. Fletcher Fund, 1932. (32.11.1) *The New York Kouros is one of many similar statues dating from about the beginning of the sixth century B.C. During that century, the male and female statues evolved from stiff and stereotyped models to natural and anatomically correct forms.*

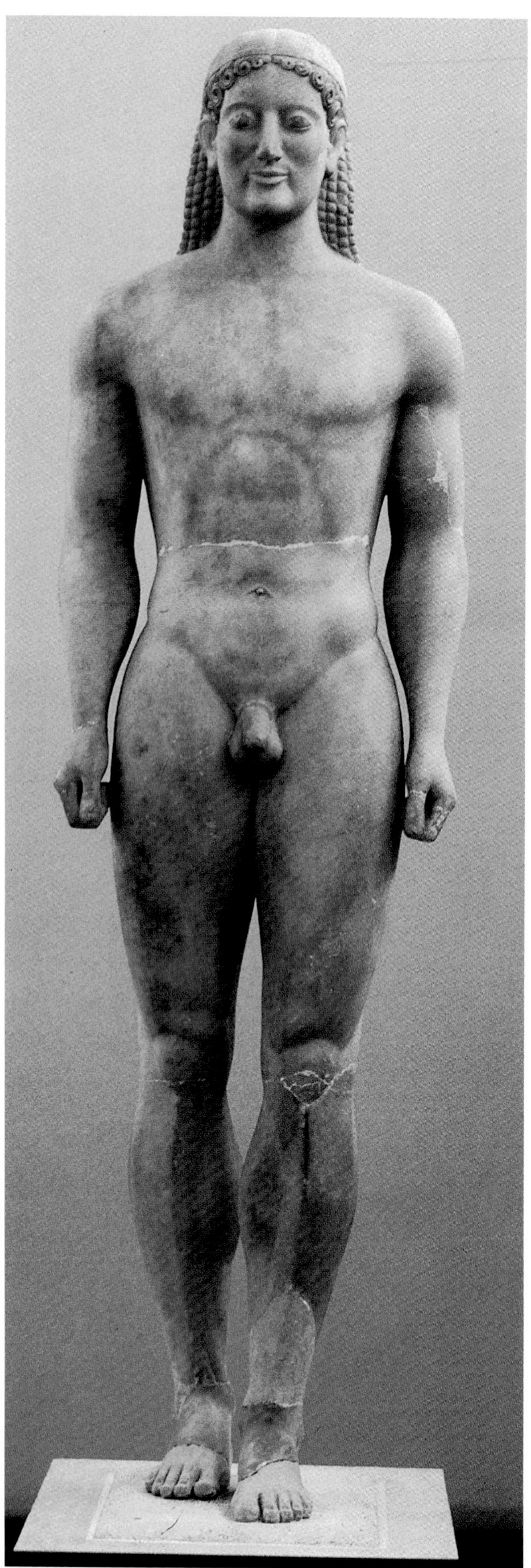

Figure 2.16 Ptoon Kouros. Ca. 540–520 B.C. Marble, ht. 76″. National Museum, Athens. *The Ptoon Kouros possesses the distinguishing characteristics of all kourai: frontality, attention to bodily details, and a general formality. However, the Ptoon Kouros's subtle innovations—more precise musculature and more liveliness, as contrasted with Figure 2.15—foreshadow the Hellenic sculpture style.*

massive torso convincingly reproduce the athletic qualities of an Olympic competitor, and the curious facial expression, known as the "archaic smile," gives an enigmatic quality to the marble figure.

The korai sculptures, like the statues of youths, evolved from a frozen, lifeless style toward a greater realism, although women were never depicted in the nude at this stage in Greek sculpture. The earliest draped korai sculptures mixed Mesopotamian and Egyptian traditions with Greek ideas, sometimes producing an interesting but awkward effect. Such an early work is the Auxerre Kore (Figure 2.17)—named for the museum in Auxerre, France—whose cylindrical shape is copied from Mesopotamian models and whose stiff pose, wiglike hair, and thin waist are borrowed from Egypt. The Greek sculptor added the broad mouth and the Greek peplos (a loose-fitting outer robe) decorated with a meander pattern, but the Auxerre Kore, despite its charming details, is rigid and inert.

The Peplos Kore (Figure 2.18), dating from about a century later, expresses beautifully the exciting changes that were taking place in late Archaic sculpture. The statue wears a chiton, or tunic, over her upper torso, and a belted peplos. The sculptor has replaced the rigidity of the Egyptian pose with a more graceful one, as shown, for example, by the way the figure holds her right arm. Traces of a painted necklace may be seen, for the Peplos Kore, like all Greek sculpture, was painted to make the figure as true to life as possible. The often awkward archaic smile is here rendered to perfection, giving this lovely maiden an aristocratic demeanor.

The Greek tradition of representing males nude and females clothed persisted throughout the Archaic Age and well into the succeeding Hellenic Age. The Greeks readily accepted male nudity, witnessing it in the army on campaigns, in the gymnasium during exercises, and in the games at Olympia and elsewhere, and this acceptance is reflected in their art. But they were much less comfortable with female nudity (except in Sparta, where women exercised in the nude), so women were usually depicted draped or robed.

The political turmoil brought on by the Persian Wars occurred simultaneously with the revolutionary changes in sculpture that were leading to a new style of art. The Temple of Aphaia at Aegina provides a lab-

Figure 2.17 Auxerre Kore. Ca. 675–600 B.C. Limestone. Louvre. *The Auxerre Kore represents a fairly early stage in the development of this female form. The small size of the sculpture (about 29½" high) suggests that it may have been part of a burial rite. Traces of red pigment on the bust indicate that this kore was once painted to make it appear more lifelike.*

Figure 2.18 Peplos Kore. Ca. 535–530 B.C. Marble, ht. 48". Acropolis Museum, Athens. *The Peplos Kore represents the highest achievement in the art of the kore. The beauty of the face, the elegance of the dress, and the expectancy of the countenance—this maiden could have been one of those who inspired Sappho's love lyrics.*

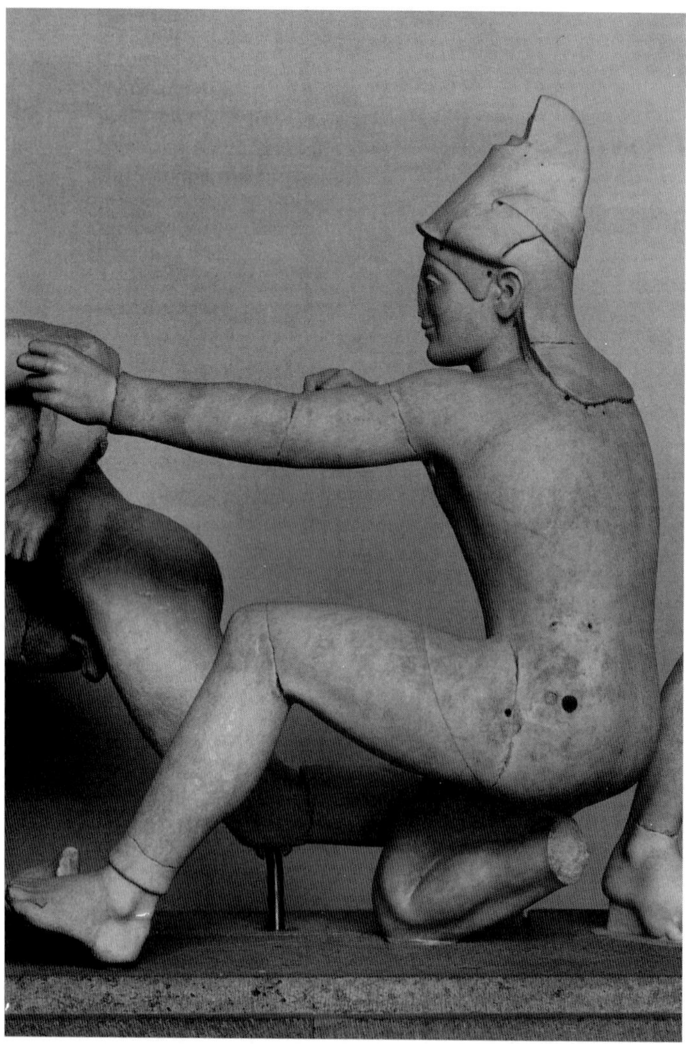

Figure 2.19 *Paris.* West pediment, Temple of Aphaia, Aegina. Ca. 500 B.C. Marble, ht. 41″. Staatliche Antikensammlungen, Munich. *The pedimental sculptures on the Temple of Aphaia illustrate the rapid changes that were occurring in artistic ideals and techniques in the period just preceding the Hellenic Age of Athens. The sculpture of Paris from the earlier west pediment is formal and stylized in comparison with its counterpart on the east pediment.*

Figure 2.20 *Herakles.* East pediment, Temple of Aphaia, Aegina. Ca. 490–485 B.C. Marble, ht. 31″. Staatliche Antikensammlungen, Munich. *The statue of Herakles from the east pediment of the Temple of Aphaia shows the advances made in sculpture in the ten to fifteen years since the figure of Paris was crafted for the west pediment. More realistic, detailed, and lifelike than Paris, Herakles is emotionally charged and tense, yet composed and restrained—a state admired and often depicted by Hellenic artists.*

oratory setting for the transition from the Archaic to the Hellenic style (480–323 B.C.) because of the different ages of the building's statues: The sculptures for the west pediment (about 500 B.C.) were made some fifteen years earlier than those for the east pediment (about 490–485 B.C.). Their stylistic differences demonstrate the changes that were under way.

An earlier statue (from the west pediment) depicts the Trojan hero Paris as a nude, somewhat sensual bowman, poised, ready to release an arrow (Figure 2.19). Paris, his body and face revealing very little tension, might have been posing, rather than preparing for action. A later sculpture (from the east pediment) portrays the legendary hero Herakles as a clothed archer, in a stance copied from the *Paris* figure (Figure 2.20). But what a contrast! Herakles' more muscular body is tensed and ready for action. Although neither face registers emotion, Herakles' gaze and set jawline convey a more lifelike image of a warrior. The *Herakles* figure is a transitional work to the next style—the Hellenic.

The Legacy of Archaic Greek Civilization

The Archaic Age in Greece was a precious moment in the story of the arts and humanities. Inheriting survival techniques from Neolithic cultures, continuing the urban ways of Mesopotamia and Egypt, and, more important, drawing spiritual and psychological sustenance from the Minoans and the Mycenaeans, the Archaic Greeks developed a unique consciousness that expressed, through original artistic and literary forms, their views about the deities and themselves and how they interacted. A mark of the creative power of the Archaic Greeks is that at the same time that they were inventing epic poetry, lyric poetry, the post-beam-triangle temple, the kore and kouros sculptures, and natural philosophy, they were involved in founding a new and better way to live in the polis.

The new way of life devised by the Archaic Greeks gave rise to what we call, in retrospect, the **humanities**—those original artistic and literary forms that made Greek civilization unique. But the cultural explosion of this brilliant age is inseparable from the Greeks' restless drive to experience life to the fullest and their deep regard for human powers. Having devised their cultural forms, the Archaic Greeks believed passionately that by simply employing these models, either through studying them or by creating new works, the individual became a better human being. In this way, the Archaic Greeks' arts and humanities were imbued with an ethical content, thus suggesting for some—notably philosophers—an alternative way of life to that offered by religion.

Wherever we look in this age, we see creative energy, a trait that has characterized Western civilization through the ages. Even though the different cultural forms did not develop at the same pace during the Archaic Age—sculpture, for example, was not as expressive as lyric poetry—these early aesthetic efforts were fundamentally different from those of the earlier Near Eastern civilizations. The touchstone of the humanistic style developed by the Archaic Greeks was their belief in human powers, both intellectual and physical. Indeed, the most powerful literary voice of this age, Homer, was quoted over and over for his claim that mortals and divinities are part of the same family. Less confident people, hearing this assertion, might have reasoned that human beings are limited in their earthly hopes. But, for the Greeks of this period, Homer meant that humans are capable of godlike actions. The reverence that the Archaic Greeks expressed for all noteworthy deeds, whether in poetry, in warfare, or in the Olympic games, attested to their belief in the basic value of human achievement.

KEY CULTURAL TERMS

frieze
fresco
Linear A
Linear B
ashlar
shaft graves
oligarchy
muse
Olympian deities
chthonian deities
hubris
epic poetry
bard
Homeric epithet
lyre
lyric poetry
post-beam-triangle construction
architrave
pediment
entablature
cornice
stylobate
cella
Doric
capital
triglyph
metope
relief
entasisx
entasis
kouros
kore
Archaic
humanities

SUGGESTIONS FOR FURTHER READING

PRIMARY SOURCES

Barnstone, W., ed. and trans. *Greek Lyric Poetry.* New York: Bantam Books, 1962. Selections from literary fragments dating from the seventh century B.C. to the sixth century A.D.; includes helpful biographical notes.

Homer. *Iliad.* Translated by R. Lattimore. Chicago: University of Chicago Press, 1962. An excellent modern translation of the story of the Trojan War.

———. *Odyssey.* Translated by R. Lattimore. New York: Harper & Row, 1968. The epic of Odysseus's adventures after the fall of Troy, again in Lattimore's lively translation.

Sappho, A Garland: The Poems and Fragments of Sappho. Translated by J. Powell. New York: Farrar, Straus & Giroux, 1993. This slim volume contains all of Sappho's existing verses, both whole and fragments, rendered into contemporary language.

Wheelwright, P., ed. *The Presocratics.* New York: Bobbs-Merrill, 1966. A collection of quotations from early philosophers that captures the flavor of sixth-century Greek thought.

Of all the many translations of Greek literature, the Loeb Classical Library (Harvard University Press) is probably the best.

3 CLASSICAL GREEK CIVILIZATION
The Hellenic Age

With the defeat of the Persians at Plataea in 479 B.C., the Greeks entered the **Hellenic** Age, a period that lasted until the death of Alexander the Great of Macedon in 323 B.C. During the more than 150 years of the Hellenic Age, the Greeks defeated the Persians for a second time and survived a century of destructive civil war, only to succumb ultimately to the Macedonians. But throughout those turbulent times, the Greeks never wavered in their supreme confidence in the superiority of their way of life.

The Greek world consisted of several hundred poleis (city-states), located on the mainland, on the Aegean Islands and the coast of Asia Minor, and in the lands bordering the Mediterranean and Black Seas (Map 3.1). Athens was the cultural center, but many poleis contributed both materially and intellectually to Hellenic civilization. The Hellenic Age is the first stage of Classical civilization, the highest achievement of the ancient Greeks. Chapter 4 describes the second stage of Classical civilization, the Hellenistic Age.

◀ **Detail** *Poseidon, Apollo, and Artemis.* Parthenon frieze. Ca. 448–442 B.C. Marble, ht. 43″. Acropolis Museum, Athens.

GENERAL CHARACTERISTICS OF HELLENIC CIVILIZATION

Despite diversity among the poleis, the Greeks of the Hellenic Age shared certain characteristics. Competitiveness and rivalry were certainly dominant features, as was an increasingly urban lifestyle (Figure 3.1). Most Greeks still lived in the countryside, but the city now dominated politics, society, and the economy.

Popular attitudes toward the Olympian deities were also changing, and public worship began to be assimilated into civic festivals. The great art of the

Map 3.1 THE ATHENIAN EMPIRE, 431 B.C.

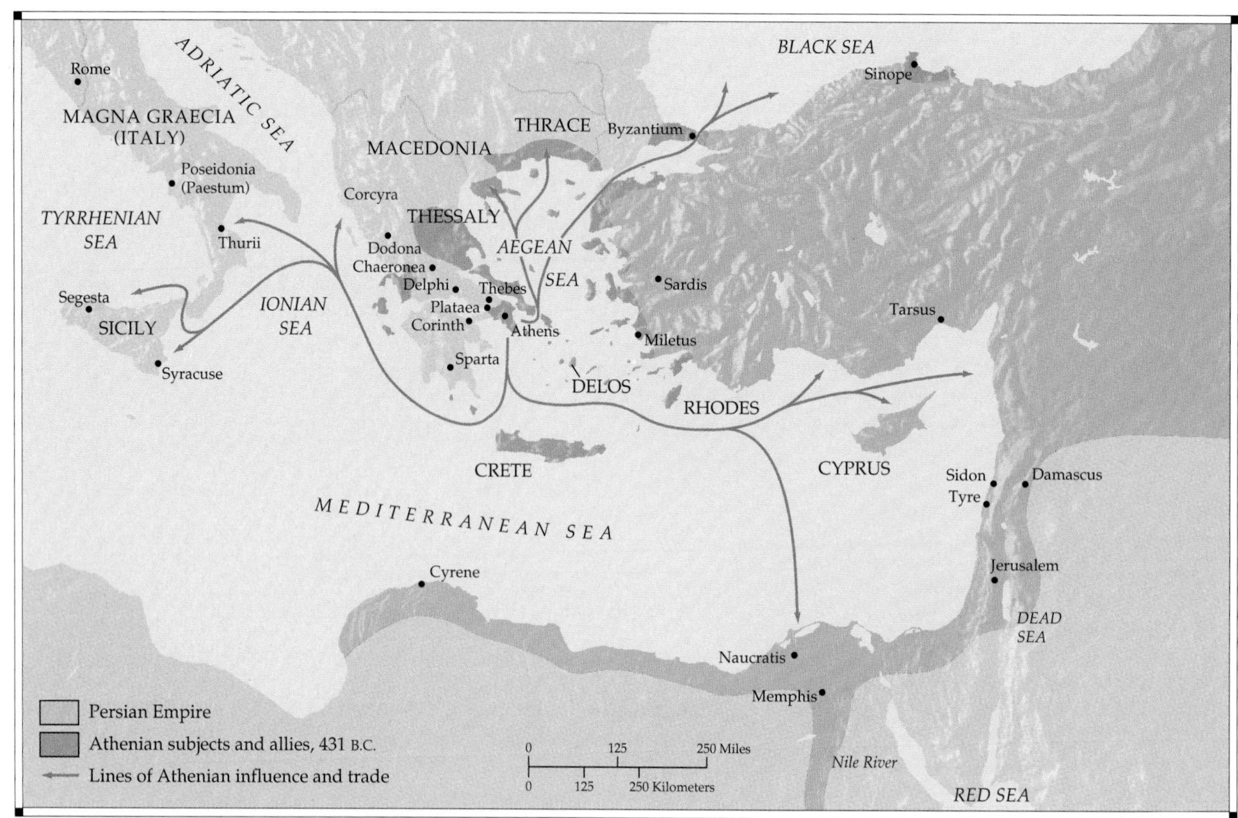

Figure 3.1 *Torch Race.* Ca. 430–420 B.C. Clay, ht. 14⅕″. Arthur M. Sackler Museum, Harvard University Art Museums, Cambridge, Mass. (Bequest of David M. Robinson). *From the dawn of the Archaic period, about 800 B.C., sports, especially competitive sports, were integral to Greek life. In the* Iliad, *which appeared about that time, Homer describes the athletic games that were played at the funeral of the warrior Patroclus. Later, in Hellenic times, artists used sports contests as subjects, as in this painting depicting a torch race, perhaps during the Panathenaea festival. This vase is executed in the red-figure style, a reversal of the black-figure style, which is illustrated in Figures 2.9 and 2.10. The relatively uncluttered design, three figures with sparse details, perfectly fits into the small panel on the krater, a mixing vessel.*

age reflected the fusion of civic and sacred in such works as the Parthenon, the temple of the goddess Athena, protector of Athens (Figure 3.2). With gods and goddesses playing increasingly ceremonial roles, religion became demystified and lost some of its personal value in people's lives. Religious dissatisfaction was also triggered by expanded civil rights: The more democratic poleis raised the collective hopes of their citizens but were unable to satisfy all their spiritual longings.

Another characteristic of Hellenic civilization was a high regard for the balanced life and for moderation in achieving it. In Athenian tragedy, a recurrent theme is the danger of great wealth and high position. According to the playwrights, riches and status bred pride and led to envy by other citizens or, worse, envy by the gods. A modest life was the safest way to avoid personal calamity.

The Greeks also sought a balance between the opposite extremes in human nature, symbolized by Apollo, god of moderation, and Dionysus, god of excess. As the god of light, Apollo embodied rational thought, ethical ideals, and aesthetic balance. Apollo's temple with its oracle at Delphi was one of the holiest shrines in Greece, second only to the island of Delos, his birthplace (Figure 3.3).

Dionysus, on the other hand, was the god of wine, drunken revelry, sexual excess, and madness. Women known as **maenads** followed and worshiped him, sometimes tearing apart beasts in their blind frenzy. By the Hellenic Age, these excesses were confined to rural areas, for the Dionysiac impulse was constantly being tamed by the Apollonian spirit and urban life. In Athens, the drunken worship of Dionysus was transformed into a civic festival, the **Dionysia,** from which tragedy, perhaps the highest expression of the Greek ethical genius, was born (Figure 3.4).

Greek citizens of Hellenic times, then, were proud of their own polis, where they participated in civic functions and religious rites. However, despite the many commonalities among the Greek poleis—language, ancestry, history, and Homer—they never shared a politically united Greek world.

Figure 3.2 *Athena Parthenos.* Marble replica based on fifth-century statue by Phidias. Ht. 3′ 5⅜″. National Museum, Athens. *Phidias's larger-than-life sculpture, which dominated the inner sanctum of the Parthenon, disappeared in ancient times, but numerous copies, such as this small figurine, have survived. Athena wears a peplos, gathered at her waist, and a helmet, ornamented with a sphinx flanked by two winged horses, and her left hand steadies a shield depicting Greek battle scenes. The statue was composed of gold and ivory sections joined together. A close examination of Athena's head demonstrates the shift from the Archaic to the Hellenic style sculpture, since it no longer has the Archaic smile and its features are idealized.*

Figure 3.3 *Apollo.* West pediment, Temple at Olympia. Ca. 460 B.C. Marble, ht. 10′ 2″. Olympia Museum. *Apollo's serene countenance in this splendidly crafted head reflects his image as the god of moderation. As the deity who counseled "Nothing in excess," Apollo was a potent force in combating the destructive urges that assailed the Greeks. This sculpture is executed in the Severe style, or the first stage of the Hellenic Classical style, which is evident by the turn of the head to the right. However, its wiglike hair indicates the lingering influence of the Archaic style.*

DOMESTIC AND FOREIGN AFFAIRS: WAR, PEACE, AND THE TRIUMPH OF MACEDONIA

On the eve of the Hellenic Age, the Greeks, having defeated the Persians, were united only in their continuing opposition to Persia and in their hostility to any polis that tried to control the others. Although they cooperated on short-term goals that served their common interests, goodwill among the poleis usually evaporated once specific ends were met.

Despite rivalries, the Greek economy expanded. A rising middle class took advantage of the economic opportunities created by the fluctuations of war and politics, causing manufacturing and commerce to flourish. Although the economic base remained agricultural, people increasingly flocked to the polis to make their fortunes, to participate in government, and to find stimulation.

The Hellenic Age can be divided into four distinct phases: (1) the Delian League; (2) wars in Greece and with Persia and the ensuing Thirty Years' Peace; (3) the Peloponnesian War; and (4) Spartan and Theban hegemony and the triumph of Macedonia (Timeline 3.1). While these conflicts raged, life within the polis went on, and in some poleis, notably Athens, extraordinary political, cultural, and intellectual changes were occurring.

After defeating the Persians, the Greeks realized that a mutual defense organization was the key to preventing further Persian attack. In 478 B.C., a number of poleis formed the Delian League, a defensive alliance, with Athens at its head. But Athens soon began to transform the league into an instrument of imperialism. As the oppressive nature of Athenian policies emerged, Athens's independent neighbors became alarmed.

Athenian power, however, was restricted by strained relations with Sparta, by the continuing menace of Per-

Figure 3.4 *Dionysus and His Followers.* Ca. 430 B.C. Staatliche Museen, Berlin. *Scrolling around a perfume vase, this painting depicts a bearded Dionysus seated on the right with his followers. Of his twelve devotees, eleven are maenads, young female revelers; the last is the bearded Silenus, the foster father and former schoolmaster of Dionysus. Silenus is depicted on the lower left in his usual drunken, disorderly state.*

Timeline 3.1 PHASES OF HELLENIC HISTORY **All dates B.C.**

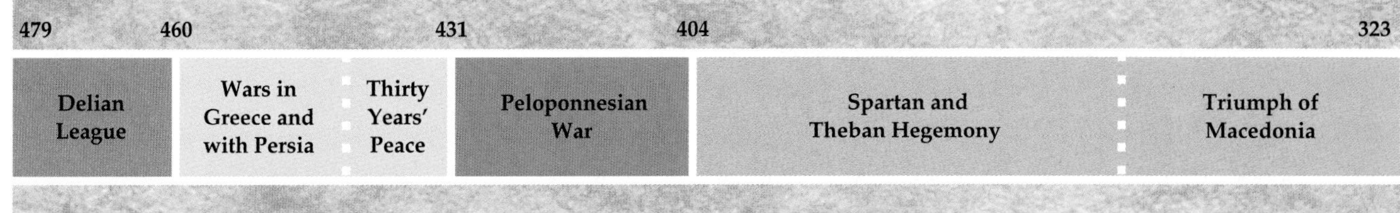

sia, and by the highly unstable Delian alliance. When a negotiated settlement finally resolved Persian claims, the Delian League fell apart, leaving Athens vulnerable to its enemies on the Greek mainland. First Thebes and then Sparta led attacks on Athens. The war dragged on, but in 445 B.C., when Sparta unexpectedly withdrew, Athens won a quick victory that forced its enemies to negotiate.

The ensuing Thirty Years' Peace (which lasted only fourteen years) brought the Hellenic Age of Athens to its zenith. Athenian democracy expanded so that even the poorest citizens were empowered with full rights (though women continued to be excluded). Artists and sculptors beautified the Acropolis, and the three great Athenian tragedians—Aeschylus, Sophocles, and Euripides—were active in the drama festivals. Drawing on the Delian treasury, Pericles [PER-uh-kleez], the popular leader and general, launched a glorious building program that was essentially a huge public works project (Figure 3.5). In a speech over Athens's war dead, Pericles offered an eloquent summation of Athenian democracy, praising its use of public debate in reaching decisions, its tolerance of diverse beliefs, it's ability to love beauty without sacrificing military strength. His conclusion boasted that Athens was the model for Greece.

However, those poleis that were not enamored of Athenian aggression became convinced that war was the only way to protect themselves. Athens's foreign policy and its expansionism had given rise to an alliance system so delicately balanced that neither side could allow the other to gain the slightest advantage. When Athens's neighbor Corinth went to war with Corcyra (present-day Corfu) in western Greece, Corcyra appealed to Athens for aid. Athens's initial victories frightened Corinth, whose leaders persuaded the Spartans to join together in the Peloponnesian League. The Peloponnesian War (431–404 B.C.) had begun.

Pericles knew the league was superior on land but thought the Athenians could hold out indefinitely within their own walls and win a war of attrition. However, a plague broke out in Athens in 430 B.C., killing many citizens, including Pericles. The first phase of the war ended in 421 B.C., when a demoralized and defeated Athens sued for peace.

The second half of the Peloponnesian War shifted from the Greek peninsula to distant Sicily and the west—a move that sealed Athens's fate. In 416 B.C., Segesta, a Sicilian polis, begged Athens for military assistance. The Athenians eventually sent help, but in trying to conduct a war so far from home, they were soundly defeated and never recovered their military and economic power.

In the early decades of the fourth century B.C., first Sparta and then Thebes emerged as the preeminent city-state, but these power struggles only further weakened the poleis and made them easy prey for an invader. At the northern edge of the civilized Greek world, that invader was gathering its forces. Macedonia was

Figure 3.5 *Pericles.* Ca. 440 B.C. Marble, ht. 19¾". Vatican Museum. *Pericles possessed a vision of Athens as the political, economic, and cultural center of the Greek world. Even though this portrait bust is a Roman copy of the Greek original, it conveys Pericles' strong sense of leadership and determination.*

Figure 3.6 *Alexander the Great.* Ca. 200 B.C. Marble, ht. 16⅛". Istanbul Museum. *Alexander's youth and fine features, idealized perhaps in this portrait bust, add to the legends that have accumulated around one of the most famous conquerors in history. Later rulers measured themselves against Alexander, whose dream of a united world was cut short by his early death.*

a primitive Greek state, governed by kings and populated with a people speaking a rough dialect of the Greek language. Their king, Philip, having been a hostage in Thebes when young, had become a *philhellene*—a lover of Greek civilization. A brilliant soldier, Philip expanded Macedonia to the east as far as the Black Sea. He then moved southward, conquering the poleis of central Greece. The poleis hastily raised an army, but Philip's well-disciplined troops crushed them at Chaeronea in 338 B.C. After establishing a league between Macedonia and the poleis, he granted the Greeks autonomy in everything except military affairs. Philip then announced an all-out war against Persia but was assassinated before he could launch his first campaign.

Philip's nineteen-year-old son, Alexander, succeeded to the throne. Tutored in philosophy by the renowned thinker Aristotle, Alexander nevertheless had the heart of a warrior. When Thebes and other poleis attempted to take control at Philip's death, Alexander burned Thebes to the ground, sparing only the house of the poet Pindar. Placing a general in command of Greece, Alexander turned his sights to the east (Figure 3.6).

Alexander dreamed of a world united under his name and of a culture fused from Hellenic and Persian roots. His armies marched into Asia Minor, Egypt, and Mesopotamia, absorbing the great Persian Empire; then they swept east through Asia to the Indus River in India. As he conquered, Alexander destroyed and looted the great centers of Eastern civilization, but he also founded new cities and spread Greek culture.

Alexander's dream ended abruptly with his death in 323 B.C. at the age of thirty-two. Seizing the opportunity presented by his sudden death, the Greeks revolted against the Macedonian oppressors, but they were quickly overwhelmed. The Macedonians then occupied Athens and installed an aristocratic government. Thus ended democracy and Hellenic civilization—in Greece.

THE PERFECTION OF THE TRADITION: THE GLORY OF HELLENIC GREECE

Throughout this era of shifting political fortunes, artistic and intellectual life flourished. Athens—bursting with creative energy—was the jewel of the Greek world. Atop its Acropolis, perfectly proportioned marble temples gleamed in the brilliant Aegean sun. Below, in the agora, philosophers debated the most profound questions of human nature. Hundreds of citizens congregated outdoors to serve in the assembly, where they passed laws or sat on juries that made legal rulings. Other citizens who were at leisure cheered on the athletes exercising in the open-air gymnasium (Figure 3.7). During drama festivals, the whole city turned out to share a gripping tragedy or to laugh uproariously at the latest comedy.

The culture that flourished in Greece at this time is known as **Classic,** or **Classical,** a term with varied meanings. *Classic* means, first of all, "best" or "preeminent," and the judgment of the Western tradition is that Greek culture was in fact the highest moment in the entire history of the humanities. *Classic* also means having permanent and recognized significance; a classic work establishes a standard against which other efforts are measured. In this second sense, the aesthetic values and forms of Greek culture have been studied and imitated in all later stages of Western history. By extension, "the classics" are the works that have survived from Greece and Rome.

Figure 3.7 *Athletes in the Palaestra.* Second quarter of the fifth century B.C. Marble, ht. 12½". National Museum, Athens. *This low-relief sculpture depicts athletes warming up in the open-air exercise area where spectators would congregate to urge on their favorites. The youth on the left is preparing for a foot race, and the one on the right tests his javelin. The pair in the center has just begun to wrestle. This relief was originally part of a sculptured base built into a wall that the Athenians constructed after the Persian Wars.*

Classic also refers to the body of specific aesthetic principles expressed through the art and literature of Greece and Rome, a system known as **Classicism.** The first stage of Classicism, which originated in the Hellenic Age, emphasized simplicity over complexity; balance, or symmetry, over asymmetry; and restraint over excess. At the heart of Classicism was the search for perfection, for the ideal form—whether expressed in the proportions of a temple constructed in marble or in the canon of the human anatomy molded in bronze or in a philosophical conclusion reached through logic. Hellenic Classicism found expression in many areas: theater, music, history, natural philosophy, architecture, and sculpture.

Theater: Tragedy

One of the most prominent institutions of Greek civilization was the theater, in which the dramatic form known as **tragedy** reached a state of perfection. Greek theater originally arose in connection with the worship of Dionysus. The word *tragedy* in Greek means "goat song," and this word may refer to a prehistoric religious ceremony in which competing male **choruses**—groups of singers—sang and danced, while intoxicated, in homage to the god of wine; the victory prize may have been a sacrificial goat. Whatever its precise origins, during the Archaic Age theater in Athens had taken the form of a series of competitive performances presented annually during the Great Dionysia, celebrated in March.

Features of the Tragic Theater At first, the chorus served as both the collective actor and the commentator on the events of the drama. Then, in the late sixth century B.C., according to tradition, the poet Thespis—from whose name comes the word *thespian,* or "actor"—introduced an actor with whom the chorus could interact. The theater was born. Initially, the main function of the actor was simply to ask questions of the chorus. During the Hellenic Age, the number of actors was increased to three, and, occasionally, late in the fifth century B.C., a fourth was added. Any number of actors who did not speak might be on the stage, but only the three leading actors engaged in dialogue. In the fifth century B.C., the chorus achieved its classic function as mediator between actors and audience. As time went on, however, the role of the chorus declined and the importance of the actors increased. By the fourth century B.C., the actor had become the focus of the drama.

Because the focus of tragedy was originally the chorus, the need for a space to accommodate their dancing and singing determined the theater's shape. The chorus performed in a circular area called an **orchestra,** or "dancing place," in the center of which was a functioning altar, serving as a reminder that tragedy was a religious rite. The audience sat around two-thirds of the orchestra on wooden bleachers or stone seats under the open sky. The other third of the orchestra was backed by a wooden or stone building called the ***skene,*** which could be painted to suggest a scene and through which entrances and exits could be made (Figure 3.8).

Figure 3.8 Theater at Epidauros. Ca. 300 B.C. *The best-preserved theater in Greece is the one at Epidauros. Although tragedy was created only in Athens, the popularity of the art form led to the construction of theaters all over Greece—a telling index of Athens's cultural imperialism. The acoustics in this ancient auditorium were remarkable. Performers' voices could be heard clearly throughout the theater even though it is in the open with fifty-four rows of seats accommodating 14,000 spectators.*

Such simple set decorations may have provided a slight bit of realism, but Greek theater was not concerned with either realism or the expressiveness of individual actors. Ideas and language were crucial. The actors—all men, even in the female roles—wore elaborate masks designed to project their voices, platform shoes, and long robes, which helped give the dramas a timeless, otherworldly quality.

Plays were performed in tetralogies (sets of four) on successive days of the Great Dionysia. Each competing playwright offered three tragedies, not necessarily related in theme or subject, that were performed during the day, and a satyr-play that was performed later. A **satyr-play** usually featured the indecent behavior and ribald speech of the satyrs—sexually insatiable half-men, half-goats—who followed Dionysus. That the Greeks liked to watch three deeply serious dramas followed by a play full of obscene high jinks demonstrates the breadth of their sensibility.

Tragic Drama The essence of Greek tragedy is the deeply felt belief that mortals cannot escape pain and sorrow. The dramatists shared with Homer the insight that "we men are wretched things, and the gods . . . have woven sorrow into the very pattern of our lives." Although terrible things happened in the tragedies—murder, incest, suicide, rape, mutilation—the attitude of the play toward these events was deeply moral. Violence for its own sake was not the concern of the playwright, and violence was never depicted onstage.

The tragedies were primarily based on the legends of royal families—usually the dynasties of Thebes, Sparta, and Argos—dating from the Age of Heroes of which Homer sang in his epics (Figure 3.9). Since the audience already knew these stories, their interest focused on the playwright's treatment of a familiar tale, his ideas about its moral significance, and how his language shaped those ideas.

The plots dealt with fundamental human issues with no easy solutions, such as the decrees of the state versus the conscience of the individual or divine law versus human law. Humans were forced to make hard choices without being able to foresee the consequences of their decisions. Nonetheless, the dramatists affirmed that a basic moral order existed underneath the shifting tide of human affairs. The political leaders of Athens recognized and accepted tragedy's ethical significance and educative function and thus made the plays into civic spectacles. For example, the audience was composed of citizens seated according to voting precincts, and Athenian warriors' orphans, who were wards of the polis, were honored at the performances.

According to the Greek philosopher Aristotle, whose immensely influential theory of tragedy, the *Poetics,* was based on his study of the dramas of the Hellenic Age, the purpose of tragedy was to work a cathartic, or purging, effect on the audience, to "arouse pity and terror" so that these negative emotions could be drained from the soul. The tragic heroes were warnings, not models; the spectators were instructed to

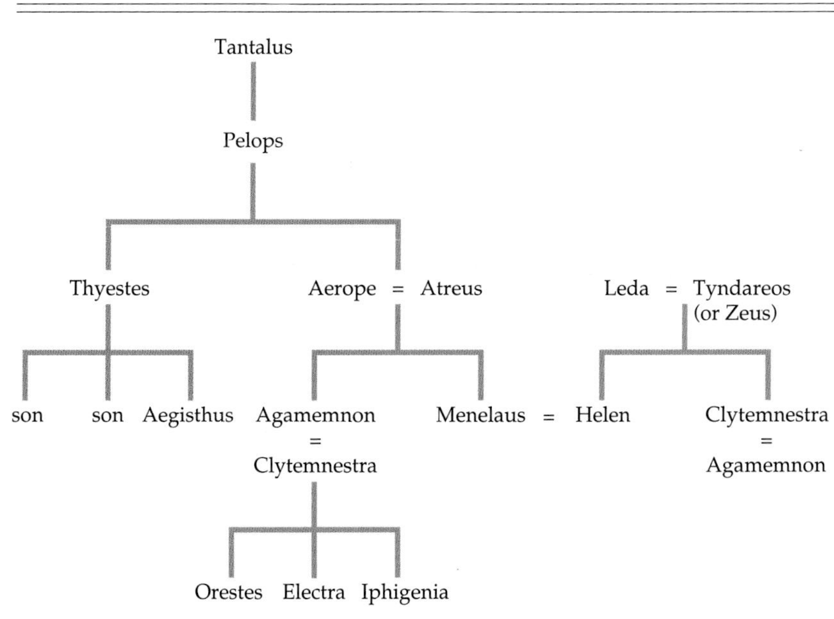

Figure 3.9 Genealogy of the House of Argos. *The tragic fate of the House of Argos (or the family of Atreus) was well under way before the opening scene of Aeschylus's tragedy* Agamemnon. *Thyestes seduced Aerope, the wife of his brother Atreus; in retaliation, Atreus killed Thyestes' two sons and served them to him in a stew. Thyestes then cursed the line of Atreus, and dire consequences followed. Most important, Agamemnon, the son of Atreus, sacrificed his own daughter to gain favorable weather for his planned invasion of Troy. Besides the* Oresteia, *three more tragedies survive that have plots based on the House of Argos*—Iphigenia in Taurus, Iphigenia in Aulis, *and* Electra, *all by Euripides—although they have no inner connection as does Aeschylus's trilogy.*

seek modest lives and not aim too high. Many tragedians pursued these themes and competed in the Dionysia, but the works of only three still survive—Aeschylus, Sophocles, and Euripides.

Aeschylus Aeschylus [ES-kuh-luhs] (about 525–about 456 B.C.), the earliest of the three dramatists, won first prize in the Great Dionysia thirteen times. He composed about ninety plays, but only seven are extant. His masterpiece, the *Oresteia,* is the only trilogy that has survived, and even here the satyr-play is missing. The framing plot is the homecoming from Troy of the Greek king Agamemnon, who had sinned by sacrificing his daughter to gain military success; his murder by his vengeful and adulterous wife, Clytemnestra; and the dire consequences of this killing.

Aeschylus's treatment of these terrible events in the *Oresteia* embodies some of the principles of Classicism. In the first place, Aeschylus shows great simplicity by avoiding distracting subplots: The first play, *Agamemnon,* tells the story of the king's death and Clytemnestra's triumph; the second, the *Libation Bearers,* relates the vengeance murder of Clytemnestra by her son, Orestes; and the third, *Eumenides,* halts—with the help of the Olympians Athena and Apollo—the cycle of revenge by instituting an Athenian court to try such cases. The trilogy is symmetrical in that Agamemnon's murder in the first play serves as punishment for the sacrifice of his daughter, Clytemnestra's death in the second avenges her slaying of Agamemnon, and the courtroom drama of the third absolves Orestes of the crime of matricide.

Finally, Aeschylus shows great restraint inasmuch as all deaths occur offstage, and the chorus or messengers only describe them. However, for the Athenian audience, the *Oresteia* had moral significance as well as stylistic power. By transforming the Furies, the blind champions of vengeance killing, into the "Kindly Ones" (*Eumenides*), Aeschylus, in effect, affirmed the ethical superiority of the rational Olympians over the earthbound chthonian divinities (see Chapter 2). In the *Oresteia,* Aeschylus confronts and resolves the opposition between several seemingly irreconcilable polarities—Olympian and chthonian gods, divine and human justice, religious cult and civic ritual, and fate and free will (Figure 3.10).

Sophocles Sophocles [SOF-uh-kleez] (about 496–406 B.C.), the most prolific of the great tragedians, wrote about 125 plays, but only 7 survive. He was popular among the Athenians, who awarded him first prize twenty-four times. Sophocles' *Antigone* (442 B.C.) expresses beautifully the principles of Classical tragedy. The simple plot treats the conflicts between King Creon and his niece Antigone. The principal, although not the sole, philosophical issue explored by the play is whether human or divine law should take precedence. Antigone's two brothers have killed each other in a dispute over the Theban crown. Creon decrees that Eteocles, who died defending the city, be buried with honor but that the body of the rebel Polyneices be left as carrion for wild beasts. Antigone, whose name in Greek means "born to oppose," defies his order and buries her brother in compliance with

Figure 3.10 *Orestes Slaying Aegisthus.* Ca. late sixth century B.C. Kunsthistorisches Museum, Vienna. *This red-figure vase painting presents a different version of events in Argos from those given by Aeschylus in the* Libation Bearers, *the second play of the* Oresteia. *The vase painter portrays Clytemnestra bearing an ax (left), a detail Aeschylus omitted, and the sister between Orestes and his mother is not named Electra as she is in the* Oresteia. *However, painter and playwright agree that Orestes killed Aegisthus, his mother's lover.*

religious teachings. Arrested and imprisoned, Antigone hangs herself, and Creon's son and wife kill themselves. Too late, King Creon sees the light; he gives up his throne saying, "There is no man can bear this guilt but I."

Several tensions are at issue here. Creon represents the typical tyrant, concerned only with "law and order." His son, Haemon, is the voice of democracy, opposing the tyrannical will of his father. Creon believes in the superiority of public power over domestic life, in the necessity of the state to seek power for its own sake, in the priority of war over the commands of love, and in the right of men to control women. When the king tries to persuade his son to renounce his love for the disobedient Antigone, they argue about all four of these issues. Whether the Athenian citizens sided with Creon or Haemon is unknown, but *Antigone* has become the classic example of a tragic dilemma where two rights confront each other. In his desire for balance, Sophocles gives equally powerful arguments to the play's opposing characters.

Sophocles returned to the history of the Theban dynasty in later plays about Antigone's ill-fated father, Oedipus. In *Oedipus the King,* he tells how the Theban ruler unwittingly kills his father and marries his mother and later blinds himself to atone for his guilt. Though fate has a pivotal role in Oedipus's story, the playwright also emphasizes the part the hero's weakness plays in his downfall. Aristotle's *Poetics* held up this work as a model of Greek tragedy. In *Oedipus at Colonus,* his last play, Sophocles portrays the former king at peace with himself and his destiny.

Euripides By the time Euripides [yu-RIP-uh-deez] (about 480–406 B.C.) was writing for the stage, Athens was fighting for its existence in the Peloponnesian War, and with him, the creative phase of Classical theater came to an end. Euripides was in tune with the skeptical mood of the later years of this struggle, and by presenting unorthodox versions of myths and legends, he exposed the foolishness of some popular beliefs and, sometimes, the emptiness of contemporary values. When he staged *The Trojan Women* in 415 B.C., the Athenians could not have missed the parallel between the cruel enslavement of the women of Troy after the Greeks destroyed their city and the fate of the women of Melos, which Athens had just subjugated.

For his ninety or more tragedies (of which eighteen survive), the Athenians awarded the first prize to Euripides only five times, perhaps because his unorthodox plays angered the audience. But later ages, far removed from the stresses of Hellenic times, found his dramas more to their liking. Among the extant works, *The Bacchae* is his masterpiece, a gruesome tale about the introduction of the worship of Dionysus into Thebes. In this play, the bacchae, or bacchantes (another name for the followers of Dionysus), blinded by religious frenzy, kill the king of Thebes under the delusion that he is a wild animal. Euripides' dark tragedy may have been a warning to the citizens of Athens about the dangers of both excess and repression in religion and politics.

Euripides followed Classical principles in *The Bacchae,* using a single plot, offstage violence, and well-defined conflict, but he also extended the range of Classical drama with his unorthodox, even romantic, language and his skeptical treatment of familiar themes. Moreover, Euripides pointed the way toward a different sort of theater by having the severed head of the hero brought onstage at the end of the tragedy.

With Euripides, the creative phase of Classical theater came to an end. The playwrights who followed him seem to have read their works aloud rather than staging them with actors and choruses. The plays of all the Greek dramatists were presented frequently throughout Greece, however, as well as later in the Macedonian and Roman Empires.

Theater: Comedy

Comedies were performed in the Great Dionysia just as the tragedies were, and they were also entered in contests in another festival known as the Lesser Dionysia, celebrated in later winter. The comedies refused to take anyone or anything seriously. They featured burlesque actions, buffoonery, slapstick, obscenity, and horseplay, and actors wore grotesque costumes with padded bellies or rumps to give a ridiculous effect. Comic playwrights invented their own plots and focused on contemporary matters: politics, philosophies, the new social classes, and well-known personalities. Even the deities were ridiculed and portrayed in embarrassing situations.

The freedom of the comic playwrights could exist only in a democracy. And yet the freedom was limited to a highly ritualized setting—the drama festivals—that allowed, even encouraged, the overturning of rules and the burlesquing of traditions. This controlled expression of the unspeakable provided a catharsis that strengthened communal bonds in the polis. At the same time, the authors demonstrated their faith in the basic good sense of the average citizen.

The comedies of Aristophanes [air-uh-STOF-uh-neez] (about 445–about 388 B.C.) are the primary source for what is known as **Old Comedy,** comic Greek plays with a strong element of political criticism. Aristophanes composed forty-four works in all, of which eleven are extant. Like Euripides, he wrote his plays for war-torn Athens, and he satirized famous contemporaries such as the thinker Socrates, depicting him as a hopeless dreamer. Aristophanes must have stepped on many toes, for the Athenians awarded him first prize only four times.

In *Lysistrata,* Aristophanes transcended the limitations of the comedic form and approached the timeless quality of the tragedies. A sexually explicit and hilarious comedy, *Lysistrata* points out the absurdity of the prolonged Peloponnesian War and, by implication, all war. In the play, Lysistrata, an Athenian matron, persuades the women of Athens and Sparta to withhold sex from their husbands until they sign a peace treaty. Filled with sexual innuendos, obscenities, and ridiculous allusions to tragic dramas, the play ends with stirring reminders to the Greeks of their common ancestry, their joint victory over the Persians earlier in the century, and their reverence for the same gods. First staged in 411 B.C., seven years before Sparta won the Peloponnesian War, this play commented on but failed to derail Athens's headlong rush to disaster (Figure 3.11).

After the Peloponnesian War and the restoration of a harsher democracy in 403 B.C., free speech was severely repressed in Athens. Comedies still relied on burlesque and slapstick, but their political edge was blunted. For all practical purposes, the great creative age of Greek theater was now over.

Music

Like other peoples of the ancient Near East, the Greeks used music both in civic and religious events and in private entertainment. But the Greeks also gave music a new importance, making it one of the humanities along with art, literature, theater, and philosophy. Music became a form of expression subject to rules, styles, and rational analysis. One reason for this was that the Greeks believed music fulfilled an ethical function in the training of young citizens. They also believed that music had divine origins and was inspired by Euterpe, one of the nine muses (thus the word *music*).

Nevertheless, the vast library of Greek music has vanished. What knowledge there is of that lost heritage, which can be only partially reconstructed from surviving treatises on musical theory and references in other writings, shows a tradition that, despite some differences, became the foundation of Western music. Greek music apparently followed the diatonic system, which had been invented by Pythagoras, using a scale of eight notes, each of which was determined by its

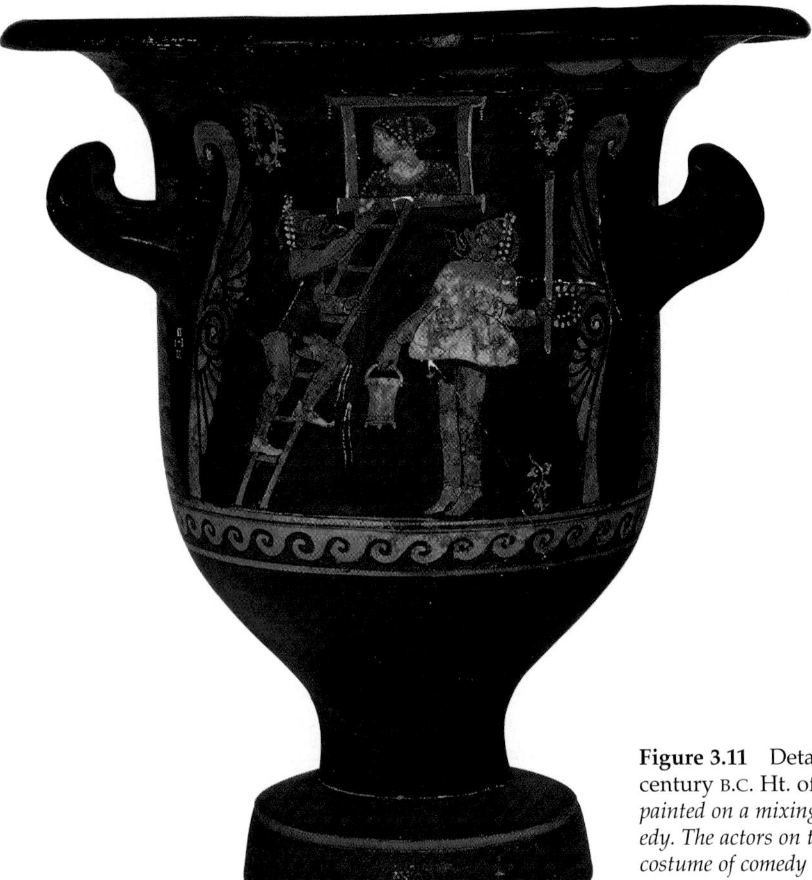

Figure 3.11 Detail, Scene from a Comedy. Mid-fourth century B.C. Ht. of vase 15⅔″. British Museum. *This scene, painted on a mixing bowl, portrays a situation from a Greek comedy. The actors on the right and left are outfitted in the grotesque costume of comedy with padded rumps and genitals. That these characters are onstage is indicated by the decorations at the bottom of the frame.*

numerical ratio to the lowest tone. The Greek composers also devised a series of scales, called **modes,** which functioned roughly like major and minor keys in later Western music. The modes, however, were not interchangeable the way keys are, because the Greeks believed that each mode produced a different emotional and ethical effect on the listener. Thus, the Dorian mode, martial and grave in its emotional impact, was thought by the Greeks to make hearers brave and dignified; the tender and sorrowing Lydian mode, to make them sentimental and weak; and the passionate and wild Phrygian mode, to make them excited and headstrong. Believing that such emotional manipulation made free citizens difficult to govern, Plato banished virtually all music from his ideal republic. Modern research has been able to reproduce all the Greek modes, but otherwise this music remains a mystery.

Despite music's high ethical status in Greece, it had no independent role in Hellenic culture. Instead, music was integrated with verse, notably in epic and lyric poetry and in tragedy and comedy, with either the lyre (a stringed instrument) or the aulos (a wind instrument) providing accompaniment.

History

The study of history began in the fifth century B.C., when inquisitive and articulate Greeks started to analyze the meaning of their immediate past and to write down in prose the results of their research, or *historia*—the Greek word for inquiry. The Greeks before the Classical period had only a dim sense of their past; what they knew came from Homer, random artifacts, and the ruins of Mycenaean grandeur. Herodotus [he-ROD-uh-tuhs] (about 484 B.C.–about 430 B.C.) was the first to approach history as a separate study and the first to practice historical writing in anything like the modern sense. He was motivated by the belief that the present had its causes in the past and could be a guide for the future. His *Histories* recorded and analyzed the Persian Wars, which Herodotus interpreted as Europe versus Asia, or West versus East. In his desire to be fair to both sides, he traveled to Persia and recorded what he learned there.

The *Histories* have been criticized for implausible and inaccurate information, but Herodotus's clear prose style, his concern for research, his efforts to be impartial, his belief in historical cause and effect, and his desire to leave a record of the past as a legacy to future generations have justly earned him the title "Father of History."

Yet, for all his excellence, Herodotus pales in comparison with Thucydides [thew-SID-uh-deez] (died about 401 B.C.). His subject was the Peloponnesian War, of which he was an eyewitness at times. Thucydides was much more skeptical and inquiring than Herodotus, and although he was an avid democrat and an admirer of Pericles, he strove to be completely fair in his account of Periclean Athens. He saw the weaknesses of his beloved polis and realized the baleful effects of imperialism. In his *History of the Peloponnesian War,* he even wrote objectively of his own role as the losing admiral in a naval battle.

Thucydides also used ordinary events to illuminate human motives and fundamental causes and effects in history. Like the Greek dramatists, he showed that human weaknesses and flaws created the real-life tragedies he observed around him. His insight into human nature was penetrating as he chronicled how individuals shift loyalties and redefine their values to justify their actions.

This masterful writer rose above his narrative to give lessons to future generations, arguing that events that happened in the past would, at some time and in similar ways, recur. Yet he denied that history repeats itself simplistically, and he warned that his book must be read closely and thoughtfully if it was to be understood wisely.

Table 3.1 PHILOSOPHY IN THE HELLENIC AGE

PHILOSOPHY	*EMPHASIS*
Pre-Socratic	The physical world; nature; debate over materialism and idealism
Sophist	Humanistic values; practical skills, such as public speaking and logic
Socratic	Enduring moral and intellectual order of the universe; the psyche (mind/soul); "Virtue is Knowledge"
Platonist	Ideas (Forms) are basis of everything; dualism, the split between the world of Ideas and the everyday world; rationalism; severe moderation in ethics
Aristotelian	Natural world is the only world; empiricism, using observation, classification, and comparison; "golden mean" in ethics

Natural Philosophy

When the Hellenic Age opened, natural philosophy remained divided into two major camps: the materialists and the idealists (see Chapter 2). The materialists, who perpetuated the inquiries of Thales and the Milesian school, believed that the world was made of some basic physical thing. The idealists, in contrast, who stemmed from Pythagoras and the Sicilian school, were nonmaterialists, reasoning that the physical world was illusory and that behind it was a spiritual force or a metaphysical power.

By the mid–fifth century B.C., this simple pattern was being challenged by new philosophies, and by 400 B.C., a revolution in thought had occurred that overshadowed everything that had gone before. The first assault came from Elea, in Sicily, where a new school of thinkers proposed to reconcile materialism and idealism. Then, in Athens, the Sophists questioned philosophical inquiry itself and the notion of absolute truth. These corrosive figures provoked Socrates, the most revolutionary thinker of the entire ancient world, to respond to their claims. Socrates' life is regarded as a watershed in Greek thought. All Greek thinkers before him are now known as Pre-Socratics, and those who came after him—chiefly Plato and Aristotle in Hellenic Greece—followed his lead in studying the human experience (Table 3.1).

The Pre-Socratics The major pre-Socratic thinkers were concerned with determining the nature of the physical world. For Parmenides [par-MEN-uh-deez] (about 515–? B.C.) and his followers in Elea, for example, the world was a single, unchanging, unmoving object whose order could be known through human reason. This attempt to reconcile materialism and idealism was modified by Parmenides' student Empedocles [em-PED-uh-kleez] (about 484–about 424 B.C.), who claimed that everything, animate or inanimate, originated in the four elements of earth, water, fire, and air. These elements were unchanging, but the opposing forces of Love and Strife could combine them in different ways, to the detriment or benefit of humans. This essentially metaphysical explanation of change later influenced Aristotle.

The Atomists, another school of pre-Socratic thinkers, believed that everything was composed of atoms—eternal, invisible bodies of varying size that, by definition, could not be divided into smaller units—and the void, the empty space between the atoms. Atomic theory was developed most fully by Democritus [de-MOK-ruht-us] of Thrace (about 460–? B.C.). The movement and shape of the atoms were sufficient to explain not only physical objects but also feelings, tastes, sight, ideas—in short, every aspect of the physical world.

Anaxagoras [an-ak-SAG-uh-ruhs] (about 500–428 B.C.), although not an Atomist, also explained the world in terms of small particles. His unique contribution was the idea that the combinations and divisions of these particles were controlled by a nonphysical agency he called *nous* (reason or mind). Socrates praised him for the originality of this conception and then faulted him for seeing *nous* only as a mechanical force without religious significance.

The Sophists The Sophists—from the Greek word *sophia,* or "wisdom"—scorned pre-Socratic speculation about atoms and elements as irrelevant and useless. These traveling teachers claimed to offer their students (for a fee) knowledge that guaranteed success in life. Their emphasis on the development of practical skills, such as effective public speaking, led their critics to accuse them of cynicism and a lack of interest in higher ethical values, but the Sophists were deeply serious and committed to humanistic values. Protagoras [pro-TAG-uh-ruhs] (481–411 B.C.), the most renowned of the Sophists, proclaimed in a dictum that "man is the measure of all things." This summed up the Sophists' argument that human beings, as the center of the universe, have the power to make judgments about themselves and their world. The Sophists helped free the human spirit to be critical and creative. If there was a danger in their teaching, it was a tendency toward unrestrained skepticism. By stressing that human beings had the power to shape the world, the Sophists opened themselves to charges of impiety and undermining traditional values, because the traditional Greek view was that the gods controlled everything.

The Socratic Revolution Socrates [SAH-kruh-teez] (about 470–399 B.C.), the thinker who launched a new era in philosophy, did not hesitate to condemn the Sophists. He claimed to oppose everything they stood for, especially what he thought was the Sophist tendency to overvalue skepticism and thus undermine values without offering new ones in their place. But Socrates shared certain traits with the Sophists, such as his rejection of philosophizing about nature, his focus on human problems, and his desire to empower individuals to make their own moral choices. What basically separated Socrates from the Sophists was his passionate conviction that an enduring moral and intellectual order existed in the universe.

Socrates' method for arriving at true moral and intellectual values was deceptively simple yet maddeningly elusive. At the heart of his thinking was the *psyche* (mind, or soul); being immortal, the psyche was deemed more important than the mortal and doomed body. Those who want wisdom must protect, nourish, and expand their psyches by giving their minds the maximum amount of knowledge, but not just any knowledge. The knowledge the psyche acquired had to be won through stimulating conversations and debates as well as by contemplation of abstract virtues and moral values. Only then could the psyche approach its highest potential.

"Virtue is Knowledge," claimed Socrates; he meant that a person who knows the truth, acquired through personal struggle to self-enlightenment, will not commit evil deeds. And this moral dictum may be reversed: Those who do wrong do so out of ignorance. If people used their psyches to think more deeply and clearly, they would lead virtuous lives. His belief in the essential goodness of human nature and the necessity of well-defined knowledge became a central tenet of Western thought.

After having pointed out the proper path to wisdom, Socrates left the rest up to his students. Bombarding inquiring youths with questions on such topics as the meaning of justice, he used rigorous logic to refute all the squirming students' attempts at precise definition. Then—as shown by Plato's dialogues, the principal source for what we know about Socrates—the students, collapsing into confusion, admitted the serious gaps in their knowledge. Socrates' step-by-step questions, interspersed with gentle humor and ironic jabs, honed his students' logical skills and compelled them to begin a quest for knowledge in light of their self-confessed ignorance. The Socratic method was adopted by many teachers in Greece and Rome and remains an honored pedagogical device.

The Athenians of this era began to perceive Socrates as a threat to their way of life. This short, homely, and rather insignificant looking man—as surviving statues reveal—aroused suspicion in the polis by his public arguments (Figure 3.12). When Athens fell to the Spartans in 404 B.C., opposition to Socrates began to swell. Many citizens now found subversion or even blasphemy in his words and in the behavior of his followers. Five years after the end of the Peloponnesian War, Socrates was accused of impiety and of corrupting the Athenian youth, and a jury declared him guilty and sentenced him to die. Plato, a former student, was so moved by Socrates' eloquent, though ineffective, defense and by the injustice of his death that the younger man dedicated the remainder of his life to righting the wrong and explaining the Socratic philosophy.

Plato also made Socrates' last days the subject of four works: the *Euthyphro* (a discussion of piety on the eve of his trial), the *Apology* (his defense before the court), the *Crito* (explanation of his willingness to die for his beliefs), and the *Phaedo* (deathbed scene with his argument in support of immortality).

Plato The spirit of Socrates hovers over the rest of Greek philosophy, especially in the accomplishments of his most famous student, Plato (about 427–347 B.C.). Plato's philosophy is the fountainhead of Western **idealism,** a thought system that emphasizes spiritual values and makes ideas, rather than matter, the basis of everything that exists. **Platonism** arose out of certain premises that were Socratic in origin—the concept of the psyche and the theory of remembrance. Like Socrates, Plato emphasized the immortal and immutable psyche over the mortal and changeful body. But Plato advanced a new polarity, favoring the invisible world of the Forms, or Ideas, in opposition to the physical world. The psyche's true home was the world of the Forms, which it inhabited before birth and after death—the time when the psyche was lost in wonder among the eternal Ideas. In contrast, the body lived exclusively in the material world, completely absorbed by the life of the senses. Once trapped inside the body, the psyche could glimpse the higher reality, or Forms, only through remembrance.

Nonetheless, Plato thought that through a set of mental exercises the psyche would be able to recall the Ideas to which it had once been exposed. The best training for the psyche was the study of mathematics, since mathematics required signs and symbols to represent other things. After the mastery of mathematics, the student proceeded, with the help of logic, to higher stages of abstract learning, such as defining the Forms of Justice, Beauty, and Love. By showing that wisdom came only after an intellectual progression that culminated in an understanding of the absolute Ideas, Plato silenced the Sophists, who claimed that knowledge was relative.

A major implication of Plato's idealism is that the psyche and the body are constantly at war. The psyche's attempts to remember the lost Ideas meet resistance from the body's pursuit of power, fame, and physical comforts. This dualism especially plagued the philosopher, the lover of wisdom; but the true philosopher took comfort in recognizing that at death the psyche would return freely to the world of the Forms.

Plato identified the Form of the Good, the ultimate Idea, with God. Yet the Platonic deity was neither the creator of the world nor the absolute and final power. Instead, Plato's deity was necessary for his idealism to function; in his thought, God was the source from which descended the imperfect objects of the natural world. In a related theological notion, he, like Socrates, attributed the presence of evil to ignorance; but Plato added the psyche's misdirected judgment and insatiable bodily appetites as other causes of evil.

Socrates' death provoked Plato to envision a perfect state where justice flourished. The book that resulted

Figure 3.12 *Socrates.* Fourth century B.C. Ht. 10½″. British Museum. *This Roman marble copy of the original Greek statue supports the unflattering descriptions of Socrates by his contemporaries. By portraying the philosopher with a receding hairline and a dumpy body, the anonymous sculptor has made one of the world's most extraordinary human beings look very ordinary.*

from Plato's speculations—the *Republic*—sets forth his model state and, incidentally, launched the study of political philosophy in the West. Plato thought that a just state could be realized only when all social classes worked together for the good of the whole, each class performing its assigned tasks. Because of the importance of the psyche, social status was determined by the ability to reason and not by wealth or inheritance. A tiny elite of philosopher kings and queens, who were the best qualified to run the state, reigned. Possessing wisdom as a result of their education in the Platonic system, they lived simply, shunning the creature comforts that corrupted weaker rulers.

The two lower ranks were similarly equipped for their roles in society by their intellects and their training: A middle group provided police and military protection, and the third and largest segment operated the economy. In Plato's dream world, both the individual and the society aimed for virtue, and the laws and the institutions ensured that the ideal would be achieved.

Aristotle Socrates may have been revolutionary; Plato was certainly poetic; but Aristotle [AIR-uh-stot-uhl] (384–322 B.C.) had the most comprehensive mind of the ancient world. His curiosity and vast intellect led him into every major field of inquiry of his time except mathematics and music. Born in Macedonia, he was connected to some of the most glittering personalities of his day. He first studied philosophy under Plato in Athens and then tutored the future Alexander the Great back at Philip's court. After Philip's conquest of Greece, Aristotle settled in Athens and opened a school, the Lyceum, that quickly rivaled the Academy, the school Plato had established.

Although his philosophy owed much to Platonism, Aristotle emphasized the role of the human senses. To Aristotle, the natural world was the only world; no separate, invisible realm of Ideas existed. Nature could be studied and understood by observation, classification, and comparison of data from the physical world—that is, through the empirical method.

Aristotle rejected the world of the Forms because he believed that Form and Matter were inseparable, both rooted in nature. Each material object contained a predetermined Form that, with proper training or nourishment, would evolve into its final Form and ultimate purpose. This growth process, in his view, was potentiality evolving into actuality, as when an embryo becomes a human or a seed matures into a plant. Thus, the philosopher could conclude that everything had a purpose, or end.

Aristotle's thought rested on the concept of God, which he equated with the First Cause. Aristotle's God was a philosopher's deity, purely rational, self-absorbed, and uncaring about the world or its inhabitants. Had this deity been anything else, Aristotle's God would not have been the supreme power or First Cause.

Rejecting Platonic dualism and its exclusive regard for the psyche, Aristotle devised a down-to-earth ethical goal—a sound mind in a healthy body—that he called happiness. To achieve happiness, he advised, in his *Nicomachean Ethics,* striking a mean, or a balance, between extremes of behavior. For example, courage is the mean between the excess of foolhardiness and the deficiency of cowardice. Noting that actions like murder and adultery are vicious by their very nature, he condemned them as being unable to be moderated. Although Aristotle disavowed many of Plato's ideas, he agreed with his former mentor that the cultivation of the higher intellect was more important than that of the body.

Aristotle's ethics are related to his politics, for he taught that happiness finally depended on the type of government under which an individual lived. Unlike Plato, who based his politics on speculative thinking, Aristotle reached his political views after careful research. After collecting over 150 state constitutions, Aristotle, in his *Politics,* classified and compared them, concluding that the best form of government was a constitutional regime ruled by the middle class. His preference for the middle class stemmed from his belief that they, exciting neither envy from the poor nor contempt from the wealthy, would honor and work for the good of all.

Aristotle's influence on Western civilization is immeasurable. His writings formed the core of knowledge that Christian scholars later studied as they struggled to keep the light of civilization burning after the collapse of the Roman Empire. Likewise, Jewish and Moslem thinkers ranked his books just below their own religious scriptures. Today, Aristotelianism is embedded in the official theology of the Roman Catholic Church, and Aristotle's logic continues to be taught in college philosophy courses.

Architecture

Of all the Greek art forms, architecture most powerfully embodied the Classical ideals of the Hellenic Age. The stone temple, the supreme expression of the Hellenic building genius, now received its definitive shape. Ironically, the Doric temple, which had originated in the Archaic Age, reached perfection in Ionian Athens. The versatile Athenians also perfected a new architectural order, the **Ionic,** which reflected more clearly their cultural tradition.

PERSONAL PERSPECTIVE

Xenophon
Secrets of a Successful Marriage

Xenophon (ca. 445–355 B.C.) was a Greek military commander, historian, essayist, and student of Socrates. In this selection from Oeconomicus, *he expounds on the secrets of a successful marriage through the characters of Socrates and Ischomachus, a rich landowner.*

I [Socrates] said, "I should very much like you to tell me, Ischomachus, whether you yourself trained your wife to become the sort of woman that she ought to be, or whether she already knew how to carry out her duties when you took her as your wife from her father and mother."

[Ischomachus replied,] "What could she have known when I took her as my wife, Socrates? She was not yet fifteen when she came to me, and had spent her previous years under careful supervision so that she might see and hear and speak as little as possible. . . .

"[A]s soon as she was sufficiently tamed and domesticated so as to be able to carry on a conversation, I questioned her more or less as follows: 'Tell me, wife, have you ever thought about why I married you and why your parents gave you to me? It must be quite obvious to you, I am sure, that there was no shortage of partners with whom we might sleep. I, on my part, and your parents, on your behalf, considered who was the best partner we could choose for managing an estate and for children. And I chose you, and your parents, apparently, chose me, out of those who were eligible. Now if some day the god grants us children, then we shall consider how to train them in the best way possible. For this will be a blessing to us both, to obtain the best allies and support in old age. But at present we two share this estate. I go on paying everything I have into the common fund; and you deposited into it everything you brought with you. There is no need to calculate precisely which of us has contributed more, but to be well aware of this: that the better partner is the one who makes the more valuable contribution. . . .

"'Because both the indoor and the outdoor tasks require work and concern, I think the god, from the very beginning, designed the nature of woman for the indoor work and concerns and the nature of man for the outdoor work. For he prepared man's body and mind to be more capable of enduring cold and heat and travelling and military campaigns, and so he assigned the outdoor work to him. Because the woman was physically less capable of endurance, I think the god has evidently assigned the indoor work to her. . . .

"'Because it is necessary for both of them to give and to take, he gave both of them equal powers of memory and concern. So you would not be able to distinguish whether the female or male sex has the larger share of these. And he gave them both equally the ability to practise self-control too, when it is needed. . . . [B]ecause they are not equally well endowed with all the same natural aptitudes, they are consequently more in need of each other, and the bond is more beneficial to the couple, since one is capable where the other is deficient.'"

Sanctuaries Before there were temples, however, Greece had sanctuaries, places considered sacred to a god or goddess. Of these sacred places, Apollo's shrine at Delphi was the oldest and the most famous (Figure 3.13). Delphi, thought to be the center of the earth, was hallowed ground to the entire Greek world, and the major poleis supported the god's priesthood there. Apollo's temple was the most splendid building on the site. Inside was Apollo's oracle—the only woman permitted at Delphi—to whom people journeyed from all over Greece with their questions.

With the rise of the poleis, the concept of a holy place set aside from the business of everyday life was adapted to the religious needs of each community. By the Hellenic Age, each polis had its own sacred area, usually built on a hill or protected by walls, which contained buildings and altars. Although each polis worshiped the entire pantheon of deities, one god or goddess was gradually singled out as a patron, and a temple was erected to house the statue of that particular divinity.

The Temple: The Perfection of the Form By Hellenic times, the Greek world was polarized between eastern (the mainland and the Aegean Islands) and western (Magna Graecia) styles of temple design, although in both styles the temples were rectilinear and of post-beam-triangle construction. Influenced by the Pythagorean quest for harmony through mathematical rules, the eastern builders had standardized six as the perfect number of columns for the ends of temples and thirteen, or twice the number of end columns plus one, as

Figure 3.13 The Delphic Sanctuary. Aerial view. Late sixth century–late fourth century B.C. *The ruins of Apollo's temple—this is an active earthquake zone—are marked by a rectangular foundation and a few standing columns. A Sacred Way, or road, zigzagged up the mountain to the temple's entrance. During the fourth century* B.C., *a gymnasium for boys and a theater were established in the sanctuary, and a stadium was constructed for athletic contests.*

Figure 3.14 Second Temple of Hera at Poseidonia. Ca. 450 B.C. Limestone. *This temple of Hera is among the best-preserved structures from the ancient world. Since Hera may have been a chthonian goddess before becoming consort to Olympian Zeus, it is appropriate that this Doric temple, with its ground-hugging appearance, be her monument.*

Figure 3.15 ICTINUS AND CALLICRATES. The Parthenon. Third quarter of the fifth century B.C. Pentelic marble. Athens. *A great humanistic icon, the Parthenon has had a long history since its days as a Greek temple. It served successively as a Christian church, a mosque, and an ammunitions depot, until it was accidentally blown up at the end of the seventeenth century A.D. Today, concerned nations are cooperating with the Greek government through UNESCO to preserve this noble ruin.*

the perfect number of columns for the sides. These balanced proportions, along with simple designs and restrained decorative schemes, made the eastern temples majestically expressive of Classical ideals.

Architects in western Greece, somewhat removed from the centers of Classical culture, were more experimental. Their buildings deviated from the eastern ideals, as can be seen in the Second Temple of Hera at Poseidonia, built of limestone in about 450 B.C. (Figure 3.14). The best preserved of all Greek temples, this Doric structure does not have the harmonious proportions of the eastern version of this style. Although the Second Temple of Hera owed much to eastern influences, including the six columns at the ends and the porches, it had too many (fourteen) columns on the sides, its columns were too thick, and the low-pitched roof made the building seem squat.

Between 447 and 438 B.C., the architects Ictinus [ik-TIE-nuhs] and Callicrates [kuh-LICK-ruh-teez] perfected the eastern-style Doric temple in the Parthenon, a temple on Athens's Acropolis dedicated to Athena (Figure 3.15). When completed, this temple established a new standard of Classicism, with eight columns on the ends and seventeen on the sides and with the numerical ratio of 9:4 used throughout, expressed, for example, in the relation of a column's height to its diameter. Inside, the builders designed two chambers, an east room for a 40-foot-high statue of Athena and a smaller room housing the Delian League treasury. The rest of the Acropolis project, finally finished in 405 B.C., included the Propylaea, the gate leading to the sanctuary; the temple of Athena Nike, a gift to Athens's patron goddess thanking her for a military victory (Figure 3.16); and the Erechtheum, a temple dedicated to three deities.

Ictinus and Callicrates introduced many subtle variations, called refinements, in their designs, so that no line is exactly straight, horizontal, or perpendicular. For example, the stepped base of the temple forms a gentle arc so that the ends are lower than the middle; the floor slopes slightly to the edges; and the columns tilt inward away from the ends. These and other refinements were no accidents but were intended to be corrections for real and imaginary optical illusions.

Figure 3.16 CALLICRATES. Temple of Athena Nike. Late fifth century B.C. Marble. Athens. *Designed by Callicrates, one of the Parthenon's architects, this miniature temple was begun after 427 B.C. and probably completed before 420 B.C. Like the Parthenon, it was dedicated to the city's patron goddess, Athena, though here she was honored as Nike, goddess of victory. This temple's simple plan includes a square cella with four Ionic columns at the front and back and a sculptural frieze, devoted to scenes of mythic and contemporary battles, encircling the upper exterior walls.*

The Parthenon's fame exerted such authority in later times that these refinements, along with harmonious proportions, became standardized as the essence of Greek architecture.

The second order of Greek architecture, the Ionic, originated in the late Archaic Age and, like the Doric, came to flower in Hellenic times. The Ionic style, freer than the Doric and more graceful, reflected its origins in the Ionian world; traditionally, the Ionians contrasted their opulence with the simplicity of the Dorians. In place of the alternating metopes and triglyphs of Doric buildings, the Ionic temple had a running frieze to which sculptured figures might be added. More decorated than the plain Doric, the Ionic columns had elegant bases, and their tops were crowned with capitals that suggested either a scroll's ends or a ram's horns. What solidified the Ionic temple's impression of elegance was its slender and delicate columns.

The Athenians chose the Ionic style for the exquisite, though eccentric, Erechtheum, the last of the great buildings erected on the Acropolis (Figure 3.17). The artistic freedom associated with the Ionic style may have led the architect, Mnesicles [NES-uh-kleez], to make the floor plan asymmetrical and to introduce so many design variations, but a more likely explanation was Mnesicles' need to integrate three existing shrines into a single building—those of the Olympians Athena and Poseidon and King Erechtheus, who introduced

Figure 3.17 MNESICLES. The Erechtheum. View from the west. Ca. 410 B.C. Marble. Athens. *The Erectheum was probably built to quiet conservatives who rejected Athena's new temple, the Parthenon, as a symbol of Athenian imperialism. Reflecting its ties with the past, the Erechtheum housed the ancient wooden cult statue of Athena, which pious Athenians believed had fallen from the sky. Its Ionic porches set the standard for the graceful Ionic order. The Porch of the Maidens (right), which was inaccessible from the outside, fronted the southern wall.*

the horse to Athens. Mnesicles took the unusual step of stressing the site's unbalanced nature by adding two Ionic porches and the temple's crowning feature, the Porch of the Maidens. By his bold design, Mnesicles created a marvelous illusion of harmony that was in keeping with the age's Classical ideals.

Sculpture

Equally impressive is the Greek achievement in sculpture. Believing that the task of sculpture was to imitate nature, the Greeks created images of gods and goddesses as well as of men and women that have haunted the Western imagination ever since. They not only forged a canon of idealized human proportions that later sculptors followed but also developed a repertoire of postures, gestures, and subjects that have become embedded in Western art.

During the Hellenic Age, Classical sculpture moved through three separate phases: The **Severe style,** which ushered in the period and lasted until 450 B.C.; the **High Classical style,** which coincided with the zenith of Athenian imperial greatness; and the **Fourth Century style,** which concluded with the death of Alexander the Great in 323 B.C.

Sculpture in the Severe style, inspired perhaps by its association with funeral customs, was characterized by a feeling of dignified nobility. The *Kritios Boy*—showing a figure fully at rest—is an elegant expression of this first phase of Classicism (Figure 3.18). Kritios [KRIT-ee-uhs], the supposed sculptor, fixed the mouth severely and altered the frontality, a feature of the Archaic style, by tilting the head subtly to the right and slightly twisting the upper torso. The flat-footed stance of the Archaic kourai has given way to a posture that places the body's weight on one leg and uses the other leg as a support. This stance is called **contrapposto** (counterpoise), and its invention, along with the mastery of the representation of musculature, helped to make the Classical revolution (Figure 3.19). Thereafter,

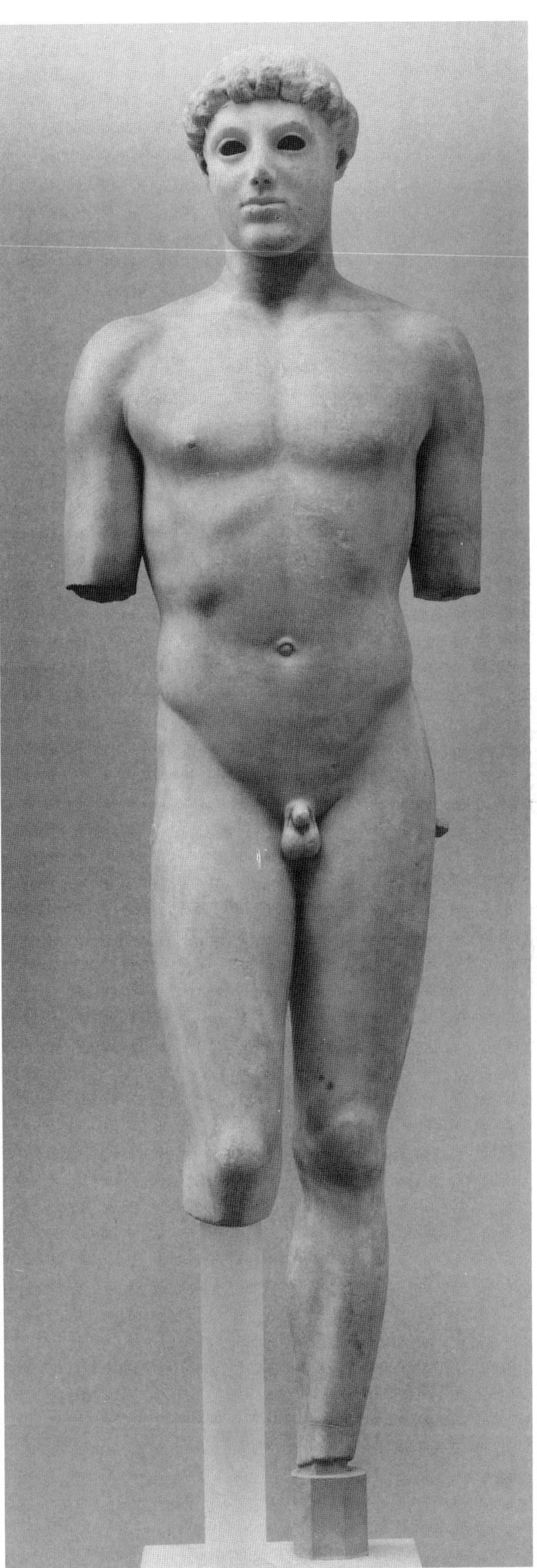

Figure 3.18 *Kritios Boy.* Ca. 480 B.C. Ht. 33″. Acropolis Museum, Athens. *This statue is carved from marble probably mined at Mt. Pentelicus in Attica. Two features—the treatment of the eyes, which were originally set with semiprecious stones, and the roll of hair—show that the Kritios sculptor was accustomed to working in bronze. The figure's beautifully rendered muscles and sense of inner life announce the arrival of the Hellenic style; the contrapposto, used sparingly here, foreshadows later developments in Greek sculpture.*

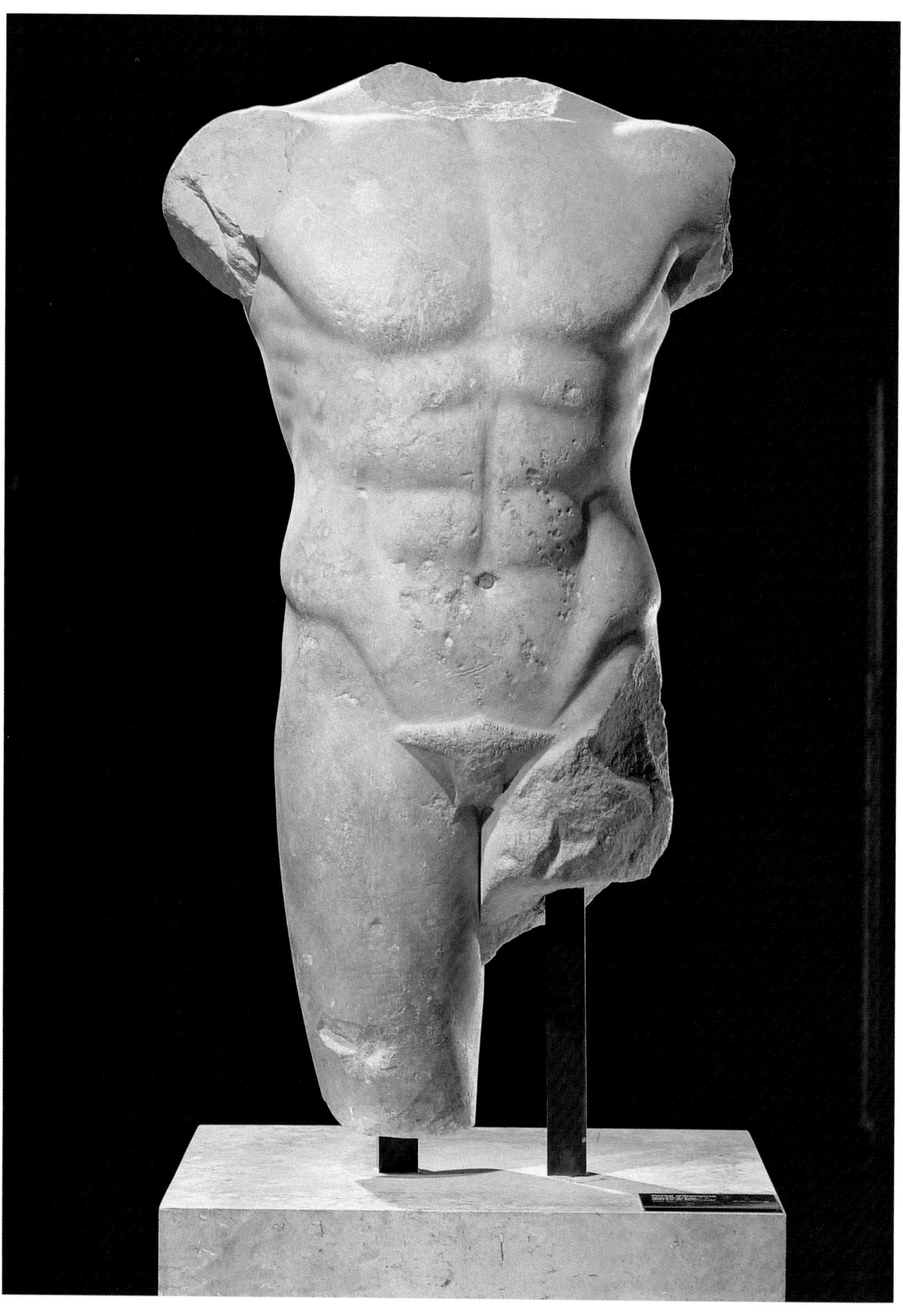

◀ **Figure 3.19** *Torso of Miletus.* Ca. 480–470 B.C. Marble, ht. 4′4″. Louvre. *The torso is all that survives from a formerly life-size statue. Scars and plaster residue indicate that it was damaged and restored in antiquity. Although little is known of its origins and first use, the statue eventually was installed in a Roman theater in Miletus, Asia Minor. The torso shows the transition from the Archaic style, marked by frontality and nudity, to Classicism, characterized by well-defined musculature and the hint of contrapposto in the lightly flexed hips.*

sculptors were able to render the human figure in freer and more relaxed poses.

The central panel of the so-called Ludovisi Throne, another sculpture from the same period, conveys an air of quiet gravity (Figure 3.20). The subject probably represents the birth of Aphrodite as she rises from the sea, indicated by pebbles under the feet of her attendants, the stooping figures on either side. This relief reflects a perfect blending of late Archaic grace (Aphrodite's stylized hair and the hint of Archaic smile) with the dignity of the Severe style (the delicate transparent draperies and the convincing realism produced by foreshortening the arms of the three figures).

In contrast to the Severe style, which accepted repose as normal, the High Classical style was fascinated with the aesthetic problem of showing motion in a static medium. The sculptors' solution, which became central to High Classicism, was to freeze the action, resisting the impulse to depict agitated movement, in much the same way that the tragic playwrights banished violence from the stage. In effect, the High Classical sculptors stopped time, allowing an ideal world to emerge in which serene gods and mortals showed grace under pressure. A striking representation of this aspect of High Classicism is the bronze statue of *Poseidon* or *Zeus,* found in the Aegean Sea off Cape Artemision. It captures to perfection High Classicism's ideal of virile grace (Figure 3.21). The mature god, signified by the beard and fully developed body, is shown poised, ready to hurl some object. In such sculptures as this, the Greeks found visual metaphors for their notion that deities and mortals are kin.

High Classical sculptors wanted to do more than portray figures in motion; some, most especially Polykleitos [pol-e-KLITE-uhs] of Argos, continued to be obsessed with presenting the ideal human form at rest. In his search for perfection, Polykleitos executed a bronze male figure of such strength and beauty—the *Doryphoros,* or *Spearbearer*—that its proportions came to be regarded as a canon, or set of rules, to be imitated by other artists (Figure 3.22). In the *Doryphoros* canon, each of the limbs bears a numerical relation to the body's overall measurements; for example, the length of the foot is one-tenth of the figure's height. Other principles of High Classicism embodied in the *Doryphoros* include the slightly brutal facial features, which were typical of this style's masculine ideal; the relaxed contrapposto; and the controlled muscles.

Greek architecture reached its zenith in the Parthenon, and, similarly, Classical Greek sculpture attained its height in the reliefs and sculptures of this celebrated temple. Under the disciplined eye of the sculptor Phidias [FIHD-e-uhs], craftspeople carved patriotic and mythological subjects destined for various parts of the building. Taken as a whole, the sculptures revealed

Figure 3.20 *The Birth of Aphrodite (?).* Ca. 460 B.C. Ht. 2′9″. Terme Museum, Rome. *The Ludovisi Throne, with its three relief panels, is a controversial work, because scholars disagree about its original function, the interpretation of its panels, and even its date. Discovered in Rome in the late nineteenth century, it probably was carved in Magna Graecia, perhaps for an altar, and brought to Rome in antiquity. The figure of Aphrodite was one of the first naked women depicted in large-scale Greek sculpture. The goddess is rendered in softly curving lines—a marked deviation from the Severe style and a forecast of the sensuous tendency of later Greek art.*

◀ **Figure 3.21** *Poseidon* (or *Zeus*). Ca. 460–450 B.C. Bronze, ht. 6′10″. National Museum, Athens. *The nobility of the Greek conception of their gods is nowhere better revealed than in this magnificent bronze sculpture of Poseidon (or Zeus). Grace, strength, and intellect are united in this majestic image of a mature deity. Poseidon's eyes originally would have been semiprecious stones, and the statue would have been painted to create a more realistic effect.*

the Parthenon to be a tribute to Athenian imperialism as much as to the goddess Athena (Figure 3.23).

On the Parthenon's metopes—the rectangular spaces on the Doric frieze—sculptors portrayed scenes in the prevailing High Classical style. In panel after panel, the metope sculptors depicted perfect human forms showing restraint in the midst of struggle, such as Amazons against men, Greeks against Trojans, and gods against giants. The south metopes portrayed the battle between the legendary Lapiths and the half-men, half-horse Centaurs (Figure 3.24). For the Greeks, the struggle between the human Lapiths and the bestial Centaurs symbolized the contest between civilization and barbarism or, possibly, between the Greeks and the Persians.

Inside the columns, running around the perimeter of the upper cella walls in a continuous band, was a low-relief frieze. Borrowed from the Ionic order, this running frieze introduced greater liveliness into High Classicism. The 525-foot-long band is filled with hundreds of men and women, walking and riding horses, along with sacrificial animals for Athena and the rest of the Olympians. The subject of this vivid scene is the procession of the Great Panathenaea festival, Athens's

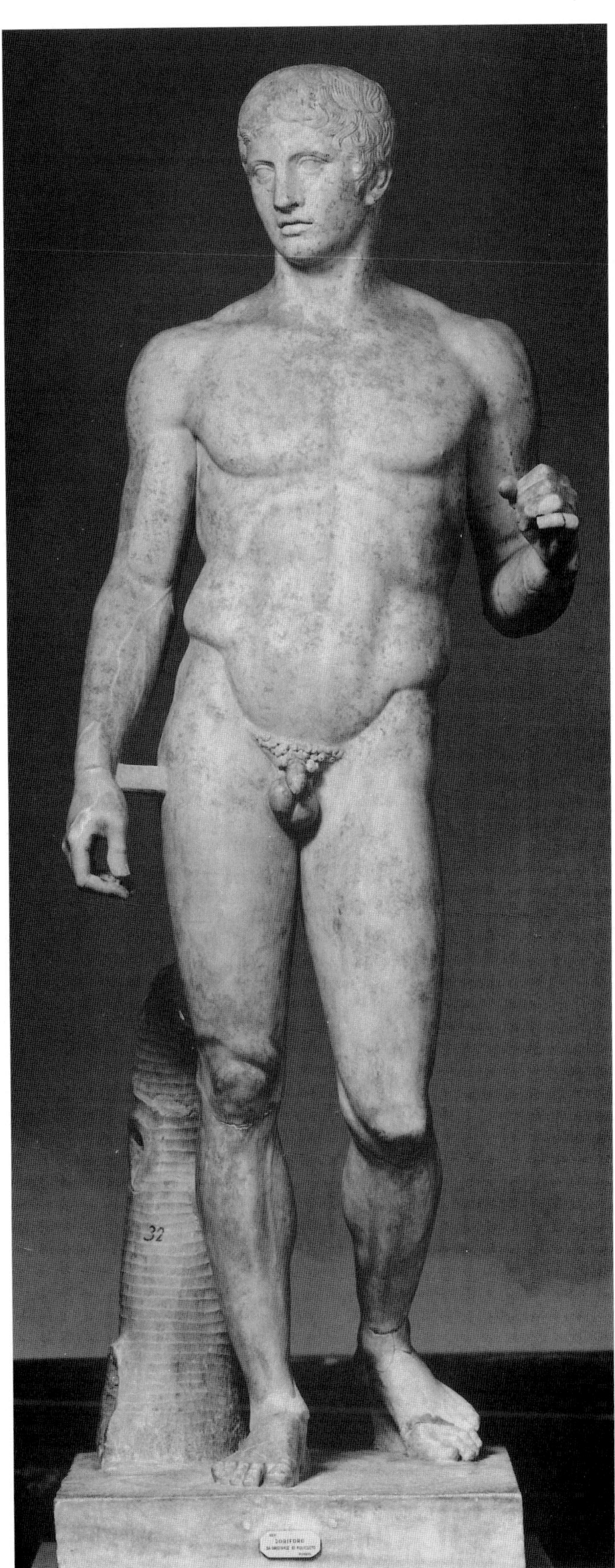

Figure 3.22 *Doryphoros*. Ca. 440 B.C. Marble copy of a bronze original by Polykleitos, ht. 6′6″. Museo Nazionale Archeologico, Naples. *The* Doryphoros *expresses the classical ideal of balanced repose. The nude figure rests his weight upon the right leg. The left arm, extended to hold the now missing spear, balances with the right leg. The left foot, barely touching the ground, balances with the relaxed right arm. Besides representing idealized repose, the* Doryphoros *was also recognized as the embodiment of human beauty with its ordered proportions, well-toned musculature, and rugged features.*

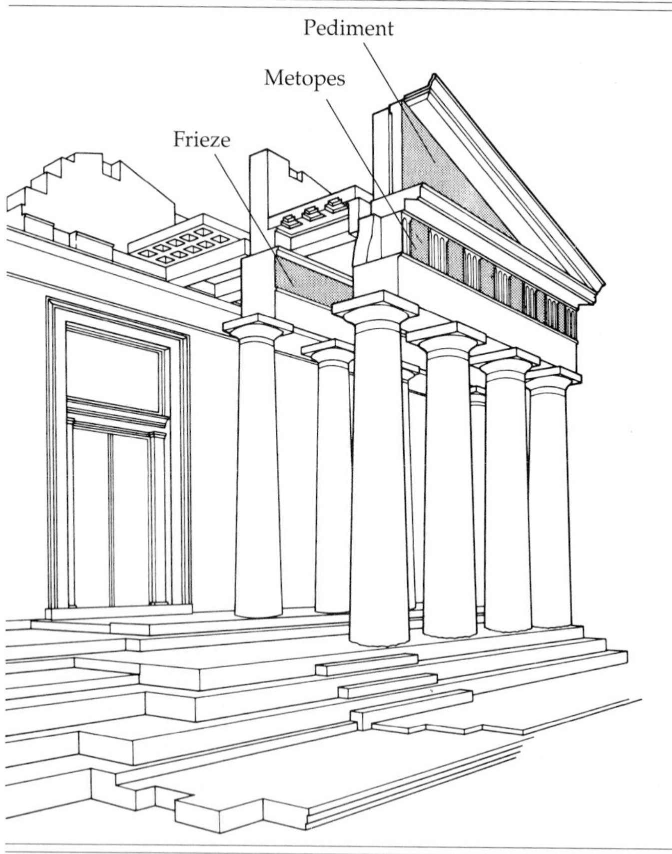

Figure 3.23 The Location of the Sculptures on the Parthenon. *This cutaway view shows the metopes, Ionic frieze, and pediments of the Parthenon, which were covered with sculptures celebrating the glory of Athens.*

most important civic and religious ritual, which was held every four years. This panoramic view of the thrilling procession concluded with a stunning group portrait of the twelve gods and goddesses, seated in casual majesty, awaiting their human worshipers. In one scene, a bearded Poseidon taps the shoulder of Apollo, which causes him to turn, while Artemis at the right absentmindedly adjusts her robe (Figure 3.25). Their tranquil faces, their sense of inner life, and the prevailing calm are the marks of mature Classicism. The entire Parthenon frieze was the most ambitious work of sculpture in the Greek tradition.

The transition to Fourth Century style coincided with the end of the creative phase of tragedy and the disintegration of the Greek world as it passed into the Macedonian political orbit. Sculpture remained innovative, since each generation seemed to produce a master who challenged the prevailing aesthetic rules, and free expression continued as a leading principle of Fourth Century style. But sculptors now expressed

Figure 3.24 *Centaur Versus Lapith.* Metope XXX, south face of the Parthenon. Ca. 448–442 B.C. Marble, ht. 56″. British Museum. *This struggling pair was designed to fit comfortably into the metope frame, and thus the proportions of the figures in relation to each other and to the small space were worked out with precision. The intertwined limbs of the warrior and the Centaur visibly demonstrate the new freedom of High Classicism. The anguished countenance of the Lapith, however, is almost unique in High Classicism and is a portent of the more emotional faces of the Hellenistic style, the next major artistic development.*

Figure 3.25 *Poseidon, Apollo, and Artemis.* Parthenon frieze. Ca. 448–442 B.C. Marble, ht. 43". Acropolis Museum, Athens. *The Hellenic style always stressed the human dimension of the Greek gods and goddesses, embodying Homer's claim that gods and humans are of the same race. In this section of the Parthenon frieze, the Homeric deities are resplendent in their beautiful bodies and are calmly serene.*

such new ideas as beauty for its own sake and a delight in sensuality. Earlier Classicism had stressed the notion that humans could become godlike, but the last phase concluded that gods and mortals alike reveled in human joys.

This new focus is apparent in Praxiteles' [prax-SIT-uhl-eez] *Hermes with the Infant Dionysus.* This sculpture, perhaps the only original work by a known sculptor that survives from Hellenic Greece, portrays two gods blissfully at play (Figure 3.26). Hermes, lounging in a casual yet dignified pose, probably dangled grapes before the attentive baby god. The contrapposto posture, beautifully defined in Hermes' stance, became widely imitated as the **Praxitelean curve.** Hermes' sensuous body, his intent gaze, and his delicate features are hallmarks of Fourth Century Classicism; by the next generation Praxiteles' treatment of the male figure had superseded the more rugged *Doryphoros* canon.

Figure 3.26 PRAXITELES. *Hermes with the Infant Dionysus.* Ca. 350–340 B.C. Marble, ht. 85". Olympia Museum. *In this statue of Hermes, Praxiteles changed the look of Classical art with his rendering of the god's body. For example, Hermes' small head and long legs contributed to the Praxitelean canon for the male figure. The sculptor has also created a dramatic contrast between Hermes' well-muscled body and his soft face. As a direct result of Praxiteles' new vision, sculptors in the Hellenistic Age became interested in more frankly sensual portrayals of the human figure, both male and female.*

The Legacy of Hellenic Civilization

Although Athens failed in its dream of political mastery of Greece, the Athenian miracle so impressed its contemporaries that Athenian culture dominated the Hellenic Age. Tragic poets, comic playwrights, and natural philosophers made the Athenian dialect the medium of expression for poetry and prose. The buildings on the Acropolis expressed visually the purity and restraint of the Athenian style. And Athenian democracy, which served as the exciting teacher of its citizens, was the envy of most of the other Greek poleis. After the fall of Greece to Macedonia, however, the idea of democracy fell into disrepute. Almost two thousand years passed before some in Europe were ready to give democracy a second chance.

But **humanism,** the other great creation of Athens, survived as a guide to refined living for the cultivated classes in the West. Athenian culture became the heart of the educational curriculum that was followed in Hellenistic civilization; that model was adopted by Rome and transmitted in the humanistic tradition to Europe. In time, the study and the practice of humanistic learning—literature, philosophy, theater, music, and the arts and architecture—became the crowning glory of Western civilization, affecting private individuals and entire societies.

Moreover, Classicism—the style of humanistic achievements in the Hellenic Age—had three great effects on the Western tradition. First, the principles of Greek Classicism—balance, simplicity, and restraint—set the standard by which the styles of other times are often measured. Second, the actual works of Classicism became basic building blocks of Western culture. In the realm of thought, the works of Plato and Aristotle quickly acquired a luster of authority and retained it until the seventeenth century A.D. Aristotle's literary criticism created a new writing genre, and his analysis of tragedy made this type of play the ultimate challenge to ambitious writers. The Greek tragedies themselves—of Aeschylus, Sophocles, and Euripides—are thought by many to be unsurpassed.

The comic plays of Aristophanes are less well known today, but their spirit still lives in period comedies and contemporary political satire. The histories of Herodotus and Thucydides retain their vitality as important sources for their respective eras, although modern research has cast doubt on some of their conclusions. Architecture has had the most potent effect of Greece's accomplishments; the ruins on the Athenian Acropolis and elsewhere are eternal reminders of this Greek heritage. Finally, the idealized statues of men and women, such as the *Doryphoros,* have inspired Western artists with their vision of noble beings alert to the rich possibilities of human life.

The third and perhaps most important contribution of Classicism to the Western tradition was a skeptical spirit that was rooted in democracy. By asserting that the purpose of human life can best be realized in cities that are shaped by the citizens' needs, as Athenian humanism claimed, the humanists declared war on all tyrants, hierarchical societies, and divinely ordered states—in other words, the prevailing order of the ancient world. Because of this critical aspect of humanism, the Greek heritage has sometimes been called into question and, during repressive periods, been subjected to attack. However, the passion for questioning, for inquiry, which characterizes the skeptical spirit, is at the core of Western consciousness.

KEY CULTURAL TERMS

Hellenic
maenad
Dionysia
Classic (Classical)
Classicism
tragedy
chorus
orchestra
skene
satyr-play
Old Comedy
modes
idealism
Platonism
Ionic
Severe style
High Classical style
Fourth Century style
contrapposto
Praxitelean curve
humanism

SUGGESTIONS FOR FURTHER READING

PRIMARY SOURCES

AESCHYLUS. *Oresteia.* Translated by R. Fagles. New York: Penguin, 1986. A good modern version of the only dramatic trilogy that survives from ancient Greece.

ARISTOPHANES. *Lysistrata.* Translated by J. Henderson. New York: Oxford University Press, 1987. This modern version captures the antiwar spirit and bawdy humor of the original comedy.

EURIPIDES. *The Bacchae and Other Plays.* Translated by P. Vellacott. New York: Penguin, 1972. An excellent collection of Euripides' dramas, in each of which strong-minded women play major roles.

HERODOTUS. *The Histories.* Translated by A. de Sélincourt. New York: Penguin, 1972. Prefaced with an informative introduction, this translation captures both the language and the narrative of the first history book in Western literature.

KAPLAN, J., ed. *The Pocket Aristotle.* New York: Washington Square Press, 1966. Edited selections from the *Physics,* the *Nicomachean Ethics, Politics,* and *Poetics* give a sense of Aristotle's method of inquiry.

ROUSE, W. H. D., trans. *Great Dialogues of Plato.* New York: New American Library, 1963. Includes the full text of the *Republic,* the *Apology, Phaedo,* and *Symposium.*

SOPHOCLES. *The Theban Plays.* Translated by E. F. Watling. New York: Penguin, 1974. The three plays about the misfortunes of King Oedipus and his family; includes *Oedipus Rex* and *Antigone.* Unlike Aeschylus's Oresteian trilogy, Sophocles' Theban plays do not constitute a unified work; each was originally performed with other plays (now lost).

THUCYDIDES. *The Peloponnesian War.* Translated by R. Warner. New York: Penguin, 1970. An updated translation that captures the sweep and drama of the original.

WINDOWS ON THE WORLD: 500–300 B.C.

HISTORY

AFRICA

Northeast Africa *Nubian culture, ca. 2000 B.C.–A.D. 350.* Capital Meroë (in modern Sudan); important trade and iron-working center.

West Africa *Nok culture, began 500 B.C.* Well-organized economy and administrative system in northern and central Nigeria; first people in sub-Saharan Africa to make iron tools and weapons. Influenced neighbors in the region.

AMERICAS

Mesoamerica *Olmec culture.* Last phase: decline followed by collapse (400 B.C.), for reasons unknown.

Andes *Chavín culture.* Final phase: noted for improved maize and the back-strap loom; spread along coastal Peru.

Native North America *Adena culture, ca. 600 B.C.–A.D. 200.* Ohio Valley; hunter-gatherers with trade network from Canada to Florida.

ART

AFRICA

West Africa *Nok culture.* Terra-cotta heads characterized black Africa's first known sculptural tradition, from ca. 500 B.C.

Jemaa Head. Ca. fifth century B.C. Tsauni Camp, Jemaa. Terra-cotta, ht. $9\frac{13}{16}$". Lagos National Museum.

AMERICAS

Mesoamerica *Olmec culture.* Carved stone figures depicting rain god with jaguar or "howling baby" features.

Andes *Chavín culture.* Gold work (in use since ca. 1900 B.C.) for cult objects and as prestige body art for the elite.

Native North America *Adena culture.* Simple pottery, carved pipes, ornaments of copper, mica, and seashells.

Olmec Statue of Priest with Supernatural "Infant." Ca. 600 B.C. Greenstone. Museo de Antropologia de la Universidad Veracruzana, Xalapa, Mexico.

ARCHITECTURE

AFRICA

Northeast Africa *Nubian culture.* About 300 pyramid tombs survive near ancient Meroë, a Kushan city of mudbrick palaces, temples, houses, and baths.

AMERICAS

Andes *Chavín culture.* Deliberately disorienting architectural style, as in Chavín's Old Temple complex: a central U-shaped platform embracing a sunken plaza, which could be reached only by a circuitous series of plazas and stairways.

Native North America *Adena culture.* Earthen pyramids and effigy mounds in the shape of sacred animals, such as Great Serpent Mound (Ohio; ca. 2nd century B.C.).

RELIGION, PHILOSOPHY, LITERATURE

AFRICA

Northeast Africa *Nubian culture.* Egyptian hieroglyphs abandoned in favor of an indigenous Meroitic script.

AMERICAS

Andes *Chavín culture.* The most common religious image was a figure (possibly a god) with jaguar fangs.

Mesoamerica *Olmec culture.* Glyphs carved on stone sculptures hint at a written language.

Gold Alloy Pectoral (with jaguar face). Found at Chavín de Huantar. Ca. 500 B.C. Former Bliss Collection, Dumbarton Oaks Research Library and Collections, Washington, D.C.

ASIA

China

Warring States period, ended 221 B.C. Endemic warfare among rival states. Spread of culture across China continued. Historic pattern of society: impoverished peasants living in villages and landowning nobility preoccupied with family, ancestor worship, and religious ritual. Iron working began. Crossbow introduced.

India

Aryan culture, ended 323 B.C. Warfare among petty kingdoms.

Japan

Jōmon culture, ended 300 B.C. Hunting, fishing, and gathering continued.

Warring States period. Decorative arts: lacquered wood, inlaid fittings, and bronze vessels. Exotic features show influence of Ch'u people assimilated into Chinese society in this period.

Monster Mask and Ring Handles. 771-221 B.C. *Bronze, mask 3 7/10" diameter, ring 3 1/2" diameter. People's Republic of China.*

Jōmon culture. Clay figurines with huge insectlike or shell-shaped eyes.

Warring States period. Ruins of rammed earth walls at Wang Ch'eng, measuring nearly 2 miles in perimeter.

Jōmon culture. Tomb burial in square pits topped by stone "sundials."

Nonakado Stone Group Above Burial Pit. Late Jōmon period. Oyu, Akita.

In philosophy, the "Hundred Schools" period (6th–3rd centuries B.C.), zenith of China's ethical tradition. Confucius (551–479 B.C.) and Confucianism: encouraged reverence for good form and the established order—the family, hierarchy, seniority. Lao-tzu (6th century B.C.) and Taoism: stressed harmony with nature and a positive acceptance of life's variety. Han Fei-tzu (?–233 B.C.) and the Legalists: taught authority of the rulers, duty of the people, and military power.

Aryan culture. India's great epic poems (about 400 B.C.): the *Rāmāyana* and the *Mahābhārata*, including the *Bhagavadgitā*. Vedism evolved into Early Hinduism, changing from a religion grounded in ritual sacrifice to one focused on asceticism and the practice of yoga. Two new religions, Buddhism and Jainism, emerged, led respectively by Siddhārtha Gautama, called Buddha ("Enlightened One"; ca. 563–ca. 483 B.C.), and Vardhamāna, called Mahāvīra ("Great Hero"; ca. 599–527 B.C.).

4 CLASSICAL GREEK CIVILIZATION

The Hellenistic Age

The Hellenistic Age covers the relatively brief period from the death of Alexander the Great in 323 B.C. to the triumph of Rome over Macedonian Greece in 146 B.C. During this time, a new urban civilization developed in the eastern Mediterranean basin. In contrast to Hellenic Greece, this new civilization was dominated by large metropolitan centers linked by trade and commerce. More racially mixed and ethnically varied than Hellenic Greece, this civilization has come to be called **Hellenistic** because of the preeminent role Greece played in its development. Greece, for example, furnished the Hellenistic world with its diplomatic and commercial language, its bureaucrats, and most of its cultural forms. And yet Hellenistic culture was eclectic, for the subjects of the various states made their presence known (Figure 4.1). Several key motifs grew from oriental roots: the concept of a ruler who is also divine, the aesthetic ideal that identifies grandiosity with earthly majesty, and new religious cults that promised immortality.

Although the Hellenistic Age is sometimes overlooked, Alexander's dream of a world community united by a common leader has had an impact reaching into modern times. The multiracial and multicultural kingdoms of the Hellenistic period are the first examples of a type whose modern versions include the United States and the former Soviet Union. And, not least, Hellenistic achievements in philosophy, art, and architecture are considerable.

This creation of a worldly Mediterranean community destroyed the Hellenic political order in which poleis were guided by their citizens. The poleis were replaced mainly by large Hellenistic kingdoms, ruled by men

◀ *Aphrodite of Melos (Venus de Milo).* Ca. 160–150 B.C. Marble, ht. 6′10″. Louvre.

Figure 4.1 Black Youth Singing. Second century B.C. Ht. 7½″. Bibliothèque Nationale, Paris. *Since the Archaic Age, Greek artists had occasionally depicted black Africans in their works. During the Hellenistic Age, with the migration of peoples and the increased use of slaves, sculptors frequently chose black figures as subjects. This small bronze statue of a young African is an illustration of the racial diversity of the Hellenistic Age. Originally, the figure held a small musical instrument—now lost—which accounts for its exaggerated pose.*

who declared themselves deities. The Hellenistic economic order rested on specialized luxury crafts and professional occupations, international trade and banking, and an abundant and cheap supply of slaves. The large ports exported and imported basic agricultural commodities such as grain, olive oil, wine, and timber, exchanging them for expensive goods like pottery, silks, jewelry, and spices.

Class divisions in Hellenistic society were pronounced. For the rich, urban life was often luxurious and cosmopolitan, but most of society remained provincial. Those in the middle social ranks, primarily tradespeople and skilled artisans, struggled to keep ahead and hoped to prosper. However, for the poorest free classes—laborers, unskilled workers, and small landowners—life offered little. Slaves, whose numbers grew during the wars of this period, were expected to bear the brunt of all backbreaking labor.

Hellenistic women were affected by the period's growing cosmopolitanism. Women, along with men, moved to the newly conquered lands and created new lives for themselves in frontier towns. In Alexandria and other large cities, some restrictions of Hellenic Greece were maintained, but others were relaxed or discarded. For example, royal and non-Greek women were able to conduct their own legal and economic affairs, though nonroyal Greek women were still forced to use a male guardian in such cases. Dowries remained the custom among Greek families, but unmarried respectable women now had the option of working in the liberal arts, as poets and philosophers, and in the professions, as artists and physicians. Hellenistic literature reflects changed mores, portraying women in carefree situations apart from the gaze of their husbands or fathers. In economic matters, some women became prosperous in their own right, and, just as men did, they made charitable bequests and erected impressive gravestones. Despite these changes, Hellenistic society was dominated by masculine thinking. The surest sign of women's subordinate role was that the Greek practice of infanticide continued as a way for families to rid themselves of unwanted females.

Timeline 4.1 THE HELLENISTIC AGE — All dates B.C.

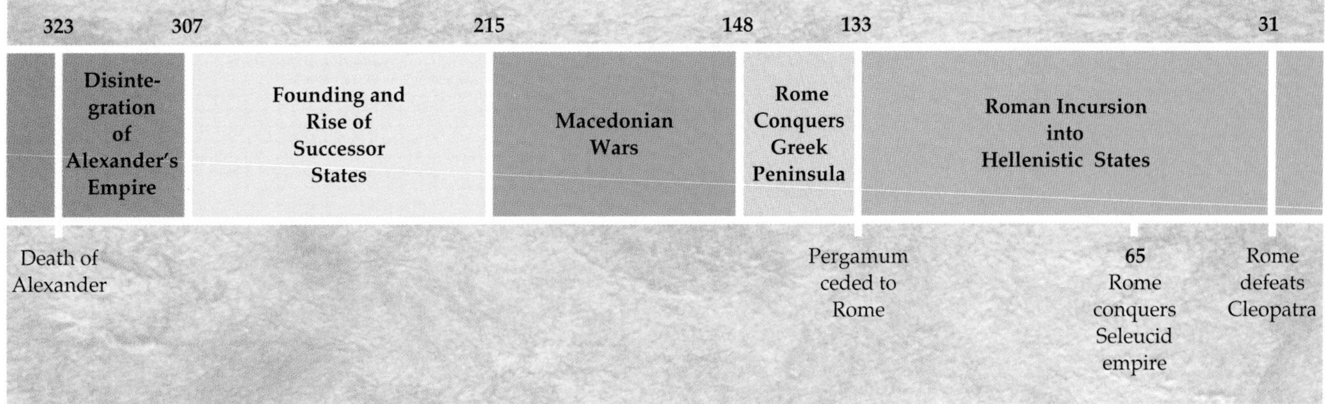

THE STAGES OF HELLENISTIC HISTORY

The shadow of Rome hung over the Hellenistic world, although the states—mired in their quarrels and jockeying for power—were unaware that their fate depended on the rising western Mediterranean power. The events of this age fall into two stages: (1) the disintegration of Alexander's empire and the rise of the successor states; and (2) the arrival and triumph of Rome (Timeline 4.1).

The End of the Empire and the Rise of the States

The years from 323 to 307 B.C. saw the shattering of Alexander's dream of a united Greek and Persian civilization. Alexander left no designated successor. After his death, his chief generals (Antigonus, Seleucus, and Ptolemy) divided his empire into three dynastic kingdoms (called the "successor states") that, along with a few minor states and leagues of Greek city-states, survived until Rome moved into the area. The era of the successor states (307 to 215 B.C.) was the zenith of Hellenistic culture. Politically the states were hardly ever at peace, but culturally they were united. Greeks and barbarians mingled freely, and an urban civilization began to emerge. A form of colloquial Greek, called ***koine,*** spread throughout the Hellenistic world and was spoken from Gaul to Syria.

The three successor states were based in Macedonia, in the former Persian Empire, and in Egypt (Map 4.1). The kingdom of Macedonia, that of Antigonus, controlled Greece until two leagues of poleis challenged Macedonian hegemony. The ensuing warfare with the Greek leagues ultimately weakened this state.

The Seleucid kingdom, that of Seleucus, was built on the ruins of the old Persian empire. At its height, Seleucid power extended east to present-day Iraq. During the mid–third century B.C., however, the eastern region of the Seleucid kingdom broke away and formed the two smaller states of Parthia and Bactria, which would later prove to be prickly adversaries of Rome. In time, the Seleucid rulers, distracted by the invading Gauls, a wandering tribe of Celtic peoples from central and eastern Europe, lost control of their kingdom and had to relinquish land in Asia Minor to a new kingdom known as Pergamum, named after an old Greek city.

The Ptolemaic kingdom, that of Ptolemy, included Egypt, the oldest civilization surviving in the ancient world. Although the Ptolemaic dynasty was marked by weak and corrupt rulers, Egypt enjoyed a resurgence as a unified and independent state. The capital, Alexandria, became the greatest urban center of the Hellenistic Age, enriched by the grains harvested in the Nile River valley and the goods and traffic that passed through its port.

The Arrival and Triumph of Rome

The second phase of Hellenistic civilization began in the late third century B.C. when Macedonia joined Carthage, a Phoenician state in North Africa, in its struggle against Rome. Thereafter, the unforgiving Romans used every opportunity to humiliate their Greek enemies. Between 215 and 148 B.C., Rome fought four wars with Macedonia, thus becoming entangled in Greek political and military squabbles. Finally, in 146 B.C., Rome brought the entire Greek peninsula under its control. The other Hellenistic kingdoms soon submitted. In 133 B.C., the ruler of Pergamum willed his state to Rome. The Seleucid kingdom was conquered by the Romans in 65 B.C. after three wars. Egypt maintained its freedom until 31 B.C., when Cleopatra and her forces were defeated by Octavian and the Roman navy.

Map 4.1 THE SUCCESSOR STATES AND THE HELLENISTIC WORLD

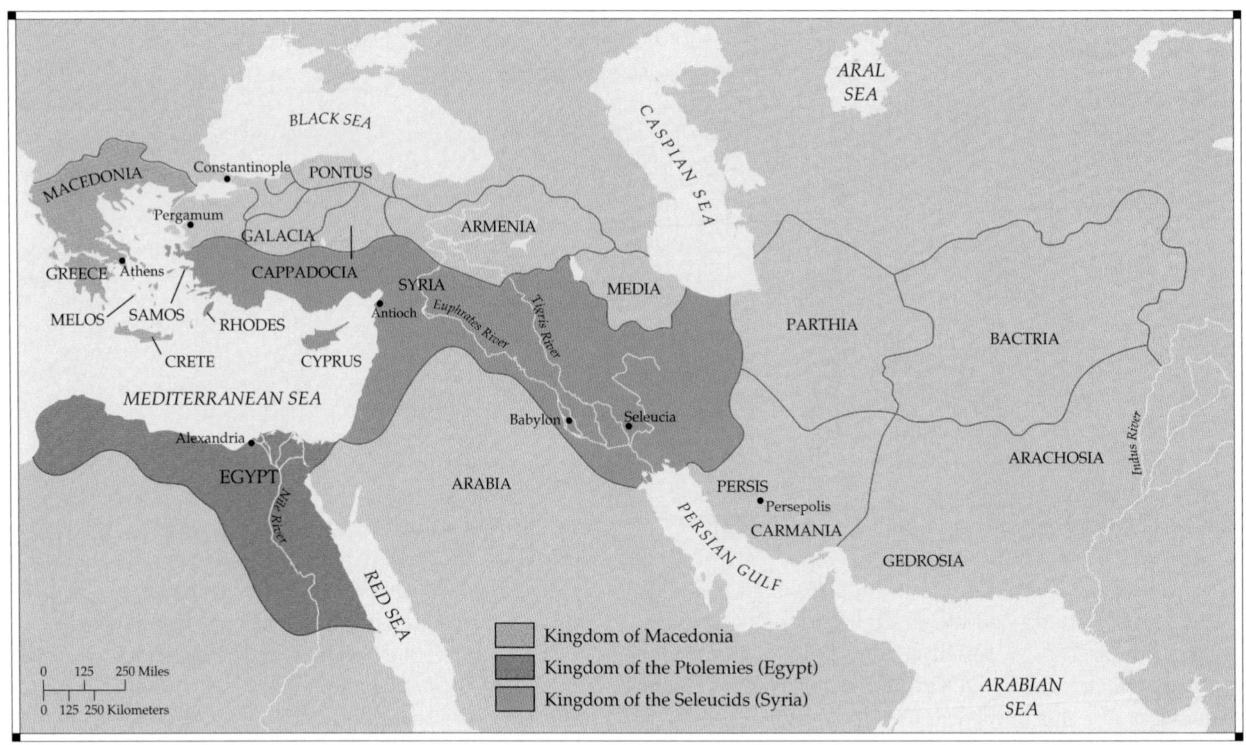

THE CITIES OF HELLENISTIC CIVILIZATION

Alexander's most enduring legacy to the Hellenistic world was his new image of the city. The city is as old as civilization, since urban life is by definition a component of civilized existence. For Alexander, cities were keystones holding together his diverse and vast empire—serving as centers of government, trade, and culture and radiating Greco-Oriental civilization into the hinterland. During his conquests, Alexander is reputed to have founded more than seventy cities, many of which were named for him.

Pergamum

During the Hellenistic period, Alexander's successors emulated him, establishing urban centers such as Antioch, on the Orontes River in southern Asia Minor, and Seleucia, the new capital of the Seleucid kingdom, near Babylon. The new city of Pergamum in western Asia Minor emerged as a brilliant center of art and thought, bringing together Greek and Persian civilizations. The Attalids, the ruling dynasty of Pergamum, decorated their city's acropolis with a splendid palace, a library second only to the one in Alexandria, and a marble temple to Athena. Scattered on the hillside beneath the acropolis were shrines, markets, and private dwellings of the more prosperous citizens. At the base of the hill, the tradespeople, artisans, and slaves lived crowded together (Figure 4.2).

Alexandria in Egypt

For all its claims to grandeur, however, Pergamum could not surpass the size, wealth, beauty, or culture of the premier Hellenistic city, Alexandria in Egypt, founded by Alexander (Figure 4.3). Under the Ptolemies, Alexandria grew to be a world city that attracted both the ambitious who sought opportunities and the apathetic who wanted to be left alone. Every desired attraction is said to have existed here, just as in the teeming cities of the twentieth century. By the end of the first century B.C., Alexandria's population was about one million, and the city was divided into five sections, including one reserved for royalty and separate residential quarters for the Egyptians and the Jews, who were attracted by the city's opportunities and tolerant atmosphere. Whereas the polis of the Hellenic Age was self-contained, with a relatively homogeneous population,

Figure 4.2 Acropolis at Pergamum. Second century B.C. Reconstruction by H. Schlief. Staatliche Museen, Berlin. *Pergamum architecture was in the Hellenic style, but the city's mixed population and economy made it the commercial and political hub of a Hellenistic kingdom. Under Eumenes II, the capital and the country reached its height of power around 160 B.C.*

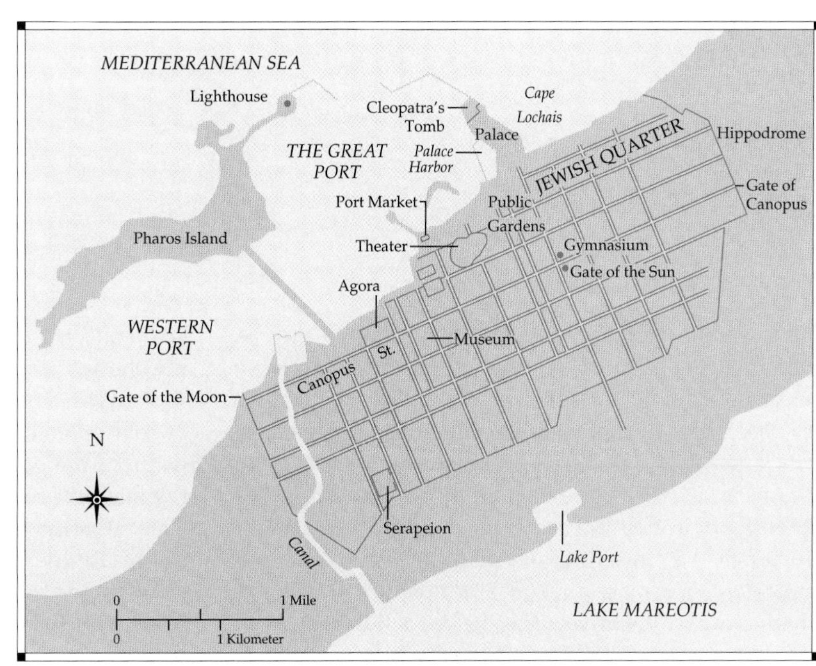

Figure 4.3 Plan of Ancient Alexandria. Third century B.C. *Designed by Deinocrates of Rhodes, Alexander's personal architect, Alexandria was laid out in a grid formed by intersecting avenues and streets. The entire city was enclosed by a wall, accessible by four massive gates at the ends of the major avenues. To the north lay two harbors that made the city the most vital port in the Mediterranean. The harbors were protected by an outer island at the point of which stood the lighthouse of Pharos—now lost. Remarkable for its colossal size, the lighthouse was considered one of the wonders of the ancient world.*

PERSONAL PERSPECTIVE

THEOCRITUS
A Street Scene in Alexandria

Two ladies, Gorgo and Praxinoa, each with her maid (Eutychis and Eunoa, respectively), make their way through the crowded streets of Alexandria, Egypt, on their way to the palace of Ptolemy II to hear a singer perform at the festival of Adonis. The passage is from Theocritus's Idylls, *dating from the third century* B.C.

[GORGO:] [C]ome, get your dress and cloak on,
and let's go to King Ptolemy's palace
and take a look at this Adonis.
The Queen, I hear, is doing things in style.
PRAXINOA: Oh, nothing but the best. Well, they can keep it.
GORGO: But when you've seen it, just think,
you can tell those who haven't all about it.
Come on, it's time we were off.
PRAXINOA: Every day's a holiday for the idle.

• • •

[*Out in the street.*]
Ye Gods, what a crowd! The crush!
How on earth are we going to get through it?
They're like ants! Swarms of them, beyond counting!
Well, you've done us many favours, Ptolemy,
since your father went to heaven.
We don't get those no-goods now, sliding up to us
in the street and playing their Egyptian tricks.
What they used to get up to, those rogues!
A bunch of villains, each as bad
as the next, and all utterly cursed!
Gorgo dear, what will become of us?
Here are the king's horses! Take care,
my good man, don't tread on me.
That brown one's reared right up!
Look how wild he is! He'll kill his groom!
Eunoa, you fool, get back!
Thank God I left that child at home.
GORGO: Don't worry, Praxinoa.
We've got behind them now.
They're back in their places.
PRAXINOA: I'm all right now.
Ever since I was a girl, two things
have always terrified me—horses,
and long, cold snakes. Let's hurry.
This great crowd will drown us.

• • •

GORGO: Look, Praxinoa! What a crowd at the door!
PRAXINOA: Fantastic! Gorgo, give me your hand.
And you, Eunoa, hold on to Eutychis.
Take care you don't lose each other.
We must all go in together. Stay close by us.
Oh no! Gorgo! My coat! It's been ripped
clean in two! My God, sir, as you hope
for heaven, mind my coat!
STRANGER: It wasn't my fault. But I'll be careful.
PRAXINOA: What a herd! They push like pigs.
STRANGER: Don't worry, madam, we'll be all right.
PRAXINOA: And may you, sir, be all right
forever and beyond, for looking after us.
What a charming man! Where's Eunoa?
She's getting squashed! Come on, girl, push!
That's it. "All safely in."

Alexandria's racially and ethnically diverse groups were held together by economic interests. With busy harbors, bustling markets, and international banks, the city became a hub of commercial and financial enterprises, similar to modern port cities.

Alexandria's economic vitality was matched by the splendor of its cultural achievements. The world's first university—a museum dedicated to the muses—was built here as a place for scholars to study and to exchange ideas. Nearby was the famed library, whose staff collected the classics of Greek civilization, including the works of Plato and Aristotle; the tragedies of Aeschylus, Sophocles, and Euripides; the comedies of Aristophanes; and the scientific treatises of Hellenistic philosophers. At the time of the Roman conquest in the late first century B.C., the library contained nearly 700,000 volumes, the largest collection in the ancient world. By then, Alexandria had become a beacon for great minds, who were attracted by the city's rich intellectual life and cosmopolitan atmosphere.

Figure 4.4 *Nike of Samothrace.* Front and side views. Ca. 190 B.C. Marble, ht. 8′. Louvre. *The* Nike of Samothrace*—commonly called the "Winged Victory" because Nike was the Greek goddess of victory—is a perfect symbol of the war-dominated Hellenistic Age. Carved to appear to be striding into the wind, with wildly agitated draperies and soaring wings, this sculpture embodies exuberant action, a defining feature of this turbulent age. Nike's costume also illustrates this age's superb virtuosity; note the transparent band of "fabric" around the navel and the draperies swathing the thighs and legs. Originally part of a sculptural group on the island of Samothrace, which included a war galley, a fountain, and a reflecting pool (now lost), the Nike gives the impression of standing on the prow of a swiftly moving ship.*

THE ELABORATION OF THE GREEK TRADITION: THE SPREAD OF CLASSICISM TO THE HELLENISTIC WORLD

The Hellenistic world to some extent rejected the simplicity, balance, and restraint that had characterized Hellenism and embraced a more emotional, theatrical view of culture (Figure 4.4). The expansiveness of Alexander's territorial conquests was echoed in the expansion of emotional and expressive content in the arts. As new energies, languages, and traditions were poured into old artistic and literary forms, the seriousness of Hellenism began to give way to a Hellenistic love of playfulness along with an interest in ordinary, everyday subjects.

Hellenistic culture also reflected the tastes and needs of the period's diverse states. Greek tragedy lost its vitality when separated from its roots in the independent polis, but comedy appealed to sophisticated urban audiences who were seeking diversion. Nondramatic literature became rather artificial as authors concentrated on perfecting their style or pursuing exotic scholarship. New philosophies and religions arose in response to the urban isolation and loneliness that many people experienced. And, finally, grandiose architecture addressed the propaganda needs of autocratic rulers, and realistic sculpture reflected the tastes of an increasingly urban, secular culture.

Nevertheless, the values of Hellenistic culture did not so much replace the standards of Hellenic Classicism as they enriched and elaborated the older ideals. Like Hellenism, the Hellenistic style depicted the realities of the physical world rather than finding truth in fantasy or abstraction. And Hellenistic artists and authors agreed with their Hellenic forebears that art must serve moral purposes, revealed through content and formal order.

Drama and Literature

In the Hellenistic Age, Greek comedy began to resemble modern productions. The grotesque padding worn by the actors gave way to realistic costumes; masks were redesigned to be representative of the portrayed characters; and the actors assumed a dominant status over the chorus. Comedies became a form of popular amusement, and Hellenistic playwrights developed a genre known as **New Comedy** to appeal to the pleasure-seeking audiences who were flocking to the theaters. Avoiding political criticism and casual obscenity, New Comedy presented gently satirical scenes from middle-class life.

The plays were generally comic romances on such themes as frustrated first love or marital misunderstandings, and although the endings were inevitably happy and there was much formula writing—somewhat like today's situation comedies on television—the plays reflected the comprehensive range of the Hellenistic style. The characters, for example, were familiar types drawn from the rich diversity of Hellenistic society—the courtesan, the slave, the fawning parasite. New Comedy remained steadfastly middle-class, however, for the traditional social order always prevailed in the end. For example, a favorite plot device of New Comedy hinged on discovering that a seemingly lowborn character was actually from a respected—and often wealthy—family.

Both ancient and modern critics tend to regard Menander [muh-NAN-duhr] (about 343–about 291 B.C.) as the leading author of New Comedy. He wrote more than one hundred plays for the Dionysia festival in Athens, winning first prize for comedy eight times, and is credited with perfecting the **comedy of manners,** a humorous play that focuses on the way people interact in society.

The Woman from Samos is a robust example of his work. Dating from about 321 B.C., this comedy concerns the identity of an orphaned baby and features stock characters: a courtesan, a young lover, an old lover, a humorous neighbor, and two comic slaves. Menander first presents a household in which the father believes that he and his son are wooing the same woman, when, in actuality, the son is involved with the girl next door. Then, when a foundling appears, absurd misunderstandings arise and false accusations are made. The play ends happily with all characters reconciled, the son wed to his true love, and the father and mistress married in a joyous ceremony—a typical New Comedy resolution. Western comedy would be inconceivable without Menander. His style was assimilated into Roman comedy, which passed the spirit of his work into the dramas of the Italian Renaissance and from there into the comedies of Shakespeare and Molière.

In nondramatic literature, the Hellenistic Age produced a style known as **Alexandrianism.** The Ptolemaic rulers who built the library and the museum in Alexandria used state subsidies to lure scholars and poets to the city to study the works that found their way, by purchase or plunder, into the library's vast collections. The writers produced works of many types—poetry, history, biography, literary criticism, and essays on geography and mathematics—but their work is generally of historical interest only. Alexandrian literature is often obscure and ornate, derivative, and scholarly.

A writer who stands apart in the Alexandrian school is the poet Theocritus [the-OCK-ruht-us] (about 310–250 B.C.), who worked within the confines of the style but achieved genuine literary distinction. He created a new poetic form, the **pastoral,** which would influence later Classical and modern European literature. These poems describe the lives of shepherds and farmers in a somewhat artificial, idealized way. Theocritus drew his images from his memory of his earlier years in rural Sicily, and his charming, nostalgic verses appealed to many who had also left the quiet rustic life for the excitement of the Hellenistic cities.

Theocritus also wrote what he called **idylls** (from the Greek meaning "little picture"), which offered small portraits, or vignettes, of Hellenistic life. Some of these poems reveal much about everyday affairs, noting the common concerns and aspirations of all generations—love, family, religion, and wealth.

Philosophy and Religion

For many people, everyday life changed drastically during the Hellenistic Age. As urban life became more multicultural, the sense of belonging that had characterized life in the Hellenic poleis was replaced by a feeling of isolation, of loneliness, even of helplessness, particularly in the urban centers. As a consequence, two seemingly contradictory points of view grew up: individualism and internationalism. Those who held these attitudes were searching for continuity in a rapidly changing world; were seeking identity for the individual through common interests, values, and hopes; and were striving to understand events that seemed unpredictable and beyond human control.

Philosophies and religions offered answers that seemed as contradictory as the problems themselves. One philosophy urged a universal brotherhood of all human beings, united regardless of race or status of birth; another, despairing of the world, excluded most people and appealed to a chosen few. Religions, similarly, provided varying answers. One faith preached salvation in a life after death, and another turned to magic to escape Fate—that blind force that controlled human life.

In the long run, such diversity of choice tended to foster tolerance, since no single set of beliefs prevailed or satisfied everyone (Figure 4.5). Having many alternatives spared society the anguish and bigotry that would have arisen had there been only two or three competing points of view. Because of the ease of communication and travel in the Hellenistic period, these new philosophies and religions quickly gained converts everywhere, regardless of class or geographic location.

The most enduring of this period's philosophies, Cynicism, Skepticism, Epicureanism, and Stoicism, attracted the better-educated and more influential groups in Hellenistic society. Of these four theories, Cynicism and Skepticism appealed to only a few, whereas Epicureanism and Stoicism had a much larger following (Table 4.1).

Figure 4.5 A Religious Ceremony. A.D. 159. Yale University Art Gallery, New Haven. *Although this relief is dated from the second century A.D., it is characteristic of Hellenistic religious practices that continued into Roman times. In the center is depicted Zeus Olympius–Baalshamin, a combination of Greek and Semitic deities. On the left is a priest burning an offering on an altar and dressed in Near Eastern garb; on the right is a priest wearing Greek clothing.*

Table 4.1 PHILOSOPHY IN THE HELLENISTIC AGE

PHILOSOPHY	*EMPHASIS*
Cynicism	True freedom arises from realizing that if one wants nothing, then one will never lack anything; *autarky* (self-sufficiency) is goal
Skepticism	Nothing can be known for certain; question all ideas; *autarky* is goal
Epicureanism	Only the atoms and void exist; pleasure is the highest good; death is final in its extinction of consciousness; the gods play no active role in human affairs
Stoicism	The world is governed by the divine *logos*, or reason, or nature; wisdom and freedom consist of living in harmony with the *logos*; all humans share in the divine *logos*; *autarky* is goal

Cynicism Of the four schools, **Cynicism** had the least impact on Hellenistic civilization. The Cynics, believing that society diverted the individual from the more important goals of personal independence and freedom, denounced all religions and governments, shunned physical comfort, and advocated the avoidance of personal pleasure. In the Cynics' logic, true freedom came with the realization that if one wanted nothing, one could not lack anything. By isolating themselves from society, they gained a type of self-sufficiency the Greeks called ***autarky.***

The most prominent Cynic, Diogenes [die-AHJ-uh-neez] (about 412–about 323 B.C.), openly scorned the ordinary values and crass materialism of his society. His contrary personality so fascinated Alexander the Great that the ruler, upon being insulted by the Cynic, is reported to have said that if he were not Alexander, he would prefer to be Diogenes (Figure 4.6)! A few Cynics earned the respect of some thinkers, but the principles of Cynicism offended the educated, and its pessimism offered no hope to the masses.

Skepticism The proponents of **Skepticism** argued that nothing could be known for certain, an extreme conclusion they were led to by their belief that the senses were unreliable sources of knowledge. Thinking that everything was relative, the Skeptics maintained that all ideas must be questioned and that no single philosophy was true. When their critics pointed out that such unrelenting questioning was clearly not a practical answer to life's uncertainties, the Skeptics

Figure 4.6 *Diogenes and Alexander the Great.* First century A.D. Villa Albani, Rome. *This Roman relief shows that Diogenes and Alexander the Great, two figures of the Hellenistic Age, were living presences for the Romans. The philosopher Diogenes is carved sitting in his famous tub, a symbol of his contempt for creature comforts. The world-conqueror Alexander is on the right, pointing his finger at the Greek thinker. The dog portrayed on top of the tub is a reference to Cynicism (the word* cynic *is from the Greek word for "dog"). Diogenes asserted that humans should live simply—like dogs.*

replied that certainty could be achieved only by admitting that truth was unknowable—a circular response. The Skeptics thought that if they recognized that intellectual inquiry was fruitless, then they could avoid frustration and achieve *autarky,* or self-sufficiency—the same goal as that of the Cynics and the Stoics.

The Skeptics, even though they attracted a smaller audience than the Cynics, had a greater impact on Western reasoning. Pyrrho [PEER-oh] of Elis founded Skepticism and pursued the native strain of Greek thinking to its logical conclusion, but he never recorded his ideas. Skepticism had some appeal for the early Romans, who brought the Greek philosopher and teacher Carneades [kar-NEE-uh-deez] (about 214–129 B.C.) to Rome in 155 B.C. Carneades shocked his pious Roman audience, who took his universal doubt as a denial of the stability and permanence of their state and its values. Although Skepticism faded after Carneades' death, the movement was revived during the Roman Empire and eventually passed into the mainstream of Western thought.

Epicureanism The strict and quiet way of life advocated by **Epicureanism** appealed to aristocrats who were more interested in learning than in politics. It began as the philosophy of the Greek thinker Epicurus [ep-uh-KYUR-uhs] (about 342–270 B.C.), who founded a school in Athens where pupils, including slaves and women, gathered to discuss ideas (Figure 4.7). For Epicurus, the best way to keep one's wants simple, and thus to achieve happiness, was to abstain from sex and focus instead on friendship. Friendship was a mystic communion, based on shared need, in which men and men, men and women, rich and poor, old and young, of all nationalities and any class supported each other in trusting relationships. This vision guided Epicurus's school, where life became a daily exercise in friendship. It was an ideal that appealed to women, since, in making them men's equals, it showed that they had more to give than bearing children and raising families.

Epicurus based his ethical philosophy on the Atomic theory of those Greek thinkers who saw the universe as completely determined by the behavior of atoms moving in empty space (see Chapter 3). Epicurus accepted this picture, but with one significant modification: He argued that because atoms on occasion swerved from their set paths and made unpredictable deviations, it was possible, even in a deterministic universe, for humans to make free choices. Like the Atomists, Epicurus also believed that the senses presented an accurate view of the physical world. Thus, by using the mind as a storehouse for sense impressions and by exercising free will in their choices, individuals could reach moral judgments and ultimately form an ethical code.

For Epicurus, the correct ethical code led to happiness, which was realized in a life of quiet—separated and withdrawn from the trying cares of the world. Furthermore, those who would be happy should keep their wants simple, not indulge excessive desires, and resist fame, power, and wealth, which only brought misery and disappointment.

Another characteristic of Epicurean happiness was freedom from fear—fear of the gods, of death, and of the hereafter. Although Epicurus believed that the gods existed, he also believed that they cared nothing about human beings, and therefore no one need be afraid of what the gods might or might not do. As for death, there was, again, nothing to agonize over because when it did occur, the atoms that made up the soul simply separated from the body's atoms and united with other particles to create new forms. With death came the end of the human capacity to feel pleasure or pain and thus the end of suffering. Consequently, death, rather than being feared, should be welcomed as a release from misfortune and trouble. Pleasure, in the Epicurean view, is the absence of pain.

Figure 4.7 *Epicurus.* Ca. 290–280 B.C. Courtesy The Metropolitan Museum of Art. Rogers Fund, 1911. (11.90) *This marble bust of Epicurus, discovered in southern Italy and inscribed with his name, is a copy of the original bronze sculpture. Many busts and likenesses of Epicurus have been found, indicating the popularity of his philosophy in Hellenistic times and especially during the Roman era.*

The happy Epicurean, standing above the cares of the world, had reached ***ataraxia,*** the desireless state that the Hellenistic Age deemed so precious.

Stoicism Both Epicureanism and **Stoicism** claimed that happiness was a final goal of the individual, and both were essentially materialistic, stressing the importance of sense impressions and the natural world. The Stoics, however, identified the supreme deity with nature, thus making the natural world divine and inseparable from the deity. The supreme being was also another name for reason, or ***logos,*** and hence nature was also rational. Since the Stoics' God was law and the author of law, this led to the notion that the workings of nature were expressed in divine laws.

The Stoics likewise discovered God in humanity. The Stoics' God, being identical with reason, gave a spark to each mortal's soul, conferring the twin gifts of rationality and kinship with divinity. The Stoics thus believed that reason and the senses could be used jointly to uncover the underlying moral law as well as God's design in the world, proving God's wisdom and power over human life and nature.

There was in Stoicism a tendency to leave everything up to God. Stoics came to accept their roles in life, whether rich or poor, master or slave, healthy or afflicted, and such a resigned and deterministic outlook could (and did) lead to apathy or unconcern. However, the ideal Stoic, the Wise Man, never became apathetic. He overcame Stoicism's fatalistic tendency by stressing his own sense of and dedication to duty. Doing one's duty was part of following the deity's plan, and the Stoic willingly performed his tasks, no matter how onerous or laborious. The reward for living a life of duty was virtue. Having achieved virtue, the Stoics were freed from their emotions, which they thought only corrupted them. The Stoics had thus achieved *autarky,* the state of existence sought by many Hellenistic philosophers.

Stoicism was unique among the Hellenistic philosophies in holding out the promise of membership in a worldwide brotherhood. Perhaps inspired by Alexander the Great's dream, the Stoics advocated an ideal state, guided by God and law, that encompassed all of humanity of whatever race, sex, social status, or nationality in a common bond of reason. As humans carried out their duties in this larger community, they would rise above local and national limitations and create a better world.

Because of their practical optimism, the Stoics drew the largest number of followers among political leaders and intellectuals, who found the Cynics, the Skeptics, and the Epicureans too pessimistic. In the end, however, all four philosophies satisfied only a small portion of the vast Hellenistic population. They failed to appeal to persons who were confused by the intellectual theories or who derived no personal satisfaction from the teachings. Instead, the bulk of the people, spurred on by a growing sense of helplessness, began to believe that Fate ruled their lives.

Fate and the Mystery Cults The belief in Fate, a concept borrowed from Babylonia, gripped the lives of many in the Hellenistic world. To them, Fate ruled the universe, controlled the heavens, and determined the course of life. Although no one could change the path of this nonmoral, predestined force, individuals could try to avoid the cruel consequences of Fate by various methods. The pseudoscience of astrology, also from Babylonia, offered one alternative. Magic was now revived, and many people used sacred objects to conjure up good spirits or to ward off evil ones. Nevertheless, it was the mystery cults—springing from the primitive chthonian religions of Greece (see Chapters 2 and 3) and elsewhere—that eventually emerged as the most popular and effective response to Fate.

During the Hellenistic Age, numerous chthonian cults spread from the Seleucid kingdom and Egypt to the Greek mainland, where they were combined with local beliefs and rituals to create religions that fused different beliefs and practices. By the second century B.C., converts were being attracted from all over the Hellenistic world to the well-established mystery cults of Orpheus and Dionysus in Greece and to the new religions from Egypt and the old Persian lands. The growth of these cults, in turn, sparked an increase in religious zeal after about 100 B.C., resulting in more ceremonies and public festivals and the revival of older faiths.

The Egyptian mystery cults grew, becoming quite popular across the Hellenistic world. Ptolemy I, the Macedonian founder of the Ptolemaic dynasty in 323 B.C., invented a new god, Serapis, in an effort to unite the Egyptians and the Greeks. Serapis became a favorite deity of the masses outside Egypt, and followers built shrines everywhere.

But the goddess Isis, already well known to the Egyptians, overshadowed the newly minted Serapis. According to her cult legend, Isis rescued her husband-brother, Osiris, from his enemies and brought him back to life with her unwavering love. This resurrection symbolized to the faithful the new life awaiting them at death. In time, Isis became associated with many foreign goddesses, fusing with them to become the most honored goddess of the ancient world (Figure 4.8).

From the Seleucid kingdom, the remnants of Babylonian and Persian cultures offered two radically different cults to the Hellenistic Age, the brutal religion of Cybele and the philosophical religion founded by Zoroaster (see Chapter 1). Cybele, the Great Mother

Figure 4.8 Isis with Her Son Harpocrates (left) and God Anubis (right). First century A.D. Terra-cotta, ht. approx. 7″. British Museum. *This small terra-cotta figurine—probably used as a votive—blends Greek sculptural style with Egyptian symbolism. The goddess is portrayed wearing an Egyptian headdress and is flanked by her son and the jackal-headed Anubis, the god of the dead. Greek features include the goddess's tightly curled hair, her slightly contrapposto pose, and the graceful drapery of her dress. The statue, fired on the Italian peninsula in the first century A.D., testifies to her popularity throughout ancient times and across the Mediterranean world.*

goddess, appealed to many women and even a few men, despite the self-mutilation that male believers had to undergo to gain the promise of a new life. Under different names, the Great Mother goddess was worshiped throughout the Hellenistic world and in Rome. Later, Mithraism, an offshoot of Zoroastrianism, with its emphasis on duty and loyalty, caught the attention of Rome's soldiers, thereby ensuring the spread of this belief wherever Roman legions were stationed.

The secret rites of the mystery cults, which communicated the thrill of initiation and the satisfaction of belonging, answered deep psychological needs in their

Hellenistic converts. This universal appeal cut across class and racial lines and attracted an ever-widening segment of the populace. With their promise of immortality, these rituals contributed to the atmosphere of the Roman world in which Christianity would later be born.

Architecture

As in Hellenic times, architecture in the Hellenistic Age reflected the central role that religion played in the life of the people. Public buildings served religious, ceremonial, and governmental purposes, and the temple continued as the leading type of structure. The altar, which had originated in Archaic Greece as a simple structure where holy sacrifices or offerings were made, now became a major structural form, second in importance only to the temple, because of its use in state rituals.

Hellenistic architecture modified the basic temple and altar forms inherited from Hellenic models to express the grandeur demanded by the age's rulers. These monarchs were mesmerized by Alexander the Great's claim to divinity, which had opened up a new vision of statecraft. As a result, Alexander's successors built temples and altars whose massive size and elaborate decoration manifested both their own earthly majesty and the divine authority of whatever deity with whom they claimed kinship.

The Corinthian Temple The **Corinthian** temple came to embody Hellenistic splendor. The Corinthian column had first appeared in the Hellenic period, when it was probably used as a decorative feature. Because it was taller, more slender, and more ornamented than either the Doric or the Ionic column, the Corinthian column was now used on the exterior of temples erected by Hellenistic builders for their kings. In time, Hellenistic taste decreed that the Corinthian column was appropriate for massive buildings. The Corinthian order later became the favorite of the Roman emperors, and it was revived in the Renaissance and diffused throughout the Western world, where it survives today as the most visible sign of Hellenistic influence.

The most outstanding Corinthian temples combined grandeur with grace, as in the Olympieum in Athens, now a ruin (Figure 4.9). Commissioned by the Seleucid king Antiochus IV [an-TIE-uh-kuhs], the Olympieum expressed his notion of a diverse, international culture united under Zeus, his divine counterpart and the lord of Mount Olympus. The temple, the

Figure 4.9 The Olympieum. Various dates: late sixth century B.C.; second quarter of second century B.C.; completed, second quarter of second century A.D. Athens. *The thirteen standing Corinthian columns were part of the original plan of the Olympieum's architect. After the temporary cessation of building in 164 B.C., some of this temple's unfinished columns were transported to Rome and reused in a building there. Their use in Rome helped to popularize the Corinthian style among political leaders and wealthy tastemakers.*

Figure 4.10 Altar of Zeus at Pergamum. (Reconstruction.) Third and second quarters of the second century B.C. Pergamum Museum, Berlin. *This masterpiece of Hellenistic architecture was erected in the 170s B.C. by Eumenes II, the king of Pergamum, to commemorate his victories over various barbarian states in Asia Minor. Eumenes believed himself to be the savior and disseminator of Greek culture, and this altar with its giant frieze was meant to suggest Hellenic monuments, such as the Athenian Parthenon.*

first to use Corinthian columns, was constructed during three different and distinct historical eras. The stylobate, or base, was laid in the late Archaic Age, but then abandoned; the Corinthian columns were raised by Antiochus IV about 175 B.C., after which work was suspended indefinitely; it was finally completed in A.D. 130 under the Roman emperor Hadrian, a great admirer of Greek culture. The temple is stylistically unified, however, because it was finished according to the surviving plans of its second-century B.C. architect. Despite its massive size and its lack of mathematical refinements, the Olympieum presented an extremely graceful appearance with its forest of delicate Corinthian columns, consisting of double rows of twenty columns each on the sides and triple rows of eight on the ends.

The Altar Before there were temples, there were altars, the oldest religious structure in the Greek world. The earliest altars were simple slabs, made wide enough to allow sacrificial animals to be slaughtered. During the Hellenistic Age, the altars were substantially enlarged. The biggest appears to have been the 650-foot-long altar, permitting the sacrifice of more than one hundred cattle at one time, funded by the tyrant of Syracuse in the third century B.C.

Although the Syracusan altar has disappeared, the dismantled altar of Zeus at Pergamum has recently been discovered and reassembled. It is easy to see why ancient travelers called it one of the wonders of the world (Figure 4.10). The actual altar, not visible in the photograph, stands lengthwise in a magnificent Ionic colonnaded courtyard. The courtyard itself is raised on a **podium,** or platform; below the courtyard, the sides of the structure are decorated with a sculptured frieze depicting the deities at war. The overall design—with the frieze below the columns—appears to be an inversion of the usual temple plan. Constructed by Eumenes II [YOU-muh-neez] of the Attalid dynasty, this altar was but one part of a concerted effort to transform Pergamum into another Athens. Thus, the idea of a "new" Athens—a recurrent motif in the humanistic tradition—had already been formulated by the Hellenistic Age.

Sculpture

Like Hellenistic architects, Hellenistic sculptors adapted many of the basic forms and ideas of the Hellenic style to meet the tastes of their day. The Hellenistic sculptors perpetuated such Hellenic principles as contrapposto and proportion as well as the Hellenic emphasis on religious and moral themes. But Hellenistic art increasingly expressed a secular, urban viewpoint, and Hellenic restraint often gave way to realism, eroticism, and violence, expressed and enjoyed for their own sake. Some of these Hellenistic qualities are apparent in the refreshingly naturalistic sculpture *Boy Struggling with a Goose* (Figure 4.11). At the same time, this work of art relates ironically to the age's values because it can be understood on two levels: Its subject is both an everyday scene and a mock-heroic battle; its playful nature masks a sense of violence; and its twisting forms and shifting planes seem overdone on such a small scale.

Between 230 and 220 B.C., King Attalos I [AT-uh-luhs] of Pergamum dedicated in Athens a group of bronze sculptures that celebrated his recent victory over the barbaric Gauls. By donating these bronzes to Athens, which was outside of Pergamum's political orbit, the Attalid ruler hoped to establish his cultural credentials as a defender of Greek culture and thus further his claims to rule over the entire Hellenistic world.

One of these pieces, *Dying Gaul* (which survives only in a Roman marble copy), shows a mortally wounded barbarian warrior (Figure 4.12). The torque, or twisted necklace, he wears identifies him as a Gaul. Lying close by are his sword and trumpet. The sculptor demonstrates his keen eye for realistic details in the open wound oozing blood from the warrior's rib cage and by the blank stare as he faces death. The Hellenis-

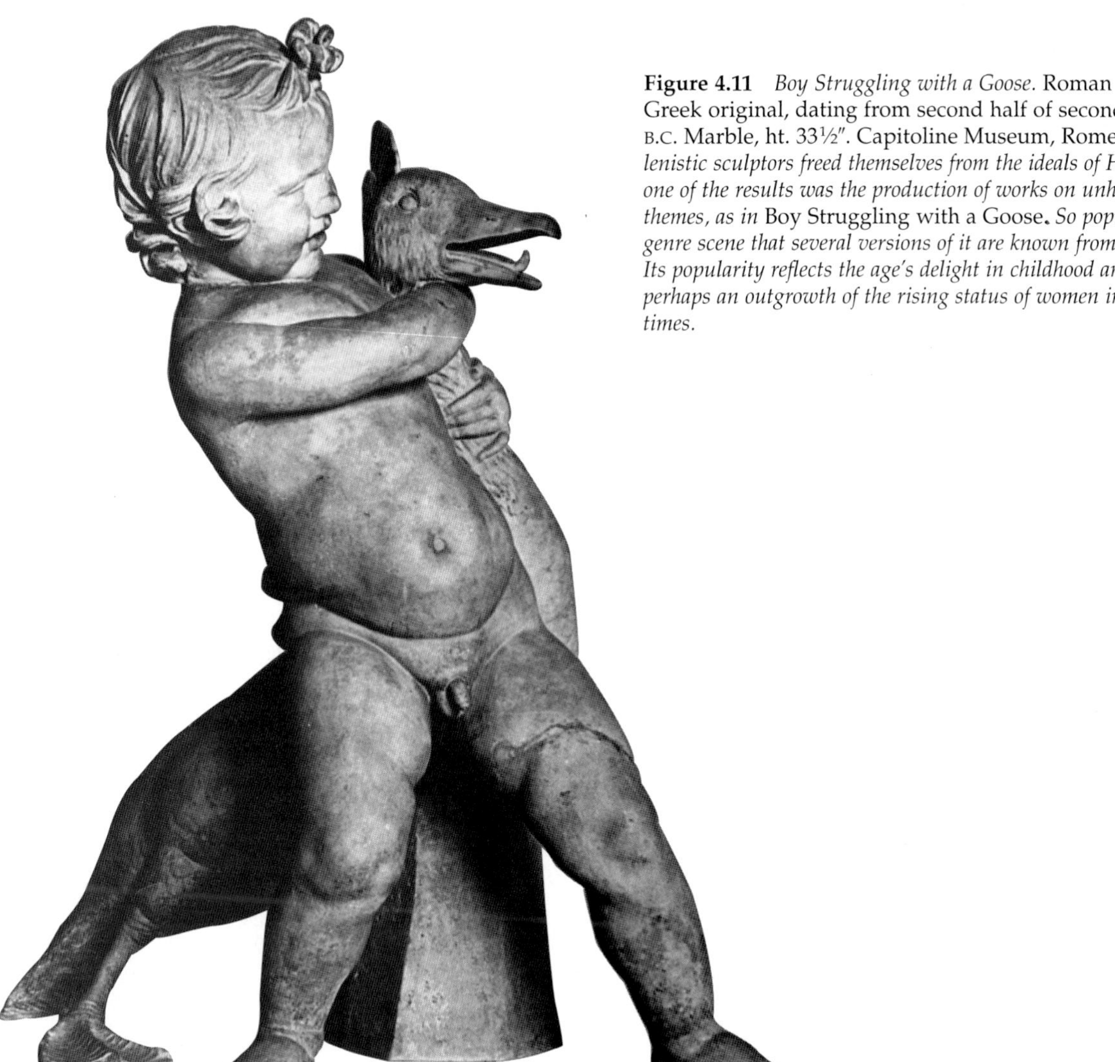

Figure 4.11 *Boy Struggling with a Goose.* Roman copy of a Greek original, dating from second half of second century B.C. Marble, ht. 33½". Capitoline Museum, Rome. *When Hellenistic sculptors freed themselves from the ideals of Hellenic art, one of the results was the production of works on unhackneyed themes, as in* Boy Struggling with a Goose. *So popular was this genre scene that several versions of it are known from antiquity. Its popularity reflects the age's delight in childhood and its joys—perhaps an outgrowth of the rising status of women in Hellenistic times.*

Figure 4.12 *Dying Gaul.* Ca. 230–220 B.C. Roman marble copy of a bronze original, ht. 3′. Capitoline Museum, Rome. *The rulers of the Hellenistic kingdom of Pergamum preferred art that was showy and overwrought, a taste that perhaps stemmed from their insecurity at being a new dynasty. A Pergamene style of sculpture developed under these kings in which gestures were theatrical and anatomical features were portrayed in exaggerated depth. The* Dying Gaul *is a superb example of this style.*

tic style's appreciation of the melodramatic is evident in the tension between the warrior's sagging body and his efforts to prop himself up. But by treating a foreign enemy with such nobility, the anonymous sculptor perpetuates the deep moral sense that was central to Hellenic art.

A radically different subject is expressed in the *Old Market Woman,* which, like a stock character from New Comedy, depicted a well-known social type (Figure 4.13). The old woman, who might have strolled out of the marketplace of any Hellenistic city, represented a **genre subject,** or a scene taken from everyday life. The original third-century B.C. bronze portrayed a stooped figure, straining under the combined weight of her groceries and her advancing years. In this Roman marble copy, the left arm is missing, but she carries a fowl and a brimming bucket. Her deeply lined and wrinkled face and her sagging breasts express the realism of Hellenistic style.

Among the masterpieces of Hellenistic art are the sculptures of the Pergamum altar frieze, which can be seen in Figure 4.10. The subject is a battle between the Olympian deities and the Giants, the monstrous race of pre-Greek gods and goddesses who were the offspring of Gaea (Earth) and Uranus (Sky, or the Heavens)—the first rulers of the universe. The Giants, having overturned their parents, are then defeated by *their* own children, the Olympian deities. To the Greeks, the final triumph of the Olympian gods and goddesses symbolized the coming of a just and moral order both in the universe and in their own society. Hence, when the Attalid rulers chose this subject for the altar frieze, they affirmed that they were continuing the values of Greek civilization. With the exception of the frieze on the Parthenon, the figures on this altar represent the most ambitious sculptural project in the ancient world.

Filled with high-powered energy, the Pergamum frieze displays figures that threaten to explode from the space in which they are barely contained. In one celebrated panel, Athena grasps the dying Giant Alkyoneus while her sacred snake bites him on the chest (Figure 4.14). Her agitated draperies appear to be billowing in a strong wind, so that the folds hang expressively rather than simply disclosing her body, as in the Hellenic style. The expression of pain on Alkyoneus's face—deeply furrowed brow and bulging eyeballs—

Figure 4.13 *Old Market Woman.* Third or second century B.C. Roman marble copy of a Hellenistic bronze, ht. 49″. Metropolitan Museum of Art. *Many Hellenistic sculptors depicted old women in pathetic situations, tired, drunk, or begging. Scholars are divided in opinion about whether these statues were meant to be admired for their truthfulness or whether they represented disdain for what Hellenistic aristocrats considered an ugly social phenomenon.*

and the straining muscles with prominent veins reflect the Pergamum school's taste for exaggeration.

The sculpture of the Hellenistic Age is also characterized by a frank appreciation of female beauty, a famous example of which is the *Aphrodite of Melos,* perhaps better known as the Venus de Milo (Figure 4.15). This original sculpture, carved from Parian marble, shows many borrowings from the tradition of Praxiteles, as shown in his *Hermes with the Infant Dionysus* (see Figure 3.26). Both Aphrodite and Hermes exhibit exaggerated contrapposto; a sensuous, even erotic, modeling of the body; and a serene countenance with an unmistakable gaze. However, the Hellenistic sculptor, demonstrating a playful flair with the rolled down draperies, calls attention to Aphrodite's exposed lower torso.

The *Aphrodite of Melos* was part of the growing influence of **Neoclassicism,** which swept the disintegrating Hellenistic world in the wake of Rome's rise to greatness. Neoclassicism, developing first in Athens in the late third century B.C. and later in Pergamum and other cities, was a kind of nostalgia for the glory days of the fifth and fourth centuries B.C. Another famous work in this style was the *Borghese Gladiator,* which combines the well-defined musculature perfected during the Hellenic period with a dramatic lunging pose

Figure 4.14 *Athena Battling with Alkyoneus.* From the Great Frieze of the Pergamum altar, east section. Second quarter of second century B.C. Marble, 7′ 6″. Pergamum Museum, Berlin. *An unusual aspect of this relief is the diversity of their bodily forms. For example, Alkyoneus's outspread wings identify him as a Giant and an offspring of Gaea, the goddess of the Earth, who is shown on the bottom right.*

so favored by Hellenistic taste (Figure 4.16). Probably commissioned by a Roman patron, this sculpture of a warrior standing on a plinth is thought to be either a copy of or inspired by a third- or second-century B.C. original. Its status as a copy is indicated by the tree trunk support—the place where the sculptor, Agasias of Ephesus (in modern Turkey), carved his name.

The *Horse and Jockey,* original bronzes that were retrieved in this century from a sunken ship in the Aegean Sea off Artemision, show Hellenistic fluidity rather than the frozen style of Hellenic art (Figure 4.17). Whether the two figures are a true ensemble is a subject of scholarly debate. Arguing against their unity is the size disparity between the small jockey and the enormous horse. But the balance seems in favor of treating them as a group, especially when the jockey is seated on the horse. In this juxtaposition, the horse's forward motion seems to cause the jockey's cloak to blow behind him. The boy, contorting his face with the strain of the race, stretches out his left hand, as if to urge his mount on to victory. This sculptured pair shows other innovations in Hellenistic art. The boy athlete, who looks rather like a ragged street urchin, represents the new interest in children that arose in Hellenistic art. And the straining horse contrasts dramatically with the serene, well-proportioned horses on the Parthenon frieze.

Rhodes: Late Hellenistic Style

Although much of the Hellenistic world, including Greece, fell into Roman hands in 146 B.C., the Aegean island of Rhodes remained free for over sixty more years (see Map 4.1). During this period, independent Rhodes became a cultural center that rivaled the older cities of Pergamum, Alexandria, and Athens in concentration of scientists, artists, and humanists. The Rhodian style, which alternated between lighthearted and gay on the one hand and colossal and theatrical on the other, was influenced by the Pergamene school and was the final stage of Hellenistic art.

A graceful example of this statuary type is a Roman copy of one figure from a Rhodian sculptural group

Figure 4.15 *Aphrodite of Melos (Venus de Milo).* Ca. 160–150 B.C. Marble, ht. 6′10″. Louvre. *This celebrated statue represents the classicizing tendency in Hellenistic art. The head is executed in the pure Hellenic style, as seen in the serene countenance, the exquisitely detailed hair, and the finely chiseled features. However, the body with its frank sensuality and its rumpled draperies is clearly in the Hellenistic style.*

Figure 4.16 AGASIAS OF EPHESUS. *Borghese Gladiator.* Ca. 100 B.C. Marble, ht. 5′6½″. Louvre. *The subject here is not a gladiator, for the Greeks were ignorant of the circus games. Instead, based on the upturned gaze and the upraised left arm, the statue depicts a warrior on foot fighting for his life against an unseen opponent on horseback. The outmatched warrior is thus a figure of pathos, a beloved theme during the Hellenistic period. Yet Agasias has injected into this theme the rugged athleticism of the fourth century B.C. Lost in antiquity, the statue was acquired by a Borghese prince on its rediscovery in the seventeenth century A.D. Today, the* Borghese Gladiator, *newly restored in 1997, stands in a place of honor in the Louvre.*

Figure 4.17 *Horse and Jockey of Artemision.* Mid-second century B.C. Bronze, ht. of jockey 33½″. National Museum, Athens. *The jockey and horse may have been intended by an athlete as a votive offering to a deity for victory in a competition. Such statues had been erected in Greece from the Archaic Age onward.*

Figure 4.18 *Muse (Melpomene* or *Polyhymnia (?)).* Roman copy, probably of a mid-second-century B.C. original by Philiskos of Rhodes. Ht. 4′ 11″ without plinth. Capitoline Museum, Rome. *The sculptor has portrayed the muse in a simple but dignified pose—leaning forward on a support, left foot upturned, chin resting on curved right hand—and swathed her in a thin mantle of fabric that falls into rhythmic folds. The contrast between the serenely meditative face and the dynamic drapery pattern is a typical effect of Hellenistic art (see Figure 4.14).*

dating from the mid–second century B.C. (Figure 4.18). The muse is probably either Melpomene, muse of tragedy, or Polyhymnia, muse of the choral hymn. She is portrayed as a young woman leaning against a support, lost in thought. Except for her left foot and left hand, she is swathed in draperies, a typically Hellenistic way of portraying women. The large number of statues of draped women surviving from the Hellenistic era reflects the rising social status of respectable women during this time.

The school of sculpture on Rhodes, even after the island's absorption into Rome, was still able to produce the sublime masterpiece of Rhodian and Hellenistic art, *The Laocoön Group* (Figure 4.19). The sculptors of this famous group, probably Hagesandros [haj-uh-SAN-drohs], Polydoros [pol-e-DOOR-uhs], and Athanadoros [ah-thay-nuh-DOOR-uhs], were all members of a local dynasty of sculptors. Their sculpture depicts the priest Laocoön and his sons. According to Vergil's *Aeneid,* the Roman epic, Laocoön, a priest of Neptune, warned the Trojans not to bring the wooden horse—which, unknown to him, concealed a party of Greek warriors—into their city. (Laocoön's admonition to beware Greeks bearing gifts has become proverbial.) As Laocoön finished his speech, sea serpents, sent by the gods, raced out of the sea and crushed him and his two sons to death. The Trojans interpreted Laocoön's speech as an impious act against the gods, and they hauled the horse into Troy.

In the *Laocoön* sculptural group, the snakes, which grasp and bite the priest and his sons, serve to integrate the three figures into an image of unrelieved horror: Laocoön's face is contorted in anguish as the serpent bites him; on the left, one of his sons is already dead; and the other son seems to be disentangling himself from the serpentine coils. This celebrated work, with its technical virtuosity and its rhetorical violence, is a fitting climax to almost four hundred years of Hellenistic art. The *Laocoön* sculptural group vanished after the fall of Rome only to be rediscovered in the early sixteenth century A.D., when it influenced the sculptor Michelangelo and the subsequent rise of Baroque art.

Figure 4.19 HAGESANDROS, POLYDOROS, AND ATHANADOROS. *The Laocoön Group.* Ca. A.D. 50. Marble, ht. 8′. Vatican Museum. *Parallels are frequently made between the distorted features of the dying Laocoön and the mortally wounded Alkyoneus from the Pergamum altar (see Figure 4.14). This similarity points to some connection between the Rhodian and Pergamene schools of sculpture, though the exact relationship is a matter of controversy.*

The Legacy of the Hellenistic World

In the Hellenistic Age, Athens and its culture achieved the status of an inspiring model to be honored and emulated. But the Hellenistic rulers had no interest in democracy; indeed, their larger political interests often conflicted with the needs of local subjects. Nor did these kings want to further humanism, which they regarded as either irrelevant to imperial goals or subversive of them. What appealed to the Hellenistic kings was a narrow, lifeless humanism, as exemplified by the dynasties of the Attalids in Pergamum and the Ptolemies in Egypt. The Hellenistic monarchs wanted to do no more than create new cultural centers that rivaled the fame of the old Athens. The great Hellenistic centers of Pergamum and Alexandria—with their libraries, poets, scientists, artists, schools of philosophy, marble buildings, and monuments—were perceived as politically useful to these ambitious rulers. In other words, they wanted to harness art to politics for propaganda purposes.

The Hellenistic world bequeathed the idea of a "new Athens" to Rome, which was, in part, inspired by its many cities, urban life, and civic culture. Rome in turn diffused the Greek heritage to the major cities of the entire Mediterranean area. After the fall of Rome, the medieval rulers adopted this tradition, making their governments responsive to the religious and, to a lesser extent, the cultural needs of their citizens. With the rise of the secular state in the eighteenth century A.D., governments began to dissociate themselves from the religious lives of their people. But state support of the arts and humanities increased and remains today a legacy of the Hellenistic Age to the modern world.

Hellenistic sculpture and architecture left their mark on later civilizations. Artists brought an invigorating realism to their genre sculpture that expressed emotions and individualism. They introduced the portrayal of female nudity, a practice that has persisted in Western art to the present day, with the exception of the Christian centuries. Their emphasis on individualism influenced Roman sculptors, who, in carving many lifelike busts during the republic, preserved this tradition in Western art. The Corinthian temple, perfected in the Hellenistic era, set the standard in decoration and proportion for Roman temples and, along with the Doric and Ionic styles, was adopted and modified for many public structures.

A final legacy of the Hellenistic Age was its schools of philosophy—Stoicism, Epicureanism, Skepticism, and Cynicism. Although contradictory of each other, these schools of thought had a common appeal: the promise of a stable belief system and inner peace in the face of a hostile and chaotic environment. From Roman times to the present, these philosophies have attracted followers, but Stoicism has had the most enduring impact (on republican Rome, early Christianity, and the Enlightenment), with Epicureanism the next most influential (on the Scientific Revolution and the twentieth century). With their advice to disengage oneself from either the world or one's own passions, these four schools have provided solace in every age marked by overwhelming events and social disorder.

KEY CULTURAL TERMS

Hellenistic
koine
New Comedy
comedy of manners
Alexandrianism
pastoral
idyll
Cynicism
autarky
Skepticism
Epicureanism
ataraxia
Stoicism
logos
Corinthian
podium
genre subject
Neoclassicism

SUGGESTIONS FOR FURTHER READING

PRIMARY SOURCES

AUSTIN, M. M., ed. *The Hellenistic World from Alexander to the Roman Conquest: A Selection of Ancient Sources in Translation.* Cambridge: Cambridge University Press, 1981. Letters, decrees, and official pronouncements from the Hellenistic period; provides a real sense of the time.

SHAPIRO, H., AND CURLEY, E., eds. *Hellenistic Philosophy: Selected Readings.* New York: Modern Library, 1965. Selections from writings on Epicureanism, Stoicism, Skepticism, and Neo-Platonism, with short introductions.

5 ROMAN CIVILIZATION
The Pre-Christian Centuries

Roman civilization is as ancient as Greek civilization, but it reached its peak later. From its legendary founding in 753 B.C., Rome grew steadily from a tiny city-state ruled by kings to a powerful republic, constantly adjusting to internal and external forces, and ultimately to a vast empire that controlled the known Western world. This chapter surveys Rome from its founding to its near collapse in A.D. 284. Chapter 7 follows the story of Rome through its rejuvenated and Christian period to the last days of the empire. Before that, Chapter 6 examines the Judeo-Christian tradition that wove itself inextricably into the Western heritage during the first centuries of imperial Rome.

THE COLOSSUS OF THE MEDITERRANEAN WORLD

In A.D. 248 the Romans celebrated the one-thousandth anniversary of the founding of their city. By that date, the Roman way of life had not only engulfed the peoples and cultures of the ancient Near East and the eastern Mediterranean but also brought the light of civilized existence to the tribes living in North Africa, in western Europe to the Rhine River, in central Europe to the Danube River, and in England (Map 5.1). So vast was Rome's dominion and so powerful its influence that until the eighteenth century, Rome was the exemplar of power and wealth, one that the nations of Europe could only dream of equaling. Roman civilization had a profound and lasting impact on life in the West (Figure 5.1).

◀ **Detail** Pantheon Interior. A.D. 126. Rome.

Map 5.1 THE ROMAN EMPIRE UNDER AUGUSTUS, A.D. 14

Figure 5.1 Porta Borsari at Verona. Mid-first century A.D. Verona, Italy. *Roman architectural innovations strongly influenced the architecture of later periods. This structure was originally attached to a building that served as a gate to the Roman city of Verona. The building itself was razed during the Renaissance, but the facade was left standing and served as a model for palaces of that era. The wall, composed of stacked, rounded arches, is a typical Roman design. Most of the wall openings are beautifully framed with triangular pediments overhead and Corinthian columns or pilasters on the sides, resulting in a visual effect of ordered diversity.*

Figure 5.2 *Statue of a Republican General.* 75–50 B.C. Marble, ht. 78″. Museo Nazionale, Rome. *This statue portrays an unknown military leader from the Late Republic. The deeply serious though realistic face is typical of the Roman style. By this time, Roman generals were imitating the custom of Hellenistic leaders of having themselves depicted as nude or seminude figures. This fashion ended abruptly with the reign of Augustus, when rulers began to be represented wearing a cuirass, or breastplate (see Figure 5.24).*

General Characteristics of Roman Civilization

Who were the Romans, and how did they create such a successful civilization? The Romans were, above all, a practical people, interested chiefly in what was useful. Possessed of a virile moral sense, they were inclined to view intellectual brilliance with suspicion. Furthermore, Roman authority figures cultivated the virtue known in Latin as *gravitas,* or gravity, meaning a deep-seated seriousness (Figure 5.2). By Greek standards, the Romans were a dull lot, too self-controlled and afraid of the imagination. But the Romans were ingenious at adapting borrowed cultural forms and had a gift for governing.

Early Rome was a minor city-state founded by herdsmen and farmers on seven low hills beside the Tiber River in central Italy. Over their long rise to world leadership, the Romans changed radically, but they never ceased to honor their agrarian roots. Roman morality and Roman law both echoed a rural ethic by stressing the importance of nature and of living within one's means. Roman literary culture was also deeply imbued with a reverence for a rustic past. When Rome became prosperous, many writers bemoaned the corrupting power of luxury and appealed to the homespun values of Rome's founders. Rome's agrarian tradition also contributed the ideal of the patriotic farmer-soldier, embodied in those early leaders who never strayed far from their farming heritage.

Another important Roman value was the sanctity of the family. Divorce was unheard of until the late republican era, and even then family values continued to be eulogized by moralists and honored by leaders. Roles were strictly defined within the Roman family, which was guided by the father, the *paterfamilias,* who exercised legal power of life and death over his entire household, including his spouse, children, relatives, servants, and slaves (Figure 5.3). The paterfamilias wielded greater authority than his Greek counterpart, but, in contrast, the Roman matron was freer and had more practical influence than did the secluded wives of Greece. In general, the Roman matron was conspicuously present in society, attending and presiding at gatherings along with her mate and supervising the education of both her female and her male offspring (Figure 5.4).

Religion permeated family life, and each Roman household kept an undying fire burning on its hearth, symbolic of the goddess Vesta, to ensure the family's continuity. Above each hearth stood statuettes of Lares, the outdoor spirits guarding fields and buildings, and Penates, the interior protectors of cupboards and barns (Figure 5.5). The family revered the deceased male ancestors, whose funeral masks adorned the walls and were regularly used in domestic rituals.

In sum, the Roman citizen was secure in the knowledge of both Rome's and his place in the world and in the cosmos. And the Roman matron, though lacking the voting rights citizenship gave to her spouse, played many roles that society and tradition demanded of her. Like her husband, she understood social rules and cultural expectations.

The Etruscan and Greek Connections

Although the Romans took great pride in their native tradition, they were receptive to change and able to assimilate the contributions of superior cultures, as their experience with the Etruscans and the Greeks demonstrates. In the late seventh century B.C., Rome, still a small city-state, was subjugated by the Etruscans, a sophisticated urban people of obscure origins in northern Italy. The Etruscans excelled at commerce and

Figure 5.3 *Patrician with Busts of Ancestors* (*Barberini* Togatus). Early first century A.D. Marble, ht. 5′5″. Palazzo dei Conservatori, Rome. *The stern and wrinkled faces of the anonymous patrician and his ancestors convey the quiet dignity and authority of the typical* paterfamilias. *Some scholars think that these portrait busts, with their unflattering realism, were modeled on death masks.*

Figure 5.4 *Eumachia.* Mid-first century A.D. Marble. Museo Nazionale, Naples. *This statue of Eumachia, which was found at Pompeii, shows that Roman matrons were involved in public life. The inscription on the statue's base praises her for having donated a building in the town's forum for the use of the fullers—workers involved in the making of woolen cloth. Her statue was paid for by the fullers' association in gratitude for her gift. Her idealized face reflects the Hellenic ideal preferred during the reign of Augustus in the first century A.D.*

Figure 5.5 Statuettes of Lares. First century B.C. Ht. approx. 8½″. Museo Nazionale, Naples. *These statuettes portray the Lares, the deities who guarded each Roman home. At first, images of the Lares were painted inside small family shrines, but wealthy citizens began to commission statuettes of these household deities. The posture of the bronze Lares—dancing on the balls of their feet and pouring wine from a drinking horn into a libation bowl—was also typical of the painted figures. The swinging skirts reflect a stylistic current that began in Hellenic art.*

conducted a brisk maritime trade with the advanced cultures of the eastern Mediterranean (Figure 5.6). Under Etruscan domination, Rome prospered and became a hub of commerce and transportation. Romans also began to put their spoken language into writing, using the Etruscan alphabet. Even what are called Roman numerals were invented by the Etruscans.

Despite their cultural gains from the Etruscans, the Romans rankled under their rule, and in 509 B.C. they expelled Tarquin the Proud, the last Etruscan king, and converted Rome into an independent republic. The Etruscan experience made the Romans intense foes of kings and monarchies, a dislike that was to play a central role in Roman history.

Whereas the Etruscans had conquered the Romans, it was the Romans who made the opening move in conquering the Greeks, beginning in 275 B.C. with the Greek colonies in southern Italy, or Magna Graecia. More conquests followed as Rome, between 146 and 31 B.C., assimilated the separate Hellenistic kingdoms into its overseas empire. Styling themselves after the defeated Hellenistic rulers, the Roman emperors eventually claimed to be immortal gods, turning the state into a divine monarchy. The emperors also adopted the civilizing mission of the Hellenistic kingdoms, thus giving Rome's domestic and foreign policies a new moral dimension.

The conquest of the Hellenistic kingdoms propelled Rome to the height of ancient civilization. However, in the end, Greek civilization conquered the conquerors, for when the Greek cultural forms (lyric and epic poetry, the arts, and architecture, among others) were imported into Rome, the Romans were forced out of their exclusively practical ways. The Romans coined the term *humanities* to refer to the artistic, literary, and philosophical activities the Greeks considered basic to civilized life. But the humanities themselves were Greek inventions, as was the belief that the study and practice of the humanities is stimulating to the soul (mind). Thus, the humanities, which originated among the artists and intellectuals of Archaic and Hellenic Greece, were preserved and transmitted by the Romans, an achievement that some historians regard as Rome's finest.

Figure 5.6 *Apollo of Veii.* Early fifth century B.C. Painted terra-cotta, ht. 70". Museo Nazionale di Villa Guilia, Rome. *This magnificent striding statue of Apollo shows strong influences from the art of Archaic Greece, such as the proportion of the torso to the limbs and the enigmatic smile. But the superb mastery of movement achieved by the Etruscan artist is well in advance of the Greek style.*

Timeline 5.1 THE ROMAN MILLENNIUM, 753 B.C.–A.D. 248

753 B.C	509 B.C	31 B.C.	A.D. 248
Monarchy	Republic	Empire	
Founding of Rome; ca. 600 Etruscan rulers	Founding of the republic	Founding of the empire	1000th birthday of Rome

The Roman Empire was centuries in the making, and pre-Christian Roman history can be divided into three periods reflecting the prevailing type of government: monarchy (753–509 B.C.), republic (509–31 B.C.), and empire (31 B.C.–A.D. 284) (Timeline 5.1). In each period, earlier traits and values endured.

Rome in the Age of Kings, 753–509 B.C.

During the Age of Kings, some basic components of Roman political, social, and economic structures were established. The city-state, although ruled by kings, had a balanced system of government in which a council of landowners helped select the ruler and the entire people ratified its choice. This system ended about 600 B.C. when the Etruscans imposed their rulers on Rome, but it became a model for government under the republic.

Also taking root at this time was another persistent feature of Roman political and economic life—class conflict. As Rome expanded, some urban dwellers, debarred from the aristocracy by poverty and birth, took advantage of commercial opportunities and began to engage in trade. The plebeians, as this class was called, accumulated wealth and began to challenge the social power of the landed aristocrats. When the aristocrats abolished the monarchy and established the republic, they safeguarded their power by denying citizenship to the plebeians. This policy of exclusion laid the groundwork for centuries of class conflict.

The Roman Republic, 509–31 B.C.

In 509 B.C., the Roman aristocrats threw off their Etruscan overlords and founded a republic. The Etruscans retreated to their lands in central Italy, where some of their small cities continued to enjoy autonomy. They tried to cling to their values, institutions, and language, but they were slowly assimilated into the Roman world, a process completed during the reign of Augustus.

Unlike the Greeks, whose political order consisted of short-lived leagues of city-states, the Romans established a republic whose provinces eventually reached the eastern Mediterranean and that lasted almost five hundred years. This republic, in contrast to Athens's direct democracy, was based on a system of representatives and a separation of powers. Rome's achievement is unsurpassed in Western history.

Rome's republic is divided into three principal periods: early, middle, and late. During these tumultuous periods, Rome became a world power. At the same time, great political and cultural changes were transforming all of Roman civilization (Timeline 5.2).

Timeline 5.2 THE ROMAN REPUBLIC, 509–31 B.C.

509	264	133	31
Early Republic	Middle Republic	Late Republic	
Rome establishes republican form of government, subdues Italian peninsula	264–241 First Punic War; 219–202 Second Punic War; 149–146 Third Punic War	133–31 Rome acquires Hellenistic kingdoms; social, political unrest	44 Julius Caesar assassinated; 44–31 civil war

The Early Republic, 509–264 B.C. Two major crises, one domestic and one foreign, faced the Early Republic and threatened to overwhelm the fledgling state. The domestic issue stemmed from the division of society into two classes—the landed, aristocratic patricians and the unorganized, disenfranchised plebeians. As the patricians dismantled the monarchy and set up a republic, they continued to exclude the plebeians from political life. They placed executive power with two consuls, each with veto power over the other. They gave legal and fiscal power to magistracies—public offices—and legislative and judicial powers to an assembly. But real power resided with the Senate, the successor to the old council of landowners that had existed under the kings. Senators served for life, and their judgments eventually achieved the force of law.

The plebeians were given no part in these reforms, and over the years jealousy and class hatred occasionally resulted in violent class struggle. But the plebeians steadily won concessions, until, by 287 B.C., they had gained all the rights of citizenship enjoyed by the ruling patricians.

The foreign crisis faced by Rome was the military conquest of the various peoples inhabiting the Italian peninsula. During these first foreign wars, the Romans originated the strategy that became the key to their military success. They permitted defeated peoples to remain self-governing, to keep their own religions, and, most especially, to satisfy obligations to Rome by providing troops for her armies instead of paying taxes. This strategy allowed the former foes some freedom and yet subtly tied them to Rome.

The Middle Republic, 264–133 B.C. Roman armies had conquered Italy, but up and down the peninsula restless tribes were not yet securely attached to Rome. The challenge was to convert them to the Roman way of life. By founding new towns and enticing settlers with offers of free land and full Roman citizenship, Rome eventually united the entire population. Roman law and the Latin language triumphed in the Italian peninsula.

Beyond the peninsula, Rome faced the challenge of Carthage, a Phoenician state in North Africa that dominated the western Mediterranean and blocked Rome's expansion into that area. In the Punic Wars (from the Latin *poeni,* "Phoenician") (264–146 B.C.), a series of three separate but related conflicts, Rome overwhelmed and finally destroyed Carthage; later, in 29 B.C., the Romans refounded Carthage as capital of the province of Africa. At the end of the Third Punic War in 146 B.C., Rome added Sicily, Corsica, Sardinia, and North Africa to its realm.

Supremacy was not without its price, however, for the wars transformed both the Roman state and the Roman character. The republic's imperialistic ambitions were emboldened by its acquisition of new territories to the west. And during the Second Punic War, the Carthaginian general Hannibal had invaded Italy and ravaged the countryside for fourteen years. His scorched-earth policy devastated Italy's farm country, and small farms began to be replaced by huge ranches worked by slaves. Italy's social fabric was permanently changed.

Having made themselves masters in the west, the Romans moved quickly to conquer the Hellenistic kingdoms to the east. The Romans granted greater freedom to these older Hellenistic cultures, but they forcefully organized and civilized the western provinces. At the end of the Middle Republic, Romans could justly call the Mediterranean Mare Nostrum—"Our Sea."

The Late Republic, 133–31 B.C. Rome in the Late Republic was ruled by an oligarchy of patrician families who dominated the Senate and clung stubbornly to their rights and privileges. Although Roman power continued to spread throughout the Mediterranean basin, economic and social problems multiplied. Despite attempts at reform, the issues proved intractable, and by 31 B.C. the republic lay in ruins.

One problem was generated by the rise of the equestrian order (*equites* in Latin), a social class who had gained wealth during the Punic Wars but who lacked the political power of the patricians. By the mid–first century B.C., open warfare had broken out between the equites and the senators, contributing to the anarchy of the period.

At the same time, the nature of the masses was changing. Increasing numbers of independent farmers were pushed off the land by large estate owners, and many of them went to Rome, where they lived in perpetual poverty and sold their votes to the highest bidders. In an effort to pacify them, the government instituted free bread and public amusements, scornfully referred to by critics as "bread and circuses." The farmer-soldier ideal of early Rome now gave way to a new mentality, one more concerned with bloody sporting events like gladiatorial contests than with political rights and duties.

The republic's last hope for substantive reform was Julius Caesar, a major figure in Roman politics from 60 to 44 B.C. Caesar had emerged as a great public hero by pacifying Gaul (France). The commander of a loyal and formidable army, he had defeated rival generals to become Rome's sole ruler in 48 B.C. He took his authority from the many titles and powers he held, including dictator for life, consul, and head of the armies. Future Roman emperors recognized him as their predecessor by calling themselves Caesar, or ruler. With the possible exception of Alexander the

Great, no other Western ruler has generated such praise or blame from philosophers, poets, and artists.

Caesar, though acting in the name of equestrian interests, held a lofty vision for Rome's future. He initiated building projects that gave work to the urban poor, allowed the Italians outside Rome more self-rule, and founded Rome's first public library. But Caesar's enemies in the Senate believed that the dictator wanted to be king—the dreaded fear dating back to Etruscan Rome. On the Ides of March (March 15) in 44 B.C., a band of senatorial assassins murdered Caesar, and Rome plunged into chaos.

A new leader emerged from the years of unrest that followed: Octavian, Caesar's great-nephew and adopted son. His accession to power in 31 B.C. marked the beginning of the Pax Romana (Roman peace), a two-hundred-year period of unprecedented tranquility and economic growth. But it also marked the gradual dismantling of the republic and the establishment of an autocratic empire.

Growing Autocracy: Imperial Rome, 31 B.C.–A.D. 284

When Octavian returned peace and order to Rome, he pledged to restore the republic. He maintained the government offices, the Senate, and the political machinery, but beneath the surface of the Roman state, power was being transferred to one man, the emperor. With no legal safeguards against the emperor's will, the citizens became subject to his personal whim, and political liberty was gradually strangled. Subsequent Roman emperors enhanced their power by stifling dissent and glorifying themselves, eventually adopting the Hellenistic practice of emperor worship.

The political structure forged by Octavian remained intact from 31 B.C. to A.D. 284. This span of almost three centuries may be broken into two parts: the two-hundred-year Pax Romana and nearly a century of civil wars.

Pax Romana, 31 B.C.–A.D. 193 Octavian, who became known as Augustus Caesar, or "revered ruler," established his power by converting Egypt—Rome's wealthiest province—into his personal property and by making the military the loyal mainstay of his rule. His armies pushed back Rome's frontiers, stopping at what he considered its natural borders, the Rhine and Danube Rivers. Augustus then extended the celebrated Pax Romana to the people whom he conquered. Governors were dispatched to rule and collect taxes, army camps were created to keep law and order, and colonies and municipalities were founded to provide more land for Romans. The amenities of urban life were also expanded: Temples, altars, schools, arenas, libraries, marketplaces, aqueducts, fountains, and baths were built, and paved roads linked each far outpost with Rome (Figure 5.7).

The rule of Augustus (31 B.C.–A.D. 14) began a long-running economic boom. Like politics, economic life became centralized under a growing imperial bureaucracy. Agriculture, industry, and trade flourished, and most social classes prospered. At the same time, Rome became a true melting pot. Except for the inhabitants of the Greek-speaking East, most people spoke Latin and followed Roman customs. Divisive social and ethnic issues had faded from memory as patrician power waned and equestrian power grew. Senators and emperors now came from the equestrian order as well as from the provinces of Greece and Spain.

Civil Wars, A.D. 193–284 Despite its economic success, however, the empire was profoundly hampered by a major problem: how to select a new emperor. Adoption and inheritance were both tried, often with disastrous results. The murder of the emperor Commodus in A.D. 193 ushered in decades of civil wars, military rule, violence, and chaos. Of the twenty-seven so-called Barrack Emperors (rulers drawn from the ranks of the Roman legions) in the third century, only four died natural deaths.

The empire was beset by problems both inside and outside its boundaries. Searching for loot, implacable Germanic tribes began crossing the northern frontiers. Runaway inflation and a debased coinage wiped out fortunes and caused a return to barter exchange. The Roman army forcibly requisitioned food and supplies from civilians. In addition, a plague ravaged the empire, killing perhaps hundreds of thousands. In A.D. 284, Diocletian, a general from Illyria (later Yugoslavia), seized power. In time, his reforms would snatch Rome from the brink of destruction, as described in Chapter 7.

THE STYLE OF PRE-CHRISTIAN ROME: FROM GREEK IMITATION TO ROMAN GRANDEUR

Hellenistic culture became the foundation of Roman civilization. Often, Rome simply expanded on Hellenistic ideas; but in areas for which the Romans had a special gift, as in lyric poetry and comedy, they created works that rivaled the Greek originals. And in architecture, the Romans made their greatest mark, because this art form naturally blends the utilitarian with the aesthetic.

As in any civilization, Roman cultural achievements were shaped by their political and social

Figure 5.7 Timgad, Algeria. Ca. A.D. 100. *Timgad, strategically located at the intersection of six Roman roads in North Africa, was typical of the towns built from scratch by the Romans during the Pax Romana and populated by ex-soldiers and their families. The town was planned as a square with two main avenues crossing in the middle where the forum stood and all other streets intersecting at right angles. The so-called Arch of Trajan in the foreground marked one of the main thoroughfares, which was lined with columns. Temples, baths, fountains, markets, a theater, and private homes gave the city the reputation of being a pleasant place to live.*

contexts. Especially notable in the long evolution of Roman culture is the shift in style that occurred as the republic gave way to the empire, a shift that can be seen in every area of cultural expression.

Under the republic, artistic achievements were inspired by the Greek model and appealed to the privileged few. Under the empire, a distinctive Roman style began to emerge in response to the tastes of the masses, and spectacle became important in Roman culture. In this atmosphere, philosophy survived mainly as an antidote to the restrictions of the imperial regime. Literature flourished among an educated elite, but flattery and propaganda crept into the works of even the greatest writers. And architecture and sculpture became increasingly monumental and theatrical.

Roman Religion

The native Roman religion was deeply affected by the cults of neighboring and conquered peoples. The **syncretism,** blending of religion, began in earliest times. After their initial contacts with the Greeks in southern Italy, the Romans started to intermingle their divinities with those of the Greek religious system, who seemed to be always either making mischief or making love (Table 5.1). Thereafter, the Greek deities enlivened Rome's religion and inspired her writers, musicians, and artists with thrilling stories. And even after the fall of Rome, the Greco-Roman gods and goddesses continued to live in the art, music, and literature of Europe.

Table 5.1 THE CHIEF ROMAN GODS AND GODDESSES AND THEIR GREEK COUNTERPARTS

ROMAN	*GREEK*
Jupiter	Zeus
Juno	Hera
Neptune	Poseidon
Pluto	Hades
Vesta	Hestia
Apollo	Apollo
Diana	Artemis
Mars	Ares
Venus	Aphrodite
Vulcan	Hephaestus
Minerva	Athena
Mercury	Hermes

From the Punic Wars onward, innovative cults sprang up in Rome. From Egypt came the worship of Isis (Figure 5.8), a religion that promised immortality, and from Asia Minor the cult of Cybele, a mother goddess. Army veterans returning from Persia brought back Mithra, the mortal son of the sun god, whose cult excluded women (Figure 5.9). Mithra's followers observed each seventh day as Sun Day and December 25 as the god's birthday; the faithful also underwent a baptism in the blood of a sacred bull.

Religious innovation was perpetuated in imperial Rome until Greek and oriental cults finally submerged

Figure 5.8 *Preparations for a Banquet.* Ca. A.D. 180–190. Detail. Mosaic, total size 7′ 4⅝″ × 6′ 10⅝″. Formerly in Carthage (Sidi-bou-Said), North Africa. Louvre. *This mosaic, depicting a slave-attendant at a banquet, probably decorated a room used by the Isis cult for ritualistic dinners, though no records have been found identifying the building in which it was discovered. The work's style, with its nearly life-size figure set against a plain white ground and the careful rendering of the human body, is typical of the mosaics of this period.*

Figure 5.9 *Mithra Slaying the Bull.* Third century A.D. Marble, ht. 2′ 10¼″. Antiquario Comunale, Rome. *This relief depicts the defining moment of the Mithra cult, a standard representation found across the Roman Empire in statues and in paintings. Mithra, dressed in Phrygian cap, tunic, trousers, and flowing cloak, presses his right knee on the bull as he slays it. The various animals and humans surrounding this dramatic scene symbolize the themes of good and evil, light and dark, life and death, which are central to the religion.*

the old Roman beliefs. Most of all, the emperor cult—the state policy of encouraging public worship of the ruler as a god—succeeded admirably, except among two groups of Roman subjects who refused to recognize the ruler's divinity—the Jews and the Christians, whose story of resistance and rebellion is told in Chapter 6.

Language, Literature, and Drama

Latin, the Roman language, was at first an unimaginative, functional language, suited only to legal documents, financial records, and military commands. But with the growth of law and oratory in the Early Republic, grammar was standardized, vocabulary was increased, and word meanings were clarified. As the Romans conquered, they made Latin the language of state, except in the Greek-speaking East. By the late empire, Latin had spread throughout the civilized world and was the common tongue for the vast majority of Roman citizens.

Latin literature began to flourish in the Middle Republic (264–133 B.C.) with lyric and epic poetry, comedy, and tragedy, all in the Greek style, although writers were beginning to develop a distinctive Roman style. Over the centuries, Roman literature changed with the changing times, evolving through several quite distinct periods.

The First Literary Period, 250–31 B.C. The writing of the first literary period was noteworthy for its strongly Greek flavor and, in some writers, its grave moral tone. This period also saw the rise of a Roman theatrical tradition influenced both by roots in boisterous Etruscan religious celebrations and by contact with the Greek theater. Many educated Romans in this period could speak Greek, and many had seen performances of tragedies and comedies during their travels.

Plautus [PLAW-tuhs] (about 254–184 B.C.), a plebeian from Italy, launched Rome's great age of comic theater with his almost 130 plays. His genius lay in breathing fresh life into the stale plots and stock characters borrowed from Menander and other Hellenistic, New Comedy playwrights. In his hands, the mistaken identities, verbal misunderstandings, and bungled schemes seemed brand new. Rome's other significant comic playwright was Terence [TAIR-ents] (about 195–159 B.C.), a Carthaginian slave who was brought to Rome, educated, and set free. Although he wrote only six plays, he won the acclaim of Rome's educated elite, perhaps because of the pure Greek tone and themes of his works. Terence's highly polished style later inspired the magisterial Cicero. When the theater revived in Renaissance Europe, playwrights first turned to Plautus and Terence for characters and plots.

As Roman comedy began to decline, superseded by the vast spectacles that the masses demanded, two major poets with distinctively different personalities and

PERSONAL PERSPECTIVE

Marcus, Son of Cicero
Letter to Tiro, Secretary to Cicero Senior

Marcus, having been accused of overspending his allowance, writes to Tiro, Cicero's secretary. In the letter, from Athens, 44 B.C., Marcus, knowing that Tiro will inform his father, gives assurances that he has reformed his ways.

I had been looking for a letter when one finally came, forty-six days out. Its arrival brought me the keenest joy; for in addition to the pleasure I got from the kind words of my father your most delightful letter filled my cup of joy to overflowing. Accordingly, I was not sorry that there had been a break in our correspondence, but rather was I glad; for I profit greatly by your writing after my long silence. Therefore I rejoice exceedingly that you have accepted my excuses.

I don't doubt, my dearest Tiro, that you are deeply gratified over the rumors that are reaching your ears, and I will guarantee and strive that with the passing days this nascent good report may be increased two-fold. You may, therefore, keep your promise of being a trumpeter of my good repute, for the errors of my youth have brought me such pain and sorrow that not only does my soul recoil at the acts themselves but my ear shrinks from the very mention of them. I know full well that you shared in the anxiety and worry of this experience.

Since I then brought you sorrow, I'll warrant that now I will bring you joy in double measure. Let me tell you that I am associated with Cratippus not as a disciple but as a son, for not only do I listen to his lectures with pleasure but also I am greatly privileged to enjoy him in person. I am with him all day and very often a part of the night since by much pleading I often succeed in getting him to dine with me. Now that he has got used to this habit, he often drops in on me at dinner time and, laying aside the severe demeanor of a college professor, he jokes with me like a human. See to it, therefore, that you embrace the earliest opportunity of meeting the eminent gentleman, of finding out what he is like, and of becoming acquainted with his merry disposition.

What now shall I say of Professor Bruttius? I keep him with me all the time. He is a regular stoic in his habits of life but a jolly good fellow withal, for he is very much of a wit both in his lectures and in his discussions. I have hired lodgings for him next door, and, as best I may, out of my slender purse I relieve him in his slender circumstances.

Besides, I am studying public speaking in Greek with Cassius. I am planning to do the same with Bruttius in Latin. On Cratippus' recommendation I am on very intimate terms with certain learned gentlemen whom he brought with him from Mytilene. I also spend a good deal of time with Epicrates, the chief Athenian, Dean Leonidas, and other men of that sort. So much for what I am doing. (Of course, I followed your suggestion as to getting rid of Gorgias, though to tell the truth he was a great help in my daily exercises.) Still I laid aside all considerations if only I might obey my father who had sent me unequivocal orders to dismiss him instanter.

I am deeply grateful to you for looking out for my commissions; please send me as soon as possible a secretary, by all means one who knows Greek; he will save me much labor in copying out my notes. Of all things, be sure to take care of yourself that we may be able to pursue our studies together. I commend you to Anterus (the postman).

talents appeared: Lucretius and Catullus. Both were heavily influenced by Greece. Lucretius [lew-KRE-shuhs] (about 94–about 55 B.C.) stands in the long line of instructive literary figures dating from Homer. A gifted poet, with his well-turned Latin phrases and imaginative and vivid language, Lucretius wrote *De Rerum Natura (On the Nature of Things)* to persuade the reader of the truth of Epicureanism, the philosophy based on scientific atomism that denied divine intervention in human affairs (see Chapter 4).

In contrast to Lucretius's lengthy poem, the verses of Catullus [kuh-TUHL-uhs] (about 84–about 57 B.C.) are characterized by brevity, one of the hallmarks of the Alexandrian school of the Hellenistic Age. Catullus's "small" epics, epigrams, and love poems also closely imitate the scholarly and romantic qualities of Alexandrianism. Catullus is best remembered for his love poems, which draw on the lives of his highborn, free-spirited circle in Rome, and which express his innermost feelings of desire, disappointment, and jealousy.

The efforts of Lucretius and Catullus pale, however, when placed beside those of their contemporary Cicero (106–43 B.C.). An equestrian from Italy, he dominated Roman letters in his own day so much that his era is often labeled the Age of Cicero. By translating Greek treatises into Latin, he created a philosophical vocabulary for the Latin language where none had

Figure 5.10 *Cicero.* First century B.C. Capitoline Museum, Rome. *The anonymous sculptor of this bust of Cicero has caught the character of the man as recalled in literary sources. Honored as one of Rome's finest intellectuals and a patriot devoted to rescuing the state from chaos, he is depicted deep in thought with stern and resolute features. This idealized portrait contributed to the mystique of Cicero as a hero of the Roman republic.*

existed before. Between the fall of Rome and A.D. 1900, Cicero's fame among educated Europeans was such that he was regarded as an authority on the order of Plato and Aristotle. For centuries, his collected speeches served as models both of public oratory and of written argument. Similarly, his philosophical tracts set the agenda for generations of thinkers and reformers. Today's readers rank Cicero's collection of letters, mostly by him, some addressed to him (a few written by his son), as his masterpiece. These nearly nine hundred letters, frank in style and language, offer an honest, unique self-portrait of a major public figure in ancient times (Figure 5.10).

The Second Literary Period: The Golden Age, 31 B.C.–A.D. 14 The second period of Roman literature coincided with the personal reign of Augustus and is considered the Golden Age of Roman letters. This period's three greatest writers, Vergil, Horace, and Ovid, captured the age's euphoric mood as peace and stability once more returned to Rome. Of the three writers, Vergil best represented the times through his vision of Rome and his stirring verses.

The works of Vergil [VUR-jill] (70–19 B.C.), an Italian plebeian, were inspired by Greek literary forms—idylls (or vignettes), didactic (instructive) poems, and epics—yet his use of native themes and his focus on the best traits in the Roman people give an authentic Roman voice to his work. Deeply moved by Augustus's reforms, he put his art in the service of the state. Vergil's pastoral poetry, the *Eclogues* and *Georgics,* celebrated rural life and urged readers to seek harmony with nature in order to find peace—advice that became a significant moral theme of the Western heritage. But Vergil is best known for the *Aeneid,* an epic poem in twelve books that he wrote in imitation of the Homeric epics. In this work, infused with Roman values and ideals, Vergil gave full voice to his love of country, his respect for Augustus, and his faith in Rome's destiny.

The *Aeneid* tells of Aeneas, the legendary Trojan hero who wandered the Mediterranean before founding Rome. In the first six books, Vergil models his tale on the *Odyssey,* writing of travel and love. The second half is modeled on the *Iliad,* stressing fighting and intrigue. The *Aeneid* became Rome's bible and its literary masterpiece. Children were often required to memorize passages from the poem to instill in them the values that had made Rome great. Aeneas served as the prototype of the faithful leader who would not be diverted from his destined path. The work's rich language led later poets to mine the *Aeneid* for expressions and images. As Homer inspired Vergil, so Vergil became the model for Western poets when imaginative literature was revived in late medieval Europe.

The second major poet of the Golden Age was Horace (65–8 B.C.), another Italian plebeian who also welcomed Augustus as Rome's savior and offered patriotic sentiments in his verses. His poems, which were written to be read aloud, use Alexandrian forms such as odes and letters in verse. He helped to create a new poetic genre, the **satire,** which rebuked the manners of the age. Horace was at his best in addressing the heartbreaking brevity of life: ". . . what has been, has been, and I have had my hour."

Ovid [AHV-uhd] (43 B.C.–about A.D. 17), the third voice of the Golden Age, was a wealthy Italian equestrian who did not devote his verses to patriotic themes or pay lip service to conventional morality. Ovid's love poems speak of the purely sensual and fleeting quality of sex and ignore the enduring value of committed love. His *Art of Love* offers advice, in a manner bordering on the scientific, on how to seduce women, whether willing or not. Such advice contrasted with Vergil's and Horace's attempts to raise the moral level of the Romans.

Ovid's masterpiece was the *Metamorphoses*, or *Transformations*. Somewhat irreverently, he breathed new life into more than two hundred Greek and Roman myths and legends that centered on the transformation of people into other forms. This work is the source of our knowledge of many Classical myths, and medieval and Renaissance poets turned to it continually for inspiration.

The Third Literary Period: The Silver Age, A.D. 14–200 In the third literary period, the patriotic style of the previous era was replaced by the critical views of writers who often satirized the Roman society and state. Lacking the originality of the Golden Age, the writers of this era looked to their predecessors for models, while they polished their phrases and reworked earlier themes. This shift in literary taste reflected a new educational ideal that stressed skills in debate and oratory. As a result, moral considerations became secondary to aesthetic effects, with writers using rhetorical flourishes and exaggerated literary conceits.

One of Rome's outstanding Silver Age talents was Seneca [SEN-e-kuh] (4 B.C.–A.D. 65). Born into a wealthy equestrian family in Spain, Seneca became a powerful senator and one of the age's chief thinkers. He is best remembered as a dramatist, though his works failed to measure up to the Greek heritage. His ten extant plays relied on emotionalism, rhetorical excess, and stage violence—the perennial traits of Roman tragedy. After his day, the staging of tragedies ceased, not to be revived for more than fifteen hundred years.

The Silver Age produced Rome's last great Latin poet, Juvenal [JOO-vuh-nuhl] (about A.D. 60–about 140), who trained his censorious gaze on the follies of the empire. Juvenal expressed his outraged observations in sixteen satires, the literary form originated by Horace and others. The voice that speaks in Juvenal's satires is embittered, perhaps a reflection of his obscure social origins. But the carefully crafted language—obscene, bilious, and evocative but always just right—made him the master of this genre in Rome if not in world letters.

The leading historian of the Silver Age was Tacitus [TASS-i-tus] (A.D. 55?–117), famed also as an orator and politician. He honored the Greek tradition of historical writing, which dictated that history must be written according to literary rules, that the proper study of history is contemporary events, and that effects in history have human, not supernatural, causes.

Tacitus acquired his knowledge of statecraft as the governor of the province of Asia (modern southwest Turkey). Among his works are two that have earned him the front rank among Roman historians. The *Annals* focus on the rulers after the death of Augustus in A.D. 14 until the murder of Nero in 68. The *Histories* then pick up the story of Rome and carry it through 96, when the tyrannical Domitian was assassinated.

Tacitus was a master of the Latin language and had a flair for dramatic narrative. Like other Roman historians, he wrote history with a moral purpose, but his critical spirit set him apart from those who had nothing but glowing praise for Rome. Instead, Tacitus's perspective is that of a proud senator who cannot conceal his distaste for Rome's loss of political freedom.

In his works, he sought to uncover the origins of the misrule that had almost destroyed Rome in his day, and he ended by concluding that tyranny was an innate flaw in the imperial office.

Philosophy

The Romans adopted the ethical aspects of Greek thought, but they rejected philosophy itself as dangerous, fearing that its study would draw their young men away from the military to lives of dreamy speculation. As a result, Roman thought stressed rules of behavior with little regard for metaphysics.

In time, Roman versions of Epicureanism and Stoicism reached a wide audience, notably among influential aristocrats. Although Epicureanism had little impact, mainly because its focus on withdrawal from worldly cares contradicted the Roman sense of duty, Stoicism's effect was potent and lasting. Stoic values seemed to confirm the farmer-soldier ideal, suggesting that the early Romans were unintentional Stoics. In addition, Stoicism under the empire caused a few aristocrats to resist, if passively, the growing menace of autocracy; these hardy Stoics, some of whom, like Seneca, willingly sacrificed their lives for their ideas, believed that the natural law was superior to the earthbound justice of the rulers.

Stoicism Although Stoicism was introduced to Rome by Greek philosophers in the Late Republic, its greatest influence was achieved later through the writings and teaching of Seneca, Epictetus, and the emperor Marcus Aurelius.

Seneca's fame as a philosopher rests on his *Letters on Morality*. These letters, which were usually written in response to pressing ethical problems, are filled with good advice, even though they break no new philosophical ground. Thus, for example, Seneca counseled a grieving acquaintance to maintain dignity and inner strength in the face of a loved one's death.

Seneca's *Letters* survived the fall of Rome in A.D. 476, but the works of most other thinkers temporarily disappeared. Consequently, he became one of the great guides for Western thought when philosophy was revived in the Middle Ages. In the modern world, however, his reputation has suffered because of his closeness to Nero, an emperor of legendary cruelty. Despite Seneca's noble philosophy, doubt has been cast on his personal morality.

No such cloud hovers over Epictetus [ep-ik-TEET-uhs] (about A.D. 55–115), who not only preached but also lived his Stoic creed. According to tradition, Epictetus, though a slave in Rome, won his freedom because of his teachings. He subsequently founded a school in Asia Minor and attracted enthusiastic converts. He did not write anything, but Arrian, a pupil, composed the *Discourses* and the *Handbook,* both in Greek, which together preserved the essence of his master's ideas.

Epictetus's philosophy reflected his own victory over personal misfortune. He advised patience in the face of trouble, indifference to material things, and acceptance of one's destiny. Although these ideas represented a rehash of basic Stoic beliefs, his moral wholeness gave them a special appeal.

Stoicism's finest hour arrived in A.D. 161 when Marcus Aurelius became emperor (Figure 5.11). Converted to Stoicism in his youth, the emperor wrote an account (in Greek) of his daily musings—called *Meditations*—while he was engaged in almost continuous warfare against Germanic invaders. His journal came to light after his death and was soon recognized as a masterpiece of Stoicism.

Like all Stoics, the emperor admonished himself to play with dignity the role that providence had assigned. If a divine plan guides the universe, then he must accept it; if, however, the world is ruled by chance, then a well-regulated mind is the best defense. Such reasoning enabled Marcus Aurelius to avoid moral confusion. Although the *Meditations* are Stoic in tone, a careful reading reveals their author to be a hardheaded Roman who was somewhat lacking in intellectual rigor. Marcus Aurelius's death in A.D. 180 signaled the end of Stoicism. The next century witnessed the swamping of all philosophies in the military anarchy and oriental cults of the times.

Neo-Platonism Some Roman thinkers adopted Greek Stoicism; others were interested in blending the various Greek schools—Platonic, Aristotelian, Stoic, among others—into a philosophic synthesis. The outstanding example of this latter trend was **Neo-Platonism,** a school of thought founded primarily by Plotinus [plo-TIE-nuhs] (A.D. 205–270) in the third century A.D. Neo-Platonism was the last major school of philosophy in the ancient world. The movement began as an attempt to correct the problem at the heart of Plato's system—the seemingly irreconcilable split between the absolute world of Ideas and the perishable material world. This Platonic dualism could and did lead to the notion that the everyday world has little purpose in the overall scheme of things. Plotinus now succeeded in bridging the two worlds with his theories, and his writings later influenced Christian thinkers in the Middle Ages and the Italian humanists of the Renaissance.

Plotinus resolved Platonic dualism not with logical analysis but with mystical insight, claiming that the union of the physical and spiritual worlds could be grasped only through an ecstatic vision. His retreat from philosophy into mysticism occurred during the turbulent era of the Barrack emperors when many people fled from urban violence to the relative peace of their villas and estates in the countryside.

Law

The most original contribution of the Roman mind was law. Rome's law created a notion of justice founded on such ideals as fairness for both citizens and subjects, as well as the presumption of innocence in criminal cases. These principles later became central to the Western legal tradition. But the most important facet of Roman law was born in Stoicism: the idea of **natural law,** or a higher justice than that made by human forces. This doctrine of natural law is the basis of the American Declaration of Independence.

Rome's law evolved over many centuries, starting in 450 B.C. with the first written code, the Twelve Tables. These tables, which represented a plebeian victory over the patricians, treated basic aspects of civil life such as personal and property rights, religious practices, and moral behavior. But this milestone did not rid Rome of class distinctions; it merely recognized conflicting rights and thus necessitated a judge above both parties. Through the years, class divisions continued to affect the way the law was applied, since the dispensing of justice always favored the rich.

The branch of Roman law dealing with property rights was called civil law and developed through the office of the *praetor.* Each praetor, at the beginning of his term, issued an edict describing the legal procedures and precedents he would follow. The body of decisions handed down by the praetors eventually came to constitute Rome's civil law.

By the Late Republic, the development of law was enhanced by the advice of legal experts, called *jurisconsults* or *jurisprudentes.* They tended to broaden Roman justice with their Stoic views. The most creative phase of Roman law occurred in the second and third centuries A.D., when eminent jurisconsults helped to codify the law and extend its principles to cover all the citizens of the empire.

Figure 5.11 *Marcus Aurelius*. Ca. A.D. 173. Bronze, ht. 16′ 8″. Piazza del Campidoglio, Rome. *The unknown artist has represented Marcus Aurelius as a warrior emperor, but the militaristic image is offset somewhat by the Stoic ruler's face. Here we see revealed a human being lost in thought and far removed from pomp and power. This magnificent equestrian statue marked the climax of sculpture in the Roman Empire.*

The Visual Arts

Architecture and sculpture dominated Rome's visual arts, but they were pressed into the service of practical needs. The Romans commissioned buildings and statues to serve the state, religion, or society, but they recognized that the practical did not have to forgo beauty, and many of Rome's engineering feats were beautiful in their functional elegance.

The early Romans learned lessons in architecture from the Etruscans, but after encountering the Greeks of Magna Graecia, they rebuilt Rome along Greek lines. By the second century B.C., wealthy Romans were collecting Greek statues in all styles—Archaic, Hellenic, and Hellenistic. Under Augustus, Hellenic style in sculpture and architecture became supreme, inching across the empire over the next two centuries. By the third century A.D., a new architectural style had arisen, blending Greek and Roman styles. This Greco-Roman style carried over into medieval civilization after the collapse of the Roman Empire in the West (see Chapter 7).

Architecture Over the years, the Romans used many types of materials in their public and private buildings. The architects of the Early Republic built with sun-dried bricks and used terra cotta, a fired clay, for roofs and decorations. As Rome's wealth grew and new materials were imported, the bricks retained an important though less visible role in buildings, chiefly in foundations and walls. By the Late Republic, two new products were adapted from the Greeks, mortar and ashlars (massive hewn stones), which, in time, revolutionized the face of Rome.

Much of the impetus for the building revolution sprang from the Romans' improvement of mortar. They produced a moldable concrete by mixing lime, sand, small rocks, and rubble, but because the concrete was visually unappealing, the builders began to cover it with slabs of expensive and highly polished marble and granite imported from Greece or quarried in Italy.

The temple became one of Rome's chief architectural forms. The basic source for the Roman temple was the Greek model with its post-beam-triangle construction, although Etruscan influence was also significant. The Romans adapted the Greek column as either support or decoration, preferring the ornamented Corinthian order to the plainer Doric and Ionic.

The Romans' most significant innovations in architecture were made with the rounded arch, which already had a long history by the time they began to experiment with it. The Mesopotamians probably invented this arch, the Greeks knew about it, and the Etruscans used it in their drainage systems. The arch's basic round form is created with wedge-shaped stones called **voussoirs.** A **keystone** at the center of the semicircle locks the arch in place. The installed arch is amazingly strong, diverting the weight of the upper walls both outward and downward onto columns or other supports (Figure 5.12).

The Romans demonstrated their inventive genius by creating ceilings, or **vaults,** from arches—by transforming the simple rounded arch into barrel vaults, groined vaults, and domes. They created the **barrel vault**—named because it looks like a barrel divided lengthwise—by building a series of contiguous arches. They intersected two barrel vaults at right angles to produce a **groined,** or **cross, vault.** Finally, the dome, the crown jewel of Rome's architectural vocabulary, was constructed essentially by rotating an arch in a full circle (see Figure 5.12). The Romans were also able to build arches more safely after they discovered the correct mathematical ratio (1:2) between the height of an arch and the width of its base.

The prototype of imperial temples is the well-preserved Maison Carrée in Nîmes, France, a major provincial city under Augustus. Built in about 16 B.C., the Maison Carrée incorporated Etruscan and Greek ideas (Figure 5.13). Raised on a platform in the Etruscan manner, this temple shows other Etruscan borrowings in the central stairway, the deep porch, and the engaged columns—that is, the columns built into the walls of the cella, the inner sanctum housing the cult statue. Greek influences are visible in the low gable—the triangular end of the building's roof—and the Corinthian columns. The Greek notion that beauty lies in mathematical harmony is also expressed in the predetermined ratio of the area of the cella to the area of the temple's porch. The aesthetic appeal of the Maison Carrée has made it one of the most famous buildings of Roman culture. In the eighteenth century, Thomas Jefferson used it as the model for the statehouse in Richmond, Virginia.

Besides perfecting their version of the rectilinear temple, the Romans also invented the round temple, as seen in the Pantheon, a sanctuary dedicated to all their deities. The Pantheon consists of three different units: the entrance porch, or portico, with its supporting columns; the huge drum, housing the sanctuary proper, which is attached to the porch; and the dome set on top of the drum (Figure 5.14). This design showed the Romans' reliance on a native heritage, because the rounded shape was probably inspired by the circular religious shrines of the pre-Romans, as modern archeology has shown. The Pantheon also combined a religious with a secular image: The dome symbolized both the heaven of the deities and the vastness of the empire.

But the Pantheon did more than reflect the deep longings of the Roman people; its rich interior illus-

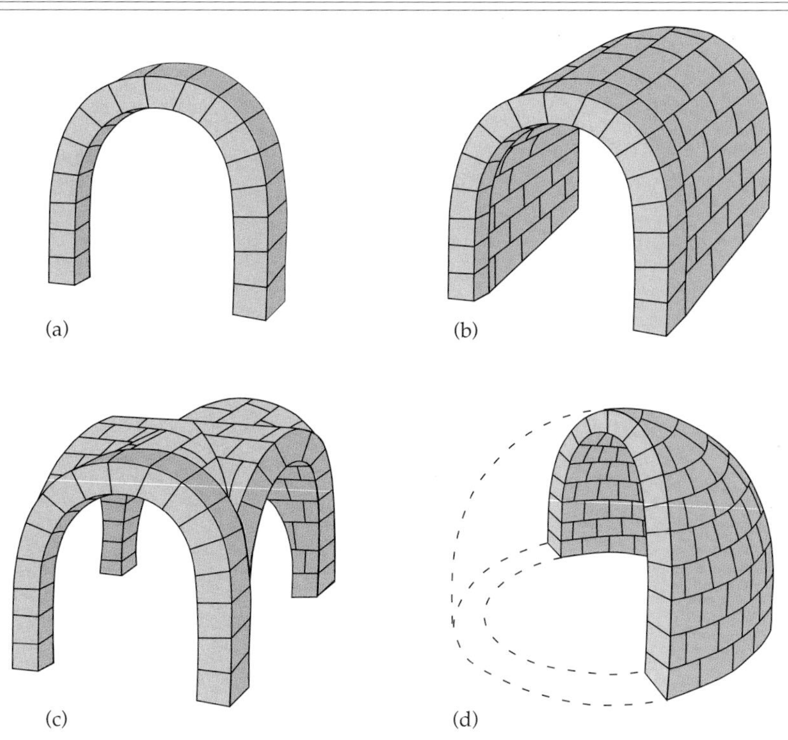

Figure 5.12 Structures Used in Roman Architecture. *Beginning with the basic arch (a), the Romans created the barrel vault (b) and the cross vault (c). These structural elements, along with the dome (d), which they formed by rotating a series of arches around a central axis, gave the Romans the architectural elements they needed to construct their innovative temples and monuments.*

Figure 5.13 Maison Carrée. Ca. 16 B.C. Base 104′ 4″ × 48′ 10″. Nîmes, France. *This temple was probably modeled on temples in Rome, since buildings with Corinthian columns and similar overall designs were being constructed in the capital at this time. Reproducing architecture in the provincial cities was another way in which the Romans spread civilization throughout their conquered lands.*

Figure 5.14 Pantheon Exterior. A.D. 126. Rome. *In modern Rome, the Pantheon is crowded into a piazza where it faces a monument topped by an Egyptian obelisk. However, when built under the emperor Hadrian, the Pantheon was part of a complex of structures that complemented each other, and the temple's facade faced a set of columns in an open forecourt. Its original setting reflected the Roman sense that urban space should be organized harmoniously.*

Figure 5.15 Pantheon Interior. A.D. 126. Rome. *The inner diameter of the dome is 144 feet. The height of the dome is 72 feet, or one half of the total height (144 feet) of the building. The sunlight sweeps around the interior and plays on the dome's decorations as the earth turns, creating constantly changing patterns of light and design.*

trated the Roman genius for decoration (Figure 5.15). A polychrome marble floor and a dome with recessed panels created a dazzling interior, and statues, decorative columns, triangular pediments, niches, and other architectural details alternated around the circular room. The most unusual effect of all was the round hole, thirty feet in diameter, called the **oculus,** or eye, which opened the dome to the sunlight and the elements. As the oldest standing domed structure in the world, the Pantheon is the direct ancestor of St. Peter's Basilica in Rome and St. Paul's cathedral in London.

Rome's architecture consisted of more than beautiful temples. The city of Rome was the center of government for the Mediterranean world, the nucleus of the state's religious system, and the hub of an international economy. And at the heart of the city was its **forum,** which functioned like the agora of Greek city-states. In the forum, citizens conducted business, ran the government, and socialized among the complex of public buildings, temples, sacred sites, and monuments (Figure 5.16). The high priest of Roman religion, the Pontifex Maximus, lived in the forum, and nearby stood the curia, or Senate house. Under the empire, the forum became a symbol of Roman power and civilization; the leading cities in each province had forums.

As part of his reforms, Augustus rebuilt and beautified much of the republican forum. Later emperors, such as Trajan (r. A.D. 98–117), constructed their own forums, which not only served as new centers for trade and government but also perpetuated their names. Trajan's forum, which originally included a library, law courts, and plazas for strolling, has vanished except for one of the most significant monuments of the Roman Empire, a column commemorating Trajan's conquest of Dacia (modern Romania) (Figure 5.17).

Another symbol of empire, the triumphal arch, originated in the republic in the second century B.C. The Romans used both single and triple arches to celebrate military victories and erected them across the empire. The style of these memorials varied until the Arch of Titus, constructed in A.D. 81, became the accepted

Figure 5.16 Roman Forum. Ca. 100 B.C.–ca. A.D. 400. *The forum was literally the center of the Roman world, for here the Romans erected the Golden Milestone from which all roads led out across the empire. The temples and public buildings, crowded together in a relatively small area, were rebuilt over several centuries as rulers added to Rome's architectural legacy.*

Figure 5.17 Trajan's Victory Column. A.D. 106–113. Ht. 125′, including base. Rome. *Borrowing the idea of a victory column from Mesopotamia, the pragmatic Trajan used art to enhance his power in the eyes of the citizens. This work commemorated his conquest of Dacia—present-day Romania. The marble column, set on a foundation, enclosed a winding stairway that led to an observation platform and a statue of Trajan. Spiraling around the column's shaft was a stone relief sculpture that told the story of Trajan's victory in lively and painstaking detail.*

Figure 5.18 Arch of Titus. Ca. A.D. 81. Marble, ht. 47′ 2″. Rome. *The Arch of Titus, like so many structures in Rome, was eventually incorporated into other buildings. Only in the early nineteenth century A.D. was the arch restored to its original splendor. Inspired by this arch, modern architects have designed similar structures throughout the Western world.*

model. This arch, which commemorated the capture of Jerusalem by the then general Titus in A.D. 70, stood at the entrance to the Via Sacra, the thoroughfare of the Roman Forum (Figure 5.18). Inscribed on the attic, or top story, of the arch is the dedication, and decorating the sides are composite columns, a Roman innovation that intertwined flowers in the capitals of Ionic columns. Inside the arch are reliefs of Titus's victorious march into Rome after subduing the Jews.

In addition to forums, columns, and arches, the emperors commissioned amphitheaters as monuments to themselves and as gifts to the citizens. The amphitheaters were the sites of the gladiatorial contests and other blood sports that were the cornerstone of popular culture in the empire. The most famous of these

Figure 5.19 Colosseum. Ca. A.D. 72–80. Ht. 166′ 6″. Rome. *Although the Flavians were a short-lived dynasty, starting with Vespasian in* A.D. *69 and ending with Domitian in 96, they left Rome this structure, one of its most enduring landmarks. The Romans created the oval amphitheater (literally "theater on both sides") by joining two semicircular Greek theaters, another example of their ingenuity and practicality.*

structures was called the Colosseum, although it was actually named the Flavian amphitheater, in honor of the dynasty that built it (Figure 5.19). The name Colosseum, dating from a later time, referred to a large statue of the emperor Nero that stood nearby.

The exterior of the Colosseum was formed by stacking three tiers of rounded arches on top of one another; Greek columns were then inserted between the arches as decorations—Doric columns on the first level, Ionic on the second, and Corinthian on the third. A concrete and marble block foundation supported this immense amphitheater. The playing area, or arena (Latin for "sand"), was made of wood and usually covered with sand. A honeycomb of rooms, corridors, and cages ran underneath the wooden floor. The Colosseum's vast size and unusual features, like its retractable overhead awning, made it one of the triumphs of Roman engineering, but the spectacular and brutal contests between men, and sometimes women, and wild beasts, in varied combinations, symbolized the sordid side of Rome.

Up and down the Italian peninsula and across the ancient world, the urban governments built forums, temples, and amphitheaters, laid roads, and engineered aqueducts in emulation of Rome. Sometimes old towns were made to conform to imperial standards. Pompeii, founded by the Greeks in southern Italy, was typical of the older provincial towns that the Romans remodeled to suit their needs. The Romans left Pompeii's earlier temples and public buildings standing, but a new forum gave the old city a modern look, with municipal offices, a business center, temples to the emperors and to Apollo, and a shrine honoring the civic deities (Figure 5.20). On the edge of town were such amenities as a palaestra—an exercise yard with swimming pool—and several markets. But disaster abruptly ended the urban renewal of Pompeii. In A.D. 79 nearby Mount Vesuvius, an active volcano, erupted and buried the city and most of its people—a horrible fate for the city, but one that produced a rich treasure for archeologists, who began excavations in the 1700s.

Like modern urban centers, Roman towns needed a continuous supply of water. In meeting the water demands of the cities, the Romans displayed their talent for organization and their preference for the practical by creating an elaborate network of aqueducts, sluices, and syphons that ran by gravity from a water source in nearby hills and culminated in a town's reservoirs and fountains.

The Romans started building underground aqueducts in about 300 B.C. and constructed the first elevated aqueduct in 144 B.C. Under Augustus, they completed an aqueduct across the Gard River near Nîmes in southern France (Figure 5.21). Known as the Pont du Gard, this aqueduct has a beautiful functional design. Six large arches form the base, and above them are eleven smaller ones supporting a third tier of thirty-five even smaller arches. Atop the third tier is the sluice through which the water flowed, by gravity, to Nîmes. This graceful structure stands today as a reminder of how the Romans transformed an ordinary object into a work of art.

Sculpture Unlike Roman architecture, Roman sculpture was deeply affected by the tastes of artists and patrons as well as by class interests. For example, certain trends in the republic ran along class lines: The patricians gravitated to the Greek styles and the plebeians favored the local art, called Italo-Roman. Under the

◀ **Figure 5.20** The Forum at Pompeii. Ca. 150–120 B.C. Pompeii, Italy. *This forum served as the civic center of this provincial town of 15,000 to 20,000 inhabitants. Four streets, from the north, south, east, and west, converged here, but no traffic was allowed in the central area.*

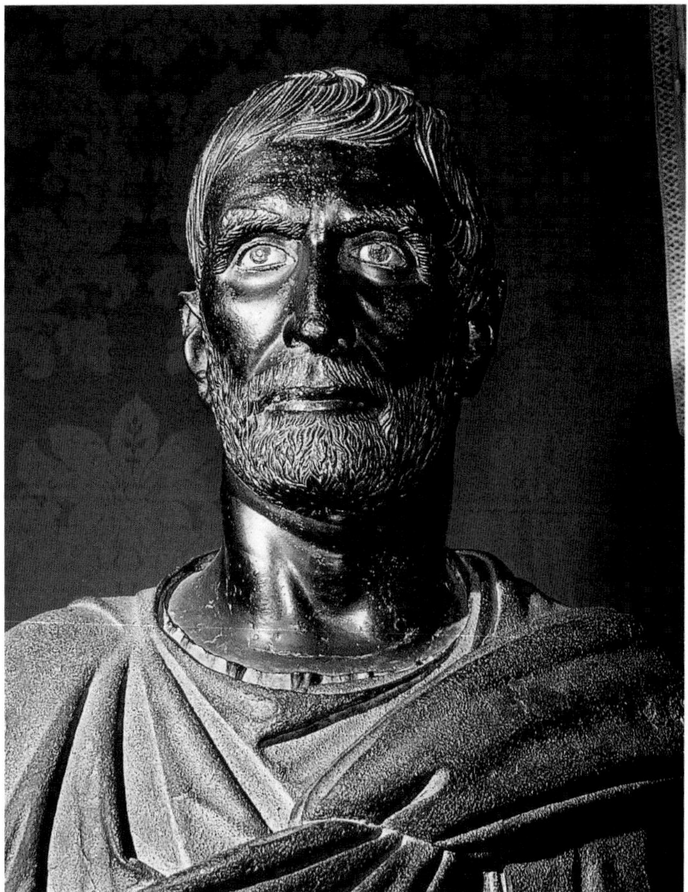

Figure 5.22 *Head of Brutus.* Ca. 350–50 B.C. Ht. 20″. Palazzo dei Conservatori, Rome. *The finely detailed hair, beard, and facial lines are the work of a skilled sculptor, perhaps a Greek from southern Italy. The broad range of possible dates for this bronze head (ca. 350–50 B.C.) indicates that scholars still disagree over when it was cast.*

empire, the same needs that gave rise to temples and amphitheaters were at work in changing the look of imperial sculpture.

Although Roman portrait sculpture never broke through to a distinct style during this period, it nevertheless passed through three definite phases. The first phase, lasting from the third to the first century B.C., was influenced by the death masks made for the family gallery as part of ancestor worship. This style can be seen in the *Head of Brutus* (Figure 5.22). Brutus, one of the great heroes who helped to turn out the last Etruscan king, is shown as a stern and resolute leader. In contrast, the artist who sculptured the *Republican Portrait of a Man* (Figure 5.23) captured the characteristic realism of sculpture in the Late Republic. The man's face, clearly troubled and aged, as indicated by the lines in his cheeks and around his eyes, was intended as a warning rather than as an inspiration to the viewer. This type of realistic sculpture, with its sense of unease, represents the second phase of Roman sculpture.

The third phase was shaped by the reign of Augustus. According to his biographer Suetonius, the emperor boasted that he found Rome a city of brick and left it a city of marble, and Augustus certainly did influence the direction of sculpture and architecture. Under his rule, imperial portraiture reverted to the idealism of Hellenic Greece, displacing the realistic art of the Late Republic. But Augustus's pure idealism did not prevail for long, for under his successors sculpture became more propagandistic—that is, more symbolic of imperial power. This move to symbolic idealism reflected the later emperors' need to find a highly visible way in which to overawe, and thus draw together, Rome's increasingly diversified masses.

Two major sculptural works associated with Augustus, the Prima Porta portrait and the Ara Pacis, or the Altar of Peace, helped to popularize the idealistic style. Augustus's statue, commissioned after his death, stood in a garden on his widow's estate, Prima Porta, just outside Rome (Figure 5.24). The pure Hellenic style is evident in Augustus's relaxed stance and idealized face, both of which were modeled on the *Doryphoros* by Polykleitos (see Figure 3.22). However, the accompanying symbols reveal the propagandistic intent of the sculpture and were portents of the path that imperial portraits would take. For example, the cupid represents Venus, the mother of Aeneas, and thus Augustus is symbolically connected to the legendary origins of Rome.

The second idealistic sculpture, the marble Ara Pacis, was funded by the Senate as an offering of thanks to Augustus for his peacekeeping missions. The entire structure was set on a platform and enclosed by three walls. On the fourth side, an entrance with steps led to the altar (Figure 5.25). Relief sculptures decorated the interior and exterior walls, some in an idealized style and others in a realistic style (Figure 5.26). The resulting tension between realism and idealism marked this altar as an early work in the imperial style.

This type of sculpture reached its highest potential as a propaganda tool on triumphal arches and victory columns, such as the Arch of Titus and Trajan's Column. One of the reliefs from the Arch of Titus, the

◀ **Figure 5.21** Pont du Gard. Ca. late first century A.D. Ht. 161′. Gard River, near Nîmes, France. *This aqueduct spanning the river was only one segment of the 31-mile system that supplied water to Nîmes. Between 8,000 and 12,000 gallons of water were delivered daily, or about 100 gallons per inhabitant.*

Figure 5.23 *Republican Portrait of a Man.* Copy of an original from about 30 B.C. Marble, ht. 13″. Museum of Art, Rhode Island School of Design, Providence, Rhode Island. *This bust reflects the upheavals of first-century* B.C. *Rome, as patricians reasserted their power over the crumbling state. Portraits of patrician leaders were characterized by wrinkled skin, clenched jaws, and determined expressions.*

Figure 5.24 *Augustus,* from Prima Porta. Ca. A.D. 14. Marble, ht. 6′7½″. Vatican Collection. *This larger-than-life statue still bears traces of bright colors. Found in Prima Porta, the villa of Augustus's wife, Livia, the statue resembled Augustus closely yet presented him as godlike. Augustus's successors commissioned similar sculptures to convey a sense of their dignity and power.*

Figure 5.25 Ara Pacis. 9 B.C. Marble, width 35′. Rome. *Like the Prima Porta statue, the Ara Pacis became a model for later emperors, who emulated its decorations, symbols, and size. The altar was rediscovered in the sixteenth century, excavated in the nineteenth and early twentieth centuries, and restored in 1938.*

Figure 5.26 *Family of Augustus,* Ara Pacis relief. 9 B.C. Marble, ht. 63″. Rome. *The figures in low relief, moving from right to left, are separated yet linked by their placement and clothing. The child to the right of center is given great prominence: He faces right while all the adults in the foreground are looking left and a man places his hand on the child's head. This singling out of the child may be an act of endearment or of recognition that he is to be the emperor.*

Figure 5.27 *March of the Legions,* from the Arch of Titus. Ca. A.D. 80. Marble relief, approx. 6 × 12½′. Rome. *This rectangular marble relief occupies the south side of the Arch of Titus. It commemorates the Roman victory in the Jewish War of A.D. 66–70, when the Romans put down a rebellion by the Jews in Judea and subsequently dispersed them across the Roman world. In the relief, the Roman soldiers hold aloft the Jewish holy relics from the Temple as they seem to press forward and pass under the arch on the right.*

March of the Legions, portrayed the army's victory march into Rome after the destruction of the Temple in Jerusalem in A.D. 70 (Figure 5.27).

The continuous frieze from Trajan's Victory Column is one of the sculptural marvels of the Roman world (Figure 5.28). This low-relief sculpture winds around the column like a long comic strip, telling the story of Trajan's campaign against Dacia. Scholars still study the carvings of campsites and fortifications on this relief, finding them a rich source for Roman military history.

The last great sculpture from this period is the equestrian statue of Marcus Aurelius (see Figure 5.11). This work reveals a falling away from Augustan idealism to a rugged, individualized style, although one that was still highly propagandistic in its use of symbols. In the Prima Porta statue, Augustus had been portrayed as a military leader; his gesture showed that he was addressing his troops. But the rest of the symbols surrounding Augustus suggested that he ruled from his capital in Rome. The symbols in the Marcus Aurelius statue, on the other hand, stress that he was a warrior emperor, even though the gesturing motion of Augustus is repeated.

Painting and Mosaics **Murals,** or wall paintings, the most popular type of painting in Rome, have been found in private dwellings, public buildings, and tem-

Figure 5.28 Detail of Trajan's Victory Column. A.D. 113. Marble, ht. of relief band approx. 36″. Rome. *Wrapped around the 100-foot-high column is the 645-foot relief carving with 2,500 figures depicting Trajan's two campaigns against the Dacians. Color was applied to heighten the realistic effect of the work, which, in its original setting, could be viewed from nearby buildings.* ▶

Figure 5.29 *Flagellation Scene.* Villa of the Mysteries. Ca. 60–40 B.C. Wall painting, ht. 60″. Pompeii, Italy. *The figures in this brilliantly colored wall frieze seem almost to be present in the room, partly because they are just under full life size and partly because the artist has placed them on a narrow painted ledge as if on a stage. The lack of depth in the mysterious scene adds to the illusion.*

ples. Surviving works hint at a highly decorative and brightly colored art. Originally the Romans applied tempera, or paint set in a binding solution directly onto a dry wall. However, this quick and easy method produced a painting that soon faded and peeled. Later they adopted fresco painting as the most practical and lasting technique. Paints were mixed and worked into a freshly plastered wall. The colors dried into the wall, resulting in a nearly indestructible painting. The Romans were inspired by many subjects: landscapes, Greek and Roman myths, architectural vistas, religious scenes, and genre scenes, or "slices of life."

Of the many paintings scattered around the Roman world, the murals in the Villa of the Mysteries at Pompeii are the most impressive. These intriguing and controversial scenes, which fill the walls in several rooms, portray twenty-nine nearly life-size figures engaged in some mystery cult rite (Figure 5.29). The grouped figures—well-balanced and separated—create tension among the participants, and the undecipherable expressions on the faces of the women heighten the sense of theater.

The Romans learned to make **mosaics** from the Hellenistic Greeks in the third century B.C. But by the third century A.D., several local Roman mosaic styles had sprung up across the empire. Although subjects varied, certain ones seemed always to be in vogue, such as still lifes, landscapes, Greek and Roman myths, philosophers and orators, and scenes from the circus and amphitheaters. A mosaic from Tunisia (North Africa) shows the intricacy of design and variety of color that artisans achieved even in the Roman provinces (Figure 5.30).

Figure 5.30 Calendar Mosaic. Late second–early third century A.D. From the Maison des Mois at El Djem. Detail of 5- by 4-foot mosaic. Sousse Museum, Sousse, Tunisia. *The El Djem Calendar comprises twelve small scenes, each representing a month, the name of which is inscribed in Latin. The Roman year began with March (top middle) and ended with February (top left corner). The months are symbolized by either religious or rural activities, such as in the September panel, which shows two figures standing in a vat crushing grapes.* ▶

MARTI
AS
IVNIVS
IVLIVS
SEP
TEM
BER
OCTO
BRES
DECEM
BER

Music

The absorption of the Greek tradition in music was so complete that later Roman music, in effect, simply perpetuated Greek forms and ideas. And yet the Romans used music only for practical purposes and rejected the Greek notion that music performed an ethical role in educating the soul or mind.

Not until imperial times did music come to play an important role in Roman life. Under the emperors, music became wildly popular, as all classes succumbed to its seductive charms. **Pantomimes**—dramatic productions with instrumental music and dances—became the spectacle favored by the Roman masses. In the long run, the pantomimes became a symbol of music's decadent trend under the empire. The largest of these productions featured three thousand instrumentalists and three thousand dancers, but the more common size was three hundred performers in each category. A more serious sort of music was kept alive by the wealthy classes, who maintained household orchestras and choruses for their private amusement. An even more cultivated audience encouraged poets such as Horace to set their verses to music, thus continuing the Greek tradition of lyric poetry.

Although what Roman music actually sounded like remains a subject of conjecture, their musical instruments, borrowed from across the Mediterranean world, can be identified with some certainty. From Greece came the stringed instruments, the lyre and the kithara, along with such woodwinds as the single **aulos,** or oboe, and the double aulos—called by the Romans the tibia (Figure 5.31). From the Etruscans came the brasses. The Romans delighted in the harsh sounds made by these instruments, incorporating them into their military music just as the Etruscans did. The hydraulic organ, or water organ, was probably perfected in Hellenistic Alexandria, but in imperial Rome it became a crowd pleaser, adding deep, voluminous sounds to the pantomimes. The taste of the imperial Roman audience is evident in the water organ, which was impressive not for its musical qualities but as a feat of engineering expertise.

Figure 5.31 *The Street Musicians.* Ca. 100 B.C. 16⅞ × 16⅛″. Museo Nazionale, Naples. *This mosaic may portray a scene from a comic play. Two masked figures dance and play the tambourine and the finger cymbals while a masked female figure plays the tibia, or double oboe. This mosaic was found in the so-called Villa of Cicero at Pompeii.*

The Legacy of Pre-Christian Rome

Western civilization is built on the ruins of Rome. Although no pre-Christian institutions survived to form a basis of European organization, other tangibles persisted in abundance, so that the mark of Rome may still be seen and heard in countless ways. The very languages of Western Europe bear the stamp of Rome, and Roman law forms the basis of the legal codes of many Western countries. Until the beginning of the twentieth century, the European educational ideal was based on the Roman curriculum, in which students studied the *trivium*—the three arts of grammar, logic, and rhetoric—and the *quadrivium*—the four sciences of arithmetic, geometry, music, and astronomy. Even today, this ideal persists at the heart of Western education.

Roman builders and engineers added to the Greek architectural tradition to create the Greco-Roman style, whose principal Roman components included domes, rounded arches, vaulting techniques, domed temples, temples on podiums, triumphal arches, amphitheaters, and victory columns. From the Renaissance, starting in 1400, until the twentieth century, the Greco-Roman style dominated Western architecture. Roman sculptors likewise helped to create the Greco-Roman style; their contributions included realistic portrait sculptures, propagandistic portraits of rulers, and equestrian statues. In literature and drama, Rome gave us the comic plays of Terence and Plautus, which influenced the rebirth of comedy in the Renaissance; the tragedies of Seneca, which inspired the tragedies of Shakespeare and other Renaissance dramatists; the contrasting satire genres invented by Horace and Juvenal, both of which spawned imitators through the ages; and the writings of Vergil, Horace, and Ovid, which became the classical standard for Europeans during the thousand years from the Fall of Rome to the Renaissance, when Latin was in the ascendant and Greek had practically disappeared. In philosophy, Cicero taught the Christian West to write and think philosophically, since his works were known to the educated for centuries. And the ideas of Greek thinkers, though in summary or corrupt form, survived through Latin translations.

Rome's greatest legacy to the Western world was its shining image of a healthy civilization: a just and well-regulated society of multiethnic, multiracial citizens. The Idea of Rome, as we may call this achievement, was adapted from the Hellenistic rulers. However, the Hellenistic cities lacked the cohesiveness and longevity—and, most important, the vision—of the Roman creation. When the ancient world was swept away, the Idea of Rome remained a beacon in the darkness that descended over Europe.

KEY CULTURAL TERMS

syncretism
satire
Neo-Platonism
natural law
voussoir
keystone
vault
barrel vault
groined vault (cross vault)
oculus
forum
mural
mosaic
pantomime
aulos

SUGGESTIONS FOR FURTHER READING

PRIMARY SOURCES

APULEIUS. *The Golden Ass.* Translated by R. Graves. New York: Farrar, Straus & Giroux, 1951. A sound translation of one of the most lively and entertaining tales in ancient literature.

HORACE. *The Complete Works of Horace.* Introduction by C. Kraemer. New York: Modern Library, 1936. Masterly translations of the works that made Horace Rome's outstanding lyric poet.

JUVENAL. *The Sixteen Satires.* Translated by P. Green. New York: Penguin, 1970. Superb vernacular versions of Juvenal's bitter works.

VERGIL. *The Aeneid.* Translated by W. F. J. Knight. New York: Penguin, 1964. A sound English prose version of Vergil's poetic epic about Aeneas, the Trojan warrior whose conquests made possible the future supremacy of Rome.

WINDOWS ON THE WORLD: 300–A.D. 500

	AFRICA	AMERICAS
HISTORY	**North Africa** *Sahara.* Camel introduced (1st century A.D.); camel caravans soon linked north Africa with the south. **Northeast Africa** *Kush culture, ended A.D. 350.* Amassed great wealth from trade in the Red Sea; conquered by King Ezana of Axum. *Axum culture, began 300 B.C.* Axum (modern Eritrea and parts of Ethiopia and Sudan) dominated trade in the region, after A.D. 200; King Ezana minted gold coins and signed a treaty with the Byzantine emperor. **West Africa** *Niger River area.* Founding (about 250 B.C.) of Jenne-jero, a farming village and iron-working center. *Nok culture, ended A.D. 200.* Mixed culture of farming, hunting, and gathering.	**Mesoamerica** *Classic period, began A.D. 150.* Teotihuacán (in modern Mexico), the first true city (125,000 at its height) in the Americas, founded A.D. 250. *Mayan culture.* Zenith: A.D. 250–900 in what is now Yucatán, Guatemala, Honduras. Ritual cities, such as Tikal and Uaxactún. *Veracruz culture.* High culture whose center was El Tajín. *Zapotec culture.* Center was Monte Albán in Oaxaca. **Andes** *Chavín culture ended 200 B.C. Paracas culture, ca. 600–175 B.C. Nasca culture, 200 B.C.–A.D. 500. Moche culture, began 200 B.C.* First organized state on North Coast. **Native North America** *Plains, from ca. 250 B.C.* Nomadic buffalo hunters began to cultivate maize, established villages. *Hopewell culture, ca. 200 B.C.–A.D. 500.* Ohio and Illinois valleys; mound builders with extensive trade network; maize cultivation ca. A.D. 100. *Southwest, ca. A.D. 100.* Migration from Mesoamerica.
ART	**Northeast Africa** *Axum culture.* Kings erected granite monuments. 	**Mesoamerica** *Classic period. Teotihuacán culture.* Frescoes, pictographic books, pottery, clay figurines, masks, and stone sculptures. *Veracruz culture.* Stone carvings and hollow clay sculptures. Wheels on toys. *Zapotec culture.* Murals, elaborate inscriptions, pottery, and bowls representing birds, fish, and jaguars. **Andes** *Paracas culture.* Ceramics, textiles, embroidery, and gold work. *Nasca culture.* Nasca Lines: carved in geometric and figural shapes, on the Nasca plains. *Moche culture.* Gold ritual objects, including necklaces, scepters, bells, and beads; invented a two-piece press mold for replicating ritual pottery forms. *Animal Figure on Wheels. Ca. A.D. 600–900. Veracruz. Ht. 7¾". American Museum of Natural History, New York.*
ARCHITECTURE	**Northeast Africa** *Axum culture.* Impressive fortresses and palaces built by kings, though little remains. **West Africa** *Nok culture.* The Nok lived in clay huts in the hills and lowlands.	**Mesoamerica** *Classic period. Teotihuacán culture.* Teotihuacán centered on Pyramids of the Sun and the Moon. *Zapotec culture.* Monte Albán with an astronomical observatory, ritual ballcourt, and necropolis (city of the dead). *Mayan culture.* The corbelled arch, made of overlapping stones. Tikal and Uaxactún: Ceremonial cities with temples, pyramids, platforms, and plazas. **Andes** *Nasca culture.* Ruins of about 40 temple mounds, at the capital Cahuachi. *Moche culture.* Forts, palaces, and pyramids, made of molded adobe brick; aqueducts and canals. **Native North America** *Plains.* Portable tepees made of poles and buffalo skins for nomadic hunters, and dome-shaped earth lodges for maize-growing tribes.
RELIGION, PHILOSOPHY, LITERATURE	**Northeast Africa** *Axum culture.* King Ezana converted to Coptic Christianity and made it the official faith of his kingdom (300s). After 451, Coptic Church separated itself from papal control and looked to the Coptic patriarch at Alexandria for new leaders. The Coptic Church is Ethiopia's state religion today. **West Africa** *Nok culture.* Polytheism and ancestor worship.	**Andes** *Paracas culture.* Elaborate burial rituals. **Mesoamerica** *Classic period.* Hieroglyphic writing, in both *Mayan* and *Zapotec cultures. Mayan culture.* Daily life and religious ritual based on coordination of the 260-day and the 365-day calendars; astronomical observation (particularly Venus); knowledge of the zero. **Native North America** *Hopewell culture.* Spread first North American pan-Indian religion from Minnesota to West Virginia. *Moche Stirrup-Spout Vessel (depicting scene of childbirth). Early Intermediate period. Ceramic. Staatliches Museum für Völkerkunde, Berlin.*

ASIA

China

Ch'in Dynasty, 221–206 B.C. Shih Huang-ti, the first emperor, united country for first time; standardized scripts, weights, and measures. The name *China* is derived from *Ch'in*. *Han Dynasty, 210 B.C.–A.D. 220.* Culturally brilliant and militarily expansive period; rule extended to Korea, Mongolia, and southern Manchuria. Trade with Rome via the Silk Road. Paper invented. *Six Dynasties, or Period of Disunity, A.D. 220–581.* Political chaos.

Ch'in Dynasty. About 6,000 life-size terracotta models of soldiers, in the burial pit of Emperor Shih Huang-ti, at the capital Ch'ang-an (206 B.C.). *Han Dynasty.* Bronze castings, jade carvings, brush-and-ink painting on paper, and paintings on silk.

Horse. Bronze, 13⅝ × 17¾". Found in a second-century tomb, Gansu, China.

Ch'in Dynasty. The Great Wall, extending for more than 1,000 miles along the northern frontier, built to keep out nomadic invaders. *Six Dynasties.* Iconography and temple and tomb building influenced by Buddhism.

Section, Great Wall of China. 215 B.C.

Ch'in Dynasty. Shih Huang-ti followed the path of Legalism and rejected the Confucian ideal. *Han Dynasty.* Ssu-ma Ch'ien's *Historical Records,* a history of early China. Hsu Shen's 10,000-character dictionary. Confucianism made an official state cult (A.D. 6) and basis of civil service examinations. Buddhism established at the royal court. Folk songs flourished, as in the *Ballad of Mu Lan* in the militant style of northern Chinese literature. Poets Tao Ch'ien and Hsieh Ling-yun explored the tension between Confucian ideal of public service and Taoist call for withdrawal.

India

Mauryan Empire, ca. 325–185 B.C. First Indian empire to include most of the subcontinent. Buddhist emperor Asoka (r. ca. 265–238 B.C.), efficient and humane ruler. The Lion Capital on Asoka's edict column became the emblem of the Republic of India. *Political disunity, 185 B.C.–A.D. 320.* Rise of regional states; foreign invasions. *Gupta Dynasty, A.D. 320–ca. 550.* A golden age. Zenith under Chandra Gupta II (r. A.D. 375–415).

Edict Column at Sarnath. Ca. 250 B.C. Archaeological Museum, Sarnath.

Mauryan Empire. Stupas (holding Buddhist relics), edict columns, and stone sculptures of divinities. *Political disunity* and *Gupta Dynasty.* Relief stone sculptures, stupas, and two schools of Buddhist art: Mathura in central India, rooted in folk art, and Gandhara (in modern Pakistan), influenced by Greco-Roman styles. The image of the Buddha in the form of a god first introduced.

Political disunity. Rock-cut sanctuaries at Bhaja (western India) became models for Jains, Buddhists, and Brahmans. *Gupta Dynasty.* Complex of 29 rock-cut sanctuaries, at Ajanta in central India, including the earliest surviving Indian paintings. *Mauryan Empire.* The capital Pataliputra, a walled city with many gates, stretched for two miles in perimeter.

Mauryan culture. A Buddhist convert, Asoka, sent Buddhist missionaries to what is now Myanmar and Sri Lanka. The policies of Asoka were guided by the *Arthashastra,* a political treatise. *Political disunity.* The *Panchatantra,* beast fables. Christianity probably arrived in western port cities. *Gupta Dynasty. Yoga Aphorisms of Patanjali,* classic yoga text; *Eight Anthologies* and *Ten Songs,* classic Tamil poetry; *Kama-sutra,* manual of sexual techniques; Bhartrihari's cynical love poems; Kālidāsa's *Shākuntalā,* first great Indian play. Invention of decimal system. Zenith of Buddhism.

Japan

Yayoi culture, ca. 300 B.C.–A.D. 300. Migrants (perhaps ancestors of modern Japanese) with new technology: bronze and iron working, wheel-thrown ceramics, and wet-rice farming. *Kofun period, began A.D. 300.* Clan rivalry. The Yamato clan (from whom later emperors claimed descent) became dominant (400s); set up a base in Korea, allowing influence from China.

Yayoi culture. Ceramics, including tableware; ceremonial objects such as bronze bells and swords, mirrors, and semiprecious stones.

Kofun period: Yamato clan built *kofun,* or mounded tombs; contained pottery figures *(haniwa).*

Kofun period. Chinese script arrived by way of Korea, and Chinese characters adapted into Japanese writing by 500.

6 JUDAISM AND THE RISE OF CHRISTIANITY

The great civilizations discussed so far—Mesopotamian, Egyptian, Greek, and Roman—were all wealthy, powerful, and culturally dynamic, and they contributed enormously to the Western heritage. Yet an even greater contribution, one that cannot be measured in buildings or governments, came from a politically insignificant people who lived in a tiny corner of the eastern Mediterranean during ancient times—the Jews. This people created a religion that helped to shape the character of the civilizations of the Western world. Through the Hebrew Bible—the Old Testament to Christians—Judaic beliefs were passed on into both Christianity and Islam and spread around the world. In addition, the fruitful interaction of the Judeo-Christian heritage with the Greco-Roman Classical ideals enriched and transformed the Western humanities.

JUDAISM

Judaism is one of the oldest living religions in the world. It originated in the third millennium B.C. among a tribal Middle Eastern people who placed themselves at the center of world history and created sacred texts for passing on their heritage. Unlike the history and religion of other ancient peoples, the history and religion of the Jews are so inextricably connected that they cannot be separated.

The People and Their Religion

About 2000 B.C., many displaced tribes were wandering throughout the Middle East because of the political upheavals that accompanied the collapse of

◀ **Detail** Synagogue. Third century A.D. Dura Europos, Syria.

Timeline 6.1 **JEWISH CIVILIZATION**

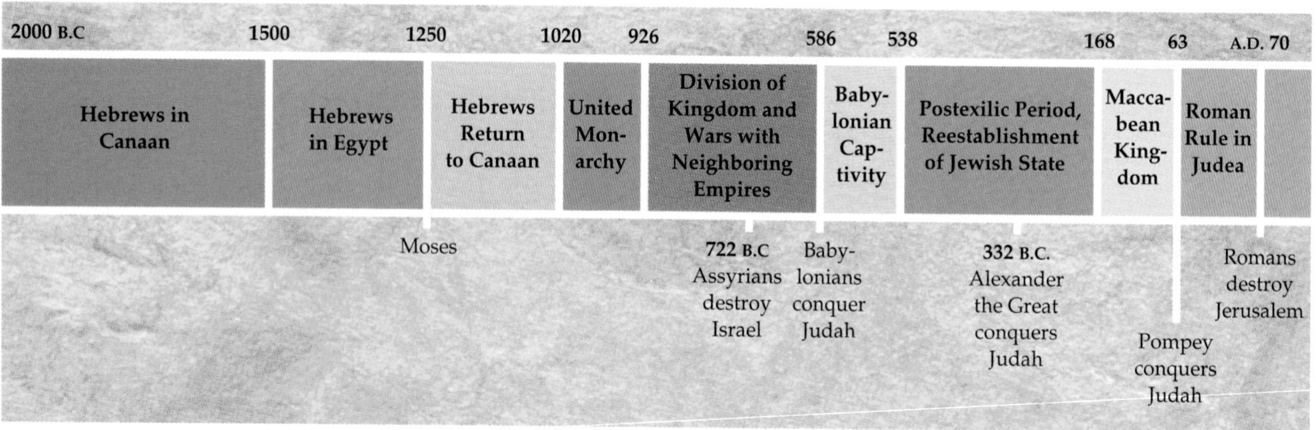

Map 6.1 **ANCIENT ISRAEL**

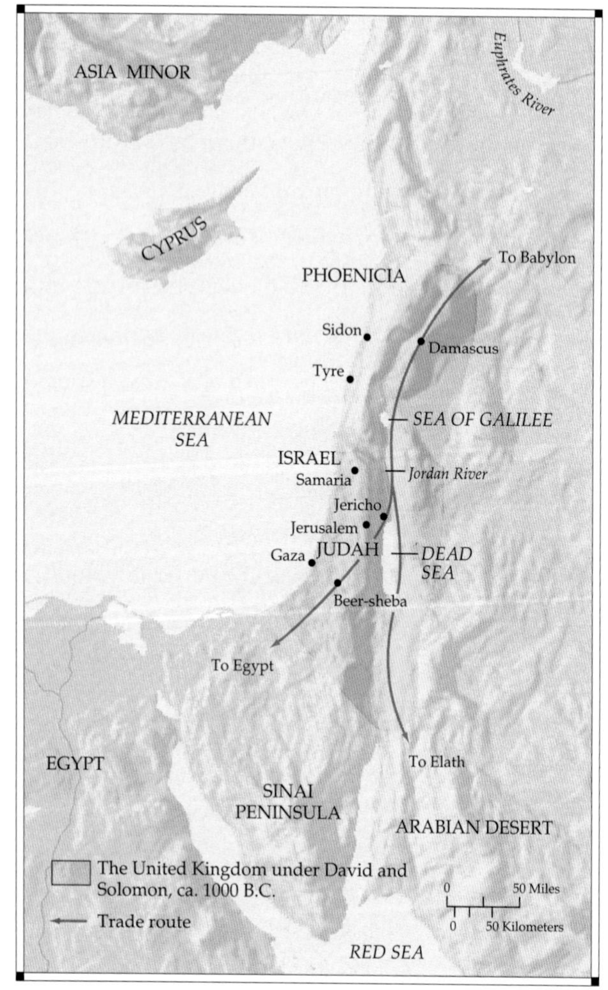

the Akkadian kingdom and the coming of the Babylonians. Some of these nomads eventually settled along the eastern coast of the Mediterranean Sea that is part of the Fertile Crescent. These patriarchal tribes, under the guidance of the oldest and most respected male members, founded communities united by bloodlines, economic interests, and folk traditions. One of these tribes, known as the Hebrews and led by the patriarch Abraham, occupied territory called Canaan, a region identified loosely with ancient Israel (Timeline 6.1). They settled in the hill country, where they tended their flocks and practiced their crafts (Map 6.1).

The Hebrews considered themselves unique, a belief based on the relationship between Abraham and a great supernatural being who spoke to him and whom he obeyed. This deity made a **covenant,** or solemn agreement (the outward sign of which was the circumcision of all male children), with Abraham to protect his family and bring prosperity to his offspring if they agreed to obey his divine commands. Although this Hebrew deity was associated with nature, he differed from other Mesopotamian deities in his commitment to justice and righteousness. He was an ethical god and sought to impose ethical principles on humans.

Egypt, Exodus, and Moses The Hebrews enjoyed many prosperous decades in Canaan, but around 1500 B.C. a group migrated south into Egypt, which had recently been overrun by the Hyksos, a Semitic people with whom the Hebrews shared language and cultural traits. Over the next few centuries, the Hebrews thrived until the Egyptians reconquered their land and enslaved both the Hyksos and the Hebrews. In about 1250 B.C., the extraordinary leader Moses rallied the Hebrews and led them on the Exodus from Egypt—one of the most significant events in Jewish history. Hebrew scriptures describe Moses as a savior sent by God.

Table 6.1 THE TEN COMMANDMENTS

1. You shall have no other gods before me.
2. You shall not make for yourself a graven image, or any likeness of any thing that is in heaven above, or that is on the earth beneath, or that is in the water under the earth. . . .
3. You shall not take the name of the Lord your God in vain. . . .
4. Observe the sabbath day, to keep it holy, as the Lord your God commanded you. . . .
5. Honor your father and your mother. . . .
6. You shall not kill.
7. Neither shall you commit adultery.
8. Neither shall you steal.
9. Neither shall you bear false witness against your neighbor.
10. Neither shall you covet your neighbor's wife . . . or anything that is your neighbor's.

Source: The Bible, Revised Standard Version, Deuteronomy 5:6–21.

As the Hebrews wandered in the desert on the Sinai peninsula, Moses molded his followers into a unified people under a set of ethical and societal laws, which they believed were received from God. The laws of Moses were unique among ancient peoples because they were grounded in the covenant between the Hebrews and God and because no distinction was made between religious and secular offenses. All crimes were seen as sins and all sins as crimes. Those who committed crimes could not simply make reparation to their victims; they also had to seek forgiveness from God. There were some crimes, such as murder, that were so offensive to God that they could not be forgiven by human beings alone. Furthermore, human life was seen as sacred, because it was given by God, who created and owned all things; and individual humans were precious because they were made in God's image.

The core of Mosaic law was the Ten Commandments, which set forth the proper behavior of human beings (Table 6.1). The commandments became the basis of a renewed covenant, which was now extended beyond Abraham and his descendants to include the entire people. The Hebrew God tolerated no rivals; he was seen as the sole, omnipotent creator and ruler of the universe. If individuals followed his laws and worshiped him alone, they would be rewarded, and if they strayed, they would be punished. Likewise, if the tribe followed the divine commands, they would prosper, and if they disobeyed, they would meet with adversity. As the mediator of the covenant between God and the Hebrew people, Moses played a crucial role in shaping Judaism into a comprehensive system of ethical monotheism.

As they wandered through the Sinai desert, the Hebrews carried with them a sacred decorated box called the Ark of the Covenant. Within were the stone tablets on which the Ten Commandments were carved. Details of how to craft the Ark and all the other sacred objects used in worship were dictated to Moses by God (Figure 6.1). In the desert, the deity also revealed a new name for himself—YHWH, a name so sacred that pious Jews never speak or write it. In the late Middle Ages, European scholars rendered YHWH as Jehovah, but today this term is generally considered a false reading of the sacred letters. In modern English, YHWH is usually rendered as Yahweh. In biblical times, Jewish priests called the deity Adonai, the Semitic term for Lord.

After forty years of wandering, followed by Moses' death, the Hebrews finally returned to Canaan, the Promised Land pledged by Yahweh to their forefathers. Over the next two centuries, the Hebrews won Canaan and became known as the Israelites.

The Kingdom of Israel In about 1000 B.C., the Israelites established a monarchy, and from the late eleventh century to the end of the tenth century B.C.,

Figure 6.1 Stone Menorah. Second century A.D. Ht. 18″. Israel Museum, Jerusalem. *Although this particular menorah dates from the second century A.D., the seven-branched candelabrum had been in use as a religious symbol for centuries. According to Jewish beliefs, God gave Moses explicit instructions on how to craft the menorah, which was made for the tabernacle, or house of prayer. Later the menorah came to symbolize knowledge and understanding as well as the light of God protecting the Jews.*

Table 6.2 HISTORICAL STAGES OF THE TEMPLE OF JERUSALEM

NAME	*CONSTRUCTION DETAILS*	*DATE DESTROYED*
Solomon's Temple. Also called First Temple	Completed under King Solomon, 957 B.C.	587/586 B.C., by the Babylonians
Second Temple. Also called Herod's Temple after being rebuilt in A.D. 26	Completed 515 B.C. Rebuilt at order of King Herod (d. 4 B.C.) between 20 B.C. and A.D. 26	A.D. 70, by the Romans. A section of the western wall (also called the Wailing Wall) survived; it was incorporated into the wall around the Muslim Dome of the Rock and al-Aqsa mosque in A.D. 691.

the nation flourished under a series of kings—Saul, David, and Solomon. The popular king David rallied the scattered Israelite tribes, centralized the government, and shifted the economy away from herding and toward commerce, trade, and farming.

Solomon, David's son, brought the Israelite kingdom to its pinnacle of power and prestige. He signed treaties with other states, expanded Israel's trade across the Middle East, and raised the standard of living for many of his subjects. He completed the building of Jerusalem begun by David, which, with its magnificent public structures and great Temple, rivaled the glory of other Middle Eastern cities. The Temple of Solomon, also known as the First Temple, housed Israel's holy relics, including the Ark of the Covenant, and became the focal point of the nation's religion, which required pilgrimages and rituals, based on the religious calendar (Table 6.2; Figure 6.2).

King Solomon considered himself a patron of literature and the arts, and under his rule Hebrew culture expanded, notably in law, writing, music, and dance. As the Hebrews' oral traditions gave way to written records, Hebrew authors wrote down their laws and

Figure 6.2 Horned Altar. Tenth century B.C. Carved limestone, ht. 26½". Oriental Institute, University of Chicago. *Middle Eastern peoples made sacrifices to their deities on altars, but the small horned altar, as pictured here, was unique to the Hebrews. Horned altars were described in the Bible, especially as a ritual object in the Temple in Jerusalem. However, this horned altar was discovered at Megiddo, one of the cities of the Hebrew kingdom.*

The Bible required ritual offerings (sacrifices of animals on large altars and wine, incense, and grain mixed with oil on small altars) twice daily. These offerings were conducted by priests in the Temple in Jerusalem as a community ritual for the entire Hebrew nation; individuals could also arrange for sacrifices to be made on their own behalf. The early Hebrews sometimes were allowed to make sacrifices outside the Temple, but this practice was later forbidden.

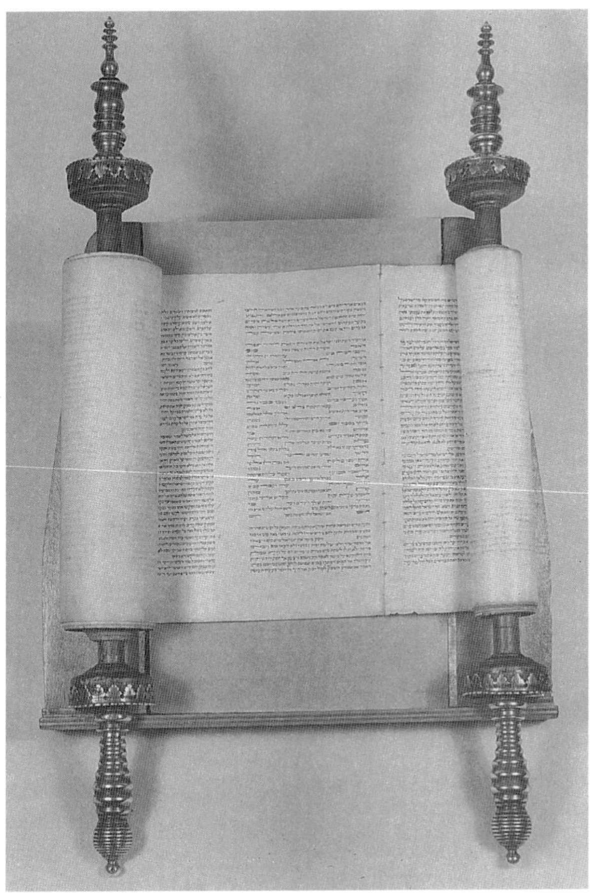

Figure 6.3 Ancient Scroll of the Pentateuch. *The ancient Hebrews recorded their scriptures on parchment scrolls. Today, a copy of the Pentateuch, or Torah, is preserved on scrolls in every synagogue.*

their earliest histories, which are preserved in the first books of the Bible (Figure 6.3). These Hebrew works predate by five centuries the writings of the great Greek historians Herodotus and Thucydides. But unlike the Greek writers, the Hebrew historians made God the central force in human history and thus transformed the unfolding of earthly events into a moral drama with cosmic significance.

Solomon's achievements came at a heavy price, however, for they undermined his people's religious foundations, intensified class divisions, and tended to divide the northern and southern tribes. When Solomon died in 926 B.C., the tensions between the regions intensified and the United Monarchy separated into two states: Israel in the north, with its capital at Samaria, and Judah in the south, with its capital at Jerusalem.

During the period of the two Hebrew kingdoms, a new type of religious leader, known as a prophet, appeared. The prophets warned of the fatal consequences of breaking Yahweh's commandments; and in predicting the downfall of surrounding non-Hebrew states, the prophets asserted that God was now using peoples other than the Hebrews to fulfill his divine plan in history. The prophets also demanded social justice for the helpless and the downtrodden. In the face of a widening gulf between rich and poor, the prophets predicted that if the well-off did not aid the less fortunate, Yahweh would bring down the evil rulers and, in the future, punish the selfish and reward the sufferers. But the words of the prophets, such as Hosea and Amos in Israel and Isaiah and Jeremiah in Judah, seemed to go unheeded.

The Babylonian Captivity and the Postexilic Period
Although Israel enjoyed its moments of prosperity and power, the larger empires, especially Egypt and Assyria, wanted to control the military and trade routes crossing this part of the Fertile Crescent. In 722 B.C., the tiny nation of Israel was destroyed by the Assyrians. Judah, to the south, endured for another two hundred years, but in 586 B.C., the Babylonians conquered Judah, destroying Solomon's Temple in Jerusalem, and deported most of the Hebrews to Babylonia. The approximately forty years of exile, known as the Babylonian Captivity, became one of the major turning points in Jewish history.

At the end of the sixth century, the Jews (as the Hebrews were called after the Babylonian Captivity) were freed by the triumphant Persians, who were sweeping across the ancient world under Cyrus (see Chapter 2). Returning to Judah, the Jews rebuilt their Temple, now known as the Second Temple, and their towns. Believing that God had rescued them, they established a theocratic state—a government ruled by those who are recognized as having special divine guidance and approval—and dedicated themselves to the correct formulation and observation of their religious beliefs. The Jews welcomed back many exiles, reestablished their commercial ties, and revived their handicraft industries. But many exiles remained outside the homeland and became known as Jews of the **Diaspora,** or the Dispersion.

After their return from Babylon, the Jews expanded their views of Yahweh. Probably under the indirect impact of the increasingly popular Persian religion, Zoroastrianism—and its description of the twin forces of good and evil or Light and Dark—the Jews began to envision a cosmic dualism in their own beliefs. The Hebrews' earlier perception of themselves as a chosen people under a universal deity was reinforced as they concluded that Yahweh had used the Persians to free them. Furthermore, the Jews started to incorporate two new features into their religion: **eschatology,** or the concern with the end of the world, and an interest in **apocalypse,** prophecies about the coming of God and a day of judgment. This future world would be led by

Figure 6.4 Model of the Reconstructed Second Temple (Herod's Temple) in Jerusalem. *This model of the Second Temple shows the strong influence of Hellenistic-style architecture, particularly in the colonnaded arcades, the decorative frieze, and the tall, slender Corinthian columns flanking the main entryway. The Second Temple was destroyed by Roman legions in* A.D. *70, but one wall was left standing.*

a **Messiah,** or Anointed One, who would bring peace and justice to all.

The Hellenistic and Roman Periods Alexander the Great conquered Judah in 332 B.C., and after his death the area became part of the Seleucid kingdom, centered in Syria. Hellenistic culture and ideas proliferated and deeply affected Jewish life. Growing tensions between the Jews and the Hellenistic leaders erupted in 168 B.C. when the Seleucid king Antiochus IV tried to impose the worship of Greek gods on the Jews, placing a statue of Zeus in the Second Temple in Jerusalem. Antiochus's violation of the sacred place enraged the Maccabean clan, whose inspired leadership and bravery led to a successful revolt and the recapture of the

Figure 6.5 Masada, Israel. *This outcropping of rock in the forbidding terrain outside Jerusalem was a natural fortress. King Herod had built one of his palace-fortresses here in the years just before the birth of Christ. For three years the Zealots occupied its ruins, holding out against the Romans after the end of the First Jewish War in* A.D. *70.*

PERSONAL PERSPECTIVE

Flavius Josephus
The Destruction of the Temple at Jerusalem

Josephus (ca. 37–ca. 100) was a Jewish soldier and historian. Captured by the Romans, he was with the general Titus when the Romans destroyed the Second Temple in Jerusalem on September 8, A.D. 70. This passage is from his History of the Jewish War.

At this moment one of the [Roman] soldiers, not waiting for orders and without any dread of such an act but driven on by some frenzy, snatched a brand from the blazing fire and, lifted up by a comrade, hurled the torch through the golden door which gave access to the buildings of the Temple Precinct from the north side. As the flames surged up, a great cry to match their feelings arose from the Jews, and they rushed to the defence, reckless of their lives and prodigal of their strength once they saw that the purpose of their previous watch was gone. . . .

As the fire gained strength, Titus found that he could not restrain the surge of his enthusiastic soldiers. . . .

Most were driven on by the hope of loot, for they thought that the inside of the building must be full of money if the outside, which they could see, was made of gold. One of those who had got in forestalled the attempts of Titus who had rushed in to check them, and hurled a brand against the hinges of the door. Suddenly flames appeared from within, which forced back Titus and his officers, leaving those outside to kindle the blaze unhindered. In this way, though much against Titus's will, the Temple was burnt. . . .

Temple. The Maccabean family ruled Judah as an independent commonwealth for approximately one hundred years. Then in 63 B.C., the Romans conquered most of the Middle East. They subsequently incorporated Judah (in what was now called Palestine) into their empire as Judea and placed the Jewish lands under client kings.

Appointed to these kingships was the Herod dynasty, a family of Jews who had gained favor with the Romans. Herod the Great, who ruled from 37 to 4 B.C., rebuilt Jerusalem, including the Second Temple, and promoted Hellenistic culture (Figure 6.4). But conditions under the Romans became unbearable to the Jews, and in A.D. 66 a rebellion broke out. After four years of fighting, called the First Jewish War, the Romans captured Jerusalem and destroyed the Second Temple (A.D. 70). A revolutionary group known as Zealots held out until 73 at Masada, a sheer-sided mesa on the shores of the Dead Sea (Figure 6.5). When their cause became hopeless, they committed suicide rather than surrender to the Romans.

One wall of the Second Temple in Jerusalem remained standing. Known as the Wailing Wall, it came to symbolize the plight of the Jewish people. As described in Chapter 5, Titus, the victorious Roman general and later emperor, returned to Rome with the holy Jewish relics (see Figure 5.27). To make sure the Jews would no longer be a problem, the Roman government in the late first century A.D. ordered the dispersal of the Jews throughout the empire. However, this second Diaspora did not end the Jews' cultural, intellectual, and religious existence. On the contrary, the Jewish way of life continued, though it changed. With the fall of the Temple in Jerusalem, Jews worshiped in synagogues, or congregations, which eventually were headed by rabbis, or teachers (Figure 6.6). Over the centuries, the rabbis' teachings evolved into Rabbinic Judaism, based on the Torah and the Talmud (from Hebrew, "learning"), a collection of legal rulings and commentaries. Rabbinic Judaism established a mode of worship and moral code that Jews worldwide have followed down to modern times.

Societal and Family Relationships From earliest times to the founding of the monarchy, Jewish families survived in an agrarian economy and society. Although the patriarchal structure set the pattern of life and ensured the dominance of the tribal chieftains, men and women shared duties and responsibilities because in a rural society a family's continuation and the preservation of its property required the efforts of all its members. Within the family, women exercised some freedom, mothers' and sisters' roles were taken seriously, and the family rights of wives and mothers were protected by law.

However, with the coming of the kingdom of Israel and during and after the Babylonian Captivity, the male leaders, in their efforts to protect the new political system, the integrity of their religion, and the Hebrew way of life, formally and informally limited the rights and powers of women. This trend accelerated in the Hellenistic period as urbanism and commercialism

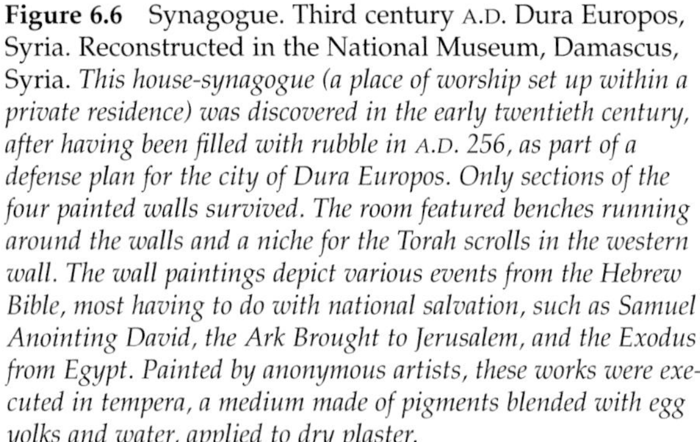

Figure 6.6 Synagogue. Third century A.D. Dura Europos, Syria. Reconstructed in the National Museum, Damascus, Syria. *This house-synagogue (a place of worship set up within a private residence) was discovered in the early twentieth century, after having been filled with rubble in A.D. 256, as part of a defense plan for the city of Dura Europos. Only sections of the four painted walls survived. The room featured benches running around the walls and a niche for the Torah scrolls in the western wall. The wall paintings depict various events from the Hebrew Bible, most having to do with national salvation, such as Samuel Anointing David, the Ark Brought to Jerusalem, and the Exodus from Egypt. Painted by anonymous artists, these works were executed in tempera, a medium made of pigments blended with egg yolks and water, applied to dry plaster.*

made inroads into the Jewish social order and family. Work was increasingly divided according to gender, with women being assigned domestic duties and subordinated and restricted within the economic, social, legal, and cultural system. The changing, and often conflicting, roles for women were reflected in the Hebrew Bible and other literature, which recorded instances of women serving as priestesses or influencing Hebrew officials, defined the qualities of a good wife, justified women's subservient status in a patriarchal order, and blamed them for human transgressions.

The Bible

The Jews enshrined their cultural developments in the Bible, their collection of sacred writings, or **scriptures.** Known as the Old Testament to Christians, the Hebrew Bible (from the Greek word for "book") contains history, law, poetry, songs, stories, prayers, and philosophical works. Evolving out of a rich and long oral tradition, the Bible probably began to take its earliest written form during the United Monarchy in the tenth century B.C. By then the Hebrews had an alphabet, which, like that of the Greeks, was probably derived from the Phoenicians. Having acquired a written language and a unified political state, the Hebrews shared a consciousness of their past and desired to preserve it. They assembled and recorded various historical accounts, songs, and stories, plus the sayings of the prophets. Sometime in the fifth century B.C., Jewish scholars and religious leaders canonized (officially accepted) parts of these writings as divinely inspired. They became the first five books of the Bible, known as the Torah or the Pentateuch. The Hebrew Bible's ultimate form was reached in A.D. 90 when a council of Jewish scholars added a last set of writings to the **canon.**

Another important development in the transmission of the Hebrew scriptures was their translation into other languages. In the third century B.C., after many Jews had been influenced by Hellenistic culture, a group of Alexandrian scholars collected all the authenticated Jewish writings and translated them into Greek. This Hebrew Greek Bible was called the Septuagint, from the Latin word for "seventy," so named because of the legend that it was translated by seventy scholars. Although traditionalist Jews initially rejected the Septuagint, it gradually was accepted as authoritative by Jewish intellectuals and early Christian scholars.

The final version of the Hebrew Bible is divided into three parts: the Law, the Prophets, and the Writings (Table 6.3). (Christians divide the Old Testament into four parts.) The Law, also called the Torah (from Hebrew, "instruction"), recounts the story of God's creation of the world and the early history of the Hebrews. More important, it details the establishment of the covenant and the foundation of the moral and ritualistic codes of personal and societal behavior that underlie Judaism.

The Prophets, canonized in the first century B.C., provide records about Israel and Judah and expand the Hebrews' ideas about God's nature and their relationship to him. They recount the conquest of Canaan, the events of the era of the Judges and the period of the United Monarchy, and the fate of Judah after the Babylonian Captivity.

Table 6.3 BOOKS OF THE HEBREW BIBLE AND THE CHRISTIAN BIBLE OLD TESTAMENT

HEBREW BIBLE		*CHRISTIAN BIBLE OLD TESTAMENT*	
The Law (Torah)		*The Pentateuch*	
Genesis	Numbers	Genesis	Numbers
Exodus	Deuteronomy	Exodus	Deuteronomy
Leviticus		Leviticus	
The Prophets		*The Historical Books*	
(Early Prophets)		Joshua	2 Chronicles
Joshua	2 Samuel	Judges	Ezra
Judges	1 Kings	Ruth	Nehemiah
1 Samuel	2 Kings	1 Samuel	Tobit*
(Later Prophets)		2 Samuel	Judith*
Isaiah	Micah	1 Kings	Esther
Jeremiah	Nahum	2 Kings	1 Maccabees*
Ezekiel	Habakkuk	1 Chronicles	2 Maccabees*
Hosea	Zephaniah	*The Poetical or Wisdom Books*	
Joel	Haggai	Job	
Amos	Zechariah	Psalms	
Obadiah	Malachi	Proverbs	
Jonah		Ecclesiastes	
The Writings		Song of Solomon (Songs)	
Psalms	Esther	Wisdom*	
Proverbs	Daniel	Sirach*	
Job	Ezra	*The Prophetical Books*	
Song of Songs	Nehemiah	Isaiah	Obadiah
Ruth	1 Chronicles	Jeremiah	Jonah
Lamentations	2 Chronicles	Lamentations	Micah
Ecclesiastes		Baruch*	Nahum
		Ezekiel	Habakkuk
		Daniel	Zephaniah
		Hosea	Haggai
		Joel	Zechariah
		Amos	Malachi

*Roman Catholics include these books in the canon and refer to them as deuterocanonical ("second canon"); Protestants sometimes place them in an appendix with other Apocrypha.

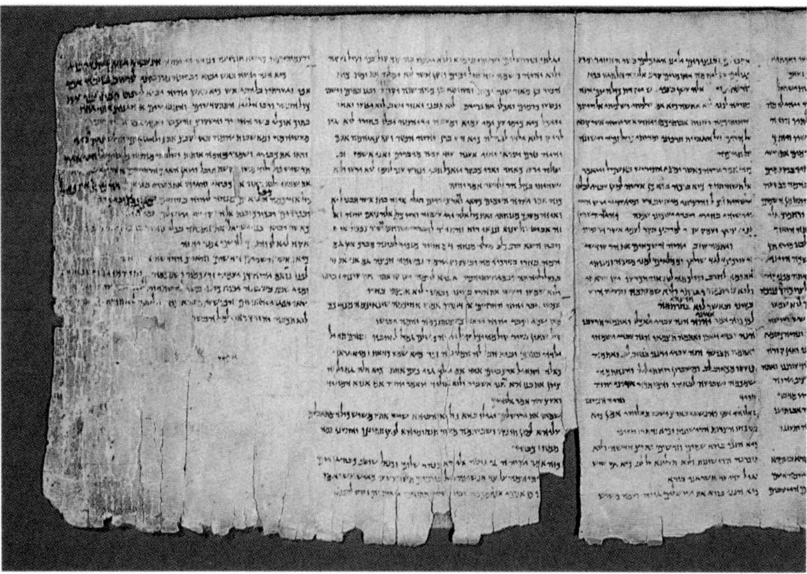

Figure 6.7 The Dead Sea Isaiah Scroll (detail). First century B.C.–first century A.D. *The Dead Sea Scrolls are believed to be the work of a Jewish sect known as the Essenes. Living in a monastic community called Qumran, this radical group rejected the leadership of the Jews in Jerusalem and practiced a militant, separatist form of Judaism. The scrolls represent their copies of the Hebrew Bible as well as previously unknown works. The Dead Sea Isaiah Scroll preserves all sixty-six chapters of the Bible's longest book.*

The Writings reflect diverse viewpoints and contain many types of literature, including poetry, wise sayings, stories, and apocalyptic visions of the end of time. Some of these books, such as Job, Ecclesiastes, and Proverbs, reflect the influence of other cultures on Jewish beliefs. The Writings were not deemed canonical until A.D. 90, with the exception of Psalms, a collection of poems, which was given sacred status by 100 B.C.

There is also a body of Jewish literature outside the canon. The Apocrypha are books written between 200 B.C. and A.D. 100 that include wisdom literature, stories, and history, including the history of the Maccabees. Though not part of the Jewish canon, these books were included in the Septuagint, the Greek translation of the Hebrew Bible, and accepted by the Roman Catholic Church as part of the Christian Old Testament.

Copies of many Jewish works, both canonical and noncanonical, were found in a cave near the Dead Sea in 1947. These documents, dating from about 200 B.C. to A.D. 100 and known as the Dead Sea Scrolls, were almost a thousand years older than any other existing manuscripts of the Bible and confirmed that the books had been transmitted faithfully for centuries (Figure 6.7). The scrolls also provided scholars with material about nonmainstream Jewish religious practices in the period before and during the earliest Christian period.

The Hebrew Bible provided Judaism with many of its beliefs and values and much of its worldview. It contrasted a changing view of God with a consistently negative opinion of human nature. Examples abound of humans who, like Adam and Eve or David, failed to uphold their side of the covenant by disobeying Yahweh, worshiping other gods, exploiting the unfortunate, or breaking moral and social codes. The Bible implied that given the weakness of human nature and Yahweh's strict demands, most mortals were unlikely to attain happiness. Perhaps happiness would be reached when Yahweh's kingdom was established on earth, but no one knew when that would happen or in what form. The individual's life was made more perplexing because no mortal could comprehend the awesome power of Yahweh. Human beings could only try to follow Yahweh's commandments—knowing that they would sin—and hope for happiness through his forgiveness.

In biblical Judaism, the hope for happiness depended on another aspect of the covenant: Jews believed that they would be forgiven for their sins. Redemption by God had occurred over and over in history, and the Bible sustained human hope while revealing Yahweh's love and mercy. Yet such qualities often seemed inconsistent with the Lord's vengeful manner. Consequently, the hearts of worshipers were torn between hope and fear. Their hope was strengthened through the covenant's promise that Yahweh would protect humanity as long as they lived just lives.

Early Jewish Art and Architecture

Jewish culture was profoundly shaped by the Second Commandment, which forbids the making of images or likenesses of God. In art, this meant that Yahweh could not, by definition, be depicted in any recognizable form. Furthermore, creation and creativity are considered the exclusive domain of God and reserved for him alone. Thus, there is no official Jewish sculpture or painting.

The scattered surviving artifacts of the Hebrews from the period before the United Monarchy can seldom be distinguished from the works of their neighbors. Because of the early Hebrews' nomadic existence, what sacred objects they had were transportable and kept in tents. These early works were not for public display because of the very holiness of Yahweh and the

Figure 6.8 Palace of John Hyrcanus. Second century B.C. Araq el Emir, Jordan. *This rendering of the palace of John Hyrcanus is based on ancient literary descriptions and recent archeological excavations. The Corinthian columns and the carved lions show Greek and Persian influences, but the lions appear more lifelike than the typically stylized Persian models.*

Hebrews' sense of their deity's power. Only a few persons were even permitted to see or be in the vicinity of these sacred objects. Once the tribes were united, however, Solomon enshrined the Ark of the Covenant and other ritualistic items in the splendid Temple that he built in Jerusalem. Solomon meant the Temple to be the central national shrine of the Hebrews and a symbol of his dynasty.

Solomon's Temple was destroyed by the Babylonians when they carried off the Jews in the early sixth century B.C. The description of the Temple in 1 Kings makes it sound similar to the "long-house" temples found in other civilizations of that time and probably indicated the influence of foreign neighbors. According to the Bible, Solomon's Temple was a rectangular building comprising three sections: a porch, a sanctuary, or main hall, and an inner sanctum that housed the Ark of the Covenant. Artists and craftspeople decorated the interior with carvings of floral designs and cherubs, highlighting these with gold. The building was made of ashlars, and two large free-standing columns were placed at the entranceway. The Temple may have been raised on a platform. A court surrounded the Temple, and a large altar stood inside the court.

When the Jews were released from the Babylonian Captivity by the Persians, they returned to their homeland and reconstructed the capital city of Jerusalem and its Temple. The Second Temple, completed in the late sixth century B.C., exhibited a simpler design and decoration scheme than did Solomon's Temple. Meanwhile, the Jews of the Diaspora gathered in Hellenistic cities to read the Torah and to pray in buildings that became synagogues, or houses of worship. No record survives of how these synagogues looked or how they might have been decorated until the third century A.D.

Greek influences became apparent in Jewish architecture during Hellenistic times. One Maccabean ruler, John Hyrcanus [hear-KAY-nuhs] (135–106 B.C.), constructed a fortress-palace at present-day Araq el Emir in Jordan that shows this influence clearly. The facade of the palace blended Greek columns and oriental carvings, typical of the Alexandrian architectural and decorative style (Figure 6.8). The edifice and its carvings were probably similar to the Second Temple in Jerusalem. One of the few decorations remaining from this palace is a lion fountain (Figure 6.9). Carved in high relief, the lion is well proportioned and conveys a sense of power, with its raised front paw and open mouth.

The lingering influence of late Greek architecture on Jewish structures is also seen in a set of tombs dug out of the soft limestone rocks east of Jerusalem in the Kidron Valley. According to the inscription, these tombs contained the remains of priests from the Hezir family (Figure 6.10). The tomb on the left displays Doric columns, and the one in the center fuses Greek Ionic columns and an Egyptian pyramidal roof. Several other tombs in the vicinity reveal a similar melding of styles.

During the reign of King Herod the Great (37–4 B.C.), architecture in Judea exhibited a further mix of Greek styles with Jewish motifs. King Herod's magnificent fortress-palace at Masada may have been a conscious blending of the two cultures in an effort to bridge the gap between the Roman and Jewish worlds (see Figure 6.5). The various buildings in Herod's complex contained many representative Greco-Roman features, including fluted Corinthian columns and marble facings (Figure 6.11). In Herod's palace, Classical patterned mosaics were combined with traditional Jewish deco-

Figure 6.9 Lion at the Palace of John Hyrcanus. Second century B.C. Araq el Emir, Jordan. *This lion, Greco-Oriental in style, was carved deeply into the stone's surface to create a high-relief work. The lion's tail, wrapped around his right rear leg, is balanced by the raised left front leg, creating a feeling of strength and agility.*

Figure 6.10 Tomb of Bene Hezir. Early first century B.C. Kidron Valley, Israel. *The Tomb of Bene Hezir (on the left) shows the influence of Greek architecture in its post-and-lintel construction and its Doric columns. Even though the area was subject to Roman impact at this time, Roman influence is not apparent in the architecture. The members of the priestly Hezir family, as recorded in 1 Chronicles 24, were buried in what has been determined to be the oldest tomb in Israel's Kidron Valley. Scholars disagree over whether the structure in the center with the pyramidal roof belonged to the Bene Hezir tomb.*

Figure 6.11 Hall of Herod's North Palace. Late first century B.C. Masada, Israel. *These Corinthian columns were originally plastered over and painted. Carved directly out of the hill's rock, they formed a natural corridor around the banqueting hall. Herod built this and other splendid palaces to impress the Jews and win their political sympathy, but he failed to do either.*

Figure 6.12 Mosaic from Herod's Palace. Late first century B.C. Masada, Israel. *The Greek practice of mosaic making was adopted by both the Romans and the Jews. The patterned designs around the borders of this mosaic from Herod's Palace are typically Greek, and the more organic image in the center is typically Jewish.* ▶

rations of flowers, fruits, and intertwined vines and branches (Figure 6.12).

Herod also built palaces at Jericho and in Jerusalem, but they were destroyed, and their remains have not been uncovered. The king also supervised the rebuilding of the Second Temple in Jerusalem, whose large dimensions and impressive features were recorded in the writings of the Jewish historian Josephus in his works *The Jewish War* and *Jewish Antiquities* (see Figure 6.4). Like the First Temple, this one contained many rooms, including the Holy of Holies with the menorah and the table where the priests placed the consecrated, unleavened bread eaten during Passover, the festival that commemorates the exodus from Egypt. Whatever may have been Herod's motives in constructing this new Temple, the results were short-lived. When the Romans finally crushed the Jewish revolt in A.D. 70, the Temple, except for the Wailing Wall, was destroyed, and its sacred objects were transported to Rome.

CHRISTIANITY

Like Judaism, Christianity rose from obscurity and gained much of its power from the tremendous moral force of its central beliefs and values. But Christianity went on to become the dominant religion of Western culture. From its origins among the Jews of Judea, Christianity slowly spread until, by the end of the fourth century A.D., it had become the official faith of Rome. When Rome lost control of the western provinces at the end of the fifth century A.D., Christianity's ideas and institutions survived as rays of hope in the surrounding darkness. In the following century, Christians gradually gained the upper hand. Their triumph was powerfully symbolized in the Early Middle Ages when church authorities revised the old Roman calendar to make the birth of Christ the pivotal event in history. Thus, the period before Jesus' birth is known as B.C., or before Christ, and the era after his birth is termed A.D., or ANNO DOMINI, Latin words meaning "in the year of the Lord," the title of respect given to Jesus by Christians. Although Christianity and the church have declined from their zenith in the Middle Ages, the Christian calendar remains in effect throughout the West as well as in many other parts of the world—a symbol of the continuing power of this creed.

The Life of Jesus Christ and the New Testament

The surviving primary sources for the origin of Christianity are writings in Greek by early believers who were openly partisan. According to them, Christianity

Timeline 6.2 CHRISTIANITY TO A.D. 284

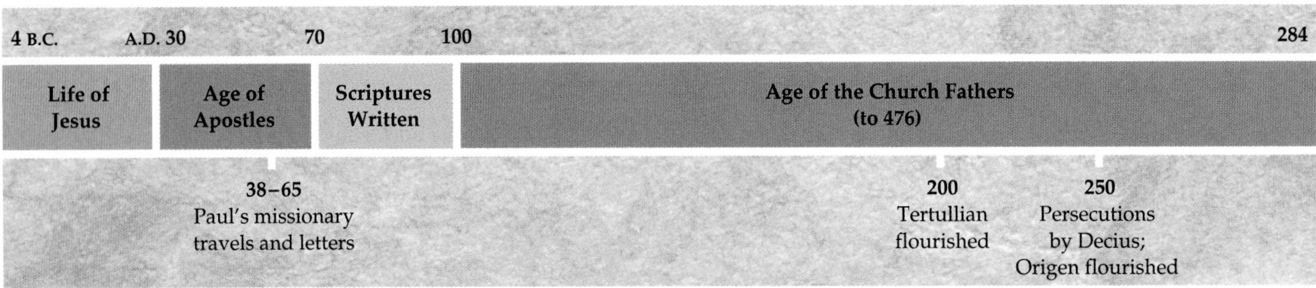

began within the Jewish faith among the followers of Jesus, a deeply pious and charismatic Jew who failed to purify his own faith but succeeded in founding a dynamic new religion.

Jesus was born to Mary and Joseph in Judea about 4 B.C. (a date that reflects changes in the Christian calendar made since its inauguration). After narrating the events surrounding his birth, the accounts of Jesus' life are almost silent until he reaches the age of about thirty, when he commenced a teaching mission that placed him squarely in conflict with prevailing Jewish beliefs and authorities. The poor and outcast in Jewish society heard Jesus' message, and he soon had a small group of followers who believed that he was the Messiah, the Anointed One who would deliver the Jews, promised by God to the prophets. He was also termed the Christ, taken from the Greek for "the anointed one." Performing miracles and healing the sick, he preached that the apocalypse, or the end of the world, was near. In anticipation of what he called the coming of the kingdom of God, he urged his followers to practice a demanding and loving ethic.

Growing discord between the Jewish establishment and this messianic band caused Roman leaders to classify Jesus as a political rebel. About A.D. 30, Jesus was crucified by the Romans (Timeline 6.2). Three days later, some of his followers reported that Jesus had risen from the dead and reappeared among them. His resurrection became the ultimate miracle associated with his teachings, the sign that immortal life awaited those who believed in him as the son of God and as the Messiah. After a few days on earth, Jesus ascended into heaven, though not before pledging to return when the world ended.

The outline of Jesus' life is set forth in the first three books, called **Gospels,** of the Christian scriptures. The early Christian community believed that the writers, known as Matthew, Mark, and Luke, were witnesses to Jesus' message; hence they were called **evangelists** after the Greek work *evangelion*—for those who preached the gospel, or the good news. The Gospels, although providing evidence for the historical Jesus, were not intended as histories in the Greco-Roman sense because they were addressed to Christian converts. Mark's Gospel was the earliest, dating from about 70; Matthew's account was written between 80 and 90; and an early version of Luke's narrative probably appeared about the same time. These three works are known as the synoptic Gospels (from the Greek *syn* for "together" and *opsis* for "view") because they take essentially the same point of view toward their subject. Between 90 and 100, a fourth, and somewhat different, Gospel appeared—that of John—which treats Jesus as a wisdom teacher, a revealer of cosmic truths. The author of the Fourth Gospel has Jesus teach the possibility of being born again to eternal life.

Despite their similarities, the synoptic Gospels reflect a schism, or split, in the early Christian church. Peter, one of Jesus' original disciples, headed a Judaizing group who stressed the necessity of first becoming a Jew before becoming a Christian. Paul, a Jew who converted to Christianity after the death of Jesus, led a group who welcomed gentile, or non-Jewish, members. Mark's Gospel was written in part to support Paul's gentile faction and therefore takes a negative tone toward Jews. Matthew was written in part as a corrective to Mark and made Peter, according to Roman Catholic doctrine, the "rock" on which the church was founded—the biblical source for the belief that Peter was the first pope. Luke's Gospel was an effort by the early Roman church to deny, after the fact, that a schism had ever existed.

Luke also wrote the Acts of the Apostles, the earliest account of the fledgling Christian community. This work records the activities of Jesus' followers immediately after his resurrection and defines some of the church's first rituals and beliefs, including a rejection of Jewish dietary laws and the practice of circumcision. Acts also affirmed the opening of Christianity to gentiles, a policy that in the future would aid in the spread of Christianity. At the time Acts was written, however, Paul and other missionaries were preaching mainly to

Map 6.2 THE EARLY CHRISTIAN WORLD

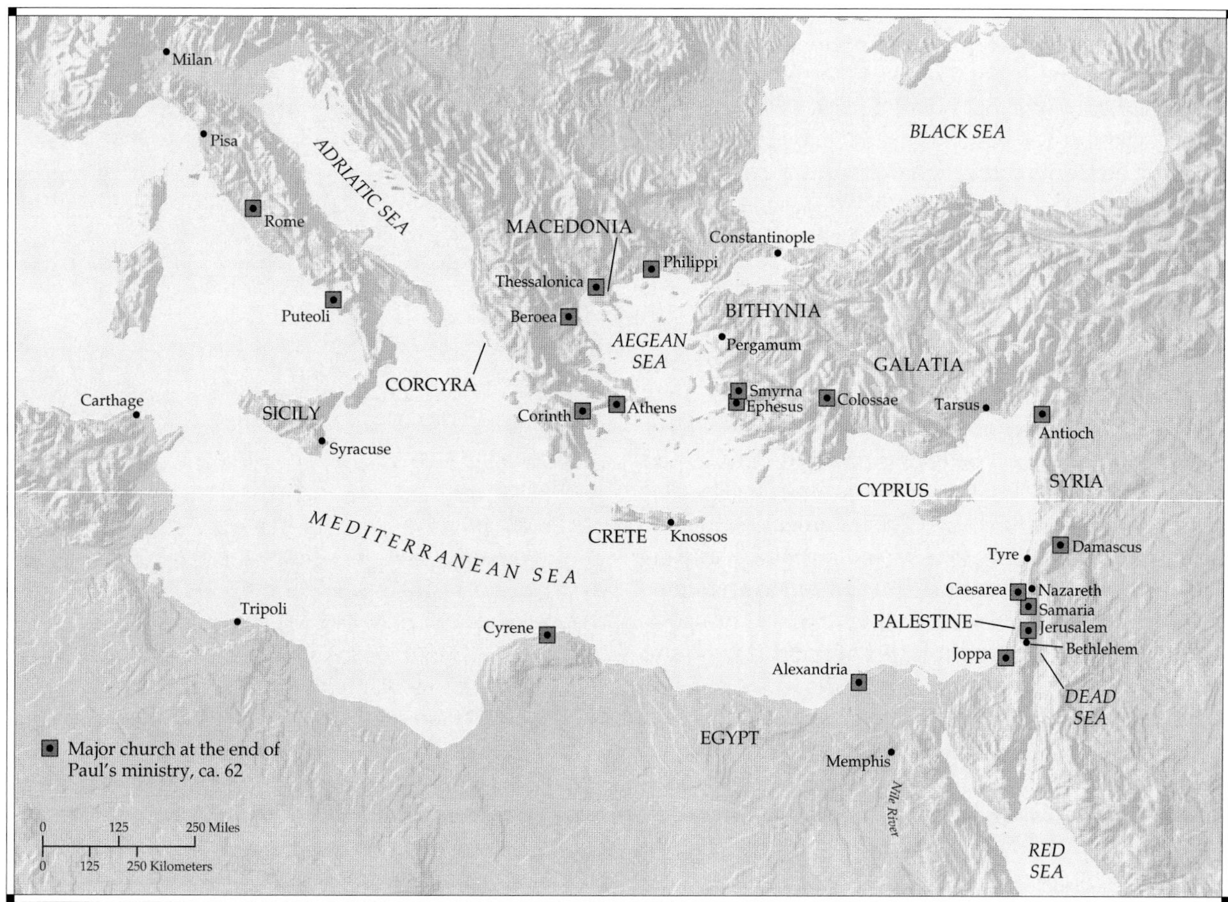

Greek-speaking Jews and Jewish converts scattered across the Roman Empire. Paul's Roman citizenship enabled him to move about freely.

The meaning of Jesus' life and teachings was further clarified by Paul, who had persecuted the Christians of Judea before joining the new faith. Between 50 and 62, Paul, who was knowledgeable of Greek philosophy, addressed both local issues and broader theological concerns in epistles, or letters, the earliest writings among the Christian scriptures, although only seven of the fourteen so-called Pauline epistles are generally recognized as being written by him. These epistles constitute Christianity's first **theology,** or the study of the nature of religious truth. Paul directed his letters to churches he either founded or visited across the Roman Empire: Ephesus and Colossae (Galatia), Philippi and Thessalonica (Macedonia), Corinth (Greece), and Rome (Map 6.2).

Paul's interpretation of the life of Jesus was based on the "Suffering Servant" section of the book of Isaiah in the Old Testament. The Suffering Servant was described as noble and guiltless but misunderstood and suffering on behalf of others. Paul set forth the doctrine of the Atonement, whereby a blameless Christ suffered on the cross to pay for the sins of humankind. Christ's life and death initiated a new moral order by offering salvation to depraved human beings who otherwise were doomed to eternal death and punishment by Adam's first sin. But, according to Paul, human redemption was not automatically given, for a sinner must have faith in Jesus Christ and his sacrifice.

Paul's teachings also stressed that Christ's resurrection, which guaranteed everlasting life for others, was the heart of Christian beliefs, an argument that echoed the synoptic Gospels. Pauline Christianity made a radical break with Judaism by nullifying the old law's authority and claiming that the true heirs of Abraham were not the Jews but the followers of Christ. Paul also affirmed that obedience to Christ led to righteousness. Such righteousness demanded ascetic living, with particular stress on sexual chastity. From Paul's writing came the Roman Catholic Church's teaching that sexuality, except for reproductive purposes, was inherently sinful.

The final section of the Christian scriptures was the Book of Revelation, dating from about 95. This apocalyptic scripture projected the end of the world and the institution of a new moral order on the occasion of Jesus' return and final judgment. Revelation's picture of Rome as a corrupt Babylon destined for destruction reflected the early church's hatred of the existing political and social order. But the book, filled with enigmatic sayings and symbols, proved controversial, and not all ancient church communities accepted its authority.

By the mid–second century, the four Gospels, the Acts of the Apostles, the fourteen Pauline epistles, the seven non-Pauline epistles, and Revelation were accepted as the canon of Christian scriptures, or New Testament (Table 6.4). Believing themselves to be the new Israel, the early Christians also retained the Hebrew scriptures, called the Old Testament. Although the spoken language of the Jews in Palestine was Aramaic, a Semitic tongue, the Christian canon was composed in Greek, like the Hebrew Septuagint. The use of Greek reflected the triumph of Paul and the gentile party as the church turned away from Jerusalem and toward the Greco-Roman world.

Table 6.4 BOOKS OF THE NEW TESTAMENT

Gospels	
Matthew	Luke
Mark	John
Acts of the Apostles	
Acts	
Epistles	
Romans	Titus
1 Corinthians	Philemon
2 Corinthians	Hebrews
Galatians	James
Ephesians	1 Peter
Philippians	2 Peter
Colossians	1 John
1 Thessalonians	2 John
2 Thessalonians	3 John
1 Timothy	Jude
2 Timothy	
Apocalypse	
Revelation	

Christians and Jews

Despite the distinctive features of early Christianity, many Jewish ideas and rituals contributed to the new religion. The Christian vision of Yahweh was rooted in Judaism: a single, creating, universal God who spoke through sacred texts (the canon) and who demanded moral behavior from all humans. Both Jewish and Christian ethical standards required social justice for individuals and for the community. Likewise, the Christian image of Jesus as Messiah was framed within the context of Jewish prophetic literature. Christian apocalyptic writing, such as Revelation, also shared a common literary form with Jewish models like the book of Daniel.

Even when Christians rejected specific Jewish ideas, such as the sanctity of the Mosaic law, the early church continued discussions on human righteousness and sin in terms familiar to Jews. The Christians probably adapted their rite of baptism from a ceremony similar to that of the Jews of the Dispersion. Christians also kept the idea of the Sabbath but changed it from Saturday to Sunday, and they transformed the festival of Passover (a celebration of the Hebrews' escape from Egypt) to Easter (a festival celebrating Jesus' resurrection). The church sanctuary as a focal point for prayer and learning evolved out of the Jewish synagogue, as did Christian priests from the Jewish elders. And the Christian **liturgy,** or the service of public worship, borrowed heavily from the Jewish service with its hymns, prayers, and Bible reading.

Judaism also influenced Christian thought by transmitting certain ideas from Zoroastrianism, including such dualistic concepts as Satan as the personification of evil, heaven and hell as the twin destinies of humankind, and a divine savior who would appear at the end of time. Jesus and the dominant Jewish sect, the Pharisees, though enemies, both integrated these Persian ideas into their religious outlooks.

Despite their common heritage, relations between Christians and Jews were stormy. After the Council at Jamnia in Judea in 90, when the Jews established the final version of their sacred canon, there was no place in Judaism for the Christian message. As revealed in Paul's letters, the Jews viewed the followers of Jesus Christ as apostates, people who had abandoned or renounced their true religion. Accordingly, the Jews tried to deny the Christians the protection that Jewish leaders had negotiated with Roman authorities regarding emperor worship and their own unique beliefs and rituals. In some cases, Jews resorted to reporting individual Christians to the Roman authorities. Until the end of the second century, Jews and Christians occasionally engaged in violent clashes. Possibly the strong anti-Jewish bias found in a few of the Christian books like the Gospel of Mark reflected these tensions.

Christianity and Greco-Roman Religions and Philosophies

Christianity also benefited from its contacts with Greco-Roman mystery cults and philosophies. Whether or not the rituals of the cults of Cybele, Isis, or Mithra directly influenced Christianity, they did share religious ideas—for example, salvation through the sacrifice of a savior, sacred meals, and hymns. Christianity, as a monotheistic religion, paralleled movements within the cults of the second and third centuries that were blending all deities into the worship of a single divinity. Among the Greco-Roman philosophies, both Stoicism and Neo-Platonism influenced Christianity as the church shifted from its Jewish roots and became hellenized; the Stoics taught the kinship of humanity, and the Neo-Platonists praised the spiritual realm at the expense of the physical world.

Christians in the Roman Empire

Eventually, the Romans viewed and treated Jews and Christians differently. The Romans initially regarded the Christians as a Jewish sect, but during the First Jewish War, the Christians evidently held aloof. The Christian attitude seemed to be that the Jews had brought calamity upon themselves through their rejection of Christ. Similarly, Christians remained untouched during later persecutions of Jews by Romans in 115–117 and in 132–135.

As their faith expanded during the first century, individual Christians began to experience trouble from the Romans, though no state policy of seizing Christians was introduced. However, if suspected Christians came to the notice of secular officials, they were punished if they did not renounce their beliefs. The same pattern of localized, random persecution continued until the mid–third century, reminding the Christians of their vulnerability. The church, having by that time increased dramatically in membership and accumulated property in buildings and cemeteries, profited from the indifference of imperial and local authorities. As long as economic prosperity and political stability lasted, the Christians seemed safe.

However, as the chaos of the third century descended on Rome, the Christians were blamed for all the empire's troubles. The emperor Decius [DEE-sheuhs] (r. 249–251) mounted a wide-ranging political test that required all citizens (men, women, and children) to make a token sacrifice to the emperor. When the Christians refused to honor the emperor in this manner, hundreds of them died, including several of their local leaders, or bishops. Decius's sudden death ended this assault, but in 257 Valerian (r. 253–260) renewed the struggle, which resulted in the martyrdom of the bishop of Rome and the age's leading intellectual, Cyprian. Christians were beheaded, buried alive, or burned alive during this persecution. The killings eventually ceased, but for the rest of the century the survival of the Christian church was uncertain and depended on a muted existence.

Despite persecutions from the authorities, the Christian church drew much sustenance from Roman culture. The language of the church in the western provinces became Latin, and in the eastern provinces the religious leaders adopted Greek. The canon law that governed the church was based on the Roman civil law. Most important, the church modeled itself on the Roman state: The bishops had jurisdiction over territories called dioceses just as the secular governors controlled administrative dioceses.

In addition, the church was moving toward a monarchical form of government. Because the authority of the officeholders was believed to descend from Jesus' faithful supporters, those bishoprics established by apostles—such as the one in Rome that tradition claimed was founded by both Peter and Paul—emerged as the most powerful.

From an insignificant number of followers at the end of the first century, the church had attained a membership of perhaps five million, or about a tenth of the population of the empire, by the end of the third century. The smallest communities were scattered along the frontiers, and the largest congregations were in Rome and the older eastern cities. Social composition of the church evolved from primarily lower-class foreign women and slaves, particularly those recruited from among the Jewish communities of the Diaspora, to progressively higher classes. By the late second century, the middle classes, especially merchants and traders, were joining the church. Aristocratic women sought membership, but men of the highest classes tended to remain unconverted, although a few aristocratic converts prepared the way for future adherents.

Christianity's appeal to women was complex, though all seemed to respond to its promise of salvation and the Apostle Paul's egalitarian vision (Galatians 3:28): "There is neither Jew nor Greek, there is neither bond nor free, there is neither male nor female: for ye are all one in Christ Jesus." Female converts also found the Christian community to be a refuge from the anonymity and cruelty of Roman society; the church formed a secret underworld of close relationships among people drawn together by an ascetic but loving way of life. That underworld promised to free women from the constraints of marriage and family life; it offered power by allowing them to influence others by their faith; it widened their horizons through intimate contacts with spiritual leaders; it gave them new iden-

PERSONAL PERSPECTIVE

VIBIA PERPETUA
Account of Her Last Days Before Martyrdom

Vibia Perpetua, an educated young woman from a wealthy Carthaginian family and a convert to Christianity, defied an edict against proselytizing issued by the emperor in A.D. 202. She was jailed and died in the arena of Carthage in 203.

A few days later we were moved to a prison [in Carthage]. I was frightened, because I had never been in such a dark place. A sad day! The large number of prisoners made the place stifling. The soldiers tried to extort money from us. I was also tormented by worry for my child. Finally, Tertius and Pomponius, the blessed deacons responsible for taking care of us, bribed the guards to allow us a few hours in a better part of the prison to regain our strength. All the prisoners were released from the dungeon and allowed to do as they wished. I gave suck to my starving child. . . . I was permitted to keep my child with me in prison. His strength came back quickly, which alleviated my pain and anguish. The prison was suddenly like a palace; I felt more comfortable there than anywhere else.

tities through foreign travel and involvement in a cause that was life-sustaining; and, for those who chose lives of chastity, it could serve as a means of birth control.

Early Christian Literature

By the late second century, the status of the church had attracted the attention of leading Roman intellectuals, such as the philosopher Celsus and the physician Galen. Celsus (second century) ridiculed the Christian notion of the resurrection of the body and the new religion's appeal to women and slaves. On the other hand, Galen (about 130–about 201) found merit in Christianity because of its philosophical approach to life and its emphasis on strict self-discipline.

Christian literature, from its birth in Paul's letters until 284, was excluded from secular public discourse. But the work of Christian writers, which addressed the evolving needs of this underground religion, began to circulate among the faithful. Of the many Christian writers active during this time, Tertullian [tehr-TULL-yuhn] (about 160–about 230) and Origen [AHR-uh-juhn] (about 185–about 254) were important because they helped to define Christianity's relation to humanistic learning.

Tertullian's life and writings showed the uncompromising nature of Christianity. Trained in Stoic philosophy in Roman Carthage, he later converted to the new faith after he witnessed the serenity of Christians dying for their religion. The strength of his beliefs made him a spokesperson for North Africa, where a cult of martyrs made the area the "Bible belt" of the Roman world. Writing in Latin, he helped to shape the Western church's voice in that language. His diatribes against the pleasures of the theaters and arenas and his intense denunciation of women as sexual temptresses became legendary. In the severest terms he rejected the Greco-Roman humanistic heritage, preferring the culture of Christianity. Such fundamentalist thinking eventually drove this restless intellect into heretical, or false, beliefs. His vehement detestation of the secular world and the institutional church proved to be an uncomfortable legacy for Christianity.

Origen of Alexandria shared Tertullian's puritanical zeal and his defiance of spiritual authority, but he did not repudiate humanistic learning. In his mature writings, composed in Greek, Origen brought Christian thought into harmony with Platonism and Stoicism. Origen's Jesus was not the redeemer of the Gospels but the *logos* of Stoicism (see Chapter 4). The *logos,* or reason, liberated the human soul so that it might move through different levels of reality to reach God. Origen's Platonism led him to reject the notion of the resurrection of the body as described in the Gospels and Paul's letters and to assert instead that the soul is eternal. Not surprisingly, Origen's ideas were condemned as heretical by later popes. Nevertheless, his philosophic writings, which were read secretly, helped free Christianity from its Jewish framework and appealed to intellectuals.

Christian women writers in this earliest period were very rare, because intellectual discourse was totally dominated by men. Women did play important roles in the new faith—such as Mary Magdalene, who waited at Jesus' empty tomb, and Lydia and Priscilla, whom Paul met on his travels—but their voices are almost always heard indirectly. In their theoretical writings, men often addressed women's issues, such as Tertullian's "The Apparel of Women." Nevertheless, the voice of one Christian woman from this period has come down to us: that of Vibia Perpetua (about A.D. 181–203) of Carthage in North Africa, one of the first female saints. An anonymous account of the Christian

Figure 6.13 The Roman Catacombs: A Narrow Corridor with Niches for Burials. *Because of their belief in a bodily resurrection, proper burial loomed large in the minds of early Christians. Roman Christians joined with other citizens in burying their dead along subterranean passages underneath the city. In 400, when Christianity triumphed in Rome, the custom of catacomb burial ceased. Knowledge of the catacombs passed into oblivion until 1578, when they were rediscovered and became subjects of study and veneration.*

martyrs' struggles includes a verbatim reproduction of Perpetua's writings in prison. Filled with heartbreaking detail, the account describes her prison ordeal as she awaited death while nursing her child. The sentence was imposed because she refused to obey an edict of the non-Christian emperor Septimius Severus.

Early Christian Art

Had Christians obeyed the Second Commandment, no Christian figurative art would have been produced. Indeed, the earliest Christian writers, including Tertullian and Origen, condemned the depiction of religious subjects as blasphemous. But pious Christians, attracted by the pull of humanism, commissioned frescoes for underground burial chambers and sculptures for their **sarcophagi,** or marble tombs. Christian painters and sculptors slowly fused their religious vision with the Greco-Roman tradition, a style that would dominate the art of the late empire. After the fall of Rome, religious values were central to Western art for almost a thousand years, until the Italian Renaissance.

In imperial Rome, citizens had the legal right to bury their dead in underground rooms beside the Appian Way, the city's chief thoroughfare (Figure 6.13). By the late second century some of the tombs displayed Christian symbols and subjects, suggesting the increased confidence of the new religion in an otherwise hostile Roman environment. In the so-called Catacomb of Callixtus, a third-century fresco depicts a shepherd as a symbol of Jesus (Figure 6.14). This depiction, which is the most popular surviving image in the Christian art of this period, is based on the idea of Jesus as the kindly shepherd of his flock of followers, an image derived from many biblical sources, including the Twenty-third Psalm: "The Lord is my shepherd." Holding a sheep across his shoulders with his right hand, the shepherd stands in the center of a circle, flanked by two sheep. This circle in turn is surrounded by eight panels with alternating depictions of orants (praying figures) and scenes from the life of Jonah.

Even though the shepherd and sheep convey a Christian message, the image adapts a familiar Greco-Roman theme—known in both art and literature—that identified such diverse figures as the philosopher Pythagoras and the Orphic cult leader Orpheus with

Figure 6.14 The Good Shepherd. Mid–third century A.D. Fresco. Crypts of Lucina, Catacomb of Callixtus, Rome. *This third-century fresco shows one of the popular religious symbols used by early Christians to disguise evidence of their faith from prying and perhaps hostile eyes. The "Good Shepherd" as an image of Jesus persisted in Christian art until the end of the fifth century.*

Figure 6.15 *Calf Bearer.* Ca. 570 B.C. Marble, ht. 65″. Acropolis Museum, Athens. *This sixth-century* B.C. *Greek statue shows a young man carrying a calf probably intended for a ritual sacrifice. The statue is executed in the kouros style, popular in the Archaic Age, as indicated by the frontality, stiffness, and stylized beard. The shepherd image later became associated with Jesus in the early Christian period.*

Figure 6.16 *Christian Good Shepherd.* Second century. Marble, ht. 39″. Vatican Museum. *This graceful statue blends Greek influences with a Christian subject. The casual pose of the shepherd with his easy contrapposto and dreamy gaze shows that the influence of Praxiteles, the fourth-century* B.C. *Greek sculptor, was still active after more than five centuries. The short cloak worn by the figure was a typical costume of shepherds in the art of the times.*

shepherds. The pose of the youth carrying an animal on his shoulders appeared in Archaic Greek sculpture as early as the sixth century B.C. (Figure 6.15). The painter of the Good Shepherd ceiling fresco portrays the shepherd as a beardless youth without distinctive, godlike traits. A statue of a shepherd from the second century attests to the widespread use of this image (Figure 6.16). By such representations as these, the artists in effect declared the limits of their art in penetrating the mystery of Jesus as both God and man.

Catacomb paintings were rich in images, however disguised, of Christian resurrection, salvation, and life after death. The Jewish Bible was a source of subjects for Christian artists, as can be seen in Figure 6.17, *Three Hebrews in the Fiery Furnace.* The youths, Shadrach, Meschach, and Abednego, were rescued from certain death by divine intervention and thus symbolize redemption (Daniel 3). In the painting, they are depicted impressionistically, floating in abstract space. Their feet are hidden in swirls of red paint, representing the fiery torment of the furnace. Their arms are upraised as if praying and constitute an additional symbol: the invocation of God's blessing.

A relief panel sculpted on the marble sarcophagus, dating from about A.D. 270, in the church of Saint Maria Antiqua, Rome, reinforces the message that the Old and New Testaments are not in conflict but exist in religious harmony (Figure 6.18). Reading from left to right on the panel is the Old Testament story of Jonah: the Prayer in the Ship, Jonah and the Whale, and Jonah Under the Gourd Vine. The three days he spent in the belly of the whale are understood as prefiguring the time Christ spent in the tomb. The rest of the panel shows Christian symbols—a praying figure (with upraised arms), a philosopher (holding a scroll), the Good Shepherd, a baptism (a standing man places his hand on a smaller figure), and a fisherman (with a net). These images, found so often in Christian funerary art, attest to the saving power of their God.

Figure 6.17 *Three Hebrews in the Fiery Furnace.* Chamber of the Velatio. Mid-third century A.D. $19\frac{1}{2} \times 34''$. Cemetery of Priscilla, Rome. *This catacomb painting of* Three Hebrews in the Fiery Furnace *illustrates the practice of early Christian artists drawing on Jewish stories to symbolize their beliefs. The rescue of the Hebrew youths, who refused to bow down to the golden image set up by the Babylonian king, becomes a symbol of Christian refusal to engage in worship of Rome's emperor. However, the Christian artist has changed the story, so that instead of being rescued by an angel, as recorded in Daniel 3:28, the Hebrews are promised salvation by means of a bird bearing leaves in its beak (above). This symbol probably derives from the Jewish story of Noah and the Flood, in which a dove with an olive leaf was a sign that the dry land had reappeared (Genesis 8:11).*

Figure 6.18 Early Christian Frieze Sarcophagus. Ca. A.D. 270 Marble. Saint Maria Antiqua, Rome. *Most sarcophagi were products of workshops; thus the artistic quality varied greatly. However, this sarcophagus, carved by anonymous artists, exhibits a fairly sophisticated artistic level in the treatment of human figures, such as the variety of poses and gestures, and the attention to detail, such as the draperies and the varied objects used to identify each person. The figures, despite their small size, possess limbs proportional to their bodies, except for the one being baptized.*

The Legacy of Biblical Judaism and Early Christianity

The entire Jewish tradition has evolved from the early history of the Hebrews—their wandering without a homeland, their role as outsiders in other cultures, their brief period in control of the promised land of Canaan, and, above all, their deep and abiding sense of being the chosen people of the almighty God, Yahweh. Under the Romans, the Jews were punished for their religious views, a portent of the anti-Semitism and violent attacks that have dogged their existence down through the twentieth century. Despite adversity, the Jews have survived and today have the longest continuous history of any group of people in Western civilization.

Unlike the Greco-Roman deities, who were seen as encouraging and supporting human achievement and excellence in many areas of life, the God of the Hebrews was primarily concerned with the ethical conduct of human beings and their obedience to his laws. Yahweh's jealousy extended to all forms of human expression insofar as they detracted from his worship. As a consequence, the arts and humanities, when allowed in Judaism, tended to be subordinated to religious concerns. Ultimately, Jewish culture found its voice in the ideals of the Bible, among the highest moral standards of any ancient people. The Jewish ethical vision, which even today drives Western reformers and revolutionaries, demanded social justice for every person, no matter how poor or powerless, within the human community.

Inheriting this conception of God and culture, the Christians reinterpreted it and gave it their distinctive stamp. After the fall of Rome, when Christianity emerged as the religion of the West, the Judeo-Christian tradition merged with the Greco-Roman heritage to form the basis of Western civilization. Following the teaching of Jesus, the early Christians perpetuated the Jewish emphasis on God's unity and omnipotence as well as the demands for stringently ethical behavior. Accordingly, Jesus' golden rule—to treat others as one would like to be treated—became the goal of devout Christians. The first Christians also laid great emphasis on taking care of the sick, the impoverished, and the homeless—a tradition that has given rise in Western civilization to a wide variety of private and public social relief programs.

The early Christians, rejecting the relatively closed nature of Judaism, turned their religion into a missionary faith; in the first generation of missionaries, Paul and other church leaders took Jesus' message to all people, addressing them as individuals regardless of their racial and ethnic backgrounds. Today, after two thousand years, nearly one-third of the world's population subscribes—at least nominally—to Christian beliefs.

Under the early Roman Empire, Christian thought also became a transnational, or international, belief system that expressed uncompromising hostility to Greco-Roman culture and to the Roman state. Those Christian writers who, like the author of the Book of Revelation, described Rome as "the great whore" and forecast that city's destruction simply expressed the collective yearnings of the faithful in the early church. Under the onslaught of the Roman persecutions, the Christians anticipated a new order ruled by God's values. Thus, early Christians adopted Greco-Roman ideas not for their own sake but for their usefulness to the Christian religion.

The hostility of the early church to humanism and secular thought was but the opening assault in a running battle between two ways of looking at the world. For the moment, in imperial Rome humanism was triumphant among the people who counted—the aristocrats, the intellectuals, and the ruling class. But by the end of the fourth century, the balance had swung over in favor of Christianity, and the non-Christian intellectuals were rapidly disappearing. This state of affairs prevailed until the Italian Renaissance; then, artists, writers, and intellectuals challenged the reigning Christian worldview by reviving humanistic learning and the Greco-Roman past. As the modern world has taken shape, Christianity has found itself assaulted from many sides and has never regained the preeminence that it held from the time of the fall of Rome to the coming of the Renaissance.

KEY CULTURAL TERMS

covenant
Diaspora
eschatology
apocalypse
Messiah
scripture
canon
Gospels
evangelists
theology
liturgy
sarcophagus

SUGGESTIONS FOR FURTHER READING

PRIMARY SOURCES

EUSEBIUS. *The History of the Church from Christ to Constantine.* Translated by G. A. Williamson. New York: Penguin, 1965. Though a partisan account written by a credulous observer, this work is the major source of early Christian history.

JOSEPHUS. *The Jewish War.* Translated by G. A. Williamson. New York: Penguin, 1974. Josephus, a Jew who served Rome, wrote one of the few surviving accounts of this period.

Holy Bible, New Testament, Old Testament. There are many translations of these sacred books, ranging from the King James version of the early seventeenth century to various twentieth-century translations based on recent scholarship. The Douay edition is the official Bible of the Roman Catholic Church.

7 LATE ROMAN CIVILIZATION

What were the forces that brought the Roman Empire to an end? This chapter focuses on Rome's final era, from 284 to 476, when political, social, and economic crises seemed increasingly beyond human control and spiritual and cultural changes indicated growing disillusionment with the old Roman ways. The chapter suggests some causes for Rome's fall after more than twelve hundred years, during the last seven hundred of which it dominated the Mediterranean basin. Since the fate of Rome was inextricably linked with the development of Christianity, the chapter also traces the growth of the church and offers reasons for its triumph. From the interweaving of Christianity and Classical humanism—the legacy of Greece and Rome—a new Western cultural ideal emerged (Figure 7.1).

THE LAST DAYS OF THE ROMAN EMPIRE

When the Roman general Diocletian [die-uh-KLEE-shun] seized power as emperor in 284, the empire appeared to be ungovernable. Twenty-seven rulers had preceded him in the previous fifty years, and most had been killed by the army. The office of emperor now depended on the army's approval, for the autocratic imperial regime had successfully stifled all other forms of political life.

Although the empire faced many dangers, Rome's military problems were the most pressing and intensified the other threats to the state. Throughout the third century, increasing numbers of soldiers were needed to defend the boundaries of the empire. Military pay for these soldiers was draining the imperial treasury, which was already threatened by inflation and a declining

◄ **Detail** *The Good Shepherd.* Ca. 450. Mausoleum of Galla Placidia, Ravenna, Italy.

Figure 7.1 *Young Christ.* Third century. Marble, ht. 27½″. Terme Museum, Rome. *Early Christian art focused on biblical scenes and especially images of Jesus Christ. Lacking a clear-cut tradition for portraying Jesus, church leaders simply borrowed from Classical art, making its tradition their own, as in this portrait of a young Christ. Like the gods on the Parthenon's frieze (see Figure 3.25), Christ is portrayed as a beardless youth, dressed in a Greek garment and seated in repose, his left foot resting against a chair leg. The image of Christ as a beardless youth persisted in the church until the fall of Rome, when it was supplanted by the image of an older, bearded man.*

economy. Urban population fell as thousands fled into the countryside to avoid military duty and burdensome taxes. Many who remained in urban areas still clamored for the amenities of Roman life, including bread and circuses, and that further drained precious state resources.

Christian converts presented yet another problem to Rome: They often refused to enroll in the military on the grounds that killing someone in battle was murder, an act forbidden by the Fifth Commandment. Given this reduction in available troops, the government recruited soldiers from among the barbarians who lived inside Roman territory—a course of action that further weakened the loyalty of the military.

Faced with these problems, Diocletian began a series of reforms that virtually refounded the Roman state. The almost-two-hundred-year period of late Roman civilization may be divided into two phases: (1) Diocletian's reforms and the triumph of Christianity, lasting from 284 to 395, and (2) Christian Rome and the end of the empire in the West, extending from 395 until 476 (Timeline 7.1).

Diocletian's Reforms and the Triumph of Christianity, 284–395

Diocletian (r. 284–305) stands as the creator of late Rome just as Augustus does of the early empire. Unlike Augustus, however, Diocletian insisted on divine

Timeline 7.1 LATE ROME, 284–476

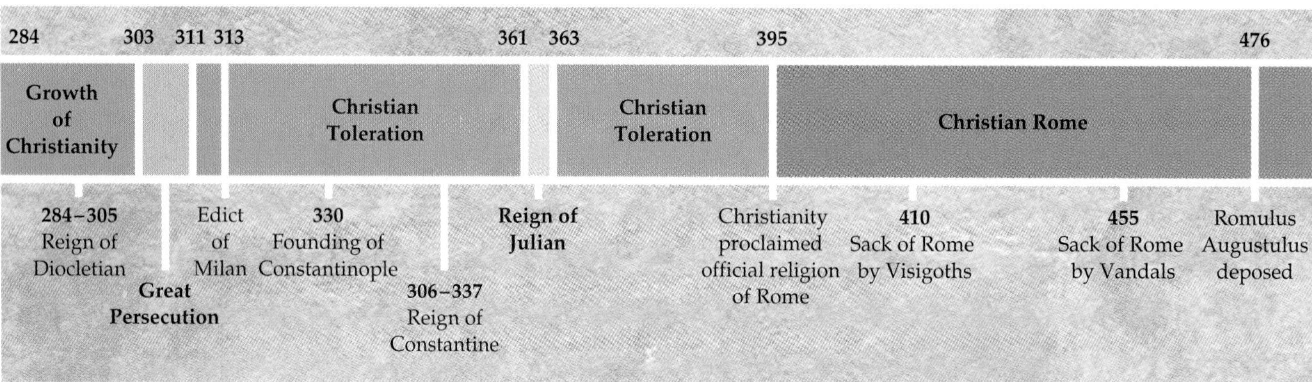

Map 7.1 THE ROMAN EMPIRE IN THE FOURTH CENTURY

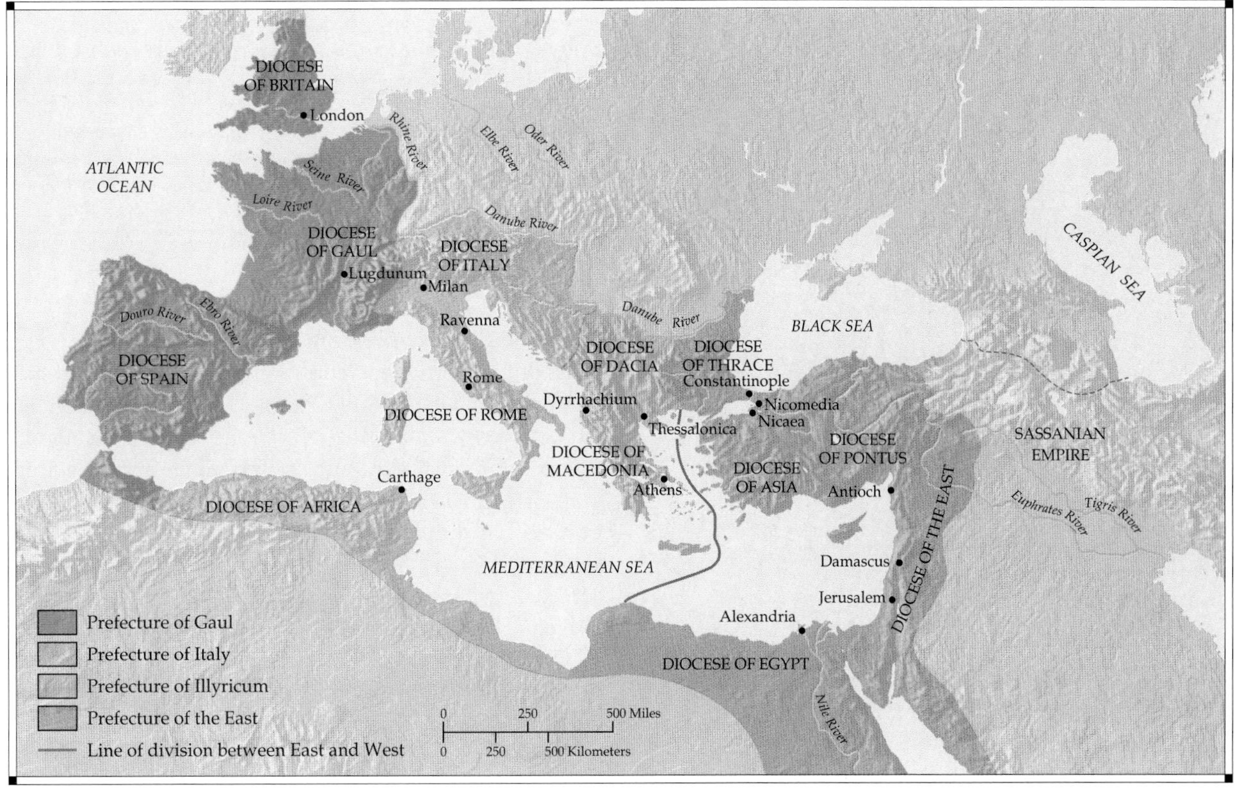

status, building on the sun god cult and inflating the image of emperor to enhance the political power of the office. But whereas Diocletian may have ruled as a god, he had the soul of a bureaucrat when he turned to the problems facing Rome. He inaugurated reforms that reined in the rebellious army, contained barbarian incursions from beyond the borders, and restored modest economic prosperity for most of the fourth century.

Diocletian's efforts to restructure the government met with mixed success. His greatest reform was the division of the empire into two separate areas. In the West, Rome still served as the ceremonial capital, although Ravenna became the imperial residence, and thus the actual capital, for several decades. The Eastern Empire was ultimately centered in Byzantium (now Istanbul, Turkey), renamed Constantinople by Diocletian's successor, Constantine (Map 7.1). Diocletian's plan for administering this vast empire under a tetrarchy, or a rule by four, proved unworkable, however. Each half of the empire was governed by two tetrarchs, an Augustus supported by a Caesar, but civil war among rival tetrarchs only made an already confused situation worse (Figure 7.2). A third reform—dividing the empire into prefectures and subdividing these into dioceses—made the vast state more centralized. But the consequences were reduced efficiency and increased bureaucracy as officials multiplied at all levels.

In addition, Diocletian could not control inflation, even by freezing wages and prices, and the old tax system could not finance the enlarged army and the expanded state bureaucracy. To ensure that taxes continued to flow into the treasury, he forced citizens to retain their occupations and sons to inherit their fathers' careers as well as their tax burdens. Rural laborers coped with this new tax code by attaching themselves to landed estates, and thus the small independent farmer disappeared—the class that had made republican Rome great. Money virtually passed out of circulation, and the economy moved toward a barter system. Citizens now paid taxes in goods or labor or supplied recruits for the army.

One of Diocletian's reforms offers insight into the position of women in Rome. Before Diocletian's reign, women, except for wealthy heiresses, were not counted in the state census, presumably because of male prejudice and because women were thought to contribute little to the overall economy. In his effort to rescue the state from chaos, Diocletian reversed that policy and began to include women and their wealth in census data. Still, old attitudes died hard, and women were not counted as the equivalent of men; in rural Thrace, for example, two women counted as one man.

Figure 7.2 *Diocletian's Tetrarchy.* Ca. 300. Porphyry, approx. 51". St. Mark's cathedral, Venice. *In this group portrait of the tetrarchs, the four rulers—two Augusti, or leaders, joined by their two Caesars, or successors—stand clasping shoulders to signify their unity and loyalty. By this time, the political leaders were no longer wearing imperial togas, as can be seen in the figures' cloaks, tunics, and hats; but the eagle-headed swords and decorated scabbards show that fine workmanship in armor was still practiced in late Rome. Despite the solidarity suggested by the sculpture, the tetrarchy was not a successful reform of the imperial administration.*

The Great Persecution and Christian Toleration For most of his reign, Diocletian ignored the growing shift from a polytheistic state to an increasingly monotheistic Christian state. But in 303 he began the Great Persecution, and although he retired in 305, for eight years the imperial policy was to stamp out Christianity. The emperors forbade Christian worship, destroyed churches and books, rebuilt pagan temples, arrested bishops, and imposed a religious test on all citizens. The number of Christians who actually died in the Great Persecution is unclear, but the government's policy ultimately failed, for the killings strengthened the church, and the courage of Christian martyrs won many converts.

The Great Persecution suddenly ceased in 311, and in 313 toleration was restored to Christians by the Edict of Milan, also known as the Peace of the Church, at the order of the emperor Constantine, a convert to Christianity (Figure 7.3). The Christian community welcomed this opportunity to advance its interests in the state. Priests joined army units, and bishops attended the imperial court. Throughout the empire, Constantine's policies expanded the restored faith, returned confiscated property to the church, built new churches, and gave tax exemptions to bishops.

Constantine, who after 324 ruled in both the East and the West, built his eastern capital, Constantinople, as a fully Christian city. Dedicated in 330 on the site of ancient Byzantium, Constantinople was endowed with churches, a Senate building, and mansions for the senators. Thick walls and water surrounded these

Figure 7.3 Colossal Statue of Constantine. Ca. 313. Marble. Palazzo dei Conservatori, Rome. *Like Diocletian, Constantine consciously nurtured the image of the emperor as a larger-than-life figure. To enhance this image, he commissioned a huge statue of himself, perhaps ten times life size, to stand in the gigantic basilica (which he had also built) in the Roman Forum. All that remains of the statue today are the head, which measures over 8 feet tall, a hand, and some pieces of the limbs. The monument signaled the climax of the emperor cult and the beginning of its decline. With the spread of Christianity, rulers were no longer viewed as gods.*

magnificent buildings, turning the city into an almost impregnable fortress. The choice of this site for the new capital also showed Constantine's recognition of the superior vitality and wealth of the East when compared with the Western Empire.

Constantine's successors supported the spread of the church, and by 395 most of the population was nominally Christian. Christianity adapted to Rome's values, promising victory to Roman armies and a bountiful life to believers. But more important, the Christian religion attracted followers who responded to its ideal of charity and its belief in the spiritual worth of the poor.

Early Christian Controversies As Christians became a majority within the empire, their success magnified the deep divisions within the faith. Unlike other cults, Christianity developed a creed, or set of authorized doctrines, which church leaders imposed on believers. Those who differed were excommunicated as heretics. Moreover, since the emperors were now Christians, the state became entangled in the new religion's problems. Distressed by church squabbles, Constantine tried to end a major controversy over the relationship of Jesus to God. The followers of the priest Arius [uh-RYE-uhs] maintained that Jesus' nature was similar to the divine, a belief that came to be known as Arianism. Those who supported deacon, later bishop, Athanasius [ath-uh-NAY-zhus] believed that the natures of Jesus and God were identical. For Christians, fundamental issues were at stake, such as whether Jesus was eternal and whether God had made the ultimate sacrifice for humanity. To reconcile the competing factions, Constantine, in 325, called a church council at Nicaea in Asia Minor. Under his guidance, the council issued the Nicene Creed, which proclaimed in favor of Athanasius.

Arianism, though condemned, divided the church for decades and remained strong in the church's ruling hierarchy. In addition, most of the Germanic tribes moving into the empire became Christians through the efforts of Ulfilas [UHL-fuh-las], a fellow German and an Arian bishop. Ulfilas's converts were treated as enemies of the true faith, for intolerant orthodox Christians recognized no difference between pagans and Christian heretics.

Despite these difficulties, Christianity continued to grow. At the same time, an ascetic Christian movement was sweeping across the empire, taking two forms. Both groups of ascetics believed that the world was evil and must be shunned, but they differed over the best way to achieve salvation. Pachomius [puh-KOH-me-uhs] founded an isolated community in which followers pursued perfection through a life of self-denial and moral rigor. His contemporary Antony chose the solitary life of a hermit, seeking union with God through his individual efforts. Ultimately the community, rather than the solitary, style became the dominant form of Christian asceticism, evolving into monasticism in succeeding decades.

Paganism lost all official support during the reign of the emperor Theodosius I [the-uh-DOH-she-uhs], called the Great (r. 379–395). The emperor and the law courts ignored the rights of non-Christians, destroyed non-Christian images and temples, and made Christianity the state religion. Although paganism was eradicated in the urban areas, it survived in the countryside, kept alive by oral traditions, protected by an ingrained conservatism, and hidden behind a Christian veneer.

Christian Rome and the End of the Western Empire, 395–476

Despite Diocletian's reforms, Rome ultimately faced insoluble problems: an increasingly non-Roman army, a growing state bureaucracy, and a shrinking tax base. When new waves of Germans began to sweep through the Western Empire in the fifth century, the Roman rulers were unable to assimilate them. The German Visigoths sacked Rome in 410, and a humbled Senate paid a hefty ransom to them.

While the Visigoths attacked Rome, the Saxons, Angles, and Jutes from the north invaded Britain, ending its ties to the empire. The Vandals raged through France and Spain, creating a North African kingdom in 442 and sacking Rome in 455. Burgundians settled in central France after 430. Elsewhere, minor tribes exploited Roman weakness.

Western society changed radically. Town life all but disappeared, leaving only noisy metropolises and the silent countryside. Powerful landowners took over many governmental functions, and their isolated and relatively secure estates attracted desperate city people seeking rural refuge. Thus began the economic and social institutions of the Middle Ages.

The Roman Senate and the church responded to the disintegrating conditions quite differently. When Ravenna became the working capital of the Western Empire in the fourth century, the Senate was reduced to the status of a ceremonial body. Yet the senators still collected rents on their estates, doubling the fees when they could. The church's response was more praiseworthy. Some church leaders used the crisis to stamp out troublesome heresies; but, more positively, others offered food and shelter to the impoverished and comfort to the grieving.

PERSONAL PERSPECTIVE

PAULINA
Epitaph for Agorius Praetextatus

Paulina, a Roman matron, composed this inscription for the tomb of her husband of forty years, Agorius Praetextatus (d. 384), an illustrious figure in religion, philosophy, letters, and public life. Although Christianity was rapidly replacing paganism at this time, Paulina praises her husband not only for his teachings but also for his spiritual guidance in pagan worship.

My parents' bright fame gave me nothing greater
than this—
that, at the time we married, I was thought worthy
of you.
Yet my whole light and glory is my husband's name,
yours, Agorius, who, born of proud ancestry,
make radiant your land, the senate, and your wife,
by your mind's integrity, your actions and
aspirations—
you who have reached the highest peak of excellence.

. . . .

[Y]ou, loyal initiate in the holy
mysteries, bury their insights deep within your mind;
instructed, you worship a manifold divinity
and generously make your wife your comrade
in rites of gods and men: faithful to you, she shares
your thought.

. . . .

Husband, by your good teaching you liberate me,
innocent and modest, from the bond of death,
you lead me into temples, dedicate me to gods;
with you as my witness, I am steeped in all the
mysteries,

. . . .

you teach me the triple secret of Hecate, whom I serve,
and make me worthy of Demeter's liturgy.
Because of you, everyone lauds me as blessed
and holy: it is you who show me to be good, and so
I who was unknown am known throughout the
world—
how could I fail to please, since you are my husband?

. . . .

How happy I'd have been had the gods let my
husband live on—yet in the end I *am* happy:
I am and have been yours, and soon, after my death,
I shall be yours.

The end of the Western Empire came swiftly when Odoacer [oh-doh-AH-suhr], the leader of a troop of Germans, defeated a Roman army in 476, deposed the young ruler, Romulus Augustulus, and sent the symbols of office to the Eastern emperor in Constantinople, thereby signaling that centralized rule had ended in the West. Odoacer prepared to rule not as a Roman emperor but as a Germanic king in northern Italy. The Western Empire was in ruins, fractured into numerous independent Germanic kingdoms.

THE TRANSITION FROM CLASSICAL HUMANISM TO CHRISTIAN CIVILIZATION

Between 284 and 476, Roman civilization moved through two stages, both of which bristled with bitter pagan and Christian tensions. The first phase, which coincided with Diocletian's reforms, was paganism's last flowering; and the second phase, which began when the empire started to break apart after Constantine's reign, was a dynamic Christian age.

Literature, Theology, and History

During Rome's last two centuries, secular writers and Christian writers competed for the hearts and minds of educated Romans through poems, treatises, letters, and essays. The secular authors, who felt threatened by Christian activity and thought, preserved Classical forms and values in their writings. They turned to the humanistic tradition for inspiration and guidance because they believed that their morals and culture were undergirded by Rome's old religion and the farmer-soldier values. Nonetheless, these writers' romantic views of the past were distorted by nostalgia and veneration for a Rome that either was no more or had never been (Figure 7.4).

Secular literature declined in the late empire, and writers did not experiment with new styles or attempt to modify established forms. No one wrote plays, novels, or epics. As a group, the secular Roman authors reflected a growing sense of a lost age. With the exception of a few poets, they seemed unable to define or to analyze the profound changes occurring in their own lifetime.

Figure 7.4 The House of Amor and Psyche (replacement copy of statuary). Fourth century. Ostia, Italy. *The non-Christian elite of late Rome still revered their Classical past, as shown by this sculpture of Amor and Psyche, the famed lovers from Greek legend, found in the private residence of a wealthy Roman. The erotic pair stood in one of four elegantly decorated, intimate bedrooms, which were dimly lit by small windows and lined in white marble. The tale still caught the fancy of sophisticated Romans living in isolated splendor, perhaps reminding them of the glories of a former age.*

The other group of writers, the Christians, looked to the future and a new world to come. They were convinced that Rome was not only dying but also not worth saving. After Constantine decreed toleration for Christians in 313, these authors moved into the mainstream and slowly began to overshadow their pagan rivals. The bitter differences of opinion between them and the pagans, which characterized the late fourth century, faded in the early fifth century. By then Christian literature had triumphed, though it remained deeply indebted to Greco-Roman thought and letters.

The Fathers of the Church By about 300, Christian writers began to find a large audience as their religion continued to win converts among the educated. Although they extolled the virtues and benefits of the new faith, they did not necessarily abandon Classical philosophy and literature; they believed that some of these writings conveyed God's veiled truth prior to the coming of Christ, and thus they combined Classical with biblical learning. No longer persecuted, these Christian writers lived either as interpreters of God's word or as bishops. Revered by later ages as the Fathers of the church, they set examples in their personal lives and public deeds. The three most renowned were Ambrose, Jerome, and Augustine. Because of their superior talents, resolute convictions, and commanding personalities, the Fathers not only were powerful figures within the church but also often intervened in secular matters, instructing the local authorities and even the emperors. Moreover, their writings laid the foundation of medieval Christian doctrine and philosophy.

The first of these men, Ambrose (about 340–397), devoted his life to affairs of the church (Figure 7.5). Born into a well-established Christian family (his sister was a nun), he was trained in the Greco-Roman classics, from which he drew material for sermons, tracts, and letters. Ambrose vigorously opposed the Arian heresy, and as bishop of Milan he aided the urban poor and the victims of barbarian assaults. In scholarly sermons, he condemned the emperors for the social injustices of their reigns. His letters shed light on problems of church government, and his treatises analyzed controversies dividing the church. Ambrose's hymns, perhaps his most memorable contribution, introduced to the Western church another way for Christians to praise their God and enrich their ceremonies.

The second major church Father, Jerome (about 340–420), wrote extensively on religious issues, but his most enduring work was his translation of the Bible into Latin from Greek and Hebrew sources. The Vulgate (from *vulgus*, "common people"), as his version is called, was composed in the common speech of his day; the mark of his Bible's success is that, with some revisions, it remains the standard of the Roman Catholic Church today. Like Ambrose, Jerome received a Classical education. Later, after settling in Bethlehem, he founded a monastery, where he devoted most of his days to his translations of the scriptures. His reclusive habits and his harshly critical opinions of Roman society made him an unattractive figure to his enemies. Yet, as with the other Fathers, Jerome's ascetic life inspired both his own generation and later Christians to emulate his strict denial of personal pleasure.

Of all the Fathers, Augustine (354–430) exercised the greatest influence on Christianity. In his youth in North Africa, he studied Classical literature and thought, including Neo-Platonism (see Chapters 5 and 6). Augustine then journeyed, via Rome, to Milan, where he met Ambrose, whose persuasive sermons assisted in his conversion. Augustine, convinced of Christianity's intellectual integrity and spiritual vitality, retired to North Africa and dedicated himself to the spread of his new faith. However, his winning personality and administrative skills soon propelled him into church politics.

Augustine joined in the debates raging in the church. During his lifetime, his writing came to repre-

Figure 7.5 *Ambrose.* Ca. 470. Church of Sant'Ambrogio, Chapel of San Vittore in Ciel d'Oro, Milan. *This portrait of Ambrose conveys some of the spiritual intensity of the powerful fourth-century bishop of Milan. The work is one of few mosaics that survived the destruction brought by Germanic assaults in northern Italy. Although the artist shows some feeling for the shape and movement of the body, the mosaic strongly reflects the artistic ideals developing in the eastern provinces: frontality, flatness, enlarged eyes, and stylized pose.*

sent the voice of orthodox beliefs. He opposed the Donatists, who claimed that a priest's sin would make the sacraments useless. Augustine's position—that each sacrament worked in and of itself—became the church's official stand. But his greatest fury was against Pelagianism, which asserted that good works could earn salvation for a sinner. Augustine's argument—that salvation can be achieved only by God's grace—rested on his rejection of free will and his insistence on original sin. Once again, he spoke for orthodoxy.

During a long, active life, Augustine wrote many kinds of religious works, but looming over them all are his two major achievements: his *Confessions* and *The City of God.* The *Confessions,* written at the end of the fourth century, trace his search for intellectual and spiritual solace and detail his dramatic conversion. In this spiritual autobiography, he castigates himself for living a sinful, sensual life. Although he was remorseful and laden with guilt for not having found God sooner, he came to believe that his efforts to understand the world by studying Greco-Roman philosophy, literature, and religion affirmed his desire to search for life's ultimate truths.

His conversion occurred in a garden in Milan, where a child's voice commanded him to read the scripture. Opening the Bible at random, he read from Paul, who directed him to arm himself with Jesus Christ as a way of combating the sins of the flesh. Upon reading this passage Augustine wrote: "The light of confidence flooded into my heart and all the darkness of doubt was dispelled." Now certain of his faith, he dedicated himself to his new mission, adopted an ascetic style of life, and, ultimately, accepted church leadership as the bishop of Hippo, in North Africa. Augustine's convictions, so forcefully expressed, helped to raise the standards of Christian literature in the final years of the Roman Empire.

In contrast to the autobiographical *Confessions, The City of God* offered a theological interpretation of history. In this work, written soon after the Visigoths sacked Rome in 410, Augustine addresses the central question confronting the Romans of that generation: Why was their empire subjected to so many catastrophes? To those who blamed the Christians, he replied that the decline of Rome was part of God's plan to prepare the world for the coming of a divine kingdom on

PERSONAL PERSPECTIVE

St. Jerome
Secular Education; The Fall of Rome

In this passage, St. Jerome defends his use of examples from non-Christian literature in his writings and describes the slide of Rome into chaos. He believed that knowledge of the classics would be necessary in the new world that was emerging.

You ask me at the close of your letter why it is that sometimes in my writings I quote examples from secular literature and thus defile the whiteness of the church with the foulness of heathenism. I will now briefly answer your question. . . . Who is there who does not know that both in Moses and in the prophets there are passages cited from Gentile books and that Solomon proposed questions to the philosophers of Tyre and answered others put to him by them. . . . That leader of the Christian army, that unvanquished pleader for the cause of Christ skillfully turns a chance inscription into a proof of the faith. For he had learned from the true David to wrench the sword of the enemy out of his hand and with his own blade to cut off the head of the arrogant Goliath. . . .

I shudder when I think of the catastrophes of our time. For twenty years and more the blood of Romans has been shed daily between Constantinople and the Julian Alps. . . . How many of God's matrons and virgins, virtuous and noble ladies, have been made the sport of these brutes! Bishops have been made captive, priests and those in minor orders have been put to death. Churches have been overthrown, horses have been stalled by the altars of Christ, the relics of martyrs have been dug up. . . .

The Roman world is falling: yet we hold up our heads instead of bowing them.

earth. If the city fell, it was best for the human race. Augustine expounded and reinforced this argument in the first ten books of *The City of God* as he attacked Greco-Roman philosophies and religions.

In the concluding twelve books of the work, he elaborated his view of world history, which relied on the Hebrew experience and Christian sources. At the heart of his argument lay what he called the two cities in history, the City of God and the City of Man. The inhabitants of the City of God were predestined to be saved, but the citizens of the City of Man were condemned to hell. Augustine predicted that the future would eventually expose the nature of the two cities: The City of Man would be destroyed, but the City of God—composed of Christians on their way to heaven—would last forever. In the City of God, the saved would enjoy an eternal happiness that paganism had promised but could not deliver.

Augustine completed *The City of God* shortly before his death and as the Vandals were approaching his city of Hippo. When Augustine's view of history seemed to be validated by the fall of Rome, his fame began to mount. For many centuries, he was venerated by Christians as the supreme authority on nearly every major theological issue.

Church History In addition to theology, early Christian writing included a new literary genre—church history. Eusebius [you-SEE-be-uhs] (about 260–about 340), bishop of Caesarea in Palestine from 314 until his death, made no claims to impartiality in his *History of the Christian Church.* It makes the bishops the heroes, for Eusebius believed that they ensured the truth of Christianity. He also charted the church's spiritual, intellectual, and institutional life in its martyrs, thinkers, and leaders from its earliest days until 324. Although he is generally reliable in his discussions, modern scholars fault him for siding with the faction that was working to make the bishop of Rome the head of the church in the West.

Written in Greek, Eusebius's history was inspired by the secular Greco-Roman historians, and he followed them in quoting from written sources. He consulted both the Old and the New Testaments, Christian scholars, and the Greek classics, including Homer and Plato. Eusebius's historical account of the early church gained authority from his background. Having been jailed twice and having survived the Great Persecution, he appeared to prove God's power in the world. He also baptized Constantine and delivered the opening oration at the Council of Nicaea.

The Visual Arts

In late Rome, secular and Christian art underwent major transformations. In terms of patronage, tastes shifted as the emperors' dictates were first challenged by the early Christian communities and then forced to bow to the triumphant church. In aesthetic terms,

Figure 7.6 Christian Orpheus with Animals. Fifth century. Ivory, 6⁵⁄₁₆ × 5⅛″. Abbey Museum, San Colombano, Italy. *This carving appears to have a secular theme: the mythological Greek figure Orpheus bringing harmony to the animal kingdom with the music he plays on his lyre. But Christians used Orpheus as a symbol of Christ, the Messiah, who brings universal peace and harmony. Because this container is intended to carry the Eucharist, it is identified as a work of Christian art.*

Classical forms and values yielded to a **symbolic realism** in imperial secular art and, later, to abstract spiritual values in Christian works. In geographic terms, church art and architecture in the Eastern Empire moved further away from Greco-Roman ideals, even though the artists and builders continued to modify Classical forms and subjects to fit their faith's themes and needs (Figure 7.6). A striking example of this trend is the art and architecture of Ravenna, the working capital of the Western Empire. Ravenna naturally had strong political ties with the East, and Ravenna's artistic monuments borrowed heavily from Eastern styles and schools.

Architecture In the late third century, Diocletian revitalized architecture, following an unproductive period during the previous fifty years of political turmoil. As a part of his efforts to restore centralized rule, Diocletian used art, specifically architecture, as a sign of his new power. Constantine followed Diocletian's lead until the Edict of Milan in 313, after which he promoted Christian architecture and art. He then launched a building campaign of churches and shrines across the empire. Except for the brief reign of Julian (360–363), who renounced Christianity and tried to restore paganism, the later emperors patronized Christian forms and styles, and pagan tastes and schools disappeared.

During the fifth century, the bishops began to vie with the emperors in erecting Christian centers of worship. The invisible forms of the underground church—rooms in private homes, isolated buildings, and converted pagan temples—were abandoned in favor of new standardized structures such as baptisteries and basilicas. Architects, craftspeople, and artists traveled throughout the empire, directing their energies into glorifying the new official religion.

As part of his imperial reforms, Diocletian built a palace on the Dalmatian coast (Croatia), where he spent the last twelve years of his life. Strategically located halfway between the Western and Eastern centers of power, his residence resembled a Roman camp in its symmetrical layout (Figure 7.7). The palace serves as a fitting monument for this soldier who re-

Figure 7.7 Floor Plan of Diocletian's Palace. Ca. 300. *The almost square enclosure of the palace, surrounded by four high walls and anchored by tall towers at each corner and at each side of the entrance gates, contained the living quarters of the emperor, his tomb, and a temple to Jupiter that was one of the last pagan shrines built before the triumph of Christianity. A thoroughfare running from the east to the west gate and intersecting the main north-south road in the center of the complex divided the fortress-palace into four sections.*

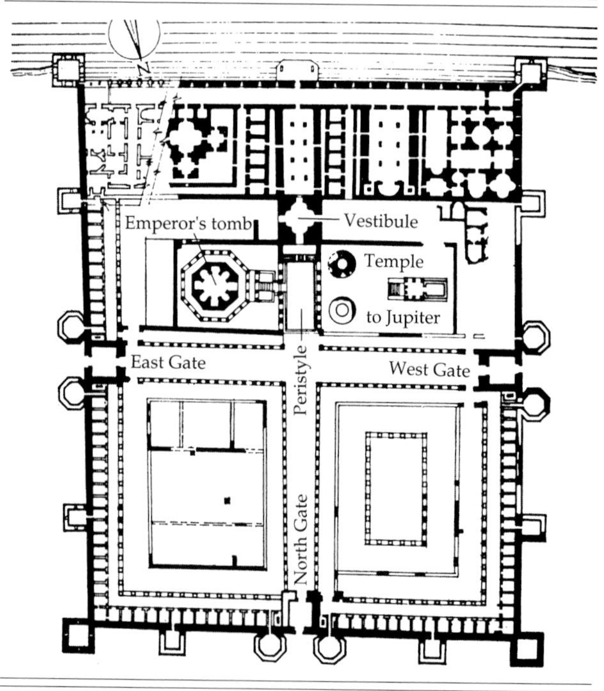

Figure 7.8 Diocletian's Palace. Ca. 300. Split, Croatia. *The peristyle, or colonnaded courtyard, screened off the buildings on the left and right, enhanced the enclosed atmosphere, and focused attention on the vestibule. Behind the peristyle, on the left, stood Diocletian's tomb (now a church) and, on the right, the Temple to Jupiter (now the Baptistery of St. John).*

Figure 7.9 Arch of Constantine. 312–315. Ht. 68′ 10″. Rome. *The frieze that winds around the monument narrates the emperor's preparations for war, his victory, and his triumphant entry into Rome. The scenes depicted on the Arch of Constantine, like those on Trajan's Column, memorialized the Roman ruler's presence at every stage of a military campaign.*

stored law and order to a world racked by civil war and incompetent rulers.

Visitors entered the palace by the main gate on the north side and walked along a path lined with columns across the central intersection and into the **peristyle,** or colonnaded courtyard (Figure 7.8). Those who traveled this far would be reminded of the emperor's presence by such architectural features as the long entranceway, the domed vestibule, and the grandiose courtyard. Beyond the vestibule, on the south side bordering the sea, were the imperial apartments, the guards' barracks, rooms for private audiences, and banquet halls. This residence incorporated nearly all the major designs and techniques, including the arch and mortar mixtures, known to Roman builders. More important, its impressive splendor symbolized divine authority combined with secular political power.

Just as Diocletian's palace was one of the last pagan edifices, the Arch of Constantine was literally the last pagan triumphal arch (Figure 7.9). The arch was erected to celebrate the emperor's victory in 312, which led to the issuing of the Edict of Milan. This well-proportioned monument with its triple arches evolved from the Arch of Titus with its single opening (see Figure 5.18). The circular **medallions** set between the detached columns on the side arches help to balance these smaller arches with the central arch. The decorated **attic,** or crown of the arch, with its statues of Germanic peoples, blends well with the lower sections. The Senate and the Roman people, according to the inscription, gratefully dedicated this arch to Constantine for his deeds as their liberator from civil war and as their new emperor.

Much of the decoration was borrowed from other monuments; for example, some of the reliefs and carvings came from works honoring the victories of Trajan, Hadrian, and Marcus Aurelius; and where a likeness of the emperor is intended, the original has been remodeled to resemble Constantine (see Figure 7.16). Despite Constantine's celebrated conversion to Christianity, however, the arch clearly reflects a strong pagan influence. The symbols and figures stress human action, and only one small frieze hints at divine intervention.

The shift from pagan to Christian architecture began after 313 under Constantine's inspiration and patronage. He ordered the building of churches as places of worship for congregations and as memorials at holy spots in Rome, Palestine, and other parts of the empire. Financed and supported by the state, this ambitious enterprise resulted not only in the spread of Christian-

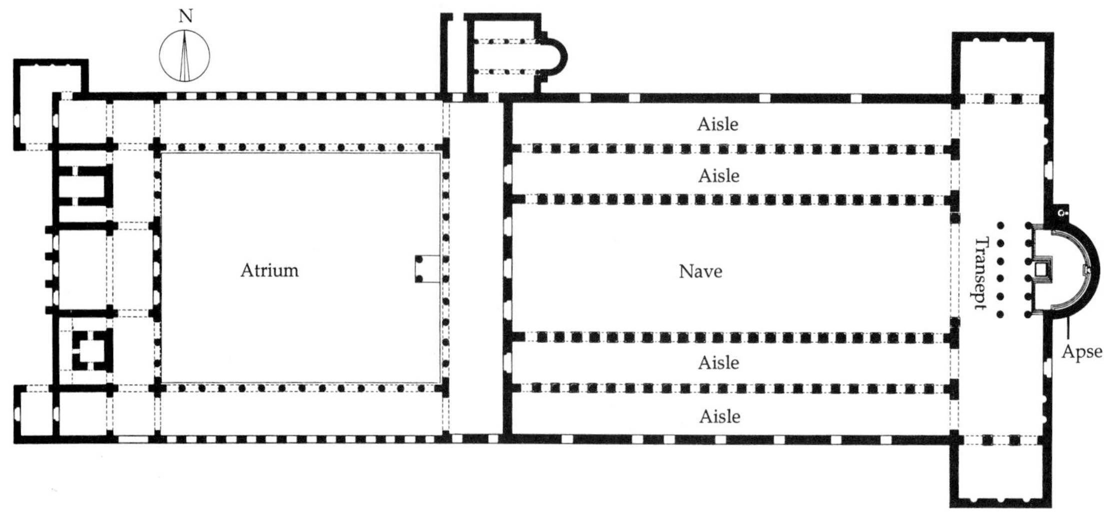

Figure 7.10 Floor Plan of Old St. Peter's Basilica. Ca. 330. Rome. *Old St. Peter's Basilica was the most important structure in Christian Europe until it was demolished in the early sixteenth century to make way for the present St. Peter's. Constantine dedicated Old St. Peter's on the spot believed to be the burial site of Peter, whom the church considered the successor to Jesus. Of the original basilica nothing remains, but sixteenth-century drawings show that it was cruciform (cross-shaped), had a wide central nave with two aisles on either side, and was fronted by an atrium, where worshipers washed their hands and faces before entering the sanctuary.*

ity but also in the founding of new artistic values and architectural forms. The basic design of the churches that Constantine had constructed was derived from the **basilica,** a large enclosed rectangular structure that dated back to the second century B.C. and by the early empire was often built to house marketplaces or public assembly halls.

Although basilicas varied in detail, the basic form used for churches was simple: an oblong hall with an **apse,** or curved wall, at the eastern end. Two rows of parallel columns usually divided the hall into a central area, or **nave,** and two side **aisles.** The roof was taller over the nave section, and **clerestory windows** were set high in the outside nave walls to let in light. The apse, where ceremonies were performed or where the holy relics were placed, was often screened off from the worshipers, who stood in the nave. In some structures, there was an **atrium,** or open courtyard, in front of the main hall.

No fourth-century Roman basilica churches remain, but drawings, such as that of the floor plan of the basilica of Old St. Peter's, suggest their appearance (Figure 7.10). St. Peter's Basilica, built to mark the grave of the apostle who, by tradition, founded the church in Rome, included a **transept,** or crossing section, that intersected the nave at the apse end of the building, making it **cruciform** (cross-shaped). This first St. Peter's Basilica served as a shrine for thousands of pilgrims and, in its early years, as a burial ground for Christians.

Constantine ordered the construction of many similar buildings around the empire. In the provincial outpost of Trier, an important administrative and commercial center on the Moselle River (in modern Germany), Constantine erected a complex of government buildings, including an imperial residence and a large basilica that was used as an assembly hall (Figure 7.11). Originally, an atrium fronted the basilica, and the hall connected to other buildings. Its heavily emphasized vertical supports, two tiers of rounded windows, and large apse established certain basic features that were incorporated into later churches, such as Sta. Maria Maggiore in Rome, built by a fifth-century pope (Figure 7.12). By this date not only had Christians taken over Classical learning as a tool for studying God's word, but they had also Christianized the pagan basilica. Sta. Maria Maggiore is typical of early churches in its Ionic columns and mosaics from the Greek tradition. By using existing models, Christians not only satisfied their own religious needs but also kept alive the Greco-Roman architectural tradition.

A second important design in Christian architecture was the round or polygonal structure topped by a dome. One of the earliest circular buildings (according to tradition, erected by Constantine as a tomb for his daughter) still stands in Rome. Now known as the Church of Sta. Costanza, the round edifice is a drum with a covering dome (Figure 7.13). As these polygonal structures evolved, they came to serve primarily as **baptisteries**—that is, places set aside for baptism. The baptistery was usually separated from the basilica be-

Figure 7.11 Constantine's Basilica in Trier. 310. Trier, Germany. *This basilica served first as an audience hall for Roman officials and then as a medieval castle; today it serves as a Lutheran church. Although it is an impressive 220 feet long, 91 feet wide, and 100 feet high, its plan is simple: a narrow hall without aisles and an apse at the eastern end. Around the exterior of the apse, two stories of round arched windows give a graceful appearance by creating the impression of an arcade. That such a monumental basilica was erected so far from the Roman capital showed the impact of imperial art in the distant provinces.*

Figure 7.12 Sta. Maria Maggiore. Interior, nave. 432–440. Rome. *As Germanic invaders were ending centralized rule in the West, Pope Sixtus III (432–440) and his successors to 470 launched a Classical revival, drawing on the designs of late Classical Roman buildings of the second, third, and fourth centuries. The basilica of Sta. Maria Maggiore is the best surviving example of this revival, as evidenced in the nave's fusion of Classical features—Ionic columns, coffered ceiling, marble floor, clerestory windows topped with rounded pediments, and Classical entablature—into a majestic, symmetrical design.*

Figure 7.13 Church of Sta. Costanza. Fourth century. Rome. *The twelve pairs of columns were carved specifically for the rotunda, the circular area beneath the dome, rather than taken from other buildings, as was often the case in late Rome. The columns support the arches, above which are windows placed in the drum.*

cause Christians believed that the unbaptized were unworthy to enter the sanctuary and mingle with the members. This design, which originated in the domed rooms of public baths and funerary architecture and whose most impressive realization was the Pantheon (see Figure 5.14), became standardized as an octagon with a domed roof (Figure 7.14).

Sculpture During Diocletian's reign and before Christianity's conquest of the Roman arts, the late empire produced some unique and monumental works, such as the group portrait of Diocletian's tetrarchy, carved in red porphyry (see Figure 7.2) and the colossal statue of Constantine, a composite of marble and metal (see Figure 7.3). The generalized features of these figures show

Figure 7.14 Baptistery at Frèjus. Fifth century. Frèjus, France. *The Baptistery at Frèjus is one of the earliest surviving examples of the octagonal building. The eight-sided structure has a central dome resting on a solidly constructed drum pierced with windows. At one time it was believed that this style was imported from the East, but now evidence indicates it originated in the West, probably in France.*

Figure 7.15 *The Last Pagan.* Ca. 380–400. Marble, ht. 66″. Museo Ostiense, Ostia, Italy. *Evidently this Roman, clad in the toga of an earlier era, has academic interests, since a set of bound books rests beside his right foot. The drapery is cut at severe angles, which increases the overall effect of this care-laden man. The statue is of Greek marble and stands just under 6 feet tall.*

the trend to symbolic representation characteristic of the art of the late empire and the movement away from the idealized or realistic faces of Classical sculpture. These public works are clearly forms of propaganda art. But Roman artists also continued to execute statues for private citizens, whose changing tastes were typified in a statue of a bedraggled scholar (Figure 7.15). Here the artist has fashioned a realistic work that delves into the psychology of his subject. The man's lined features, worried look, and weary slouch convey resignation and defeat. Symmachus, one of the last learned non-Christians, often visited Ostia, where this statue was found; the sculptor may have been depicting this Roman intellectual.

In addition to free-standing sculptures, relief sculptures continued to be popular in late Roman art. In the Western Empire, the best of these surviving reliefs are the original carvings on the Arch of Constantine. The carvings, coarse and yet stylized, reflect the impact of provincial art on Rome and signify a marked change in the long tradition of secular sculpture in the West. In one of the reliefs, Constantine and those around him are portrayed as distributing the fruits of the empire—a typical theme in Roman art (Figure 7.16). But the figures are depicted more as stereotypes than as real individuals.

Christian sculpture was undergoing aesthetic changes similar to those taking place in secular art. By the end of the third century, Christian art was symbolic in content and **impressionistic** in style (see Chapter 6). Simple representations of Jesus and the apostles had become common in the underground church. In 313, when the Peace of the Church brought Christian art literally aboveground, artists began to receive the support of the Roman state.

Christian Rome's reshaping of the humanistic tradition can be seen in the carvings on sarcophagi. The Roman anxiety about life after death and the pursuit of intellectual matters easily evolved into Christian images and themes. The growing acceptance of burial rather than cremation and the resultant increased demand for sarcophagi afforded many artists new opportunities to express themselves. After about the second century, rich Roman families commissioned artists to decorate the sides of these marble boxes with images of Classical heroes and heroines, gods and goddesses, military and political leaders, and scenes of famous events and battles. The Christians borrowed

Figure 7.16 *The Imperial Bounty,* from the Arch of Constantine. 312–315. Marble, ht. 4′ 3″. Rome. *The style for this relief derived from Trier in Gaul. Unlike Classicism, this provincial style conveyed its message with cartoonlike directness. Constantine, enthroned in the center, divides the panel in two, and officials above dispense coins to the citizens below. Some of the crowd show their eagerness through their upturned heads and reaching hands.*

Figure 7.17 The Plotinus Sarcophagus. Late third century. Marble, ht. 4′ 11″. Lateran Museum, Rome. *This relief may depict Plotinus, a founder of Neo-Platonism, and his admirers. If so, then the scene is ironic, for Neo-Platonist philosophy rejected realistic art, claiming that art should be viewed with the inner eye. This Neo-Platonist belief influenced Christian mysticism, which in turn helped to create the symbolic art of the Middle Ages, an art that used traditional images to express religious faith.*

many of these subjects and transformed them into religious symbols pertaining to salvation and life after death. Thus, although the content of sarcophagus art became Christian after the Peace of the Church, the style remained Classical for some time.

Roman sarcophagi also depicted abstract concepts. For example, a carving of a seated philosopher, surrounded by attentive men and women, represents the life of the mind, its attention directed toward more important matters than earthly delights (Figure 7.17). The carvings, finely executed and well-balanced, capture this philosophical idea through superbly realized human characters. On either side of the philosopher is a female follower. Neo-Platonism appealed to women because it welcomed them equally with men as students of philosophy. Women also responded favorably to its harsh moral code (sparse vegetarian diet, limited sleep, chastity) because it suited their intellectual striving and made them independent of men's sexual control.

Biblical scenes from both the Old and New Testaments continued to appear on sarcophagi throughout

Figure 7.18 Junius Bassus Sarcophagus. Ca. 359. Marble, 8′ long, 5′ wide, 6′ high (including lid). Treasury Museum, St. Peter's, the Vatican. *Called a double-register columnar sarcophagus, this stone coffin is divided into two levels, with each level's sculpture displayed in five niches framed by columns. This sarcophagus with its fine-quality sculpture reflects the high status of the deceased, Junius Bassus, who died while serving as city prefect, the highest official residing in Rome, the head of the Senate. Bassus, as identified on the inscription on the upper edge of the sarcophagus, was also a Christian; he was baptized on his deathbed, a common practice at the time.*

Figure 7.19 Illumination from Vergil's *Aeneid.* Fifth century. 6 × 6″. Vatican Library. *This page from an illustrated manuscript of Vergil's* Aeneid *shows an episode from Book IV. Dido, the Queen of Carthage, and Aeneas seek shelter in a cave from a thunderstorm caused by the goddess Juno, who is plotting to bring them together. Outside the cave wait two guards and their horses. A delightful touch is that one of the guards has turned his shield over his head, using it as an umbrella. Although a charming image, this illumination shows a decline in Classical artistic standards, in the lack of balance and perspective in the design, the absence of structure and proportion in the figures, the masklike faces, and the awkwardly placed arms and hands.*

the empire, illustrating the complex themes and messages of the new faith. One relief, from the Junius Bassus Sarcophagus, is especially rich in biblical imagery (Figure 7.18). The top register, left to right, consists of the sacrifice of Isaac, the arrest of Peter, Christ enthroned over Coelus (the Roman personification of the universe) and giving the Law to two apostles, the arrest of Christ, and the judgment of Pilate. The lower register, left to right, includes the poverty of Job, Adam and Eve, the triumphal entry of Christ into Jerusalem, Daniel in the lions' den, and the arrest of Paul. Christ in all three scenes is portrayed beardless, his typical representation in ancient Christian art. In this relief, the emphasis on Old Testament suffering (Job, Isaac, Adam and Eve, and Daniel) and New Testament martyrdom (Peter and Paul), when viewed within the context of Christ's sacrificial death, points to the belief in salvation through grace.

Painting and Mosaics Unlike architecture and sculpture, painting exhibited no changes directly caused by the Peace of the Church. In the fourth century, Christian frescoes flourished in the Roman catacombs and continued the symbolic, impressionist style of the previous era (see Chapter 6). Non-Christian paintings are extremely scarce from the fifth century, except for a few works such as a collection of illustrations for Vergil's *Aeneid*, probably painted for a wealthy patron. This extensive picture cycle (Figure 7.19), numbering over 225 scenes, recalls the style of earlier paintings, but it is also an early example of a new medium, the illustrated book. Books were now written on vellum, a parchment made from animal skins, and bound in pages rather than written on scrolls. In the Middle Ages, this type of decorated, or illuminated, book became a major art form. In the late empire, however, the form was in its infancy.

A more vital art form was the mosaic, which, as in other art forms, Christians ultimately turned to their

Figure 7.20 *Female Athletes.* Detail from mosaic. 350–400. Villa at Piazza Armerina, Sicily. *This scene may show a female version of games that continued to be conducted in the Christian empire. The mosaic conveys a grace and lightheartedness somewhat at odds with this troubled age and with the changing artistic ideals of Christian art.*

own ends. Pagans continued to place mosaics on both floors and walls, but Christians more often put them on the walls. Christian artists also replaced the stone chips with bits of glass that reflected light, thus adding a glittering, ethereal quality to the basilicas and other buildings.

In the late Roman mosaics, pagan and Christian subjects stand in sharp contrast. Among the many pagan mosaics that survive, one depicting young female athletes from a country villa in Sicily indicates the continued interest of the Romans in the body as the temple of the mind and as an object of admiration (Figure 7.20). The artist has captured the energy and playfulness of these (probably professional) performers in a variety of feats: dancing, running, and exercising. Their movements are realistic, graceful, and strikingly modern. The pagans also liked pictures of young children, or ***putti,*** in the role of adults at work or play or even in religious scenes. In the very first Christian art, some artists adopted this playful genre for scenes of grape harvesting, as in a mosaic from the Church of Sta. Costanza, Rome (Figure 7.21). In Christian art, however, the scene was a disguised representation of the Christian communion, in which wine made from grapes became the blood of Christ.

The *putti* genre proved not to be popular with Christians. More acceptable was art emphasizing the spiritual and otherworldly qualities of saintly figures, such as the mosaic of the church father Ambrose (see Figure 7.5). Where the *putti*'s movements are fluid, his pose is static, and where their bodies are celebrated, the shape of his body is completely concealed under his clothing, in accordance with the church teaching that the body is sinful and should be hidden from view.

Mosaics became one of the dominant art forms in the Eastern Empire and areas influenced by the Eastern rulers, beginning late in the fifth century. In Ravenna, the small cruciform tomb of Galla Placidia [GALL-uh pluh-SID-e-uh], daughter of Theodosius the Great, contains some splendid mosaics that prefigured the Byzantine style, which in succeeding centuries would dominate Christian art in the Eastern Empire. In the mosaics in the tomb of Galla Placidia, scrolls of vines and leaves wind around the ceiling; large flowers, or rosettes, decorate other sections; and animals and saints adorn parts of the curved walls. Over the entranceway stands the youthful shepherd watching over his flock (Figure 7.22). By the fifth century, the rich and the powerful, such as the relatives of Galla Placidia, were honoring the Good Shepherd in their sanctuaries as the giver of eternal life. The mosaics in the tomb of Galla Placidia clearly show the adaptation of Classical models to Christian purposes.

Figure 7.21 Putti *Harvesting Grapes.* Mosaic. Fourth century. Church of Sta. Costanza, Rome. *Besides alluding to communion, this scene illustrates the Christian scripture John 15:1, in which Jesus says, "I am the true vine, and my Father is the vinedresser."* Putti *are depicted trampling grapes and loading grapes into carts pulled by oxen; the rest of the scene is a labyrinth of vines, making up an arbor, amid which other* putti *are gathering grapes. This scene harkens back to representations of the cult of Dionysus; we know it is Christian only because it is in a Christian church.*

Figure 7.22 *The Good Shepherd.* Ca. 450. Mausoleum of Galla Placidia, Ravenna, Italy. *The young, beardless Christ, which was still the accepted image of the Christian savior in the fifth century, supports himself with the cross and feeds the sheep, the symbol of the church, with his right hand. Foliage and plants in the background tie in with similar decorations on the mausoleum's ceilings and walls. Upon entering the small tomb, worshipers would immediately be confronted with this large figure of Christ.*

Music

The music of late Rome was in decline, but Christian music was just beginning to take shape. The Christians took the principles of Greco-Roman music and integrated them with the Jewish tradition of singing the psalms and the liturgy to make music a dynamic part of their church rituals. In later times, this Christian practice gave birth to a rich body of sacred music that included both singers and instrumentalists.

In late Rome, however, sacred music was limited to chanting and unaccompanied singing. The Antioch church, inspired by the congregational singing in Jewish synagogues, developed a new musical genre, the hymn, a song of praise to God. From Antioch the practice of hymn singing spread to Constantinople and Milan and eventually was integrated into the Christian liturgy everywhere. A few hymns survive from the period before Constantine, but only a fragment of musical notation has come to light. As with other ancient music, how it actually sounded can only be a matter of speculation.

Ambrose, bishop of Milan and a powerful influence at the imperial court, stands out among the earliest hymn writers as one of the founders of the Western sacred song. His hymns, which were written in Latin, coincided with a new era in the church; up until the fourth century, the liturgy of the early church was in Greek. Ambrose's Latin hymns were probably meant to be sung antiphonally—that is, with lines sung alternately between a leader and a chorus.

WHY DID ROME FALL?

When the Western Empire collapsed in 476, many forces had been at work in undermining Rome since the end of the second century. During those three centuries, the mounting pressures from the Germanic tribes, the incompetence of the bureaucracy, the politically inert masses, the rampant inflation, the crushing and inequitable tax system, and, above all, the problems associated with a heterogeneous and uncontrollable army had together wrought havoc on the state and society. Considering all these difficulties, the wonder is that the empire was able to be propped up by Diocletian after 284 and to last as long as it did.

Nevertheless, all the foregoing forces, although important, were not as significant a cause of Rome's decline and fall as was the change in the Roman constitution from a republic to an empire. This theory—first advanced by the French philosopher and historian Montesquieu in the eighteenth century—blamed Rome's fall on the moral consequences of the constitutional shift. According to Montesquieu, under the healthy republic, with its separation of political powers, the citizens actively decided their own future. But pressed down by a diseased empire, with power centered in one man in one city, the citizens became pawns of the ruling autocrat. Consequently, toward the end of the empire, corruption engulfed all elements of society, from megalomaniacal emperors, to aristocrats wallowing in luxury, to the masses clamoring for handouts, to the aliens selling their votes for favors.

What effect did the triumph of Christianity have on the fall of Rome? This issue was first raised in the eighteenth century by English historian Edward Gibbon in his *Decline and Fall of the Roman Empire.* Gibbon's thesis was that the coming of Christianity was a major contributing factor in Rome's fall. Gibbon blamed the Christians for focusing on life in heaven rather than on earth and for sapping the military will of the Roman people. A careful review of Rome's last years reveals that Gibbon oversimplified events. Some Christians did avoid military service because of their pacifist ideas, and few Christians felt loyalty to the forms of pagan life. But by the time Christianity was firmly fixed as the official religion, in 395, the empire was already tottering on the brink of annihilation. Thus, there was very little that the Christians, or for that matter any other group, could have done to prevent the fall of Rome.

The Legacy of Late Roman Civilization

Late Roman civilization, as we have described it, constituted the legacy of the ancient world to the next era, the Middle Ages. That legacy was neither the unadulterated humanism of Greece nor the Idea of Rome as formulated in the pre-Christian centuries. Rather, late Roman culture reflected a synthesis of Christian and Greco-Roman values achieved in a changing world. Christian intellectuals valued Greco-Roman thought for the support it lent to the spiritual values that were now considered primary. Late Roman art and architecture also reflected this synthesis of traditions.

This late Roman synthesis of Christian and Greco-Roman values was supremely embodied in the Christian church, including its monastic system. From the fall of Rome until the 1800s, and particularly in the Middle Ages, the church's culture was nearly synonymous with the West's wider culture; to be Western was to be Christian. Church leaders were now the chief patrons of culture, and, as such, they commanded artists to create only religious works, using a symbolic, impressionistic style; they commissioned architects to build churches in the form of Roman basilicas adapted to religious needs and baptisteries based on round, or polygonal, designs; they asked composers to write music for the church liturgy; they authorized scholars to harmonize faith with Greco-Roman thought; and they ordered sacred books to be decorated—manuscript illumination—by gifted artist-clergy. Most notably, church leaders known as the Fathers left an impressive array of writings, including Jerome's Vulgate Bible, Augustine's vast theological works, and Ambrose's hymns, which soon became authoritative. A final church leader with an important legacy was Eusebius, who established the literary form of church history, a popular genre throughout the Middle Ages.

Besides the amalgam of Christianity and humanism, the late Roman period also contributed much of the structure of everyday life to the medieval world. From late Rome came the sharp division of society into aristocratic landowners and dependent agricultural laborers, the emergence of the church in society as a state within the state, the rise of a barter economy, the development of the military power of large-scale landed proprietors, and the ideal of a multiethnic but Christian society. In effect, the late Classical world was the womb from which would emerge the next incarnation of Western institutions as well as the Western humanities.

KEY CULTURAL TERMS

symbolic realism
peristyle
medallion
attic
basilica
apse
nave
aisles
clerestory windows
atrium
transept
cruciform
baptistery
impressionistic
putti

SUGGESTIONS FOR FURTHER READING

PRIMARY SOURCES

St. Augustine. *Confessions.* Translated by R. S. Pine-Coffin. New York: Penguin, 1966. One of the enduring books of Western literature; reveals the anguish and achievements of this influential thinker.

———. *The City of God.* Edited by D. Knowles. New York: Penguin, 1972. A monumental work that illustrates Augustine's blending of Classical and Christian thought.

Staniforth, M., trans. *Early Christian Writings: The Apostolic Fathers.* New York: Penguin, 1968. Useful introduction to the issues and personalities of the early Christian church.

8 THE SUCCESSORS OF ROME

Byzantium, Islam, and the Early Medieval West

When Rome fell in 476, a power vacuum developed in the western Roman lands. Gradually, three new civilizations—Byzantium, Islam, and the Early Medieval West—emerged to compete for control of the Mediterranean basin. Although none succeeded in reviving Roman grandeur or uniting the Mediterranean world, these three contrasting civilizations developed religious and cultural values that today dominate half the globe.

Of the three, the Byzantine Empire (the former Eastern Roman Empire) seemed in 476 to have the greatest prospects for dominance and longevity, with its autocratic government, stable farm economy, Greek intellectual heritage, and what came to be called Orthodox Christianity. (The Eastern Empire is called "Byzantine" because its capital, Constantinople, was founded on the site of the ancient Greek city of Byzantium.) In contrast, Islam did not appear until the seventh century, when it began a meteoric rise and quickly spread across the Mediterranean world. Building on Arabic roots and the new faith propounded by Muhammad, Islamic civilization borrowed freely from the Greco-Roman and Persian heritages to attain a brilliant culture superior in many respects to the cultures of Byzantium and Western Europe.

At the same time, civilization in the West was all but eclipsed, its political and economic systems in disarray and its people huddled in wooden huts beside armed fortresses. In the midst of this chaos, however, a new world was being born, built on Classical ruins, spurred by Germanic energies, and animated by the new Christian ethos. This chapter traces the development of these three varied civilizations (Map 8.1).

◀ The Tomb of Timur Lenk (Tamerlane). Ca. 1403. Samarkand, Uzbekistan.

Map 8.1 THE BYZANTINE, CAROLINGIAN, AND ISLAMIC EMPIRES IN 814, THE YEAR OF CHARLEMAGNE'S DEATH

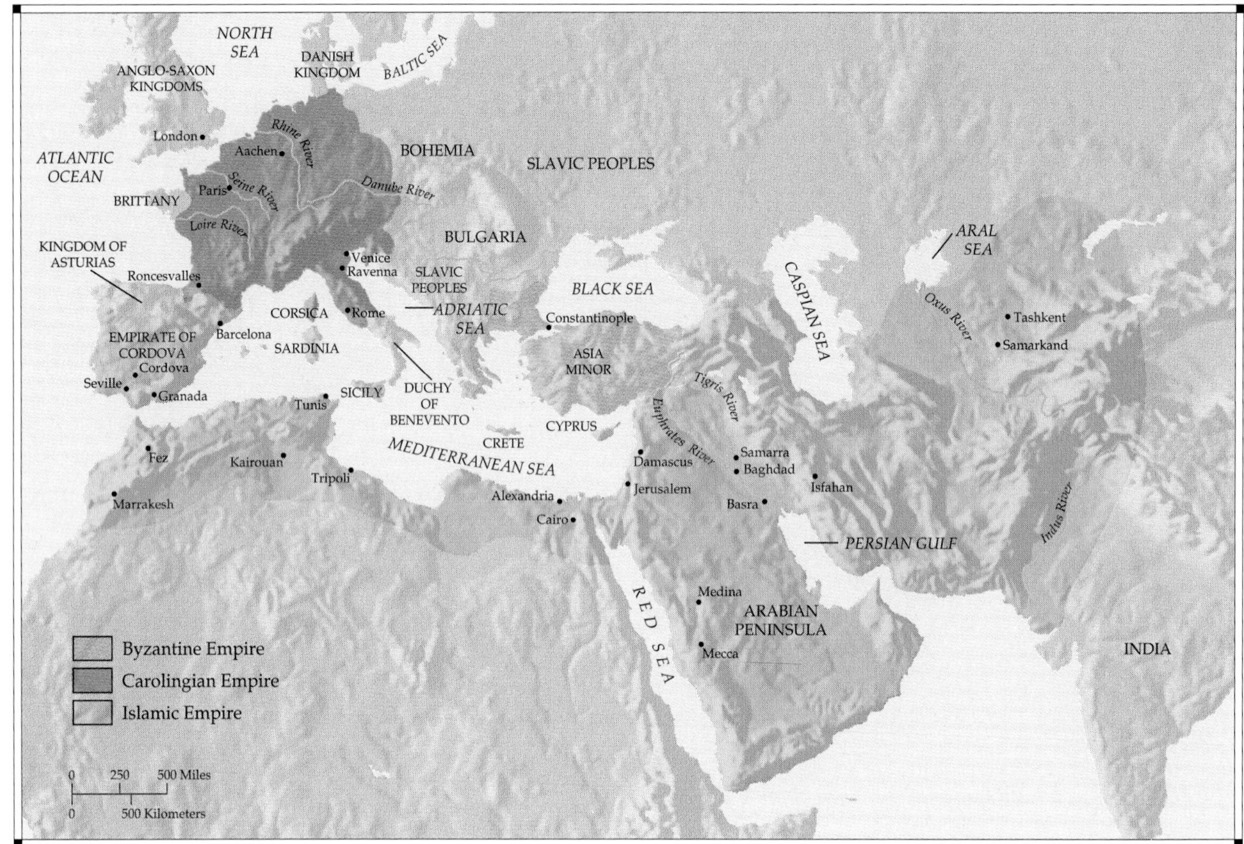

THE EASTERN ROMAN EMPIRE AND BYZANTINE CIVILIZATION, 476–1453

The end of centralized rule in Rome's western lands in 476 had little effect on the Eastern Roman Empire. Diocletian's division of the empire into two administrative halves in the third century had already set the eastern region on a different path. During its one-thousand-year existence, the empire took its Roman heritage and became an autocratic, static entity in a world of great upheaval and movement of populations. The changing boundaries of the Byzantine world tell the story of an empire under continual siege. Byzantium's borders reached their farthest western limits in the sixth century and then contracted over the next eight hundred years. The empire lost territory to the Arabs in the east and to the Bulgars and other groups in the west. Finally, no longer able to defend even the city of Constantinople itself, the empire fell to the Ottoman Turks in 1453.

Although Byzantium was buffeted by rapid and sometimes catastrophic upheavals, great wealth and economic resources allowed the state to survive. The rulers tightly controlled their subjects' economic affairs, a policy that placed state interests above individual gains. A stimulating urban life developed, centered especially in Constantinople, the empire's capital and preeminent city (Figure 8.1). Beyond Constantinople, the countryside was dotted with walled towns and vast farming estates owned by aristocrats and tilled by *coloni,* or serfs. Agriculture remained Byzantium's basic source of wealth.

Even though the frontiers of the empire expanded and contracted over the centuries, its heartland in Greece and Asia Minor remained basically stable. Here, a relatively uniform culture evolved that differed markedly from late Rome and the Medieval West. The Byzantine world gave up its pagan and Latin roots to become a Christian, Greek civilization. The Orthodox Church, led by the patriarch of Constantinople, emerged as a powerful force, but without the independence from secular rulers enjoyed by the Western church and the pope. Greek became the language of church, state, and scholarship, just as Latin served those functions in the West. But, like late Rome and unlike the Medieval West, Byzantium remained characterized by ethnic and racial diversity; new peoples, such as the Serbs and the Bulgarians, helped to ensure

Figure 8.1 Isidore of Miletus and Anthemius of Tralles. Hagia Sophia, Exterior. 532–537. 270′ long × 240′ wide, ht. of dome 180′. Istanbul. *The Byzantine emperors transformed their capital into a glittering metropolis that easily outshone ravaged Rome. The most magnificent building in the city was Hagia Sophia ("Holy Wisdom"), originally built by Justinian as a church. The building's 101-foot diameter makes it the largest domical structure in the world. Two half-domes at either end double the interior length to more than 200 feet. The beauty of Hagia Sophia made the domed church the ideal of Byzantine architecture.*

this diversity as they were slowly assimilated into the Byzantine way of life.

History of the Byzantine Empire

Throughout its history, the Byzantine Empire's fortunes fluctuated depending on its relations with its hostile neighbors. From 476 to 641, the emperors made a valiant but ultimately futile effort to recover the lost western provinces and revive the empire (Timeline 8.1). The memorable emperor Justinian (r. 527–565) conquered several of the Germanic kingdoms that had arisen in the former Western Empire and extended the empire's borders to encompass Italy, southern Spain, and North Africa (Figure 8.2). Justinian's wars exhausted the state treasury, however, leaving his successors unable to maintain the empire.

Between 641 and 867, the second period of Byzantine history, a series of weak rulers lost all the western lands that Justinian had recovered. The emperors were also forced to yield much of Asia Minor to their Arab foes, and in 687 a Bulgarian kingdom was carved out of Byzantine territory in the Balkans. To repel these enemy assaults, Byzantium became more militarized. In the provinces, generals were given vast military and civil powers, and they began to replace the aristocrats as landowners. A style of feudalism—vast estates protected by private armies—slowly arose. Despite the changes in the social structure, important cultural developments occurred, including a major revision of the law code and the establishment of a second university in Constantinople.

With the reign of Basil I (867–886), a new dynasty of capable Macedonian rulers led Byzantium into the Golden Age (867–1081). These rulers again expanded the borders of the empire and restored the state to economic health. Orthodox missionaries eventually tied the peoples of eastern Europe to the religion and civilization of Byzantium, and in the late tenth century they introduced Christianity to Russia. As a result, after the fall of Constantinople in 1453, the Russian state claimed to be the principal heir to the spirituality and culture of Byzantine civilization.

In 1081 an exceptional feudal general, Alexius Comnenus [kahm-NEE-nuhs] (r. 1081–1118), seized the throne, and thus began a new period, characterized by increasing pressure from the West (1081–1261). Despite the energy of Comnenus and his successors, they were unable to solve the empire's social problems. Under the Comneni dynasty, Byzantium became fully militarized and feudalized. The free peasantry disappeared, having been transformed into a vast population of serfs forced to labor on the landlords' estates.

The Comneni rulers tried vainly to win allies, but they were surrounded by enemies—Normans, Seljuk Turks, Hungarians, Serbs, Bulgars, and, after 1095, even the European Crusaders on their way to the Holy Land. In 1204 the soldiers of the Fourth Crusade conquered Constantinople and took over the remaining lands. The empire appeared to be finished except for some scattered holdings in Asia Minor. But, in 1261 Michael Palaeologus [pay-lee-AHL-uh-guhs] (r. 1261–1282) regained Constantinople and breathed some new life into the feeble empire.

The Palaeologian dynasty ruled over the Byzantine world during the fifth and last phase of its history (1261–1453), but eventually it was forced to recognize that the empire was but a diminished Greek state. From 1302 onward, the Ottoman Turks—named for their leader Osman—built an empire on the ruins of the Byzantine Empire. By 1330 this new state had absorbed Asia Minor, and by 1390 Serbia and Bulgaria were Turkish provinces. In 1453 the Turks took Constantinople, ravaging the city for three days, searching for booty and destroying priceless art treasures. Thus ended the last living vestige of ancient Rome. From the ashes of Byzantium rose the Ottoman Empire, which

Timeline 8.1 THE BYZANTINE EMPIRE

476	641	867	1081	1261	1453
Revival of Empire	Withdrawal and Renewal	The Golden Age	The Challenge from the West	Palaeologian Emperors	

- 476: Fall of Rome
- 726–843: Iconoclastic Controversy
- 1054: Schism between Orthodox and Roman churches
- 1453: Fall of Constantinople

Figure 8.2 *Justinian and His Courtiers.* Sixth century. Ravenna, Italy. *This mosaic represents a contemporary portrait of Justinian with his courtiers, including the patriarch of Constantinople, who is holding the bejeweled cross. The luxurious trappings of office—purple robes, jeweled crown, and golden scepter—were calculated to enhance the emperor's earthly dignity. The Byzantine Empire's union of church and state is symbolized by the juxtaposition of the soldiers on the emperor's right with the ecclesiastical officials on his left.*

anchored the southeastern corner of Europe for nearly five hundred years until 1912, when revolutions and wars destroyed it.

Byzantine Culture: Christianity and Classicism

From Rome, Byzantium inherited a legacy of unresolved conflict between Christian and Classical ideals. In the wider Byzantine culture, this conflict was revealed in the division between secular forms of expression, which showed a playful or humorous side of Byzantine life, and religious forms, which were always deeply serious. However, Byzantine culture, whether secular or religious, tended to stress Classical values of serenity, dignity, and restraint. This timeless and even majestic quality was cultivated, perhaps, in compensation for the beleaguered nature of the Byzantine state.

The Orthodox Religion While the bishop of Rome (the pope) was the head of the Christian church in the West, the bishop (or patriarch) of Constantinople was the spiritual and doctrinal head of the Eastern (Orthodox) Church in Byzantium. Many differences existed between the two Christian churches. They disagreed over the issue of whether the pope or a patriarch should lead the church; they also differed in language (Latin in the West, Greek in the East), religious practices (Roman Catholic priests were celibate, Orthodox priests could marry), and fine points of religious doctrine. In 1054 the patriarch of Constantinople refused to yield to the Roman church's demand for submission, and a permanent schism, or split, ended all ties between the two faiths.

The patriarch of Constantinople had to deal with challenges from the pope, rival patriarchs in other Eastern cities, and the Byzantine emperors, who viewed the church as an extension of the government (the patriarchs never had the kind of power enjoyed by the popes). The Eastern Church was also plagued by internal dissension and a variety of heresies.

The most serious issue to confront the Orthodox Church was the Iconoclastic Controversy (726–843), which erupted when the emperor Leo III commanded the removal and destruction of all religious images (Figure 8.3). The iconoclasts, or image-breakers, claimed that the devotion paid to sacred pictures was blasphemous and idolatrous, a belief perhaps inspired by Judaism or Islam, which both strongly condemned the use of religious images. Siding with the iconoclastic emperors were the bishops, the army, and the civil service; opposed were the monks, many of whom lost their lives in the civil unrest that seized the empire. In the West, the papacy refused to join the iconoclastic frenzy. The controversy lasted for over one hundred years, and by the time the Byzantine rulers restored the veneration of icons, nearly all religious pictures had been destroyed by zealous reformers.

Figure 8.3 An Iconoclast Breaking an Image. Miniature from the Studion or Theodore Psalter. 1066. British Library, London. *This miniature painting illustrating the period of the Iconoclastic Controversy is historically inaccurate. It portrays an iconoclast attired as a monk, wearing a flowing robe and sporting a beard. In reality, the monks favored icons and protested their destruction. That the artist has depicted a monk desecrating a religious picture may indicate that the manuscript was commissioned by a patron from the imperial circle, where images were despised.*

Monasticism, which furnished the chief foes of the iconoclastic emperors, was a basic expression of Orthodox piety. Monastic practices began in late Roman Egypt and quickly spread across the Roman world, adapting to local conditions (see Chapter 7). Like Western asceticism, Byzantine monasticism took two forms, hermitic (or isolated) and communal. The monastic communities were basically places where people retreated from the world to lead strictly disciplined lives. For centuries, the monasteries received immense gifts of land and wealth from rulers, merchants, and peasants alike, and eventually they achieved a powerful economic position in Byzantine society.

The most important monastic complex in Byzantium was at Mount Athos, founded in 963 (Figure 8.4). This mountain retreat in northern Greece, which housed about eight thousand monks in the thirteenth century, achieved relative independence from the secular authorities, which may explain how it survived into the twentieth century. The style of Mount Athos—self-governing, self-contained, and committed to study and prayer—influenced monastic development in the Orthodox world.

Law and History From the viewpoint of Western culture, Byzantium's greatest accomplishment was the codification of the Roman law made under the emperor Justinian in the sixth century. The Justinian Code, which summarized a thousand years of Roman legal developments, not only laid the foundation of

Figure 8.4 Mount Athos, Greece. *Since the tenth century, Mount Athos, located on a 40-mile-long peninsula in northern Greece, has been the site of a thriving monastic community. Throughout its history, the monks have enforced a strict code that excludes females, whether human or animal. Within the Mount Athos complex, each monastery is a self-governing unit that maintains order over its inmates, houses, and lands.*

Byzantine law but also later furnished the starting point for the revival of Roman law in the West. This law code preserved such legal principles as requiring court proceedings to settle disputes, protecting the individual against unreasonable demands of society, and setting limits to the legitimate power of the sovereign. Through the Justinian Code, these Roman ideals permeated Byzantine society and served as a restraint on the autocratic emperors. When the West revived the study of the Roman law in the Middle Ages, these principles were adopted by the infant European states. Today, in virtually all the Western states, these principles continue to be honored.

From the viewpoint of world culture, Byzantium was noteworthy for contributing one of the first known works of history by a woman: the *Alexiad*, by Anna Comnena [kawm-NEE-nuh] (1083–about 1153), daughter of Emperor Alexius I Comnenus. Joining Christian and Classical knowledge and following the rigorous method pioneered by the Greek historian Thucydides (see Chapter 3), the *Alexiad* is a scholarly study of the reign of Anna's father, Alexius. Despite the author's obvious bias toward her father and confused chronology, the work is the best source for this period in Byzantine history. Especially valuable for Western readers is its portrait of the soldiers, saints, and hangers-on of the First Crusade (1096) passing through Constantinople on the way to Jerusalem. To Anna Comnena's non-Western eyes, the European Crusaders were a crude, violent bunch, more greedy for loot than concerned about salvation.

Architecture and Mosaics Besides law and history, architecture was the great achievement of the Byzantine world. Byzantine architecture was committed to glorifying the state and the emperors and to spreading the Christian message. Most of the Byzantine palaces and state buildings either were destroyed in the fifteenth century or have since fallen into ruins, but many churches still survive and attest to the lost grandeur of this civilization.

By the seventh century, the **Byzantine style** had been born, a style that drew from Greek, Roman, and oriental sources. The Greco-Roman tradition supplied the basic elements of Byzantine architecture: columns, arches, vaults, and domes. Oriental taste contributed a love of rich ornamentation and riotous color. Christianity fused these ingredients, provided wealthy patrons, and suggested subjects for the interior decorations. The **Greek cross,** which has arms of equal length, came to be the preferred floor plan for most later Byzantine churches.

Despite their borrowings, the Byzantines made one significant innovation that became fundamental in their architecture: They invented **pendentives**—supports in the shape of inverted concave triangles—that allowed a dome to be suspended over a square base (Figure 8.5). As a result of this invention, the domed building soon became synonymous with the Byzantine style, notably in churches.

The Byzantine obsession with the dome probably stemmed from its central role in the magnificent church Hagia Sophia, or Holy Wisdom, in Constantinople (see Figures 8.1 and 8.5). The dome had been employed in early Christian architecture (see Figure 7.14) and in important Roman temples like the Pantheon (see Figure 5.14). Erected by Justinian, Hagia Sophia was intended to awe the worshiper with the

Figure 8.5 ISIDORE OF MILETUS AND ANTHEMIUS OF TRALLES. Hagia Sophia, Interior. 532–537. Istanbul. *Hagia Sophia was the mother church of the Orthodox faith. After the Ottoman conquest, the church became an Islamic mosque, and some of the trappings, such as the calligraphic writings, still survive from this stage of the building's life. Today, Hagia Sophia is a museum, and its striking mixture of Byzantine and Islamic elements makes it a vivid symbol of the meeting of West and East.*

twin majesties of God and the emperor. The central dome measures more than 101 feet in diameter and rests on four pendentives that channel the weight to four huge pillars. Half-domes cover the east and west ends of the aisles.

In the vast interior, the architects showed that they were divided about the Classical legacy. On the one hand, they used such Classical features as vaulted aisles, well-proportioned columns, and rounded arches. But they ignored the basic rules of Classical symmetry; for example, they failed to harmonize the floor columns with the columns in the second-story gallery. Their goal was not to produce a unified effect but rather to create an illusion of celestial light. Glittering walls covered with polychrome marbles and brilliant mosaics, which have since disappeared or been covered with whitewash, suggested shimmering cloth to early viewers and contributed to the breathtaking effect of this magnificent church.

Although many later Byzantine architects adopted Hagia Sophia as their model—a floor plan that unites the early Christian longitudinal basilica with a central square surmounted by a dome or domes set upon drums—they also built churches without a dome, particularly in Ravenna on Italy's northeast Adriatic coast. Protected by marshes on the land side and with an escape route to the sea, Ravenna enjoyed the best of both Roman worlds. The Western emperors began to rule from there in 404 and to turn their new capital into an artistic jewel. In the late fifth century, Ravenna fell into the hands of Germanic invaders, who continued to add to the city's splendor.

When the city became a Byzantine outpost under Justinian, two new churches were built, San Vitale and Sant' Apollinare in Classe (Ravenna's port). San Vitale was domed (Figure 8.6), but Sant' Apollinare in Classe imitated late Roman styles with its basilica shape and its symbolic mosaics (Figure 8.7). The Western Classical ideal was visible in the harmonious nave of this church, where twenty-four perfectly proportioned columns were echoed above by precious marbles, which no longer exist. But the architect turned to oriental sources for his imaginative treatment of the columnar capitals in the nave. Instead of using stylized Corinthian capitals, he twisted and curled the acanthus leaves into fanciful shapes, as if blown by a stiff wind. The overall result was an artful blending of the Western and Eastern traditions.

Mosaic making had experienced a lively flowering in late Rome, and in Byzantium it became a major form of artistic expression. Unlike the Roman mosaics, which were of stone and laid in the floor, the Byzantine mosaics were usually of glass and set into the walls. Of the Byzantine mosaics, the most beautiful and the most perfectly preserved are those in the churches of Ravenna.

The church of San Vitale is home to a pair of impressive mosaics, one depicting Justinian and his courtiers (see Figure 8.2), the other depicting Justinian's empress, Theodora, and her retinue (Figure 8.8).

Figure 8.6 San Vitale, Exterior. 526–547. Ravenna, Italy. *Ravenna's church of San Vitale, with its octagonal plan and domed central core, is the prototype of the domed church that became standard in Byzantine civilization. From the outside, San Vitale's dome is not visible because it is covered by a timber and tile roof. This church inspired Charlemagne's Royal Chapel in Aachen (see Figure 8.23).*

Figure 8.7 Sant' Apollinare in Classe, Nave. Ca. 549. Classe, near Ravenna, Italy. *Dedicated in 549 by the bishop of Ravenna, the church of Apollinare was built about 3 miles outside the walled city of Ravenna at the local port of Classe. Today, the harbor has long since silted up, and the church presides like a sentinel over the surrounding farmlands. Sant' Apollinare's glittering interior mosaics and splendid marble columns remind the visitor that this country church was once at the center of the Byzantine world.*

Figure 8.8 *Theodora and Her Attendants.* Ca. 547. San Vitale, Ravenna. *This mosaic featuring the empress Theodora faces the panel of her husband, Justinian, with his courtiers (see Figure 8.2). Together, these mosaics communicate the pageantry and the luxury of this age. The man on Theodora's right draws back a curtain, inviting the imperial party into some unseen interior. His gesture may mean that this scene was part of a religious procession.*

In these mosaics, debts to late Roman art may be seen in the full frontal presentation of each figure, their large and staring eyes, and their long gowns. But the two-dimensional rendering of the figures reveals the new Byzantine aesthetic; the rulers and their companions seem to float in space, their feet pointing downward and not touching any surface. In various ways, the mosaics compare Justinian and Theodora to Christ and the Virgin Mary. For example, Justinian is surrounded by twelve companions, and the lower edge of Theodora's robe shows the three Wise Men bearing gifts to the Christ child.

During the Iconoclastic Controversy, the emperors destroyed virtually all figurative religious art that was under their control. After the conclusion of the controversy, a formalized repertory of church decoration evolved that characterized Byzantine art for the rest of its history. The aim of this religious art was strictly

Figure 8.9 *Christ Pantocrator.* Central dome, Church of Dafni. 1100. Dafni, near Athens. *In early Christian art, Christ had been portrayed as a beardless youth, often in the guise of the Good Shepherd (see Figure 7.22) or Orpheus. In Byzantine art, starting in the seventh century, Christ began to be depicted as a mature man with a full beard, as in this mosaic. Part of the change was a result of a fashion for full beards at this time, but, more important, the bearded figure reflected Orthodox theology's focus on Christ as the stern judge of the world.*

theological. For instance, Christ Pantocrator (Ruler of All) dominated each church's dome (Figure 8.9). In these portraits, Christ was presented as the emperor of the universe and the judge of the world. Accordingly, Byzantine art came to picture him with a stern and forceful countenance, in contrast to Western portrayals, which increasingly focused on his suffering.

THE ISLAMIC WORLD, 600–1517

Islamic civilization was born at approximately the same time as Byzantine culture and in the same part of the world, the eastern Mediterranean. In Arabic, the word *islam* means "submission" (to God); a *muslim* is "one who has submitted." Arabic religion and culture are known collectively as Islam, and those who practice the faith are known as Muslims. At its height, about 900, Islamic civilization extended over an enormous area that included southern Spain, Sicily, North Africa, Syria, Palestine, Mesopotamia, Persia, and the Arabian peninsula (see Map 8.1). The peoples living in these areas retained many elements of their native traditions but adopted the Islamic religion. These territories have remained Islamic to the present day, with the exceptions of southern Italy and Sicily, which the Normans conquered in the eleventh century; Spain, which the Christians won in the fifteenth century; and Palestine, which became the Jewish state of Israel after World War II.

The pre-Islamic Arabs inhabited the Arabian peninsula, a dry land wedged between the Red Sea and the Persian Gulf. Their tradition traces their ancestry to Abraham and the Hebrew patriarchs, and their Semitic tongue, Arabic, is related to Hebrew and to Syriac and Coptic, the chief languages of Syria and Egypt, respectively, at this time.

Geography accounted for the differences between the two major groups of pre-Islamic Arabs on the Arabian peninsula. In the north, nomadic Bedouins lived in the desert, herding sheep and goats, their tribal membership providing identity and cohesion. The southern Arabs lived in cities and traded with their neighbors. Caravan routes crossed Arabia, connecting India and the Roman world; local Arab merchants benefited from the passing traffic, sometimes accumulating great fortunes.

Jews and Christians settled in southern Arabia and served as major sources for cultural interchange. From them the Arabs acquired knowledge of weaponry, textiles, food and wine, and writing. The Arabs also learned that their polytheism conflicted with Jewish and Christian monotheism. A meeting place for all these peoples was Mecca, the leading commercial city of southern Arabia, centrally located on the rich overland route between the Indian Ocean and the Mediterranean.

History of Islam

At the beginning of the seventh century, Mecca was dominated by a wealthy merchant aristocracy of the Quraish tribe (Timeline 8.2). Into this Quraish society in about 570 was born Muhammad, the founder of Islam and one of the most commanding figures in history. At the age of forty, after becoming a wealthy merchant, he had a vision in which he felt himself called by God to be a prophet to the Arab people, just as Moses and Jesus had been prophets before him. Declaring that there was but one God (Allah), Muhammad attacked the polytheistic beliefs of his fellow Arabs and condemned the Kaaba, a local pagan shrine that housed a sacred black stone.

Timeline 8.2 THE WORLD OF ISLAM, 600-1517

500	600	632	800	1000	1258	1517
Pre-Islamic Culture	600-632 Age of Muhammad	Islamic Empire			Decline and Disintegration	Triumph of the Ottoman Turks

The Kaaba was a source of revenue from the thousands of pilgrims who visited it every year, so the Quraish leaders reacted to Muhammad's message with alarm. When he began converting others to his views, notably the poorer Arabs, Quraish hostility changed to persecution. Under these threats, Muhammad and his followers fled in 622 to Yathrib, a neighboring city. This historic flight, or Hegira, transformed Muhammad's message of reform into a call for a new religion, and the date marks the beginning of the Arab calendar. Yathrib was later renamed Medina, "the city of the Prophet."

In Yathrib, Muhammad's followers began to record the religious messages he received from Allah, and these writings became the Koran, the sacred book of Islam. Prominent among the divine words given to Muhammad was the *jihad*, the command to "holy war." Armed with this sacred order, Muhammad launched a religious and military movement that quickly brought both urban Arabs and desert Bedouins under his authority. In 630 his forces defeated the Quraish, and a triumphant Muhammad reentered Mecca, making it his capital. The Kaaba shrine, now purified of pagan and other religious images, kept its sacred rock and thus remained an object of veneration for Muslims; this action ensured the willing cooperation of the newly converted business community, which had at first bitterly opposed him. When Muhammad died in 632, he left an Arab state united around his prophecies.

From 632 to 750, the energies awakened by Muhammad's mission were unleashed in a series of military campaigns. Motivated by the lure of plundered wealth, the pressures of overpopulation, and the command to make holy war, the Arabs built a world state whose extent rivaled that of the Roman Empire. By 650 the Arabs ruled Syria, Mesopotamia, Egypt, and Persia, and, by 740, North Africa and most of Spain. Only the militant kingdom of the Franks in the west and the impregnable Constantinople in the east were able to withstand the Arabs.

During the Abbasid dynasty (754–1258), Islamic civilization attained its Golden Age. There was a gradual fusion of conquerors and conquered as the Arabs adapted other cultures to their own needs, and Arabic became the common cultural language throughout the empire. Millions converted to Islam, although Jews and Christians were allowed to retain their beliefs because they, like Muslims, were "people of the book." Trade with Europe, China, Russia, and Scandinavia generated great wealth for merchants and aristocrats, though the mainstay of the economy was agriculture, supported by the peasant labor on small farms. This vast Islamic empire was a theocracy, autocratically ruled by a caliph, or deputy, of the prophet Muhammad.

After the Abbasid era, the Islamic world declined as feudal agriculture replaced the commercial economy. In place of a united caliphate, mutually hostile Islamic states confronted one another, and after 1453 the eastern Mediterranean area and the Balkan region were clearly ruled by the Ottoman Turks from Constantinople. Eventually, in 1517, the Turks added Egypt and Syria to their holdings.

Islamic Religious and Cultural Developments

The Islamic civilization that flowered from the ninth to the twelfth century was brilliant. Original learning flourished in science, mathematics, and law. Arab medicine was recognized in the West and in Byzantium as superior, and Islamic scholars made their civilization a successor to the Hellenic tradition by translating Greek philosophy, mathematics, and science into Arabic. Nevertheless, religion, then as now, dominated Islamic life. The Koran not only served as a guide for public and private morality but also influenced the creation of major cultural forms such as history and jurisprudence. To the fundamentalist Muslim, religion, science, history, law, architecture, and theology

Figure 8.10 The Great Mosque of Kairouan, Tunisia. Ninth century. Stone, approx. 395 × 230′; ht. of minaret without finial 103′. *As in the other civilizations of this period, the dominant building type in Islam was the house of worship. The Great Mosque of Kairouan in Tunisia, with its plain walls and square tower for calling the faithful to prayer, reflects the simple style of early Islam. Inside the walls, a large unadorned courtyard serves as a praying area.*

were all different aspects of the same thing: God's divine word (Figure 8.10).

One area of life deeply affected by the rise of Islam was the status of women, notably in family life, divorce, and economic activity. Muhammad's teachings gave a definite normative and legal status to women's rights and duties and thus enhanced the general status of women, in contrast to their fluid and ambiguous situation in pre-Islamic Arabia. Yet the Koran explicitly gave superior rights to fathers and husbands and allowed polygamy and divorce at the instigation of the husband under specified conditions. There were mixed attitudes toward economic activity for women. Society in general viewed commerce with respect and manual labor with contempt. Hence, Muslim women who were commercially active had legal protection, but women who engaged in manual trades, such as textile weavers, were treated like outcasts.

Islamic Religion There are two central beliefs in Islam: There is but one God, and Muhammad is his prophet. Muslims worship the same God as Jews and Christians, but the Muslims alone recognize Muhammad as the *final* prophet of a tradition that goes back to Abraham and Moses in Judaism and that includes Jesus Christ as the giver of the Christian message. For the devout Muslim, Muhammad's voice is the culminating revelation from God that continues and perfects his earlier messages to Jews and Christians.

Muhammad's prophecies were recorded in the Koran during the generation after his death. Following no chronological pattern, this sacred book divides his revelations into chapters and verses beginning with the longest chapters and ending with the shortest. Muhammad's utterances reveal him as a master of literary expression and of rhetorical skills. Within a century of Muhammad's death, a collection of his sayings and practices, preserved by the faithful, appeared. This collection came to be known as the Hadith, or the Tradition. Together, the Tradition and the Koran became the infallible guide to God's will on earth for Muslims.

The core of Muslim religious life rests on the five Pillars of the Faith, which include one affirmation and four required devotional practices. The affirmation of faith states: "There is but one God, Allah, and Muhammad is his Prophet." The four acts of devotion are to pray five times a day facing Mecca, to fast during the lunar month of Ramadan, to give alms to the poor, and to make the pilgrimage to Mecca. Islam, like Christianity, promises salvation in heaven for the good and damnation in hell for the wicked. Besides the five Pillars of the Faith, the Muslim who desires God's favor has to meet many other religious, ethical, legal, and social obligations that form the basis of the *Sharia,* or holy law, which is rooted in the Koran and the Tradition.

History Because of Muhammad's supreme significance to Islam, lives of the Prophet and histories of his era appeared soon after his death. In time the Islamic world developed a great demand for historical writings, and diverse historical genres appeared, including accounts of territorial conquest, family genealogies, and town histories. The greatest Islamic historian was Ibn Khaldun [ib-uhn kal-DOON] (1332–1406). His fame rests on the three-volume *Muqaddima,* or Prolegomena, which sets forth his scientific theory of history. In this work, he reasons that the best history should downplay the role of divine forces and instead focus on the role of human activity. He believed that historians who probed beneath the surface explanations would discover that human beings are motivated not by religious or idealistic impulses but by status concerns and desires to identify with certain groups. One of the founders of modern scientific history, Ibn Khaldun deserves wider recognition.

Science Muslim scientists form a link in the cultural chain that connects the ancient Greek thinkers to modern science. Not only did Muslim intellectuals translate the Greek texts into Arabic and thus preserve them for later medieval and Renaissance scholars, but they also used the Greek heritage to lay the foundation for Muslim mathematics, astronomy, physics, geography, chemistry, and medicine. During Islam's Golden Age, its scholars made more scientific advances than had been made since the Hellenistic period.

The outstanding areas of Muslim science were medicine and mathematics. Many works of Islamic scholars were translated into Latin by Western writers, an indication of the deep respect Christians accorded these Muslim specialists. Muslim doctors obtained their medical knowledge from the ancient Greek texts and from their training in the hospitals that dotted the Islamic world. Islamic medicine's commitment to observation and experimentation extended the frontiers of medical science. For example, Muslim doctors added many new drugs to the pharmacopeia, stressed the role of diet in the treatment of various illnesses, and were the first to make the clinical distinction between measles and smallpox.

In mathematics, however, the Muslims did their most original work, the greatest figure being al-Khwarizmi [al-KWAHR-iz-me] (780–850). Al-Khwarizmi (from whose name the word *algorithm* is derived) founded the algebraic system by adopting and expanding the hints thrown out by a Hellenistic Greek thinker. Al-Khwarizmi's study of quadratic equations introduced algebra to the West, and in translation this work became a standard textbook used in Western universities from the twelfth to the eighteenth century. His celestial observations were used for centuries. Finally, al-Khwarizmi took from Hindu mathematics the idea of zero and the numeration system that became more widely known as arabic numerals.

Art and Architecture Islamic art and architecture borrowed freely from other cultures, but the borrowings were always adapted to Arabic tastes in complex and exotic ways. From Greco-Roman architecture came the column and the **arcade.** From Byzantine architecture came the pendentive, which allowed the dome to become a prominent feature of the Islamic style. And from Persian art and architecture came the miniature painting, the vaulted hall, the pointed arch, and floral and geometric ornamentation.

Figure 8.11 Arabesque Detail. Great Mosque of Cordoba. 785–987. Cordoba, Spain. *This arabesque is used as a decorative feature above the portal of the Great Mosque of Cordoba. It had its origins in the Arabic world's love of designs. These elaborate and elegant decorations were constructed either from geometric features or from floral motifs. The geometric features, as seen here, were rarely based on nature but were meant to make viewers think of values other than those of their surrounding world.*

The course of Islamic art was dramatically affected by the Koran's prohibition against the representation of living creatures. Large-scale paintings and sculptures were not produced, and lifelike figures, whether of humans or animals, largely disappeared from art. In compensation, perhaps, artists were abundantly inventive in the use of nonrepresentational forms. The **arabesque**—a complex figure made of intertwined floral, foliate, or geometrical forms—became a highly visible sign of Islamic culture (Figure 8.11). Geometric

بسم الله الرحمن الرحيم
الم ذلك الكتاب لا ريب فيه هدى للمتقين
الذين يؤمنون بالغيب ويقيمون الصلوة ومما
رزقناهم ينفقون والذين يؤمنون بما انزل اليك
وما انزل من قبلك وبالاخرة هم يوقنون اولئك

Figure 8.12 Arabic Calligraphy. Page of a Koran in Naskhi script, by the calligrapher Yaquat al-Musta'simi (d. 1298). Turkish Islamic Art Museum, Istanbul. *Because Islam forbade the representation of figures in art, artisans focused on decoration, design, and other nonrepresentational forms of expression. Besides the popular arabesques, Arabic calligraphy was the major form available to Muslim artists. This handwritten page from a fifteenth-century Koran shows the exquisite beauty of this painstaking art.*

Figure 8.13 The Tomb of Timur Lenk (Tamerlane). Ca. 1403. Samarkand, Uzbekistan. *Islamic architects imposed domes not only over prayer halls in mosques but also over the tombs of rulers and holy men. The dome of Timur Lenk's tomb has the characteristic high melon shape of Islamic architecture; in addition, the dome is decorated with ribs that break up the play of light on its surface. Below the dome on the cylindrical drum are letters in Kufic (Timur Lenk's language) that say, "Allah [alone] is permanent." Some of the Kufic characters are 34 feet high.*

shapes, floral forms, and **calligraphy,** or writing, decorated walls, books, and mosaics (Figure 8.12).

In architecture, the dominant structure was the **mosque.** Plain in exterior decoration and rectangular in shape, mosques were distinguished from secular buildings by their interior features and spaces—basins and fountains for ritual hand washing, porticoes for instruction, and an open area for the group prayers. Sometimes the mosque was crowned with a dome, as in the Byzantine churches, but the Islamic dome's high melon shape distinguished it from the more spherical Byzantine form (Figure 8.13). The mosque was also identified by a thin pointed tower, or **minaret,** from whose top a Muslim official called the faithful to prayer five times a day. Inside the mosque, from the earliest times, rich decorations assaulted the eyes of the worshipers, reminding them of the beauty of paradise. Brilliant mosaics and oriental carpets emblazoned the floors, facings and calligraphic friezes beautified the walls, and overhead metal lamps cast a twilight glow onto the faithful at night (Figure 8.14). Richly decorated minbars, or portable pulpits, were used by the local prayer leader to address worshipers during Friday services (Figure 8.15).

In early Islam, the congregational mosque developed in response to the devotional practices and ritualistic needs. It housed the Friday worshipers in a central courtyard with a domed fountain for ablutions. The ninth-century Ibn Tulun mosque at Cairo is an imposing example of the congregational type of mosque (Figure 8.16). Four rows of arcades stand between the faithful and the east wall (the direction of Mecca), and portals of pointed arches open into the arcaded area (Figure 8.17). A minaret with a winding stair rises just beyond the mosque, which is built of brick faced with stucco. In later Islamic mosques, the pointed arches

Figure 8.14 *The "Ardebil" Carpet.* Formerly in the Mosque of Ardebil, Iran. 1539–1540. Woolen knotted carpet, 37′9½″ × 17′6″. Victoria and Albert Museum, London. *Praised as "the greatest example of carpet weaving in the world," the "Ardebil" carpet was woven for the Ardebil mosque in Persia. It is noted for its luxurious texture, subtle use of color, and harmonious design. Typical of carpets made for holy places, it has a silk warp and weft (the lengthwise and horizontal threads, respectively), though its pile, or surface, is wool, numbering about 350 knots to the square inch. The ground is midnight blue with a floral design in light blue, turquoise, light green, cream, yellow, salmon, plum, and black. Dominating the carpet's center is a yellow medallion filled with scrolling tendrils, which end in arabesque leaves. The medallion is surrounded by sixteen ogees (pointed ovals), and a red mosque lamp appears at either end of the carpet. A fourth of the medallion with respective ogees but without the mosque lamp fills each corner. A rare feature of this work is that it is signed (top): "The work of the slave of the threshold Maqsud Kashani in the year 946 [A.D. 1540]." However, because thirty-two million knots or more were needed to complete this project, most scholars believe it was too arduous for one artisan and thus must be the product of team effort. If so, then Maqsud may have been head of the workshop where it was made.*

Figure 8.15 *Kutubiyya Minbar.* Ca. 1137–1145. Bone and colored woods, ht. 12′10″, width, 2′10¼″, depth, 11′4¼″. Kutubiyya Mosque, Marrakesh, Morocco. Islamic. Three quarter view from the right. Photography by Bruce White. Photograph © 1998, The Metropolitan Museum of Art. *Commissioned in 1137 by Sultan Ali Ibn Yusuf of the Almoravid Dynasty, this minbar, or portable pulpit, was built by craftspeople in Cordoba, Spain. The minbar is basically a wooden staircase on wheels, with a seat at the top of the stairs for the prayer leader. Intricately detailed, it was assembled from perhaps a million pieces of bone and fine African woods, many of them carved into such shapes as stars, hexagons, arabesques, pine cones, and Arabic letters. Used for eight centuries in the Kutubiyya mosque, it fell into disrepair in this century. Recently, it was restored by the Metropolitan Museum of Art.*

and decorated stucco work became basic features of this style. Later, during the Christian Middle Ages, Western architects adapted the pointed arch to their own needs, using it to perfect the Gothic style of architecture.

In the eleventh century, the mosque evolved from a place for group prayer to a place for teaching, but the basic rectangular shape remained the same. In the teaching mosque, four large enclosed teaching halls with vaulted ceilings replaced the covered arcades on the perimeter of the courtyard, each opening into the central space.

Islamic artisans also excelled in palace architecture, and no more beautiful example exists than the Alhambra in Granada, the residence of the last Muslim rulers of Spain. Its exterior of plain red brick contrasts dramatically with its interior of restless splendor. The palace's asymmetrical plan includes ornately decorated rooms, splendid courts, and formal gardens. The decoration of the Alhambra—variegated marbles, lustrous tiles, and painted stucco—creates a fantastic illusion of airiness. The Court of the Lions illustrates vividly the meaning of the term *arabesque,* with its calligraphic carvings, slender columns, geometric and floral shapes, and lacy decoration (Figure 8.18). The fountain surrounded by stone lions is a rare example of Islamic representational sculpture.

Notwithstanding the Koranic prohibition, one branch of Islamic art, Persian **miniatures,** usually depicted realistic scenes. After the thirteenth century, illustrated manuscripts were produced in Persia under the patronage of the Mongol sultans, who had replaced the caliphs as rulers. Although the Mongols brought Chinese influences to the Persian miniatures, the Muslim artists rejected the openness of Chinese space and created their own ordered reality, as shown in a superb example from the fifteenth century (Figure 8.19). The painter records each object with painstaking naturalistic detail. The painting's high horizon and its rectangular format put the two figures in a precise setting. Like all Persian miniatures, this exquisite work is characterized by fine detail, naturalistic figures and landscape, and subtle colors.

Figure 8.16 Ibn Tulun Mosque, Cairo. 876–879. Red brick covered with white stucco, exterior 531 × 532½′. *Ibn Tulun, a governor who founded a short-lived Egyptian dynasty independent of the caliphate in Baghdad, built this mosque in the congregational style created by Muhammad. The view is from inside the courtyard, with a domed fountain, used for ritual washing, standing in the foreground. Outside the walls rises the spire of a four-story minaret, set on a square base with a cylindrical second story and an exterior staircase. The finest surviving example of this style, the Ibn Tulun mosque was imitated throughout the Muslim world.*

THE EARLY MEDIEVAL WEST

Since the Italian Renaissance, scholars have described the fall of Rome as the end of the ancient world and the beginning of the thousand-year era known as the medieval period, or the Middle Ages. Although Renaissance intellectuals used the word *medieval* as a negative term, today's scholars believe the civilization of the Middle Ages to be as worthy of study as the ancient and modern worlds. This section is devoted to the first phase of this era, the Early Medieval period, dating from about 500 to about 1000.

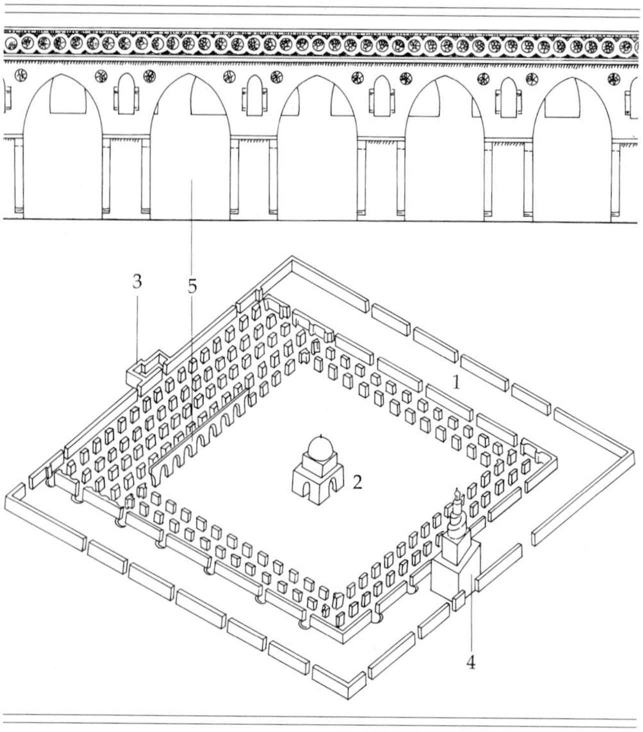

Figure 8.17 Floor Plan of Ibn Tulun Mosque. *This diagram shows the main features of the Ibn Tulun mosque, a prototype of the congregational mosque that flourished early in Islamic civilization. Constructed basically as an open rectangular area, the mosque has passageways (1) on three sides that lead through an arcaded area (5) into a central courtyard dominated by a domed fountain (2). In the middle of the eastern wall is the mihrab (3), a decorated niche indicating the direction of Mecca. Opposite the mihrab, on the western side, stands a minaret (4), a tower used by an official for calling the faithful to prayer.*

Figure 8.18 Court of the Lions. The Alhambra. Thirteenth and fourteenth centuries. Granada, Spain. *The Alhambra is the only Muslim palace surviving from the medieval period. Because of its location in the West, this fairy-tale palace has made Granada a popular destination for tourists. As a result, the ornate Alhambra has played a pivotal role in developing a taste for the arabesque among many Westerners.*

Figure 8.19 Scene from the *Khamsah (Five Poems)* of Amir Khosrow. 1485. 6¾ × 4½″. Chester Beatty Library, Dublin. *The art of Persian miniatures achieved its classic expression during the fifteenth century, the age of the Mongol rulers in Persia. These small works are immediately recognizable by their rectangular designs, their representation of the human figure as about one-fifth the height of the painting, and their use of extremely refined detail.*

The Early Middle Ages: A Romano-Germanic Christianized World

After the fall of Rome, life in the West was precarious for most people. There was a return to an essentially agrarian existence, accompanied by a decline in commerce and in the standard of living. Village life was simple and barter the primary medium of exchange. The little security that people had was provided by the Christian church, with its bishops and priests, its increasingly powerful pope in Rome, and its spreading network of monasteries and convents.

By about 500, Western life had stabilized to some degree. Three Germanic tribes occupied and ruled vast parts of the old Western Roman Empire: the Visigoths in Spain, the Ostrogoths in Italy and southern Germany, and the Franks in France and western Germany. The Angles and Saxons were dominant in England, the Vandals in North Africa, and the Burgundians in southern France; other Germanic tribes claimed land in central Europe, on the Scandinavian peninsula, and along the Baltic Sea. In Gaul (modern-day France), especially, life was being redefined in ways that would have a profound impact on Western civilization.

While a Germanic tribe known as the Lombards was gaining control of the Italian peninsula, the Franks were centralizing rule in Roman Gaul under Clovis, the

Timeline 8.3 THE KINGDOM OF THE FRANKS

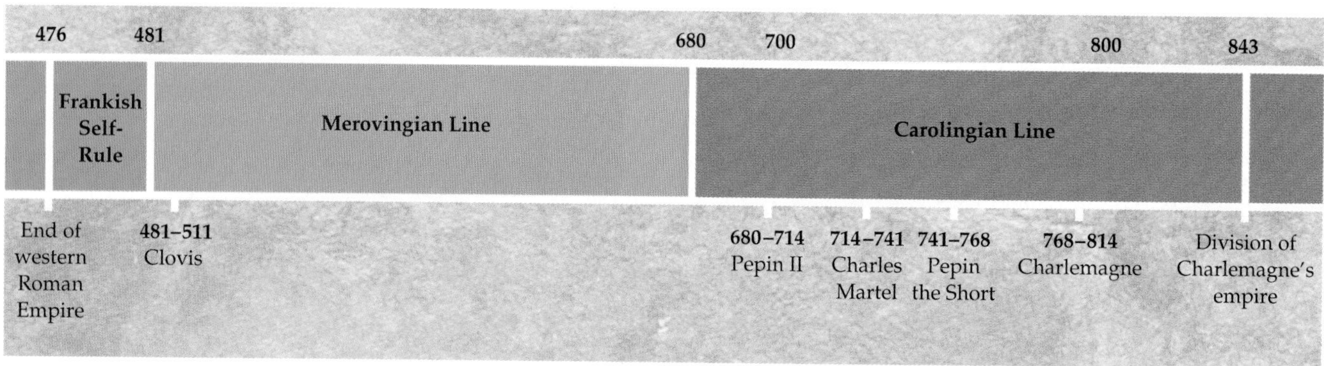

first important ruler of the Merovingian dynasty (Timeline 8.3). An early convert to Latin Christianity, through the persuasion of his wife, Clotilda, Clovis supported missionaries in newly conquered territories, strengthening political ties between Gaul and the pope.

During these years of political expansion in the Frankish kingdom, some security and order gradually developed, especially around the rulers' fortress-palaces. As the barbarian invasions subsided in the late sixth century, manorialism developed as a new economic system. Most of the Germanic invaders settled on the manors, or landed estates, of the Frankish warrior class. There they became serfs, indentured servants who were bound to the land. Their value as workers earned them the protection of the lord of the manor in time of war.

Frankish society was composed of three well-defined ranks: those who fought, those who prayed, and those who worked. Each social rank had a rigidly defined hierarchy of subgroups. The warrior class, headed by the king, consisted of the lords of the great manors and their families and, under them, their courtiers, the less wealthy knights, and the lords of small manors. The upper clergy, who shared the high social status of warriors, consisted of the archbishops, bishops, and abbots; the lower clergy comprised priests, monks, nuns, and clerical scribes and secretaries. The working ranks consisted of free farmers, artisans, and a few merchants; the vast population of peasants, serfs, and a few slaves were at the bottom.

In Frankish society, the status of women declined sharply from what it had been in the Roman world. On the manors, noblewomen enjoyed few personal or property rights, since, under Frankish law, land was passed through the male line. The noblewoman's primary function was the bearing of sons, and the peasant woman was simply another laborer. The only leadership role for women was in the nunneries, for women traditionally ruled themselves in these religious institutions.

After 700 the Merovingians gradually lost control of the Frankish kingdom to the Carolingian dynasty. Under Charles Martel ("Charles the Hammer"), Carolingian troops halted the advance of the Muslims at the Battle of Tours in southern France in 732, thereby ensuring the future of Europe as a Christian land. In 751, Pepin the Short (r. 751–768), the son of Charles Martel, was declared king of the Franks, with the approval of the pope and the votes of the Frankish nobles. Three years later, a new pope crowned Pepin and anointed him as defender of the church. This ceremony, cementing an alliance between the popes and the Franks, set the course for church-state relationships in the West.

In exchange for papal recognition of his royal title, Pepin conquered the Lombards, who ruled most of Italy, and gave their lands in central Italy to the pope. These lands, which later became known as the Papal States, were conveyed in one of the most important documents of the Early Middle Ages, the Donation of Pepin. The alliance symbolized by the Donation of Pepin benefited both parties: The pope's authority and the church's economic foundation were enhanced, and the Frankish kings gained legitimacy and a claim to be the hereditary protectors of Rome. This alliance also redirected the church's interests away from the Eastern Empire and linked Rome's destiny with western Europe.

Charlemagne ("Charles the Great") (r. 768–814), the son of Pepin the Short, established the first real empire in medieval Europe and challenged the Byzantine rulers' claims to the western Roman lands. Because Charlemagne was the most powerful ruler in the Early Middle Ages, historians have named a dynasty and an age for him—Carolingian, from *Carolus,* Latin for Charles. Charlemagne fought the Lombards in Italy, the Saxons in Germany, and the Muslims in Spain, colonizing most of these areas and converting the populace to Christianity. To reward Charlemagne's military and religious triumphs, Pope Leo III crowned him "Charles Augustus, Emperor of the Romans" on Christmas Day, 800. With this act, Leo may have hoped to assert the authority of the church over the state, but Charlemagne continued to believe in the supremacy of the state. The coronation enhanced Charlemagne's reputation, but it also widened the rift between Byzantium and the West.

Charlemagne created an efficient bureaucracy, instituted a fair judicial system, and brought learned people to his court as part of a revival of the arts and humanities. He granted large tracts of land to local warriors and then held them responsible for maintaining law and order in their domains. This administrative system fused the Roman approach to governing an empire with the Germanic warrior tradition, and it worked efficiently as long as Charlemagne lived.

The end of the Carolingian era began in 843 when Charlemagne's grandsons divided the empire into three parts, hastening the splintering of western Europe into smaller kingdoms. In the ninth and tenth centuries, a final wave of invaders entered western Europe—the Vikings from Scandinavia and the Magyars from the Hungarian plains. By the late tenth century, however, two new kingdoms—later to become modern France and Germany—were emerging from the political chaos.

France developed from the ambitions of Hugh Capet (r. 987–996), a noble landowner who was crowned king of the western Franks. From their power base in Paris, the Capetian kings consolidated their grip over the other feudal lords and their lands. The other emerging kingdom was that of Otto the Great (r. 936–973), who was elected king of the Germans and Saxons. A superb military leader and dedicated church reformer, Otto extended his kingdom into Italy. There he released the papacy from the control of corrupt Roman families and forced the pope, in return, to recognize him as emperor. Otto was clearly following the dream of Charlemagne—to restore the lost Roman world (Figure 8.20).

Figure 8.20 Church of St. Pantaleon. 966–980, restored 1890–1892. Cologne, Germany. *Otto the Great founded this church for a Benedictine monastery in Cologne where his brother was archbishop. As a builder of churches, Otto was following in Charlemagne's footsteps, identifying himself as God's chosen instrument intent on expanding both the Christian faith and his own empire. Of the original fortresslike church, only the westworks with three towers survive. Like many tenth-century churches, St. Pantaleon was flanked by two tall towers and an enclosed entrance. The rest of the church was restored in the late nineteenth century.*

Religion and Culture in the Early Middle Ages

During the Early Middle Ages, literature, art, and architecture degenerated from the already low standards of late Rome. There was a brief, bright moment in the early ninth century under Charlemagne and his successor when literature, learning, and the arts flourished, but by the middle of the ninth century this renaissance had faded in the wake of political disintegration and foreign invasions. Later, Otto the Great encouraged the cultivation of letters within his empire. Notwithstanding their sporadic nature, these intellectual and artistic developments helped to blend the Germanic and Greco-Roman worlds into an emerging Christian Europe.

Christianity: Leadership and Organization Regardless of internal dissension and external foes in the period between 500 and 1000, Christianity strengthened itself and its hold on society. The early popes faced heresy, disorganization, and a vast world of unbaptized men and women. The energetic and dedicated Pope Gregory the Great (pope 590–604) was the most successful of the early medieval pontiffs. He reformed the clergy, whose poor training and lax habits, in particular their sexual behavior, worked against the church's efforts to set high moral standards. Tradition claims he standardized the use of music in the service of worship, so that the Gregorian chants became synonymous with the medieval church. He encouraged the founding of new monasteries among the Germanic

PERSONAL PERSPECTIVE

Anna Comnena
The Arrival of the First Crusade in Constantinople

Mutual suspicion, prejudice, and hostility characterized relations among the three civilizations that succeeded Rome. This first selection is from Byzantine historian Anna Comnena's Alexiad *and recounts the arrival of the First Crusade (1096) in Constantinople; the Frankish Crusaders, led by Peter the Hermit, were on their way to Jerusalem to recover Christian holy places from the Muslim Turks.*

Before he [Emperor Alexius I] had enjoyed even a short rest, he heard a report of the approach of innumerable Frankish armies. Now he dreaded their arrival for he knew their irresistible manner of attack, their unstable and mobile character and all the peculiar natural and concomitant characteristics which the Frank retains throughout. . . .

. . . [Peter the Hermit had] contrived to assemble the Franks from all sides, one after the other, with arms, horses and all the other paraphernalia of war. And they were all so zealous and eager that every highroad was full of them. And those Frankish soldiers were accompanied by an unarmed host more numerous than the sand or the stars, carrying palms and crosses on their shoulders, women and children, too, came away from their countries. And the sight of them was like many rivers streaming from all sides, and they were advancing towards us through Dacia generally with all their hosts. Now the coming of these many peoples was preceded by a locust which did not touch the wheat, but made a terrible attack on the vines. This was really a presage as the diviners of the time interpreted it, and meant that this enormous Frankish army would, when it came, refrain from interference in Christian affairs, but fall very heavily upon the barbarian Ishmaelites [Muslim Turks] who were slaves to drunkenness, wine, and Dionysus.

Usamah
The Curious Medicine of the Franks

In The Memoirs of Usamah, *a twelfth-century Arab writer living in Palestine describes Westerners as "animals possessing the virtues of courage and fighting, but nothing else." He includes the following description of their "curious medicine."*

The lord of al-Munaytirah wrote to my uncle asking him to dispatch a physician to treat certain sick persons among his people. My uncle sent him a Christian physician named Thabit. Thabit was absent but ten days when he returned. So we said to him, "How quickly hast thou healed thy patients!" He said:

"They brought before me a knight in whose leg an abscess had grown; and a woman afflicted with imbecility. To the knight I applied a small poultice until the

peoples. Abroad, he sent missionaries to England, thus ensuring the triumph of Christianity among the Anglo-Saxons. Despite their successes and reforms, however, Gregory and the later popes could not break the grip of secular power over church affairs, a thorny problem that awaited solution in the High Middle Ages.

The church found a new source of strength in monasticism. Western monks followed the guidelines that were laid down by St. Benedict (480–543) and observed in the Benedictine order's first monastery at Monte Cassino, south of Rome. Benedictines, after a period of rigorous intellectual training and self-denial, vowed to lead lives of chastity, obedience, and poverty. They divided their days into alternating periods of work, prayer, and study. The monks were known as the regular clergy, because they followed a *regula,* or rule. After the seventh century, women became part of the monastic system, using the Benedictine rules and sharing with monks the same facilities, then known as double monasteries. By the tenth century, separate facilities for women—nunneries—were being established by noblemen and noblewomen. Supervised by an abbess, some of these convents became important centers for women's concerns, and nearly all served as refuges for the devoted or for those forced by their families to take the veil as brides of Christ.

The monasteries and nunneries that spread across Europe served many purposes. They were havens for the populace during invasions. They were centers for copying ancient literary and philosophical texts, which were then studied in their libraries. The monks often established schools for the local young men, and the abscess opened and became well; and the woman I put on diet and made her humour wet. Then a Frankish physician came to them and said, 'This man knows nothing about treating them'. . . . He then examined the woman and said, 'This is a woman in whose head there is a devil which has possessed her. Shave off her hair.' Accordingly they shaved it off and the woman began once more to eat their ordinary diet—garlic and mustard. Her imbecility took a turn for the worse. The physician then said, 'The devil has penetrated through her head.' He therefore took a razor, made a deep cruciform incision on it, peeled off the skin at the middle of the incision until the bone of the skull was exposed and rubbed it with salt. The woman . . . expired instantly. Thereupon I asked them whether my services were needed any longer, and when they replied in the negative I returned home, having learned of their medicine what I knew not before."

Liudprand of Cremona
A Mission to the Byzantine Court

Bishop Liudprand of Cremona, emissary of the German ruler Otto I (the Great), traveled (968) to Constantinople to arrange a marriage between Otto's son and a Byzantine princess. Here he describes his reception to Otto.

On the fourth of June we arrived at Constantinople, and after a miserable reception, meant as an insult to yourselves, we were given the most miserable and disgusting quarters. . . .

On the sixth of June, which was the Saturday before Pentecost, I was brought before the emperor's brother Leo, marshal of the court and chancellor; and there we tired ourselves with a fierce argument over your imperial title. He called you not emperor, which is Basileus in his tongue, but insultingly Rex, which is king in yours. I told him that the thing meant was the same though the word was different, and he then said that I had come not to make peace but to stir up strife. Finally he got up in a rage, and really wishing to insult us received your letter not in his own hand but through an interpreter. . . .

On the seventh of June, the sacred day of Pentecost, I was brought before Nicephorus himself in the palace called Stephana, that is, the Crown Palace. He is a monstrosity of a man. . . . He began his speech as follows:—

> It was our duty and our desire to give you a courteous and magnificent reception. That, however, has been rendered impossible by the impiety of your master, who in the guise of an hostile invader has laid claim to Rome; . . . has tried to subdue to himself by massacre and conflagration cities belonging to our empire. . . .

To him I made this reply: "My master did not invade the city of Rome by force nor as a tyrant; he freed her from a tyrant's yoke, or rather from the yoke of many tyrants. . . . Your power, methinks, was fast asleep then; and the power of your predecessors, who in name alone are called emperors of the Romans, while the reality is far different. . . .

nuns for young women. These self-sufficient monasteries and nunneries were models of agricultural productivity and economic resourcefulness (Figure 8.21).

Literature, History, and Learning Writers during this period were more interested in conserving the past than in composing original works. Consequently, literature—all of it written in Latin—was eclectic, blending Christian ideas with Classical thought and often mixing genres, such as history, biography, science, philosophy, and theology.

The most highly educated scholar of the Early Middle Ages was Boethius [bo-E-the-uhs] (about 480–524), a Roman aristocrat and a courtier of Theodoric, the Ostrogoth king in Italy. A rarity in this age, an intellectual who knew Greek, Boethius translated much of Aristotle's vast writings into Latin. In the later Middle Ages, all that Latin scholars knew of Aristotle was through Boethius's translations.

Boethius fell from favor in Theodoric's court and was eventually executed. While in prison, he wrote the *Consolation of Philosophy,* a work widely read throughout the Middle Ages and beyond. In it he described his mental struggle with despair at life's cruel turn of events. He personified Philosophy as a learned woman with whom he argued many issues in search of the meaning of happiness. In the face of imminent death, Boethius finally concluded that true contentment was reserved for those who combined intellectual inquiry with Christian beliefs.

Although several scholars wrote historical chronicles, only Gregory of Tours and Bede can be classified

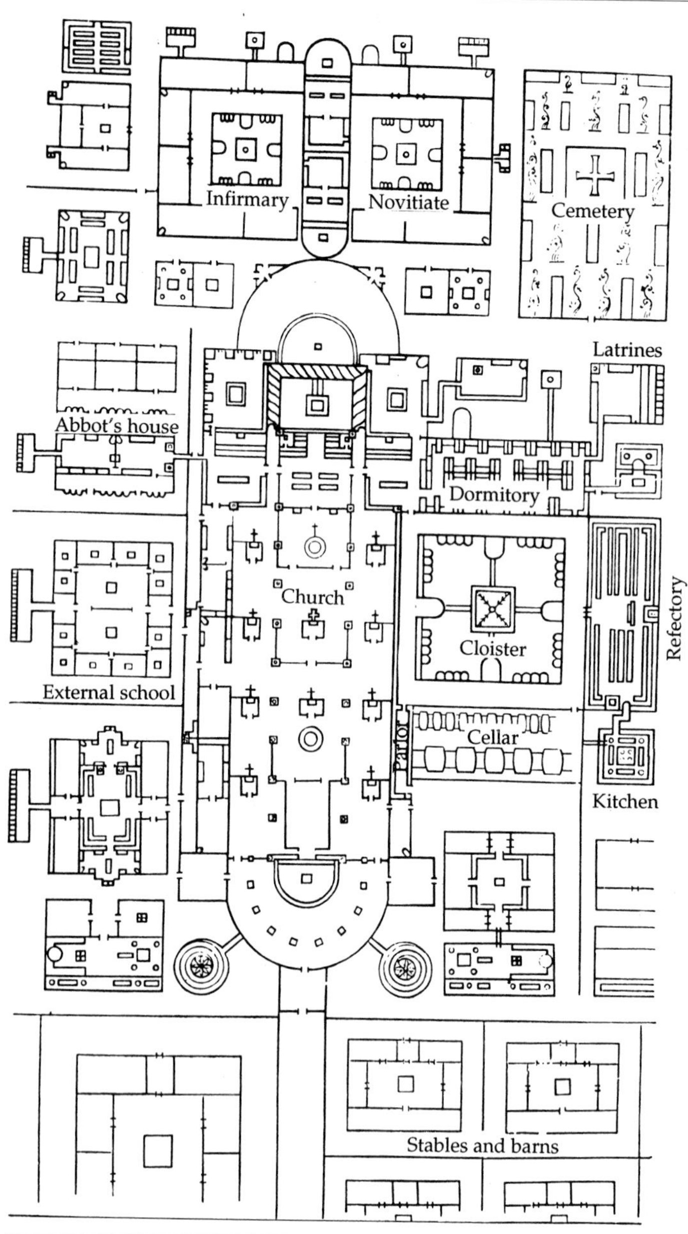

Figure 8.21 Plan of St. Gall Monastery. Ca. 820. *One of the most prominent ninth-century monasteries was the Benedictine House at St. Gall in Switzerland. Although the monastery no longer exists, its original plan, perhaps by Linhard, has been preserved. The plan reveals the self-sufficient system of the monastery, with its school, hospital, dormitories, poorhouse, and various buildings and plots of land.*

as historians. Both consulted written documents and other sources and in general strove for (but did not always achieve) objectivity and historical accuracy. Gregory of Tours (about 538–593) left the single surviving record of the sixth-century Merovingian kingdom in his *History of the Franks.* Gregory's account lacks historical cohesion and shows stylistic confusion, but he manages to capture the flavor of his times in his lively and humane character sketches of the Frankish rulers. In Anglo-Saxon England, Bede [BEED] (673–735), an English monk and scholar, composed *A History of the English Church and People,* which described the missionary activities that led to the founding of the English church. Written in a pure Latin style, his *History* is a major source for the chronology of this troubled age.

When Charlemagne came to power, cultural life enjoyed its greatest flowering in the Early Middle Ages. The Carolingian Renaissance, which represented Europe's first genuine rebirth of Classical studies within the context of Christian beliefs, had its roots in educational reform. Recognizing that ignorance posed a threat to his regime, Charlemagne founded a palace school at his residence at Aachen, in present-day western Germany. He invited the most learned men of the day to train his own staff and to teach the sons of the nobility. Leading scholars from England, Ireland, and Italy settled in Aachen, where they pursued their scholarship. Foremost among them was Alcuin [AL-kwin] of York (735–804), who led the palace school, giving instruction in Latin, composing his own textbooks, and overseeing the copying of manuscripts.

Another important scholar and adviser at Aachen was Einhard [INE-hart] (about 770–840), who came from Gaul. His lasting contribution was his brief and simple biography of Charlemagne, the *Vita Caroli* (the *Life of Charles*). Modeled on the lives of the Caesars by the Roman historian Suetonius, this work is a major literary achievement of the Early Middle Ages and still gives today's readers a vivid portrait of Charlemagne and his times.

One of the important achievements of the palace school was a significant innovation in handwriting. Trained scribes developed a flowing style consisting primarily of rounded lowercase letters that became the standard form for all later handwriting styles in the West. With the development of this legible and uniform Latin script, known as Carolingian minuscule, educated men and women gained access to written material and monks, in transcribing books, were liable to fewer errors (Figure 8.22).

During the turbulent ninth and tenth centuries, the light of civilization seemed to grow dimmer, except in monasteries in Ireland and Germany, where many monks and nuns kept the humanities alive. Especially noteworthy among the monastic scholars who bal-

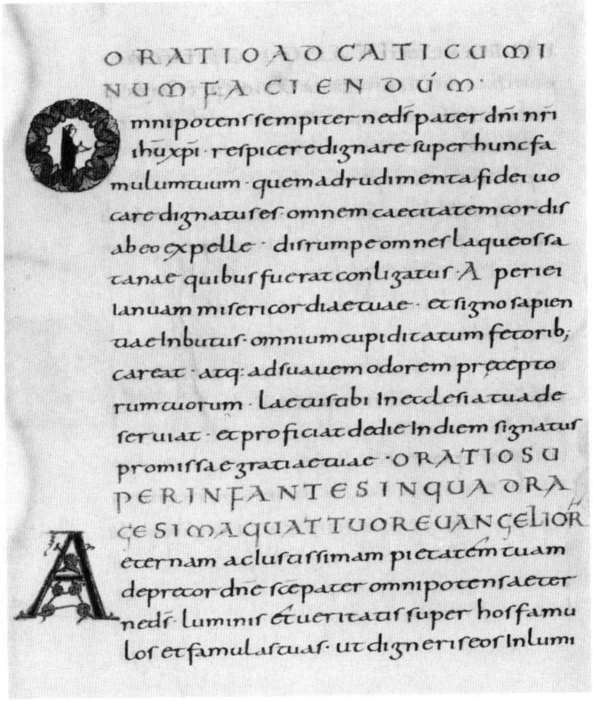

Figure 8.22 Carolingian Minuscule. Ninth century. Bibliothèque Nationale, Paris. *Because Christianity relied heavily on written works, legible texts were important; but the prevailing style of writing, which used separately formed lowercase letters, was almost impossible to read. To overcome this difficulty, scribes during Charlemagne's reign perfected a new style of writing—the Carolingian minuscule—characterized by clearly formed letters linked into words, spaces between words, and capital letters at the beginning of sentences, as shown here. All subsequent Western handwriting styles follow from this tradition.*

anced Christian faith with the Classics was Hrotswitha [rawts-VEE-tar] (about 935–about 975), a canoness (a nunlike vocation that did not require vows for life) at Gandersheim convent in Saxony. The first German playwright, Hrotswitha wrote six plays, in Latin, modeled on those of Terence, the Roman dramatist (see Chapter 5), but infused with erudite religious ideas. Rejecting the themes of Roman comedy as spiritually unhealthy, these Christian dramas focused on fall and conversion themes, as in *Abraham,* which tells of a prostitute rescued by a saintly monk. Literary exercises, these plays were probably never performed, except perhaps as recitations with mimed action. Hrotswitha's writings, forgotten until the Renaissance, were rediscovered about 1500 by German humanists who recognized them as major monuments of medieval drama.

Music Music became integral to the church liturgy during the Early Middle Ages and kept alive the Greek heritage of music as an art form. From this religious foundation ultimately arose all of the sacred and secular music of the modern West. The name of Pope Gregory the Great is preserved in the early medieval musical form, the **Gregorian chant,** which became the official liturgical music of the early church—used in the Mass (the celebration of the Eucharist) and other services of the yearly cycle of public worship. The chants consisted of a single melodic line sung in unison, without instrumental accompaniment, by male voices. They had an impersonal, nonemotional quality and served religious rather than aesthetic or emotional purposes. Notwithstanding this aim, the chants cast a spell over their listeners, evoking in them feelings of otherworldliness, peace, and purity.

In the ninth century, one of the most important advancements in music history occurred, the rise of polyphony—two lines of melody sounded at the same time. Polyphony, unlike the monophonic Gregorian chants, gave music a vertical as well as a horizontal quality. But further musical developments would have to await more settled social and political conditions.

Architecture The overall decline of living conditions in western Europe took its toll in architecture and art as patronage evaporated, skills fell into disuse, and artistic talents were necessarily directed to more pragmatic ends. The few artisans and builders who were still in business traveled across western Europe constructing churches and chapels in protected places.

Charlemagne gave full support to the construction of impressive churches and palaces, especially his own royal residence. Today, most of the original apartments and offices of his palace are restored rather than original, but the Palace Chapel remains largely as it was first built (Figure 8.23). Inspired by the design of San Vitale in Ravenna, this magnificent room reflects the architect's reinterpretation of the graceful Byzantine style to incorporate the massive solidity of Roman monuments and the vigor of Germanic taste. The octagonal chapel stands two stories high, and heavy square pillars support the second level, where galleries are framed by graceful arches and columns from Italy. The bronze gratings and mosaic floor were also brought to Aachen from Italy. An **ambulatory,** or passageway for walking, extends around the circumference of the central space behind the pillars. Spiral steps lead to the upper floor, where the tribune, or emperor's throne, was located. From here, Charlemagne observed and participated in church services and ceremonies and was in turn observed by his subjects, enthroned as Christ's representative on earth.

Painting: Illuminated Manuscripts Although nearly all the murals, frescoes, and mosaics from this period have vanished, the surviving **illuminated manuscripts** offer an excellent view of the Early Medieval painting ideal. The art of manuscript illumination was influenced by the Germanic practice of decorating

Figure 8.23 Charlemagne's Palace Chapel. Ca. 792–805. Diameter over 50′. Aachen, Germany. *Odo of Metz designed the Royal Chapel for Charlemagne, and Pope Leo III probably dedicated it in 805. Although the chapel is inspired by Byzantine architecture, the decorative scheme and the roof design make it principally a Roman building. From the tenth to the sixteenth century, the Germans crowned their kings in this chapel.*

Figure 8.24 *St. Mark,* from the Gospel Book of St. Medard of Soissons. Early ninth century. Painted on vellum, 14 × 10″. Bibliothèque Nationale, Paris. *The so-called Italo-Alpine style of painting is evident in this portrait of St. Mark because it includes Roman decorations, in particular the columns derived from the Corinthian order. Although this gospel book was made for Charlemagne, it was given to the abbey of St. Medard by Louis the Pious, Charlemagne's heir.*

small objects and the Classical tradition of fine metalwork that had been maintained in Italy. During the Early Middle Ages, gifted artists and dedicated monks joined these disparate artistic elements to produce richly illustrated books and bejeweled book covers. Most of these decorated books were used in the liturgy of the Mass, such as the psalters, the collections of the psalms, and the gospel books, which were the texts of the first four books of the New Testament. For three centuries, in monasteries and abbeys from Ireland to Germany, scribes copied the Bible and their fellow artists adorned the pages with geometric and foliage designs, mythical animals, Christian symbols, and portraits of biblical characters and saints.

Manuscript illumination became both more symbolic and more realistic in the Carolingian Renaissance, partly because Italian artists were now influencing Frankish tastes. For example, the Gospel Book of St. Medard of Soissons follows Italian practice in being filled with Christian symbols and religious icons as well as making visual references to Classical architecture. In a portrait of St. Mark, the painter decorates the page with the lion, St. Mark's symbol, and frames the saint with a rounded arch, Corinthian columns, and folded curtains (Figure 8.24). In this small work, the figure of St. Mark exhibits a dynamic sense of life in his energetic body and tilted head.

Perhaps the most impressive of the Carolingian illuminated manuscripts was the St. Paul Bible, one of the presents Charles the Bald (r. 840–877), the grandson of Charlemagne, gave to win the pope's approval

Figure 8.25 *Adam and Eve.* Genesis, from the St. Paul Bible. Ca. 870. San Paolo Fuori le Mura, Rome. *This miniature painting of Adam and Eve was intended to introduce the Book of Genesis. Divided into three bands, the painting presents, from left to right, the story of the first man and woman, beginning with the creation of Adam and ending with the exile of both from Eden. The decoration is brilliantly colored and extremely inventive, as in the final episode, where Adam is shown digging while Eve stands by suckling her firstborn, Cain. The treatment of the human figures, with carefully modeled limbs and appropriate expressions, shows a full mastery of the human form. The only sour note in the painting is the way the artist has rendered Eve's breasts as pendulous—perhaps a reflection of the artist's lack of access to live models or a conventional depiction of Eve copied by the artist.*

for his coronation as emperor in 875. Produced in an unidentified scriptorium in the city of Reims by a team of scribes and illuminators, the St. Paul Bible originally contained twenty-four (today, twenty-three) decorated full-page miniature paintings to introduce some of the books in the Old and New Testaments (Figure 8.25). It also included a dedicatory miniature of Charles the Bald and his wife; a miniature based on the life of St. Jerome, translator of the Vulgate Bible; and a treasure trove of decorated title pages and initial letters. The luxurious style of the St. Paul Bible was typical of the works commissioned by Charles the Bald, who is recognized today as the most important patron of the Carolingian Renaissance.

At the end of the Early Middle Ages, the style of manuscript illumination became even more elaborate and richer in tone, as in the Gospel Book of Otto III, a product of the German Reichnau school. This manuscript represents the enthroned figure of St. Luke in a state of religious ecstasy. The saint supports a host of Jewish prophets and heavenly messengers; books from the Old Testament are stacked in his lap. Hovering above St. Luke's head is his symbol, the ox (Figure 8.26).

Figure 8.26 *St. Luke,* from the Gospel Book of Otto III. Ca. 1000. About 13 × 9⅜". Bayerische Staatsbibliothek, Munich. *In this illumination from a gospel book, the biblical symbols and images above St. Luke dominate the earthly and human forms. The unnatural colors and placement of the figures suggest a mystical meaning.*

The Legacy of Byzantium, Islam, and the Early Medieval West

When Constantinople fell, Byzantine civilization left a profound legacy to the West, some of which is alive today. In Eastern Europe, the Orthodox church continues to influence the Slavic population. Western law owes a great debt to the Code of Justinian, which became the standard legal text studied in medieval universities. Elements of Byzantine art appeared in Renaissance art in Italy, and the Italian cities of Venice, Genoa, and Pisa became major cultural centers in the fifteenth century because of the wealth they had accumulated from Byzantine trade.

Byzantium also served conserving functions for the West. The Byzantine state acted as a buffer against the militant Arabs in the seventh century and against the Seljuk Turks in the twelfth century. Byzantine scholars preserved the ancient Greek texts, many of which were carried to Italy, England, and elsewhere in the mid–fifteenth century. When these works were reintroduced into the West, they intensified the cultural revival already under way.

Islamic civilization's impact on Western culture has been significant, though not as direct as that of Byzantium. Of all of the benefits passed on from Islam, the transmission of the basic philosophical and scientific texts from the ancient world is probably the most important. Original Muslim contributions in algebra and other mathematical concepts have also been central to the rise of the modern scientific tradition in the West.

The civilization of the Early Medieval West, of course, has been most decisive for the direction of Western culture. Most of the heritage from this first medieval period was simply a transmission of what had been formed earlier in the ancient world: the Christian church, the papacy, the Latin language, the educational ideal embodied in the arts and the sciences, building and artistic techniques, Greek thought, and Greco-Roman literary and artistic forms. Most of these ancient legacies were reshaped in some way, such as the reform of monasticism along Benedictine lines and the spread of female monasticism.

What was added to the Western legacy in the Early Middle Ages was basically the uniting of Classical, Germanic, and Christian elements into a new civilization centered in Europe rather than in the Mediterranean basin. This new version of Western culture was born in the reign of Charlemagne, and its memory lingered on in the monasteries and other isolated quarters. When the barbarian invasions were over, a more enduring Western culture was born.

KEY CULTURAL TERMS

Byzantine style
Greek cross
pendentive
arcade
arabesque
calligraphy
mosque
minaret
miniature
Gregorian chant
ambulatory
illuminated manuscript

SUGGESTIONS FOR FURTHER READING

PRIMARY SOURCES

BEDE. *A History of the English Church and People.* Translated by L. Sherley-Price. New York: Penguin, 1955. Written in 731, this account of the church in Saxon England is an important source for understanding early Christian society and attitudes in England.

BOETHIUS. *The Consolation of Philosophy.* Translated by V. E. Watts. New York: Penguin, 1969. An account, combining verse and prose and written in the early sixth century, that shows how Christian faith and pagan philosophy enabled the author to accept both his fall from power and death.

COMNENA, ANNA. *The Alexiad of Anna Comnena.* Translated and with a brief introduction by E. R. A. Sewter. New York: Penguin, 1979. A fresh, modern translation of this Byzantine classic work of history, with notes, a map, appendices, and genealogical tables; some of the author's digressions are consigned to footnotes.

EINHARD AND NOTKER THE STAMMERER. *Two Lives of Charlemagne.* Translated by L. Thorpe. New York: Penguin, 1969. A useful introduction and many footnotes enlighten the student about these two brief but important contemporary biographies by, respectively, the head of Charlemagne's palace school and a monk.

GREGORY, BISHOP OF TOURS. *History of the Franks.* Translated by L. Thorpe. New York: Penguin, 1974. An engrossing account of this chaotic time by an eyewitness.

HROTSWITHA. *The Plays of Hrotsvit [Hrotswitha] of Gandersheim.* Translated and with an introduction by K. Wilson. New York: Garland, 1989. A lively and authoritative translation of these early medieval plays, with scholarly notes.

WINDOWS ON THE WORLD: 500–1000

HISTORY

AFRICA

East Africa *Madagascar.* Settlement by Southeast Asians; introduced new crops (bananas, plantains, and papayas).

North Africa Egypt and the Maghreb (modern Libya, Tunisia, Algeria, and Morocco) conquered by Arab Muslims (late 7th century).

West Africa *Ghana (West Sahara).* Rise of kingdom of Ghana; controlled gold and salt caravan trade. Black and Berber population. *Niger Delta.* Jenne-jero, a mudbrick town of about 10,000, flourished; wealth based on gold and salt trade.

Northeast Africa *Axum culture.* Controlled western Arabia for short time (6th century). Ended 1000.

AMERICAS

Andes *Moche culture.* Collapse ca. 600. *Sicán culture (North Coast), began 700.* Wide-ranging trade network. *Tiwanaku (Lake Titicaca)* and *Wari cultures, 500–800.* Warrior theocracies; long-distance trade; raised-field farming.

Mesoamerica *Classic period, ended 900. Mayan culture (zenith: 600–900).* Modern Chiapas, Belize, and southern lowlands. *Teotihuacán culture.* Collapse ca. 650. *Zapotec culture.* Strong trading economy. *Early Postclassic period, began 900. Mayan culture.* General decline; Toltecs seized Chichén Itzá in Yucatán ca. 900. *Toltec culture.* Tula (north of Mexico City) and Chichén Itzá. Iron introduced. *Zapotec culture.* Loss of population and abandonment.

Native North America *Hohokam (ca. 200–1450; Arizona).* Canal irrigation systems and ritual ballcourts. *Anasazi (ca. 400–1300; Arizona, Colorado).* Pueblos connected by road system; dominated turquoise trade.

ART & MUSIC

AFRICA

South Africa Rock art in Cedar Mountains (Republic of South Africa), painted by hunter-gatherers.

West Africa *Nigeria, at Igbo-Ukwu.* Terra-cotta and bronze sculptures entombed with dignitaries.

AMERICAS

Andes *Sicán culture.* Silver, gold, and bronze funerary objects; textiles with abstract patterns of deities. *Tiwanaku culture.* Stylized monolithic stone figures, ceramics, metalwork, and pottery. *Wari culture.* Textiles, ceramics, goldwork, and monumental sculpture.

Mesoamerica *Classic period. Mayan culture.* Various styles of art. Sculptural friezes. *Zapotec culture.* Tomb paintings and ritual clay urns.

Native North America *Southwest. Mogollon (ca. 200–1250; New Mexico, Arizona).* Mimbres pottery (stylized figurative designs in black on white). *Hohokam.* Etched shells, fine pottery, turquoise mosaics.

The Friar. Carved monolith. Red sandstone, ht. 8′. Tiwanaku, Bolivia.

ARCHITECTURE

AFRICA

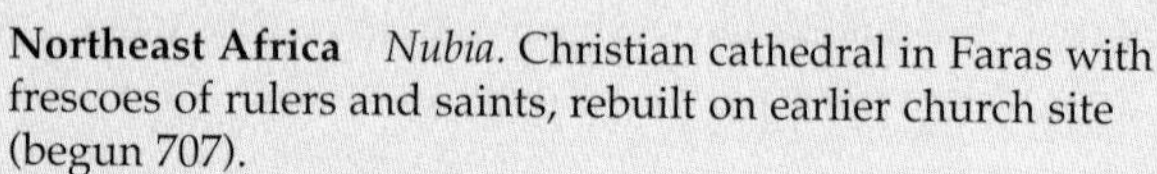

Northeast Africa *Nubia.* Christian cathedral in Faras with frescoes of rulers and saints, rebuilt on earlier church site (begun 707).

South Africa *Bantu culture.* Egalitarian society with people grouped into villages of conical thatched huts (6th century). By 10th century, chiefs lived separately, behind high-walled enclosures.

AMERICAS

Andes *Tiwanaku culture.* Ceremonial centers with palaces, pyramids, plazas, and sunken courtyards; elaborate post-and-lintel portals. Use of the grid in city design.

Mesoamerica *Mayan culture.* Palenque Palace; Temple of the Inscriptions, tomb of King Pacal. *Zapotec culture.* Mile-long stone wall around center of Monte Albán; underground tombs.

Native North America *Anasazi.* Chaco Canyon multistory "apartment" complexes around plazas with ceremonial subterranean kivas. Cliff-house villages.

Temple of the Inscriptions, Ca. 750. Palenque, Mexico.

RELIGION, PHILOSOPHY, LITERATURE

AFRICA

North Africa Islam spreads across the region.

Northeast Africa *Nubia (Kush).* Converted to Christianity (about 540).

West Africa *Nigeria.* Elaborate burial rituals.

Altar Stand. Found in Igbo-Ukwu tomb. Ninth century. Bronze, ht. 11¾″. Nigerian Museum, Lagos.

AMERICAS

Andes *Sicán culture.* Sicán Precinct, a religious and funeral site. *Tiwanaku culture.* Religious images suggestive of sun worship. *Wari culture.* Agrarian motifs (especially maize) in religion.

Mesoamerica *Classic period. Mayan culture.* Inscriptions on stone slabs. *Zapotec culture.* Glyph writing on tombs and in paintings. *Early Postclassic period. Toltec culture.* Ritual sacrifice of defeated enemies; practice also adopted by the Mayas.

Native North America *Southwest. Anasazi.* Petroglyphs on cliffs depicting historical events, migration routes, astronomical patterns.

ASIA

China

Sui Dynasty, 581–618. China reunited; strong centralized state. *T'ang Dynasty, 618–906.* A culturally vibrant and militarily expansionist period. World's largest empire. *Five Dynasties, 907–960.* End of centralized rule. *Sung Dynasty, began 960.* China reunited; capital Kaifeng, in the north.

India

Northern. Gupta Dynasty fell to the Huns (about 550). *Post–Gupta period.* Rival dynasties; most successful was the Buddhist Pala Dynasty (8th–10th centuries). Feudal society. *Southern.* Region controlled by the Hindu Pallava Dynasty (4th–9th centuries); growth of Aryan culture. Built navy and dockyards; rich sea trade. Pallavas defeated (ca. 900) by Cholas and Pandyas (Tamil Dynasties).

Japan

Asuka to Nara periods, 552–794. Height of Chinese influence. The first fixed capital Nara (710–794) modeled after the T'ang capital Ch'ang-an (now Xi'an). A more centralized regime emerged. *Heian period, began 794.* Chinese-style government failed, and capital moved to Heian (modern Kyoto). The apogee of aristocratic Japan. Emperor's power in decline (950) and warrior class (samurai) ascending.

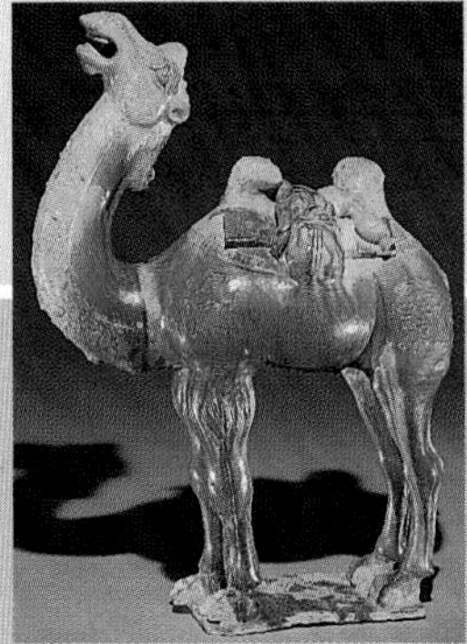

Tomb Model of Camel. Eighth century. Glazed pottery. British Museum.

T'ang Dynasty. Relief carvings in Buddhist cave shrines; marble figures of Buddha and bodhisattvas; landscape painting; ceramics, often placed in tombs. A rich period in music.

Northern. Pala Dynasty. Complex stone sculptures, in response to a new form (Vajrayana) of Buddhism. *Southern. Pallava Dynasty.* Larger-than-life stone sculptures of animals, humans, and gods. Kings were music patrons.

Asuka to Nara periods. Narrative painting, lacquered wood, and embroidery; zenith of Buddhist sculpture. *Heian period.* Huge stone and wood religious sculptures; scroll and screen paintings, in both Chinese and Japanese style. *Gagaku,* court music, based on Chinese models.

Sui Dynasty. Great Wall rebuilt and realigned. *T'ang Dynasty.* Cave temples.

Northern. Pala Dynasty. Buddhist stupas. *Southern. Pallava Dynasty.* Free-standing stone temples at Mamallapuram, a coastal city.

Shore Temple, Mamallapuram. Early eighth century.

Asuka to Nara periods. The Hōryūji, a walled compound at Nara, enclosing several wooden buildings; except for a pagoda derived from Buddhist architecture, the buildings were based on the T'ang Chinese temple. *Heian period.* The Shingon temple of Murōji (near Nara), a five-story pagoda with broad overhanging shingle roof. Buddhist monastery complex (more than 300 buildings) on a mountain near Heian.

Sui Dynasty. Hsieh Ho's *Old Record of the Classifications of Painters,* a classic of art criticism. Spread of Mahayana Buddhism and the cult of bodhisattvas ("enlightened" disciples). *T'ang Dynasty.* Golden Age of poetry. Woodblock printing invented; mass production of Buddhist and Taoist texts.

Northern. Pala Dynasty. University of Nalanda in Bihar flourished; Buddhism spread to Tibet. *Sind (modern Pakistan).* Conquered by Arab Muslims (712).

Asuka to Nara periods. The history *Kojiki* (*Records of Ancient Matters,* 712), the earliest work of Japanese literature. Chinese Buddhism arrived (552) by way of Korea. Chinese calendar adopted. Japanese National University founded. *Heian period. Kokinshū,* a collection of 1,111 poems (905). New school of Buddhism (Tendai), imported from China; offered hope to ordinary men and women.

CARROLVS
CAROLVS
CAROLVS
CAROLVS
CAROLVS
CAROLVS

9 THE HIGH MIDDLE AGES
The Christian Centuries

Although Charlemagne's ambitious hopes for Europe were thwarted by the invasions of the ninth and tenth centuries, society had grown more settled by the early eleventh century, and a brighter era began to unfold in the West. Between 1000 and 1300—the period called the High Middle Ages—a new foundation was laid that would support the future development of Western civilized life.

During this time, the Christian church became the dominant institution of the medieval world. At the same time, feudalism was established as the principal military, economic, and political system, and feudal monarchies in France, England, and central Europe were beginning to form what would become European states. Town life also revived in the West, and a new urban class was born. Situated midway between the feudal aristocrats and the peasants, this middle class included merchants, moneylenders, and skilled artisans—virtually all free persons associated with town life.

These momentous political, social, and economic changes were reflected in cultural interests. Theologians, writers, and architects worked to harmonize the two opposing trends of the time, the secular and the spiritual. They achieved a stunning but short-lived synthesis. Moving from rugged warrior values, supreme between 1000 and 1150, Western culture became more refined, more learned, and increasingly secular between 1150 and 1300. The earlier 150-year period is associated with monastic and feudal themes in literature and the Romanesque style in architecture. The later period saw a growing trend toward urban and courtly themes in literature and the rise of Gothic architecture, the most spectacular realization of which was the Gothic cathedral.

◀ **Detail** *Charlemagne Panels.* Stained-glass window, Chartres cathedral. Ca. 1220–1225. Chartres, France.

Figure 9.1 *Count Eckhart and Uta.* Naumburg cathedral. Ca. 1245. Limestone, life-size. Naumburg, Germany. *In this representation of a feudal lord and lady, the most striking features are the woman's chaste beauty, reflecting her role as the queen of chivalry and linking her to the Virgin Mary, and the man's great heraldic shield and sword, symbolizing his position as an aristocratic warrior and defender of honor. These two figures are among several that stand in Naumburg cathedral, representing noble men and women associated with the founding of the cathedral. The Naumburg statues are considered among the most beautiful sculptures from this period.*

FEUDALISM

Out of feudalism—a military and political system based on personal loyalty and kinship—arose a new social order, a code of conduct, and an artistic and literary tradition. In the beginning, feudalism restored law and order to western Europe, even though local lords often exploited those under them. But during the High Middle Ages, the feudal nobility slowly lost power to the feudal kings, who laid the foundations of the early modern national monarchies. By the early 1300s, feudalism no longer served its original function and was being superseded in many areas by different political, social, and economic forms.

The Feudal System and the Feudal Society

Feudalism evolved in the Early Middle Ages under the Franks and expanded under Charlemagne. As a military system, it offered some protection from invaders but at the cost of fragmenting society into rival states. As the feudal chiefs began to pass their lands on to their eldest sons, Europe became dominated by a military aristocracy (see Chapter 8).

Feudal wealth was reckoned in land; the feudal estate included lands, manor houses, and the serfs who worked the land. The feudal lords attracted warriors, called vassals, to their private armies by offering them estates, and thus feudalism depended on the manorial economy. The feudal estate, called a fief, provided the warrior with the means to outfit himself with the proper military equipment and attendants and to live in an aristocratic style.

Over the generations, feudalism became a complex web of agreements, obligations, and rituals. A written agreement spelled out the mutual duties and obligations of the lord and the vassal. Typically, the lord gave military protection to his vassal and settled quarrels among his supporters through his court. The vassal in turn furnished military or financial aid and sat as counsel in the lord's court. Conflicts between a lord and his vassal were sometimes settled by peers in the lord's court, but more often they escalated into civil wars.

The vassal–lord relationship was the heart of feudalism, but the form of the institution varied geographically. Feudalism's prototype was that of northern France, around Paris, but each area modified the French form to suit its local needs. Those who profited from feudalism retained the institution as long as possible, so that well into the twentieth century its vestiges were evident in central Europe and Russia and were eliminated only by revolution.

The hierarchical feudal social order was defined and elaborated in the unwritten rules of conduct known as the **chivalric code.** In the early eleventh century, chivalry (from the French word *cheval,* meaning "horse") was largely a warrior code, although one rooted in Christian values. More an ideal than a reality, it nevertheless inspired the vassal to honor his lord and to respect his peers. He was also expected to protect the weak from danger and to practice his ideals—bravery, strength, and honesty—with all members of society. The French clergy refined the chivalric code by initiating the Peace of God, a call for an end to fighting at specified times, and other clerics encouraged the knights to treat women, clergy, and peasants more humanely.

By the twelfth century, both the Peace of God and the notion of protected classes—notably women—had been incorporated into the heart of a more refined and courtly version of the chivalric code. Especially influential in altering the status of women was the rise of courtly love, a movement that began in the aristocratic courts of southern France. The love of a lord for a lady (usually an unattainable lady, such as another man's wife) was seen as an ennobling emotion, encouraging the man to ever greater deeds. Aristocratic ladies were idealized and venerated with an almost holy respect, resembling that shown for the Virgin Mary (Figure 9.1). (However, a contemporaneous countertrend also identified women with Eve, who, by tempting Adam to eat the forbidden fruit, brought the burden of original sin to humanity.) Courtly love, one of the greatest contributions of medieval civilization, provided inspiration for much of the secular literature, art, and music of the High Middle Ages because it encouraged the intermingling of men and women in social settings, where dancing, music, and conversation were enjoyed in accordance with the rules of courtesy.

Whatever the image of woman in medieval society, however, on a practical level her position was determined by the social status of her husband or her father or by the support of a powerful family. A few women—such as Eleanor of Aquitaine, wife of King Henry II of England, in the twelfth century—sometimes influenced a spouse's decisions or wielded power on behalf of a son. But their rarity as rulers in their own right testifies to how little power women had in the Middle Ages, despite their exalted image.

Peasant Life

Feudalism and chivalry served the interests of the small noble classes. Life was quite different for the peasants, who constituted the vast majority of the population. Some were free, but many were bound in service. The two most common forms of servitude, slavery and serfdom, were legacies from Rome. Slaves were the personal property of the lord, whereas serfs were half-free but tied to the land. Serfs worked for the lord in exchange for living on his land. In eleventh-century Europe, slavery was dying out because the church's teachings had largely convinced the feudal lords of its inhumanity, but serfdom was firmly entrenched.

The routine of the serfs and the free peasants was dictated by custom and regulated by daily and seasonal events (Figure 9.2). With men and women occasionally working together in the fields, they eked out a bare subsistence from their tiny plots of land; they lived in wooden huts, raised their children, and found relief in the church's frequent Holy Days and feast days. As farming innovations were introduced (such as three-field crop rotation, which allowed the land to replenish itself), the plight of the serfs improved. Increasing the productivity of the soil brought economic benefits to the lord, who could then, if he wished, pay the peasants in coin and sell them tracts of land.

Figure 9.2 *Labors of the Months.* Amiens cathedral. Ca. 1220–1230. Amiens, France. *The labors of the months—threshing and fruit-picking—are shown beneath their respective zodiacal signs—Cancer (late June to late July) and Leo (late July to late August). These carefully observed scenes of peasant life from the western portals of Amiens cathedral show peasants engaged in their seasonal tasks. The labors of the months and the zodiacal signs are framed in quatrefoils—four-leafed shapes—which are typical decorative devices in medieval art.*

As serfs gained a few legal rights, they could become economically independent and gain their freedom from the manorial system. These trends, however, were confined to western Europe, notably England and France. In some areas of central and eastern Europe, serfs continued to be exploited for centuries.

The Rise of Towns

A new trend began to counter the dominance of the feudal system: the rise of urban areas where free individuals pursued their own economic goals. Although rural manors provided work and security for 90 percent of the population at the beginning of the High Middle Ages, the population of Europe nearly doubled between 1000 and 1300, from thirty-five million to almost seventy million, and an increasing number of people sought economic opportunities in the new and revitalized urban areas (Figure 9.3). From this point on, the future of the West lay with town dwellers.

As towns grew larger and urban life became more competitive, the residents formed associations, called guilds, to protect their special interests. The artisan and craft guilds, for example, regulated working conditions, created apprenticeship programs, and set wages; the merchant and banking guilds approved new businesses and supervised trade contracts. These guilds often quarreled over issues inside the town walls, but they joined hands against the intrusions of the church and the local nobility.

Because urban economic life conflicted with the interests of the feudal system, urban dwellers, led by the

Figure 9.3 *Street Scene in a Medieval Town.* Bibliothèque Nationale, Paris. *Four businesses are crowded together into this narrow street. In the background, three furriers await customers. Other merchants have hung out signs to advertise their trades, such as the barber who displays four "barber bowls"—a device placed over the head during a haircut. In the left foreground, tailors stitch clothing, and, on the right, a storekeeper arranges goods in front of his shop. Most tradesmen lived above their stores, which meant that the town was filled with people both day and night.*

guilds, founded self-governing towns, called communes, often with written charters that specified their rights in relation to the feudal lords. By about 1200, many towns in northern and western Europe had charters, and their political independence spurred economic growth.

Artisans and merchants needed buyers, secure trade routes, and markets for their products if they were to prosper. The earliest trade routes were the rivers and the old Roman roads. As demand increased in the West for luxury items from the East, new trade routes opened. Italian cities led this international commerce, trading the luxurious woolen cloth of Flanders for the silks of China and the spices of the Middle East (Map 9.1). Along the overland routes in Europe, local lords guaranteed traders safe passage through their territory for a fee. Some nobles and towns along the way sponsored fairs to lure this rich international trade.

As on the feudal manor, the position of women in the medieval urban world was still subordinate to that of men, even though urban women often worked closely with their husbands in trade or crafts. Indeed, in this hierarchical society gender roles became in-

Map 9.1 PRINCIPAL TRADING ROUTES AND TOWNS OF EUROPE, 1300

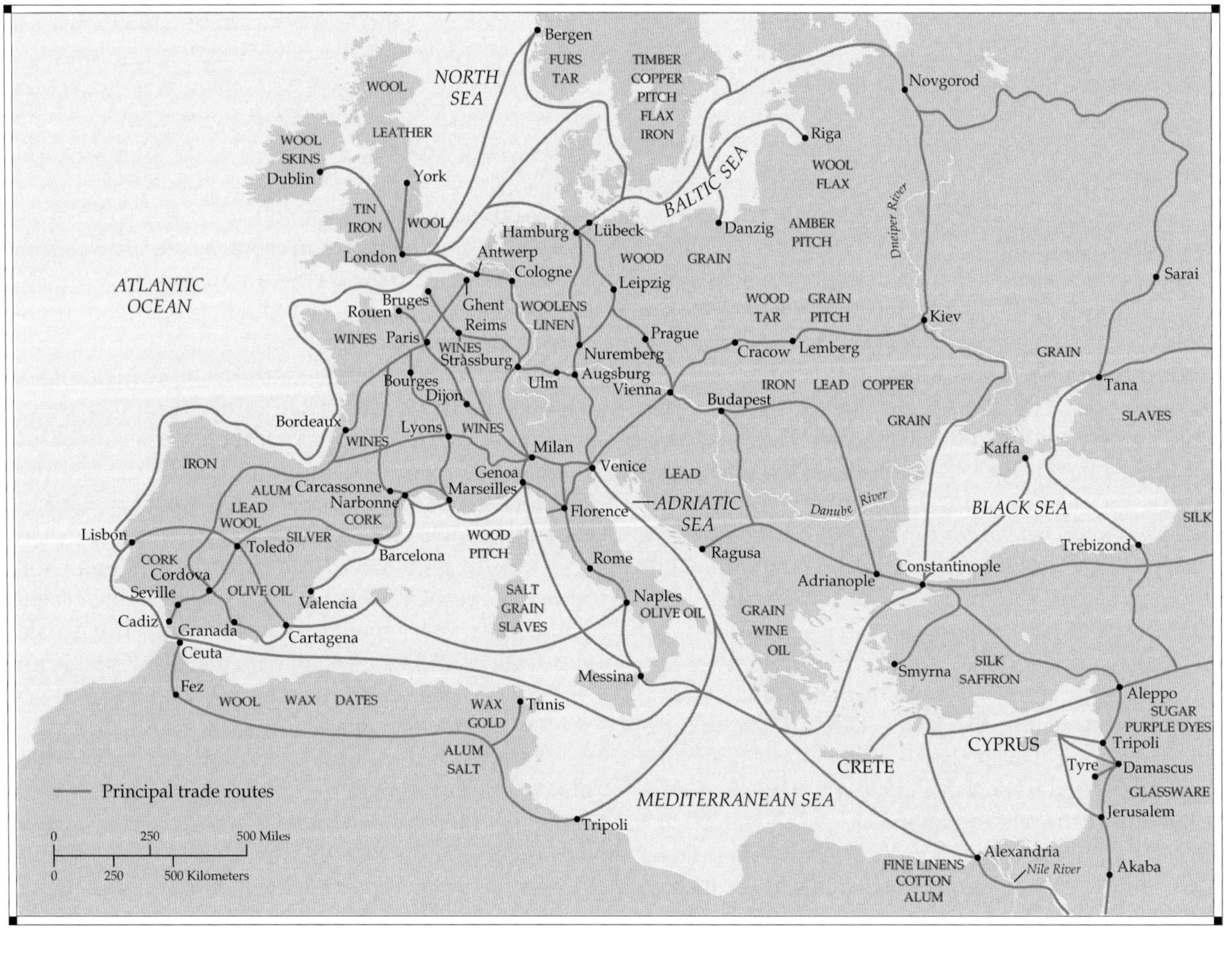

creasingly differentiated through custom and legislation. As a consequence, females could neither hold governmental office nor have any public voice in politics. The few women with economic power—such as those directly involved in manufacturing and trade or the occasional rich widow who kept her husband's business afloat—were exceptions to this general exclusionary rule.

The Feudal Monarchy

Politically, feudalism was leading to a new form of rule. By about 1100, some powerful feudal lords had begun to expand their holdings into larger kingdoms. As these ambitious noblemen subdued weaker ones, they often sealed their victories through marriages with the conquered family. Over the ensuing generations, their heirs extended and consolidated their lands, always seeking to win the loyalty of their new subjects. The greatest problem a feudal monarch faced was building a centralized rule to keep the kingdom from disintegrating into a set of separate, warring states. During the High Middle Ages, four feudal monarchies dominated the West: France, England, the Holy Roman Empire, and the papacy, which was politically similar to the three secular monarchies (Timeline 9.1).

The French Monarchy The origins of modern France stem from the reign of Hugh Capet (r. 987–996), the first of the Capetian rulers, who exercised power over a part of the old Frankish kingdom (see Chapter 8). By the early eleventh century, the Capetians, having defeated their rivals, had founded a feudal monarchy in central France, with Paris as its center.

During the twelfth and thirteenth centuries, a series of able monarchs managed to consolidate and expand the Capetian power base and control the great vassals by forming alliances with the lesser nobles, the middle class, the clergy, and the popes. The establishment of central authority in France was a slow process, but by the beginning of the reign of Philip IV in 1285, France was the most powerful feudal kingdom in Europe and the French tradition of royal absolutism was well established.

The English Monarchy The English monarchs also amassed power at the expense of the feudal landowners, but the English rulers never controlled their kingdom to the same degree as the Capetians. Moreover, because some English kings made grievous mistakes, England's feudal barons won pivotal battles against the monarchy. In addition, judicial reforms and advisory councils tended to limit, not to expand, the English kings' power.

Three major events determined English history during the High Middle Ages. The first was the Norman invasion of England. For five centuries, England had been ruled by an Anglo-Saxon monarchy, and when the king died in 1066 without a clear successor, Duke William, the ruler of the duchy of Normandy in northern France, invaded England to claim the throne. At the Battle of Hastings, in 1066, William conquered the Anglo-Saxon contender, Harold, and became king of England (Figure 9.4). For the rest of the High Middle Ages, England was ruled by Norman kings and their French (Angevin) successors, and conquerors and conquered were blended into one nation and one culture.

The second major event occurred in 1215 when the English feudal barons forced King John (r. 1199–1216) to sign the Magna Carta ("great charter"), a document that limited royal authority and gave the barons certain financial and governmental controls over the crown. In the long run, the Magna Carta was also a victory for all freemen because it gave them certain judicial rights, such as trial by jury.

The third event was the creation of Parliament, which occurred during the reign of Henry III (r. 1216–1272). Faced with renewed hostility from his English barons, Henry agreed to convene the ancient but little-used Great Council, comprising representatives from every county and town. This body became Parliament (from the French word *parler,* "to talk") and began to advise the king. Initially, Parliament was part of the royal government, but in time it represented the people against the crown, as England moved further toward a limited feudal monarchy.

The Holy Roman Empire Whereas France and England grew into unified feudal monarchies, the Holy Roman Empire, which began as the Saxon dynasty of Otto I in the late tenth century, failed to achieve a centralized state. From the early eleventh to the early twelfth century, the empire prospered and trade expanded, but a conflict with the papacy arose that would undermine the empire. It concerned the European-wide practice of lay investiture—the appointment of priests, bishops, and archbishops by local lords and nobles, often for money. Such appointments allowed the secular rulers some control over the wealth and influence of the church within their own territories. The central issue in the long and complicated conflict was whether the bishops and archbishops were the servants of the pope or of the secular rulers.

The issue of lay investiture was settled by the Concordat of Worms in 1122, which allowed the pope to confer spiritual authority on the clergy and the emperor to invest them with land and secular authority. But the rivalry between the Holy Roman rulers and the popes would not die. Under the Hohenstaufen

Timeline 9.1 THE FEUDAL MONARCHIES IN THE HIGH MIDDLE AGES

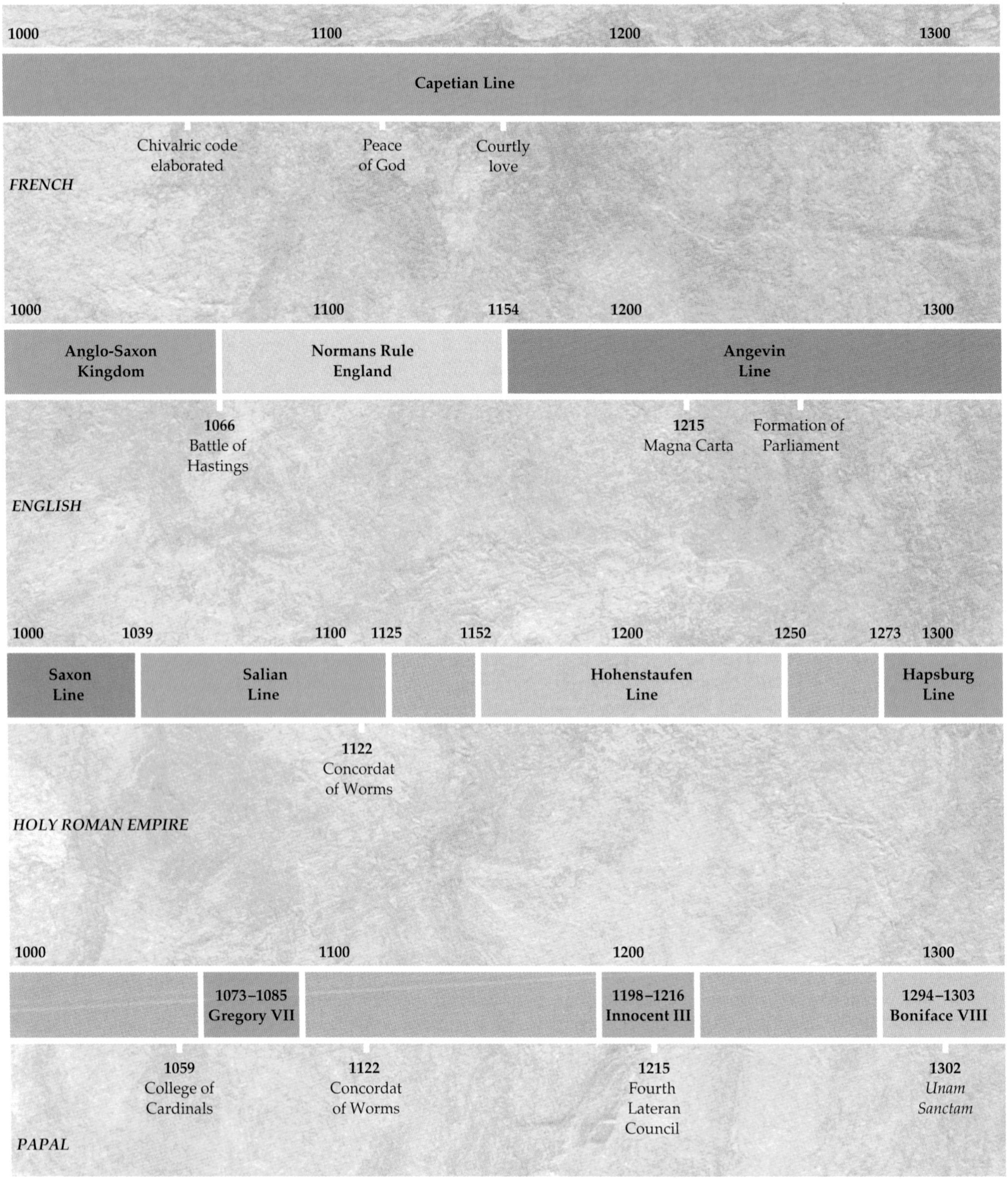

FRENCH

1000 | 1100 | 1200 | 1300

Capetian Line

Chivalric code elaborated

Peace of God

Courtly love

ENGLISH

1000 | 1100 | 1154 | 1200 | 1300

Anglo-Saxon Kingdom | **Normans Rule England** | **Angevin Line**

1066 Battle of Hastings

1215 Magna Carta

Formation of Parliament

HOLY ROMAN EMPIRE

1000 | 1039 | 1100 | 1125 | 1152 | 1200 | 1250 | 1273 | 1300

Saxon Line | **Salian Line** | **Hohenstaufen Line** | **Hapsburg Line**

1122 Concordat of Worms

PAPAL

1000 | 1100 | 1200 | 1300

1073–1085 Gregory VII | **1198–1216 Innocent III** | **1294–1303 Boniface VIII**

1059 College of Cardinals

1122 Concordat of Worms

1215 Fourth Lateran Council

1302 *Unam Sanctam*

Figure 9.4 *These Men Wonder at the Star. Harold.* Panel from the Bayeux Tapestry. Third quarter of the eleventh century. Wool embroidery on linen, ht. 20″. Bayeux, France. *Today housed in the cathedral of Bayeux, this famous embroidery provides an important historic record of the events leading up to the Battle of Hastings and presents a justification for the Norman conquest of England. Harold is cast as a villain who breaks his oath of allegiance to William and loses the English crown as a result of this treachery.*

Halley's comet, interpreted as an evil omen, appeared over England in February 1066. The comet is shown in the center of the upper border. On the left, men point to the comet, and on the right Harold also seems upset by the comet. Beneath Harold and his adviser are outlines of boats, implying a possible invasion by the Normans.

dynasty, Frederick Barbarossa and Frederick II temporarily created an empire in central Europe, which included Italy. Their successors failed to maintain this empire, and the popes resumed their sway over Italian politics. The Holy Roman emperors ceased playing a major role in European affairs until after the coming of the Hapsburg line in 1273.

The Papal Monarchy The papacy during the High Middle Ages closely resembled the feudal monarchies in Europe, except that it was guided by the ideal of Christendom—a universal state ruled by the popes under God's law. The church's most powerful claim to authority was that only through the clergy—those trained and ordained to administer the sacraments—could a Christian hope to gain everlasting life. The church defined society's moral standards at the same time that it participated in the politics of the period.

The key to the church's power was a reform movement that originated in the Benedictine monastery at Cluny, France, and swept through Europe in the 900s. Before this movement, the church had been riddled with scandal and corruption, and many clergy were poorly trained and lived less than exemplary lives. Because of lay investiture, bishops often acted as vassals of feudal lords rather than as agents of the church. The buying and selling of church offices, a practice known as simony, meant that positions often went to the highest bidder. Worst of all, many clergymen expressed blatant disregard for the sacraments.

The monks at Cluny, however, were free of feudal obligations and loyal only to the pope. Little by little, the Cluniacs impressed Europe with their spirituality, and as they established new monasteries and reformed others, the church began to revive, to eliminate corrupt practices, and to reimpose celibacy on the clergy. In 1059 the College of Cardinals was founded to elect the popes, thus freeing the papacy from German and Italian politics. By the late eleventh century, the political power of the reformed popes rivaled that of the feudal monarchs.

Of the great medieval popes, the two most powerful were Gregory VII and Innocent III. Gregory VII (pope 1073–1085), brought to the papacy by the Cluniac revival, purified the wayward clergy, demanding full obedience to canon law. Innocent III (pope 1198–1216) was probably the most powerful pontiff in the history of the church. He excommunicated kings; intervened in the secular affairs of England, France, and the Holy Roman Empire; and advocated crusades against the Muslims abroad and the heretics at home. Motivated by the ideal of Christendom, his aim was to unite Europe under the papal banner.

By his extravagant claims, Pope Boniface VIII (pope 1294–1303) unwittingly undid the three centuries' work of his predecessors to build papal power (Figure 9.5). In 1302 he issued the papal bull (from the Latin word *bolla,* "seal") known as *Unam sanctam,* a proclamation of papal superiority over all secular rulers. The French crown swiftly sent an army to arrest the pope, and an unnerved Boniface VIII had to flee and died soon thereafter. This episode precipitated a decline in the prestige of the papacy from which it did not fully recover until the sixteenth century.

MEDIEVAL CHRISTIANITY AND THE CHURCH

In addition to its political significance, the institution of the church had incalculable influence in the High Middle Ages, bringing Christian values to bear on virtually all of medieval life. The church owed its influence not only to the maneuverings of the popes but also to the tireless work of the clergy and the powerful effect of Christian beliefs.

Figure 9.5 Arnolfo di Cambio. *Pope Boniface VIII.* Early fourteenth century. Museo dell'Opera del Duomo, Florence, Italy. *Boniface VIII is portrayed in his crown and vestments—the rich trappings of papal monarchical power. The sculptor, Arnolfo di Cambio, who was also the first architect of the Florentine cathedral (see Chapter 10), has depicted Boniface VIII in the elongated Late Gothic style with sagging draperies.*

By this time in its history, the church had evolved an elaborate organization to carry out its work. The pope, as the spiritual leader of Christianity, stood at the head of a strict hierarchy. Supporting him was the papal curia—a staff of administrators, financial experts, secretaries, clerics, and legal advisers. A system of ecclesiastical courts handled the church's judicial functions and interpreted canon law, the church's law code based on the Bible. These courts were technically restricted to cases involving clerical personnel, but in actuality their jurisdiction was broader because of the huge number of people enmeshed in the workings of the church. The church's judicial branch rivaled the feudal courts in jurisdiction, and canon law sometimes challenged the authority of feudal law.

Tithes, taxes, and special collections provided funds for the church's daily operations and its charitable obligations. The system was relatively efficient, and as long as the church spent the funds wisely, the populace kept up its generous contributions.

Christian Beliefs and Practices

A great part of the immense authority of the church sprang from the belief shared by the overwhelming majority of the medieval population that the church held the keys to the kingdom of heaven and provided the only way to salvation. By attempting to adhere to the Christian moral code and by participating in the rituals and ceremonies prescribed by the church and established by tradition, Christians hoped for redemption and eternal life after death.

These rituals and ceremonies were basically inseparable from the doctrines of the religion. They had been derived from the teachings of Jesus and Paul, clarified by the church fathers, particularly Augustine, and further defined by medieval theologians. Finally, the Fourth Lateran Council of 1215, under Pope Innocent III, officially proclaimed the sacraments as the outward signs of God's grace and the only way to heaven.

As established by the council, the sacraments numbered seven: baptism, confirmation, the Eucharist (Holy Communion), penance, marriage, last rites, and ordination for the priesthood. Baptism, the Eucharist, and penance were deemed of primary importance. In baptism, the parents were assured that the infant had been rescued from original sin. In the Eucharist, the central part of the Mass, the church taught that a miracle occurred whereby the priest turned the bread and wine into the body and blood of Jesus. That the outer appearance of the bread and wine remained the same while their inner nature changed was explained by medieval philosophers in the doctrine of transubstantiation. For the uneducated congregation, however, the

Mass and the miracle were simply another sign of the church's spiritual power.

Penance evolved into a rather complicated practice. First, sinners confessed their sins individually to a priest; the priest conveyed God's forgiveness for the mortal penalties of sin so that hell could be avoided; the priest then directed that an earthly punishment—the penance—be carried out in an effort to erase the effects of the sin. Depending on the severity of the sin, penance could range from a few prayers to a pilgrimage or a crusade. This sacrament was made even more complex by its association with purgatory.

With the groundwork laid by Augustine in the fifth century and Pope Gregory the Great in the sixth century, the doctrine of purgatory was given more explicit form by the papacy and scholastic thinkers of the High Middle Ages. Neither hell nor heaven, purgatory was a third place, where those who had died in a state of grace could avoid damnation by being purged, or purified, from all stain of sin. All souls in purgatory were ultimately destined for heaven; penance was a means of reducing time in purgatory. Thus the living could do penance on earth in hope of spending less time in purgatory.

Confession and penance became widespread practices of the eleventh-century church. By 1300, both were integral to Christian rituals and beliefs. In political terms, penance, along with the Mass, was an effective means for controlling the moral behavior of church members.

Religious Orders and Lay Piety

Crucial to the workings of the church were the clergy, who were the most visible signs of the church's presence in everyday life. The "secular" clergy (from *saeculum,* Latin for "world") moved freely in society, and the "regular" clergy lived apart from the world in monasteries under a special rule (*regula* in Latin). The monasteries served as refuges from the world, as schools, and as places of study where manuscripts could be copied and traditional learning maintained. They also gave rise to the reform movements that periodically cleansed the church of corruption.

As noted earlier, the Cluniac monks originated the reform movement that helped to establish the moral and political authority of the medieval church. Other waves of reform followed, the most important of which was represented by the founding of the Cistercian order in the twelfth century. Bernard of Clairvaux [klair-VOE] (1090–1153), a saint, a mystic, and one of the most forceful personalities of the period, personally founded over 160 Cistercian abbeys. Unlike the moderate Cluniacs, the Cistercians observed a severe rule, living usually in isolated monasteries where the brothers worked with the local peasants. The Cistercians also simplified their worship services, eliminating elaborate ceremonies.

For women, the religious impulse found an outlet in convents and nunneries. Here, women could devote themselves to Christ and follow ascetic lives filled with prayer, contemplation, and service. Convents had existed since the time of Charlemagne, although seldom with the large endowments monasteries enjoyed or with as much influence in local affairs.

Convent life nevertheless did nurture several gifted women who influenced this age, most notably Hildegard of Bingen (1098–1179), founder and abbess of the Benedictine house of Rupertsberg near Bingen (in what today is Germany). Her writing and preaching attracted scores of supporters in Germany, France, and Switzerland, including most of her male superiors. She was highly influential with major figures of the time, as evidenced by her correspondence with Eleanor of Aquitaine, the Holy Roman emperor Frederick Barbarossa (r. 1152–1190), and various popes. She wrote in the medical arts, theology, and the history of science, but it was mainly through visionary tracts that she had the most impact on her contemporaries. Her first book, entitled *Scivias* (translated variously as *May You Know* or *Know the Way*), included descriptions of her visions, the texts of liturgical songs, and a sung morality play, *Ordo Virtutatum (The Company of the Virtues),* the first of its kind. She also illuminated manuscripts (Figure 9.6) and composed sacred poetry, which has survived in monophonic musical settings and has found new audiences today. Hildegard was a bold talent and left a superb legacy, especially given the belief of the time that it was dangerous to teach a woman to read and write.

Besides convents and nunneries, another type of religious order appeared in the thirteenth century with the rise of two major mendicant, or begging, orders, the Franciscans and the Dominicans. These new churchmen, called **friars,** were originally dedicated to working among the urban poor, but by 1250 most of them were also priests and they dominated higher education. For example, Thomas Aquinas, the age's leading scholar, was a Dominican friar. Although both orders made important contributions, the Franciscans had a greater impact on medieval society, largely because of the gentle nature of the order's sainted founder, Francis (1182–1226). Many people still find Francis's piety, selflessness, and legendary humility the personification of a sublime Christian (Figure 9.7).

As monastic reform slowed in the late twelfth century, a wave of lay piety swelled up from the lower ranks of society, triggered by a mixture of religious protest and social and economic causes. Typical of

Figure 9.6 Hildegard's Awakening: A Self-Portrait from *Scivias.* Ca. 1150. *Hildegard's description of the moment when she received the word of God is effectively captured in this illumination: a "burning light coming from heaven poured into my mind." The Holy Spirit inflames her mind as she etches the word of God on a tablet; Volmar, the priest of the abbey and her loyal secretary, gazes at the event. The simplistic sketch of the towers and building is typical of similar twelfth-century illuminated manuscripts.*

these unorthodox movements were the beguines, independent communities of laywomen dedicated to good works, poverty, chastity, and religious devotion. Unlike nuns, who isolated themselves from the world, the beguines had regular contact with society—caring for the sick at home and in hospitals, teaching in both girls' and boys' schools, and working in the textile industry. The beguines first established themselves in northern France and then, along with male lay brethren called beghards, spread to Germany and the Netherlands, usually in proximity to Dominican monasteries. These lay communities became centers of freethinking, as some members turned their intellectual gifts to spiritual matters. For example, Mechthild of Magdeburg (about 1207–about 1282) wrote *The Flowing Light of the Godhead,* a mystical account of her religious odyssey. The beguine and beghard communities also provided the audience for medieval Germany's finest devotional writer and a great mystic of the Christian tradition, Meister Eckhart (about 1260–1328), who composed tracts and sermons to guide these laypeople's religious piety into orthodox ways.

Despite a reputation for freethinking, the beguines and the beghards won approval from religious authorities, but other lay groups were condemned as heretics, probably because they failed to amass enough property to found permanent residences and, hence, appeared to the church to be uncontrollable. The most powerful of these heretical sects was the Albigensian, which was centered at Albi in southern France. The Albigensians were also known as the Cathari, from the Greek word for "pure." Their unorthodox beliefs were derived partly from Zoroastrianism, the source of their

Figure 9.7 *St. Francis of Assisi.* Ca. 1274. Attributed to school of Berlinghieri. Tempera on panel, 31 × 20". Accademia, Florence. *Many miraculous events were reported to have occurred in the life of Francis, the founder of the Franciscan order. In this painting, completed some fifty years after the saint's death, he is portrayed as receiving the stigmata, or the wounds of Christ —a sign to Christians that Francis was a man marked in a special way by God.*

PERSONAL PERSPECTIVE

Hildegard of Bingen
From *Scivias*

Hildegard of Bingen experienced visions that revealed to her the most profound meanings of religious texts and scriptures. Bernard of Clairvaux and other church figures, including the pope, confirmed the truth of her writings. In this excerpt, she describes one of her experiences.

And Behold! In the forty third year in my course of time, while gazing at a heavenly vision with much fear and trembling, I saw great splendor from which a voice was formed that said to me from heaven: O fragile human, dust of dust, filth of filth, say and write what you hear and see. But as you are fearful in speaking, and simple in explaining, and ignorant in writing, say and speak not according to a human mouth, nor according to the mind of human invention, nor according to the conventions of human writing, but according to that which you see and hear among the wonders of God in high heaven. . . .

. . . [A] fiery light of greatest brilliance coming from above transfused my whole brain and heart and breast with a flame that did not burn so much as warmed, as the sun warms all it touches with its rays. And I suddenly knew the meaning of the books, such as the psalter and the gospels and I understood other catholic volumes from both Old and New Testaments but not by way of interpreting the words of their texts, nor dividing the syllables, nor did I have knowledge of the cases and tenses. . . .

concept of a universal struggle between a good God and an evil deity, and partly from Manichaeism, the source of their notion that the flesh is evil. The Albigensians stressed that Jesus was divine and not human, that the wealth of the church was a sign of its depravity, and that the goal of Christian living was to achieve the status of Cathari, or perfection.

These unorthodox beliefs spread rapidly across much of southern France, permeating the church and the secular society. In 1214 Pope Innocent III called for the destruction of the hated beliefs. His message appealed to the feudal nobles who were greedy for the heretics' lands. The Albigensians were repressed with incredible ferocity and cruelty. Many Cathari were slaughtered and their property was confiscated; others were tried by the Inquisition and burned at the stake. Such actions reflected the less benign face of the medieval church and its immense power.

THE AGE OF SYNTHESIS: EQUILIBRIUM BETWEEN THE SPIRITUAL AND THE SECULAR

Between 1000 and 1300, Christian values permeated European cultural life. The Christian faith was a unifying agent that reconciled the opposing realms of the spiritual and the secular, the immaterial and the material—as symbolized in many cities and towns by the soaring spires of the **cathedral** (Figure 9.8). Medieval culture drew from the arts and humanities of the Classical world, the heritage of the various European

Figure 9.8 Auxerre Cathedral. Begun ca. 1225. Auxerre, France. *Looming over the town and dominating the countryside for miles around, the Gothic cathedral symbolized the preeminent role of the Christian church in medieval life. No other building could soar past its spires, either literally or figuratively. People worshiped inside it, built their houses right up to its walls, and conducted their business affairs within the shadows of its towers. Thus, the cathedral also symbolized the integration of the secular and the sacred in medieval life.*

peoples, and, to a lesser extent, the traditions of Byzantium and Islam. Because of these diverse influences, the culture of the High Middle Ages was by no means uniform. What many writers, thinkers, and artists shared was a set of common concerns and interests, most notably the quest for forms that could transcend the contradictions of the age.

A historical watershed occurred in the mid–twelfth century that was reflected in architecture, sculpture, music, learning, and literature. Before 1150 Western culture tended to express the rugged virtues of the feudal castle and the cloistered monastery; the militant warrior and the ascetic monk were the social ideals; and women were treated as chattel, or property. After 1150 the urban values of the new towns became paramount along with a more courtly attitude toward women. The church indirectly encouraged this trend with the rise of the cult of the Virgin Mary; Mary's status became so great that she was revered almost as much as Christ.

Learning and Theology

From about 1000 onward, scholars revived the school system that had flourished briefly under Charlemagne in the Early Middle Ages. These monastic schools—along with many new cathedral schools—appealed to an age that was hungry for learning and set Europe's intellectual tone until about 1200. During these two centuries, the only serious rival to the schools was a handful of independent scholars who drew crowds of students to their lectures in Paris and elsewhere. By 1200 new educational institutions arose—the universities—that soon surpassed the monastic and cathedral schools and forced the independent masters out of business. Since then, the universities have dominated intellectual life in the West.

Cathedral Schools and the Development of Scholasticism During the twelfth century, the new cathedral schools reached the height of their power, as Chartres and Paris led the way. Schooling, with rare exceptions, was the exclusive province of men who were preparing for careers in either the church or the dynastic states. For the next three hundred years, the curriculum stayed the same as that codified by Boethius in the sixth century: the trivium (grammar, logic, and rhetoric) and the quadrivium (arithmetic, astronomy, geometry, and music)—the seven liberal arts—which in turn were based on the works of the Classical authors and the early church fathers. Teachers and pupils communicated in Latin, and students read the Christian works in the original Latin. In contrast, Classical writings were known only from misleading Latin summaries until they were replaced in the twelfth century with more accurate Latin versions made from Arabic translations.

The introduction of the new versions of the Classical texts, notably those of Aristotle, caused a revolution in education and elevated the Greek thinker to the status of an authority whose word could not be questioned. By 1300 Aristotle's writings virtually monopolized the curriculum at every educational level. The revival of Aristotle contributed to the development of **scholasticism.** In general, the aim of a scholastic thinker was to bring Aristotle's thought into harmony with the Christian faith. Scholasticism was also a system of reasoning that had been perfected in oral debates in the schools. In the scholastic method, a scholar divided each problem into three parts. First, a question was set forth for intellectual analysis; next, a discussion thoroughly summarized the arguments for and against the question, usually citing the Bible, the church fathers, Aristotle, and other ancient authors; finally, a solution was offered, reinforced with support from religious and secular sources.

The scholastic method was not meant to discover new knowledge; rather, it used deductive logic to clarify existing issues and to explore the intellectual ramifications of a topic. This method, which tended to uphold rather than to question religious beliefs, was discarded in favor of an inductive, mathematically based style of reasoning in the seventeenth century.

Peter Abelard The primacy of the cathedral schools of Chartres and Paris in the twelfth century was challenged by a few independent masters who pitted their intellects against the authority of the faculty of these institutions. Of this daring breed of scholars, Peter Abelard [AB-uh-lard] (in French, Pierre Abélard) (1079–1142) was the most brilliant and controversial. More important, he was one of the first medieval thinkers to proclaim a clear distinction between reason and faith. Intellectually curious and reveling in provocative disputes, Abelard attended the lectures of William of Champeaux [shahm-POE] (about 1070–1121), the most revered teacher in the cathedral school of Paris. Dissatisfied with what he was hearing, Abelard began his own lecture series. He quickly became the sensation of Paris and his words found eager listeners. A master logician, Abelard demolished William's arguments and drove his rival into a monastery.

What divided Abelard and William of Champeaux was the problem of universals, the supreme intellectual issue between 1050 and 1150. This controversy revolved around the question of whether or not universals, or general concepts, such as "human being" and "church," truly exist. At stake in this dispute between the two schools of thought, known as **Realism** and

Nominalism, were basic Christian ideas, such as whether Jesus' sacrifice had removed the stain of original sin from each individual. The Realists, following Plato, reasoned that universals do exist independently of physical objects and the human mind. Hence, "humanity," for example, is constantly present in every individual. In opposition, the Nominalists denied the existence of universals and claimed that only particular objects and events are real. Hence, "church" and "human being" exist only in particular instances.

In these debates, Abelard showed that William of Champeaux's extreme Realism denied human individuality and was thus inconsistent with church teachings. For his part, Abelard taught a moderate Realism that held that the universals existed, but only as mental words, and hence could be used as an intellectual convenience. Later in the century, when new translations of Aristotle became available, thinkers discovered that Abelard and the Greek genius agreed about universals, a discovery that further enhanced Abelard's fame. In the next century, Abelard's moderate Realism was adopted by Thomas Aquinas, the greatest mind of the High Middle Ages.

The Rise of the Universities After 1100 a period of cultural ferment erupted that brought forth some of the finest achievements of medieval times, including the founding of the universities. By 1200 conditions were ripe for the rise of universities at Bologna, Paris, and Oxford, the first Western schools of higher education since the sixth century. Unlike the ancient universities in Athens and Alexandria, these medieval institutions were organized into self-governing corporations with charters. A century later, similar centers of learning were springing up elsewhere in Italy, France, and England, as well as in Spain, Portugal, and Germany. The University of Paris was the most celebrated institution of advanced learning during the High Middle Ages. Divided into faculties by specialization, it awarded degrees in civil law and canon law, medicine, theology, and the liberal arts. The liberal arts degree was basically devoted to mastering the new translations of Aristotle. Other universities taught a similar curriculum, but their faculties lacked the international renown of the Parisian professors.

Intellectual Controversy and Thomas Aquinas More and more of Aristotle's works became available in the late twelfth and early thirteenth centuries. Between 1150 and 1200, a few hardy Christian scholars traveled to remote centers of learning, such as Muslim Sicily and Toledo, Spain, to meet Islamic and Jewish scholars and study Aristotle's writings. There they learned Arabic and translated the Greek and Arabic philosophical and scientific works into Latin, the form in which they entered the mainstream of European medieval thought.

At the University of Paris, the introduction of these improved and more complete versions divided the intellectual community. On one side was the theological faculty, who welcomed the Arabic writings but wanted to reconcile them to Christian thinking. Arrayed against them were the members of the arts faculty, who advocated that reason be fully divorced from faith or, in other words, that philosophy be separated from theology. The leaders of the arts faculty were called Latin Averroists because they claimed inspiration from the Arabic philosopher Ibn Rushd [ib-uhn RUSHT], known in the West as Averroës [uh-VER-uh-weez].

Faced with the skeptical Latin Averroists, the Parisian theologians devised two ways to relate the new learning to orthodox beliefs. The more traditional view was set forth by Bonaventure [bahn-uh-VEN-chur] (1221–1274), who was later made a saint. Denying that knowledge was possible apart from God's grace, Bonaventure, following Augustine's mode of reasoning, argued that truth had to begin in the supernatural world and thus could not arise in the senses, as Aristotle had argued. A new and brilliant theological view, and the one that carried the day, was set forth by Thomas Aquinas [uh-KWI-nus] (1226–1274), a Dominican friar who taught at Paris from 1252 to 1259 and again from 1269 to 1272. Within a generation of his death, he was made a saint, and six hundred years later, in 1874, the papacy declared his thought the official basis of Roman Catholic beliefs. Avoiding the pure rationalism of the Latin Averroists and the timidity of Bonaventure, Thomas Aquinas steered a middle path, or ***via media,*** which gave Aristotle a central role in his theology while honoring traditional Christian beliefs. Known as Thomism, this theological system in its complex design and sheer elegance remains one of the outstanding achievements of the High Middle Ages.

Of Thomas Aquinas's two monumental *summas*—comprehensive summaries of Christian thought—the *Summa Theologica* is his masterpiece. In this work, he showed that God had given human beings two divine paths to truth: reason and faith. Following Aristotle, he made the senses the only source for human knowledge—a bold step that sharpened the difference between reason and faith. At the same time, Thomism escaped the strict rationalism of the Latin Averroists by denying that philosophy, or reason, could answer all theological questions. Aquinas claimed that reason based on sensory knowledge could prove certain truths, such as the notions that God exists and that the soul exists, but that reason had limits and that faith was necessary for those truths that were beyond sensory proof, such as the beliefs in the soul's immortality and the holy Trinity.

Dante Vernacular writing appeared late in Italy; not until the thirteenth century did Italian poetry begin to emerge. But, despite its later start, Italy had brought forth by 1300 the greatest literary figure of the High Middle Ages, Dante Alighieri [DAHN-tay ahl-egg-YEH-ree] (1265–1321). A native of Florence, in the province of Tuscany, Dante was the first of a proud tradition that soon made the Tuscan dialect the standard literary speech of Italy.

Born into a minor aristocratic family, Dante was given an excellent education with a thorough grounding in both Greco-Roman and Christian classics. Attracted to the values of ancient Rome, he combined a career in public office with the life of an intellectual—a tradition of civic duty inherited from the ancient Roman republic. When Dante's political allies fell from office in 1301, he was exiled from Florence for the rest of his life. During these years, poor and wandering about Italy, he composed the *Commedia,* or *Comedy,* which stands as the culmination of the literature of the Middle Ages. The *Comedy*'s sublime qualities were immediately recognized, and soon its admirers attached the epithet "divine" to Dante's masterpiece.

Divided into three book-length parts, the *Divine Comedy* narrates Dante's fictional travels through three realms of the Christian afterlife. Led first by the ghost of Vergil, the ancient Roman poet, Dante descends into hell, where he hears from the damned the nature of their various crimes against God and the moral law. Vergil next leads Dante into purgatory, where the lesser sinners expiate their guilt while awaiting the joys of heaven. At a fixed spot in purgatory, Vergil is forced to relinquish his role to Beatrice, a young Florentine woman and Dante's symbol of the eternal female. With Beatrice's guidance, Dante enters paradise and even has a vision of the almighty God.

The majestic complexity of Dante's monumental poem, however, can scarcely be conveyed by this simple synopsis. Written as an allegory, the *Divine Comedy* was meant to be understood on several levels. Read literally, the poem bears witness to the author's personal fears as a moral sinner yet affirms his hope for eternal salvation. Read allegorically, the poem represents a comprehensive synthesis of the opposing tendencies that characterized medieval culture, such as balancing the Classical with the Christian, Aristotle with Aquinas, the ancient with the new, the proud with the humble, and the secular with the spiritual.

Of the great cultural symbols that abound in the *Divine Comedy,* the richest in meaning are the central figures of Vergil and Beatrice, who represent human reason and divine revelation, respectively. In the poem, Vergil is made inferior to Beatrice, thus revealing Dante's acceptance of a basic idea of Thomas Aquinas—reason can lead only to awareness of sin; revelation is necessary to reach God's ultimate truth. Besides this fundamental Christian belief, the two figures convey other meanings. Vergil stands for Classical civilization and the secular literary life; Beatrice (Italian for "blessing") symbolizes spiritualized love and Christianized culture. By turning Beatrice into an image of God's grace, Dante revealed that the High Middle Ages were open to new symbols of Christian truth. (By the time of the Catholic Counter-Reformation in the sixteenth century, however, Dante's image was considered blasphemous and was censured by religious critics.)

Dante's spiritual odyssey is set during the season of Easter. The poet's journey through hell coincided with Jesus' descent into hell on Good Friday, and Dante's ascent up the Mount of Purgatory happens at Easter dawn—the time of Jesus' resurrection; the visit to heaven occupies the rest of Easter week. Thus Dante's allegory has the religious aim of forcing his readers to meditate on the fate of their own immortal souls.

Dante's vision of the afterlife underscored his belief that humans have free will. Predestination had no place in his system, as his picture of hell shows. With one exception, all of the damned earned their fate by their deeds on earth. Excepted were the people consigned to Limbo—the pious pagans who lived before Jesus and thus were denied his message of hope. Moreover, those in Limbo, such as Aristotle and Plato, were not subjected to any punishment other than being removed from God's presence.

The intricate structure of Dante's massive poem owes much to numerology, a pseudoscience of numbers that absorbed the medieval mind. The numbers three and nine, for example, occur prominently in the *Divine Comedy.* Three is a common symbol of the Christian Trinity (the union of the Father, the Son, and the Holy Ghost in one God), and the poem is written in a three-line verse form called ***terza rima*** (an interlocking rhyme scheme in three-line stanzas, as *aba, bcb, cdc, ded,* and so on, ending in a rhyming couplet), which was Dante's invention. The other number, nine, symbolizes the Trinity squared. More important, Dante identified the number nine with the dead Beatrice, whose soul lived on in the ninth heaven, the one nearest to God. He also divides hell, purgatory, and paradise into nine sections each.

Despite its allegorical and theological features, the *Divine Comedy* is a deeply personal poem. Dante rewards and punishes his Florentine friends and foes by the location that he assigns each in the afterlife. He also reveals his private feelings as he enters into discussions with various saints and sinners along the way. Beyond his desire for salvation, his most cherished idea is to bring about a harmony between the church and the secular state on earth.

Figure 9.10 Christ in Glory with Four Evangelist Symbols. Tympanum of the royal portal, Chartres cathedral. Twelfth century. Stone. Chartres, France. *The Romanesque sculptures in this tympanum portray Christ in glory, indicated by the cross-shaped nimbus behind his head and the oval in which he sits. He is surrounded by the four evangelist symbols, which are, moving counterclockwise from upper left: man (Matthew), winged lion (Mark), winged bull (Luke), and eagle (John). These four images originated in Mesopotamia and were taken up by Judaism (Ezekiel 1:4–10). They became the standard representation of the authors of the Christian Gospels, the first four books of the New Testament.*

Architecture and Art

Just as scholars and writers devoted their efforts to exploring religious concerns and Christian values, artists, artisans, and architects channeled their talents into glorifying the Christian house of worship. Because the dominating physical presence of the church made it a ubiquitous symbol in both the countryside and the towns, architecture ranked higher than the other arts in medieval life. Indeed, the arts lacked an independent status, for they were regarded as mere auxiliary sources of church decoration—wall paintings, statues, and **stained-glass** windows, most of which portrayed saints and biblical heroes (Figures 9.10 and 9.11). In this respect, these art forms conformed to the church's teachings that the purpose of art was to represent Christian truth.

Even though the church dominated art and architecture, it did not prevent architects and artists from experimenting. In about 1000 an international style called the **Romanesque** emerged. The first in a succession of uniform styles to sweep over Europe, the Romanesque was carried along by the monastic revival until about 1200. But by 1150 the **Gothic** style was developing in Paris; it was to become the reigning style of the towns for the remainder of the Middle Ages, succumbing finally to Renaissance fashion in about 1500.

Figure 9.11 Scenes from the Life of Christ. Detail. Ca. 1150–1170. Stained-glass windows, each panel: 40⅛″ wide × 41⅓″ high. West facade. Chartres cathedral. *The stained-glass windows of Chartres cathedral are renowned as the most beautiful examples of this craft to survive from the Gothic period. Of Chartres's windows, those in the west facade have been much praised for the brilliant effects created by their jewel tones of red, blue, and gold, as well as white, with small areas of green and lemon yellow. Taken from the central window of the west facade, this detail shows fifteen of its twenty-four panels, treating the life of Christ. Visible in the detail are panels depicting the annunciation (bottom left row), the visit of the three wise men (left and right, third row from bottom), and the flight into Egypt (left and right, sixth row from bottom). In the design, square panels alternate with roundel forms to frame each scene; red is the ground color for the squares and blue for the roundels. The windows can be awe-inspiring, as in the reaction of the scholar Henry Adams, who described the cathedral's interior as a "delirium of coloured light."*

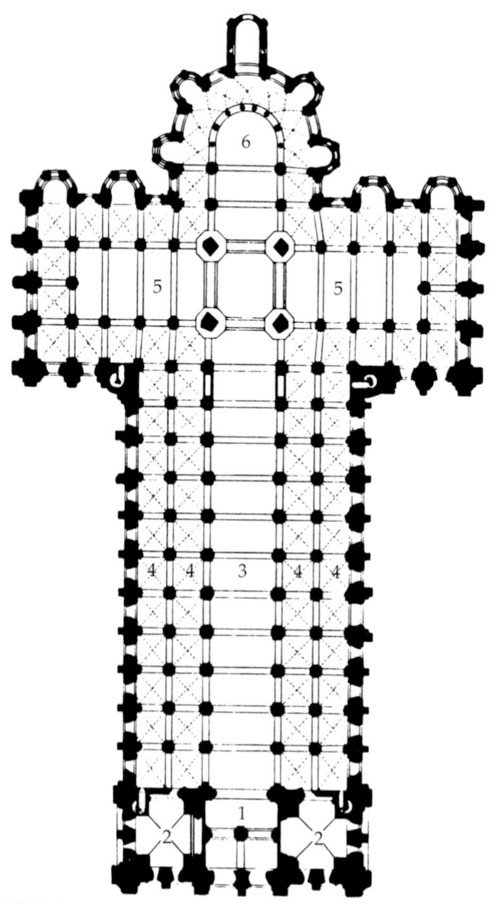

Figure 9.12 Floor Plan of a Typical Romanesque Church. *This floor plan identifies the characteristic features of a Romanesque church with its cruciform floor plan: (1) narthex, (2) towers, (3) nave, (4) side aisles, (5) transept, and (6) apse.*

Romanesque Churches and Related Arts The Romanesque style earned its name from the ancient Roman building features that had characterized the churches of the Early Middle Ages. These Roman features, along with Christian influences, had flourished briefly in some churches built during the Carolingian era (see Figure 8.23). The Romanesque church architects revived such basic Roman elements as the basilica plan and employed rounded arches, vaulted ceilings, and columns for both support and decoration (see Figure 7.10). They also perpetuated early Christian ideas by pointing each basilica toward Jerusalem in the east and curving the building's eastern end into an apse to house the altar. A transept, or crossing arm, was added at the church's eastern end to convert the floor plan into a cruciform shape to symbolize the cross (Figure 9.12). Other Christian beliefs dictated such practices as having three doorways in the western facade, which symbolized the Trinity, and building the baptistery apart from the church to keep the unbaptized out of sacred space.

In its origins, the Romanesque is associated with the Cluniac monastic order because the headquarters church at Cluny in eastern France was built in this style. The extravagant success of the Cluniac movement in the eleventh century led to the spread of the Romanesque style over the map of Europe. In appearance, the Romanesque style reflected both the needs of the monastic communities and the physical demands created by the unsettled conditions of the day. These churches were sturdy and earth hugging, with massive walls and very few windows. They looked like the spiritual fortresses that they indeed were (Figure 9.13).

Many Romanesque churches were pilgrimage churches—destinations for pilgrims traveling vast distances to see and venerate holy relics, very often the supposed bones of saints. The foremost pilgrimage churches had to be built to accommodate the hordes of religious tourists, and this was usually done by build-

Figure 9.13 Church of Sainte-Marie-Madeleine, Vézelay, France. View from the west. Ca. 1089–1206. *This church conveys the fortresslike quality that was typical of Romanesque architecture and reflects the harsh style of life of twelfth-century Europe. The church's facade is massive, pierced only by doorways at ground level and arched openings above. Highlighting its impressively stark exterior is a simple plan of decoration consisting largely of sculptures over the central portal and on pillars and in niches in the central upper section.*

Figure 9.14 View of Nave, Looking East. Church of Sainte-Marie-Madeleine, Vézelay, France. Ca. 1089–1206. *Vézelay's nave was made unusually long so that religious pilgrims might make solemn processions along its length. A reliquary, or an area for displaying holy relics, was later set aside in the choir. Within the choir, the design of the ambulatory provided ample space for masses of pilgrims to view all the relics at one time.*

ing ambulatories, semicircular or polygonal aisles behind the apse.

A celebrated pilgrimage church in the Romanesque style is Sainte-Marie-Madeleine in Vézelay, France. Attached to a Cluniac convent, this church attracted penitents eager to view the bones of Mary Magdalene. Vézelay's builders followed a basilica design with a cruciform floor plan. Inside, the most striking feature is the nearly 200-foot-long nave, which could hold a large number of pilgrims as well as allow religious processions (Figure 9.14). Typical of the Romanesque style, the nave is divided into sections called **bays.** Each bay is framed by a pair of rounded arches constructed from blocks of local pink and grey stones. These colors alternate in the overhead arches and create a dazzling effect for which this church is famous. The ceiling of each bay is a groin vault—a Roman building technique. The support system for the tall nave walls was also taken from Roman architecture—a series of arches resting on clusters of columns.

Vézelay's Romanesque builders used sculpture to provide "sermons in stone" for illiterate visitors. Symbolic rather than idealistic or realistic, the Romanesque figures were designed to convey religious meanings. For example, instead of copying the ancient Greco-Roman columns, the artisans created their own style of decorated column. The capitals, or tops, of the interior columns are sculptured with religious scenes and motifs, such as one that shows Jacob, one of the Hebrew patriarchs (on the left), wrestling with the angel (Figure 9.15). The angel, clutching his robe in his left hand, raises his right hand to bless Jacob. The simple figures with their dramatic gestures and expressive faces accurately convey the message in Genesis (32: 24–30) that Jacob has been chosen by God to lead the Hebrew people. The art is typically Romanesque: The feet point downward, the limbs are placed in angular positions, and the drapery folds are depicted in a stylized manner.

Figure 9.15 *Jacob Wrestling with the Angel.* Decorated column capital. Church of Sainte-Marie-Madeleine, Vézelay, France. Ca. 1089–1206. *The Vézelay capitals survive in near-immaculate condition. Late medieval moralists considered their vivacity and gaiety inappropriate in God's house, and the offending sculptures were plastered over. When they were uncovered during a nineteenth-century restoration of the church's interior, the capitals were revealed in their charming originality.*

Figure 9.16 *The Ascension and the Mission to the Apostles.* Tympanum over central portal. Church of Sainte-Marie-Madeleine. Vézelay, France. 1125–1135. *The subject of this tympanum, Jesus' missionary charge to his disciples, was especially appropriate for Sainte-Marie-Madeleine. Two crusades against the Muslims who occupied the holy places in the Middle East were preached and begun from this church.*

Other carvings in this church, however, show a more mature art. The stone **tympanum** over the central doorway in the **narthex** depicts Jesus' ascension into heaven and a symbolic rendering of his mission to the apostles (Figure 9.16). Jesus' lively draperies and pose reflect the dynamism and stress on mystical truth that were typical of Romanesque art. Each apostle, feet pointing downward, holds a gospel, showing that he accepts his missionary role. On the lintel below are depicted various real and legendary peoples, the recipients of the Christian message. Above the semicircular panel in framed units are portrayed biblical events, zodiac signs, and peasant scenes—a visual symbol of the integration of sacred and profane learning.

Besides church building and church decoration, the Romanesque style was used in manuscript illumina-

Figure 9.17 *Moses Expounding the Law of the Unclean Beasts.* The Bury Bible. 1130–1140. Approx. 20 × 14″. Bury St. Edmunds, England. Master and Fellows of Corpus Christi College, Cambridge. *These panels depict Moses delivering the dietary laws to the ancient Hebrews. The responses of his audience reveal the sure hand of the artist, known only as Master Hugo. For example, in the upper panel one figure pulls at his nose, while a nearby companion looks skeptical. Moses' head is depicted with horns, which reflected a biblical mistranslation of the term for the radiance that surrounded him after receiving God's law.*

tion. Originated in late Rome and developed in the Early Middle Ages, this art remained a cloistered activity in this age of monasticism (see Chapter 8). Perhaps only cloistered painters had the leisure to pursue this painstaking skill. During the High Middle Ages, new local styles arose, inspired by regional tastes and by a knowledge of Byzantine painting brought from the East by Crusaders. The English monks probably developed the finest of these local styles.

The Bury Bible, painted at Bury St. Edmunds monastery, reflects an English taste that is calmer and less exuberant than Continental styles. Two panels from the Bury manuscript, set off by a border of highly colored foliage, show an episode in Moses' life (Figure 9.17). Borrowings from Byzantine art may be detected in the elongated figures, the large eyes, the flowing hair, and the hanging draperies. The naturalness of these scenes presented a vivid contrast with the spirited agitation of French Romanesque art.

Figure 9.18 Principal Features of a Typical Gothic Church. *In this schematic drawing, the features are numbered from the nave outward: (1) nave arcade, (2) pointed arch, (3) vault, (4) clerestory, (5) flying buttress, (6) buttress, and (7) gargoyle.*

Gothic Churches and Related Arts The word *Gothic* was invented by later Renaissance scholars who preferred Greco-Roman styles. They despised medieval architecture, labeling it *Goth-ic*—meaning a barbaric creation of the Goths, or the Germanic peoples. Modern research, however, has shown that this Renaissance view is false. In fact, the Gothic grew out of the Romanesque and was not a German art. Nevertheless, the term *Gothic* is still used today, although its negative connotation has long since been discarded.

Gothic architecture sprang from the religious revival of the twelfth century, when the clergy wanted to bring God's presence more tangibly to their urban congregations. As a result, clerics began to demand taller churches with more windows than were available in the relatively dark Romanesque churches. To the medieval mind, height and light were symbols of the divine. Another impetus behind the Gothic was the rise of the middle class, who wanted churches that reflected their growing economic power. Thus spiritual and economic forces were united in pushing architects to seek a new kind of architecture.

Two problems with the Romanesque stood in the way: The groin vaults were so heavy that the nearly windowless walls had to be extremely thick to support their great weight, and the rounded arches limited the building's height to less than 100 feet. During the early twelfth century, builders constantly sought solutions to these problems.

Eventually, between 1137 and 1144, the Gothic style was created by Suger [sue-ZHAY] (about 1081–1151), the abbot of the royal Abbey Church of St. Denis, near Paris, and an adviser to the French kings. Suger's approach to architecture grew out of his religious faith, as in his words, "Through the beauty of material things we come to understand God." The brilliant innovation employed by Suger and the architects and artisans he hired was to change the vaulting problem from one of weight to one of stress. First, they replaced the groin vault with a **ribbed vault;** this step allowed lighter materials to be placed between the stone ribs, thus reducing the weight. Next, they abandoned the rounded arch in favor of the Muslim pointed arch. The combination of pointed arch and ribbed vault permitted an increase in the building's height as well as a rechanneling of the ceiling's stresses downward and outward to huge **piers** internally and, in later buildings, to **flying buttresses** externally, which formed a bridge between the upper nave walls and the nearby tall pillars (Figure 9.18). With the support skeleton transferred to the building's exterior, the builders could easily insert stained-glass windows into the non-weight-bearing walls.

Figure 9.19 Ambulatory. Church of St. Denis, Paris. Ca. 1145. *This view of the choir of St. Denis shows a portion of the ambulatory that allowed pilgrims to view the chapels in the apse. The evenly spaced support columns and the pointed arches create this flowing, curved space. The ribbed arches in the ceiling are also central to the Gothic skeletal construction.*

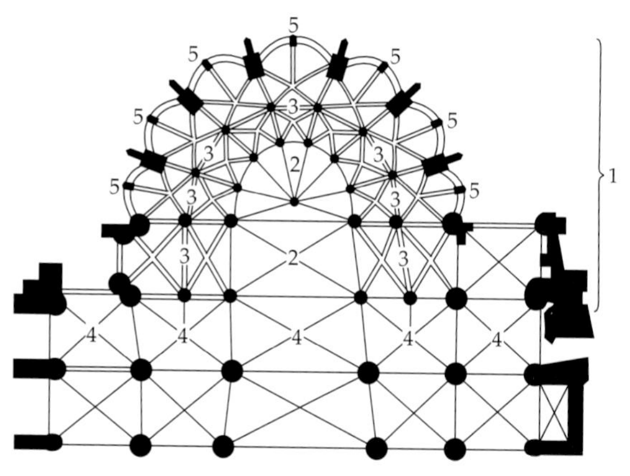

Figure 9.20 Floor Plan, Ambulatory. Church of St. Denis, Paris. Ca. 1145. *This floor plan, based on a similar design used in the pilgrimage churches, became the basis for the reordering of interior space in the Gothic choirs. The features include (1) choir, (2) apse, (3) ambulatory, (4) transept, and (5) chapel.*

The glory of the Gothic church—the **choir**—was all that remained to be built. The plan and inspiration for the choir (the part of the church where the service was sung) were the pilgrimage churches, like Vézelay, that had enlarged their apses to accommodate religious tourists. In Suger's skillful hands, the east end of St. Denis was now elaborated into an oval-shaped area—the choir—ringed with several small chapels (Figure 9.19). At the heart of the choir was the apse, now arcaded; a spacious ambulatory area divided the apse from the chapels (Figure 9.20).

St. Denis gave only a foretaste of the triumphant art that was called Gothic. Between 1145 and 1500, the Gothic style presented an overwhelming image of God's majesty and the power of the church. A Gothic exterior carried the eye heavenward by impressive vertical spires. A Gothic interior surrounded the daytime worshiper with colored, celestial light; the soaring nave ceiling, sometimes rising to more than 150 feet, was calculated to stir the soul. In its total physicality the Gothic church stood as a towering symbol of the medieval obsession with the divine.

During the High Middle Ages, the Gothic style went through two stages, the Early and the High. The Early Gothic style lasted until 1194 and was best represented by Notre Dame cathedral in Paris. The High Gothic style flourished until 1300 and reached perfection in the cathedral at Amiens, France.

EARLY GOTHIC STYLE, 1145–1194 The cathedral of Notre Dame ("Our Lady," the Virgin Mary) in Paris made popular the Early Gothic style, making it a fashion for other cities and towns. Begun in 1163, the cathedral was the most monumental work erected in the West to this time. Its floor plan was cruciform, but the length of the transept barely exceeded the width of the aisle walls (Figure 9.21).

Part of Notre Dame's beauty stems from the rational principles applied by the builders, notably the ideal of harmony, best expressed in the integration of sculpture and decorative details with building units. For instance, the west facade is divided into three equal horizontal bands: the three doorways, the **rose window** and **blind arcades,** and the two towers (Figure 9.22). Within each subdivision of this facade, figurative sculpture or architectural details play a harmonizing role, from the rows of saints flanking each of the portals to the **gargoyles,** or grotesque demons, peering down from the towers.

Inside Notre Dame, the spectacular nave reveals the awe-inspiring effects of Early Gothic art at its best (Figure 9.23). The strong vertical lines and the airy atmosphere represent the essence of this taste. With its ribbed vaults and pointed arches, the nave rises to a height of 115 feet from the pavement to the roof. Like the harmonious west facade, the nave is divided into three equal tiers: the nave and double aisles, the open

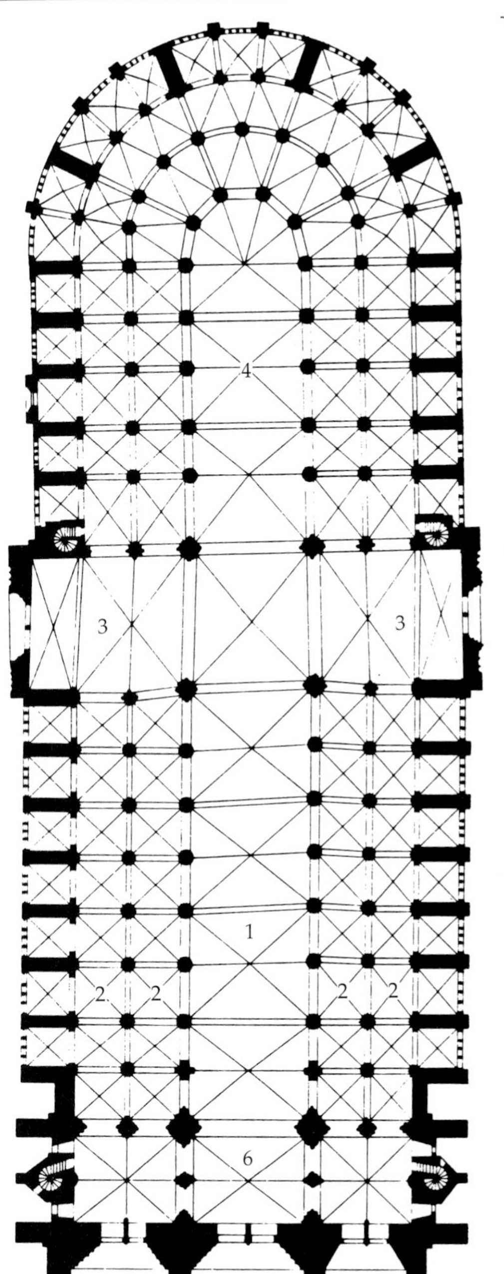

Figure 9.21 Floor Plan of Notre Dame. Paris. 1163–ca. 1250. *This drawing shows the principal features of Notre Dame cathedral: (1) nave, (2) aisle, (3) transept, (4) apse, (5) choir, and (6) narthex.*

Figure 9.22 Western Facade. Notre Dame. Paris. 1220–1250. *In the gallery above the western portals are twenty-eight images of the kings of Judah, including David and Solomon. These sculptures, which are typical of Gothic churches, are more than decorations: They are reminders that Mary and Jesus were descended from royalty. In the medieval mind, this religious idea was meant to buttress the monarchical style of government.*

Figure 9.23 Nave. Notre Dame. Paris. View from the height of the western rose window. 1180–1250. Ht. floor to summit of roof 115′. *The nave is clearly not aligned properly. The choir bends perceptibly to the north, which probably reflected the different building times for various parts of the cathedral. The transept and the choir were finished first, after which the nave and the double aisles were added. The western facade was completed last.*

Figure 9.24 Notre Dame. Paris. View from the east. 1163–1182. *Notre Dame's choir, shown on the right, was originally built without chapels and flying buttresses—a sign of its Early Gothic origins. Paris's greatest church caught up with the High Gothic style in the four-teenth century, when these architectural features were added.*

spectator **gallery** above the aisles, and, at the top, the clerestory, as the window area is called.

Notre Dame reveals that the choir was coming to dominate the entire Early Gothic church. Notre Dame's choir is almost as long as the nave, so that the transept virtually divides the church into two halves. At first, the choir's walls had no special external supports, but as cracks began to appear in the choir's walls during the thirteenth century, flying buttresses were added to ensure greater stability—a feature that would later characterize High Gothic churches (Figure 9.24).

The Gothic sculptures that decorate Notre Dame differ from the exuberant Romanesque style. The Romanesque's animated images of Jesus have given way to the Gothic's more sober figures. In addition, the Gothic figures are modeled in three dimensions, and their draperies fall in natural folds (Figure 9.25). At the same time, the rise of the cult of the Virgin meant an increased number of images of Mary as well as of fe-

Figure 9.25 *The Last Judgment.* Central portal, west facade. Notre Dame, Paris. Ca. 1210. *This tympanum represents Jesus enthroned and presiding over the Last Judgment. Surrounding him are the apostles, the prophets, the church fathers, and the saints—arranged in descending order of their importance in relation to Jesus. Like all the sculptures of Notre Dame's first story, the entire scene was gilded with gold paint until the mid–fifteenth century.*

Figure 9.26 North Rose Window of Notre Dame. Paris. Ca. 1255. *This masterwork by Jehan de Chelles is the only original of Notre Dame's three rose windows. The nineteenth-century restoration genius Viollet-le-Duc re-created the other two. Measuring 43 feet in diameter, the window was installed after workers first removed sections of the existing wall. The bits of predominantly blue glass, encased in iron settings, were then placed inside the stone frame.*

male saints. The name "Notre Dame" itself testifies to the appeal of the Virgin cult. Despite these visual differences, however, the Gothic remained true to the symbolic purposes of Romanesque art.

Before Notre Dame was finished, its architects began to move in new directions, refining the traditional features into a new style, called **Rayonnant,** or Radiant. In the Rayonnant style, the solid walls gave way to sheets of stained glass framed by elegant **traceries,** or rich ornamentation, of stone. This radiant effect was especially evident in the north transept facade, which was rebuilt in this new style. With the addition of this transept's imposing rose window, designed to suggest the rays of the sun, the cathedral's interior was bathed in constantly shifting colors, giving it a mystical atmosphere (Figure 9.26).

Figure 9.27 Amiens Cathedral. Amiens, France. Ca. 1220–1270. *This photograph shows the brilliantly articulated exterior skeleton of Amiens cathedral. The Gothic churches openly displayed the exterior support system that made their interior beauty possible. In the Renaissance, this aspect of Gothicism was decried for its clumsiness. Renaissance architects preferred Classical structures that hid their stresses and strains.*

HIGH GOTHIC STYLE, 1194–1300 The High Gothic style is a tribute to the growing confidence of the builders of the thirteenth century. These builders took the Gothic ingredients and refined them, creating grander churches than had been erected earlier. In comparison with Early Gothic architecture, High Gothic churches were taller and had greater volume; artistic values now stressed wholeness rather than the division of space into harmonious units. Rejecting the restrained decorative ideal used in the Early Gothic style, the High Gothic architects covered the entire surface of their churches' western facades with sculptural and architectural designs.

The cathedral in Amiens is a perfect embodiment of the High Gothic style. Amiens was planned so that flying buttresses would surround its choir and march along its nave walls (Figure 9.27). Instead of trying to disguise these supports, the architect made the exterior skeleton central to his overall plan. As a result, more spacious window openings could be made in the nave and the choir walls than had been the case in Notre Dame. Furthermore, the design of Amiens's nave was also changed so that the entire space was perceived as a homogeneous volume. The division of the nave walls into three equal horizontal bands was eliminated, and the system of arches and bays overhead became less emphatic (Figure 9.28). Amiens's overall floor plan was conservative, however, for it resembled that of Notre Dame; for example, its transept bisected a choir and a nave of equal length (Figure 9.29).

Figure 9.28 Nave. Amiens cathedral. View from the west. ▶ Amiens, France. Ca. 1220–1236. Ht. floor to summit of vault, 139′. *Gothic architecture was built to appeal to the emotions. The overwhelming height and the celestial light were intended to create a spiritual environment. This spiritual feeling may be sensed even in a photograph. The dramatic contrast between the human elements—the chairs—and the voluminous space is a reminder of the frailty of mortals.*

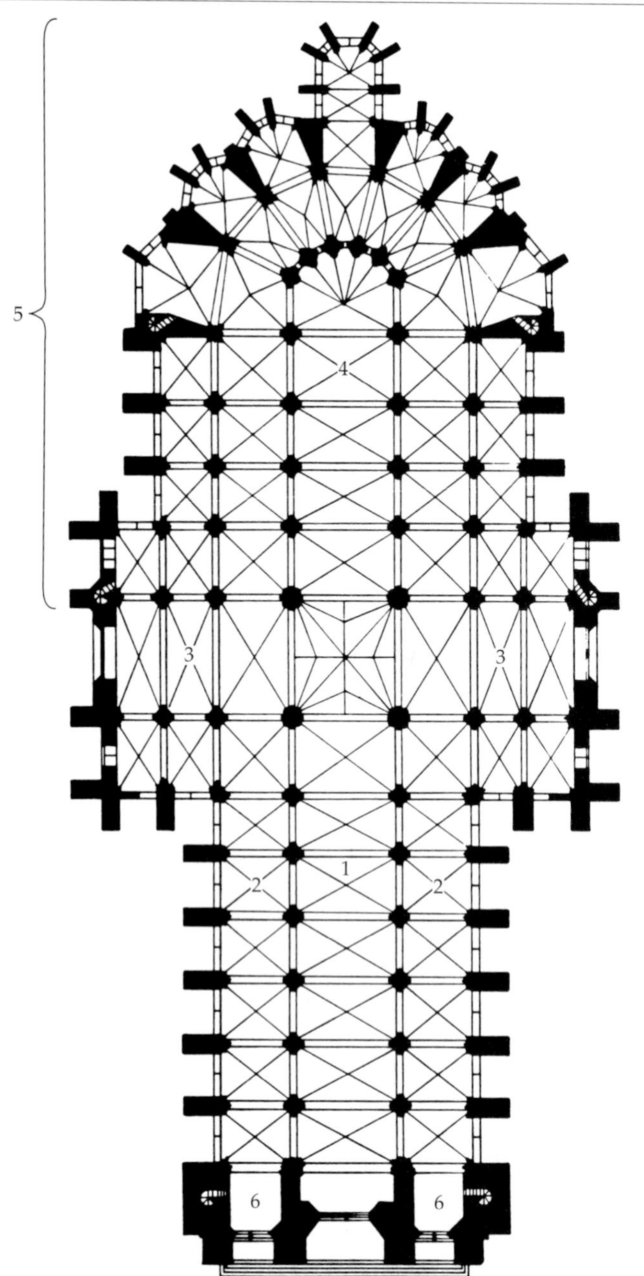

Figure 9.29 Floor Plan of Amiens Cathedral. Amiens, France. Ca. 1220–1236. *This drawing shows the principal features of Amiens cathedral: (1) nave, (2) aisle, (3) transept, (4) apse, (5) choir, and (6) narthex.*

The western facade of Amiens shows how decoration changed in the High Gothic style (Figure 9.30). Amiens's western wall and towers are pierced with rich and intricate openings. The elegant tracery has the effect of dissolving the wall's apparent solidity. What surface remains intact is covered with an elaborate tapestry of architectural devices and sculptural figures (Figure 9.31).

The finest stained glass from the High Gothic era is from the cathedral in Chartres, a bishopric in Hugh Capet's old lands. Indeed, Chartres's windows are often recognized as the most exquisite of all Gothic stained glass. Chartres has 176 windows, and most are the thirteenth-century originals. Outstanding examples of this art are the Charlemagne panels depicting scenes from the *Song of Roland*, illustrated earlier in this

Figure 9.30 Western Facade. Amiens cathedral. Amiens, France. Ca. 1220–1236. *Comparison of Amiens's facade with that of Notre Dame in Paris (see Figure 9.22) shows how the High Gothic differs from the Early Gothic. The basic form remains the same, but Amiens's surface is richer in detail and more splendid overall. The pointed features, such as the arches over the portals and over the openings in the towers, are the most characteristic visual element in the High Gothic style.*

chapter (see Figure 9.9). Each figure is precisely rendered, though many are cropped off at the edge of the pictorial space. The glass itself is brilliant, notably in the dominant blue tones.

High Gothic painting survives best in the manuscript illuminations of the late thirteenth century. By this time, these small paintings were being influenced by developments elsewhere in Gothic art. The Gothic illuminators abandoned the lively draperies of the Romanesque and instead showed gowns hanging in a natural manner. More important, they sometimes allowed the architectural frame to dominate the painting, as in the Psalter of St. Louis IX of France. Commissioned by the sainted French king (r. 1226–1270), this volume contains seventy-eight full-page paintings of scenes from the Old Testament. Of these paintings, "Balaam and His Ass" is a typical representation of the anonymous painter's style (Figure 9.32). The scene unfolds before a High Gothic church; two gables with rose windows are symmetrically balanced on the page. Although this painting owes much to changes in Gothic sculpture, the animated figures of the men, the angel, and the ass are reminiscent of the exuberant Romanesque style.

Figure 9.31 *Golden Virgin.* Amiens cathedral. Amiens, France. Ca. 1260. *The* Golden Virgin *of Amiens, so called because it was originally covered with a thin layer of gold, is one of the most admired works of Gothic art. The artist has depicted Mary as a loving earthly mother with fine features, a high forehead, and a shy smile. This sculpture shows the new tenderness that was creeping into art during the High Middle Ages as part of the rise of the cult of the Virgin.*

Figure 9.32 *Balaam and His Ass.* Psalter of St. Louis IX. 1252–1270. Bibliothèque Nationale, Paris. *The architectural details in this miniature painting show a correspondence with the Rayonnant architectural style: the two gabled roofs, the two rose windows with exterior traceries, the pointed arches, and the pinnacles. Just as Gothic architects emphasized the decorative aspects of their buildings, so did this anonymous miniature painter. The story of Balaam and his ass (from Numbers 22:22–35 in the Old Testament) was a beast fable—a popular literary genre in the Middle Ages. In the biblical story, the ass could speak and see things of which his master, Balaam, was ignorant. In the painting, the ass turns his head and opens his mouth as if to speak.*

Music

As with the other arts, the purpose of music during the High Middle Ages was the glorification of God. At the beginning of this period the monophonic (single-line) Gregorian chants were still the main form of musical expression, but two innovations—the introduction of tropes and the development of polyphony—led the way to a different sound in the future.

The **tropes,** or turns, were new texts and melodies inserted into the existing Gregorian chants. Added for both poetic and doctrinal reasons, these musical embellishments slowly changed the plainchants into more elaborate songs. Culminating in about 1150, this musical development coincided with the appearance of the richly articulated Gothic churches.

The tropes also gave a powerful impetus to Western drama. From the practice of troping grew a new musical genre, the **liturgical drama,** which at first was sung and performed in the church but gradually moved outdoors. From the twelfth century onward, these works were staged in the area in front of the church as sacred dramas or mystery plays (*mystery* is derived from the Latin *ministerium,* "handicraft" or "occupation"). As their popularity increased, they began to be sung in the vernacular instead of Latin. Ultimately, the liturgical drama supplied one of the threads that led to the revival of the secular theater.

Gregorian chants were also being modified by the development of **polyphony,** in which two or more lines of melody are sung or played at the same time. In the early eleventh century, polyphony was extremely simple and was known as **organum.** It consisted of a main melody, called the *cantus firmus,* accompanied by an identical melody sung four or five tones higher or lower. By about 1150, the second line began to have its own independent melody rather than duplicating the first. During the thirteenth century, two-voiced organum gave way to multivoiced songs called **motets,** which employed more complex melodies. In the motets, the main singer used the liturgy as a text while up to five other voices sang either commentaries or vernacular translations of the text. The result was a complex web of separate voices woven into a harmonious tapestry. By about 1250, the motet composers had laid the foundations of modern musical composition.

Notwithstanding these developments in sacred music, the church could not stop the rise of secular music any more than it could prevent the spread of courtly love. Indeed, the first secular music was associated with the same feudal courts where the *chansons de geste* and the troubadour songs flourished in the twelfth century. At first, France was the center of this musical movement, but in the early thirteenth century, German poets took the lead. At the same time, music began to be practiced not just by aristocratic poets but also by middle-class minstrels, and new musical instruments—some, such as the **lute** (a multistringed instrument with neck and soundbox) and the bagpipe, banned by the church—started to find their way into secular music (Figure 9.33).

The High Middle Ages also gave rise to some innovations that made modern music possible. Guido of Arezzo [GWEE-doe/uh-RET-so] (about 995–about 1050), an Italian monk, modernized musical notation by his invention of the music staff, the set of five horizontal lines and four intermediate spaces on which notes may be drawn. Guido also began the practice of naming the musical tones by the syllables *ut* (or *do*), *re, mi, fa, sol,* and *la,* a step that greatly simplified the teaching of music. The music composed according to Guido's system can be reproduced by today's music historians; thus, Western music may be said to descend in an unbroken line from the music of this period.

Figure 9.33 Embellished Letter *B.* Psalter from Würzburg-Ebrach. Early thirteenth century. Universitäts Bibliothek, Munich. *In illuminated manuscripts, the initial letter of a sentence was often embellished with intricate details, drawn from the artist's imagination and experience. In this example from a thirteenth-century German psalter, the letter* B *is interwoven with a band of musicians playing instruments typical of the era: organ (with bellows), bells, ivory horn, flute, stringed instruments, and an instrument for bows. The artist who painted this miniature scene has captured the liveliness of a musical performance, depicting several players singing.*

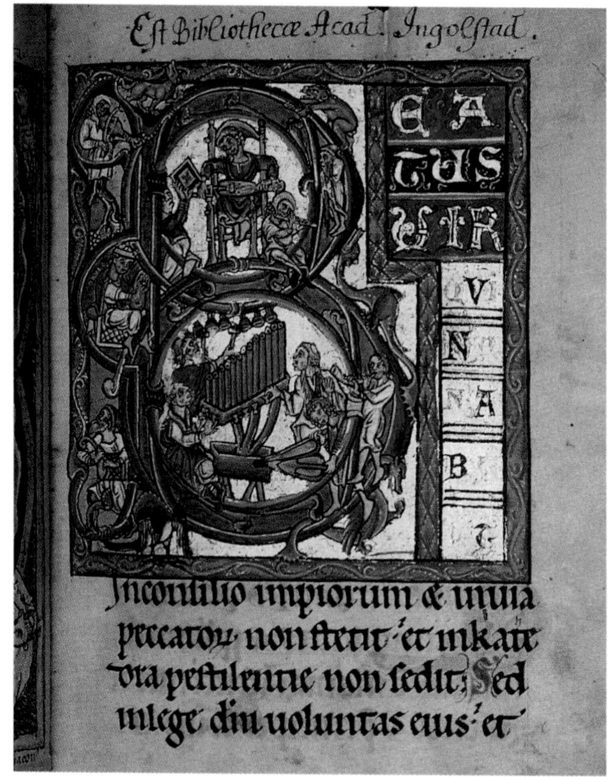

The Legacy of the Christian Centuries

The grandeur of this age of synthesis declined after 1300, when the secular and the spiritual began to go their separate ways. But the legacy of the Christian centuries survives, particularly in the writings of Dante, the theology of Thomas Aquinas, and the Gothic cathedrals. Of Dante's works, the *Divine Comedy* is his most enduring gift to world literature; his poetic style and literary forms influenced Italian writers for centuries. Furthermore, Dante's love for Beatrice has deeply influenced Western literature by encouraging poets to seek inspiration from a living woman.

The Roman Catholic world is the most significant beneficiary of the philosophy of Thomas Aquinas. Since the late nineteenth century, Thomism has been regarded as the basis of orthodox beliefs. As for the Gothic style, it ceased to be practiced after about 1500, although it was revived in the nineteenth century as part of the Romantic movement, and even today universities often adopt Gothic elements in their official architecture.

Besides these great gifts, the Christian centuries have left the modern world other significant cultural legacies. First and foremost was the birth of the courtly love movement that glorified individual romantic affection—the idea that *this* man loves *this* woman. Vernacular literature finally found its voice during this time in the first European poetry. Of special note, the vernacular writers created one of the richest literary traditions in the West through the stories of King Arthur and the knights of the Round Table. The basic theoretical system for composing music was developed during this period under the auspices of the church. Outside the church, the ancestor of all Western love songs was invented by the Provençal poets. In Gothic sculpture, artists began to move away from symbolic representation to a more realistic art.

Notwithstanding these innovations, the Christian centuries transmitted many of the legacies that had been received from ancient and other sources. The liberal arts, the Christian religion, the rationalist tradition, Muslim science, and the entire Greco-Roman heritage are only the major ingredients of this invaluable legacy to later ages.

KEY CULTURAL TERMS

chivalric code
friars
cathedral
scholasticism
Realism
Nominalism
via media
goliard
chanson de geste
vernacular language
canzone
minstrel
troubador
romance
lay
terza rima
stained glass
Romanesque style
Gothic style
bay
tympanum
narthex
ribbed vault
pier
flying buttress
choir
rose window
blind arcade
gargoyle
gallery
Rayonnant
tracery
trope
liturgical drama
polyphony
organum
motet
lute

SUGGESTIONS FOR FURTHER READING

PRIMARY SOURCES

CHRÉTIEN DE TROYES. *Arthurian Romances.* Translated by W. W. Comfort. New York: Everyman's Library, 1955. A good prose version of Chrétien's romances, including *Lancelot.*

DANTE. *The Divine Comedy. The Inferno. The Purgatorio. The Paradiso.* Translated by J. Ciardi. New York: New American Library, 1982. The best contemporary English translation.

HILDEGARD OF BINGEN. *Scivias* or *May You Know* or *Know the Way.* Translated by M. Fox. Santa Fe: Bear, 1986. The most accessible edition of Hildegard's writings.

The Lais of Marie de France. Translated and with an introduction by R. Hanning and J. Ferrante. Durham: Labyrinth Press, 1982. A modern, free-verse translation of these Old French poems; with notes and an extremely useful introductory essay.

The Song of Roland. Translated by F. Golden. New York: Norton, 1978. A readable and modern translation that still captures the language and drama of the original.

ST. THOMAS AQUINAS. *Summa Theologica.* 3 vols. Translated by Fathers of the English Dominican Province. New York: Benziger, 1947. A good English version of St. Thomas's monumental work, which underlies Roman Catholic theology.

TIERNEY, B. *The Crisis of Church and State, 1050–1300.* Englewood Cliffs, N.J.: Prentice-Hall, 1964. Primary documents linked together by sound interpretations and explanations.

WINDOWS ON THE WORLD: 1000–1300

HISTORY

AFRICA

East Africa Swahili-speaking coastal city-states, with black African and Arab Muslim traders; trading links with Far East and Middle East.

North Africa *Maghreb.* Islamized Berber dynasties, from about 1050. Settled farming society became tribal and nomadic. *Egypt.* Arab Muslim dynasties.

Northeast Africa *Axum culture.* Collapse, ca. 1000. *Ethiopia. Zagwe Dynasty, 1137–1270.* Evolved from Axum empire. Kings extended the Christian faith inland. *Solomonic Dynasty, began 1270.*

West Africa *Ghana Empire.* Traded slaves for salt and cloth. Muslim invaders sacked capital (1076). Fell to Mali Empire, led by Sundiata (1235). *Mali Empire.* Covered 1,000 miles from Atlantic to Middle Niger River. *Yoruba culture.* Ife, the political and religious center.

AMERICAS

Andes *Late Intermediate period, 900–1400.* Chimú, north and central coasts; Ica, south coast. Sicán fell under the sway of Chimú about 1100.

Mesoamerica *Early Postclassic period, 900–1200. Toltec culture.* The capital, Tula, abandoned about 1200, though its art, architecture, and myths influenced the Aztecs. *Zapotec culture.* Ritual city of Mitla. *Late Postclassic period, began 1200. Toltec culture.* Sack and abandonment of Chichén Itzá (early 1300s). *Mayan culture.* Loose confederation of cities on Yucatán peninsula, centered on Mayapán.

Native North America *Mississippian culture, ca. 700–1500.* Theocratic village-states, mainly along Mississippi River and tributaries; trade network thoughout continent. Cahokia (Illinois) was major urban and ceremonial center (ca. 900–1200).

ART & MUSIC

AFRICA

North Africa *Morocco* and *Tunisia.* Under the Almohad Dynasty (about 1121–1269), Berber power and culture at its zenith. Urban life and the arts flourished.

West Africa *Yoruba culture.* Ife sculptural arts in bronze and terra cotta (1100s); two distinct styles: idealized naturalism and extreme stylization.

An Oni (Local Priest-King) of Ife. Twelfth century or earlier. Brass, ht. 18³/₈" Ife Museum, Nigeria.

AMERICAS

Andes *Chimú culture.* Mass-produced art objects for the elite, displayed in residences and buried in tombs; long-distance trade to import emeralds and amber. *Sicán culture.* Gold and silver metalwork, ceramics, textiles.

Mesoamerica *Early Postclassic period. Toltec culture.* Plumbate pottery, made to look like metal.

Native North America *Mississippian culture.* Elaborate headdresses, wooden masks, effigy pottery; motifs included feathered serpent, human figures, geometric shapes.

Ceremonial Tumi *Knife. About 1250. Gold, silver, and turquoise. Sicán. Royal Ontario Museum, Toronto.*

ARCHITECTURE

AFRICA

Northeast Africa *Ethiopian culture.* Eleven churches carved from native rock at Roha.

West Africa *Ghana culture.* The capital Koumbi Saleh (in modern Mauritania) laid out in two towns: round mud huts where the ruler lived in a palace encircled by a wall; stone houses for the Muslim merchants.

AMERICAS

Andes At the Chimú capital Chan Chan (pop. about 30,000), a complex of adobe buildings, consisting of royal compounds, palaces, and home workshops.

Mesoamerica *Early Postclassic period. Zapotec culture.* Mitla: palaces, open plazas, and buildings faced with geometric mosaics and stonework. *Toltec culture.* Tula: pyramids linked by spacious courtyards and colonnades. Chichén Itzá: pyramids, temples, courtyards, an observatory, and the largest ballcourt in Mesoamerica.

Native North America *Mississippian culture.* Ceremonial plazas bordered by pyramidal or oval earth mounds with temple or palace on top. Monks Mound (ca. 1100), the largest in Cahokia.

RELIGION, PHILOSOPHY, LITERATURE

AFRICA

North Africa *Egypt.* Saladin, a mythic hero to Muslims and Christians, founded the Ayyubid Dynasty. *Morocco* and *Tunisia.* Ibn Rushd (Averroës, 1126–1198), Islamic philosopher and court physician. The Almohads swept to power based on Sufism, a mystical form of Islam.

Northeast Africa *Ethiopian culture.* Geez language used by clerical elite; Amharic language spoken by ordinary people. The Solomonic Dynasty claimed descent from the marriage of biblical King Solomon and the Queen of Sheba.

Western Africa Islam spread into Ghana about 1050. Elsewhere, various African religions prevailed. Among the Yoruba, oracles were used to forecast the future through poems that became sacred texts.

AMERICAS

Mesoamerica *Early Postclassic period. Toltec culture.* Rise of the cult of Quetzalcoatl; the legend forecasting his return helped Cortés's conquest of the Aztecs in 1519. *Late Postclassic period. Mayan culture.* Four books (codices) survive, covering mathematics and astronomy, prophecies, ritual observances, and a table of movements of the planet Venus.

Native North America *Mississippian culture.* Religion centered around sun worship; high chief's title was the Great Sun. Ceremonies included ritual ballgames.

The Caracol (Astronomical Observatory). After 1000. Chichén Itzá.

ASIA

China

Sung Dynasty, ended 1279. Turkic invaders (the Chin) conquered north China (1127); made Beijing the capital. Southern Sung state founded (1128), with Hangzhou as capital. Advances in medicine and technology. *Yüan Dynasty, 1260–1368.* China united under its first foreign dynasty (Mongol), founded by Kublai Khan; capital, Beijing; peace established, trade expanded, and links renewed with the West.

India

Chola Dynasty, 907–1279. Dominated south India, including Sri Lanka and Malay Archipelago; defeated by two rival dynasties, the Pāndyas and the Hoysalas. *Medieval period, began 550.* In north India, Hindu dynasties fought for control, as Muslim power moved into the region. *Delhi Sultanate, began 1192.* Delhi, the capital of six successive Muslim dynasties.

Japan

Heian period, ended 1185. Imperial family weakened; power shifted to Fujiwara clan (after 897). Onset of feudalism. *Kamakura period, 1185–1333.* Clan warfare (1156–85) over the office of shōgun (military dictator); shōgun's headquarters moved to Kamakura; emperor remained in Kyōto (pop. [1185]: 500,000). Samurai increased power.

Jōchō. Amida, Buddha of the Western Paradise. *1053. Gold leaf and lacquer on wood, ht. 116". Phoenix Hall. Byōdōin, Kyōto.*

Sung Dynasty. A golden age of calligraphy and ink painting. Three ink-painting styles: Northern Sung (mountain landscape), Southern Sung (romantic landscape), and the Ch'an (Zen) Buddhist style of sophisticated "simplicity." Woven and embroidered silks, tapestry, lacquer, carved jades, and ivory. Music: the *tz'u* genre blended poetry and song.

Chola Dynasty. Bronze sculptures of deities, such as Shiva Nataraja, the Lord of the Dance, both creator and destroyer of the universe.

Kamakura period. Revitalization of art: portrait sculpture, portrait painting, and sword making. Buddhist-influenced art.

Sung Dynasty. Lin Chieh's *Ying-tsao fa-shih,* the oldest treatise on Chinese architecture. *Yüan Dynasty.* Tibetan-style White Pagoda in Beijing's royal gardens, built (1272) by Kublai Khan.

Chola Dynasty. The Hindu Rajarajeshvara Temple, the supreme expression of the South Indian style, built by King Rājarāja I in his capital, Tanjore (about 1000). *Delhi Sultanate.* Islamic mosques.

View of the Phoenix Hall, Byōdōin. 1053. Uji, Kyōto.

Heian period. The Byōdōin, the private chapel of the regent Fujiwara Yorimichi (994–1074). *Kamakura period.* After civil war, Buddhist monasteries rebuilt in many styles. A secular "warrior style" emerged: buildings and training grounds surrounded by narrow moats or stockades.

Sung Dynasty. Li Ch'ing-chao, composer of *tz'u,* one of China's greatest female poets. Southern Sung scholars influenced by Ch'an Buddhism. *Yüan Dynasty.* Golden era of the dramatic form *tsa-chü,* such as Wang Shih-fu's *The Pavilion of the West.* Short stories and novels. *Marco Polo's Travels,* an account of the Venetian's years at the Mongol court. Toleration for many faiths, such as Tibetan lamaism, Islam, and Nestorian Christianity.

Shiva Nataraja. *Eleventh–twelfth centuries (Chola Dynasty). Bronze, ht. 32¼". Von der Heydt Collection, Museum Rietberg, Zurich.*

Chola Dynasty. Hinduism, the official faith. *Medieval period.* Buddhism introduced into Tibet under the Pala Dynasty.

Heian period. Perfection of *kana*-style calligraphy. Women writers flourished: Lady Murasaki's classic, *The Tale of Genji,* and *The Pillow-Book of Sei Shōnagon,* the diary of a lady-in-waiting. Chinese-style Buddhism, especially the Amida Pure Land Paradise cult, adopted by the ruling class. *Kamakura period. The Confessions of Lady Ñyō,* a novel of a court lady's love affairs; and *An Account of My Hut,* by Kamo no Chōmei, a Buddhist poet disenchanted with the world. Samurai warriors sought support either in the native Shinto religion or Zen Buddhism, imported from China. Zen monks adopted the ritual tea ceremony.

10 THE LATE MIDDLE AGES 1300–1500

Many who lived during what a modern historian has termed the "calamitous" fourteenth century believed that the biblical apocalypse had arrived, attended by plague, famine, and war. Amid this turbulence, the unique culture of the High Middle Ages, which blended the spiritual with the secular, began to unravel. In the Late Middle Ages, the church had to relinquish its dream of a united Christendom when faced with the reality of warring European states. New military tactics and weapons rendered chivalry obsolete, and the chivalric code began to seem a romantic fiction. In the universities, new intellectual currents drove a wedge between philosophy and theology, which had been so carefully integrated by Thomas Aquinas. And the balanced High Gothic style in art and architecture gave way to the florid Late Gothic style.

This chapter examines the third and final period of medieval civilization, between 1300 and 1500. It also explores the rise of secularism in this contradictory age and the technological and artistic innovations that were guiding the Western world in a new direction. The specific developments in the 1400s that ushered in the Renaissance and the modern era will be the focus of the next chapter.

◀ **Detail** *Wine-Making.* Fifteenth century. Tapestry. Cluny Museum, Paris.

HARD TIMES COME TO EUROPE

Shortly after the opening of the fourteenth century, Europe entered a disastrous period of economic depression, accompanied by soaring prices and widespread famine. Against the backdrop of the Hundred Years' War between England and France (1337–1453), social unrest increased and renegade feudal

Map 10.1 PROGRESS OF THE BLACK DEATH ACROSS EUROPE IN THE FOURTEENTH CENTURY

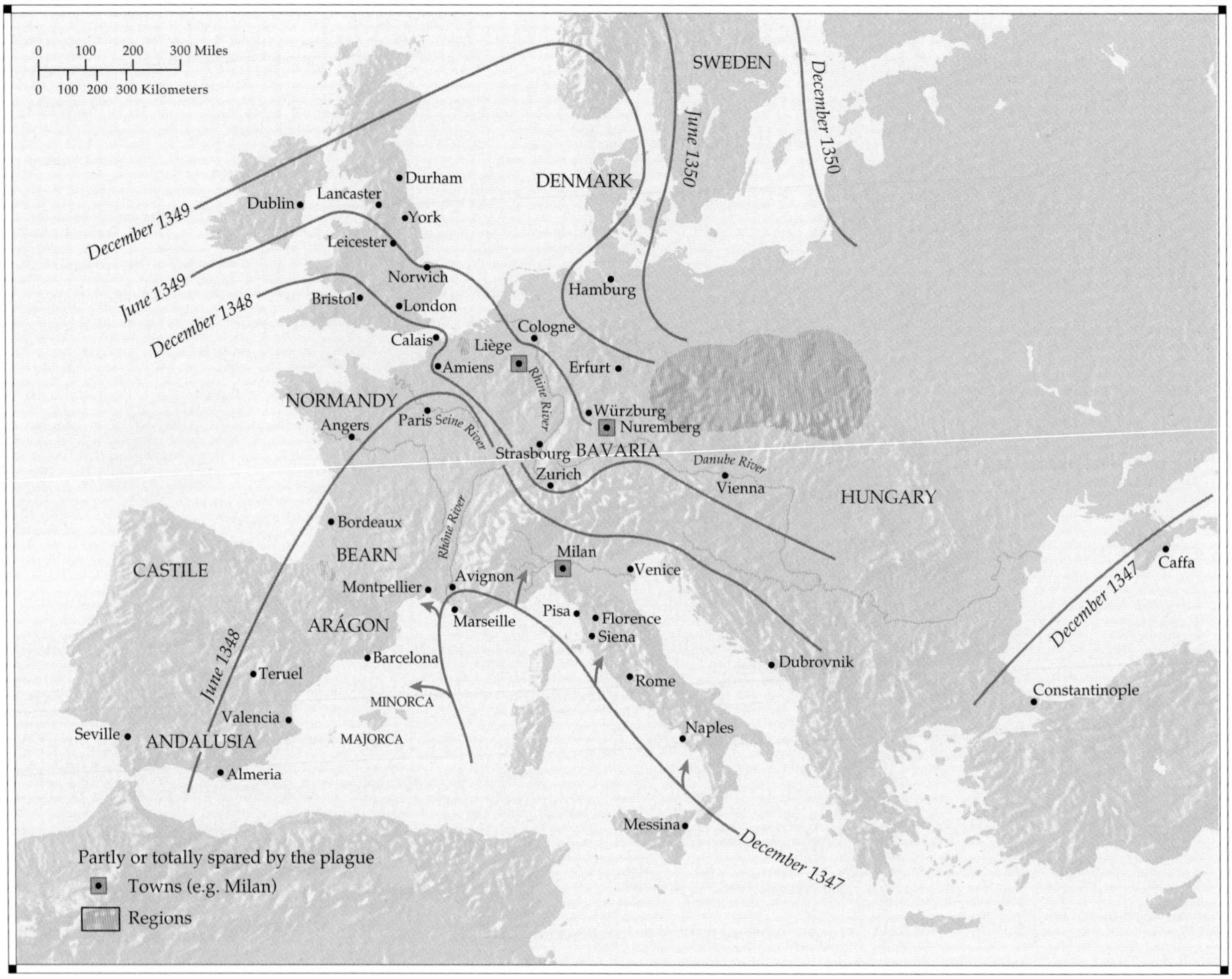

0 100 200 300 Miles
0 100 200 300 Kilometers
SWEDEN
December 1350
June 1350
DENMARK
December 1349
June 1349
December 1348
Dublin
Lancaster
Durham
York
Leicester
Norwich
Bristol
London
Hamburg
Calais
Cologne
Liège
Amiens
Erfurt
Rhine River
NORMANDY
Angers
Paris
Seine River
Würzburg
Nuremberg
Strasbourg
BAVARIA
Zurich
Danube River
Vienna
HUNGARY
Bordeaux
Rhône River
BEARN
CASTILE
Milan
Venice
Caffa
December 1347
Montpellier
Avignon
ARÁGON
Marseille
Pisa
Florence
Siena
June 1348
Barcelona
Dubrovnik
Teruel
Rome
Constantinople
MINORCA
Valencia
Naples
Seville
ANDALUSIA
MAJORCA
Almeria
Messina
December 1347
Partly or totally spared by the plague
Towns (e.g. Milan)
Regions

Figure 10.1 *The Dance of Death.* Fifteenth century. *In the wake of the Black Death, art and literature became filled with themes affirming the biblical message that life is short and death certain. A vivid image of this theme was the* Danse Macabre, *or Dance of Death, which took many artistic and literary forms. In this example, a miniature painting taken from a fifteenth-century Spanish manuscript, the corpses are shown nude, stripped of their human dignity, and dancing with wild abandon.*

armies ravaged much of western Europe. The church, in disgrace and disarray for much of this period, was unable to provide moral or political leadership. As old certainties evaporated, the optimistic mood of the High Middle Ages gave way to a sense of impending doom.

Ordeal by Plague, Famine, and War

Of all the calamities that now befell Europe, the worst was the plague, which first appeared in northern Italy in 1347. Imported from the East along newly opened trade routes, the plague bacillus was carried over sea and land by fleas, which in turn were transported by rats (Map 10.1). From Italy, the disease spread rapidly over most of Europe, halted by the frost line in the north. A few cities and areas—such as Milan and central Germany—were free of plague, but elsewhere it raged from 1348 until 1351, and further onslaughts occurred at random into the next century. So deadly was the disease that more than a third of Europe's seventy million people died in the first epidemic alone.

The mechanism of disease transmission was not fully understood, and the plague created panic. Using medieval accounts of the disease, modern researchers have detected three forms of plague: bubonic (infected lymph nodes), pneumonic (infected lungs), and septicemic (blood poisoning). All three forms were extremely painful, and death could result in a matter of hours or days. People in the Late Middle Ages referred to these disease types collectively as "the plague"; in the sixteenth century, historians began to label the epidemic the "Black Death," which has become the common term.

The Black Death cast a long shadow over the Late Middle Ages. Many writers and artists reflected the melancholy times, occasionally brightening their dark works with an end-of-the-world gaiety. The age's leading image became the Dance of Death, often portrayed as a skeleton democratically joining hands with kings, queens, popes, merchants, peasants, and prostitutes as they danced their way to destruction. In the direct manner of medieval thinking, this symbol forcefully showed the folly of human ambition and the transitory nature of life (Figure 10.1).

The plague was compounded by growing famine conditions across the European continent. Starting in 1315, agricultural harvests failed with some regularity for more than a century. Besides raising the death rate, these famines weakened the populace and made them more susceptible to diseases.

War also disrupted the pattern of social and economic life. By 1450 the kings of Aragon in eastern Spain had defeated and replaced the French rulers of Naples, Sicily, and Sardinia. The increasingly powerful northern Italian cities waged war among themselves for commercial and political advantage. Farther east, from 1347 on, the Ottoman Turks had been on the move, occupying Greece and the Balkan peninsula, conquering Constantinople in 1453 and menacing Bohemia and Hungary as the century ended. During the same period in the west, England and France fought the seemingly endless Hundred Years' War, while the dukes of Burgundy attempted to carve out a "middle kingdom" between France and the German empire.

One consequence of this almost constant warfare was a growing number of renegade soldiers who wandered the land. The countryside was filled with bands of roving knights—nobles, younger sons or bastards of aristocratic families, and outlaws—who blackmailed both landowners and peasants. Throughout Europe, these dangerous circumstances compelled town dwellers to retreat behind their city walls.

Depopulation, Rebellion, and Industrialization

The chief consequence of the plagues, famines, and wars was depopulation, which affected the commercial centers of Europe. In general, the regions hardest hit economically were those that had benefited most in the earlier boom, particularly France. New centers rose to economic importance, including Bohemia, Poland, Hungary, Scandinavia, and Portugal. The northern Italian cities of Florence, Genoa, and Venice, the largest cities in Europe, rallied from the plague's devastating losses in the fifteenth century to make a remarkable economic recovery.

Population decline also caused dramatic social dislocations. Plague-free regions lost population as healthy people flocked to plague-stricken areas, where laborers were in great demand. The rural population decreased, and thousands of villages simply disappeared as peasants abandoned their farms and settled in the towns. A short-term effect of the population shift was the widening of the gap between rich and poor. As a once relatively homogeneous population began to split into antagonistic classes, the established social order broke down, and society experienced warfare between peasants and landowners, guildsmen and merchants, and town laborers and middle-class elites. These social uprisings often had an anticlerical element, with the rebels attacking church property and denouncing the collection of tithes.

Starting in Flanders in 1296, social unrest mounted across Europe. In 1358 the French Jacquerie, or rural renegades, made common cause with Parisian workers and killed many nobles. In England during the brief Peasants' Revolt in 1381, insurgents seized and occupied

London. Among their demands was that the English king abolish the nobility. In the end, these uprisings failed to remedy the inequalities in the social order.

Although the immediate consequence of the demographic crisis was increased social unrest, the long-term effect was a higher standard of living for the survivors (Figure 10.2). Peasants in western Europe found their labor more in demand and their bargaining positions with the landowners improved. Many broke free from servitude and became rent-paying farmers. Others, less fortunate, moved from the status of serf to that of sharecropper. As a result of all these changes, manorialism was dying out in most of western Europe by 1500. But in central and eastern Europe, where the plague had been less devastating and the landlords could hold firm, estate owners bound the serfs ever more tightly to their farm labors.

As farming changed, so did Europe's fledgling industrial life. Hand-loomed textile manufacturing remained the leading industry, but its production and distribution centers shifted. Cut off by war from their former wool supplies and their retail markets, the Flemish and French weavers were challenged by woolen manufacturers from northern Italy, the Rhineland, and Poland. The greatest change in textile manufacturing, however, was ultimately precipitated by England's shift from the export of raw wool to the export of finished cloth, a change that disrupted the traditional rural way of life.

New industries also developed around the production of rag paper, a Chinese invention perfected by the Arabs and manufactured widely in Spain after 1300; of salt, distributed by Venice and Lisbon and used in tanning leather and preserving food; and of iron, in demand for weapons, armor, and horseshoes. New technology, such as the suction pump and the spinning wheel, increased productivity in other industries, and older inventions, such as eyeglasses, clocks, and gunpowder, were perfected in this age of rapid change. The development of movable type in the mid–fifteenth century was the most significant technological innovation of the Late Middle Ages; it gave rise to the printing and publishing industries and had enormous repercussions on education and literature.

The Secular Monarchies

France and England maintained their leading positions in Europe, but they exhausted their economies with wasteful wars. The Hundred Years' War, as the group of conflicts between the mid–fourteenth and the mid–fifteenth centuries is called, arose over feudal and military rivalries dating from the High Middle Ages

Figure 10.2 *Wine-Making*. Fifteenth century. Tapestry. Cluny Museum, Paris. *Wine production became a specialty of certain regions in the Late Middle Ages. This tapestry records the typical wine-making process on a fifteenth-century manor. In the lower left, a peasant carries grapes on his back. In the center, two means of wine-making are shown: above, a wine press, and, below, the more traditional stomping of the grapes in a vat. In the upper right corner, two peasants pour wine, through a funnel, into a barrel. And, in the left foreground, the lord and lady of the manor, recognizable by their rich gowns, supervise the making of the wine.*

Timeline 10.1 ROYAL DYNASTIES IN LATE MEDIEVAL FRANCE AND ENGLAND

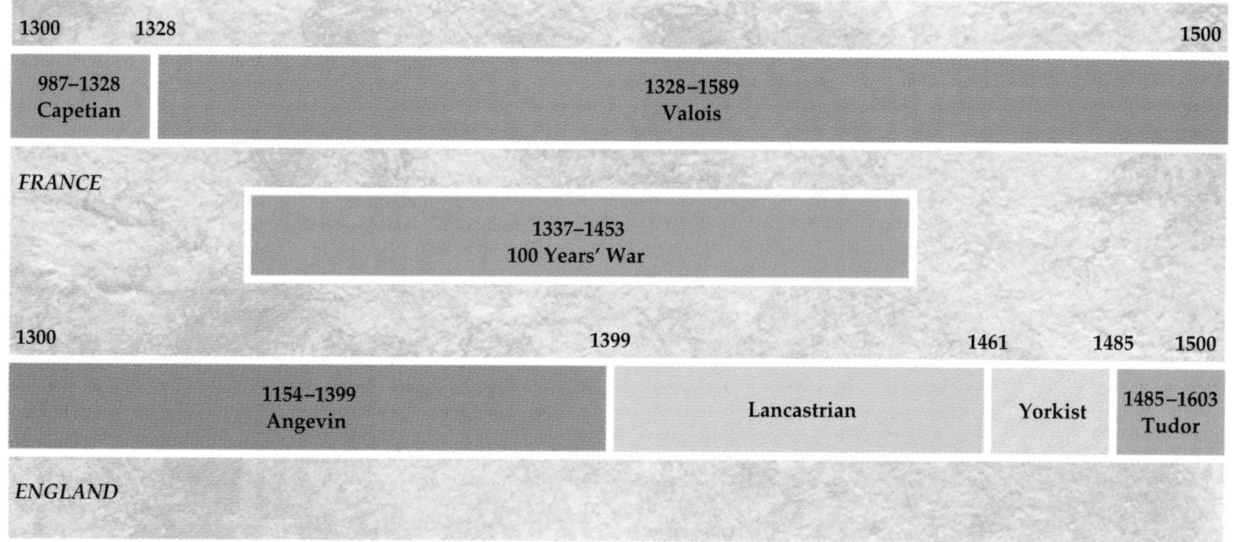

(Timeline 10.1). The war was fought entirely on French soil. The Valois dynasty had to contend not only with England but also with the dukes of Burgundy, who threatened to break their ties with the French crown and establish an independent kingdom on the northeast border of France. The Burgundian court at Dijon was the most brilliant in northern Europe, attracting the leading artists and humanists of the age. A heroic figure who emerged from this war was Joan of Arc (1412–1431), who rallied the French to victory, only to be burned at the stake by the English; in modern times, she became one of France's national heroines and a Roman Catholic saint.

Despite the ravages of the Hundred Years' War, the Valois kings ultimately increased their territory. Except for the port of Calais in northern France, England was forced to cede its overseas lands to the French crown. The dukes of Burgundy were brought under French control. And the northwestern region of Brittany, the last major territory that had escaped the French crown, was acquired through marriage. The contour of modern France was now complete.

While the Hundred Years' War raged on the Continent, life in England was disrupted by feudal rebellion, peasant unrest, and urban strife. Like France, England was emerging from the feudal system, but it was moving in a different direction. The English Parliament, which represented the interests of the nobles, the towns, and the rural counties, gained power at the expense of the king. Parliament also reflected popular feeling when it passed laws curbing papal power in England.

When Henry VII (r. 1485–1509) became king, however, it became apparent that a key reason for the dominance of Parliament had been the weakness of the kings. This founder of England's brilliant Tudor dynasty avoided the quarrels his predecessors had had with Parliament by abandoning foreign wars, living off his own estates, and relying on his own advisers. Henry VII's policies deflated parliamentary power and made him as potent as his contemporaries in France.

The success of the French and the English kings in centralizing their states attracted many imitators. Their ruling style—with royal secretaries, efficient treasuries, national judiciaries, and representative assemblies—was adopted in part by other states. Spain was the most successful in achieving unity. Dynastic politics and civil war kept central Europe and Scandinavia from becoming strong and centralized. The Holy Roman Empire was the least successful of these political entities, and Germany remained divided into combative states.

The Papal Monarchy

From its pinnacle of power and prestige in 1200 under Pope Innocent III, the church entered a period of decline in about 1300, and for the next century it was beset with schism and heresy. For most of the fourteenth century, the seat of the papacy was located in Avignon, a papal fief on the Rhône River, to escape from Rome's factional politics. Opponents of the relocation of the papacy, which had never happened before, claimed

Figure 10.3 Jacques Coeur's House. 1443–1451. Bourges, France. *Coeur was an immensely successful entrepreneur who at one point bankrolled the French kings. His magnificent mansion at Bourges spawned many imitations among wealthy businessmen across Europe. The building's spiky turrets, fanciful balconies, and highly decorated windows are all secular adaptations of the Late Gothic style more commonly seen in church architecture. Coeur conducted his European-wide financial and commercial dealings from this house, sending messages by carrier pigeons released through holes on the roof.*

these popes were in the pocket of the French king. The chief success of the Avignonese popes was to centralize the papacy, an accomplishment comparable to what was happening in the secular kingdoms. These popes reorganized the church's financial system and changed payments from kind to money. At the same time, unfortunately, they rarely made moral reforms. Their reigns lapsed into worldliness and greed, which made the papacy more vulnerable to criticism.

The Avignonese papacy had barely ended in 1378 when a new calamity, the Great Schism, threw the church into even more confusion. Under Pope Gregory XI, the papacy had returned to Rome in 1377, and the cardinals had elected an Italian pope when Gregory died. The French cardinals did not approve of this pope, and they elected another pontiff to rule from Avignon. Western Christendom was thus divided into two obediences with two popes, two colleges of cardinals, two curias, and two church tax systems. The rising power of the secular states became evident as rulers cast their support along political lines. France, Sicily, Scotland, Castile, Aragon, and Portugal rallied behind the Avignon pope; England, Flanders, Poland, Hungary, Germany, and the rest of Italy stayed loyal to the Roman pope. The papal office suffered the most; the pope's authority diminished as pious Christians became bewildered and disgusted.

The worst was yet to come. In 1409 both sets of cardinals summoned a church council in Pisa to heal the fissure. The Pisan Council elected a new pope and called on the other two to resign. They refused, and the church was faced with *three* rulers claiming papal authority. The Great Schism was finally resolved at the Council of Constance (1414–1418), which deposed the Avignon ruler, accepted the resignation of the Roman claimant, ignored the Pisan Council's choice, and elected a new pope, Martin V.

With the success of the Council of Constance, conciliar rule (rule by councils) as a way of curbing the power of the popes seemed to be gaining support in the church. But Martin V (pope 1417–1431) rejected this idea as soon as he was elected to the papal throne. Nevertheless, the conciliar movement remained alive until the mid–fifteenth century, when strong popes reasserted the monarchical power of their office. Although powerful, these popes failed to address pressing moral and spiritual concerns, for they were deeply involved in Italian politics and other worldly interests, ruling almost as secular princes in papal states.

THE CULTURAL FLOWERING OF THE LATE MIDDLE AGES

The calamitous political, social, and economic events of the Late Middle Ages were echoed in the cultural sphere by the breakdown of the medieval synthesis in religion, in theology, in literature, and in art. New secular voices began to be heard, challenging traditional views, and the interests of the bourgeoisie started to have an impact on art and architecture. Although the church remained the principal financial supporter of the arts, rich town dwellers, notably bankers and merchants, were emerging as the new patrons of art (Figure 10.3). Conspicuous art patronage made them the equals of the most powerful figures in society, but they still had few political rights.

Religion

Monastic reform had been a major force within the church in the High Middle Ages, but such collective acts of piety were largely unknown in the Late Middle Ages. Dedicated and virtuous monks and nuns were increasingly rare, and their influence was waning. Innovative forms of religious expression did not come from members of religious orders but from laypeople, inspired perhaps to protest and react against what they perceived as the increasing worldliness of the church and the declining commitment of many clergy.

Lay piety was thus one of the most significant developments in the religious landscape. By 1400 the Brethren and Sisters of the Common Life and the Friends of God were rising in the Rhineland, the Low Countries, and Flanders. This lay movement constituted the ***devotio moderna,*** or the "new devotion," with its ideal of a pious lay society. Disappointed with traditionally trained priests, members of these groups often rejected higher education and practiced the strict discipline of the earlier monastic orders, but without withdrawing into a monastery. Among the most important expressions of this new devotion was *The Imitation of Christ,* by Thomas à Kempis (1380–1471). His manual, with its stern asceticism, reflected the harsh ideals of the Brethren of the Common Life, the group of which Kempis was a member.

Within the pietistic movement, extreme ascetic practices that verged on heresy increased in these turbulent years. The bizarre behavior of the flagellants, for example, was triggered by the plague. They regarded this disease as God's way to judge and punish an evil society. The flagellants staged public processions in which they engaged in ritual whippings in an attempt to divert divine wrath from others (Figure 10.4).

The flagellants managed to escape official censure, but those more openly critical of the church did not. The leaders who attempted to reform the church in England and Bohemia met stout resistance from the popes. The English reform movement sprang from the teachings of John Wycliffe (about 1320–1384), an Oxford teacher whose message attracted both nobility and common folk. Wishing to purify the church of worldliness, Wycliffe urged the abolition of ecclesiastical property, the subservience of the church to the state, and the denial of papal authority. The most lasting achievement of Wycliffe's movement was the introduction of the first complete English-language Bible, produced by scholars inspired by his teaching. After his followers (known as Lollards) were condemned as heretical, the secular officials launched savage persecutions that resulted in the murder of those supporters who did not recant.

The Bohemian reformers in the Holy Roman Empire were indebted to Wycliffe, whom some had met at Oxford; but, more important, their strength was rooted in the popular piety and evangelical preachers of mid-fourteenth-century Prague. The heresy became identified with Jan Hus (about 1369–1415), a Czech theologian who accepted Wycliffe's political views but rejected some of his religious teachings. Hus was invited to the Council of Constance in 1415, where his ideas were condemned, and he was burned at the stake by state authorities. His death outraged his fellow Czechs, many of whom, including the powerful and wealthy, now adopted his views. Hussite beliefs became a vehicle for Czech nationalism, as his ethnic comrades fought against German overlords and attacked church property. Because of the backing of powerful lay leaders, the Hussites survived into the next century. They gained more followers during the Protestant Reformation and exist today as the Moravian Brethren.

Although the secular authorities, instigated by the church, could usually be counted on to put down the heresies, the church had a more powerful internal weapon at its disposal: the Inquisition (from the Latin *inquisitio,* meaning "inquiry"). Born in the aftermath of the Albigensian heresy in the twelfth century (see Chapter 9), the Inquisition was a religious court for identifying and condemning heretics. The Inquisition reached its cruel height during the Late Middle Ages, particularly in Italy and Spain.

Because of its procedures, the Inquisition became the most notorious instrument ever created by the

Figure 10.4 *Flagellation Scene. Annales of Gilles Le Muisit.* Bibliothèque Royale Albert Ier, Brussels. *This miniature painting represents a familiar scene across Europe during the plague years. The penitents, depicted with bare backs and feet, marched through towns scourging themselves with whips. By this self-punishment, they hoped to atone for their own and society's sins and thus end the plague.*

PERSONAL PERSPECTIVE

Henry Knighton
From the ***Chronicle***

An excellent source for the Late Middle Ages in England is the Chronicle *of the cleric Henry Knighton (?–1396). An attentive observer of public affairs, he recorded the political and religious unrest of his age. He lived mainly in Leicestershire, far from London, but he had well-placed contacts and reliable sources. In the first excerpt, Knighton details events of the 1381 rebellion of Wat Tyler. The second excerpt records an instance of religious unrest, which may be related to the Lollards, who believed that women could be priests.*

1

The next day, which was Saturday [15 June 1381], they all came together again in Smithfield, where the king [Richard II] came early to meet them, and showed that although he was young in years he was possessed of a shrewd mind. He was approached by their leader, Wat Tyler, who had now changed his name to Jack Straw. He stood close to the king, speaking for the others, and carrying an unsheathed knife, of the kind people call a dagger, which he tossed from hand to hand as a child might play with it, and looked as though he might suddenly seize the opportunity to stab the king if he should refuse their requests, and those accompanying the king therefore greatly feared what might come to pass. The commons asked of the king that all game, whether in waters or in parks and woods should become common to all, so that everywhere in the realm, in rivers and fishponds, and woods and forests, they might take the wild beasts, and hunt the hare in the fields, and do many other such things without restraint.

And when the king wanted time to consider such a concession, Jack Straw drew closer to him, with menacing words, and though I know not how he dared, took the reins of the king's horse in his hand. Seeing that, [William] Walworth, a citizen of London, fearing that he was about to kill the king, drew his basilard and ran Jack Straw through the neck. Thereupon another esquire, called Ralph Standish, stabbed him in the side with his basilard. And he fell to the ground on his back, and after rising to his hands and knees, he died.

2

A woman in London celebrates mass. At that time there was a woman in the city of London who had an only daughter whom she taught to celebrate the mass; and she privily set up and furnished an altar in her own bedroom, and there she caused her daughter on many occasions to dress as a priest and in her fashion to celebrate mass, though when she came to the sacramental words she prostrated herself before the altar and did not complete the sacrament. But then she would rise for the rest of the mass and recite it to the end, her mother assisting her and showing her devotion.

That nonsense went on for some time, until it was revealed by a neighbour who had been admitted to the secret, when it came to the ears of the bishop of London. He summoned them to his presence and showed them the error of their ways, and compelled them to display the child's priestly tonsure in public, for her head was found to be quite bald. The bishop greatly deplored and bewailed such misconduct in the church in his time, uttering many lamentations, and put an end to it by enjoining penance upon them.

Christian church. Ignoring the basic ideals of Roman law, this church court allowed suspects to be condemned without ever facing their accusers. Confessions made under torture were also allowed to serve as evidence against other persons. Forbidden by the Bible to shed blood, the leaders of the Inquisition turned convicted heretics over to the state authorities, who then executed them by burning. By modern estimates, thousands of men and women perished in this way.

The Inquisition was also used to rid society of women—and to a lesser extent of men—who were suspected of being in league with the devil. The belief in witchcraft, an occult legacy of the ancient world, was next to universal during the Middle Ages. Many educated people sincerely believed that certain women were witches and that magical devices could protect the faithful from their spells. Consequently, hundreds of suspected individuals were killed by the Inquisition or by unruly mobs. Fear of witchcraft persisted as a dangerous part of popular lore into the eighteenth century.

Theology, Philosophy, and Science

Although the popes betrayed their spiritual mission in these years, the church was not without dedicated followers who cared deeply about theological issues. Many of these clerical thinkers were affiliated with the universities, principally in Paris and at Oxford. Their major disputes were over Thomism, the theological system of Thomas Aquinas, which in the Late Middle Ages was losing supporters and coming increasingly under attack. At the same time, the ongoing philosophical struggle between Realism and Nominalism finally ended with a Nominalist victory. In the long run, those who questioned Thomism and those who accepted Nominalism set philosophy and theology on separate paths and thus paved the way to the Renaissance and the Scientific Revolution.

***The* Via Antiqua *Versus the* Via Moderna** The opening round in the theological war against Thomism began soon after the death of Thomas Aquinas in 1274 and before the High Middle Ages was over. In 1277 church officials in Paris condemned the Latin Averroists at the local university for their rationalist ideas. As part of their attack on extreme rationalism, the church authorities rejected some of Aquinas's arguments. The censure of Thomism led to a heated controversy that raged for much of the Late Middle Ages among university scholars. In particular, Thomas's fellow Dominican friars waged an acrimonious battle with the Franciscan masters, their great rivals in theological studies.

During these theological debates, new labels were invented and assumed by the opposing sides. Aquinas's *via media* came to be termed by his opponents the ***via antiqua,*** or the old-fashioned way. Broadly speaking, the *via antiqua* followed Thomism in urging that faith and reason be combined as the correct approach to divine truth. In contrast, the ***via moderna,*** or the modern way, made a complete separation of biblical beliefs and rationalism. In time the *via moderna* prevailed, driving the *via antiqua* underground until it was rescued from oblivion in the modern period.

Duns Scotus and William of Ockham The conflict between the *via antiqua* and the *via moderna* was best exemplified in the writings of John Duns Scotus and William of Ockham, respectively. The first of these commentators was sympathetic to the theology of Thomas Aquinas, but the second scholar was unmistakably hostile and tried to discredit Thomism.

Duns Scotus [duhnz SKOAT-us] (about 1265–1308), the most persuasive voice of the *via antiqua,* was a Scottish thinker who was trained as a Franciscan and lectured at the universities in Oxford, Paris, and Cologne. Even though he was a supporter of Thomism, Duns Scotus unwittingly undermined Aquinas's synthesis by stressing that faith was superior to reason, a shift in focus that arose from his belief in God's absolute and limitless power. Pointing out that God's existence could not be proven either through the senses or by reason, he asserted that only faith could explain the divine mystery. Furthermore, Duns Scotus concluded that because the theologian and the philosopher have different intellectual tasks, theology and science (that is, the study of nature) should be independent fields of inquiry.

What Duns Scotus unintentionally began, William of Ockham (about 1300–about 1349) purposely completed. Under the assaults of Ockham's keen intellect, the Thomist theological edifice collapsed. An Oxford-trained theologian, he recognized the importance of both reason and faith; but, like Scotus, he did not see how reason could prove God's existence. Both thinkers believed that only personal feelings and mystical experiences could reveal God and the divine moral order. Yet Ockham went further than Scotus by asserting that reason, the senses, and empirical evidence could enable human beings to discover and hence understand the natural world. To Ockham, faith and reason were both valid approaches to truth, but they should be kept apart so that each could achieve its respective end.

In the seemingly endless medieval debate between the Realists and the Nominalists, Ockham's reasoning swept Nominalism to its final victory. Like the Nominalists of the twelfth century, Ockham denied the existence of universals and claimed that only individual objects existed. He concluded that human beings can have clear and distinct knowledge only of specific things in the physical world; no useful knowledge can be gained through reason or the senses about the spiritual realm. Ockham's conclusion did not mean that human beings were cast adrift without access to the world of God. A corollary of his approach was that understanding of the spiritual realm rested solely on the truths of faith and theology.

In his reasoning, William of Ockham asserted a principle of economy that stripped away all that was irrelevant: Arguments should be drawn from a minimum of data and founded on closely constructed logic. "It is vain to do with more what can be done with fewer," he says in one of his works. Ockham's "razor" of logic eliminated superfluous information that could not be verified, thus enabling a student to cut to the core of a philosophical problem. The Ockhamites, following their mentor's logic and empiricism, challenged the Realists and dominated the intellectual life of the universities for the next two hundred years.

Developments in Science Ockham's ideas broadened the path to modern science that had been opened by two thirteenth-century thinkers. In that earlier time, Robert Grosseteste [GROAS-test] (about 1175–1253), a Franciscan at Oxford University, had devised a scientific method for investigating natural phenomena; using step-by-step procedures, he employed mathematics and tested hypotheses until he reached satisfactory conclusions. Roger Bacon (about 1220–1292), another Franciscan and a follower of Grosseteste, advocated the use of the experimental method, which he demonstrated in his studies of optics, solar eclipses, and rainbows and in his treatises on mathematics, physics, and philosophy. From the modern standpoint, Bacon was perhaps the most original mind of this generally barren period in the history of science.

In the fourteenth century, other thinkers, with Grosseteste and Bacon as guides and Ockham's logic as a weapon, made further contributions to the advance of science. Outstanding among these men was one bold Parisian scholar who took advantage of the growing interest in the experimental method, Nicholas Oresme [O-REM] (about 1330–1382). Oresme answered all of Aristotle's objections to the idea that the earth moved. Using pure reason and applying theoretical arguments, he concluded that it was as plausible that the earth moved around the sun as that it was fixed. Having used reason to show that the earth may move, however, Oresme then chose to accept church doctrine, denying what he had demonstrated. Nevertheless, Oresme's arguments, along with Ockham's separation of natural philosophy from theology and Bacon's formulation of the experimental method, foreshadowed the end of the medieval concept of the physical and celestial worlds.

Literature

The powerful forces that were reshaping the wider culture—the rising new monarchies, the growing national consciousness among diverse peoples, the emerging secularism, and the developing urban environment—were also transforming literature in the Late Middle Ages. The rise of literacy produced a growing educated class who learned to read and write the local languages rather than Latin, and a shift to vernacular literature began to occur. Two new groups—the monarchs and their courts and the urban middle class—started to supplant the nobility and the church as patrons and audiences. And, ultimately most important of all, in the mid-fifteenth century Johann Gutenberg developed a practicable method of using movable type to print books. This invention helped to seal the doom of medieval civilization and signaled the commencement of the modern world.

Northern Italian Literature: Petrarch and Boccaccio

New literary forms emerged in the areas where the chivalric and feudal modes were weakest—northern Italy and England. Petrarch and Boccaccio, both Florentines, like Dante, grew up in a Christian world that was rapidly being secularized. These two writers captured the mood of this transition era as Florence and the other Italian city-states shed their medieval outlook. Both authors looked back to the Classical world for inspiration, and yet both found in the bustling world of the nearby towns the materials and characters for their stories. Of the two, Petrarch was the more dedicated Classicist and often used ancient themes in his writings.

Francesco Petrarch [PEE-trark] ("Petrarca" in Italian) (1304–1374), though Florentine by birth and in spirit, flourished in Avignon amid the splendor and learning of the papal court. As a diplomat for popes and Italian princes, he won fame and wealth, but his reputation arose from his career as a professional man of letters. Rejecting the age's trend toward the vernacular, he dedicated his life to Latin writing and to the recovery of ancient manuscripts, although the work for which he is most renowned, a collection of love lyrics and sonnets called *Canzoniere,* or *Songbook,* is written in Italian. His devotion struck a responsive chord among his fellow Italians, who in 1341 proclaimed him poet laureate for his lyrics, sonnets, treatises, and epics. In many ways, Petrarch, despite a clerical training, shows the typical secular interests of his times. A conventional Christian, he only occasionally addressed religious issues in his works.

A religious theme is touched on in *Secretum,* or *My Secret,* in which Petrarch deals with the state of his soul. In this dialogue, "Augustinus," or St. Augustine, hounds "Franciscus," or Petrarch, about his innermost thoughts and desires, charging him with all the deadly sins. Freely admitting his moral lapses, Franciscus pleads that he is the same as any other man—driven by a love of learning, a weakness for fleshly attractions, and an appetite for personal comforts. Despite this confession, with its modern overtones, the dialogue shows that Petrarch could not liberate himself fully from medieval values.

Even more than his lifelong friend Petrarch, Giovanni Boccaccio [bo-KACH-e-o] (1313–1375) was a man of the world. The son of a banker, Boccaccio began his literary career by penning prose romances along with poetic pastorals and sonnets, many of which were dedicated to Fiammetta, a young woman who was both his consuming passion and his literary muse. His early efforts, however, were overshadowed by his Italian prose masterpiece, *The Decameron.* Written in about 1351, this work reflects the grim conditions of the Black Death, which had just swept through Florence (Figure 10.5). In *The Decameron* (from the Greek for "ten days"), Boccaccio describes how ten young men and women, in their efforts to escape the plague, flee the city to a

Figure 10.5 FRANCESCO TRAINI. *Triumph of Death.* Detail. Ca. 1350. Entire fresco 18′6″ × 49′2″. Pisa, Italy. *Like the storytellers in* The Decameron, *these well-dressed travelers have left their plague-stricken city, perhaps in search of safety or hoping for a day's pleasant diversion in the countryside. Instead, they come on three corpses rotting in coffins—even the dogs are afraid—and a hermit who points out the lesson: Death triumphs over all. This detail is from a huge fresco painted on the wall of the cemetery next to the Pisa cathedral.*

country villa, where they pass the time, each telling a story a day for ten days. Most of their one hundred tales were based on folk stories and popular legends. Although some tales deal lightly with social mores and a few contain moral messages, the majority simply entertain the listener. Boccaccio, speaking through a cross section of urban voices and relying on well-known stories, helped develop a form of literature that eventually led to the modern short story.

English Literature: Geoffrey Chaucer Like its Italian counterpart, English literature rapidly matured into its own forms during the Late Middle Ages. The development of an English literary style was aided immensely by the evolution of a common language. Until this time, most educated English people read and spoke French, but a rising sense of national consciousness, triggered by the Hundred Years' War and by an emerging educated urban class, hastened the spread of English as the native tongue. England's kings came to see themselves as different from their French ancestors and purposely began to speak English instead of French; they also made English the official language of government.

By 1300 important works in English were beginning to appear, such as *The Vision of Piers Plowman,* a moral allegory, probably written by William Langland (about 1332–1400), that graphically exposes the plight of the poor and calls for a return to Christian virtues. This work provides insight into England's social and economic system and, through the author's anguish, reveals the social tension around the time of the Peasants' Revolt in 1381.

English literature was still establishing its own identity and a common language was slowly emerging when Geoffrey Chaucer (about 1340–1400) appeared on the scene. He wrote in an East Midland dialect of English that became the standard form for his generation as well as the foundation of modern English. The son of a wealthy London merchant, Chaucer spent his professional life as a courtier, a diplomat, and a public servant for the English crown. The profession of "writer" or "poet" was unknown in Chaucer's day. But his poetry brought him renown, and when he died he was the first commoner to be buried in Westminster Abbey, a favored burial spot for English royalty.

Chaucer began composing his most famous work, *The Canterbury Tales,* in 1385. He set the tales in the context of a pilgrimage to the tomb of Thomas à Becket, the twelfth-century martyr. Even though the journey has a religious purpose, Chaucer makes it plain that the travelers intend to have a good time along the way. To make the journey from London to Canterbury more interesting, the thirty-one pilgrims (including Chaucer himself) agree to tell tales—two each going and returning—and to award a prize for the best story told.

Chaucer completed only twenty-three tales and the general Prologue, in which he introduces the pilgrims. Each person on the pilgrimage not only represents an English social type but also is a unique and believable human being. In this poetic narrative about a group of ordinary people, the spiritual is mixed with the temporal and the serious with the comic.

Chaucer drew his pilgrims from nearly all walks of medieval society. The Knight, in this late stage of feudalism, personified much that was noble and honorable in the chivalric code; his bravery could not be questioned, but he was also a mercenary and cruel to his enemies. Certain representatives of the church are also somewhat skeptically treated. The Prioress, the head of a convent and from the upper class, is more concerned about her refined manners and polished language than the state of her soul. Similarly, the Monk lives a life of the flesh and enjoys good food, fine wines, and expensive clothing. The Friar seems the very opposite of his sworn ideals; he is eager to hear a confession for a fee, and he never goes among the poor or aids the sick. However, in the country Parson, Chaucer portrays a true servant of God who preaches to his parish, looks after the infirm and dying, and never takes more than his share from his religious flock.

Among the secular travelers, the most vivid is the Wife of Bath. A widow five times over, this jolly woman is full of life and loves to talk. She has been on many pilgrimages and not only knows about foreign places but also has a keen insight into people (Figure 10.6).

As for the tales they tell, the pilgrims' choices often reflect their own moral values. The worthy Knight tells a chivalric love story, but the Miller, a coarse, rough man well versed in lying and cheating, relates how a young wife took on a lover and deceived her husband—an example of the popular medieval tale known as a *fabliau.* Thus the pilgrims' stories, based on folk and fairy tales, romances, classical stories, and beast fables, reveal as much about the narrators as they do about late medieval culture.

Figure 10.6 *The Wife of Bath.* Ellesmere Manuscript. Early fifteenth century. Bancroft Library, University of California at Berkeley. *In the Ellesmere Manuscript, an early edition of* The Canterbury Tales *issued soon after Chaucer's death, each story was accompanied by a sketch of the pilgrim who was narrating it. This portrait of the Wife of Bath shows her riding an ambler, a horse that walks with an easy gait, and wearing a wimple, the typical headdress of nuns as well as laywomen of the period.*

French Literature: Christine de Pizan France was also touched by the winds of change blowing through Europe during the Late Middle Ages. Christine de Pizan, the leading French writer of the day, began to explore in her works the status and role of women, giving voice in the process to one of the most prominent issues in the Post-Modern world (see Chapter 21). She also contributed to the triumph of vernacular over Latin language by writing in a graceful French with the learnedness of Latin.

Christine de Pizan (sometimes written as "de Pisan," or "of Pisa") (1364–about 1430) was by birth an Italian whose literary gifts blossomed under the patronage of the French kings and dukes of Burgundy. She began a life of study and learning after the death of her husband, a royal official, in 1389, left her with a family to support. The first known Western woman to earn a living through her writings, de Pizan was a pioneer who blazed the trail for women authors.

De Pizan wrote on diverse topics, working within the well-established literary genres of her day, including love poems, lays, biography, letters, political tracts, and moral proverbs. Two themes dominate her writing: calls for peace and appeals for the recognition of women's contributions to culture and social life. Both themes reflect the era in which she lived—an age beset by civil strife due to the Hundred Years' War and a time in which women were scarcely allowed to express an opinion in public.

The work of de Pizan's that has excited the most interest among modern readers is *The Book of the City of Ladies* (1405), a book that forcefully tries to raise the status of women and to give them dignity. Offering one of the first histories of women and arguing that women have the right to be educated, based on her premise that women are moral and intellectual equals of men, this book seems almost feminist in a modern sense; however, a close reading shows that de Pizan is writing within a medieval framework. Nowhere in this book or in any other writings does she advocate that women abandon their traditional roles and strike out on a new path. It is proper nevertheless to claim that de Pizan is the first Western writer to raise the issue of women's rights in society and culture.

Art and Architecture

The Gothic style continued to dominate architecture throughout this period (see Chapter 9), but the balanced and unified High Gothic of the thirteenth century was now replaced with the ornate effects of the **Late Gothic style.** Virtuosity became the chief aesthetic goal, as the architects took basic forms and pushed them to the stylistic limits.

Late Gothic sculpture and painting also became more virtuosic. Statues and sculptured figures were given willowy, swaying bodies, rendered in exquisite detail, and illuminated manuscripts and painted wooden panels became ever more refined. At the same time, Giotto, an early-fourteenth-century Florentine painter, was revolutionizing art with a new approach to painting. The trend toward naturalism embodied in his works was the most significant new artistic development of this period and was destined to be the wave of the future.

Figure 10.7 The Church of St. Maclou. 1435–ca. 1514. Rouen, France. *St. Maclou's exterior illustrates the ornate Late Gothic style. Its west facade, unlike a square High Gothic front, fans out to form a semicircular entrance. There are five portals (rather than the usual three), two of which are blind, and set above them are steeply pitched stone arches of intricate design.*

Late Gothic Architecture France—the home of the Gothic style—remained a potent source of architectural innovation. French architects now abandoned the balanced ideal of the High Gothic and made extravagance their guiding principle, creating a Late Gothic style typified by ever greater heights and elaborate decoration. In the fifteenth century, this tendency culminated in the **Flamboyant style,** so named for its flamelike effects. French churches built in this style had sky-piercing spires, and their facades were embroidered with lacy or wavy decorations that obscured the buildings' structural components (Figure 10.7).

During the fourteenth century, the Late Gothic spread, becoming an international style. All across Europe, the focus shifted to fanciful designs: The churches were smaller, the roofs and towers taller, the naves wider, and the decorations more luxuriant. Regional tastes, however, made for local variations in the general style.

In England, the Late Gothic was called **Perpendicular** because of its dramatic emphasis on verticality. This Perpendicular style was characterized by an increased use of paneled decorations on the walls and overhead

Figure 10.8 Choir of Gloucester Cathedral. Ca. 1330–1357. Gloucester, England. *The choir and apse of Gloucester cathedral were rebuilt in the Perpendicular Gothic style in about 1330, when King Edward III chose the church as the burial shrine for his murdered father, Edward II. The architects made the earlier Norman apse into a square and filled the east end with glass panels. Inside, the builders redesigned the support system, using thin vertical piers; these piers were attached to the walls and laced together on the ceiling, creating elaborate patterns that complemented the glass decorations.*

Figure 10.9 South Cloister of Gloucester Cathedral. Ca. 1370. Gloucester, England. *Fan vaulting, an intricate pattern in which ribs arch out from a single point in the ceiling, first appeared at Gloucester cathedral and inspired many imitations. Although the ribs may appear to be structurally necessary, they are really a richly decorative device carved from stone. In Gloucester's south cloister, the tracery fans out from the top of each column and then merges in the center of the ceiling, giving the impression of a delicate screen.*

vaults, resulting in a variation of rib vaulting, called **fan vaulting,** in which stone ribs arch out from a single point in the ceiling to form a delicate pattern. This style also increased the number of window openings, which necessitated additional flying buttresses. The best example of the English Perpendicular is the cathedral in Gloucester.

In the choir, the vertical lines, extending from the floor to the ceiling, where the tracery is interwoven, unite the building's interior into an upward-moving volume (Figure 10.8). Just as impressive as the interior is the nearby cloister with its fan tracery vaulting that weaves a pattern overhead while tying the walls and ceiling into a complex unit (Figure 10.9).

In Italy, the Gothic had put down only shallow roots because the Italians felt that the French builders had little to teach them about architecture. Italian Gothic has strong affinities with the Romanesque style—the large hall with its basilica floor plan and massive walls. In addition, most of the key Gothic features are missing from the Italian Gothic, such as the flying buttresses, the twin towers, and the vast numbers of stained-glass windows.

A key example of the Late Italian Gothic is the cathedral in Siena. Filled with civic pride, Siena's citizens urged their leaders to build a cathedral more splendid than those of their neighbors. Begun in the mid–thirteenth century, the cathedral was constructed over the next hundred and fifty years, and, as a result, the building complex shows a mixture of styles: The **campanile,** or bell tower, is executed in the Italian Romanesque, but the overall cathedral complex is Italian Gothic (Figure 10.10). The facade, for the first time in Italy, incorporated nearly life-size figures into the total design, thus heightening its resemblance to the French Gothic. However, many features distinguish the style of Siena from the French style. For example, the decorative statues on Siena's facade were placed above the gables and not set in niches. Furthermore, the Sienese builders put mosaics into the spaces in the gables and above the central rose window.

Florence, Siena's greatest military and trade rival, refused to be outdone by its nearby competitor. The Florentine city fathers asked Giotto [JAWT-toe] (about 1276–1337), the city's most renowned painter, to design a campanile for their own cathedral. Today, the

Figure 10.10 Siena Cathedral. 1250–1400. Siena, Italy. *Extant records and floor plans show that the Sienese changed their minds several times before deciding on the cathedral's final shape. At one time, in about 1322, a commission of architects advised that the existing cathedral be demolished because the foundations and walls were not strong enough to support new additions. Nonetheless, construction went forward, and the cathedral is still standing after more than six hundred years.*

first story of the bell tower—with its carvings, interlaced patterns of pink and white marble, and hexagonal inlays—still stands as conceived by Giotto (Figure 10.11). Giotto's plan, as left in a drawing, called for an open tower with a spire on top, as in a French Gothic tower. But later architects constructed a rectangular top instead and decorated it with marble—making it distinctively Italian rather than reminiscent of the French.

Late Gothic Sculpture During the Late Middle Ages, sculpture, like architecture, continued to undergo stylistic changes, among which two general trends may be identified. One trend centered in Italy, notably in Siena, where the Pisano [pee-SAHN-o] family began to experiment with sculptural forms that foreshadowed Renaissance art, with its return to Classical themes and values (see Chapter 11). Outstanding among the members of the gifted Pisano family was Giovanni Pisano (1245–1314), who designed the intricate Late Gothic facade of the Siena cathedral (see Figure 10.10). Giovanni's great artistic reputation is largely based on the massive marble pulpit that he carved for the cathedral at Pisa. Using Classical themes derived from Roman art (as Renaissance artists were to do), he designed the pulpit to rest on acanthus leaves at the top of eight Corinthian columns (Figure 10.12). The lions that

Figure 10.11 GIOTTO. Campanile of the Florentine Cathedral. Ca. 1334–1350. Ht. approx. 200′. Florence, Italy. *Giotto's Tower, as this campanile is known in Florence, is one of the city's most cherished landmarks. Today, its bells still toll the time. The two sets of windows in the central section and the taller openings at the top give the campanile a strong sense of balanced proportion. Thus, despite being built in the fourteenth century, the tower anticipates the Classical ideal that was revived in the Renaissance.*

Figure 10.12 GIOVANNI PISANO. Pulpit in the Pisa Cathedral. Ca. 1302–1310. Pisa, Italy. *Pisano built and carved this massive (17-foot-high) pulpit at the height of his reputation. A superb artist but a quarrelsome man, Pisano recorded his frustrations in the lengthy inscription around the pulpit's base. In it he claimed that he had achieved much, had been condemned by many, and took full responsibility for this work of art. Pisano's advance from anonymity to a position of great artistic repute was typical of a new breed of artist appearing in fourteenth-century Italy.* ▶

COMITE TUNC DICO MONTISFELTRI FREDERICO HIC ASSISTENTE NECTO
NUNC CLAMAT NON BENE CAVI : DUM PLUS MONSTRAVI : PLUS HOSTICA DAMNA PROBAVI : CORDE SED IGNAVI

Figure 10.13 GIOVANNI PISANO. Nativity Scene. Pulpit in the Pisa cathedral. Ca 1302–1310. 33½ × 44½". Pisa, Italy. *In this Late Gothic sculpture, Pisano cut deeply into the marble's surface to give a nearly three-dimensional effect. His many figures seem involved in their own tasks but are nevertheless linked with one another around the Madonna and child. For example, the two shepherds (the head of one has been lost) in the upper right corner appear to be listening to the angels approaching from the left, while at the far right, sheep rest and graze. Such balanced placements are evidence of Pisano's classicizing tendencies. Pisano's relief retains a prominent Gothic feature, however, by presenting the Virgin and child twice—in the central scene and in the lower left corner, where a seated Mary, balancing the baby Jesus on her right leg, stretches her left hand to test the temperature of the water in an elaborate basin.*

support two of the columns were modeled on those on an ancient Roman sarcophagus. Just as late Roman art blended Christian and Classical symbols, so Giovanni's treatment of the pulpit's base mixed images of the cardinal virtues, such as Justice and Temperance, with the figure of the Greek hero Herakles.

Pisano's octagonal pulpit includes eight panels in high relief that depict scenes from the lives of either John the Baptist or Christ. Of these panels, the scene depicting the Nativity ranks as his finest work. In this scene, he portrays a natural vitality through the careful balance and orderly spacing of the animals and people (Figure 10.13). The placement and the calm actions of the surrounding figures frame the Virgin and child so that the viewer's attention is focused on these two central figures. Giovanni's swaying figures with their smooth draperies were rooted in Late Gothic art, but their quiet serenity attested to his classicizing manner.

The other trend in sculpture during this time centered in Burgundy, where Philip the Bold (r. 1364–1404) supported scholars and artists at his ducal court in Dijon. Preeminent among these was Claus Sluter [SLUE-tuhr] (about 1350–1406), a sculptor of Netherlandish origin who helped to define this last phase of Gothic art. Sluter's masterly sculptures are still housed in a monastery near Dijon, and his most famous work, *The Well of Moses,* was commissioned for the cloister of this monastic retreat.

The Well of Moses, which was designed as a decorative cover for an actual well in a courtyard, is surrounded at its base with Old Testament prophets symbolizing the sacraments of communion and baptism. The most beautifully rendered of the surviving life-size statues is Moses, encased in a flowing robe and standing erect with a finely chiseled head (Figure 10.14). Sluter's sense of the dramatic moment, of the prophet's personal emotions, and of the individual features makes the statue nearly an individual portrait. Sluter rendered Moses' beard and the unfurled scroll in precise detail and carved the figure with the head turned to the side, eyes looking into the future.

Late Gothic Painting and the Rise of New Trends Of all the arts, painting underwent the most radical changes in the Late Middle Ages. Illuminated manuscripts maintained their popularity, but their themes became more secular under the patronage of titled aristocrats and wealthy merchants. At the same time, painters of frescoes and wooden panels introduced new techniques for applying paint and mixing colors. Stylistically, painters preferred to work in the extravagant Late Gothic manner with its elegant refinement and its undulating lines. Nevertheless, as mentioned earlier, Giotto and other Italian painters discovered fresh ways of depicting human figures that started to revolutionize art.

ILLUMINATED MANUSCRIPTS The Burgundian court played a pivotal role in the production of one of the outstanding illuminated manuscripts of the medieval period, the *Très Riches Heures du Duc de Berry.* This famous collection of miniatures was painted by the three Limbourg brothers for the duke of Berry, brother of Philip the Bold of Burgundy. These illustrations stand above the others of their time for their exquisite detail, general liveliness, and intricately designed crowd scenes—some of the marks of the Late Gothic style.

The *Très Riches Heures,* or the *Very Rich Hours,* represents a type of small prayer book that was a favorite of nobles and businessmen. These personal books of worship, with their litanies and prayers, were often handsomely hand-illustrated to enhance their value. The duke of Berry's prayer book contained some 130 miniature paintings, including scenes from the life of Christ and the calendar cycle. In the calendar series, each tiny painting, finely detailed and colored in jewel-like tones, notes a seasonal activity appropriate for the month. Some represent the brilliant court life of the duke, and others depict the drudgery of peasant life, sharply differentiated from the court scenes by their action and color. The illustration for January shows the duke of Berry surrounded by his well-dressed courtiers and enjoying a sumptuous feast (Figure 10.15).

THE PRINT The print, a new artistic medium, developed in the Late Middle Ages in the Austrian-Bavarian regions, eastern France, and the Netherlands. Sparked by the growth of lay piety, the earliest prints were devotional woodcuts to be used as aids to personal meditation. The prints initially featured scenes from the lives of the Virgin and Christ. For the **woodcut print,** the artist drew an image on a woodblock, which was then cut by a woodcutter and printed by the artist; some were then hand-tinted by a colorist. By 1500 the new techniques of **engraving** (using a sharp tool to draw an image onto a metal plate overlaid with wax, dipping the plate in acid, and then printing it) and **drypoint** (marking an image onto a copper plate with a metal stylus and then printing it) were becoming increasingly popular.

Probably the outstanding set of prints dating from this period was that in the Medieval Housebook, a late-fifteenth-century German manuscript. The so-called Medieval Housebook was a gathering of 192 prints, of which only 126 remain. Most of the prints are in black and white, though a few are partially colored. The printing techniques vary from drypoint and engraving to simple drawings on vellum. Stylistic differences indicate that at least three artists contributed to the work, thus suggesting that the Housebook may have been produced in a workshop. For convenience, however, the painter is called simply the Housebook Master.

Of the surviving 126 prints, the subjects range over late medieval life, from the workaday world to jousting scenes to court life. Some offer realistic views of medieval buildings, including barnyards, private dwellings, and palaces; most are highly detailed, showing hair and clothing styles. Others are lively and playful, depicting relations between the sexes and the classes (Figure 10.16).

NEW TRENDS IN ITALY: GIOTTO While the illuminated manuscript and the print were popular in northern Europe, a revolution in painting was under way in Italy. The paintings of Giotto are generally recognized as having established a new direction in Western art, one that led into the Renaissance. In Giotto's own day,

◀ **Figure 10.14** CLAUS SLUTER. *Moses*, from *The Well of Moses*. Ca. 1395–1406. Ht. of full figure approx. 6′. Chartreuse de Champmol, Dijon, France. *Sluter followed the allegorical tradition of medieval art in this portrait of the Hebrew prophet Moses. The book in Moses' right hand and the scroll over his left shoulder symbolize the Word of God. Sluter also depicted Moses with "horns" growing out of his forehead, as was characteristic in medieval representations.*

Figure 10.15 LIMBOURG BROTHERS. Month of January, from the *Très Riches Heures du Duc de Berry*. 1413–1416. Approx. 8½ × 5½″. Musée Condé, Chantilly, France. *This miniature painting provides insightful social history in its exquisite details. The duke, seated in the right center, is dressed in a blue patterned cloak and is greeting his guests for what was probably a New Year's celebration. Behind the duke stands a servant, over whose head are written the words "aproche, aproche," a welcome that is the equivalent of "Come in, come in." Above this festive scene, the zodiac signs of Capricorn and Aquarius identify the month as January.*

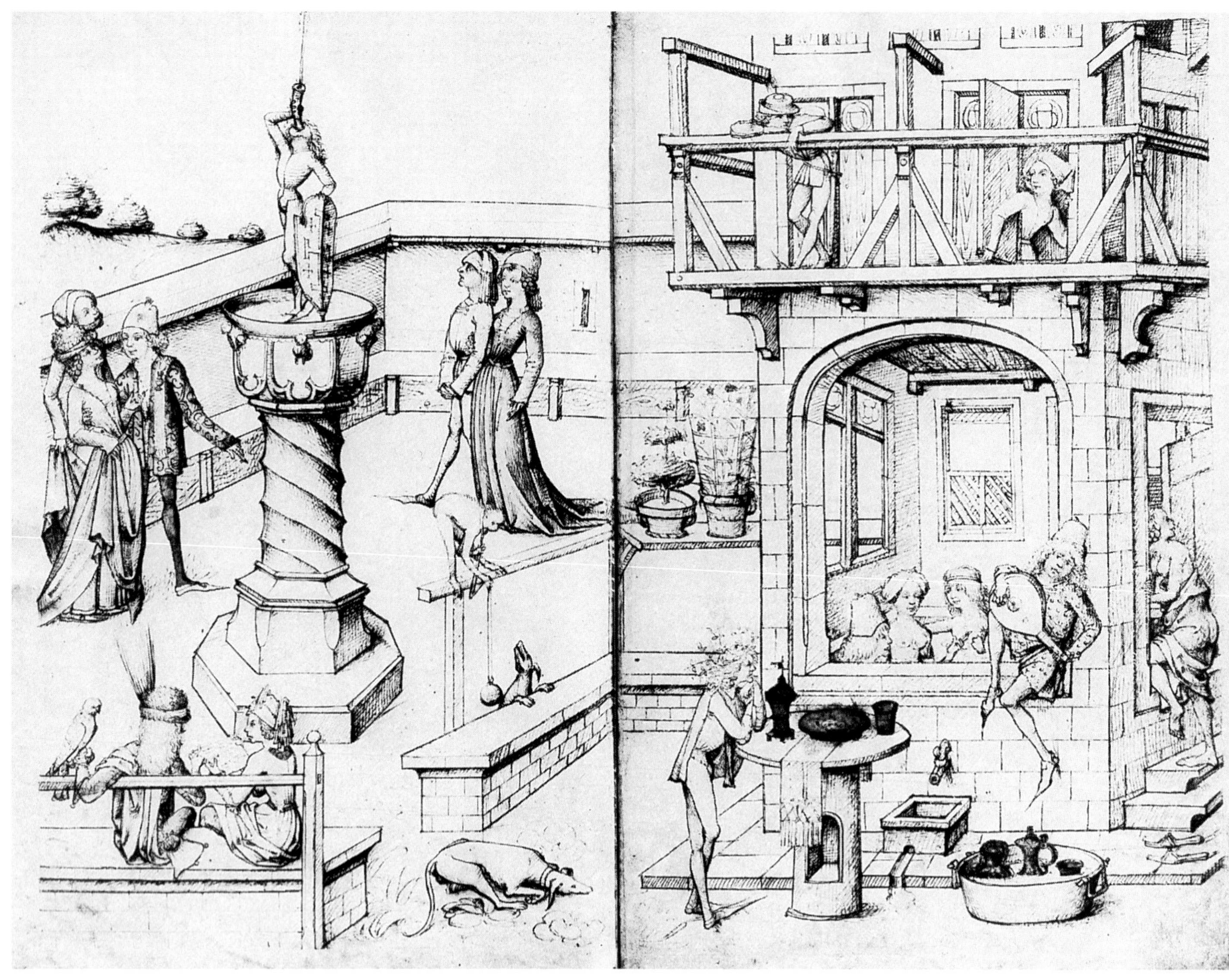

Figure 10.16 HOUSEBOOK MASTER. *Leisure Time at the Bath.* Ca. 1475–1490. Ink on vellum drawing, partially colored. Private collection. *This print reveals the upper classes at play as well as the strict social order. On the left, young couples converse or flirt around a fountain in a courtyard; the pets (a falcon, two dogs, and a monkey) are indicators of the high status of their owners; a lady-in-waiting holds the skirt of her mistress. On the right, young aristocrats (a man and two women) enjoy bathing, while a third woman is entering the bathhouse. A servant serenades the bathers on a stringed instrument, as another waits in attendance. On the balcony, two servants enjoy a flirtatious moment. This Chaucerian-like scene, with its frank sensuality, indicates that within the increasingly secular world of the Late Middle Ages the pleasures of the flesh could be a fit subject for an artist.*

Dante praised him and the citizens of Florence honored him. Later, Vasari, the famous sixteenth-century painter and biographer, declared that Giotto had "rescued and restored" painting.

Giotto's revolution in painting was directed against the prevailing **Italo-Byzantine style,** which blended Late Gothic with Byzantine influences. He turned this painting style, with its two-dimensional, lifeless quality, into a three-dimensional art characterized by naturalism and the full expression of human emotions. Partly through the innovative use of light and shade and the placement of figures so as to create nonmathematical **perspective,** or depth, Giotto was able to paint realistic-looking figures, rather than the flat, ornamental depictions found in most illuminated manuscripts or the Italian altar paintings.

A painting by one of Giotto's contemporaries, Cimabue [chee-muh-BU-a] (about 1240–1302), the *Madonna Enthroned,* reveals the state of Italian painting at this time (Figure 10.17). The angels on the side are

Figure 10.17 CIMABUE. *Madonna Enthroned.* Ca. 1280. Tempera on panel, 12′7½″ × 7′4″. Uffizi Gallery, Florence. Although *Cimabue was experiencing the same desire for freedom in art as the sculptor Giovanni Pisano, this painting of the Madonna shows that he still was strongly under the spell of the Italo-Byzantine tradition. Rather than showing the intense feeling of Giotto's portraits, Cimabue's Virgin and child remain medieval and mystical.*

◀ **Figure 10.18** GIOTTO. *Madonna Enthroned.* Ca. 1310. Tempera on panel, 10′8″ × 6′8″. Uffizi Gallery, Florence. *Giotto's* Madonna Enthroned, *so revolutionary in its composition and spatial dimensions, has been called the most influential painting of the fourteenth century. Especially innovative in this altarpiece is the realistic treatment of the Virgin's eyes. They are shaped like ordinary eyes and peer out at the viewer rather than gazing into the distance, as in the Italo-Byzantine style.*

rendered stiffly, aligned vertically without any sense of space between them, and placed flat on the wood panel without any precise relationship with the four prophets below them. Although Cimabue's angels were balanced in their placement and the depiction of the figures of the Madonna and Christ child offered some sense of rounded form, the overall effect of the work confirms its debt to the two-dimensional tradition of Italo-Byzantine art.

In contrast, Giotto's *Madonna Enthroned,* painted about twenty years after Cimabue's, shows how Giotto was transforming Florentine art (Figure 10.18). His Madonna seems to be actually sitting on her throne, and the four angels on either side of her chair are placed to give a sense of spatial depth, or perspective. The angels' distinctive gazes are highly expressive, suggesting feelings of wonder and respect. The Virgin resembles an individual woman and Christ a believable child, not a shrunken adult. Although Giotto uses Gothic touches—the pointed arch, the haloes, and the applied gold leaf—the natural rendering of the figures foreshadows great changes in art.

Giotto was a prolific artist whose paintings adorned churches in Florence and cities all over Italy. At the Arena Chapel in Padua, Giotto painted his masterpiece, two sets of frescoes, one of the life of the Virgin and the other of the life of Christ. These thirty-eight scenes show Giotto at the height of his powers, rendering space with a sense of depth and organizing figures so as to create dramatic tension. An outstanding scene from the Padua frescoes is the *Pietà,* or *Lamentation* (Figure 10.19). This scene, which portrays the grief for the dead Christ, expresses total despair through the mourners' faces and gestures, from Mary, who cradles the body of Jesus, to John, who stands with arms outstretched, to the hovering angels. In the fresco's stark and rugged landscape, even nature seems to mourn, notably in the barren tree that symbolizes the wood of the cross on which Jesus was crucified. After Giotto died in 1337, no painter for the rest of the century was able to match his remarkable treatment of nature and human emotions.

FLEMISH PAINTING: JAN VAN EYCK AND HANS MEMLING When Philip the Good (r. 1419–1467) became duke of Burgundy, he expanded his territories to include the wealthy counties of Holland, Zeeland, and Luxembourg. Philip was the greatest secular patron of the arts of his day. Of the artists encouraged by his patronage, the brothers Jan and Hubert van Eyck are the most famous, and their religious works and portraits established the Flemish style of art. Little is known of Hubert, but Jan van Eyck [YAHN van IKE] (about 1370–1441) is considered the founder of the Flemish school.

As a general principle, Flemish art sought reality through an accumulation of precise and often symbolic details, in contrast to Italian art, which tended to be more concerned with psychological truth, as in Giotto's frescoes in the Arena Chapel. This national style, expressed primarily through painting with oils on wood panels, turned each artwork into a brilliant and precise reproduction of the original scene. The finest detail in a patterned carpet, the reflected light on a copper vase, or the wrinkled features of an elderly patron were laboriously and meticulously recorded. The Flemish style, with its close attention to detail, was widely appreciated and quickly spread to Italy and England.

Jan van Eyck, probably with his brother's help, painted an altarpiece for the cathedral at Ghent, Belgium (Figure 10.20). This large work—originally commissioned to beautify the high altar—still remains in its original place. The twenty panels are hinged together so that when opened twelve are visible. These twelve panels are divided into two levels—heavenly figures and symbols on the upper level and earthly figures on the lower level. On the ends of the upper level are nude portraits of Adam and Eve, next to angels singing and playing musical instruments. Mary on the left and John the Baptist on the right flank a portrayal of God the Father, resplendent in a jewel-encrusted robe and triple crown (Figure 10.21). Below, on the lower level, are human figures who are depicted as moving toward the center panel. On the left, knights and judges ride on horseback, while, on the right, pilgrims and hermits approach on foot.

The focus of the *Ghent Altarpiece,* when opened, is the lower center panel, the *Adoration of the Lamb.* In this work, the sacrificial death of Jesus is symbolized by the cross, the baptismal font in the foreground, and the blood issuing from the lamb into the communion chalice. The surrounding worshipers include holy virgins, martyrs, and prophets, plus the four evangelists and the Twelve Apostles, who stand and kneel in groups amid plants and trees (Figure 10.22).

In contrast to this mystical work, Jan van Eyck painted a decidedly secular but still symbolic work in his *Arnolfini Wedding Portrait* (Figure 10.23). In this

◄ **Figure 10.19** GIOTTO. *Lamentation*. Ca. 1305–1310. Fresco, 7′7″ × 7′9″. Arena Chapel, Padua, Italy. *Such works gained Giotto his reputation as the modern reviver of realistic art—a tradition that had been lost with the fall of ancient Rome. In this fresco, he created three-dimensional space in ways that even the Greeks and the Romans had not used. Giotto's illusion of depth was conveyed by surrounding the dead Christ with numerous figures and, in particular, by placing two mourners in the foreground with their backs to the viewer. Giotto's use of perspective was convincing to his generation even though it lacked mathematical precision.*

Figure 10.20 HUBERT AND JAN VAN EYCK. *Ghent Altarpiece*. Ca. 1432. Oil on panel, 11′3″ × 14′5″. St. Bavo cathedral, Ghent, Belgium. *This large altarpiece may seem to be a collection of separate paintings, but the work is united in themes and symbolism. What links the panels is their portrayal of Christ's redemption of humanity. From "The Sin of Adam and Eve" to the mystic "Adoration of the Lamb," all the paintings touch in some manner on Christ's sacrifice.*

Figure 10.21 *Mary, God the Father, and John the Baptist.* From the *Ghent Altarpiece.* Ca. 1432. St. Bavo cathedral, Ghent, Belgium. *Van Eyck portrays his saintly subjects as if they were conducting an earthly royal court. All three wear rich robes of varying colors with jewel-encrusted borders and sit in thrones whose golden backs bear biblical verses. Mary wears a twelve-point, gem-studded crown, a sign that she is Queen of Heaven. God the Father in the image of Jesus wears the bejeweled papal crown while an earthly crown rests at his feet—symbols that he wields both spiritual and secular power. The theme of royalty reflects the theological point that, with the redemption of humankind (the general theme of the* Ghent Altarpiece*), a new order will begin in the world, the New Jerusalem.*

Figure 10.23 Jan van Eyck. *Arnolfini Wedding Portrait.* 1434. Oil on wood, 33 × 22½". Reproduced by courtesy of the Trustees, National Gallery, London. *This work is a perfect expression of the symbolic realism that dominated northern European painting in the Late Middle Ages. The wedding is celebrated in a room filled with religious symbols of the marriage rite. For example, the bride and groom stand shoeless, indicating that they are in holy space, and above them is a chandelier with a single lighted candle, a sign of God's presence.* ▶

Figure 10.22 Hubert and Jan van Eyck. *Adoration of the Lamb.* Detail of the *Ghent Altarpiece.* Ca. 1432. St. Bavo cathedral, Ghent, Belgium. *This lower center section of the opened altarpiece dramatically shows how the Flemish school could use religious symbolism to evoke a mystical effect. The refined details, which derived from the tradition of manuscript painting, make this scene both credible and otherworldly.*

painting, nearly every object—the lighted candle, the shoes, the fruit, the dog—refers to a wedding custom or belief. Yet, the details—for example, the mirror on the rear wall reflecting the couple's backs, the artist, and a fourth person—create a worldly setting. Van Eyck's painting is not an imaginary scene but a recording of an actual event, for Arnolfini was an Italian businessman who lived in Bruges. Thus, the commerce and wealth of Burgundy and the Italian cities are symbolically united by van Eyck in this wedding portrait.

A second outstanding artist working in Flanders during the Late Middle Ages was Hans Memling (about 1430–1494), the most popular painter of his day in Bruges. Long a northern commercial center, Bruges was now entering a period of decline, hastened by the displacement of the Burgundian ruling house by that of the Hapsburgs. Before settling in Bruges, the German-born Memling studied painting in Cologne and the Netherlands, where he fully absorbed the northern tradition. Memling's painting style, which borrowed heavily from that of Jan van Eyck and his generation, was characterized by serenity and graceful elegance, traits that stand in marked contrast to this turbulent era. After starting his workshop in Bruges, Memling grew wealthy from commissions, mainly for altarpieces and portraits, paid for by church leaders, local businesspeople, and resident foreign merchants. More than eighty of his works have survived.

Memling was particularly celebrated for the piety of his Madonna paintings, such as the *Madonna and Child with Angels* (Figure 10.24). Following the Flemish tradition, this painting is filled with religious symbolism, which reinforces the message that Christ died to atone for the sins of humankind. The baby Christ reaches for an apple held by an angel, the fruit symbolizing original sin. The second angel, dressed in a vestment associated with the High Mass, plays a harp, possibly a reference to heavenly music. A carved vine of grapes, depicted on the arch, is an emblem of Holy Communion. On the left column stands David, an ancestor of Christ, and on the right column stands Isaiah, a prophet who foretold the birth of the Messiah.

The format and the details of Memling's enthroned Madonna harken back to Jan van Eyck, but without the intensity or sense of reality. Memling's style is static and somewhat artificial. The painting space is clearly arranged, but the landscape and architectural background function as a stage set; the figures are so composed that they constitute a veritable *tableau vivant*, a staged scene in which costumed actors remain silent as if in a picture. Each of the three figures is treated in similar fashion—thin bodies; oval faces; blank, emotionless stares. Adding to the air of artificiality is the absence of shadows, for the painting is bathed in unmodulated light.

Figure 10.24 HANS MEMLING. *Madonna and Child with Angels.* After 1479. Oil on panel, 23⅛ × 18⅞". Andrew W. Mellon Collection. National Gallery of Art, Washington, D.C. (1937.1.41) Photograph © Board of Trustees. *Memling, though part of the Flemish tradition, appeared to be aware of developments in Renaissance Italy. He introduced some Italian elements into this painting, such as the putti, or small angels (used as decorations on the columns and arch), and the stringed musical instruments held by the angels.* ▶

The Legacy of the Late Middle Ages

All historical eras are periods of transition, but the changes of the Late Middle Ages were especially momentous. The medieval world was dying, and the modern era was struggling to be born. Dating from this turbulent period were many of the cultural tensions that defined the history of Europe for the next four hundred years.

The most revolutionary happening in the Late Middle Ages was the release of a powerful secular spirit that began to make its presence felt everywhere. The upsurge of vernacular literature, the rise of literary themes questioning the low status of women, and the divergence of philosophy and theology are three examples of this new development. But the greatest impact of the rise of secularism on cultural life was that painting and sculpture began to be liberated from the service of architecture. The first stirrings of this change were expressed in the works of Giotto and other Italian and Flemish artists. By the next century, painting in Italy had freed itself from the tutelage of architecture and become the most important artistic genre in the West.

This period also saw the emergence of a new breed of secular ruler who was prepared to mount a sustained drive against the church's combined political and spiritual powers. The victories of the English and the French kings over the papacy—each ruler was able to secure control over his national church—were signs of the breakup of Christendom.

Another important legacy of these years is that the towns, led by their bourgeois citizens, began to exercise their influence over the countryside. From today's perspective, the growth of the middle class as a dominant force in society was perhaps the most critical development of this age. Finally, this period witnessed the unusual spectacle of the common people revolting against the aristocratic control of the culture and society. Their sporadic efforts failed, but the seeds of future revolution were planted.

KEY CULTURAL TERMS

devotio moderna
via antiqua
via moderna
Late Gothic style
Flamboyant style
Perpendicular style
fan vault
campanile
woodcut
engraving
drypoint
Italo-Byzantine style
perspective

SUGGESTIONS FOR FURTHER READING

PRIMARY SOURCES

BOCCACCIO, G. *The Decameron.* Translated by M. Musa and P. E. Bondanella. New York: Norton, 1977. An updated translation of the hundred stories—some learned, some coarse, but all humorous—that make up this work; first published about 1351.

CHAUCER, G. *The Canterbury Tales.* Edited by N. Coghill. New York: Penguin, 1978. Of many versions of these bawdy and lighthearted tales, Coghill's is one of the most readable and enjoyable; the original work dates from 1385.

CHRISTINE DE PIZAN. *The Book of the City of Ladies.* Translated by E. J. Richards. New York: Persea Books, 1982. An accessible, modern translation of this Late Medieval work, which argues that the political and cultural dignity of women depends on their being educated properly, just as men are; first published in 1405.

LANGLAND, W. *The Vision of Piers Plowman.* Translated by H. W. Wells. New York: Sheed and Ward, 1959. A good modern version of Langland's work criticizing the religious establishment of his day and calling for a new order; written between 1362 and 1394.

WINDOWS ON THE WORLD: 1300–1500

HISTORY

AFRICA

East Africa *Coastal trading states.* Arab-Swahili society; trade with inland peoples and Ming China. *Zimbabwe.* Bantu state; based on gold; height of Great Zimbabwean civilization. *Zambezi Valley.* Rival states fought to control trade.

North Africa *Egypt.* Mameluke Dynasty, ended 1517. *Morocco.* Merinid Dynasty lost Atlantic port to Portuguese.

West Africa *Songhai Empire.* Successor to Ghana and Mali; controlled salt and gold through Timbuktu, Jenne-jero, and Gao. *Kongo Kingdom.* Bantu trading state; under Portuguese influence (1482). *Yoruba culture.* Ife, a religious center; Benin and Oyo, trading states; Benin dominant (after 1440) and free of European control.

South Africa Portuguese made contact with Bushmen, Hottentots, and Bantu-speaking peoples.

AMERICAS

Andes *Sicán culture.* Ended 1400. *Inca culture.* Conquered Chimú and Ica (ca. 1460). Empire ranged from Peru to Chile.

Mesoamerica *Late Postclassic period, ended 1519. Mayan culture.* Faded away after peasant revolt in Mayapán (about 1460). *Aztec culture.* Began 1426. Capital Tenochtitlán (Mexico City); ruled much of modern Mexico, Guatemala, and El Salvador. Warrior culture devoted to conquest and ritual sacrifice of captured enemies.

Native North America *Southwest.* Descendants of Anasazi (including Hopi, Zuni, Acoma tribes) migrated to river areas (1300–1700). *Eastern woodlands.* Five Lake Ontario tribes formed Iroquois League (ca. 1390).

Caribbean Arawaks greeted Columbus when he landed on Hispaniola (1492); decimated by epidemics in wake of contact with Europeans (1508–11).

ART & MUSIC

AFRICA

West Africa *Yoruba culture.* Ife bronzes: naturalistic life-size heads of kings and queens. Benin bronzes: life-size and miniature statues of people and animals; portrait heads; influenced by Nok and Ife art. *Oriki,* or praise song, flourished, encompassing daily chores and life's passages.

Bronze Head. Benin. Fifteenth century. British Museum.

AMERICAS

Andes *Chancay culture.* Textiles (ponchos and clothing) and ceramics (figurines and whistling pots). *Inca culture.* Tapestries and ceramics. *Colombia.* Jewelry and pectorals, made from alloys of copper, silver, and gold.

Mesoamerica *Late Postclassic period. Mayan culture.* At Mayapán: stone stelae depicting gods; at Tulum: polychrome, ceramic figures, especially images of the deity Chac. *Aztec culture.* Clay figurines of deities. Monumental stone sculptures.

Native North America *Koniag culture, Alaska.* Wooden masks representing real people. *Mississippian culture. Calusa culture, Florida.* Wooden feline figurines. *Southwest. Pueblo.* Elaborate kachina masks representing supernatural beings in ritual ceremonies.

ARCHITECTURE

AFRICA

East Africa *Coastal trading states.* Mosques and palaces. *Zimbabwe.* Mortarless stone buildings, built for Bantu kings, priests, and ruling class. Round mud huts with pole-and-thatch roofs for ordinary Bantu.

AMERICAS

Andes *Inca culture.* The mountaintop fortress city of Machu Picchu, built of massive interlocked stones fitted together without mortar.

Mesoamerica *Late Postclassic period. Mayan culture.* Walled city of Mayapán. *Aztec culture.* Tenochtitlán, modeled on Teotihuacán, laid out on a grid dominated by two pyramids; Tlatelolco, largest trading center in the Americas.

North America *Iroquois culture, northeastern U.S.* Communal longhouses, made of poles covered with sheets of bark.

General View. Machu Picchu, Peru. Fifteenth century.

RELIGION, PHILOSOPHY, LITERATURE

AFRICA

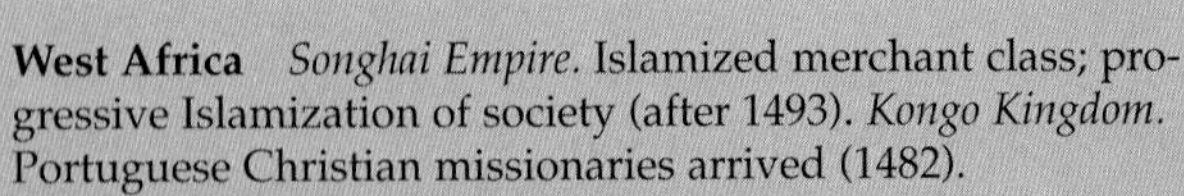

West Africa *Songhai Empire.* Islamized merchant class; progressive Islamization of society (after 1493). *Kongo Kingdom.* Portuguese Christian missionaries arrived (1482).

AMERICAS

Andes *Inca culture.* Daily and periodic offerings (a llama, a fine textile, a child) to the gods. Royal mummies ritually fed, dressed, consulted, and carried in processions.

Mesoamerica *Late Postclassic period. Aztec culture.* Tenochtitlán's twin pyramids dedicated to the chief gods. At Tepeyacac: worship of mother goddess Tonantzín; site later identified with Virgin of Guadalupe.

Aztec Calendar Stone. Fifteenth century. Basalt, diam. 360″. Tenochtitlán. National Museum of Anthropology, Mexico City.

ASIA

China	India	Japan
Ming Dynasty. At first, expanded influence, forcing tribute from Mongolia, Japan, and Korea and sending maritime expeditions to Southeast Asia and East Africa. Later, turned inward to support farming, commerce, and social change. Zenith: Yung-lo (r. 1402–24).	*Medieval period.* Hindu and Muslim states at war: Vijayanagar Empire (1336–1565), the most successful Hindu state; Bahmani Kingdom (about 1347–1518), the strongest Islamic state. *Delhi Sultanate, ended 1526.* Political instability: three dynasties between 1413 and 1451, when the Lodis brought stability and territorial expansion.	*Muromachi period, began 1333.* Weak shōguns; continual warfare among the *daimyō* (feudal lords) and their samurai retainers.
Ming Dynasty. Height of blue and white porcelain; silk brocades. Two schools of landscape painting: the court artists, or Zhe School, centered in province of Zhejiang; the Wu School, based in Suzhou, the cultural capital. A Wu School legacy: poem painting (including a complementary poem in a painting).	*Medieval period.* In Vijayanagar Empire: carved stone figures of deities on Hindu temples.	*Muromachi period.* Chinese (Yüan, Ming, and Zen Buddhist) influences; silk paintings, fine arts, decorations, and ink paintings (landscape, poem, and portrait). Chinese art collected by shōguns and the ruling class.
Ming Dynasty. Splendid imperial tombs with many above-ground rooms. Emperor Yung-lo made Beijing the capital (1403); built the Forbidden City, a 250-acre compound containing the administrative center of the country and palaces, temples, and tombs for the royal family; style characterized by wooden beams and pillars and wide tile roofs.	*Vijayanagar Empire.* Lotus Mahal, a two-story pavilion. *Delhi Sultanate.* Persian-style buildings (low domes and thick walls).	*Muromachi period.* Chinese-style pavilions built by shōguns, often as retreats; teahouses; and rock and dry landscape gardens.
Yüan Dynasty. First color printing in the world. *Ming Dynasty.* Definitive Confucian texts, arranged by Emperor Yung-lo. Encyclopedia (about 11,000 volumes) began to be issued (1403).	*Delhi Sultanate.* Lodi rulers cultivated a transplanted Persian culture. One of India's greatest Persian writers, the poet and historian Amir Khosrow (see Figure 8.19).	*Muromachi period.* Nō drama created: Nobumitsu's classic play *Ataka* and 240 plays by Motokiyo Zeami. *Tsurezuregusa* (casual jottings), the period's chief prose genre.

The Forbidden City, Beijing. General view of one of the inner courtyards of the palace. Fifteenth. century.

Golden Pavilion, Kyōto. General view. 1398; rebuilt, 1964.

11 THE EARLY RENAISSANCE
Return to Classical Roots
1400–1494

Believing they had broken radically with the past, Italian artists and intellectuals in the fifteenth century began to speak of a rebirth of civilization. Since the nineteenth century, the term ***Renaissance*** (meaning "rebirth") has described the cultural and artistic activities of the fifteenth and sixteenth centuries that began in Italy and spread northward. The Renaissance profoundly altered the course of Western culture, although scholars have differing interpretations of the significance of this first modern period.

THE RENAISSANCE: SCHOOLS OF INTERPRETATION

In the 1860s, Swiss historian Jacob Burckhardt, agreeing with the fifteenth-century Italians, asserted that the Renaissance was a rebirth of ideas after centuries of cultural stagnation. He maintained that a new way of understanding the world had emerged, as the Italians looked back to ancient Greece and Rome for inspiration and declared themselves part of a revitalized civilization that was distinctive and superior to the immediate past.

By the mid–twentieth century, Burckhardt's interpretation began to be viewed as too simplistic. According to some scholars, the Italians, after the fall of Rome, never lost sight of their Classical roots. These historians considered the revival of learning in the fifteenth century to be more of a shift in educational and cultural emphasis than a rediscovery of antiquity. They also noted that the Renaissance had at least two phases, the Early and the High, each with different contributions.

◀ **Detail** FRA ANGELICO. *Annunciation.* 1438–1445. Fresco, 7′6″ × 10′5″. Monastery of San Marco, Florence.

Figure 11.1 DOMENICO GHIRLANDAIO. *Old Man with a Child.* Ca. 1480. Panel, 24½ × 18". Louvre. *This double portrait by the Florentine artist Ghirlandaio summarizes many of the new secular values of the Early Renaissance, such as its human centeredness and its preference for simple scenes. Further, the work's subject, possibly a man with his grandchild, indicates the important role that the family played in the life of the times. In addition, the age's commitment to direct observation of the physical world is evident in the treatment of the man's diseased nose (acne rosacea) and the landscape glimpsed through the open window. Finally, the painter has made the exterior scene realistic by using linear and atmospheric perspective—two new techniques invented during the period.*

Since the 1960s, a third interpretation has dominated Renaissance studies. In this view, the Renaissance label should be used cautiously and only to describe what was happening in learning and the arts, not in politics and society. The authors of this book tend to agree with this third interpretation. In politics, economics, and society, Italy in the 1400s differed little from Italy in the 1300s; however, the Italians of the 1400s did start down a new *cultural* path (Figure 11.1).

This chapter examines the first phase of this new cultural style, the Early Renaissance (1400–1494); Chapter 12 is devoted to the brief High Renaissance (1494–1520) and to Early Mannerism (1520–1564), an anti-Classical phase of the Renaissance. Chapter 13 considers Northern Humanism, the Northern Renaissance, the early-sixteenth-century religious reformations, and Late Mannerism (1564–1603), when Renaissance style was slowly undermined by new trends (Timeline 11.1).

EARLY RENAISSANCE HISTORY AND INSTITUTIONS

For most of the fifteenth century, the city-states of northern Italy were prosperous and peaceful enough to sustain upper-class artists and writers. This supportive climate encouraged the innovations of Renaissance culture. By the end of the century, however, disputes among Italy's city-states and a shift in maritime trade from the Mediterranean to the Atlantic, coupled with the French invasion of Florence in 1494, had dimmed northern Italy's cultural preeminence.

Italian City-States During the Early Renaissance

The erratic fortunes of Italy's economy were a major factor in the region's politics in this period. The northern Italian city-states had emerged from the High Middle Ages in 1300 as Europe's leading commercial center and manufacturer of finished woolens (see Chapter 9), but by 1500 they had been eclipsed by various European nations to the north. In the 1300s, Italian population, productivity, and prosperity declined because

Timeline 11.1 STAGES OF THE ITALIAN RENAISSANCE

1400	1494	1520	1600
Early Renaissance	High Renaissance	Late Renaissance	

of the Black Death and the birth of the English woolen industry. Although the Italians made a limited economic recovery in the 1400s, history was moving against them. Even their domination of international banking was challenged by German businessmen.

During the Early Renaissance, five Italian states competed for dominance: the Republic of Venice, the Duchy of Milan, the Republic of Florence, the Papal States, and the Kingdom of Naples. Other small states, such as the artistic and intellectual centers of Ferrara and Modena, played minor but crucial roles (Map 11.1). In the first half of the fifteenth century, the Italian states waged incessant wars among themselves, shifting sides when it was to their advantage.

The continuous warfare and the uncertain economy provided the conditions for the emergence of autocratic rulers called *signori,* who were from ruling families or elitist factions. Taking advantage of economic and class tensions, these autocrats pledged to solve local problems, and in so doing they proceeded to accumulate power in their own hands. What influence the guilds, business leaders, and the middle class had wielded in the fourteenth century gave way to these despots, ending the great medieval legacy of republicanism in Venice, Milan, and Florence.

Under the *signori,* the conduct of warfare also changed. Technological developments changed weaponry, and battles were fought with mercenary troops led by *condottieri,* soldiers of fortune who sold their military expertise to the highest bidder. But the most significant change in Renaissance warfare was the emergence of diplomacy as a peaceful alternative to arms, a practice that gradually spread throughout the continent. The Italian regimes began sending representatives to other states, and it soon became customary for these diplomats to negotiate peace settlements. In turbulent fifteenth-century Italy, these agreements seldom lasted long—with the notable exception of the Peace of Lodi. This defensive pact, signed in 1454 by Milan, Florence, and Venice, established a delicate balance of power and ensured peace in Italy for forty years.

The Peace of Lodi came apart in 1494, when a French army led by Charles VIII entered Italy in the hope of promoting French monarchic ambitions.

Map 11.1 THE STATES OF ITALY DURING THE RENAISSANCE, CA. 1494

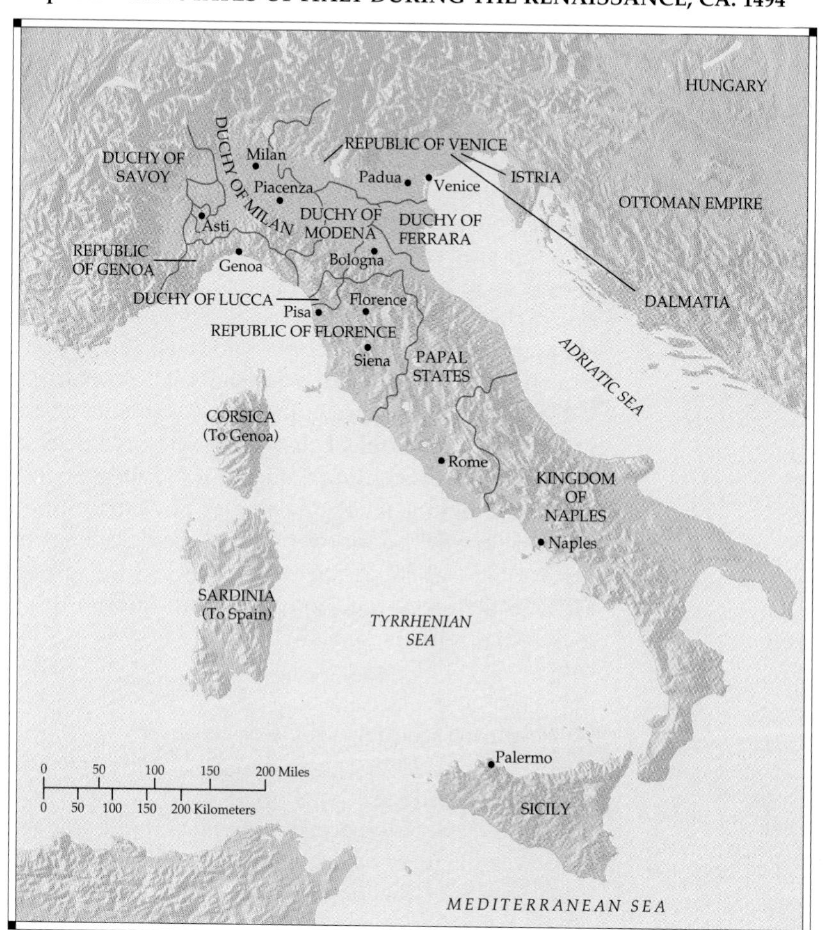

Figure 11.2 PEDRO BERRUGUETE (?). *Federico da Montefeltro and His Son Guidobaldo.* Ca. 1476–1477. Oil on panel, 4′5⅛″ × 2′5⅞″. Galleria Nazionale della Marche, Urbino. *Urbino, under the Montefeltro dynasty, was transformed from a sleepy hill town with no cultural history into a major center of Renaissance life. Federico, the founder of the dynasty and one of the greatest* condottieri *of his day, was created duke of Urbino and captain of the papal forces by Pope Sixtus IV in 1474. Federico then devoted his energies to making Urbino a model for Italian Renaissance courts. In this portrait, the seated Federico wears the armor of a papal officer while reading a book—symbols that established him as both a soldier and a scholar, later the ideal of Castiglione's Courtier. At the duke's right knee stands his son and heir, Guidobaldo, wearing an elaborate robe and holding a scepter, a symbol of power. Federico's dream ended with his son, the last of the Montefeltro line.*

At the Urbino court, artists combined Flemish and Italian styles, as in this double portrait. The internal lighting, emanating from some unseen source on the left, is adopted from the tradition pioneered by Jan van Eyck; the profile portrait of the duke follows the Italian practice, based on portrait heads rendered on medals. This double portrait was probably painted by Pedro Berruguete, Spain's first great Renaissance artist, who studied painting in Naples and worked briefly in Urbino before returning to his homeland.

Outside Italy, three events further weakened the region's prospects for regaining its position as a major economic power: the fall of Constantinople in 1453, Portugal's opening of the sea route around Africa to India at the end of the century, and Columbus's Spanish-sponsored voyage to the New World.

These three events shifted the focus of international trade from the Mediterranean to the Atlantic. The fall of Constantinople to the Ottoman Turks in 1453 temporarily closed the eastern Mediterranean markets to the Italian city-states. At the same time, by virtue of the wide-ranging global explorations they sponsored, some European powers—most notably Portugal and Spain—were extending their political and economic interests beyond the geographical limits of continental Europe.

Before the Italian city-states were eclipsed by other European powers, however, upper-class families enjoyed unprecedented wealth, which they used to cultivate their tastes in literature and art and thus substantially determine the culture of the Early Renaissance (Figure 11.2). One reason for the importance these families gave to cultural matters is that they put high value on family prestige and on educating their sons for their predestined roles as head of the family business and their daughters as loyal wives and successful household managers. The courts of the local rulers, or *grandi,* became places where educated men—and, on occasion, women—could exchange ideas and discuss philosophical issues.

Although the status of women did not improve appreciably, more were educated than ever before. Many ended up behind the walls of a convent, however, if their parents could not afford the costly dowry expected of an upper-class bride (Figure 11.3). The few upper-class women with an independent role in society were those who had been widowed young. The women at the ducal courts who exercised any political influence did so because of their family alliances. One of the most powerful of these women was Lucrezia Borgia [loo-KRET-syah BOR-juh] (1480–1519), the illegitimate daughter of Pope Alexander VI. Married three times before the age of twenty-one, she held court in Ferrara and was the patron of many writers and artists. Most women who tried to exercise real power, however, found it unattainable.

Florence, the Center of the Renaissance

Amid the artistic and intellectual activity occurring throughout Italy, Florence, the capital of the Tuscan region, was the most prominent of the city-states. After 1300 Florence's political system went through three phases, evolving from republic to oligarchy to family

Figure 11.3 GIOVANNI TOSCANI. *The Palli* Cassone *(Chest)*. Ca. 1430. Bargello, Florence. *Richly decorated* cassoni, *or wedding chests, which held a prospective bride's clothing and linens, became a popular piece of furniture among wealthy Italian families. The painted panel on this* cassone *illustrates the annual procession of the Feast of John the Baptist and shows Florentine nobles carrying banners, or "palli," emblazoned with coats of arms and guild emblems, toward the Florentine Baptistery (on the left). The chest embodies the Florentine ethos of family, city, and church.*

rule. During these turbulent political times, however, Florentine artists and writers made their city-state the center of the Early Renaissance (Timeline 11.2).

The republic, which began in the fourteenth century with hopes for political equality, fell into the hands of a wealthy oligarchy. This oligarchy, composed of rich bankers, merchants, and successful guildsmen and craftsmen, ruled until the early fifteenth century, when the Medici family gained control. The Medicis dominated Florentine politics and cultural life from 1434 to 1494, sometimes functioning as despots.

The Medicis rose from modest circumstances. Giovanni di Bicci de' Medici [jo-VAHN-nee dee BEET-chee day MED-uh-chee] (1360–1429) amassed the family's first large fortune through banking and close financial ties with the papacy. His son Cosimo (1389–1464) added to the Medicis' wealth and outmaneuvered his political enemies, becoming the unacknowledged ruler of Florence. He spent his money on books, painting, sculptures, and palaces, and, claiming to be the common man's friend, he was eventually awarded the title *Pater patriae,* Father of His Country—a Roman title revived during the Renaissance.

Cosimo's son, Piero, ruled for only a short time and was succeeded by his son Lorenzo (1449–1492), called the Magnificent because of his grand style of living.

Timeline 11.2 THE EARLY RENAISSANCE IN FLORENCE, 1400–1494

1400 — **1494**

Early Renaissance

- **1403–1424** Ghiberti's north doors, Florentine Baptistery
- **1425** Invention of linear perspective (Brunelleschi)
- **1425–1428** Masaccio's frescoes for Santa Maria Novella
- **1429–1437** Ghiberti's east doors, Florentine Baptistery
- **1430–1432** Donatello's *David*
- **1435** Alberti's *On Painting*
- **1438–1445** Fra Angelico's *Annunciation*
- **1461** Completion of Pazzi Chapel by Brunelleschi
- **1462** Founding of Platonic Academy, Florence
- **1473–1475** Verrocchio's *David*
- **1480s** Botticelli's *Primavera* and *The Birth of Venus*
- **1483** Leonardo da Vinci's *The Virgin of the Rocks*

Lorenzo and his brother Giuliano controlled Florence until Giuliano was assassinated in 1478 by the Pazzi family, rivals of the Medicis. Lorenzo brutally executed the conspirators and then governed autocratically for the next fourteen years.

Within two years of Lorenzo's death, the great power and prestige of Florence began to weaken. Two events are symptomatic of this decline in Florentine authority. The first was the invasion by Charles VIII's French army in 1494. The invasion initiated a political and cultural decline that would eventually overtake Italy, whose small city-states could not withstand the incursions of the European monarchies. The French army drove the Medici family from Florence; they remained in exile until 1512.

The second event was the iconoclastic crusade against the city led by the Dominican monk Fra Savonarola [sav-uh-nuh-ROH-luh] (1452–1498). He opposed the Medicis' rule and wanted to restore a republican form of government. In his fire-and-brimstone sermons, he denounced Florence's leaders and the city's infatuation with the arts. He eventually ran afoul of the papacy and was excommunicated and publicly executed, but not before he had had an enormous effect on the citizens—including the painter Botticelli, who is said to have burned some of his paintings while under the sway of Savonarola's reforming zeal.

The Resurgent Papacy, 1450–1500

The Great Schism was ended by the Council of Constance in 1418, and a tattered Christendom reunited under a Roman pope (see Chapter 10). By 1447 the so-called Renaissance popes were back in command and had turned their attention to consolidating the Papal States and pursuing power. Like the secular despots, these popes engaged in war and, when that failed, diplomacy. They brought artistic riches to the church but also lowered its moral tone by accepting bribes for church offices and filling positions with kinsmen. But above all, these popes patronized Renaissance culture.

Three of the most aggressive and successful of these church rulers were Nicholas V (pope 1447–1455), Pius II (pope 1458–1464), and Sixtus IV (pope 1471–1484). Nicholas V, who had been librarian for Cosimo de' Medici, founded the Vatican Library, an institution virtually unrivaled for its holdings of manuscripts and books. He also continued the rebuilding of Rome begun by his predecessors. Pius II, often considered the most representative of the Renaissance popes because of his interest in the Greek and Roman classics and in writing poetry himself, rose rapidly through the ecclesiastical ranks. This clever politician practiced both war and diplomacy with astounding success. As a student of the new learning and as a brilliant writer in Latin, Pius II attracted intellectuals and artists to Rome. His personal recollections, or *Commentaries*, reveal much about him and his turbulent times.

Sixtus IV came from the powerful and scheming della Rovere family, and he increased his personal power through nepotism, the practice of giving offices to relatives. He continued the papal tradition of making Rome the most beautiful city in the world. The construction of the Sistine Chapel, later adorned with paintings by Botticelli and Michelangelo, was his greatest achievement (see Chapter 12).

THE SPIRIT AND STYLE OF THE EARLY RENAISSANCE

Drawing inspiration from ancient Greek and Roman models, the thinkers and the artists of the Early Renaissance explored such perennial questions as, What is human nature? How are human beings related to God? and What is the best way to achieve human happiness? Although they did not reject Christian explanations outright, they were intrigued by the secular and humanistic values of the Greco-Roman tradition and the answers they might provide to these questions. They also rightfully claimed kinship with certain fourteenth-century predecessors such as the writer Petrarch and the artist Giotto (see Chapter 10).

Those artists, scholars, and writers who are identified with the Early Renaissance and who embodied its spirit were linked, through shared tastes and patronage, with the entrepreneurial nobility, the progressive middle class, and the secular clergy. Until about 1450, most artistic works were commissioned by wealthy patrons for family chapels in churches and for public buildings; later, patrons commissioned paintings and sculptures for their private dwellings.

Even though artists, scholars, and writers stamped this age with their fresh perspectives, some of the old cultural traits remained. Unsettling secular values emerged in the midst of long-accepted religious beliefs, creating contradictions and tensions within the society. In other ways, however, the past held firm, and certain values seemed immune to change. For example, Early Renaissance thought made little headway in science, and church patronage still strongly affected the evolution of the arts and architecture, despite the growing impact of the urban class on artistic tastes.

The artists, scholars, and writers who flourished in the Early Renaissance were almost exclusively men, in contrast with the Middle Ages, when women occasionally played cultural roles. Recent scholarship has pointed out that women living in the Italian Renaissance were subjected to new constraints, especially in well-to-do families. For example, the learned Laura Cereta [che-RAY-tah], daughter of a physician in Brescia, was silenced at eighteen years of age for her outspokenness, though not before she had published a defense of herself, asserting the right of women to be educated the same as men.

Humanism, Scholarship, and Schooling

Toward the end of the 1300s, Italy's educated circles became fascinated by ancient Roman civilization. Inspired by Petrarch's interest in Latin literature and language, scholars began to collect and translate Roman manuscripts uncovered in monastic libraries and other out-of-the-way depositories. There was a shift in emphasis from the church Latin of the Middle Ages to the pure Latin style of Cicero, the first-century B.C. Roman writer whose eloquent essays established a high moral and literary standard.

In the 1400s, these scholars spoke of their literary interests and new learning as ***studia humanitatis.*** They defined this term, which may be translated as humanistic studies, as a set of intellectual pursuits that included moral philosophy, history, grammar, rhetoric, and poetry. At first, the men who studied these disciplines read the appropriate works in Latin, but after the Greek originals began to appear about 1400 and the study of ancient languages spread, they learned from the Greek texts as well.

In response to the demand for humanistic learning, new schools sprang up in most Italian city-states. In these schools was born the Renaissance ideal of an education intended to free or to liberate the mind—a liberal education. To that end, study was based on the recently recovered Latin and Greek works rather than on the more narrowly defined curriculum of scholasticism and Aristotelianism that had been favored in the Middle Ages.

The first Renaissance scholars, who were primarily searching for original Latin manuscripts, were philologists—that is, experts in the study of languages and linguistics. In time, they came to call themselves humanists because of their training in the *studia humanitatis.* These early humanists created a branch of learning, now called textual criticism, that compares various versions of a text to determine which one is most correct or authentic. They recognized that knowledge of the evolution of language was necessary to make a critical judgment on the authenticity of a text. As a result of their studies, they revealed writing errors committed by medieval monks when they copied ancient manuscripts—revelations that, in the case of religious documents, raised grave problems for the church.

The most spectacular application of textual criticism was made by Lorenzo Valla (1406–1457), who exposed the Donation of Constantine as a forgery. Throughout the Middle Ages, this famous document had been cited by the popes as proof of their political authority over Christendom. By the terms of the document, the Roman emperor Constantine gave the popes his western lands and recognized their power to rule in them. But by comparing the Latin of the fourth century, when Constantine reigned, with the Latin of the eighth century, when the document first came to light, Valla concluded that the Donation must have been produced then and not in the fourth century.

Other humanists played an active role in the life of their states, modeling themselves on the heroes of the Roman republic. Outstanding among them is Leonardo Bruni (1374–1444), who typifies the practical, civic humanist. A one-time chancellor, or chief secretary, of Florence's governing body, or *signoria,* Bruni also worked for both the Medicis and the papacy and wrote the *History of the Florentine People.* This work reflected his humanistic values, combining as it did his political experience with his knowledge of ancient history. To Bruni, the study of history illuminated contemporary events. Bruni and the other civic humanists, through their writings and their governmental service, set an example for later generations of Florentines and helped infuse them with love of their city. Moreover, by expanding the concept of humanistic studies, they contributed new insights into the ongoing debate about the role of the individual in history and in the social order.

An important consequence of humanistic studies was the rise of educational reforms. Vittorino da Feltre [veet-toe-REE-no dah FEL-tray] (1378–1446) made the most significant contributions. Vittorino favored a curriculum that exercised the body and the mind—the ideal of the ancient Greek schools. His educational theories were put into practice at the school he founded in Mantua at the ruler's request. At this school, called the Happy House, Vittorino included humanistic studies along with the medieval curriculum. A major innovation was the stress on physical exercise, which arose from his emphasis on moral training. At first, only the sons and daughters of Mantuan nobility attended his school, but gradually the student body became more democratic as young people from all classes were enrolled. Vittorino's reforms were slowly introduced into the new urban schools in northern Europe, and their model—the well-rounded student of sound body, solid learning, and high morals—helped to lay the foundation for future European schools and education.

PERSONAL PERSPECTIVE

Laura Cereta
Defense of the Liberal Instruction of Women

In this letter, dated January 13, 1488, the young Laura Cereta responds fiercely to a critic who admired her writing by wondering how it could possibly be the work of a woman.

My ears are wearied by your carping. You brashly and publicly not merely wonder but indeed lament that I am said to possess as fine a mind as nature ever bestowed upon the most learned man. You seem to think that so learned a woman has scarcely before been seen in the world. You are wrong on both counts. . . .

I would have been silent, believe me, if that savage old enmity of yours had attacked me alone. . . . But I cannot tolerate your having attacked my entire sex. For this reason my thirsty soul seeks revenge, my sleeping pen is aroused to literary struggle, raging anger stirs mental passions long chained by silence. With just cause I am moved to demonstrate how great a reputation for learning and virtue women have won by their inborn excellence, manifested in every age as knowledge. . . .

Only the question of the rarity of outstanding women remains to be addressed. The explanation is clear: women have been able by nature to be exceptional, but have chosen lesser goals. For some women are concerned with parting their hair correctly, adorning themselves with lovely dresses, or decorating their fingers with pearls and other gems. Others delight in mouthing carefully composed phrases, indulging in dancing, or managing spoiled puppies. Still others wish to gaze at lavish banquet tables, to rest in sleep, or, standing at mirrors, to smear their lovely faces. But those in whom a deeper integrity yearns for virtue, restrain from the start their youthful souls, reflect on higher things, harden the body with sobriety and trials, and curb their tongues, open their ears, compose their thoughts in wakeful hours, their minds in contemplation, to letters bonded to righteousness. For knowledge is not given as a gift, but [is gained] with diligence. The free mind, not shirking effort, always soars zealously toward the good, and the desire to know grows ever more wide and deep. It is because of no special holiness, therefore, that we [women] are rewarded by God the Giver with the gift of exceptional talent. Nature has generously lavished its gifts upon all people, opening to all the doors of choice through which reason sends envoys to the will, from which they learn and convey its desires. The will must choose to exercise the gift of reason. . . .

I have been praised too much; showing your contempt for women, you pretend that I alone am admirable because of the good fortune of my intellect. . . . Do you suppose, O most contemptible man on earth, that I think myself sprung [like Athena] from the head of Jove? I am a school girl, possessed of the sleeping embers of an ordinary mind. Indeed I am too hurt, and my mind, offended, too swayed by passions, sighs, tormenting itself, conscious of the obligation to defend my sex. For absolutely everything—that which is within us and that which is without—is made weak by association with my sex.

Thought and Philosophy

The Italian humanists were not satisfied with medieval answers to the perennial inquiries of philosophy because those answers did not go beyond Aristotelian philosophy and Christian dogma. Casting their nets wider, the Renaissance thinkers concluded that the ancients had given worthwhile responses to many of the same issues as Christians and that they should not be dismissed simply because they were non-Christian.

Renaissance scholars came to advocate more tolerance toward unorthodox beliefs and began to focus on the important role played by the individual in society. Individual fulfillment became a leading Renaissance idea and remains a central notion in Western thought today. During the Renaissance, the growing emphasis on the individual resulted in a more optimistic assessment of human nature—a development that in time led to a rejection of Christianity's stress on original sin.

After the fall of Constantinople in 1453 and the flight of Byzantine scholars bearing precious manuscripts, the humanists began to focus increasingly on Greek literature, language, and, in particular, philosophy. The philosophy of Plato found a home in Italy in 1462 when Cosimo de' Medici established the Platonic Academy at one of his villas near Florence. Here, scholars gathered to examine and to discuss the writings of Plato as well as the Neo-Platonists, whose reinterpreted Platonism had influenced early Christian theology. The academy was under the direction of the brilliant humanist Marsilio Ficino [mar-SILL-e-o fe-CHEE-no] (1433–1499), whom Cosimo commissioned to translate Plato's works into Latin.

In two major treatises, Ficino made himself the leading voice of Florentine Neo-Platonism by harmonizing Platonic ideas with Christian teachings. Believing that

Figure 11.4 SANDRO BOTTICELLI. *The Birth of Venus.* 1480s. Tempera on canvas, 5′8″ × 9′1″. Uffizi Gallery, Florence. *With the paintings of Botticelli, the nude female form reappeared in Western art for the first time since the Greco-Roman period. Botticelli's* Venus *contains many Classical echoes, such as the goddess's lovely features and her modest pose. But the artist used these pre-Christian images to convey a Christian message and to embody the principles of Ficino's Neo-Platonist philosophy.*

Platonism came from God, Ficino began with the principle that both thought systems rested on divine authority. Like Plato, Ficino believed that the soul was immortal and that complete enjoyment of God would be possible only in the afterlife, when the soul was in the divine realm. Ficino also revived the Platonic notion of free will. In Ficino's hands, free will became the source of human dignity because human beings were able to choose to love God.

Ficino had the most powerful impact on the Early Renaissance when he made Plato's teaching on love central to Neo-Platonism. Following Platonism, he taught that love is a divine gift that binds all human beings together. Love expresses itself in human experience by the desire for and the appreciation of beauty in its myriad forms. Platonic love, like erotic love, is aroused first by the physical appearance of the beloved. But Platonic love, dissatisfied by mere physical enjoyment, cannot rest until it moves upward to the highest spiritual level, where it finally meets its goal of union with the Divine. Under the promptings of Platonism, the human form became a metaphor of the soul's desire for God. Many Renaissance writers and artists came under the influence of Ficino's Neo-Platonism, embracing its principles and embodying them in their works. Sandro Botticelli, for example, created several allegorical paintings in which divine love and beauty were represented by an image from pre-Christian Rome—Venus, goddess of love (Figure 11.4).

Ficino's most prized student, Pico della Mirandola [PEE-koh DAYL-lah me-RAHN-do-lah] (1463–1494), surpassed his master's accomplishments by the breadth of his learning and the virtuosity of his mind. Pico—a wealthy and charming aristocrat—impressed everyone with his command of languages, his range of knowledge, and his spirited arguments. His goal was the synthesis of Platonism and Aristotelianism within a Christian framework that also encompassed Hebraic, Arabic, and Persian ideas. Church authorities and traditional scholars attacked Pico's efforts once they grasped the implication of his ambitious project—that all knowledge shared basic common truths and that Christians could benefit from studying non-Western, non-Christian writings.

Pico's second important contribution—the concept of individual worth—had been foreshadowed by Ficino. Pico's *Oration on the Dignity of Man* gives the highest expression to this idea, which is inherent in the humanist tradition. According to Pico, human beings, endowed with reason and speech, are created as a microcosm of the universe. Set at the midpoint in the scale of God's creatures, they are blessed with free will—the power to make of themselves what they wish—which enables them either to raise themselves to God or to sink lower than the beasts. This liberty to determine private fate makes human beings the masters of their individual destinies and, at the same time, focuses attention on each human being as the measure of all things—a Classical belief now reborn.

Figure 11.5 LEONE BATTISTA ALBERTI. Tempio Malatestiano (Malatesta Temple) (Church of San Francesco). Ca. 1450. Rimini, Italy. *Although unfinished, this church strikingly demonstrates the revolution in architecture represented by Early Renaissance ideals. Nothing could be further from the spires of Late Gothic cathedrals than this simple, symmetrical structure with its plain facade, post-and-lintel entrance, rounded arches, and Classical columns. Designed by the leading theoretician of the new style, the Malatesta Temple served as a model for artists and architects of the later Renaissance.*

Architecture, Sculpture, and Painting

It was in architecture, sculpture, and painting that the Renaissance made its most dramatic break with the medieval past. The **Early Renaissance style** was launched in Florence by artists who wanted to make a complete break with the Late Gothic style (Figure 11.5). Led by the architect Filippo Brunelleschi [bru-nayl-LAYS-kee] (1377–1446), this group studied the ruins of Classical buildings and ancient works of sculpture to unlock the secrets of their harmonious style. They believed that once the Classical ideals were rescued from obscurity, new works could be fashioned that captured the spirit of ancient art and architecture without slavishly copying it.

Artistic Ideals and Innovations Guided by Brunelleschi's findings, architects, sculptors, and painters made the Classical principles of balance, simplicity, and restraint the central ideals of the Early Renaissance style. The heaviest debt to the past was owed by the architects, for they revived the Classical orders—the Doric, the Ionic, and the Corinthian. The new buildings, though constructed to accommodate modern needs, were symmetrical in plan and relied on simple decorative designs. The theoretician of Early Renaissance style and its other guiding light was Leone Battista Alberti [ahl-BAIR-tee] (1404–1472), who wrote at length on Brunelleschi's innovations and published a highly influential book on the new painting. Alberti believed that architecture should embody the humanistic qualities of dignity, balance, control, and harmony and that a building's ultimate beauty rested on the mathematical harmony of its separate parts.

Sculpture and painting, freed from their subordination to architecture, regained their ancient status as independent art forms and in time became the most cherished of the visual arts. Renaissance sculptors and painters aspired to greater realism than had been achieved in the Gothic style, seeking to depict human musculature and anatomy with a greater degree of credibility. Sculptors, led by this period's genius Donatello [dah-nah-TEL-lo] (about 1386–1466), revived Classical practices that had not been seen in the West for more than a thousand years: the free-standing figure; the technique of contrapposto, or a figure balanced with most of the weight resting on one leg (see Figure 3.22); the life-size nude statue; and the equestrian statue.

Whereas architecture and sculpture looked back to ancient Greek and Roman traditions, developments in painting grew from late medieval sources. In the early fourteenth century, Giotto had founded a new realistic and expressive style (see Chapter 10), on which Florentine painters began to build at the opening of the fifteenth century. Much of Giotto's genius lay in his ability to show perspective, or the appearance of spatial depth, in his frescoes, an illusion he achieved largely through the placement of the figures (see Figure 10.19). Approximately one hundred years after Giotto, painters learned to enhance the realism of their pictures by the use of linear perspective, the most significant artistic innovation of the age.

The invention of linear perspective was another of Brunelleschi's accomplishments. Using principles of architecture and optics, he conducted experiments in 1425 that provided the mathematical basis for achieving the illusion of depth on a two-dimensional surface (and, coincidentally, contributed to the enhancement of the status of the arts by grounding them in scholarly learning). Brunelleschi's solution to the problem of linear perspective was to organize the picture space around the center point, or **vanishing point.** After determining the painting's vanishing point, he devised a structural grid for placing objects in precise relation to each other within the picture space. He also computed the ratios by which objects diminish in size as they recede from view, so that pictorial reality seems to correspond visually with physical accuracy. He then subjected the design to a mirror test—checking its truthfulness in its reflected image.

When the camera appeared in the nineteenth century, it was discovered that the photographic lens "saw" nature according to Brunelleschi's mathematical rules. After the 1420s, Brunelleschi's studies led to the concept of Renaissance space, the notion that a composition should be viewed from one single position. For four hundred years, or until first challenged by Manet in the nineteenth century, linear perspective and Renaissance space played a leading role in Western painting (see Chapter 18).

A second type of perspective, atmospheric or aerial, was perfected by painters north of the Alps in the first half of the fifteenth century, although the Italian painter Masaccio was the first to revive atmospheric perspective in the 1420s, based on the Roman tradition. Through the use of colors, these artists created an illusion of depth by subtly diminishing the tones as the distance between the eye and the object increased; at the horizon line, the colors become grayish and the objects blurry in appearance. When atmospheric perspective was joined to linear perspective, as happened later in the century, a greater illusion of reality was achieved than was possible with either type used independently.

Again commenting on the innovations of Brunelleschi was Alberti, who published a treatise in 1435 that elaborated on the mathematical aspects of painting and set forth brilliantly the humanistic and secular values of the Early Renaissance. Alberti was an aristocratic humanist with both a deep knowledge of Classicism and a commitment to its ideals. In his treatise, he praised master painters in rousing terms, comparing their creativity to God's—a notion that would have been considered blasphemous by medieval thinkers. He asserted that paintings, in addition to pleasing the eye, should appeal to the mind with optical and mathematical accuracy. But paintings, he went on, should also present a noble subject, such as a Classical hero, and should be characterized by a small number of figures, by carefully observed and varied details, by graceful poses, by harmonious relationships among all elements, and by a judicious use of colors. These Classical ideals were quickly adopted by Florentine artists eager to establish a new aesthetic code.

Architecture In the High Middle Ages, most architects were stonemasons and were regarded as artisans, like shoemakers or potters. But by the fifteenth century, the status of architects had changed. Because of the newly discovered scientific aspects of their craft, the leading architects were now grouped with those practicing the learned professions of medicine and law. By 1450 Italian architects had freed architecture from Late Gothicism, as well as from the other arts. Unlike Gothic cathedrals adorned with sculptures and paintings, these new buildings drew on the Classical tradition for whatever simple decorative details were needed. This transformation became the most visible symbol of Early Renaissance architecture.

Although Brunelleschi established the new standards in architecture, most of his buildings have been either destroyed or altered considerably by later hands. However, the earliest work to bring him fame still survives in Florence largely as he had planned it—the dome of the city's cathedral (Figure 11.6). Although the rest of the cathedral—nave, transept, and choir—was finished before 1400, no one had been able to devise a method for erecting the projected dome until Brunelleschi received the commission in 1420. Using the learning he had gained from his researches in Rome as well as his knowledge of Gothic building styles, he developed an ingenious plan for raising the dome, which was virtually completed in 1436.

Faced with a domical base of 140 feet, Brunelleschi realized that a hemispheric dome in the Roman manner, like the dome of the Pantheon, would not work (see Figure 5.14). Traditional building techniques could not span the Florentine cathedral's vast domical base, nor could the cathedral's walls be buttressed to support a massive dome. So he turned to Gothic methods, using diagonal ribs based on the pointed arch. This innovative dome had a double shell of two relatively thin walls held together by twenty-four stone ribs, of which only eight are visible. His crowning touch was to add a lantern that sits atop the dome and locks the ribs into place (Figure 11.7). The dome's rounded windows echo the openings in the upper nave walls, thereby ensuring that his addition

Figure 11.6 FILIPPO BRUNELLESCHI. Cathedral Dome, Florence. 1420–1436. Ht. of dome from floor 367′. *After the dome of the Florence cathedral was erected according to Brunelleschi's plan, another architect was employed to add small galleries in the area above the circular windows. But the Florentine authorities halted his work before the galleries were fully installed, leaving the structure in its present state.*

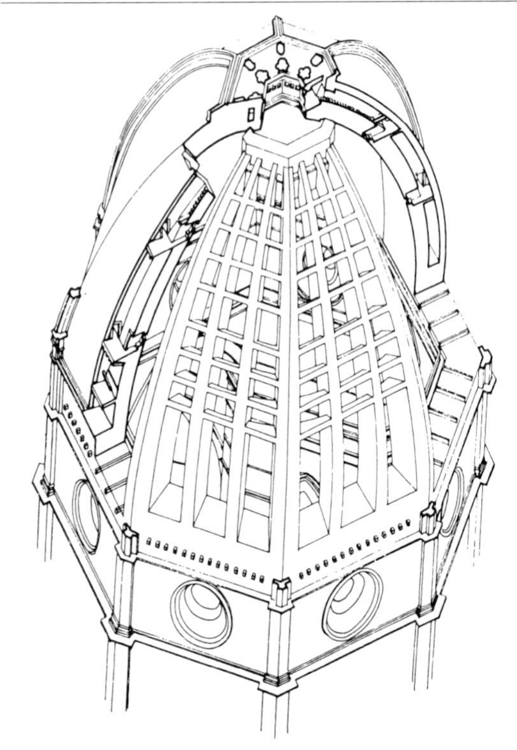

Figure 11.7 FILIPPO BRUNELLESCHI. Design for Construction of Dome of Florence Cathedral. *Brunelleschi designed the dome of the Florence cathedral with an inner and an outer shell, both of which are attached to the eight ribs of the octagonal-shaped structure. Sixteen smaller ribs, invisible from the outside, were placed between the shells to give added support. What held these elements together and gave them stability was the lantern, based on his design, that was anchored to the dome's top sometime after 1446.*

would harmonize with the existing elements. But the octagonal-shaped dome was Brunelleschi's own creation and expresses a logical, even inevitable, structure. Today, the cathedral still dominates the skyline of Florence, a lasting symbol of Brunelleschi's creative genius.

Brunelleschi's most representative building is the Pazzi Chapel, as the chapter house, or meeting room, of the monks of Santa Croce is called. This small church embodies the harmonious proportions and Classical features that are the hallmark of the Early Renaissance style. In his architectural plan, Brunelleschi centered a dome over an oblong area whose width equals the dome's diameter and whose length is twice its width and then covered each of the chapel's elongated ends with a barrel vault. Double doors opened into the center wall on one long side, and two rounded arch windows flanked this doorway. A loggia, or porch, which Brunelleschi may not have designed, preceded the entrance (Figure 11.8). Inside the chapel, following the Classical rules of measure and proportion, Brunelleschi employed medallions, rosettes, **pilasters** (or applied columns), and square panels. In addition to these Classical details, the rounded arches and the barrel vaults further exemplify the new Renaissance style (Figure 11.9). His Classical theories were shared by Florence's humanist elite, who found religious significance in mathematical harmony. Both they and Brunelleschi believed that a well-ordered building such as the Pazzi Chapel mirrored God's plan of the universe.

The other towering figure in Early Renaissance architecture was Alberti. Despite the influence of his ideas, which dominated architecture until 1600, no completed building based on his design remains. A splendid unfinished effort is the Tempio Malatestiano in Rimini (see Figure 11.5), a structure that replaced the

Figure 11.8 (Inset), FILIPPO BRUNELLESCHI AND OTHERS. Exterior, Pazzi Chapel, Santa Croce Church. 1433–1461. Florence. *The Pazzi Chapel's harmonious facade reflects the Classical principles of the Early Renaissance style: symmetry and simplicity. By breaking the rhythm of the facade with the rounded arch, the architect emphasizes its surface symmetry so that the left side is a mirror image of the right side. Simplicity is achieved in the architectural decorations, which are either Greco-Roman devices or mathematically inspired divisions.* ▶

Figure 11.9 FILIPPO BRUNELLESCHI. Interior. Pazzi Chapel, Santa Croce Church. Ca. 1433–1461. 59′ 9″ long × 35′ 8″ wide. Florence. *Decorations on the white walls of the Pazzi Chapel's interior break up its plain surface and draw the viewer's eye to the architectural structure: pilasters, window and panel frames, medallions, capitals, and dome ribs. The only non-architecturally related decorations are the terra-cotta sculptures by Luca della Robbia of the four evangelists and the Pazzi family coat of arms, mounted inside the medallions.*

Figure 11.10 DONATELLO. *The Feast of Herod.* Ca. 1425. Gilt bronze, 23½″ square. Baptismal font, San Giovanni, Siena. *The first low-relief sculpture executed in the Early Renaissance style,* The Feast of Herod *is a stunning example of the power of this new approach to art. Its theatrical force arises from the successful use of linear perspective and the orderly placement of the figures throughout the three rooms.*

existing church of San Francesco. Rimini's despot, Sigismondo Malatesta, planned to have himself, his mistress, and his court buried in the refurbished structure, and he appointed Alberti to supervise the church's reconstruction.

Alberti's monument represents the first modern attempt to give a Classical exterior to a church. Abandoning the Gothic pointed arch, he designed this church's unfinished facade with its three rounded arches after a nearby triumphal arch. He framed the arches with Corinthian columns, one of his favorite decorative devices. Although the architect apparently planned to cover the church's interior with a dome

Figure 11.11 DONATELLO. *David.* Ca. 1430–1432. Bronze, ht. 62¼″. Bargello, Florence. *The David and Goliath story was often allegorized into a prophecy of Christ's triumph over Satan. But Donatello's sculpture undermines such an interpretation, for his* David *is less a heroic figure than a provocative image of refined sensuality, as suggested by the undeveloped but elegant body, the dandified pose, and the incongruous boots and hat. Donatello's* David *is a splendid modern portrayal of youthful male power, self-aware and poised on the brink of manhood.*

comparable to Brunelleschi's on the Florentine cathedral, Malatesta's fortunes failed, and the projected temple had to be abandoned. Nevertheless, Alberti's unfinished church was admired by later builders and helped to point the way to the new Renaissance architecture.

Sculpture Like architecture, sculpture blossomed in Florence in the early 1400s. Donatello, the leader of the sculptural revival, was imbued with Classical ideals but obsessed with realism. He used a variety of techniques—expressive gestures, direct observation, and mathematical precision—to reproduce what his eyes saw. Donatello accompanied Brunelleschi to Rome to study ancient art, and he adapted linear perspective as early as 1425 into a small **relief** called *The Feast of Herod* (Figure 11.10).

The subject is the tragic end of John the Baptist, Florence's patron saint, as recounted in Mark 6:20–29. In Donatello's square bronze panel, the saint's severed head is being displayed on a dish to King Herod at the left, while the scorned Salome stands near the right end of the table. A puzzled guest leans toward the ruler, who recoils with upraised hands; two children at the left back away from the bloody head; and a diner leans back from the center of the table—all depicted under the rounded arches of the new Brunelleschian architecture. The sculpture's rich details and use of linear perspective point up the horror of the scene and thus achieve the heightened realism that was among the artistic goals of this era. The scene's vanishing point runs through the middle set of arches, so that the leaning motions of the two figures in the foreground not only express their inner turmoil but also cause them to fall away from the viewer's line of sight.

Donatello also revived the free-standing male nude, one of the supreme expressions of ancient art. Donatello's bronze *David,* probably executed for Cosimo de' Medici, portrays David standing with his left foot on the severed head of the Philistine warrior Goliath—a pose based on the biblical story (Figure 11.11). This sculpture had a profound influence on later sculptors, who admired Donatello's creation but produced rival interpretations of David (Figure 11.12). Donatello and his successors used the image of David to pay homage to male power—a major preoccupation of Renaissance artists and intellectuals.

Like other Renaissance masters, Donatello owed debts to Classical artists, but he also challenged them by adapting their principles to his own times. For example, the Roman statue of Marcus Aurelius (see Figure 5.11) inspired Donatello's bronze called the *Gattamelata,* the first successful equestrian sculpture in over twelve hundred years (Figure 11.13). As Donatello's *David* portrays the subtleties of adolescent male beauty, his *Gattamelata* pays homage to mature masculine power. This work honored the memory of Erasmo da Narni, a Venetian *condottiere* nicknamed Gattamelata, or "Honey Cat." The warrior's pose resembles the Roman imperial style, but in almost every other way, the sculptor violates the harmonious ideas of ancient art.

Figure 11.12 ANDREA DEL VERROCCHIO. *David.* 1473–1475. Bronze, ht. 4′ 2″. Bargello, Florence. *Verrocchio's* David *inaugurated the tradition in Renaissance Florence of identifying the Jewish giant-killer with the city's freedom-loving spirit. A masterpiece of bravado, Verrocchio's boyish hero stands challengingly over the severed head of Goliath. In its virility, this work surpasses the sculpture that inspired it, Donatello's* David *(see Figure 11.11). Florence's ruling council liked Verrocchio's statue so much that they placed it in the Palazzo Vecchio, the seat of government, where it remained until Michelangelo's* David *(see Figure 12.19) displaced it.*

Most significant, the rider's face owes its sharp realism—firm jawline, bushy eyebrows, widely set eyes, and close-cropped hair—to fifteenth-century sources, especially to the cult of the ugly, an aesthetic attitude that claimed to find moral strength in coarse features that did not conform to the Classical ideals (Figure

Figure 11.13 DONATELLO. *Equestrian Monument of Erasmo da Narni, Called "Gattamelata."* 1447–1453. Bronze, approx. 11 × 13′. Piazza del Santo, Padua. *This equestrian statue of the* condottiere *was funded by his family but authorized by a grateful Venetian senate in honor of his military exploits. Conceiving of the dead military leader as a "triumphant Caesar," Donatello dressed him in Classical costume and decorated his saddle and armor with many allusions to antique art, such as flying cupids and victory depicted as a goddess.*

Figure 11.14 DONATELLO. Detail of *"Gattamelata."* 1447–1453. Piazza del Santo, Padua. *Donatello deliberately designed the monument's stern, deeply lined, and serious face to conform to the Renaissance ideal of a strong military commander.*

11.14). Since this work was commissioned after the hero's death and since Donatello had no way of knowing how the soldier looked, he sculptured the face to conform to his notion of a strong-minded general. The massive horse, with flaring nostrils, open mouth, and lifted foreleg, seems to be an extension of the soldier's forceful personality.

The only serious rival to Donatello in the Early Renaissance was another Florentine, Lorenzo Ghiberti [gee-BAIR-tee] (about 1381–1455), who slowly adapted to the new style of art. In 1401 he defeated Brunelleschi in a competition to select a sculptor for the north doors

Figure 11.15 LORENZO GHIBERTI. *The Annunciation.* Panel from the north doors of the Baptistery. 1403–1424. Gilt bronze, 20½ × 17¾". Florence. *Ghiberti's rendition of the Annunciation was typical of his panels on the north doors. Mary and the angel are placed in the shallow foreground and are modeled almost completely in the round. The background details, including a sharply foreshortened representation of God on the left, are scarcely raised from the metal. The contrast between these design elements enhances the illusion of depth.*

of Florence's Baptistery. The north doors consist of twenty-eight panels, arranged in four columns of seven panels, each depicting a New Testament scene. These doors, completed between 1403 and 1424, show Ghiberti still under the influence of the International Gothic style that prevailed in about 1400. Illustrative of this tendency is the panel of *The Annunciation* (Luke 1:26–38), which depicts the moment when Mary learns from an angelic messenger that she will become the mother of Christ (Figure 11.15). The Gothic quatrefoil, or four-leafed frame, was standard for these panels, and many of Ghiberti's techniques are typical of the Gothic style—the niche in which the Virgin stands, her swaying body, and the angel depicted in flight. Nevertheless, Ghiberti always exhibited a strong feeling for Classical forms and harmony, as in the angel's well-rounded body and Mary's serene face.

The artistic world of Florence was a rapidly changing one, however, and Ghiberti adapted his art to conform to the emerging Early Renaissance style of Donatello. Between 1425 and 1452, Ghiberti brought his mature art to its fullest expression in the east doors, the last of the Baptistery's three sculptured portals. These panels, larger than those on the north doors, depict scenes from the Old Testament, such as the story of Cain and Abel from Genesis (Figure 11.16). Most of the Gothic touches are eliminated, including the framing quatrefoils, which are now replaced with rectangular panels. In many other ways, the Cain and Abel panel on the east doors shows Ghiberti's growing dedication to Classical ideals: the graceful contrapposto of the standing figures and their proportional relationships, for example. This work translates Albertian aesthetics into bronze by creating an illusion of depth. But according to Ghiberti's *Commentaries,* the sculptor's purpose was not illusion for its own sake but, rather, a clear presentation of the biblical story. Five incidents from the story of Cain and Abel are illustrated: (1) Cain and Abel as children with their parents, Adam and Eve, at the top left; (2) Cain and Abel making sacrifices before an altar, at the top right; (3) Cain plowing with oxen and Abel watching his sheep, in the middle and foreground, respectively, on the left; (4) Cain slaying Abel with a club, in the right middle; and (5) Cain being questioned by God, in the right foreground. So sublime was Ghiberti's accomplishment that Michelangelo, in the next century, is said to have referred to these doors as "the Gates of Paradise."

Figure 11.16 LORENZO GHIBERTI. *The Story of Cain and Abel.* Detail from the east doors of the Baptistery (the "Gates of Paradise"). 1425–1452. Gilt bronze, 31¼ × 31¼". Florence. *This exquisite panel from the Florence Baptistery's east doors is a testament to Ghiberti's absorption of Early Renaissance taste. He followed Brunelleschi's new rules for linear perspective by placing the vanishing point in the middle of the tree trunks in the center of the panel, and he adhered to Alberti's principle of varied details by adding the oxen, sheep, and altar.*

Figure 11.17 MASACCIO. *The Holy Trinity*. 1427 or 1428. Fresco, 21′ 10½″ × 10′ 5″. Santa Maria Novella, Florence. *Masaccio achieved a remarkable illusion of depth in this fresco by using linear and atmospheric perspective. Below the simulated chapel he painted a skeleton in a wall sarcophagus (not visible in this photograph) with a melancholy inscription reading, "I was once that which you are, and what I am you also will be." This* memento mori, *or reminder of death, was probably ordered by the donor, a member of the Lenzi family. His tomb is built into the floor and lies directly in front of the fresco.*

Painting The radical changes taking place in architecture and sculpture were minor compared with the changes in painting. Inspired by Classicism though lacking significant examples from ancient times, painters were relatively free to experiment and to define their own path. As in the other arts of the 1400s, Florentine painters led the way and established the standards for the new style—realism, linear perspective, and psychological truth. This movement climaxed at the end of the century with the early work of Leonardo da Vinci.

After 1450 Florence's dominance was challenged by Venetian painters, who were forging their own artistic tradition. Venice, having won its freedom from the Byzantine Empire only in the High Middle Ages, was still in the thrall of Byzantine culture (see Chapter 8). As a result, Venetian painters and their patrons showed a pronounced taste for the stylized effects and sensual surfaces typical of Byzantine art. However, a distinct school of Venetian painters emerged, which eventually was to have a major impact on the course of painting in the West.

North of the Alps, a third Early Renaissance development was taking place in Burgundy and the Low Countries. There, the painters pursued an art more religious than that of Italy and closer in spirit to the Late Gothic. The northern artists concentrated on minute details and landscapes rather than on the problems of depth and composition that concerned Italy's painters. This survey confines itself to the major figures in the Florentine school, which is divided into two generations, and to the founder of the Venetian school.

The guiding genius of the revolution in painting in the earlier Florentine school was the youthful Masaccio [mah-ZAHT-cho] (1401–1428), whose career was probably cut short by the plague. He adopted mathematical perspective in his works almost simultaneously with its invention by Brunelleschi. In the history of Western painting, Masaccio's *Holy Trinity* fresco, painted in 1425, is the first successful depiction in painting of the new concept of Renaissance space.

Masaccio's design for this fresco in the church of Santa Maria Novella, Florence, shows that he was well aware of the new currents flowing in the art of his day. The painting offers an architectural setting in the style of Brunelleschi, and the solidity and vitality of the figures indicate that Masaccio had also absorbed the values of Donatello's new sculpture. Masaccio's fresco portrays the Holy Trinity—the three divine beings who make up the Christian idea of God—within a simulated chapel (Figure 11.17). Jesus' crucified body appears to be held up by God the Father, who stands on a platform behind the cross; between the heads of God and Jesus is a dove, symbolizing the Holy Spirit and completing the Trinitarian image. Mary and Saint John, both clothed in contemporary dress, flank the holy trio. Mary points dramatically to the Savior. Just outside the chapel's frame, the donors kneel in prayer—the typical way of presenting patrons in Renaissance art.

In the Trinity fresco, Masaccio uses a variety of innovations. He is the first painter to show light falling from a single source, in this instance, from the left, bathing the body of Christ and coinciding with the actual light-

Figure 11.18 MASACCIO. *The Tribute Money.* Ca. 1425. Fresco, 8′2⅜″ × 19′8¼″. Santa Maria del Carmine, Florence. *This fresco represents the highest expression of the art of Masaccio, particularly in his realistic portrayal of the tax collector. This official, who appears twice, first confronting Christ in the center and then receiving money from Peter on the right, is depicted with coarse features—a typical man of the Florentine streets. Even his posture, though rendered with Classical contrapposto, suggests a swagger—a man at home in his body and content with his difficult occupation.*

ing in Santa Maria Novella. This realistic feature adds to the three-dimensional effect of the well-modeled figures. The use of linear perspective further heightens the scene's realism. Finally, the perspective, converging to the midpoint between the kneeling donors, reinforces the hierarchy of beings within the fresco: from God the Father at the top to the human figures at the sides. In effect, mathematical tidiness is used to reveal the divine order—an ideal congenial to Florence's intellectual elite.

A second fresco by Masaccio, *The Tribute Money,* painted in the Brancacci Chapel of the church of Santa Maria del Carmine, Florence, is recognized as Masaccio's masterpiece (Figure 11.18). This fresco illustrates the Gospel account (Matthew 17:24–27) in which Jesus advises Peter, his chief disciple, to pay the Roman taxes. Because this painting depicts a biblical subject virtually unrepresented in Christian art, it was probably commissioned by a donor to justify a new and heavy Florentine tax. Whether the fresco had any effect on tax collection is debatable, but other artists were captivated by Masaccio's stunning technical effects: the use of perspective and **chiaroscuro,** or the modeling with light and shade.

The Tribute Money fresco follows the continuous narrative form of medieval art. Three separate episodes are depicted at the same time—in the center, Jesus is confronted by the tax collector; on the left, Peter, as foretold by Jesus, finds a coin in the mouth of a fish; and, on the right, Peter pays the coin to the Roman official. Despite this Gothic effect, the fresco's central section is able to stand alone because of its spatial integrity and unified composition. Jesus is partially encircled by his apostles, and the tax gatherer, viewed from the back, stands to the right. In this central group, the heads are all at the same height, for Masaccio aligned them according to Brunelleschi's principles. Fully modeled in the round, each human form occupies a precise, mathematical space.

Painters like the Dominican friar Fra Angelico (about 1400–1455) extended Masaccio's innovations. Fra Angelico's later works, painted for the renovated monastery of San Marco in Florence and partially funded by Cosimo de' Medici, show his mature blending of biblical motifs in Renaissance space. *The Annunciation* portrays a reflective Virgin receiving the angel Gabriel (Figure 11.19). Mary and Gabriel are framed in niches in the Gothic manner, but the other elements—the mastery of depth, the simplicity of gestures, the purity of colors, and the integrated scene—are rendered in the new, simple Renaissance style. The painting's vanishing point is placed to the right of center in the

Figure 11.19 FRA ANGELICO. *Annunciation.* 1438–1445. Fresco, 7′6″ × 10′5″. Monastery of San Marco, Florence. *Fra Angelico's portrayal of the Virgin at the moment when she receives the news that she will bear the baby Jesus is a wonderful illustration of the painter's use of religious symbols. Mary's questioning expression and her arms crossed in a maternal gesture help to establish the painting's subject. Moreover, the physical setting of the scene, bare except for the rough bench on which she sits, suggests an ascetic existence—an appropriate detail for the painting's original setting, a monastery.*

small barred window looking out from the Virgin's bedroom. The loggia, or open porch, in which the scene takes place was based on a new architectural fashion popular among Florence's wealthy elite. Religious images abound in this painting; the enclosed garden symbolizes Mary's virginity, and the barred window attests to the purity of her life. Because of his gracious mastery of form and space, Fra Angelico's influence on later artists was pronounced.

One of those he influenced was Piero della Francesca [PYER-o DAYL-lah frahn-CHAY-skah] (about 1420–1492), a great painter of the second Florentine generation, who grew up in a Tuscan country town near Florence. His panel painting *The Flagellation* shows the powerful though mysterious aesthetic effects of his controversial style (Figure 11.20). The sunlight flooding the scene unites the figures, but the composition places them in two distinct areas. At the extreme left sits Pilate, the judge, on a dais. The painting's subject—the scourging of Christ before his crucifixion—is placed to the left rear. Reinforcing this odd displacement are the figures on the right, who are apparently lost in their own conversation. Aesthetically this strange juxtaposition arises because della Francesca has placed the horizon line around the hips of the figures beating Christ, causing the three men on the right to loom in such high perspective; thus the men in the foreground appear to be indifferent to Christ and unaware of his importance. The effect is distinctly unsettling in a religious scene. The modern world, which loves conundrums, has developed a strong passion for the private vision of della Francesca as represented in his art.

Sandro Botticelli [baht-tuh-CHEL-lee] (1445–1510) is the best representative of a lyrical aspect of this second generation and one of the most admired painters

Figure 11.20 PIERO DELLA FRANCESCA. *The Flagellation.* 1460s. Oil on panel, 23 × 32". Galleria Nazionale della Marche, Palazzo Ducale, Urbino. *A secondary religious message may be found in this work. In 1439 the Orthodox Church discussed union with Rome at the Council of Florence but later repudiated the merger when the Byzantine populace rioted in favor of Turkish rule. The hats on Pilate (seated at the left) and the third man from the right are copies of Greek headdresses that were worn at the council. In effect, these figures suggest that the Greek Church is a persecutor of true Christianity, for the papacy regarded the Greek Orthodox faith as schismatic.*

in the Western tradition. One of the first Florentine artists to master both linear and atmospheric perspective, he was less interested in the technical aspects of painting than he was in depicting languid beauty and poetical truth.

Until the 1480s, Botticelli's art was shaped by the Neo-Platonic philosophy of the Florentine Academy, and thus he often allegorized pagan myths, giving them a Christian slant. Especially prominent in Neo-Platonic thought was the identification of Venus, the Roman goddess of love, with the Christian belief that "God is love." Botticelli, with the support of his patrons, notably the Medici family, made the Roman goddess the subject of two splendid paintings, the *Primavera* and *The Birth of Venus.* In this way, female nudes once again became a proper subject for art, though male nudes had appeared earlier, in Donatello's generation (see Figure 11.11).

Botticelli's *Primavera,* or *Allegory of Spring,* presents Venus as a Christianized deity, dressed in a revealingly transparent gown (Figure 11.21). At first glance, the goddess, standing just slightly to the right of center, appears lost amid the general agitation, but on closer view she is seen to be presiding over the revels. Venus tilts her head coyly and holds up her right hand, establishing by these commanding gestures that this orange grove is her garden and the other figures are her familiars, or associates, all of them symbolically linked with divine love.

Even though the *Primavera* is one of the most beloved works of Western art, in technical terms the painting shows that Botticelli was out of step with the Early Renaissance. He has placed the scene in the near foreground, stressing this area's extreme shallowness by the entangled backdrop of trees and shrubs. The figures

Figure 11.21 SANDRO BOTTICELLI. *Primavera.* Ca. 1482. Tempera on panel, 6′8″ × 10′4″. Uffizi Gallery, Florence. *Botticelli's lyricism is evident in his refined images of human beauty. His figures' elegant features and gestures, such as the sloping shoulders and the tilted heads, were copied by later artists. The women's blond, ropelike hair and transparent gowns are typical of Botticelli's style.*

are flattened, and the background appears more decorative than real.

An even more famous work by Botticelli, and one of the great landmarks of Western art, is *The Birth of Venus* (see Figure 11.4). Painted in an even more flattened style than the *Primavera,* this masterpiece was probably intended as a visual complement to it. In Neo-Platonic terms, Venus is an image of beauty and love as it is born and grows in the human mind; the birth of Venus corresponds to the baptism of Jesus, because baptism is a symbol of rebirth.

In the 1480s, Florentine art was moving toward its culmination in the early works of Leonardo da Vinci (1452–1519). Leonardo is the quintessential representative of a new breed of artist: the Renaissance man, who takes the universe of learning as his province. Not only did he defy the authority of the church by secretly studying human cadavers, but he also rejected the Classical values that had guided the first generation of the Early Renaissance. He relied solely on empirical truth and what the human eye could discover. His notebooks, encoded so as to be legible only when read in a mirror, recorded and detailed his lifelong curiosity about both the human and the natural worlds. In his habits of mind, Leonardo joined intellectual curiosity with the skills of sculptor, architect, engineer, scientist, and painter.

Among his few surviving paintings from this period, the first version of *The Virgin of the Rocks* reveals both his scientific eye and his desire to create a haunting image uniquely his own (Figure 11.22). In this scene, set in a grotto or cave, Mary is portrayed with the infant Jesus, as a half-kneeling infant John the Baptist prays and an angel watches. The plants underfoot and the rocks in the background are a treasure of precise documentation. Nevertheless, the setting is Leonardo's own invention—without a scriptural or a traditional basis—and is a testimony to his creative genius.

Leonardo's plan of *The Virgin of the Rocks* shows the rich workings of his mind. Ignoring Brunelleschian

Figure 11.22 LEONARDO DA VINCI. *The Virgin of the Rocks.* 1483. Oil on panel, approx. 6′ 3″ × 3′ 7″. Louvre. *Two slightly different versions of this work exist, this one dating from 1483 and a later one done in 1506 and on view in the National Gallery in London. The Louvre painting, with its carefully observed botanical specimens, is the culmination of the scientific side of the Early Renaissance. The painting's arbitrary features—the grotto setting and the unusual perspective—point ahead to the High Renaissance; the dramatic use of chiaroscuro foreshadows the "night pictures" of the Baroque period (see Figure 14.8).*

perspective, he placed the figures his own way. He also developed a pyramid design for arranging the figures in relation to one another; Mary's head is the pyramid's apex, and her seat and the other three figures anchor its corners. Within this pyramid, Leonardo creates a dynamic tension by using gestures to suggest a circular motion: The angel points to John the Baptist, who in turn directs his praying hands toward Jesus. A second, vertical, line of stress is seen in the gesturing hands of Mary, the angel, and Christ. Later artists so admired this painting that its pyramidal composition became the standard in the High Renaissance.

No prior artist had used chiaroscuro to such advantage as Leonardo does in this work, causing the figures to stand out miraculously from the surrounding gloom. And unlike earlier artists, he colors the atmosphere, softening the edges of surfaces with a fine haze called ***sfumato.*** As a result, the painting looks more like a vision than a realistic scene. Leonardo's later works are part of the High Renaissance (see Chapter 12), but his early works represent the fullest expression of the scientific spirit of the second generation of Early Renaissance painting.

While the Florentine painters were establishing themselves as the driving force in the Early Renaissance, a rival school was beginning to emerge in Venice. The Venetian school, dedicated to exploring the effects of light and air and re-creating the sensuous effects of textured surfaces, was eventually to play a major role in the history of painting in Italy and the West. Founded by Giovanni Bellini, a member of a dynasty of painters, the Venetian school began its rise to greatness.

Giovanni Bellini (about 1430–1516), who trained in the workshop of his father, the Late Gothic painter Jacopo Bellini (about 1400–about 1470), made Venice a center of Renaissance art comparable to Florence and Rome. Ever experimenting, always striving to keep up with the latest trends, he frequently reinvented himself. Nevertheless, there were constants in his approach to painting. He combined the traditions of the Florentine school (the use of linear perspective and the direct observation of nature) and the Flemish school (the technique of oil painting, the use of landscape as background, and the practice of religious symbolism). Made aware of the importance of atmosphere by the Venetian setting, Bellini also experimented with a range of colors, variations in color intensity, and changes in light. In particular, Bellini perfected the landscape format as a backdrop for foreground figures. A great teacher, Bellini founded a workshop where his methods were taught to young painters, including Giorgione and Titian (see Chapter 12).

An excellent example of Bellini's use of landscape may be seen in *St. Francis in Ecstasy* (Figure 11.23). This work, which depicts an ecstatic St. Francis displaying the stigmata, shows Bellini's typical treatment of landscape. He divides the painting surface into zones, beginning with the area around the saint in the foreground, continuing through a second zone occupied by a donkey and a crane, to a third zone featuring Italian castles nestled into a hillside, and concluding with a fourth zone marked by a fortress and the sky. To heighten the realism, Bellini uses both a rich palette of colors and numerous objects to lead the viewer's eye into the vast distance. He adds to the realism by suffusing the scene

Figure 11.23 GIOVANNI BELLINI. *St. Francis in Ecstasy.* 1470s. Oil in tempera on panel, 49 × 55⅞". Frick Collection, New York. *In the foreground, Bellini renders his vision of the grotto at Alvernia, a mountain retreat near Assisi, where St. Francis went to pray and fast for forty days, in imitation of Christ's forty days in the wilderness. The artist reinforces the scene's religious significance through various symbols, such as the grapevine and the stigmata, alluding to the sacrifice of Christ, and the donkey (in the middle distance), emblematic of Jesus' entry into Jerusalem prior to the Crucifixion.*

with natural light. The landscape, with its vivid rendering of flora and fauna, expresses the Franciscan belief that humankind should live in harmony with the natural world (see Chapter 9).

Music

The changes affecting the cultural life of fifteenth-century Europe naturally also affected the music of the time. The impetus for a new musical direction, however, did not spring from Classical sources, because ancient musical texts had virtually perished. Instead, the new music owed its existence to meetings between English and Continental composers at the church councils that were called to settle the Great Schism (see Chapter 10) and the Continental composers' deep regard for the seductive sound of English music. The English composer John Dunstable [DUHN-stuh-bull] (about 1380–1453) was a central figure in the new musical era that began with the opening of the fifteenth century. Working in England and in France, he wrote mainly religious works—motets for multiple voices and settings for the Mass—that showed his increasingly harmonic approach to polyphony. The special quality of his music is its freedom from the use of mathematical proportion—the source of medieval music's dissonance.

Dunstable's music influenced composers in France, in Burgundy, and in Flanders, known collectively as the Franco-Netherlandish school. This school, which became the dominant force in fifteenth-century music, blended Dunstable's harmonics with northern European and Italian traditions. The principal works of this group were Latin **Masses,** or musical settings of the most sacred Christian rite; motets, or multivoiced songs set to Latin texts; and secular ***chansons,*** or songs, with French texts, including such types as the French ballade and the Italian madrigal, poems set to music for two and six voices, respectively. Together, these polyphonic compositions established the musical ideal of the Early Renaissance: multiple voices of equal importance singing ***a cappella*** (without instrumental accompaniment) and stressing the words so they could be understood by listeners.

Between 1430 and 1500, the continent's musical life was guided by composers from the Franco-Netherlandish school, the most important of whom was the Burgundian Josquin des Prez [zho-SKAN day PRAY] (about 1440–1521). Josquin was influential in his day and is now recognized as one of the greatest composers of all time. He was the first important composer to use music expressively so that the sounds matched the words of the text, thereby moving away from the abstract church style of the Middle Ages. One of his motets was described at the time as evoking Christ's suffering in a manner superior to painting. Josquin also began to organize music in the modern way, using major and minor scales with their related harmonies. All in all, he is probably the first Western composer whose music on first hearing appeals to modern ears.

The Legacy of the Early Renaissance

Today, modern times are considered to begin with the Early Renaissance in Italy. This period saw the rebirth of the study and practice of the arts and the humanities and the rise of the idea of the "Renaissance man," the supreme genius who makes all of human knowledge his province. Under the powerful stimulus of humanism, the liberal arts were restored to primacy over religion in the educational curriculum, a place they had not held for a thousand years, or since the triumph of Christianity in the fourth century. With humanism also came a skeptical outlook that expressed itself in a new regard for the direct role of human causality in history and the rise of textual criticism. A new ingredient in Renaissance humanism was the drive to individual fulfillment, perhaps the defining trait of Western civilization from this point onward.

The greatest cultural changes took place in the arts and in architecture, largely under the spell of humanistic learning. Now freed from subordination to architecture, sculpture and painting became independent art forms. Fifteenth-century architects, inspired by the Greco-Roman tradition, adapted Classical forms and ideals to their own needs. For the next four hundred years, until the Gothic revival in the nineteenth century, Classicism was the ruling force in a succession of architectural styles. Sculpture also used its Classical roots to redefine its direction, reviving ancient forms and the practice of depicting male and female nudes. Of all the visual arts, painting was least influenced by the Classical tradition, except for its ideals of simplicity and realism. Perhaps as a consequence of its artistic freedom, painting became the dominant art form of this era and continues to hold first rank today.

KEY CULTURAL TERMS

Renaissance
studia humanitatis
Early Renaissance style
vanishing point
pilaster
relief
chiaroscuro
sfumato
Mass
chanson
a cappella

SUGGESTIONS FOR FURTHER READING

PRIMARY SOURCES

CASSIRER, E., KRISTELLER, P. O., AND RANDALL, J., eds. *The Renaissance Philosophy of Man.* Chicago: University of Chicago Press, 1948. Selections from Pico, Valla, and other Renaissance scholars accompanied by a useful text.

PICO DELLA MIRANDOLA. *On the Dignity of Man.* Indianapolis: Bobbs-Merrill, 1956. A succinct statement on Renaissance thought by one of its leading scholars.

SUGGESTIONS FOR LISTENING

DUNSTABLE (or DUNSTAPLE), JOHN (about 1380–1453). Dunstable's sweet-sounding harmonies helped inaugurate Early Renaissance music. Predominantly a composer of sacred music, he is best represented by motets, including *Veni Sancte Spiritus—Veni Creator Spiritus* and *Sancta Maria, non est similis.* He also wrote a few secular songs of which the two most familiar are *O Rosa bella* and *Puisque m'amour.*

JOSQUIN DES PREZ (1440–1521). Josquin's Masses, motets, and *chansons* all illustrate his skill at combining popular melodies with intricate counterpoint and his use of harmonies commonly heard today. The motet *Ave Maria,* the *chanson Faulte d'argent,* and the Mass *Malheur me bat* are good examples of his style.

12 THE HIGH RENAISSANCE AND EARLY MANNERISM

1494–1564

Between 1494 and 1564, one of the most brilliantly creative periods in Western history unfolded in Italy. During this span of seventy years, there flourished three artists—Leonardo da Vinci, Raphael, and Michelangelo—and a writer—Machiavelli—whose achievements became legendary. The works of these geniuses, and of other talented but less well known artists and intellectuals, affected the basic Western concept of art and fundamentally influenced how we understand ourselves and the world.

The **High Renaissance,** lasting from 1494 to 1520, was the first phase of this creative period and was a time when the Classical principles of beauty, balance, order, serenity, harmony, and rational design reached a state of near perfection. The center of culture shifted from Florence, the heart of the Early Renaissance, to Rome, where the popes became the leading patrons of the new style in their desire to make Rome the world's most beautiful city. Florence even had to yield the services of Michelangelo, its favorite son, to the wealthy and powerful Roman pontiffs (Figure 12.1).

After 1520, however, the Renaissance veered away from the humanistic values of Classicism toward an antihumanistic vision of the world, labeled **Mannerism** because of the self-conscious, or "mannered," style adopted by its artists and intellectuals. Mannerist art and culture endured from 1520 until the end of the century, when the style was affected by religious controversy. This chapter covers the High Renaissance style and the Mannerist style through the end of its first phase in 1564, with the death of Michelangelo.

◀ **Detail** LEONARDO DA VINCI. *The Last Supper*. 1495–1498. Oil tempera on wall, 13′ 10″ × 29′7½″. Refectory, Santa Maria delle Grazie, Milan.

THE RISE OF THE MODERN SOVEREIGN STATE

The most important political development in the first half of the sixteenth century was the emergence of powerful sovereign states in the newly unified and stabilized nations of France, England, and Spain. This process was already under way in the late fifteenth century (see Chapter 10), but it now began to influence foreign affairs. The ongoing rivalries of these aggressive national kingdoms led to the concept of balance of power—a principle that still dominates politics today.

From 1494 to 1569, Europe's international political life was controlled, either directly or indirectly, by France and Spain. France's central role resulted from the policies of its strong Valois kings, who had governed France since the early fourteenth century. Spain's fortunes soared during this period, first under the joint rule of Ferdinand V and Isabella and then under Charles I. In 1519 Charles I was also elected Holy Roman Emperor as Charles V (he was of the royal house of Hapsburg), thus joining the interests of Spain and the Holy Roman Empire until his abdication in 1556. England kept aloof from Continental affairs during this time.

After 1591 the French and the Spanish rulers increasingly dispatched their armies and allies into the weaker states, where they fought and claimed new lands. As the sovereign monarchs gained power, the medieval dream of a united Christendom—pursued by Charlemagne, the popes, and the Holy Roman emperors—slowly faded away. These new states were strong because they were united around rulers who exercised increasing central control. Although most kings claimed to rule by divine right, their practical policies were more important in increasing their power. They surrounded themselves with ministers and consultative councils, both dependent on the crown. The ministers were often chosen from the bourgeois class, and they advised the rulers on such weighty matters as religion and war and also ran the developing bureaucracies. The bureaucracies in turn strengthened centralized rule by extending royal jurisdiction into matters formerly administered by the feudal nobility, such as the justice system.

Figure 12.1 MICHELANGELO. *Dying Slave.* 1513–1516. Marble, approx. 7′ 5″. Louvre. *Michelangelo's so-called* Dying Slave *embodies the conflicting artistic tendencies at work between 1494 and 1564. The statue's idealized traits—the perfectly proportioned figure, the restrained facial expression, and the body's gentle* S*-curve shape—are hallmarks of the High Renaissance style. But the figure's overall sleekness and exaggerated arm movements—probably based on one of the figures in the first-century* A.D. Laocoön Group *(see Figure 4.19), which had recently been rediscovered—were portents of Early Mannerism.*

The crown further eroded the status of the feudal nobles by relying on mercenary armies rather than on the warrior class, a shift that began in the Late Middle Ages. To pay these armies, the kings had to consult with representative bodies, such as Parliament in England, and make them a part of their regular administration.

The Struggle for Italy, 1494–1529

Italy's relative tranquility, established by the Peace of Lodi in 1454, was shattered by the French invasion in 1494. For the next thirty-five years, Italy was a battleground where France, Spain, and the Holy Roman Empire fought among themselves, as well as with the papacy and most of the Italian states.

The struggle began when France, eager to reassert a hereditary claim to Naples, agreed to help Milan in a controversy involving Naples, Florence, and the pope. The French king, Charles VIII (r. 1483–1498), took Florence in 1494 and then advanced to Rome and Naples. But the Italians did not relinquish ground easily. Joined by Venice and the pope and supported by the Holy Roman emperor and the Spanish monarch, they drove out the French. In 1499 the French returned to Italy to activate their claim to Milan, and the Spanish and the Germans joined with the Italians to drive them out. Over the next several decades, however, France continued to invade Italy intermittently. In the course of their campaigns, the French rulers, who were enamored of the Italian Renaissance, brought its artistic and intellectual ideals to northern Europe (Figure 12.2).

Figure 12.2 JEAN CLOUET. *Francis I.* Ca. 1525. Oil on panel, 37¾ × 29⅛". Louvre. *During his thirty-two-year-long reign, Francis I was a major force in sixteenth-century European affairs. He also embarked on an extensive artistic program, inspired by the Italian Renaissance, to make his court the most splendid in Europe. Under his personal direction, Italian artworks and artists, including Leonardo da Vinci, were imported into France. Ironically, this rather stylized portrait by Jean Clouet, Francis's chief court artist, owes more to the conventionalized portraits of the Gothic style than it does to the realistic works of the Italian Renaissance.*

In 1522 full-scale hostilities broke out between France and the Holy Roman Empire over Italy's future, a struggle that pitted the old Europe against the new. The Holy Roman Empire, ruled by Charles V, was a decentralized relic from the feudal age. France, under the bold and intellectual leadership of Francis I (r. 1515–1547) of the royal house of Valois, was the epitome of the new sovereign state.

The first Hapsburg-Valois war was the only one fought in Italy. In 1527 the troops of Charles V ran riot in Rome, raping, looting, and killing. This notorious sack of Rome had two major consequences. First, it cast doubt on Rome's ability to control Italy—long a goal of the popes—for it showed that the secular leaders no longer respected the temporal power of the papacy. Second, it ended papal patronage of the arts for almost a decade, thus weakening Rome's role as a cultural leader. It also had a chilling effect on artistic ideals and contributed to the rise of Mannerism.

In 1529 the Treaty of Cambrai ended this first phase of the Hapsburg-Valois rivalry. Years of invasions and wars had left most of Italy divided and exhausted. Some cities had suffered nearly irreparable harm. Florence, because it had so much to lose, fared the worst. In the 1530s, the Medici rulers resumed ducal power, but they were little more than puppets of the foreigners who controlled much of the peninsula. The only Italian state to keep its political independence was Venice, which became the last haven for artists and intellectuals in Italy for the rest of the sixteenth century.

Charles V and the Hapsburg Empire

By 1530 the struggle between the Valois and the Hapsburgs had shifted to central Europe. The French felt hemmed in by the Spanish in the south, the Germans to the east, and the Dutch to the north—peoples all ruled by the Hapsburg emperor Charles V. In French

Map 12.1 EUROPEAN EMPIRE OF CHARLES V, CA. 1556

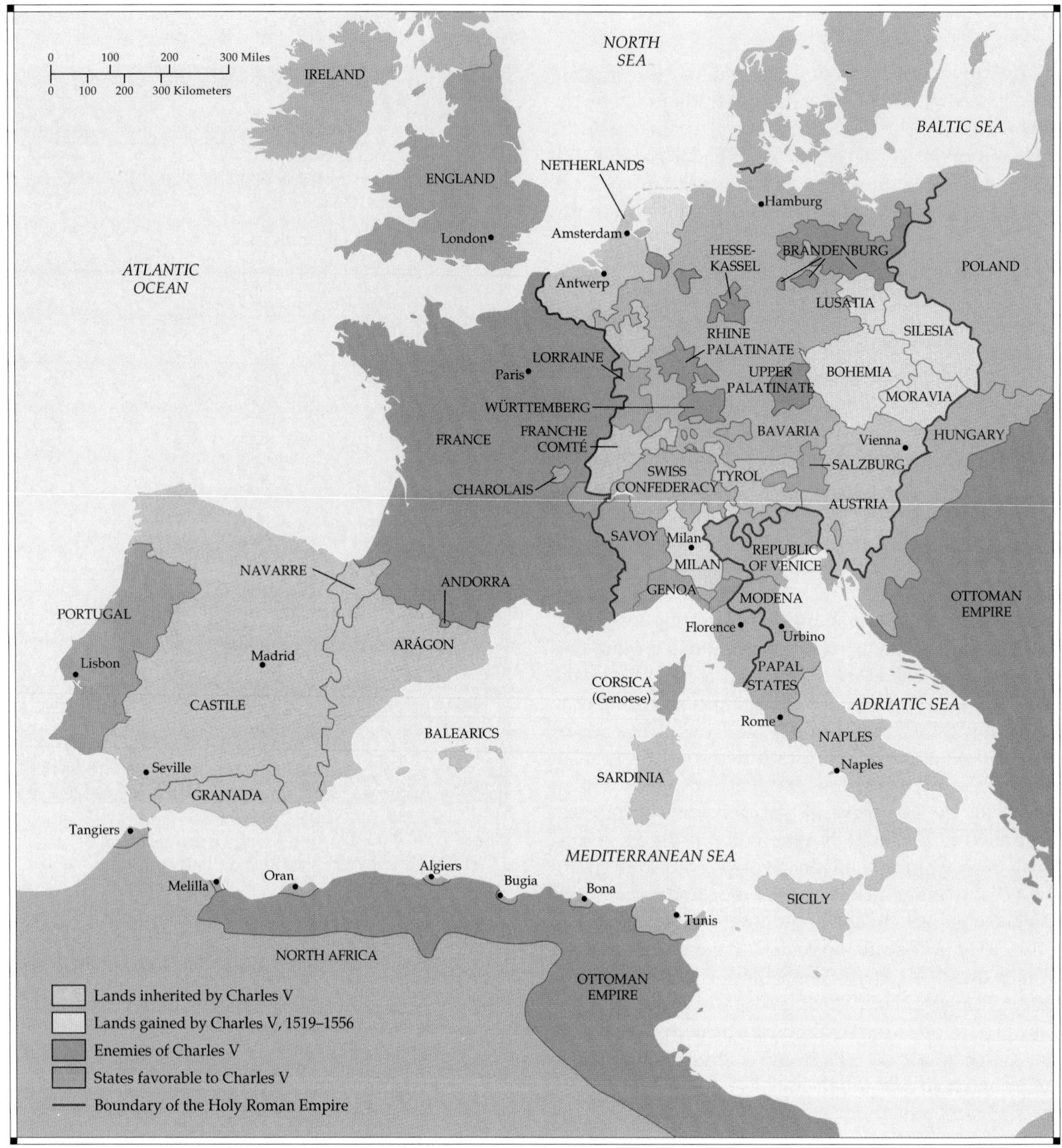

eyes, Charles had an insatiable appetite for power and for control of the Continent. In turn, the Hapsburg ruler considered the French king a land-hungry upstart who stood in the way of a Europe united under a Christian prince—in other words, the dream of Christendom. In 1559, after a number of exhausting wars and a series of French victories, the belligerents signed the Treaty of Cateau-Cambrésis, which ushered in a brief period of peace (Map 12.1).

Charles V, the man at the center of most of these events, lived a life filled with paradoxes (Figure 12.3). Because of the size of his empire, he was in theory one of the most powerful rulers ever to live; but in actuality, again because of the vastness of his lands, he never quite succeeded in gaining complete control of his empire. In some ways, he was the last of medieval kings; in other ways, he foreshadowed a new age driven by sovereign kings, standing armies, diplomatic agreements, and strong religious differences.

Charles V's unique position at the center of Europe's political storm was the result of a series of timely deaths and births and politically astute arranged marriages. These circumstances had permitted the Hapsburg rulers to accumulate vast power, wealth, and land. Charles was born in 1500 to a German father and a Spanish mother, and he was the grandson of both the

Holy Roman emperor Maximilian I and the Spanish king Ferdinand V. He held lands in present-day Spain, France, Italy, Germany, and Austria—along with the unimaginable riches of the recently acquired lands in the New World. By 1519 Charles V—simultaneously Charles I of Spain—ruled the largest empire the world has ever known.

For most of his life, Charles traveled from one of his possessions to another, fighting battles, arranging peace treaties, and attempting to unify his empire by personal control and compromise. His attention was often divided, and he found himself caught between two powerful foes—especially the French to the west and the Ottoman Turks in the east—who drained both his personal energies and his imperial resources.

Within the Holy Roman Empire, the princes of the German principalities often took advantage of his prolonged absences and his preoccupation with the French and the Turks. Their ability to gain political power at the emperor's expense increased after Martin Luther's revolt and the beginning of the Protestant Reformation (see Chapter 13). Charles also weakened his own position by his contradictory policies. At times he angered the disaffected German princes by meddling in their affairs and condemning Lutheran doctrines, and at other times he angered the popes by making concessions to the Protestants.

Exhausted and disillusioned by his inability to prevail in Europe, Charles abdicated in 1556 and retired to a monastery. His brother Ferdinand took control of the German-Austrian inheritance and was soon elected Holy Roman emperor. His son Philip assumed control of the Spanish Hapsburg holdings, including Spain, the New World territories, and the Netherlands. Thus ended Charles's vision of a united Europe and Christendom, which had turned into a nightmare of endless meetings, gory battles, and false hopes of peace and unity.

Figure 12.3 TITIAN. *Charles V with a Dog*. Ca. 1533. Oil on canvas, 6′3″ × 3′8″. Prado, Madrid. *Titian's full-length, standing portrait of Charles V was painted when the Hapsburg emperor was at the height of his power. By rendering the "ruler of the world" in contrapposto, his fingers casually holding the collar of his dog, Titian endows the emperor with a natural grace. The lighting that illuminates Charles from the dark background and the breathless hush that seems to envelop the man and dog are trademarks of Titian's style.*

ECONOMIC EXPANSION AND SOCIAL DEVELOPMENTS

By the end of the fifteenth century, Europe had nearly recovered from the impact of the plague; the sixteenth century continued to be a time of growing population and increasing prosperity. The center of commerce shifted from the Mediterranean to the Atlantic coast, making cities like London and Antwerp financial and merchandising centers. Skilled craftspeople turned out quality products, and enterprising merchants distributed these finished goods across much of northwestern Europe. The daring sailing expeditions and discoveries of the late fifteenth and early sixteenth centuries provided new raw materials from America. Innovative manufacturing methods spurred economic growth and expanded worldwide markets.

Although the data are scattered and often unreliable, evidence indicates that the population of Europe increased from about 45 million in 1400 to 69 million in 1500 and to about 89 million by 1600. There was a major population shift from rural to urban areas, and the number of cities with populations over 100,000 grew from five to eight between 1500 and 1600. Rome, for example, grew from about 50,000 in 1526—the year before the sack—to 100,000 by the end of the century.

Timeline 12.1 ITALIAN CULTURAL STYLES BETWEEN 1494 AND 1564

1494		1520				1564
	High Renaissance		Early Mannerism			
French invasion of Italy	**1508–1512** Michelangelo's Sistine Chapel ceiling frescoes	**1519** Death of Leonardo da Vinci **1520** Death of Raphael	**1532** Publication of Machiavelli's *Prince*	**1536–1541** Michelangelo's *Last Judgment* fresco	**1550** Palladio's Villa Rotonda	**1564** Death of Michelangelo

Prosperity brought a higher standard of living to most of the urban middle class, but throughout much of the century prices rose faster than wages. Those who were not profiting from increased economic growth, such as poor peasants or impoverished nobility living on unproductive farms, suffered the most. In areas of Europe hardest hit by inflation or agricultural and commercial stagnation, economic crises often became intertwined with social and religious matters that intensified long-standing regional and local differences.

Yet the boom offered economic opportunities to some. Many merchants made fortunes and provided employment for others. These merchants and the bankers who offered loans were also accumulating capital, which they then invested in other types of commercial activity. The campaigns of Charles V were financed by wealthy bankers operating in a well-organized money market. The amassing of surplus capital and its reinvestment ushered in the opening phase of commercial capitalism that laid the foundation for Europe's future economic expansion.

During the first half of the sixteenth century, the abundance of raw materials and the vast market potential of the New World had just begun to affect Europe's economy. South American gold and silver played an important role in the upward price spiral. After 1650 New World agricultural products, such as tobacco, cotton, and cocoa, were used in new manufactured goods and profoundly altered consumer habits.

In the late 1500s, a major economic change had occurred that would make it possible to bring the natural resources of the New World to Europe. Some Europeans, taking advantage of the institution of slavery and the existing slave trade in western Africa, mercilessly exploited the local Africans by buying them and shipping them to European colonies in the New World. The Africans were forced to work in the gold and silver mines of Central and South America and on the cotton and sugarcane plantations in the West Indies, where they became a major factor in the production of these new forms of wealth.

FROM HIGH RENAISSANCE TO EARLY MANNERISM

The characteristics of High Renaissance style were largely derived from the visual arts. Led by painters, sculptors, and architects who worshiped ancient Classical ideals, notably those of late-fifth-century B.C. Greece, the High Renaissance was filled with images of repose, harmony, and heroism. Under the spell of Classicism and the values of simplicity and restraint, artists sought to conquer unruly physical reality by subjecting it to the principle of a seemingly effortless order.

Although the visual arts dominated the High Renaissance, literary figures also contributed to this era. From Classicism, the High Renaissance authors appropriated two of their chief aesthetic aims, secularism and idealism. Like their ancient predecessors, historians showed that contemporary events arose from human causes rather than from divine action—unmistakable evidence of a mounting secular spirit. Actually, secularism more deeply affected the writing of history than it did the arts and architecture, where church patronage and religious subjects still held sway. A rising secular consciousness can also be seen in the popular handbooks on manners that offered advice on how to become a perfect gentleman or lady. Although they have no counterpart in ancient literature, these books nevertheless have the Classical quality of treating their subject in idealized terms.

What distinguished the High Renaissance preoccupation with the Classical past from the Early Renaissance's renewed interest in ancient matters was largely a shift in creative sensibility. The Early Renaissance artists, in the course of growing away from the Late Gothic style, had invented new ways of recapturing the harmonious spirit of ancient art and architecture. The geniuses of the next generation, benefiting from the experiments of the Early Renaissance, succeeded in creating masterpieces of disciplined form and idealized beauty. The High Renaissance masters' superb confidence allowed them to produce works that were

Figure 12.4 *Pope Clement VII Besieged in Castel Sant' Angelo.* 1554. Engraving, 6⅙ × 9″. Kunsthalle, Hamburg. *This engraving shows the imperial army of Charles V besieging Castel Sant' Angelo, one of the pope's palaces, during the sack of Rome in 1527. The engraver's sympathies with the pope are revealed by the huge statues of St. Peter (with keys, on the right) and St. Paul (with sword, on the left), who look on disapprovingly. Pope Clement VII, imprisoned in his own fortress, peers down on the scene from a balcony at the center top.*

in harmony with themselves and the physical world—a hallmark of Classical art.

In spite of its brilliance, the High Renaissance existed for only a fleeting moment in the history of Western culture—from the French invasion of Italy in 1494 until the death of Raphael in 1520 (preceded by the death of Leonardo in 1519) (Timeline 12.1). In this era, the Renaissance popes spared no expense in their patronage of the arts and letters. After the disasters of the fourteenth century, the papacy seemed to have restored the church to the vitality that it had enjoyed in the High Middle Ages. In reality, however, the popes of the early sixteenth century presided over a shaky ecclesiastical foundation. To the north, in Germany, a theological storm was brewing that would eventually split Christendom and destroy the papacy's claim to rule over the Christian world. This religious crisis, coupled with increasing tendencies to exaggeration in High Renaissance art and with the sack of Rome in 1527, contributed to the development of Mannerism and its spread through Italy and later across western Europe (Figure 12.4).

Mannerist painters, sculptors, and architects moved away from two of the guiding principles of the High Renaissance: the imitation of nature and the devotion to Classical ideals. In contrast to the High Renaissance masters, Mannerist painters deliberately chose odd perspectives that called attention to the artists' technical effects and their individual points of view. Mannerist sculptors, rejecting idealism, turned and twisted the human figure into unusual and bizarre poses to express their own notions of beauty. Likewise, Mannerist architects toyed with the emotions and expectations of their audience by designing buildings that were intended to surprise. Behind the Mannerist aesthetic lay a questioning or even a denial of the inherent worth of human beings and a negative image of human nature, along with a sense of the growing instability of the world.

Literature

The leading writers of the High Renaissance in Italy drew their themes and values from the Greco-Roman classics. Their artistic vision sprang from the Classical virtue of *humanitas*—a term coined by Cicero in antiquity (see Chapter 5) that can be translated as "humanity," meaning the wisdom, humor, tolerance, and passion of the person of good sense. With some reservations, they also believed in Classicism's basic tenet that human nature is inherently rational and good. One of the finest expressions of Classicism in Renaissance literature was the poetry of the Venetian Gaspara Stampa, whose lyric verses, though devoted to obsessive sexual love, asserted the moral worth of the lover.

But even as High Renaissance literature was enjoying its brief reign, the Mannerist works of the Florentine author Niccolò Machiavelli began to appear, and at the heart of his thought is an anti-Classical spirit. Despite his education in Classicism and his strict rationalism, Machiavelli concluded that the human race was irremediably flawed. The contrast between the idealizing spirit of the High Renaissance and the antitraditionalist views of Mannerism can be clearly seen by placing the work of the diplomat and courtier Baldassare Castiglione beside that of Machiavelli. Each wrote a book that can fairly be described as a manual of behavior—but there the resemblance ends.

Gaspara Stampa Gaspara Stampa (about 1524–1554) embraced the classical tradition renewed by Petrarch in the 1300s; her work is thus typical of High Renaissance poetry. She adopted the Petrarchan sonnet as the preferred vehicle for her thoughts, and, like the earlier poet, she used her poetic gifts to investigate the byways of love. Rather than glorifying the distant beloved, however, she asserted the moral worth of the suffering lover, thus transforming the essentially male Petrarchan ideal into a female point of view. Stampa poured out her heart in her verses, confessing vulnerability and lamenting abandonment. She portrayed the abandoned one as superior to the unresponsive loved one—the same lesson taught by Socrates in one of Plato's dialogues (see Chapter 3).

That Gaspara Stampa became a poet at all is testimony to the changing mores of Renaissance Venice, a city fabled for its love of luxury and pleasure. Her autobiographical poetry grew out of her situation in Venice's marginal world of writers, musicians, and artists, including aristocrats and high officials of church and state, who were notably indifferent to Christian values. As a courtesan, or kept woman, she was a welcome member of this twilight world where sexuality was fused with art. Although she seems to have had several liaisons in her brief life, it was Count Collaltino di Collalto, a soldier, who won her heart. In time, Collaltino wearied of her, but Stampa transformed her hopeless love into some of the West's most touching poetry.

Castiglione The reputation of Castiglione [kahs-teel-YOH-nay] (1478–1529) rests on *The Courtier,* one of the most influential and famous books of the High Renaissance. Intended for Italian court society, *The Courtier* was published in 1528 and translated into most Western languages by the end of the century. It quickly became the bible of courteous behavior for Eu-

Figure 12.5 RAPHAEL. *Baldassare Castiglione.* 1514. Oil on canvas, 32¼ × 26½″. Louvre. *Castiglione was memorialized in this handsome portrait by Raphael, one of the great portrait painters of the High Renaissance. Raphael's debt to Leonardo's portrait style, especially as represented by the* Mona Lisa, *is evident in the half-length, seated pose and the direct gaze of the subject. Elegantly groomed and completely at ease, Castiglione appears here as the age's ideal courtier.*

rope's upper classes and remained so over the next two hundred years. Even today, at the beginning of the twenty-first century, Castiglione's rules for civilized behavior are still not completely outmoded.

A Mantuan by birth, Castiglione (Figure 12.5) based his guide to manners on life at the north Italian court of Urbino, where, between 1504 and 1517, he was the beneficiary of the patronage of its resident duke, Guidobaldo da Montefeltro (see Figure 11.2). Impressed by the graceful conversations of his fellow courtiers and most especially taken with the charms of Urbino's duchess, Elisabetta, Castiglione was moved to memorialize his experiences in writing. *The Courtier* is composed as a dialogue, a literary form originated by Plato and favored by Cicero. Castiglione's dialogue is set in Urbino over a period of four evenings and peopled with actual individuals for whom he invents urbane and witty conversations that suit their known characters. Despite this realistic touch, his book's overall tone is definitely idealistic and hence expressive of High Renaissance style.

Castiglione's idealism shines forth most clearly in the sections in which the invited company try to define the perfect courtier, or gentleman. Under Duchess Elisabetta's eye, the guests cannot agree on which aspect of the ideal gentleman's training should take precedence: education in the arts and humanities or skill in horsemanship and swordplay. Some claim that a gentleman should be first a man of letters as well as proficient in music, drawing, and dance. In contrast, others believe that a courtier's profession is first to be ready for war, and hence athletics should play the central role. At any rate, both sides agree that the ideal courtier should be proficient in each of these areas. A sign that the Renaissance had raised the status of painting and sculpture was the group's expectation that a gentleman should be knowledgeable about both of these art forms.

The Courtier also describes the perfect court lady. In the minds of the dialogue participants, the ideal lady is a civilizing influence on men, who would otherwise be crude. To that end, the perfect lady should be a consummate hostess, charming, witty, graceful, physically attractive, and utterly feminine. She ought to be well versed in the same areas as a man, except for athletics and the mastery of arms. With these social attributes, the cultivated lady can then bring out the best in a courtier. But she must not seem his inferior, for she contributes to society in her own way.

Castiglione's book turned away from medieval values and led his followers into the modern world. First, he argued that social relations between the sexes ought to be governed by Platonic love—a spiritual passion that surpassed physical conquest—and thus he rejected medieval courtly love and its adulterous focus. Second, he reasoned that women in society should be the educated equals of men, thereby sweeping away the barrier that had been erected when women were excluded from the medieval universities. In the short run, the impact of Castiglione's social rules was to keep women on a pedestal, as courtly love had done. But for the future, his advice allowed women to participate actively in every aspect of society and encouraged their education in much the same way as men's.

Machiavelli In contrast to Castiglione's optimism, the Florentine Machiavelli [mak-ee-uh-VEL-ee] (1469–1527) had a negative view of human nature and made human weakness the central message of his writings. If *The Courtier* seems to be taking place in a highly refined never-never land where decorum and gentility are the primary interests, Machiavelli returns the reader to the solid ground of political reality. His Mannerist cynicism about his fellow human beings sprang from a wounded idealism, for life had taught him that his early optimism was wrong. His varied works, by means of their frank assessments of the human condition, were meant to restore sanity to a world that he thought had gone mad.

Except for Martin Luther, Machiavelli left a stronger imprint on Western culture than any other figure who lived between 1494 and 1564. His most enduring contribution was *The Prince,* which inaugurated a revolution in political thought. Rejecting the medieval tradition of framing political discussions in Christian terms, Machiavelli treated the state as a human invention that ought not necessarily conform to religious or moral rules. He began the modern search for a science of politics that has absorbed political thinkers and policymakers ever since.

Machiavelli's career in sixteenth-century Italy, like that of many writers in antiquity, was split between a life of action and a life of the mind. Between 1498 and 1512, he served the newly reborn Florentine republic as a senior official and diplomat, learning statecraft firsthand. During these turbulent years, he was particularly impressed by the daring and unscrupulous Cesare Borgia, Pope Alexander VI's son. In 1512, after the fall of the Florentine republic to the resurgent Medici party, Machiavelli was imprisoned, tortured, and finally exiled to his family estate outside the city. There, as he recounts in one of his famous letters, he divided his time between idle games with the local farmers at a nearby inn and nightly communion with the best minds of antiquity in his study. From this background emerged in 1513 the small work known as *The Prince,* which circulated in manuscript until after his death. In 1532 it was finally published.

Machiavelli had several motives in writing this masterpiece. Despairing over Italy's dismemberment by

Figure 12.6 LEONARDO DA VINCI. *The Last Supper.* Restored. 1495–1498. Oil-tempera on wall, 13′ 10″ × 29′ 7½″. Refectory, Santa Maria delle Grazie, Milan. *Classical restraint is one of the defining characteristics of this High Renaissance masterpiece. Instead of overwhelming the viewer with distracting details, Leonardo reduces the objects to a minimum, from the austere room in which the meal is being celebrated to the simple articles on the dining table. The viewer's gaze is thereby held on the unfolding human drama rather than on secondary aspects of the scene.*

the French and the Spanish kings, he hoped the book would inspire an indigenous leader to unify the peninsula and drive out the foreigners. Enlightened by his personal experience in Florence's affairs, he wanted to capture in writing the truth of the politics to which he had been a witness. And, of equal importance, by dedicating *The Prince* to the restored Medici ruler, he hoped to regain employment in the Florentine state. Like other writers in this age, Machiavelli could not live by his wits but had to rely on secular or religious patronage.

Machiavelli's work failed to gain its immediate objectives: The Medici despot brushed it aside, and Italy remained fragmented until 1870. But as a work that exposed the ruthlessness needed to succeed in practical politics, *The Prince* was an instant, though controversial, success. The book was denounced by religious leaders for its amoral treatment of political power and read secretly by secular rulers for its sage advice. In the prevailing climate of opinion in the sixteenth century, which was still under the sway of Christian ideals, the name "Machiavelli" became synonymous with dishonesty and treachery, and the word **Machiavellianism** was coined to describe the amoral notion that "the end justifies any means."

From the modern perspective, this negative valuation of Machiavelli is both too simplistic and too harsh. Above all else he was a clear-eyed patriot who was anguished by the tragedy unfolding in Italy. *The Prince* describes the power politics that the new sovereign states of France and Spain were pursuing in Italian affairs. Machiavelli realized that the only way to rid Italy of foreigners was to adopt the methods of its successful foes. Seeing his countrymen as cowardly and greedy, he had no illusions that a popular uprising would spring up and drive out Italy's oppressors. Only a strong-willed monarch, not bound by a finicky moral code, could bring Italy back from political chaos.

The controversial heart of Machiavelli's political treatise was the section that advised the ruler on the best way to govern. He counseled the prince to practice conscious duplicity, since that was the only way to maintain power and to ensure peace—the two basic goals of any state. By appearing virtuous and upright while at the same time acting as the situation demanded, the prince could achieve these fundamental ends. Machiavelli's startling advice reflected both his involvement in Italian affairs and his own view of human nature.

Painting

In the arts, the period between 1494 and 1564 was preeminently an age of painting, though several sculptors and architects created major works in their respective fields. The Classical values of idealism, balance, and restraint were translated by High Renaissance painters into harmonious colors, naturally posed figures with serene faces, realistic space and perspectives, and perfectly proportioned human bodies. After 1520 Mannerist tendencies became more and more evident, reflected in abnormal subjects, contorted figures with emotionally expressive faces, and garish colors.

Leonardo da Vinci The inauguration of the High Renaissance in painting is usually dated from Leonardo's *The Last Supper,* which was completed between 1495 and 1498 (Figure 12.6). Painted for the Dominican friars of the church of Santa Maria delle Grazie in Milan, *The Last Supper* heralded the lucidity and harmony that were the essence of High Renaissance style. In executing the fresco, Leonardo unfortunately made use of a flawed technique, and the painting began to flake during his lifetime. Over the centuries, the work has been touched up frequently and restored seven times, with the most recent restoration completed in 1999. Nevertheless, enough of his noble intention is evident to ensure the reputation of *The Last Supper* as one of the best-known and most beloved paintings of Western art.

Leonardo's design for *The Last Supper* is highly idealized—a guiding principle of the High Renaissance. The fresco depicts the moment when Jesus says that one of the twelve disciples at the table will betray him. Ignoring the tradition that integrated this symbolic meal into an actual refectory, Leonardo separated the scene from its surroundings so that the figures would seem to hover over the heads of the clergy as they ate in their dining room. Idealism is also evident in Leonardo's straightforward perspective. The artist makes Jesus the focal center by framing him in the middle window and locating the vanishing point behind his head. In addition, the arrangement of the banqueting party—Jesus is flanked by six followers on either side—gives the painting a balanced effect. This harmonious composition breaks with the medieval custom of putting the traitor Judas on the opposite side of the table from the others.

A final idealistic touch may be seen in the way that Leonardo hides the face of Judas, the third figure on Jesus' right, in shadow while illuminating the other figures in bright light. Judas, though no longer seated apart from the rest, can still be readily identified, sitting cloaked in shadows, reaching for the bread with his left hand and clutching a bag of silver—symbolic of his treason—in the other hand. For generations, admirers have found Leonardo's fresco so natural and inevitable that it has become the standard version of this Christian subject.

Leonardo's setting and placement of the figures in *The Last Supper* are idealized, but his depiction of the individual figures is meant to convey the psychological truth about each of them. Jesus is portrayed with eyes cast down and arms outstretched in a gesture of resignation, while on either side a tumultuous scene erupts. As the disciples react to Jesus' charge of treason, Leonardo reveals the inner truth about each one through bodily gestures and facial expressions: Beneath the visual tumult, however, the artistic rules of the High Renaissance are firmly in place. Since neither biblical sources nor sacred tradition offered an ordering principle, Leonardo used mathematics to guide his arrangement of the disciples. He divides them into four groups of three figures; each set in turn is composed of two older men and a younger one. In his conception, not only does each figure respond individually, but also each interacts with other group members.

Besides mastering a narrative subject like *The Last Supper,* Leonardo also created a new type of portrait when he painted a half-length view of the seated *Mona Lisa* (Figure 12.7). As the fame of this work spread, other painters (and later, photographers) adopted Leonardo's half-length model as a basic artistic format for portraits. This painting, perhaps the most famous portrait in Western art, was commissioned by a wealthy Florentine merchant. Avoiding the directness of *The Last Supper,* Leonardo hints at the sitter's demure nature through her shy smile and the charmingly awkward gesture of having the fingers of her right hand caress her left arm. In her face, celebrated in song and legend, he blends the likeness of a real person with an everlasting ideal to create a miraculous image. Further heightening the painting's eternal quality, the craggy background isolates the figure in space and time, in much the same way that the grotto functioned in Leonardo's *Virgin of the Rocks* (see Figure 11.22). Finally, he enhances the *Mona Lisa*'s mystery by enveloping the subject in the smoky atmosphere called *sfumato*—made possible by the oil medium—that softens her delicate features and the landscape in the background.

During the High Renaissance, Leonardo's great works contributed to the cult of genius—the high regard, even reverence, that the age accorded to a few select artists, poets, and intellectuals. *The Last Supper* earned him great fame while he was alive. The history of the *Mona Lisa* was more complicated, since it was unseen while he lived and found among his effects when he died in 1519. After his death, as the *Mona Lisa* became widely known, first as a possession of the king of France and later as a jewel in the Louvre collection, Leonardo was elevated to membership among the immortals of Western art.

Michelangelo While Leonardo was working in Milan during most of the 1490s, Michelangelo Buonarroti [my-kuh-LAN-juh-lo bwo-nahr-ROH-tee] (1475–1564) was beginning a career that would propel him to the

Figure 12.7 LEONARDO DA VINCI. *Mona Lisa*. 1503. Oil on panel, 30¼ × 21″. Louvre. *Leonardo's* Mona Lisa, *a likeness of the wife of the merchant Giocondo, illustrates the new status of Italy's urban middle class. This class was beginning to take its social cues from the fashionable world of the courts, the milieu described by Castiglione. Leonardo treats his middle-class subject as a model court lady, imbuing her presence with calm seriousness and quiet dignity.*

forefront of first the Florentine and later the Roman Renaissance, making him the most formidable artist of the sixteenth century. Michelangelo's initial fame rested on his sculptural genius, which manifested itself at the age of thirteen when he was apprenticed to the Early Renaissance master Ghirlandaio and then, one year later, taken into the household of Lorenzo the Magnificent, the Medici ruler of Florence. In time, Michelangelo achieved greatness in painting and architecture as well as in sculpture, but he always remained a sculptor at heart.

Michelangelo's artistic credo was formed early, and he remained faithful to it over his long life. Sculpture, he believed, was the art form whereby human figures were liberated from the lifeless prison of their surrounding material. In this sense, he compared the sculptor's creativity with the activity of God—a notion that would have been judged blasphemous in prior Christian ages. Michelangelo himself, unlike the skeptical Leonardo, was a deeply pious man given to bouts of spiritual anxiety. His art constituted a form of divine worship.

Central to Michelangelo's artistic vision was his most celebrated image, the heroic nude male. Like the ancient Greek and Roman sculptors whose works he studied and admired, Michelangelo viewed the nude male form as a symbol of human dignity. In the High Renaissance, Michelangelo's nudes were based on Classical models, with robust bodies and serene faces. But in the 1530s, with the onset of Mannerism, the growing spiritual crisis in the church, and his own failing health, Michelangelo's depiction of the human figure changed. His later nudes had distorted body proportions and unusually expressive faces.

In 1508 Michelangelo was asked by Pope Julius II to decorate the Sistine Chapel ceiling. Michelangelo tried to avoid this commission, claiming that he was a sculptor and without expertise in frescoes, but the pope was unyielding in his insistence. The chapel had been built by Julius II's uncle, Pope Sixtus IV, in the late 1400s, and most of the walls had already been covered with frescoes. Michelangelo's frescoes were intended to bring the chapel's decorative plan closer to completion.

The challenge of painting the Sistine Chapel ceiling was enormous, for it was almost 70 feet from the floor, its sides were curved downward, necessitating numerous perspective changes, and its area covered some 5,800 square feet. Michelangelo overcame all these difficulties, teaching himself fresco technique and working for four years on scaffolding, to create one of the glories of the High Renaissance and unquestionably the greatest cycle of paintings in Western art (Figure 12.8).

Michelangelo, probably with the support of a papal adviser, designed a complex layout (Figure 12.9) for the ceiling frescoes that combined biblical narrative, theology, Neo-Platonist philosophy, and Classical allusions. In the ceiling's center, running from the altar to the rear of the chapel, he painted nine panels that illustrate the early history of the world, encompassing the creation of the universe, the fall of Adam and Eve, and episodes in the life of Noah. Framing each of these biblical scenes were nude youths, whose presence shows Michelangelo's belief that the male form is an expression of divine power.

On either side of the center panels, he depicted Hebrew prophets and pagan sibyls, or oracles—all foretelling the coming of Christ (Figure 12.10). The pagan sibyls represent the Neo-Platonist idea that God's word was revealed in the prophecies of pre-Christian seers. At the corners of the ceiling, he placed four Old Testament scenes of violence and death that had been allegorized as foreshadowing the coming of Christ. Michelangelo unified this complex of human and divine figures with an illusionistic architectural frame, and he used a plain background to make the figures stand out.

The most famous image from this vast work is a panel from the central section, *The Creation of Adam* (Figure 12.11). In the treatment of this episode from the book of Genesis, Michelangelo reduces the scene to a few details, in accordance with the High Renaissance love of simplicity. Adam, stretched out on a barely sketched bit of ground, seems to exist in some timeless space. Michelangelo depicts Adam as a pulsing, breathing human being. Such wondrous vitality in human flesh had not been seen in Western art since the vigorous nudes of ancient Greek art. In a bold move, Michelangelo ignored the Genesis story that told of God's molding Adam from dust. Instead, the artist paints Adam as half-awakened and reaching to God, who will implant a soul with his divine touch—an illustration of the Neo-Platonic idea of flesh yearning toward the spiritual.

By the 1530s, Michelangelo was painting in the Mannerist style, reflecting his disappointment with Florence's loss of freedom and his own spiritual torment. In this new style, he replaced his heroic vision with a fearful view of the world. A compelling example of this transformation is *The Last Judgment,* painted on the wall behind the Sistine Chapel's altar. This fresco conveys his own sense of sinfulness as well as humanity's future doom (Figure 12.12). Executed twenty-five years after the ceiling frescoes, *The Last Judgment,* with its images of justice and punishment, also reflects the crisis atmosphere of a Europe divided into militant Protestant and Catholic camps. In the center of the fresco, Michelangelo depicts Jesus as the divine and final judge, with right arm raised in a commanding gesture. At the bottom of the fresco, the open graves yield up the dead, and the saved and the damned (on Jesus' right and left, respectively) rise to meet their fate.

In this painting, Michelangelo abandons the architectural framework that had given order to the ceiling frescoes. Instead, the viewer is confronted with a chaotic surface on which a circle of bodies seems to swirl around the central image of Jesus. Michelangelo elongates the bodies and changes their proportions by reducing the size of the heads. There is no classical serenity here; each figure's countenance shows the anguish provoked by this dreaded moment. Faced with judgment, some gesture wildly while others look beseechingly to their Savior. In this Mannerist masterpiece, simplicity has been replaced by exuberant abundance, and order has given way to rich diversity.

Raphael The youngest of the trio of great High Renaissance painters is Raphael [RAFF-ee-uhl] Santi (1483–1520). Lacking Leonardo's scientific spirit and Michelangelo's brooding genius, Raphael nevertheless

Figure 12.8 MICHELANGELO. Sistine Chapel Ceiling. (Restored.) 1508–1512. Full ceiling 45 × 128′. The Vatican. *Michelangelo's knowledge of architecture prompted him to paint illusionistic niches for the Hebrew prophets and the pagan sibyls on either side of the nine central panels. Neo-Platonism inspired his use of triangles, circles, and squares, for these geometric shapes were believed to hold the key to the mystery of the universe. These various framing devices enabled him to give visual order to the more than three hundred figures in his monumental scheme.*

Figure 12.9 Plan of Ceiling Frescoes, Sistine Chapel. 1508–1512. *The paintings on the Sistine Chapel ceiling may be grouped as follows: (1) the central section, which presents the history of the world from the creation (called "The Separation of Light from the Darkness") through the "Drunkenness of Noah"; (2) the gallery of portraits on both sides and at either end, which depict biblical prophets and pagan oracles; and (3) the four corner panels depicting Jewish heroes and heroines who overcame difficulties to help their people survive.* ▶

Judith and Holofernes	Delphica	Josiah	Isaiah	Ezekias	Cumaea	Asa	Daniel	Jesse	Libyca	Moses and the Serpent of Brass
Zechariah	Drunkenness of Noah	The Flood	Sacrifice of Noah	Temptation and Expulsion	Creation of Eve	Creation of Adam	Separation of Land from Water	Creation of Sun, Moon, Plants	Separation of Light from Darkness	Jonah
David and Goliath	Joel	Zorobabel	Erythraea	Ozias	Ezekiel	Roboam	Persica	Salmon	Jeremiah	The Death of Haman

Figure 12.10 MICHELANGELO. *The Delphic Oracle* (Delphica). Detail of the Sistine Chapel ceiling. 1508–1512. The Vatican. *Michelangelo, despite his manifold gifts as painter, sculptor, architect, and poet, always thought of himself as a sculptor, and this is nowhere more evident than in his portrait of the Delphic Oracle from the Sistine Chapel ceiling frescoes. The oracle, or Delphica (her Latin name), is painted to resemble a sculpture, seated on an illusory throne and holding an open scroll, from whose reading she appears interrupted. Delphica's muscular body is a deviation from Classical sculptural ideals of feminine beauty and reflects, instead, Michelangelo's practice of using male models for female subjects. He was also fascinated by the anatomy of position, as in the effect on Delphica's body of her head turned to the left and of one arm upraised and the other at rest. In symbolic terms, Delphica, according to the ceiling's Neo-Platonic plan, represented the pagan Greek prophetess foretelling the coming of Jesus Christ.*

Figure 12.11 MICHELANGELO. *The Creation of Adam*. Detail (restored) of the Sistine Chapel ceiling. 1511. 9′ 5″ × 18′ 8″. The Vatican. *One of the most celebrated details of this fresco is the outstretched fingers of God and Adam that approach but do not touch. By means of this vivid symbol, Michelangelo suggests that a divine spark is about to pass from God into the body of Adam, electrifying it into the fullness of life. The image demonstrates the restraint characteristic of the High Renaissance style. The Vatican's ongoing restoration of the Sistine Chapel frescoes has revealed the brilliant colors of the original, apparent in this detail.*

Figure 12.12 MICHELANGELO. *The Last Judgment*. 1536–1541. 48 × 44′. Sistine Chapel, the Vatican. *This* Last Judgment *summarizes the anti-Classicism that was sweeping through the visual arts. Other painters studied this fresco for inspiration, borrowing its seemingly chaotic composition, its focus on large numbers of male nudes, and its use of bizarre perspective and odd postures as expressions of the Mannerist sensibility. This fresco was recently restored, its colors returned to the vivid primary colors of Michelangelo's original design and the draperies removed (they had been added during the Catholic Reformation).*

had such artistry that his graceful works expressed the ideals of this style better than did those of any other painter. Trained in Urbino, Raphael spent four years (from 1504 to 1508) in Florence, where he absorbed the local painting tradition, learning from the public works of both Leonardo and Michelangelo. Inspired by what he saw, Raphael developed his artistic ideal of well-ordered space in which human beauty and spatial harmony were given equal treatment.

Moving to Rome, Raphael had an abundance of patrons, especially the popes. At the heart of Raphael's success was his talent for blending the sacred and the secular, and in an age when a pope led troops into battle or went on hunting parties, this gift was appreciated and rewarded. Perhaps Raphael's most outstanding work in Rome was the cycle of paintings for the *stanze,* or rooms, of the Vatican apartment—one of the finest patronage plums of the High Renaissance. Commissioned by Julius II, the *stanze* frescoes show the same harmonization of Christianity and Classicism that Michelangelo brought to the Sistine Chapel ceiling.

Raphael's plan for the four walls of the Stanza della Segnatura in the papal chambers had as its subjects philosophy, poetry, theology, and law. Of these, the most famous is the fresco devoted to philosophy called *The School of Athens* (Figure 12.13). In this work, Raphael depicts a sober discussion among a group of ancient philosophers drawn from all periods. Following Leonardo's treatment of the disciples in *The Last Supper,* Raphael arranges the philosophers in groups, giving each scholar a characteristic gesture that reveals the essence of his thought. For example, Diogenes sprawls on the steps apart from the rest—a vivid symbol of the arch Cynic's contempt for his fellow man. In the right foreground, Euclid, the author of a standard text on geometry, illustrates the proof of one of his theorems. In his careful arrangement of this crowd scene, Raphael demonstrates that he is a master of ordered space.

The School of Athens has a majestic aura because of Raphael's adherence to Classical forms and ideas. The architectural setting, with its round arches, medallions, and coffered ceilings, is inspired by Classical architectural ruins and also perhaps by contemporary structures. Perfectly balanced, the scene is focused on Plato and Aristotle, who stand under the series of arches at the painting's center. Raphael reinforces their central position by placing the vanishing point just above and between their heads. The two thinkers' contrasting gestures symbolize the difference between their philosophies: Plato, on the left, points his finger skyward, suggesting the world of the Forms, or abstract thought, and Aristotle, on the right, motions toward the earth, indicating his more practical and empirical method. Raphael also uses these two thinkers as part of his ordering scheme to represent the division of philosophy into the arts and sciences. On Plato's side, the poetic

◄ **Figure 12.13** RAPHAEL. *The School of Athens.* 1510–1511. Fresco, 18 × 26′. Stanza della Segnatura, the Vatican. *Much of Raphael's success stemmed from the ease with which he assimilated the prevailing ideas of his age. For instance, the posture of the statue of Apollo in the wall niche on the left is probably derived from Michelangelo's* Dying Slave *(see Figure 12.1). For all his artistic borrowings, however, Raphael could be very generous, as indicated by the conspicuous way he highlights Michelangelo's presence in this fresco: The brooding genius sits alone in the foreground, lost in his thoughts and oblivious to the hubbub swirling about him.*

thinkers are gathered under the statue of Apollo, the Greek god of music and lyric verse; Aristotle's half includes the scientists under the statue of Athena, the Greek goddess of wisdom.

Of even greater fame than Raphael's narrative paintings are his portraits of the Virgin Mary. They set the standard for this form of portraiture with their exquisite sweetness and harmonious composition. The *Sistine Madonna* is probably the best known of this group (Figure 12.14). This painting shows Raphael at his best, borrowing from several sources yet creating his own convincing style. It is composed in the pyramid shape first popularized by Leonardo da Vinci (see Figure 11.22). The Virgin's head forms the apex of the pyramid, Pope Julius II (whose death the painting commemorates) stands bareheaded on her right, and St. Barbara, the patron saint of the arrival of death, on her left; the drape of the curtains underscores the pyramidal design. Raphael relieves the scene's somber mood by painting below the hovering figures two mischievous *putti,* or angels, who look upward, unimpressed with the scene-stealing baby Jesus. Raphael's assurance in handling these complex effects makes the *Sistine Madonna* a glowing masterpiece of the High Renaissance.

Figure 12.14 RAPHAEL. *Sistine Madonna.* 1513. Oil on canvas, 8′8½″ × 6′5″. Gemäldegalerie, Dresden. *Raphael's adherence to the rules of Classical art in the* Sistine Madonna *is nowhere more evident than in the painting's balanced composition. Bracketing the central image of the Virgin and child are a variety of pairings: At the top, two curtains are drawn open; toward the middle, two human figures kneel in prayer; and the open space between the draperies above is echoed by the two angels below. These artful pairings not only give visual variety to the simple scene but also outline and define the sacred space surrounding the Virgin and child.*

The Venetian School: Giorgione and Titian Venice maintained its autonomy during the High Renaissance both politically and culturally. Despite the artistic pull of the Roman and Florentine schools, the Venetian artists stayed true to their Byzantine-influenced tradition of sensual surfaces, rich colors, and theatrical lighting. The two greatest painters of the Venetian High Renaissance were Giorgione [jor-JO-na] (about 1477–1510), who was acknowledged to be Venice's premier artist at the end of his life, and Titian [TISH-uhn] (about 1488–1576), who in his later years was revered as Europe's supreme painter.

Little is known of Giorgione's life until the last years of his brief career. A student of Bellini, he won early fame, indicated by the rich private and public commissions he was awarded. Although only a few of his works survive, Giorgione's influence on the course of European art was substantial. His two major innovations, the female nude and the landscape, contributed to the growing secularization of European painting. These developments helped to make Venetian art distinctive from that of Rome and Florence.

The Tempest (Figure 12.15) is probably his best-known work. Breaking free of Bellini's influence, Giorgione created a dramatic landscape, framed on the left by a soldier and on the right by a partly clothed mother nursing a child, which did not allude to mythology, the Bible, or allegorical stories. While Bellini's *St. Francis in Ecstasy* (see Figure 11.23) made the saint the focus of the painting, in *The Tempest* the framing figures are overshadowed by the menacing storm. Thus, Giorgione's landscape, freed of storytelling elements, becomes the subject and should be appreciated on its own terms.

Titian's paintings were prized not only for their easy grace and natural lighting—characteristics of the Venetian High Renaissance—but also for the masterful

Figure 12.15 GIORGIONE. *The Tempest.* 1505. Oil on canvas, 31¼ × 28¾". Galleria dell'Accademia, Venice. *Giorgione's mysterious painting evokes the period—called an "anxious hush"—that sometimes attends the prelude to a violent thunderstorm He creates this tense mood through atmospheric effects that suggest a gathering storm: billowing clouds; a flash of lightning and its watery reflection; and, in particular, the stark color contrasts between the harshly lighted buildings and the somber hues of earth, sky, and river. The mood is also heightened by the presence of two vulnerable figures, especially the nursing mother who gazes quizzically at the viewer, about to be engulfed by the storm. The painting has a typical Venetian feature in its carefully rendered textures—flesh, cloth, wood, stone, and foliage. Giorgione's painting blazed the path for later artists, chiefly in northern Europe, who took the landscape as a subject.*

use of rich color to create dramatic effects (see Figure 12.3). Titian's adherence to the principles of High Renaissance style is evident in such narrative paintings as his *Presentation of the Virgin in the Temple,* a subject based on a legendary account of the life of Mary (Figure 12.16). Titian's careful arrangement of this complicated scene—with its landscape, classicizing architecture, and gathering of accessory figures—reflects his commitment to the principles of simplicity and naturalism. He conceived of the scene as a sweeping pageant, starting on the left with the pious procession and culminating with the young Mary, standing on the temple stairs in the middle right. Waiting to greet her at the head of the stairs are the high priest and other officials.

One deviation from Classical principles in this painting is the asymmetry of the closed architectural forms on the right set against the open landscape on the left. Instead of symmetry, Titian uses color as a unifying element. Cool colors, primarily blue, are prominent in the sky and the mountains on the left; warm

Figure 12.16 TITIAN. *Presentation of the Virgin in the Temple.* 1534–1538. 11′ 4″ × 25′ 5″. Originally in the Scuola Grande di Santa Maria della Carità, now part of the Accademia di Belle Arte, Venice. *Titian's painting is filled with symbols conveying Christian ideas. The Virgin is bathed in an oval of light of which she is the source; light is a traditional symbol of God's presence. On the left, the tall, thin pyramid alludes to Mary's divine status; it is a Renaissance symbol of Holy Wisdom, an attribute of the Virgin. The large cumulus cloud in the distance refers to the Holy Spirit, and the begging woman at the rear of the procession symbolizes Charity, or Almsgiving. Most complex of all are the two images in front of the stairway: the old egg seller who appears oblivious to the momentous event taking place above her head, and, to the right of the door, an ancient bust. Scholars identify these two images, respectively, with Judaism and paganism, both of which were to be superseded by the coming of Christ.*

Figure 12.17 PARMIGIANINO. *Madonna with the Long Neck.* 1534–1540. Oil on panel, 7′ 1″ × 4′ 4″. Uffizi Gallery, Florence. *This Madonna by Parmigianino is one of the landmark works in the rise of the Mannerist style. Ignoring Classical ideals, Parmigianino exaggerates the Virgin's body proportions, especially the slender hands and long neck, and elongates the body of the sleeping Jesus. This anti-Classical portrait was greatly at odds with the prevailing High Renaissance image of the Madonna established by Raphael.*

Figure 12.18 MICHELANGELO. *Pietà.* 1498–1499. Marble, ht. 5′ 8½″. St. Peter's, the Vatican. *This* Pietà *is the only one of Michelangelo's sculptures to be signed. Initially, it was exhibited without a signature, but, according to a legend, when Michelangelo overheard spectators attributing the statue to a rival sculptor, he carved his signature into the marble strap that crosses Mary's chest.*

colors, mainly brown and pink, are the primary hues of the buildings and the vestments of the temple leaders on the right. Because he used subtle modulations of color to create harmony in his works, Titian became the leading "colorist"—as opposed to those more concerned with form—to future generations of painters.

The School of Parma: Parmigianino Parma, in northern Italy, was another center of High Renaissance art, but the city's best-known artist is a founder of Mannerism, Parmigianino [pahr-mee-jah-NEE-noh] (1503–1540). The *Madonna with the Long Neck* shows Parmigianino's delight in ambiguity, distortion, and dissonance and his love of eccentric composition (Figure 12.17). Mary is portrayed with sloping shoulders and long arms in the manner of Botticelli, and her sensuous figure is not quite hidden under diaphanous draperies—a disturbing mix of sacred and profane love. A similar confusion exists in the depiction of the infant Christ: The bald baby Jesus appears more dead than alive, so that the subject invokes the Pietà image of the dead Christ stretched on his mother's lap along with the image of the Virgin and child. On the left, five figures stare in various directions. In the background, unfinished columns and an old man reading a scroll, perhaps an allusion to biblical prophecies of Jesus' birth, add to the feeling of multiple focuses and contradictory scales. Unlike the art of the High Renaissance, which offered readily understood subjects, this Mannerist painting, with its uneasy blend of religious piety and disguised sexuality, is enigmatic.

Sculpture

Michelangelo's art is as central to the High Renaissance style in sculpture as it is in painting. An early sculpture that helped to inaugurate this style was the *Pietà,* executed when he was twenty-one (Figure 12.18). The touching subject of the **Pietà**—Mary holding the body

Figure 12.19 MICHELANGELO. *David.* 1501–1504. Marble, ht. 14′ 3″. Accademia, Florence. *Michelangelo's colossal* David*—standing more than 14 feet tall—captures the balanced ideal of High Renaissance art. The "closed" right side with its tensed hanging arm echoes the right leg, which supports the figure's weight; in the same way, the "open" left side with its bent arm is the precise counterpart of the flexed left leg. Further tension arises from the contrast between David's steady stare and the readiness of the right fist, which holds the stone. Through these means, Michelangelo reinforces the image of a young man wavering between thought and action.*

PERSONAL PERSPECTIVE

Giorgio Vasari
Lives of the Most Eminent Painters, Sculptors, and Architects

Vasari (1511–1574) actually studied painting under Michelangelo, but he is known today for his accounts of the lives of Renaissance artists, sculptors, and architects. In this excerpt, he describes how Michelangelo executed his most famous work, the David.

Some of his [Michelangelo's] friends wrote to him from Florence urging him to return there as it seemed very probable that he would be able to obtain the block of marble that was standing in the Office of Works. Piero Soderini, who about that time was elected Gonfalonier for life [head of the Florentine republic], had often talked of handing it over to Leonardo da Vinci, but he was then arranging to give it to Andrea Contucci of Monte Sansovino, an accomplished sculptor who was very keen to have it. Now, although it seemed impossible to carve from the block a complete figure (and only Michelangelo was bold enough to try this without adding fresh pieces) Buonarroti had felt the desire to work on it many years before; and he tried to obtain it when he came back to Florence. The marble was eighteen feet high, but unfortunately an artist called Simone da Fiesole had started to carve a giant figure, and had bungled the work so badly that he had hacked a hole between the legs and left the block completely botched and misshapen. So the wardens of Santa Maria del Fiore (who were in charge of the undertaking) threw the block aside and it stayed abandoned for many years and seemed likely to remain so indefinitely. However, Michelangelo measured it again and calculated whether he could carve a satisfactory figure from the block by accommodating its attitude to the shape of the stone. Then he made up his mind to ask for it. Soderini and the wardens decided that they would let him have it, as being something of little value, and telling themselves that since the stone was of no use to their building, either botched as it was or broken up, whatever Michelangelo made would be worthwhile. So Michelangelo made a wax model of the young David with a sling in his hand; this was intended as a symbol of liberty for the Palace, signifying that just as David had protected his people and governed them justly, so whoever ruled Florence should vigorously defend the city and govern it with justice. He began work on the statue in the Office of Works of Santa Maria del Fiore, erecting a partition of planks and trestles around the marble; and working on it continuously he brought it to perfect completion, without letting anyone see it. . . .

When he saw the David in place Piero Soderini was delighted; but while Michelangelo was retouching it he remarked that he thought the nose was too thick. Michelangelo, noticing that the Gonfalonier was standing beneath the Giant and that from where he was he could not see the figure properly, to satisfy him climbed on the scaffolding by the shoulders, seized hold of a chisel in his left hand, together with some of the marble dust lying on the planks, and as he tapped lightly with the chisel let the dust fall little by little, without altering anything. Then he looked down at the Gonfalonier, who had stopped to watch, and said:

"Now look at it."

"Ah, that's much better," replied Soderini. "Now you've really brought it to life."

And then Michelangelo climbed down, feeling sorry for those critics who talk nonsense in the hope of appearing well informed.

of the dead Christ—struck a responsive chord in Michelangelo, for he created several sculptural variations on the Pietà theme during his lifetime.

The first *Pietà,* executed in 1498–1499, about the same time as Leonardo's *Last Supper,* shows Michelangelo already at the height of his creative powers. He has captured completely a bewildering sense of loss in his quiet rendering of Mary's suffering. Everything about the sculpture reinforces the somber subject: the superb modeling of Jesus' dead body, with its heavy head and dangling legs; Mary's outstretched gown, which serves as a shroud; and Mary's body, burdened by the weight of her son. Like some ancient funeral monument, which the *Pietà* brings to mind, this sculpture of Mary and Jesus overwhelms the viewer with its sorrowful but serene mood.

In 1501, two years after finishing the *Pietà,* Michelangelo was given the commission by the city of Florence for the sculpture that is generally recognized as his supreme masterpiece, the *David* (Figure 12.19). Michelangelo was eager for this commission because it allowed him to test himself against other great sculptors who had tackled this subject, such as Donatello in the Early Renaissance (see Figure 11.11). Moreover, Michelangelo, a great Florentine patriot, identified David with the aggressive spirit of his native city.

Figure 12.20 MICHELANGELO. *Pietà.* Before 1555. Marble, ht. 7′8″. Santa Maria del Fiore, Florence. *The rage that seemed to infuse Michelangelo's Mannerist vision in* The Last Judgment *appears purged in this* Pietà—*the work he was finishing when he died at the age of eighty-eight. Mannerist distortions are still present, particularly in the twisted body of the dead Christ and the implied downward motion of the entire ensemble. But the gentle faces suggest that serenity has been restored to Michelangelo's art.*

Michelangelo's *David* was instantly successful, and the republic of Florence adopted the statue as its civic symbol, placing the work in the open square before the Palazzo Vecchio, the town hall. Damage to the statue through weathering and local unrest caused the civic leaders eventually to house Michelangelo's most famous sculpture indoors, where it remains today.

Michelangelo's *David,* rather than imitating Donatello's partly clothed and somewhat effete version, portrays the young Jewish warrior as a nude, Classical hero. Taking a damaged and abandoned block of marble, Michelangelo carved the colossal *David* as a muscular adolescent with his weight gracefully balanced on the right leg, in Classical contrapposto. The *David* perfectly represents Michelangelo's conception of sculpture; imaging a human figure imprisoned inside marble, he simply used his chisel to set it free.

Michelangelo also made minor deviations from Classical principles in his rendition of David in the name of higher ideals, just as ancient artists had done. David's large hands, for example, are outside Classical proportions and suggest a youth who has yet to grow to his potential. And his furrowed brow violates the Classical ideal of serene faces but reflects his intense concentration.

Michelangelo's later sculpture is Mannerist in style, as are his later paintings. A second *Pietà* group—with Christ, Mary, Mary Magdalene, and Joseph of Arimathea—shows the change in his depiction of the human form (Figure 12.20). In this somber group, Michelangelo's anti-Classical spirit is paramount. Jesus' body is elongated and unnaturally twisted in death; the other figures, with great difficulty, struggle to support his dead weight. But rather than detracting from the sculpture's impact, the awkward body adds to the scene's emotional interest—an aim of Mannerist art, which did not trust the viewer to respond to more orderly images. Joseph, the rich man who, according to the Gospel, donated his own tomb to Jesus, has Michelangelo's face—a face that is more a death mask than a human countenance.

Architecture

The architectural heir to Alberti in the early sixteenth century was Donato Bramante [brah-MAHN-tay] (1444–1514), who became the moving force behind the High Renaissance in architecture. Trained as a painter, Bramante rejected the reigning building style, called **scenographic,** in which buildings are composed of discrete, individual units. Instead, by concentrating on space and volume, Bramante created an architecture that was unified in all its components and that followed the rules of the Classical orders.

The clearest surviving expression of Bramante's architectural genius is the Tempietto, or little temple, in Rome (Figure 12.21). This small structure was designed both as a church, seating ten worshipers, and as a building marking the site of the martyrdom of St. Peter. Copied from the circular temples of ancient Rome, this small domed building became the prototype of the central plan church popularized in the High Renaissance and later.

Bramante's design for the Tempietto sprang from ancient Classical principles. Foremost was his belief that architecture should appeal to human reason and that a building should present a severe appearance and not seek to please through specially planned effects. Further, he thought that a building should be unified like a piece of sculpture and that ornamentation should be restricted to a few architectural details.

In accordance with this artistic credo, the Tempietto functions like a work of sculpture; it is raised on a pedestal with steps leading up to its colonnaded porch. In the absence of sculptural decorations, the temple's

Figure 12.21 BRAMANTE. Tempietto. After 1502. Marble, ht. 46′; diameter of colonnade 29′. San Pietro in Montorio, Rome. *Bramante's Tempietto is the earliest surviving High Renaissance building and an exquisite example of this style. Fashioned from pure Classical forms, the building is almost devoid of decoration except for architectural features, and the separate parts—dome, cylindrical drum, and base—are brought into a harmonious whole. The only significant missing feature (since High Renaissance buildings were always planned in relation to their enveloping space) is the never-finished courtyard.*

Figure 12.22 MICHELANGELO. Dome of St. Peter's. View from the southwest. 1546–1564. (Completed by Giacomo della Porta, 1590.) Ht. of dome 452′. Rome. *Its harmonious design and its reliance on Classical forms made Michelangelo's dome an object of universal admiration when it was completed in 1590, after his death. From then to the present day, other architects have used his dome as a model, hoping to reproduce its Classical spirit.*

exterior is accented with architectural details: the columns; the **balustrade,** or rail with supporting posts; and the dome with barely visible ribs. The proportions of its various features, such as the ratio of column widths to column heights, were based on ancient mathematical formulas. Unfortunately for Bramante's final conception, the plan to integrate the small temple into a circular courtyard of a nearby church was never completed. Despite the absence of this crowning touch, the Tempietto is one of the jewels of the High Renaissance.

Bramante had been commissioned by Pope Julius II to rebuild St. Peter's Basilica, the world's most famous church, but he died before his plans could be carried out. The supervision of the rebuilding of St. Peter's fell to other architects; eventually Michelangelo, at the age of seventy-one, was given this vital task. From 1546 until his death in 1564, Michelangelo, among his other artistic tasks, was occupied with St. Peter's, especially with the construction of the dome. Over the years, other building projects had come his way, but nothing could compare with the significance of this one. Although the dome was completed after his death and slightly modified, it remains Michelangelo's outstanding architectural monument and a splendid climax to his career.

Michelangelo's sculptural approach to architecture was similar to that of Bramante. In an attempt to integrate the dome of St. Peter's with the rest of the existing structure, Michelangelo used double Corinthian columns as a unifying agent. Because the facade of St. Peter's was altered in the 1600s, Michelangelo's dome is best observed from the southwest (Figure 12.22). Beginning at ground level, the Corinthian order provides the artistic cement that pulls the entire building together. Sometimes as columns, sometimes as pilasters, and sometimes as ribs, the double Corinthian units move up the walls, eventually up the dome's drum, and up the dome itself.

This plan for St. Peter's shows that Michelangelo the architect differed from Michelangelo the painter and sculptor. In painting and sculpture, he had by the 1530s become a Mannerist in his use of exaggeration and expressive effects. But in architecture, he stayed faithful to the High Renaissance and its ideal of harmonious design.

The preeminent architect of the Mannerist style was Andrea di Pietro (1508–1580), known as Palladio [pah-LAHD-yo], whose base of operations was Vicenza, in northern Italy. The name Palladio derives from Pallas, a name for Athena, the goddess of wisdom. Palladio's artistic creed was rooted in Classicism, but his forte was the richly inventive way in which he could arrange the Classical elements of a building to guarantee surprise. He played with the effects of light and shadow, adding feature on top of feature, to create buildings that possess infinite variety in the midst of a certain decorative solemnity.

Palladio's most influential domestic design was the Villa Capra, more commonly called the Villa Rotonda because of its central circular area and covering dome (Figure 12.23). Inspired by ancient Roman farmhouses, the Villa Rotonda is a sixteenth-century country house

Figure 12.23 PALLADIO. Villa Rotonda (Villa Capra). Begun 1550. (Completed by Vincenzo Scamozzi.) Ht. of dome 70′, villa 80′ square. Vicenza. *Despite its harmonious proportions and Classical features, the Villa Rotonda belongs to the Mannerist style. Unlike High Renaissance buildings, which were designed to be integrated with their settings, this boxlike country house stands in an antagonistic relationship to its surrounding garden space. Furthermore, the Mannerist principle of elongation is apparent in its four long stairways. But the Villa Rotonda's most striking Mannerist feature is the surprise inherent in a plan that includes four identical porches.*

built of brick and faced with stucco and located on a rise overlooking Vicenza. A dome provides a central axis from which four symmetrical wings radiate. Each of the four wings in turn opens to the outdoors through an Ionic-style porch raised on a pedestal. The porticoes, or covered porches supported by columns, then lead to the ground level through deeply recessed stairways. Statues stand on the corners and peak of each of the four pediments, and others flank the four stairways.

Palladio's Mannerist spirit can be seen at work in the design of this building. Although the coldly formal porches are Classical in appearance, no Greek or Roman temple would have had four such identical porches, one on each side of the building (Figure 12.24). Palladio's design incorporates the unexpected and the contradictory within an apparently Classical structure.

Besides designing buildings, Palladio also wrote about architecture in his treatise *Quattro libri dell' architettura*, or *The Four Books of Architecture*. Through its

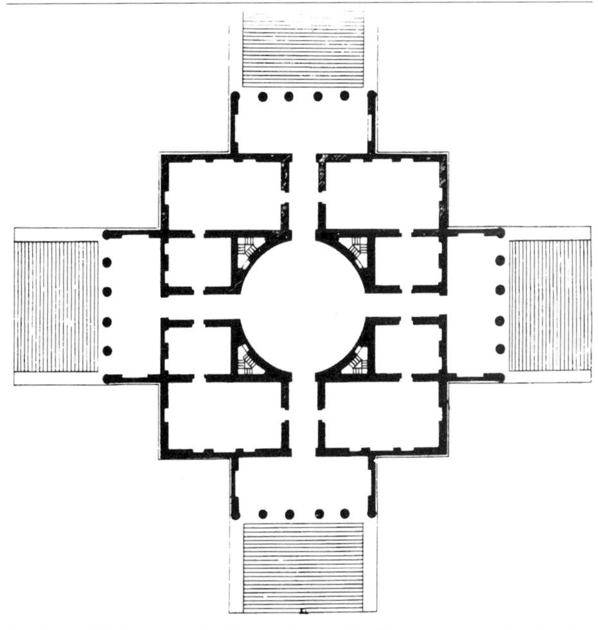

Figure 12.24 PALLADIO. Floor Plan of the Villa Rotonda. *Palladio designed the Villa Rotonda to further the social ambitions of its wealthy Venetian owner, so he made its most prominent interior feature a central circular area, or rotunda. Surmounted by a dome, this area was ideal for concerts, parties, and other entertainments. Palladio surrounded the rotunda with four identically shaped sets of rooms on two levels, where the family lived and guests were housed. Passageways led to the four porches, where villa residents could obtain relief from the summer's heat and enjoy diverting views of the surrounding countryside.*

English translation, this work gained wide currency and led to the vogue of Palladianism in the English-speaking world. English aristocrats in the eighteenth century commissioned country houses built on Palladian principles, as did plantation owners in America's antebellum South.

Music

No radical break separates the music of the High Renaissance from that of the Early Renaissance. Josquin des Prez, the leading composer of the dominant Franco-Netherlandish school, had brought to a climax the Early Renaissance style of music while he was employed in Italy by the popes and the local aristocrats (see Chapter 11). Josquin's sixteenth-century pieces, which consist chiefly of religious Masses and motets along with secular *chansons*, or songs, simply heightened the ideal already present in his earlier works: a sweet sound produced by multiple voices, usually two to six, singing *a cappella* and expressing the feelings described in the text. Despite his interest in music's emotional power, Josquin continued to subordinate the song to the words—thus reflecting the needs of the church, the foremost patron of the age. This balancing act between the music and the words, resulting in a clearly sung text, was also evidence of the Classical restraint of his High Renaissance style. A striking feature of this style was the rich multichoral effect produced when the singing group was subdivided into different combinations of voices.

Experimentation with choral effects was carried into the next generation by Adrian Willaert [VIL-art] (about 1490–1562), a member of the Netherlandish school and a disciple of Josquin's. After the death of his mentor, Willaert was probably Europe's most influential composer. He made his mark on musical history from his post as chapel master of the cathedral of St. Mark's in Venice, and he is considered the founder of the Venetian school of music. Taking advantage of St. Mark's two organs and the Venetian practice of blending instruments with voices, he wrote music for two choirs as well. By a variety of musical mechanisms, such as alternating and combining voices, contrasting soft and loud, and arranging echo effects, Willaert created beautiful and expressive sounds that were the ancestor of the splendid church concertos of the Baroque era. A benefit of Willaert's innovations was that the organ was released from its dependence on vocal music.

Except for the stylistic perfection achieved by Josquin and Willaert, the musical scene during this period witnessed only minor changes from that of the Early Renaissance. Instrumental music still played a secondary role to the human voice, though Josquin and Willaert composed a few pieces for specific instruments, either transposing melodies that originally had been intended for singers or adapting music forms from dance tunes.

The development that had the most promise for the future was the invention of families of instruments, ranging from the low bass to the high treble, which blended to make a pleasant sound (Figure 12.25). In most cases, these families, called **consorts,** consisted of either recorders or viols. The consorts represented the principle of the mixed instrumental ensemble, and from this beginning would emerge the orchestra. Recorders and viols could also be blended to make an agreeable sound; when human voices were added to the mixture, the conditions were ripe for opera.

Figure 12.25 HANS BURGKMAIR. *Maximilian with His Musicians.* Illustration from *Der Weisskunig.* Sixteenth century. Woodcut. Courtesy of the Metropolitan Museum of Art. Gift of William Loring Andrews, 1888. (88.1 fol. 142b). *This woodcut depicts the Holy Roman emperor Maximilian surrounded by his court musicians. Among the instruments being played are an organ, a flute, a harp, and a harpsichord-type instrument. On the tabletop at the right are a viol, recorders, and a cromorne (a curved instrument with a double reed), and piled together in the right foreground are a lute, drums, a kettledrum, and an ancestor of the slide trombone. Rounding out this musical scene is the quartet of singers in the upper left.*

The Legacy of the High Renaissance and Early Mannerism

From a contemporary perspective, the seventy-year period during which the High Renaissance and Early Mannerism flourished is the Golden Age of the West in certain artistic and humanistic areas. In the visual arts—painting, sculpture, and architecture—standards were set and indelible images created that have not been surpassed. In political theory, this age produced the Mannerist thinker Machiavelli, who is the founder of modern political thought.

Beyond those achievements, two other important steps were being taken on the road to the modern world. On a political level, the beginnings of the modern secular state may be seen in the changes taking place in France, Spain, and England. What was innovative, even revolutionary, for these countries in the early sixteenth century has become second nature to the states of the twenty-first century, both in the Western world and beyond. On a social level, a new code of behavior appeared in the Italian courts and was in time adopted throughout Europe. Not only did the rules of courtesy finally penetrate into the European aristocracy and alter their behavior, but also they eventually trickled down to the middle classes. By our day, the behavior of Castiglione's courtier and lady, though in diluted form, has become the model for all Western people with any shred of social ambition.

Another new idea was beginning to develop now as well. The Classical and the medieval worlds had praised what was corporate and public, in conformity with traditional, universal values. But in the 1500s a few artists and humanists, along with their patrons, began to revere what was individual and private. The supreme example of free expression and of the "cult of genius" in the High Renaissance was Leonardo da Vinci, whose encoded notebooks were meant for his personal use and not for general publication. Early Mannerism carried individual expression to extremes by finding merit in personal eccentricities and unrestrained behavior. That patrons supported the new works of these artists and humanists demonstrates the rise of the belief that free expression is both a social and a private good. Both the High Renaissance and Early Mannerism encouraged the daring idea of individualism and thereby introduced what has become a defining theme of Western culture.

KEY CULTURAL TERMS

High Renaissance
Mannerism
Machiavellianism
Pietà
scenographic
balustrade
consort

SUGGESTIONS FOR FURTHER READING

PRIMARY SOURCES

CASTIGLIONE, B. *The Book of the Courtier.* Translated by G. Bull. New York: Penguin, 1967. A flowing translation; includes a helpful introduction and descriptions of characters who participate in the conversations recorded by Castiglione; first published in 1528.

MACHIAVELLI, N. *The Prince.* Translated by G. Bull. New York: Penguin, 1971. The introduction covers Machiavelli's life and other writings to set the stage for this important political work; written in 1513.

SUGGESTIONS FOR LISTENING

WILLAERT, ADRIAN (about 1490–1562). Willaert is particularly noted for his motets, such as *Sub tuum praesidium,* which reflect the Renaissance humanist ideal of setting the words precisely to the music. His *Musica nova,* published in 1559 and including motets, madrigals, and instrumental music, illustrates the complex polyphony and sensuous sounds that made him a widely imitated composer in the second half of the sixteenth century.

1500
Albertus Durerus Noricus
ipsum me propriis sic effin-
gebam coloribus ætatis
anno XXVIII.

APPENDIX

Writing for the Humanities: Research Papers and Essay Examinations

The most important part of a man's education is the ability to discuss poetry intelligently.

—PROTAGORAS, FIFTH CENTURY B.C.

I would have the ideal courtier accomplished in those studies that are called the humanities.

—CASTIGLIONE, SIXTEENTH CENTURY A.D.

The idea of "writing for the humanities" has a long history, extending back over twenty-five centuries to ancient Greece. There, in fifth-century-B.C. Athens, the Sophists invented what we today call a "liberal education." These philosophers, who could be termed the first humanists, taught literature, the arts, music, and philosophy, along with what we call political science, anthropology, psychology, and history, to young Athenians, particularly those who hoped to play a leading role in politics. Not only did the Sophists demand that their students master a specific body of knowledge, but they also took care to instruct them in putting the humanistic disciplines into practice. They believed that individuals who had honed their analytical skills in the study of the humanities would be able to make wise judgments in private and public matters and to contribute to the community's political affairs.

The Sophists' educational ideal—training for good citizenship—was later adopted by the Romans, who transmitted it to the medieval West, where it became a guiding principle of university education down to the present. Today, college humanities professors give writing assignments because of their belief in the liberal education ideal as well as because of their conviction that writing, despite the spread of mass media technology, remains an essential tool of private and public communication and the hallmark of the truly educated person.

AN INTEGRATIVE APPROACH TO WRITING ABOUT THE HUMANITIES

In your study of the humanities, you will probably be given writing assignments that reflect the integrative approach of *The Western Humanities* (see the Introduction). This means that your papers and examinations will not be limited to a single humanistic discipline. Instead, you will be expected to draw information from all the humanities as well as other disciplines that help illuminate the historical setting, such as political science, economics, and psychology. For example, if you were assigned a term paper on some aspect of nineteenth-century Europe, you would have to consider the civilization as a whole, both its material and its cultural developments, and at the same time bring into clearer focus such specific factors as the impact of the ruling middle class on stylistic changes in the arts and literature or the influence of the rise of nationalism on cultural developments. This integrative approach to writing reinforces the message of the textbook—that the humanities are best understood when studied holistically in their historical setting.

GENERAL RULES FOR WRITING

Typically, writing assignments for a college-level humanities course are out-of-class research or term papers and in-class essay examinations. Regardless of the writing format, keep in mind three general rules. First, think of writing as an exercise in persuasion. Assume the teacher is unfamiliar with the topic, and write to demonstrate your mastery of the material. Second, follow basic principles of good grammar and punctuation. Some teachers will penalize you for mistakes in grammar and punctuation. Even if that is not the case, instructors cannot help but be skeptical of your learning if your writing is riddled with errors. Third, accept criticism and learn from past mistakes. Few individuals are born with a gift for writing; most have to struggle to reach a writing level that is personally satisfying. Even many authors, including famous ones, still find the writing process itself deeply frustrating. Like swimming, writing cannot be learned by talking about it; it is a skill you acquire through experience. Writing well requires patience, practice, and the willingness to learn from mistakes.

RESEARCH AND TERM PAPERS

Learning to write well starts with good work habits. Establish a quiet and comfortable work space, such as a table at a library, a desk in a dormitory room, a computer station, or a desk in an empty classroom. A computer is necessary, as is access to references, such as dictionaries, biographical books and the Internet. Develop an orderly schedule of study; plan ahead so things are not left until the last minute. Balancing work and play is a prelude to writing well, since you need brief respites from intense study to rest and refresh your mind. If you arm yourself with good work habits, you will be ready to face the challenge of writing a research or term paper.

Steps in Writing a Paper

The first step in writing a research or term paper is to pick a topic. Choose a topic that is interdisciplinary, involving at least two humanistic fields of study, such as the arts and literature of a specific historical period. Make sure your topic is manageable, neither too narrowly nor too broadly focused for your paper's length. Above all, select a topic that sparks some intellectual interest in you. Otherwise, your finished paper, even if it is carefully researched, may turn out to be uninspired and pedestrian. If you cannot find something that appeals to you on a list of suggested topics, consult with your instructor about a new subject satisfactory to both of you. As part of choosing a topic, you should also decide what approach to use in your paper, such as analytical, impressionistic, overview, or other. These approaches are described in detail in the next section.

The next step is to establish a basic bibliography. Scan your school library's holdings, either through the card catalogue system or by computer, to identify books and articles relevant to your topic. Once you have accumulated a bibliography of perhaps twenty to thirty sources, check the library stacks for additional books with appropriate call numbers that you may have overlooked in your search thus far. Then survey all these sources, treating them as background reading. At this preparatory level, take some notes on file cards and draw up a fuller list of secondary and, if needed, primary sources, such as diaries or documents, from the bibliographies in the books you are examining. After completing this survey, you are ready to make an outline.

The outline—whether for a five-page paper or a major research project—is mandatory. The outline is a memory device that serves several functions: It forces you to stick to the main topics, keep an accurate perspective, incorporate relevant information, follow the framing narrative, and proceed in an orderly fashion from the opening to the conclusion. Rework your outline until it includes all relevant points and ideas. Think of it as the framework on which you raise your final piece of writing, molded into a coherent shape.

With the outline set, you are ready to make a first draft of your paper. One approach is to expand each section of the outline into a paragraph, incorporating your ideas, the facts, your examples, and your references into a narrative. Be sure to relate each paragraph to both the preceding and the succeeding paragraphs, keeping in mind the overall organization of the paper. Each paragraph should begin with a topic sentence, include examples and references to support the topic, and conclude with a summary sentence or an idea that leads into the next paragraph. Strive to remain invisible in the narrative except where a personal observation might be helpful, and try to write in the active rather than the passive voice. At times you will have to search for the word or phrase that best expresses your thought, perhaps with the help of a dictionary or a thesaurus.

The next step is to edit and re-edit your work until it sounds right. When you reread a first draft, it usually sounds like a first draft, tentative and filled with half-finished thoughts. A good test of your first draft is to read it aloud, either to yourself or to a fellow student. You will be more likely to notice gaps in logic, infelicitous words or phrases, and obvious errors in fact when you hear them out loud. At this point your good work habits will pay off, because you should now have time to polish and improve the text. Don't forget to proof the papers for misspelled words, typographical errors, and misstatements. Attention to literary style and correctness makes the difference between a satisfactory and an excellent paper.

Especially critical in writing a research paper is the citation of sources, or footnotes. Instructors have their varying policies about the use of footnotes, but the following rules apply in most situations. Short quotations (that is, a phrase or one or two sentences) may be cited in the text if the proper recognition is given. Sources for longer quotations (that is, three or more sentences) should be placed in a footnote. A full bibliography listing all books consulted, whether cited directly in the paper or not, should be included at the end of the paper. Regardless of the style you use, make sure the citation forms for footnotes are consistent throughout the paper. You should purchase a writing and style manual; often the instructor will tell you which one to buy. Two of the most frequently used manuals are the following:

Gibaldi, J. *MLA Handbook for Writers of Research Papers.* 5th ed. New York: Modern Language Association of America, 1999.

Turabian, K. Revised by J. Grossman and A. Bennett. *Student's Guide to Writing College Papers.* 6th ed. Chicago: University of Chicago Press, 1996.

Types of Term Papers Assigned in the Humanities

In your humanities course you may be assigned any one of various types of research or term papers, reflecting the breadth of the disciplines that are covered under the humanities rubric. The most common types are the impressionistic paper, the analytical paper, the historical overview, and the integrative paper. Each type requires a different approach, even though the basic writing techniques described above are valid for all.

The Impressionistic Paper In this type of paper you offer a personal, though informed, reaction to some aspect of culture, such as the Gothic style or Post-Modernist art and architecture. Despite its focus on subjective feelings, the impressionistic paper nevertheless has to be documented with specific information, such as key historical events, biographical data, and details about particular works of art, literature, and music.

The Analytical Paper Here, you compare and contrast two creative works. More strictly scholarly than an impressionistic paper, the analytical research paper usually requires that you study both the original works and the leading secondary sources that provide critical commentaries. Using this approach, you might examine two works within the same historical period, such as Aeschylus's tragedy *Agamemnon* and Sophocles' tragedy *Oedipus Rex;* or works across historical periods, such as Aeschylus's tragedy *Agamemnon* and Shakespeare's tragedy *Hamlet;* or works across genres, such as Aeschylus's tragedy *Agamemnon* and Verdi's opera *Rigoletto.*

The Historical Overview In this type of paper you survey a specific time period to establish or explain a particular outcome, such as the prevailing worldview, or the leading cultural characteristics, or the impact of a particular social class. For example, if your topic were the role of aristocratic courts in the arts of the Italian Renaissance, you would have to survey fifteenth- and sixteenth-century Italian history and culture as well as the history of specific courts, such as that of the Medici in Florence and the Sforza in Milan.

The Integrative Paper This type of paper offers a versatile approach, since it allows for a combination of many topics. For example, if you wanted to write on Freudian theory and its application to culture, you would have to research the principles of Freudian theory and discuss Freudian interpretations of specific examples of art and literature. Or, if your topic were the Classical ideal of restraint in the late eighteenth century, you would have to research the period's music, art, literature, economic theory, and political theory.

ESSAY EXAMINATIONS

Besides research papers, you will also have to write essay tests in most college-level humanities courses. The purpose of such tests is to allow you to demonstrate how well you comprehend the course lectures and readings. To succeed on essay tests, you must learn to take notes efficiently during class and while reading out-of-class assignments and to analyze the assigned material in study sessions.

The following steps will help you write better essays on examinations:

1. Before the exam, master the assigned material through sound and productive work habits. This means keeping up with daily assignments, rereading and studying lecture notes, and reviewing study materials over a four- to five-day period before the test.
2. During the exam, read the entire test carefully before beginning to write. This will ensure that you understand all the questions and allow you to set a time frame for completing each section of the exam. If you are unsure about the meaning of a question, do not hesitate to ask the instructor for a clarification.
3. If there are choices, answer those questions first that seem the easiest. This rule simply reflects common sense; it is always best to lead with your strength.
4. Briefly outline the answer to each question. The outline should include an introduction, a section for each part of the question, and a conclusion. If time permits, it is also helpful to include the major points you want to cover, specific examples or illustrations, and ideas for topic sentences and conclusions of paragraphs. The outline will help you stick to the main topics and finish the exam on time. It can also trigger more ideas while you are writing it.
5. Follow sound writing rules in composing each essay. Begin each paragraph with a topic sentence; then give examples from a wide range of sources in the humanities to support the opening statement; and conclude with a paragraph that pulls the main arguments together. Take nothing for granted. Be concise but specific. Unless they are asked for, keep your own opinions to a bare minimum.
6. Review the exam. Before turning in the exam to the monitor, review your test to correct errors, give added examples, and clarify arguments, where needed. Always allow time to proofread an essay exam.

If you score poorly on the first essay exam in a course, consult with the instructor about how to improve your performance. But remember that improvement is seldom instantaneous and good writing is achieved only after practice. Old habits die hard; the only way to do better on papers and essay exams is to keep on writing.

Glossary

Italicized words within definitions are defined in their own glossary entries.

abstract art Art that presents a subjective view of the world—the artist's emotions or ideas—or art that presents *line*, *color*, or shape for its own sake.

Abstract Expressionism Also known as Action Painting, a nonrepresentational artistic style that flourished after World War II and was typified by randomness, spontaneity, and an attempt by the artist to interact emotionally with the work as it was created.

abstraction In Modern art, nonrepresentational or nonobjective forms in sculpture and painting that emphasize shapes, *lines*, and *colors* independent of the natural world.

a cappella [ah kuh-PEL-uh] From the Italian, "in chapel style"; music sung without instrumental accompaniment.

aesthete One who pursues and is devoted to the beautiful in art, music, and literature.

aisles The side passages in a church on either side of the central *nave*.

Alexandrianism [al-ig-ZAN-dree-an-ism] A literary style developed in the *Hellenistic* period, typically formal, artificial, and imitative of earlier Greek writing.

ambulatory [AM-bue-la-tor-e] A passageway for walking found in many religious structures, such as outdoors in a cloister or indoors around the *apse* or the *choir* of a church.

Anglicanism The doctrines and practices of the Church of England, which was established in the early sixteenth century under Henry VIII.

anthropomorphism [an-thro-po-MOR-fizm] The attributing of humanlike characteristics and traits to nonhuman things or powers, such as a deity.

apocalypse [uh-PAHK-uh-lips] In Jewish and early Christian thought, the expectation and hope of the coming of God and his final judgment; also closely identified with the last book of the New Testament, Revelation, in which many events are foretold, often in highly symbolic and imaginative terms.

apse In architecture, a large projection, usually rounded or semicircular, found in a *basilica*, usually in the east end; in Christian *basilicas*, the altar stood in this space.

arabesque [air-uh-BESK] Literally, "Arabian-like"; decorative lines, patterns, and designs, often floral, in Islamic works of art.

arcade A series of arches supported by *piers* or columns, usually serving as a passageway along a street or between buildings.

Archaic style The style in Greek sculpture, dating from the seventh century to 480 B.C., that was characterized by heavy Egyptian influence; dominated by the *kouros* and *kore* sculptural forms.

architrave [AHR-kuh-trayv] The part of the *entablature* that rests on the *capital* or column in Classical *post-beam-triangle construction*.

aria [AH-ree-uh] In music, an elaborate *melody* sung as a solo or sometimes a duet, usually in an *opera* or an *oratorio*, with an orchestral accompaniment.

art song *(lied)* In music, a *lyric* song with *melody* performed by a singer and instrumental accompaniment usually provided by piano; made popular by Schubert in the nineteenth century.

ashlar [ASH-luhr] A massive hewn or squared stone used in constructing a fortress, palace, or large building.

assemblage art An art form in which the artist mixes and/or assembles "found objects," such as scraps of paper, cloth, or junk, into a three-dimensional work and then adds paint or other decorations to it.

ataraxia [at-uh-RAK-see-uh] Greek, "calmness"; in *Hellenistic* philosophy, the state of desiring nothing.

atonality [ay-toe-NAL-uh-tee] In music, the absence of a *key* note or tonal center and the use of the *tones* of the chromatic *scale* impartially.

atrium [AY-tree-uhm] In Roman architecture, an open courtyard at the front of a house; in Christian *Romanesque* churches, an open court, usually colonnaded, in front of the main doors of the structure.

attic The topmost section or crown of an arch.

audience The group or person for whom a work of art, architecture, literature, drama, film, or music is intended.

aulos In music, a reed woodwind instrument similar to the oboe, usually played in pairs by one player as the double aulos; used in Greek music.

autarky [AW-tar-kee] Greek, "self-sufficient"; in *Hellenistic* thought, the state of being isolated and free from the demands of society.

avant-garde [a-vahn-GARD] French, "advanced guard"; writers, artists, and intellectuals who push their works and ideas ahead of more traditional groups and movements.

baldacchino [ball-duh-KEE-no] An ornamental structure in the shape of a canopy, supported by four columns, built over a church altar, and usually decorated with statues and other ornaments.

balustrade In architecture, a rail and the row of posts that support it, as along the edge of a staircase or around a dome.

baptistery A small, often octagonal structure, separated from the main church, where baptisms were performed.

bard A tribal poet-singer who composes and recites works, often of the *epic poetry* genre.

Baroque [buh-ROKE] The prevailing seventeenth-century artistic and cultural style, characterized by an emphasis on grandeur, opulence, expansiveness, and complexity.

barrel vault A ceiling or *vault* made of sets of arches placed side by side and joined together.

basilica [buh-SILL-ih-kuh] A rectangular structure that included an *apse* at one or both ends; originally a Roman building used for public purposes, later taken over by the Christians for worship. The floor plan became the basis of nearly all early Christian churches.

bay A four-cornered unit of architectural space, often used to identify a section of the *nave* in a *Romanesque* or *Gothic* church.

bel canto [bell KAHN-toe] Italian, "beautiful singing"; a style of singing characteristic of seventeenth-century Italian *opera* stressing ease, purity, and evenness of tone along with precise vocal technique.

blank verse Unrhymed iambic pentameter (lines with five feet, or units, each consisting of an unaccented and an accented syllable).

blind arcade A decorative architectural design that gives the appearance of an open *arcade* or window but is filled in with some type of building material such as stone or brick.

blues A type of music that emerged around 1900 from the rural African American culture, was originally based on work songs and religious spirituals, and expressed feelings of loneliness and hopelessness.

Byzantine style [BIZ-uhn-teen] In painting, decoration, and architecture, a style blending Greco-Roman and oriental components into a highly stylized art form that glorified Christianity, notably in domed churches adorned with *mosaics* and polished marble; associated with the culture of the Eastern Roman Empire from about 500 until 1453.

Cajun A descendant of French pioneers, chiefly in Louisiana, who in 1755 chose to leave Acadia (modern Nova Scotia) rather than live under the British Crown.

calligraphy Penmanship or handwriting, usually done with flowing lines, used as a decoration or as an enhancement of a written work; found in Islamic and Christian writings.

Calvinism The theological beliefs and rituals set forth in and derived from John Calvin's writings, placing emphasis on the power of God and the weakness of human beings.

campanile From the Latin "campana," bell; a bell tower, especially one near but not attached to a church; an Italian invention.

canon A set of principles or rules that are accepted as true and authoritative for the various arts or fields of study; in architecture, it refers to the standards of proportion; in painting, the prescribed ways of painting certain objects; in sculpture, the ideal proportions of the human body; in literature, the authentic list of an author's works; in religion, the approved and authoritative writings that are accepted as divinely inspired, such as the *Scriptures* for Jews and Christians; and in religious and other contexts, certain prescribed rituals or official rules and laws. In music, a canon is a *composition* in which a *melody* sung by one voice is repeated exactly by successive voices as they enter.

canzone [kan-ZOH-nee] Latin, "chant"; a type of love poem popular in southern France during the twelfth and thirteenth centuries.

capital In architecture, the upper or crowning part of a column, on which the *entablature* rests.

cathedral The church of a bishop that houses a cathedra, or throne symbolizing the seat of power in his administrative district, known as a diocese.

cella [SELL-uh] The inner sanctum or walled room of a *Classical* temple where sacred statues were housed.

chanson [shahn-SAWN] French, "song"; a fourteenth- to sixteenth-century French song for one or more voices, often with instrumental accompaniment. Similar to a *madrigal.*

chanson de geste [shahn-SAWN duh zhest] A poem of brave deeds in the *epic* form developed in France during the eleventh century, usually to be sung.

character A person in a story or play; someone who acts out or is affected by the *plot.*

chiaroscuro [key-ahr-uh-SKOOR-oh] In painting, the use of dark and light contrast to create the effect of modeling of a figure or object.

chivalric code The rules of conduct, probably idealized, that governed the social roles and duties of aristocrats in the Middle Ages.

chivalric novel A late medieval literary form that presented romantic stories of knights and their ladies; the dominant literary form in Spain from the Late Middle Ages into the Renaissance.

choir In architecture, that part of a *Gothic* church in which the service was sung by singers or clergy, located in the east end beyond the *transept;* also, the group of trained singers who sat in the choir area.

chorus In Greek drama, a group of performers who sang and danced in both *tragedies* and *comedies,* often commenting on the action; in later times, a group of singers who performed with or without instrumental accompaniment.

Christian humanism An intellectual movement in sixteenth-century northern Europe that sought to use the ideals of the *Classical* world, the tools of ancient learning, and the morals of the Christian *Scriptures* to rid the church of worldliness and scandal.

chthonian deities [THOE-nee-uhn] In Greek religion, earth gods and goddesses who lived underground and were usually associated with peasants and their religious beliefs.

civilization The way humans live in a complex political, economic, and social structure, usually in an urban environment, with some development in technology, literature, and art.

Classic, or **Classical** Having the forms, values, or standards embodied in the art and literature of Greek and Roman *civilization;* in music, an eighteenth-century style characterized by simplicity, proportion, and an emphasis on structure.

Classical Baroque style A secular variation of the *Baroque* style that was identified with French kings and artists, was rooted in *Classical* ideals, and was used mainly to emphasize the power and grandeur of the monarchy.

Classicism A set of aesthetic principles found in Greek and Roman art and literature emphasizing the search for perfection or ideal forms.

clavier [French, KLAH-vyay; German, KLAH-veer] Any musical instrument having a keyboard, such as a piano, organ, or harpsichord; the term came into general usage with the popularity of Bach's set of studies entitled *The Well-Tempered Clavier.*

clerestory windows [KLEER-stor-ee] A row of windows set along the upper part of a wall, especially in a church.

collage [koh-LAHZH] From the French "coller," to glue, a type of art, introduced by Picasso, in which bits and pieces of materials such as paper or cloth are glued to a painted surface.

color Use of the hues found in nature to enhance or distort the sense of reality in a visual image.

comedy A literary genre characterized by a story with a complicated and amusing *plot* that ends with a happy and peaceful resolution of all conflicts.

comedy of manners A humorous play that focuses on the way people in a particular social group or class interact with one another, especially regarding fashions and manners.

composition The arrangement of constituent elements in an artistic work; in music, composition also refers to the process of creating the work.

concerto [kuhn-CHER-toe] In music, a composition for one or more soloists and *orchestra,* usually in a symphonic *form* with three contrasting movements.

consort A set of musical instruments in the same family, ranging from bass to soprano; also, a group of musicians who entertain by singing or playing instruments.

Constructivism A movement in nonobjective art, originating in the Soviet Union and flourishing from 1917 to 1922 and concerned with planes and volumes as expressed in modern industrial materials such as glass and plastic.

content The subject matter of an artistic work.

context The setting in which an artistic work arose, its own time and place. Context includes the political, economic, social, and cultural conditions of the time; it can also include the personal circumstances of the artist's life.

contrapposto [kon-truh-POH-stoh] In sculpture and painting, the placement of the human figure so the weight is more on one leg than the other and the shoulders and chest are turned in the opposite direction from the hips and legs.

convention An agreed-upon practice, device, technique, or form.

Corinthian The third Greek architectural order, in which temple columns are slender and *fluted,* sit on a base, and have *capitals* shaped like inverted bells and decorated with carvings representing the leaves of the acanthus bush; this style was popular in *Hellenistic* times and widely adopted by the Romans.

cornice In architecture, the crowning, projecting part of the *entablature.*

Counter-Reformation A late-sixteenth-century movement in the Catholic Church aimed at reestablishing its basic beliefs, reforming its organizational structure, and reasserting itself as the authoritative voice of Christianity.

covenant In Judaism and Christianity, a solemn and binding agreement or contract between God and his followers.

Creole An ambiguous term, sometimes referring to descendants of French and Spanish settlers of the southern United States, especially Louisiana; used by Kate Chopin in her short stories and novels in this sense. In other contexts, *Creole* can refer either to blacks born in the Western Hemisphere (as distinguished from blacks born in Africa) or to residents of the American Gulf States of mixed black, Spanish, and Portuguese ancestry.

cruciform [KROO-suh-form] Cross-shaped; used to describe the standard floor plan of a church.

Cubism A style of painting introduced by Picasso and Braque in which objects are broken up into fragments and patterns of geometric structures and depicted on the flat canvas as if from several points of view.

culture The sum of human endeavors, including the basic political, economic, and social institutions and the values, beliefs, and arts of those who share them.

cuneiform [kue-NEE-uh-form] Wedge-shaped characters used in writing on tablets found in Mesopotamia and other ancient *civilizations.*

Cynicism A *Hellenistic* philosophy that denounced society and its institutions as artificial and called on the individual to strive for *autarky.*

Dada [DAH-dah] An early-twentieth-century artistic movement, named after a nonsense word that was rooted in a love of play, encouraged deliberately irrational acts, and exhibited contempt for all traditions.

Decadence A late-nineteenth-century literary style concerned with morbid and artificial subjects and themes.

deductive reasoning The process of reasoning from the general to the particular—that is, beginning with an accepted premise or first statement and, by steps of logical reasoning or inference, reaching a conclusion that necessarily follows from the premise.

Deism [DEE-iz-uhm] A religion based on the idea that the universe was created by God and then left to run according to *natural laws,* without divine interference; formulated and practiced in the eighteenth century.

de Stijl [duh STILE] Dutch, "the style"; an artistic movement associated with a group of early-twentieth-century Dutch painters who used rectangular forms and primary colors in their works and who believed that art should have spiritual values and a social purpose.

devotio moderna [de-VO-tee-oh mo-DER-nuh] The "new devotion" of late medieval Christianity that emphasized piety and discipline as practiced by lay religious communities located primarily in northern Europe.

Diaspora [dye-AS-puhr-uh] From the Greek, "to scatter"; the dispersion of the Jews from their homeland in ancient Palestine, a process that began with the Babylonian Captivity in the sixth century B.C. and continued over the centuries.

Dionysia [DYE-uh-NYSH-ee-ah] Any of the religious festivals held in ancient Athens honoring Dionysus, the god of wine; especially the Great Dionysia, celebrated in late winter and early spring in which *tragedy* is thought to have originated.

Doric The simplest and oldest of the Greek architectural orders, in which temple columns have undecorated *capitals* and rest directly on the *stylobate.*

drypoint In art, the technique of incising an image, using a sharp, pointed instrument, onto a metal surface or block used for printing. Also, the print made from the technique.

Early Renaissance style A style inspired by *Classical* rather than *Gothic* models that arose among Florentine architects, sculptors, and painters in the late fourteenth and early fifteenth century.

empiricism The process of collecting data, making observations, carrying out experiments based on the collected data and observations, and reaching a conclusion.

engraving In art, the technique of carving, cutting, or etching an image with a sharp, pointed instrument onto a metal surface overlaid with wax, dipping the surface in acid, and then printing it. Also, the print made from the technique.

Enlightenment The eighteenth-century philosophical and cultural movement marked by the application of reason to human problems and affairs, a questioning of traditional beliefs and ideas, and an optimistic faith in unlimited progress for humanity, particularly through education.

entablature [en-TAB-luh-choor] In architecture, the part of the temple above the columns and below the roof, which, in *Classical* temples, included the *architrave,* the *frieze,* and the *pediment.*

entasis [EN-ta-sis] In architecture, convex curving or enlarging of the central part of a column to correct the optical illusion that the column is too thin.

epic A poem, novel, or film that recounts at length the life of a hero or the history of a people.

epic poetry Narrative poetry, usually told or written in an elevated style, that recounts the life of a hero.

epic theater A type of theater, invented by Brecht, in which major social issues are dramatized with outlandish props and jarring dialogue and effects, all designed to alienate middle-class audiences and force them to think seriously about the problems raised in the plays.

Epicureanism [ep-i-kyoo-REE-uh-niz-uhm] A *Hellenistic* philosophy, founded by Epicurus and later expounded by the Roman Lucretius, that made its highest goals the development of the mind and an existence free from the demands of everyday life.

eschatology [es-kuh-TAHL-uh-jee] The concern with final events or the end of the world, a belief popular in Jewish and early Christian communities and linked to the concept of the coming of a *Messiah.*

evangelists From the Greek *evangelion,* a term generally used for those who preach the Christian religion; more specifically, the four evangelists, Matthew, Mark, Luke, and John, who wrote about Jesus Christ soon after his death in the first four books of the New Testament.

evolution The theory, set forth in the nineteenth century by Charles Darwin, that plants and animals, including humans, evolved over millions of years from simpler forms through a process of natural selection.

existentialism [eg-zi-STEN-shuh-liz-uhm] A twentieth-century philosophy focusing on the precarious nature of human existence, with its uncertainty, anxiety, and ultimate death, as well as on individual freedom and responsibility and the possibilities for human creativity and authenticity.

Expressionism A late-nineteenth-century literary and artistic movement characterized by the expression of highly personal feelings rather than of objective reality.

fan vault A decorative pattern of *vault* ribs that arch out or radiate from a central point on the ceiling; popular in English *Perpendicular* architecture.

Faustian [FAU-stee-uhn] Resembling the character Faust in Goethe's most famous work, in being spiritually tormented, insatiable for knowledge and experience, or willing to pay any price, including personal and spiritual integrity, to gain a desired end.

Fauvism [FOH-viz-uhm] From the French "fauve," wild beast; an early-twentieth-century art movement led by Matisse and favoring exotic colors and disjointed shapes.

fête galante [fet gah-LAHNN] In *Rococo* painting, the *theme* or scene of aristocrats being entertained or simply enjoying their leisure and other worldly pleasures.

Flamboyant style [flam-BOY-uhnt] A Late French *Gothic* architectural style of elaborate decorations and ornamentation that produce a flamelike effect.

Florid Baroque style A variation of the *Baroque* style specifically identified with the Catholic Church's patronage of the arts and used to glorify its beliefs.

fluting Decorative vertical grooves carved in a column.

flying buttress An external masonry support, found primarily in *Gothic* churches, that carries the thrust of the ceiling or *vault* away from the upper walls of the building to an external vertical column.

forms In music, particular structures or arrangements of elements, such as *symphonies*, songs, concerts, and *operas*.

forum In Rome and many Roman towns, the public place, located in the center of the town, where people gathered to socialize, transact business, and administer the government.

Fourth Century style The sculptural style characteristic of the last phase of the *Hellenic* period, when new interpretations of beauty and movement were adopted.

fresco A painting done on wet or dry plaster that becomes part of the plastered wall.

friars Members of a thirteenth-century mendicant (begging) monastic order.

frieze [FREEZ] A band of painted designs or sculptured figures placed on walls; also, the central portion of a temple's *entablature* just above the *architrave*.

fugue [fewg] In music, a *composition* for several instruments in which a *theme* is introduced by one instrument and then repeated by each successively entering instrument so that a complicated interweaving of themes, variations, imitations, and echoes results; this compositional technique began in the fifteenth century and reached its zenith in the *Baroque* period in works by Bach.

gallery In architecture, a long, narrow passageway or corridor, usually found in churches and located above the *aisles*, and often with openings that permit viewing from above into the *nave*.

gargoyle [GAHR-goil] In architecture, a water spout in the form of a grotesque animal or human, carved from stone, placed on the edge of a roof.

genre [ZHON-ruh] From the French, "a kind, a type, or a class"; a category of artistic, musical, or literary composition, characterized by a particular *style*, *form*, or *content*.

genre subject In art, a scene or a person from everyday life, depicted realistically and without religious or symbolic significance.

geocentrism The belief that the earth is the center of the universe and that the sun, planets, and stars revolve around it.

glissando [gle-SAHN-doe] (plural, **glissandi**) In music, the blending of one *tone* into the next in scalelike passages that may be ascending or descending in character.

goliards [GOAL-yuhrds] Medieval roaming poets or scholars who traveled about reciting poems on topics ranging from moral lessons to the pains of love.

Gospels The first four books of the New Testament (Matthew, Mark, Luke, and John) that record the life and sayings of Jesus Christ; the word itself, from Old English, means good news or good tales.

Gothic style A *style* of architecture, usually associated with churches, that originated in northern France and whose three phases—Early, High, and Late—lasted from the twelfth to the sixteenth century. Emerging from the *Romanesque* style, Gothic is identified by pointed arches, *ribbed vaults*, *stained-glass* windows, *flying buttresses*, and carvings on the exterior.

Greek cross A cross in which all the arms are of equal length; the shape used as a floor plan in many Greek or Eastern Orthodox churches.

Gregorian chant A style of *monophonic* church music sung in unison and without instrumental accompaniment and used in the *liturgy*; named for Pope Gregory I (590–604).

groined vault, or **cross vault** A ceiling or *vault* created when two *barrel vaults*, set at right angles, intersect.

harmony The simultaneous combination of two or more *tones*, producing a chord; generally, the chordal characteristics of a work and the way chords interact.

heliocentrism The belief that the sun is the center of the universe and that the earth and the other planets revolve around it.

Hellenic [hell-LENN-ik] Relating to the time period in Greek civilization from 480 to 323 B.C., when the most influential Greek artists, playwrights, and philosophers, such as Praxiteles, Sophocles, and Plato, created their greatest works; associated with the *Classical* style.

Hellenistic [hell-uh-NIS-tik] Relating to the time period from about 323 to 31 B.C., when Greek and oriental or Middle Eastern cultures and institutions intermingled to create a heterogeneous and cosmopolitan *civilization*.

hieroglyphs [HI-uhr-uh-glifs] Pictorial characters used in Egyptian writing, which is known as hieroglyphics.

High Classical style The *style* in Greek sculpture associated with the ideal physical form and perfected during the zenith of the Athenian Empire, about 450–400 B.C.

higher criticism A rational approach to Bible study, developed in German Protestant circles in the nineteenth century, that treated the biblical *Scriptures* as literature and subjected them to close scrutiny, testing their literary history, authorship, and meaning.

High Renaissance The period from about 1495 to 1520, often associated with the patronage of the popes in Rome, when the most influential artists and writers of the *Renaissance*, including Michelangelo, Raphael, Leonardo da Vinci, and Machiavelli, were producing their greatest works.

high tech In architecture, a *style* that uses obvious industrial design elements with exposed parts serving as decorations.

Homeric epithet A recurring nickname, such as "Ox-eyed Hera," used in Homer's *Iliad* or *Odyssey*.

hubris [HYOO-bris] In Greek thought, human pride or arrogance that leads an individual to challenge the gods, usually provoking divine retribution.

humanism An attitude that is concerned with humanity, its achievements, and its potential; the study of the *humanities*; in the *Renaissance*, identified with *studia humanitatis*.

humanities In the nineteenth century, the study of Greek and Roman languages and literature; later set off from the sciences and expanded to include the works of all Western peoples in the arts, literature, music, philosophy, and sometimes history and religion; in *Post-Modernism* extended to a global dimension.

hymn From the Greek and Latin, "ode of praise of gods or heroes"; a song of praise or thanksgiving to God or the gods, performed both with and without instrumental accompaniment.

idealism in Plato's philosophy, the theory that reality and ultimate truth are to be found not in the material world but in the spiritual realm.

idée fixe [ee-DAY FEEX] French, "fixed idea"; in music, a recurring musical *theme* that is associated with a person or a concept.

ideogram [ID-e-uh-gram] A picture drawn to represent an idea or a concept.

idyll A relatively short poem that focuses on events and themes of everyday life, such as family, love, and religion; popular in the *Hellenistic Age* and a standard form that has been periodically revived in Western literature throughout the centuries.

illuminated manuscript A richly decorated book, painted with brilliant colors and gold leaf, usually of sacred writings; popular in the West in the Middle Ages.

illusionism The use of painting techniques in *Florid Baroque* art to create the appearance that decorated areas are part of the surrounding architecture, usually employed in ceiling decorations.

impasto [ihm-PAHS-toe] In painting, the application of thick layers of pigment.

Impressionism In painting, a *style* introduced in the 1870s, marked by an attempt to catch spontaneous impressions, often involving the play of sunlight on ordinary events and scenes observed outdoors; in music, a style of *composition* designed to create a vague and dreamy mood through gliding melodies and shimmering tone colors.

impressionistic In art, relating to the representation of a scene using the simplest details to create an illusion of reality by evoking subjective impressions rather than aiming for a totally realistic effect; characterized by images that are insubstantial and barely sketched in.

inductive reasoning The process of reasoning from particulars to the general or from single parts to the whole and/or final conclusion.

installation art A boundary-challenging type of art born in the 1960s that creates architectural tableaux, using objects drawn from and making references to artistic sources (such as music, painting, sculpture, and theater) and the workaday world (such as everyday tasks, media images, and foodstuffs) and that may include a human presence. Associated with the work of Ann Hamilton.

International style In twentieth-century architecture, a *style* and method of construction that capitalized on modern materials, such as ferro-concrete, glass, and steel, and that produced the popular "glass box" skyscrapers and variously shaped private houses.

Ionic The Greek architectural order, developed in Ionia, in which columns are slender, sit on a base, and have *capitals* decorated with scrolls.

Italo-Byzantine style [ih-TAL-o-BIZ-uhn-teen] The *style* of Italian *Gothic* painting that reflected the influence of *Byzantine* paintings, *mosaics,* and icons.

jazz A type of music, instrumental and vocal, originating in the African American community and rooted in African, African American, and Western musical forms and traditions.

Jesuits [JEZH-oo-its] Members of the Society of Jesus, the best-organized and most effective monastic order founded during the *Counter-Reformation* to combat Protestantism and spread Roman Catholicism around the world.

key In music, a tonal system consisting of seven *tones* in fixed relationship to a tonic, or keynote. Since the Renaissance, *key* has been the structural foundation of the bulk of Western music, down to the *Modernist* period.

keystone The central stone at the top of an arch that locks the other stones in place.

koine [KOI-nay] A colloquial Greek language spoken in the *Hellenistic* world that helped tie together that *civilization.*

kore [KOH-ray] An *Archaic* Greek standing statue of a young draped female.

kouros [KOO-rus] An *Archaic* Greek standing statue of a young naked male.

Late Gothic style A *style* characterized in architecture by ornate decoration and tall cathedral windows and spires and in painting and sculpture by increased refinement of details and a trend toward naturalism; popular in the fourteenth and fifteenth centuries in central and western Europe.

Late Mannerism The last stage of the *Mannerist* movement, characterized by exaggeration and distortion, especially in painting.

Late Modernism The last stage of *Modernism,* characterized by an increasing sense of existential despair, an attraction to non-Western cultures, and extreme experimentalism.

lay A short *lyric* or narrative poem meant to be sung to the accompaniment of an instrument such as a harp; based on Celtic legends but usually set in feudal times and focused on courtly love themes, especially adulterous passion. The oldest surviving lays are those of the twelfth-century poet Marie de France.

leitmotif [LITE-mo-teef] In music, and especially in Wagner's *operas,* the use of recurring *themes* associated with particular characters, objects, or ideas.

liberalism In political thought, a set of beliefs advocating certain personal, economic, and natural rights based on assumptions about the perfectibility and autonomy of human beings and the notion of progress, as first expressed in the writings of John Locke.

libretto [lih-BRET-oh] In Italian, "little book"; the text or words of an *opera,* an *oratorio,* or a musical work of a similar dramatic nature involving a written text.

line The mark—straight or curved, thick or thin, light or dark—made by the artist in a work of art.

Linear A In Minoan civilization, a type of script still undeciphered that lasted from about 1800 to 1400 B.C.

Linear B In Minoan civilization, an early form of Greek writing that flourished on Crete from about 1400 until about 1300 B.C. and lasted in a few scattered places on the Greek mainland until about 1150 B.C.; used to record commercial transactions.

liturgical drama Religious dramas, popular between the twelfth and sixteenth centuries, based on biblical stories with musical accompaniment that were staged in the area in front of the church, performed at first in Latin but later in the *vernacular languages;* the mystery plays (*mystery* is derived from the Latin for "action") are the most famous type of liturgical drama.

liturgy A rite or ritual, such as prayers or ceremonies, practiced by a religious group in public worship.

local color In literature, the use of detail peculiar to a particular region and environment to add interest and authenticity to a narrative, including description of the locale, customs, speech, and music. Local color was an especially popular development in American literature in the late nineteenth century.

logical positivism A school of modern philosophy that seeks truth by defining terms and clarifying statements and asserts that metaphysical theories are meaningless.

logos [LOWG-os] In *Stoicism,* the name for the supreme being or for reason—the controlling principle of the universe—believed to be present both in nature and in each human being.

lute In music, a wooden instrument, plucked or bowed, consisting of a sound box with an elaborately carved sound hole and a neck across which the (often twelve) strings pass. Introduced during the High Middle Ages, the lute enjoyed a height of popularity in Europe from the seventeenth to eighteenth century.

Lutheranism The doctrine, liturgy, and institutional structure of the church founded in the sixteenth century by Martin Luther, who stressed the authority of the Bible, the faith of the individual, and the worshiper's direct communication with God as the bases of his new religion.

lyre In music, a hand-held stringed instrument, with or without a sound box, used by ancient Egyptians, Assyrians, and Greeks. In Greek culture, the lyre was played to accompany song and recitation.

lyric A short subjective poem that expresses intense personal emotion.

lyric poetry In Greece, verses sung and accompanied by the *lyre;* today, intensely personal poetry.

Machiavellianism [mahk-ih-uh-VEL-ih-uhn-iz-uhm] The view that politics should be separated from morals and dedicated to the achievement of desired ends through any means necessary ("the end justifies the means"); derived from the political writings of Machiavelli.

madrigal [MAD-rih-guhl] A *polyphonic* song performed without accompaniment and based on a secular text, often a love *lyric;* especially popular in the sixteenth century.

maenad [MEE-nad] A woman who worshiped Dionysus, often in a state of frenzy.

magic realism A literary and artistic *style* identified with Latin American *Post-Modernism* that mixes realistic and supernatural elements to create imaginary or fantastic scenes.

Mannerism A cultural movement between 1520 and 1600 that grew out of a rebellion against the *Renaissance* artistic norms of symmetry and balance; characterized in art by distortion and incongruity and in thought and literature by the belief that human nature is depraved.

Mass In religion, the ritual celebrating the Eucharist, or Holy Communion, primarily in the Roman Catholic Church. The Mass has two parts, the Ordinary and the Proper; the former remains the same throughout the church year, whereas the latter changes for each date and service. The Mass Ordinary is composed of the Kyrie, Gloria, Credo, Sanctus, and Agnus Dei; the Mass Proper includes the Introit, Gradual, Alleluia or Tract, Sequence, Offertory, and Communion. In music, a musical setting of certain parts of the Mass, especially the Kyrie, Gloria, Credo, Sanctus, Benedictus, and Agnus Dei. The first complete Mass Ordinary was composed by Guillaume de Machaut [mah-SHOH] (about 1300–1377) in the fourteenth century.

mass culture The tastes, values, and interests of the classes that dominate modern industrialized society, especially the consumer-oriented American middle class.

medallion In Roman architecture, a circular decoration often found on triumphal arches enclosing a scene or portrait; in more general architectural use, a tablet or panel in a wall or window containing a figure or an ornament.

medium The material from which an artwork is made.

melody A succession of musical *tones* having a distinctive shape and rhythm.

Messiah A Hebrew word meaning "the anointed one," or one chosen by God to be his representative on earth; in Judaism, a savior who will come bringing peace and justice; in Christianity, Jesus Christ (*Christ* is derived from a Greek word meaning "the anointed one").

metope [MET-uh-pee] In architecture, a panel, often decorated, between two *triglyphs* on the *entablature* of a *Doric* Greek temple.

minaret In Islamic architecture, a tall, slender tower with a pointed top, from which the daily calls to prayer are delivered; located near a *mosque*.

miniature A small painting, usually of a religious nature, found in *illuminated manuscripts;* also, a small portrait.

minstrel A professional entertainer of the twelfth to the seventeenth century; especially a secular musician; also called "jongleur."

Modernism A late-nineteenth- and twentieth-century cultural, artistic, and literary movement that rejected much of the past and focused on the current, the secular, and the revolutionary in search of new forms of expression; the dominant style of the twentieth century until 1970.

modes A series of musical *scales* devised by the Greeks and believed by them to create certain emotional or ethical effects on the listener.

monophony [muh-NOF-uh-nee] A *style* of music in which there is only a single line of melody; the *Gregorian chants* are the most famous examples of monophonic music.

monotheism From the Greek *monos*, single, alone, and the Greek *theos*, god; the belief that there is only one God.

mood In music, the emotional impact of a *composition* on the feelings of a listener.

mosaic An art form or decoration, usually on a wall or a floor, created by inlaying small pieces of glass, shell, or stone in cement or plaster to create pictures or patterns.

mosque A Muslim place of worship, often distinguished by a dome-shaped central building placed in an open space surrounded by a wall.

motet A multivoiced song with words of a sacred or secular text, usually sung without accompanying instruments; developed in the thirteenth century.

mural A wall painting, usually quite large, used to decorate a private or public structure.

muse In Greek religion, any one of the nine sister goddesses who preside over the creative arts and sciences.

music drama An *opera* in which the action and music are continuous, not broken up into separate *arias* and *recitatives,* and the music is determined by its dramatic appropriateness, producing a work in which music, words, and staging are fused; the term was coined by Wagner.

narrator The speaker whose voice we hear in a story or poem.

narthex The porch or vestibule of a church, usually enclosed, through which worshipers walk before entering the *nave.*

Naturalism In literature, a late-nineteenth-century movement inspired by the methods of science and the insights of sociology, concerned with an objective depiction of the ugly side of industrial society.

natural law In *Stoicism* and later in other philosophies, a body of laws or principles that are believed to be derived from nature and binding on human society and that constitute a higher form of justice than civil or judicial law.

nave The central longitudinal area of a church, extending from the entrance to the *apse* and flanked by *aisles.*

Neoclassical style In the late eighteenth century, an artistic and literary movement that emerged as a reaction to the *Rococo* style and that sought inspiration from ancient *Classicism.* In the twentieth century, between 1919 and 1951, *Neoclassicism* in music was a style that rejected the emotionalism favored by Romantic composers as well as the dense orchestral sounds of the Impressionists; instead, it borrowed features from seventeenth- and eighteenth-century music and practiced the ideals of balance, clarity of texture, and nonprogrammatic works.

Neoclassicism In the late third century B.C., an artistic movement in the disintegrating Hellenistic world that sought inspiration in the Athenian Golden Age of the fifth and fourth centuries B.C.; and, since 1970, *Neoclassicism* has been a highly visible submovement in *Post-Modernism*, particularly prominent in painting and architecture, that restates the principles of *Classical* art—balance, harmony, idealism.

Neoexpressionism A submovement in *Post-Modernism,* associated primarily with painting, that offers social criticism and is concerned with the expression of the artist's feelings.

Neolithic Literally, "new stone"; used to define the New Stone Age, when human *cultures* evolved into agrarian systems and settled communities; dating from about 10,000 or 8000 B.C. to about 3000 B.C.

Neo-Platonism A philosophy based on Plato's ideas that was developed during the Roman period in an attempt to reconcile the dichotomy between Plato's concept of an eternal World of Ideas and the ever-changing physical world; in the fifteenth-century *Renaissance,* it served as a philosophical guide for Italian humanists who sought to reconcile late medieval Christian beliefs with *Classical* thinking.

Neorealism A submovement in *Post-Modernism* that is based on a photographic sense of detail and harks back to many of the qualities of nineteenth-century *Realism.*

New Comedy The style of comedy favored by *Hellenistic* playwrights, concentrating on gentle satirical themes—in particular, romantic *plots* with stock *characters* and predictable endings.

Nominalism [NAHM-uh-nuhl-iz-uhm] In medieval thought, the school that held that objects were separate unto themselves but could, for convenience, be treated in a collective sense because they shared certain characteristics; opposed to *Realism.*

Northern Renaissance The sixteenth-century cultural movement in northern Europe that was launched by the northward spread of Italian *Renaissance* art, culture, and ideals. The Northern Renaissance differed from the Italian Renaissance largely because of the persistence of the *Late Gothic style* and the unfolding of the *Reformation* after 1520.

octave In music, usually the eight-tone interval between a note and a second note of the same name, as in C to C.

oculus [AHK-yuh-lus] The circular opening at the top of a dome; derived from the Latin word for "eye."

Old Comedy The style of *comedy* established by Aristophanes in the fifth century B.C., distinguished by a strong element of political and social satire.

oligarchy From the Greek *oligos,* few; a state ruled by the few, especially by a small fraction of persons or families.

Olympian deities In Greek religion, sky gods and goddesses who lived on mountaintops and were worshiped mainly by the Greek aristocracy.

opera A drama or play set to music and consisting of vocal pieces with *orchestral* accompaniment; acting, scenery, and sometimes *choruses* and dancing are used to heighten the dramatic values of operas.

oratorio A choral work based on religious events or *scripture* employing singers, *choruses,* and *orchestra* but without scenery or staging and performed usually in a church or a concert hall.

orchestra In Greek theaters, the circular area where the *chorus* performed in front of the audience; in music, a group of instrumentalists, including string players, who play together.

organum [OR-guh-nuhm] In the ninth through the thirteenth centuries, a simple and early form of *polyphonic* music consisting of a main melody sung along with a *Gregorian chant;* by the thirteenth century it had developed into a complex multivoiced song.

Paleolithic Literally, "old stone"; used to define the Old Stone Age, when crude stones and tools were used; dating from about 2,000,000 B.C. to about 10,000 B.C.

pantheism The doctrine of or belief in multitudes of deities found in nature.

pantomime In Roman times, enormous dramatic productions featuring instrumental music and dances, favored by the masses; later, a type of dramatic or dancing performance in which the story is told with expressive or even exaggerated bodily and facial movements.

pastoral A type of *Hellenistic* poetry that idealized rural customs and farming, especially the simple life of shepherds, and deprecated urban living.

pavane [puh-VAHN] A sixteenth- and seventeenth-century English court dance of Italian origin; the dance is performed by couples to stately music. Ravel based *Pavane for a Dead Princess* (1899) on this *Baroque* dance form.

pediment In *Classical*-style architecture, the triangular-shaped area or gable at the end of the building formed by the sloping roof and the *cornice.*

pendentive [pen-DEN-tiv] In architecture, a triangular, concave-shaped section of *vaulting* between the rim of a dome and the pair of arches that support it; used in Byzantine and Islamic architecture.

performance art A democratic type of mixed media art born in the 1960s that ignores artistic boundaries, mixing high art (such as music, painting, and theater) and popular art (such as rock and roll, film, and fads), to create a unique, nonreproducible, artistic experience. Associated with the work of Laurie Anderson.

peristyle [PAIR-uh-stile] A colonnade around an open courtyard or a building.

Perpendicular style The highly decorative style of *Late Gothic* architecture that developed in England at the same time as the *Late Gothic* on the European continent.

perspective A technique or formula for creating the illusion or appearance of depth and distance on a two-dimensional surface. **Atmospheric perspective** is achieved in many ways: by diminishing color intensity, by omitting detail, and by blurring the lines of an object. **Linear perspective,** based on mathematical calculations, is achieved by having parallel lines or lines of projection appearing to converge at a single point, known as the *vanishing point,* on the horizon of the flat surface and by diminishing distant objects in size according to scale to make them appear to recede from the viewer.

philosophes [FEEL-uh-sawfs] A group of European thinkers and writers who popularized the ideas of the *Enlightenment* through essays, novels, plays, and other works, hoping to change the climate of opinion and bring about social and political reform.

phonogram A symbol used to represent a syllable, a word, or a sound.

Physiocrats [FIZ-ih-uh-kratz] A group of writers, primarily French, who dealt with economic issues during the *Enlightenment,* in particular calling for improved agricultural productivity and questioning the state's role in economic affairs.

pianoforte [pee-an-o-FOR-tay] A piano; derived from the Italian for "soft/loud," terms used to describe the two types of sound emitted by a stringed instrument whose wires are struck with felt-covered hammers operated from a keyboard.

picaresque novel From the Spanish term for "rogue." A type of literature, originating in sixteenth-century Spain, that recounted the comic misadventures of a roguish hero who lived by his wits, often at the expense of the high and mighty; influenced novel writing across Europe, especially in England, France, and Germany, until about 1800; the anonymous "Lazarillo de Tormes" (1554) was the first picaresque novel.

pictogram A carefully drawn, often stylized, picture that represents a particular object.

pier In architecture, a vertical masonry structure that may support a *vault,* an arch, or a roof; in *Gothic* churches, piers were often clustered together to form massive supports.

Pietà [pee-ay-TAH] A painting or sculpture depicting the mourning Virgin and the dead Christ.

pilaster [pih-LAS-tuhr] In architecture, a vertical, rectangular decorative device projecting from a wall that gives the appearance of a column with a base and a *capital;* sometimes called an applied column.

Platonism The collective beliefs and arguments presented in Plato's writings stressing especially that actual things are copies of ideas.

plot The action, or arrangement of incidents, in a story.

podium In architecture, a low wall serving as a foundation; a platform.

poetry Language that is concentrated and imaginative, marked by meter, rhythm, rhyme, and imagery.

Pointillism [PWANT-il-iz-uhm] Also known as Divisionism, a style of painting, perfected by Seurat, in which tiny dots of paint are applied to the canvas in such a way that when they are viewed from a distance they merge and blend to form recognizable objects with natural effects of color, light, and shade.

polyphony [puh-LIF-uh-nee] A style of musical *composition* in which two or more voices or melodic lines are woven together.

polytheism [PAHL-e-the-iz-uhm] The doctrine of or belief in more than one deity.

Pop Art An artistic *style* popular between 1960 and 1970 in which commonplace commercial objects drawn from *mass culture,* such as soup cans, fast foods, and comic strips, became the subjects of art.

portico In architecture, a covered entrance to a building, usually with a separate roof supported by columns.

post-and-lintel construction A basic architectural form in which upright posts, or columns, support a horizontal lintel, or beam.

post-beam-triangle construction The generic name given to Greek architecture that includes the post, or column; the beam, or lintel; and the triangular-shaped area, or *pediment.*

Post-Impressionism A late-nineteenth-century artistic movement that extended the boundaries of *Impressionism* in new directions to focus on structure, composition, fantasy, and subjective expression.

Post-Modernism An artistic, cultural, and intellectual movement, originating in about 1970, that is more optimistic than *Modernism,* embraces an open-ended and democratic global civilization, freely adapts elements of high culture and *mass culture,* and manifests itself chiefly through revivals of earlier styles, giving rise to *Neoclassicism, Neoexpressionism,* and *Neorealism.*

Praxitelean curve [prak-sit-i-LEE-an] The graceful line of the sculptured body in the *contrapposto* stance, perfected by the *Fourth Century style* sculptor Praxiteles.

primitivism In painting, the "primitives" are those painters of the Netherlandish and Italian schools who flourished before 1500, thus all Netherlandish painters between the van Eycks and Dürer and all Italian painters between Giotto and Raphael; more generally, the term reflects modern artists' fascination with non-Western art forms, as in Gauguin's Tahitian-inspired paintings. In literature, primitivism has complex meanings; on the one hand, it refers to the notion of a golden age, a world of lost innocence, which appeared in both ancient pagan and Christian writings; on the other hand, it is a modern term used to denote two species of cultural relativism, which either finds people isolated from civilization to be superior to those living in civilized and urban settings, as in the cult of the Noble Savage (Rousseau), or respects native peoples and their cultures within their own settings, yet accepts that natives can be as cruel as Europeans (the view expressed by Montaigne).

problem play A type of drama that focuses on a specific social problem; the Swedish playwright Ibsen was a pioneer of this *genre,* as in *A Doll's House* (1879), concerning women's independence.

program music Instrumental music that depicts a narrative, portrays a *setting,* or suggests a sequence of events; often based on other sources, such as a poem or a play.

prose The ordinary language used in speaking and writing.

Puritanism The beliefs and practices of the Puritans, a small but influential religious group devoted to the teachings of John Calvin; they stressed strict rules of personal and public behavior and practiced their beliefs in England and the New World during the seventeenth century.

putti [POOH-tee] Italian, plural of *putto;* in painting and sculpture, figures of babies, children, or sometimes angels.

ragtime A type of instrumental music, popularized by African Americans in the late nineteenth and early twentieth centuries, with a strongly syncopated rhythm and a lively *melody.*

Rayonnant [ray-yo-NAHNN] A decorative *style* in French architecture associated with the High *Gothic* period, in which walls were replaced by sheets of *stained glass* framed by elegant stone *traceries.*

Realism In medieval philosophy, the school that asserted that objects contained common or universal qualities that were not always apparent to the human senses but that were more real or true than the objects' physical attributes; opposed to *Nominalism.* In art and literature, a mid- to late-nineteenth-century style that focused on the everyday lives of the middle and lower classes, portraying their world in a serious, accurate, and unsentimental way; opposed to *Romanticism.*

recitative [ress-uh-tuh-TEEV] In music, a rhythmically free but often stylized declamation, midway between singing and ordinary speech, that serves as a transition between *arias* or as a narrative device in an *opera.*

Reformation The sixteenth-century religious movement that looked back to the ideals of early Christianity, called for moral and structural changes in the church, and led ultimately to the founding of the various Protestant churches.

regalia Plural in form, often used with a singular verb. The emblems and symbols of royalty, as the crown and scepter.

relief In sculpture, figures or forms that are carved so they project from the flat surface of a stone or metal background. **High relief** projects sharply from the surface; **low relief,** or **bas relief,** is more shallow.

Renaissance [ren-uh-SAHNS] From the French for "rebirth"; the artistic, cultural, and intellectual movement marked by a revival of *Classical* and *humanistic* values that began in Italy in the mid–fourteenth century and had spread across Europe by the mid–sixteenth century.

representational art Art that presents a likeness of the world as it appears to the naked eye.

Restrained Baroque style A variation of the *Baroque* style identified with Dutch and English architects and painters who wanted to reduce Baroque grandeur and exuberance to a more human scale.

revenge tragedy A type of play popular in sixteenth-century England, probably rooted in Roman *tragedies* and concerned with the need for a family to seek revenge for the murder of a relative.

ribbed vault A masonry roof with a framework of arches or ribs that reinforce and decorate the *vault* ceiling.

rocaille [roh-KYE] In *Rococo* design, the stucco ornaments shaped like leaves, flowers, and ribbons that decorate walls and ceilings.

Rococo style [ruh-KOH-koh] An artistic and cultural *style* that grew out of the *Baroque* style but that was more intimate and personal and that emphasized the frivolous and superficial side of aristocratic life.

romance A story derived from legends associated with Troy or Celtic culture but often set in feudal times and centered on themes of licit and illicit love between noble lords and ladies.

Romanesque style [roh-muhn-ESK] A *style* of architecture, usually associated with churches built in the eleventh and twelfth centuries, that was inspired by Roman architectural features, such as the *basilica,* and was thus Roman-like. Romanesque buildings were massive, with round arches and *barrel* or *groined vaulted* ceilings, and had less exterior decoration than *Gothic* churches.

Romanticism An intellectual, artistic, and literary movement that began in the late eighteenth century as a reaction to *Neoclassicism* and that stressed the emotional, mysterious, and imaginative side of human behavior and the unruly side of nature.

rose window A large circular window, made of *stained glass* and held together with lead and carved stones set in patterns, or *tracery,* and located over an entrance in a *Gothic* cathedral.

sacred music Religious music, such as Gregorian chants, *masses,* and hymns.

sarcophagus [sahr-KAHF-uh-guhs] From the Greek meaning "flesh-eating stone"; a marble or stone coffin or tomb, usually decorated with carvings, used first by Romans and later by Christians for burial of the dead.

satire From the Latin, "medley"—a cooking term; a literary *genre* that originated in ancient Rome and that was characterized by two basic forms: (a) tolerant and amused observation of the human scene, modeled on Horace's style, and (b) bitter and sarcastic denunciation of all behavior and thought outside a civilized norm, modeled on Juvenal's style. In modern times, a literary work that holds up human vices and follies to ridicule or scorn.

satyr-play [SAT-uhr] A comic play, often featuring sexual themes, performed at the Greek drama festivals along with the *tragedies*.

scale A set pattern of tones (or notes) arranged from low to high.

scenographic [see-nuh-GRAF-ik] In *Renaissance* architecture, a building style that envisioned buildings as composed of separate units; in the painting of stage scenery, the art of *perspective* representation.

scherzo [SKER-tso] From the Italian for "joke"; a quick and lively instrumental *composition* or movement found in *sonatas* and *symphonies*.

scholasticism In medieval times, the body or collection of knowledge that tried to harmonize Aristotle's writings with Christian doctrine; also, a way of thinking and establishing sets of arguments.

Scientific Revolution The seventeenth-century intellectual movement, based originally on discoveries in astronomy and physics, that challenged and overturned medieval views about the order of the universe and the theories used to explain motion.

scripture The sacred writings of any religion, as the Bible in Judaism and Christianity.

secular music Nonreligious music, such as *symphonies*, songs, and dances.

serial music A type of musical composition based on a *twelve-tone scale* arranged any way the composer chooses; the absence of a tonal center in serial music leads to *atonality*.

setting In literature, the background against which the action takes place; in a representational artwork, the time and place depicted.

Severe style The first sculptural style of the *Classical* period in Greece, which retained stylistic elements from the *Archaic* style.

sfumato [sfoo-MAH-toh] In painting, the blending of one tone into another to blur the outline of a form and give the canvas a smokelike appearance; a technique perfected by Leonardo da Vinci.

shaft graves Deep pit burial sites; the dead are usually placed at the bottom of the shafts.

skene [SKEE-nee] A small building behind the *orchestra* in a Greek theater, used as a prop and as a storehouse for theatrical materials.

Skepticism A *Hellenistic* philosophy that questioned whether anything could be known for certain, argued that all beliefs were relative, and concluded that *autarky* could be achieved only by recognizing that inquiry was fruitless.

slave narrative A literary *genre*, either written by slaves or told by slaves to secretaries, which emerged prior to the American Civil War; the genre was launched by the *Narrative of the Life of Frederick Douglass, an American Slave* (1845); the harsh details of the inhumane and unjust slave system, as reported in these narratives, contributed to *Realist* literature.

social contract In political thought, an agreement or contract between the people and their rulers defining the rights and duties of each so that a civil society might be created.

socialism An economic and political system in which goods and property are owned collectively or by the state; the socialist movement began as a reaction to the excesses of the factory system in the nineteenth century and ultimately called for either reforming or abolishing industrial capitalism.

Socialist Realism A Marxist artistic theory that calls for the use of literature, music, and the arts in the service of the ideals and goals of socialism and/or communism, with an emphasis in painting on the realistic portrayal of objects.

sonata [soh-NAH-tah] In music, an instrumental *composition*, usually in three or four movements.

sonata form A musical *form* or structure consisting of three (or sometimes four) sections that vary in *key*, *tempo*, and mood.

stained glass An art form characterized by many small pieces of tinted glass bound together by strips of lead, usually to produce a pictorial scene of a religious theme; developed by *Romanesque* artists and a central feature of *Gothic* churches.

stele [STEE-lee] A carved or inscribed vertical stone pillar or slab, often used for commemorative purposes.

Stoicism [STO-ih-sihz-uhm] The most popular and influential *Hellenistic* philosophy, advocating a restrained way of life, a toleration for others, a resignation to disappointments, and a resolution to carry out one's responsibilities; Stoicism appealed to many Romans and had an impact on early Christian thought.

stream-of-consciousness A writing technique used by some modern authors in which the narration consists of a *character's* continuous interior monologue of thoughts and feelings.

structuralism In *Post-Modernism*, an approach to knowledge based on the belief that human behavior and institutions can be explained by reference to a few underlying structures that themselves are reflections of hidden patterns in the human mind.

studia humanitatis [STOO-dee-ah hu-man-ih-TAH-tis] **(humanistic studies)** The Latin term given by *Renaissance* scholars to new intellectual pursuits that were based on recently discovered ancient texts, including moral philosophy, history, grammar, rhetoric, and poetry. This new learning stood in sharp contrast to medieval *scholasticism*.

Sturm und Drang [STOORM oont drahng] German, "Storm and Stress"; a German literary movement of the 1770s that focused on themes of action, emotionalism, and the individual's revolt against the conventions of society.

style The combination of distinctive elements of creative execution and expression, in terms of both form and *content*.

style galant [STEEL gah-LAHNN] In *Rococo* music, a *style* of music developed by French composers and characterized by graceful and simple *melodies*.

stylobate [STY-luh-bate] In Greek temples, the upper step of the base that forms a platform on which the columns stand.

Sublime [suh-BLIME] In *Romanticism*, the term used to describe nature as a terrifying and awesome force full of violence and power.

Suprematism [suh-PREM-uh-tiz-uhm] A variation of abstract art, originating in Russia in the early twentieth century, characterized by the use of geometric shapes as the basic elements of the composition.

Surrealism [suh-REE-uhl-iz-uhm] An early-twentieth-century movement in art, literature, and theater, in which incongruous juxtapositions and fantastic images produce an irrational and dreamlike effect.

symbolic realism In art, a *style* that is realistic and true to life but uses the portrayed object or person to represent or symbolize something else.

symphony A long and complex *sonata,* usually written in three or four movements, for large *orchestras;* the first movement is traditionally fast, the second slow, and the third (and optional fourth) movement fast.

syncopation [sin-ko-PAY-shun] In music, the technique of accenting the weak beat when a strong beat is expected.

syncretism [SIN-kruh-tiz-uhm] The combining of different forms of religious beliefs or practices.

synthesizer [SIN-thuh-size-uhr] An electronic apparatus with a keyboard capable of duplicating the sounds of many musical instruments, popular among *Post-Modernist* composers and musicians.

tabula rasa [TAB-yuh-luh RAH-zuh] "Erased tablet," the Latin term John Locke used to describe the mind at birth, empty of inborn ideas and ready to receive sense impressions, which Locke believed were the sole source of knowledge.

technique The systematic procedure whereby a particular creative task is performed.

tempo In music, the relative speed at which a composition is to be played, indicated by a suggestive word or phrase or by a precise number such as a metronome marking. (A metronome is a finely calibrated device used to determine the exact tempo for a musical work.)

terza rima [TER-tsuh REE-muh] A three-line stanza with an interlocking rhyme scheme (*aba bcb cdc ded,* and so on), used by Dante in his *Divine Comedy.*

texture In a musical composition, the number and nature of voices or instruments employed and how the parts are combined.

theater of the absurd A type of theater that has come to reflect the despair, anxieties, and absurdities of modern life and in which the characters seldom make sense, the plot is nearly nonexistent, bizarre and fantastic events occur onstage, and tragedy and comedy are mixed in unconventional ways; associated with *Late Modernism.*

theme The dominant idea of a work; the message or emotion the artist intends to convey.

theocracy From the Greek *theos,* god; a state governed by a god regarded as the ruling power or by priests or officials claiming divine sanction.

theology The application of philosophy to the study of religious truth, focusing especially on the nature of the deity and the origin and teachings of an organized religious community.

tone A musical sound of definite pitch; also, the quality of a sound.

tracery Ornamental architectural work with lines that branch out to form designs, often found as stone carvings in *rose windows.*

tragedy A serious and deeply moral drama, typically involving a noble protagonist brought down by excessive pride (hubris) and describing a conflict between seemingly irreconcilable values or forces; in Greece, tragedies were performed at the festivals associated with the worship of Dionysus.

transept In church architecture, the crossing arm that bisects the *nave* near the *apse* and gives the characteristic *cruciform* shape to the floor plan.

triglyph [TRY-glif] In Greek architecture, a three-grooved rectangular panel on the frieze of a *Doric* temple; triglyphs alternated with *metopes.*

triptych [TRIP-tik] In painting, a set of three hinged or folding panels depicting a religious story, mainly used as an altarpiece.

trope [TROHP] In *Gregorian chants,* a new phrase or melody inserted into an existing chant to make it more musically appealing; also called a turn; in literature, a figure of speech.

troubador [TROO-buh-door] A composer and/or singer, usually an aristocrat, who performed secular love songs at the feudal courts in southern France.

twelve-tone scale In music, a fixed *scale* or series in which there is an arbitrary arrangement of the twelve *tones* (counting every half-tone) of an *octave;* devised by Arnold Schoenberg.

tympanum [TIM-puh-num] In medieval architecture, the arch over a doorway set above the lintel, usually decorated with carvings depicting biblical themes; in *Classical*-style architecture, the recessed face of a *pediment.*

ukiyo-e [oo-key-yoh-AY] A type of colorful Japanese print, incised on woodblocks, that is characterized by simple design, plain backgrounds, and flat areas of color. Developed in seventeenth-century Japan; admired by late-nineteenth-century Parisian artists, who assimilated it to a Western style that is most notable in the prints of Mary Cassatt.

Utilitarianism [yoo-til-uh-TARE-e-uh-niz-uhm] The doctrine set forth in the social theory of Jeremy Bentham in the nineteenth century that the final goal of society and humans is "the greatest good for the greatest number."

vanishing point In linear *perspective,* the point on the horizon at which the receding parallel lines appear to converge and then vanish.

vault A ceiling or roof made from a series of arches placed next to one another.

vernacular language [vuhr-NAK-yuh-luhr] The language or dialect of a region, usually spoken by the general population as opposed to the wealthy or educated elite.

vernacular literature Literature written in the language of the populace, such as English, French, or Italian, as opposed to the language of the educated elite, usually Latin.

via antiqua [VEE-uh ahn-TEE-kwah] The "old way," the term used in late medieval thought by the opponents of St. Thomas Aquinas to describe his *via media,* which they considered outdated.

via media [VEE-uh MAY-dee-ah] The "middle way" that St. Thomas Aquinas sought in reconciling Aristotle's works to Christian beliefs.

via moderna [VEE-uh moh-DEHR-nah] The "new way," the term used in late medieval thought by those thinkers who opposed the school of Aquinas.

video art A type of art made with a video monitor, or monitors; produced using either computerized programs or handheld cameras; can be ephemeral or permanent.

virtuoso [vehr-choo-O-so] An aristocratic person who experimented in science, usually as an amateur, in the seventeenth century, giving science respectability and a wider audience; later, in music, a person with great technical skill.

voussoir [voo-SWAR] A carved, wedge-shaped stone or block in an arch.

woodcut In art, the technique of cutting or carving an image onto a wooden block used for printing; originated in the Late Middle Ages. Also, the print made from the technique.

word painting In music, the illustration of an idea, a meaning, or a feeling associated with a word, as, for example, using a discordant *melody* when the word *pain* is sung. This technique is especially identified with the sixteenth-century *madrigal;* also called word illustration, or madrigalism.

ziggurat [ZIG-oo-rat] A Mesopotamian stepped pyramid, usually built with external staircases and a shrine at the top; sometimes included a tower.

TEXT CREDITS

Chapter 1 Page 9, Samuel N. Kramer, "Sumerian Text of Father Rebuking Son," from *History Begins at Sumer*. Doubleday Anchor, 1959, pp. 12–16. Reprinted by permission of Mildred Kramer; page 19, Miriam Lichtheim, "Troubled Times" from "The Man Who Was Tired of Life" in *Ancient Egyptian Literature. Three Volumes*. Volume I, pp. 166–169. Copyright © 1973–1980 Regents of the University of California. Reprinted by permission. **Chapter 2** Page 45, Solon, "Political Verses: The Ten Ages of Man" from David Milroy, *Early Greek Lyric Poetry*, 1992, pp. 68–69. Reprinted by permission of the University of Michigan Press; Sappho, "He Seems to Be a God" from *7 Greeks*, translated by Guy Davenport. Copyright © 1995 by Guy Davenport. Reprinted by permission of New Directions Publishing Corporation. **Chapter 3** Page 71, Xenophon, "Secrets of a Successful Marriage," from *Oeconomicus: A Social and Historical Commentary*. Translated by S. B. Pomeroy, pp. 139–141, 143, 145. Copyright © 1994 Clarendon, a division of Oxford University Press. Reprinted by permission of the translator. **Chapter 4** Page 92, Theocritus, from *The Idylls of Theocritus: A Verse Translation*, translated by Thelma Sargent. Translation copyright © 1982 by Thelma Sargent. Reprinted by permission of W. W. Norton & Company, Inc. **Chapter 6** Page 151, Flavius Josephus, "The Destruction of the Temple at Jerusalem" from *The Jewish War* by Josephus. Translated by G. A. Williamson (Penguin Classics 1959). Copyright © 1959 G. A. Williamson. Reprinted by permission of Penguin Books, Ltd.; page 162, Perpetua, "Perpetua's Vision" from *The Acts of the Christian Martyrs*. Edited by Herbert Musurillo, 1972, pp. 109–111, 125–126, 129, 131. Reprinted by permission of Oxford University Press (Oxford, England). **Chapter 7** Page 174, Paulina, "Epitaph for Agorius Praetextatus" from Peter Dronke, *Women Writers of the Middle Ages*, 1984. Reprinted by permission of Cambridge University Press (New York). **Chapter 8** Page 208, Usamah, "The Curious Medicine of the Franks" from *Memoirs of Usamah*. Translated by Philip K. Hitti. Copyright © 1929 by Columbia University Press. Reprinted with permission of the publisher; Anna Comnena, "The Arrival of the First Crusade in Constantinople," from *The Alexiad of the Princess Anna Comnena*. Translated by Elizabeth A. S. Dawes. Originally published by Routledge & Kegan Paul, London; page 209, Liudprand of Cremona, excerpt from "A Mission to the Byzantine Court" in *The Works of Liudprand of Cremona*. Translated by F. A. Wright, 1930. Reprinted by permission of Routledge (Hampshire, UK). **Chapter 9** Page 229, Hildegard of Bingen, "Scivias" from *Cry Out and Write*, by Edward Peter Nolan, 1994, p. 46. Reprinted by permission of the Continuum Publishing Group. **Chapter 11** Page 296, Laura Cereta, excerpt from "Defense of the Liberal Instruction of Women," January 13, 1488. From *Her Immaculate Hand: Selected Works by and about the Women Humanists of Quattrocento Italy*. Edited by Margaret King & Albert Rabil, 1992. Pegasus Press, #13. Reprinted by permission of MRTS, SUNY Binghamton, NY. **Chapter 12** Page 337, Georgio Vasari, "Michelangelo Sculpting David" from *Lives of the Artists Volume I*. Translated by George Bull (Penguin Classics, 1965, Revised Edition 1971). Copyright © 1965 George Bull. Reprinted by permission of Penguin Books, Ltd. **Chapter 20** Page 547, Elie Wiesel, excerpt from *Night*, translated by Stella Rodway. Copyright © 1960 by MacGibbon & Kee. Copyright renewed © 1988 by the Collins Publishing Group. Reprinted by permission of Hill and Wang, a division of Farrar, Straus and Giroux, LLC. **Chapter 21** Page 592, Bill Moyers, excerpts from "Bill Moyers: A World of Ideas II." Copyright © 1990 by Public Affairs Television, Inc. Used by permission of Doubleday, a division of Random House, Inc.

PHOTO AND ILLUSTRATION CREDITS

P. xxii, © Erich Lessing/Art Resource, NY; **p. xxiii**, The Museum of Modern Art, New York. Acquired through the Lillie P. Bliss Bequest. Photograph © 2000 The Museum of Modern Art, New York. © 2000 Estate of Pablo Picasso/Artists Rights Society (ARS), New York; **p. xxviii**, Georgia O'Keeffe, American, 1887–1986, *Cow's Skull with Calico Roses*, oil on canvas, 1932, 92.2 x 61.3 cm, Gift of Georgia O'Keeffe, 1947.712. Photograph © 2000 The Art Institute of Chicago, All Rights Reserved. © 2000 The Georgia O'Keeffe Foundation/Artists Rights Society (ARS), New York. **Chapter 1 CO-1**, © The British Museum; **1.1**, © The British Museum; **1.2**, © Jean-Marie Chauvet/Sygma; **1.3**, © Naturhistorisches Museum, Wien; **1.5**, © The British Museum; **1.6**, © Erich Lessing/Art Resource, NY; **1.7**, © The British Museum; **1.8**, © Hirmer Fotoarchiv, Munich; **1.9**, © Hirmer Fotoarchiv, Munich; **1.10**, © P & G Bowater/The Image Bank; **1.12**, © Tim Schermerhorn; **1.13**, © Inge Morath/Magnum Photos, Inc.; **1.14**, © AKG London; **1.15**, Harvard University, Museum of Fine Arts Expedition. (11.1738). Courtesy Museum of Fine Arts, Boston. Reproduced with permission. © 2000 Museum of Fine Arts, Boston. All rights reserved; **1.16**, Courtesy The Metropolitan Museum of Art, Rogers Fund and contribution from Edward S. Harkness, 1929. (29.3.2); **1.17**, © Margarete Büsing/Bildarchiv Preussischer Kulturbesitz; **1.18**, © C. M. Dixon; **1.19**, © The British Museum; **1.20**, © The British Museum; **1.21**, © Boltin Picture Library; **1.22**, © The British Museum; **1.23**, Persepolis, Iran/© Bridgeman Art Library; **p. 28T**, © David Coulson/Robert Estall Photograph Library; **p. 28B**, © Robert & Linda Mitchell; **p. 29L**, British Museum, London, UK/ © Bridgeman Art Library; **p. 29R**, © J. M. Kenoyer/Harappa. **Chapter 2 CO-2**, © George Grigoriou/ Tony Stone Images; **2.1**, © C. M. Dixon; **2.2**, © Ronald Sheridan/Ancient Art & Architecture Collection; **2.3**, © Erich Lessing/Art Resource, NY; **2.4**, © Gordon Gahan/National Geographic Image Collection; **2.5**, © Hirmer Fotoarchiv, Munich; **2.6**, © Ira Block/National Geographic Image Collection; **2.7**, © Erich Lessing/Art Resource, NY; **2.8**, © George Grigoriou/Tony Stone Images; **2.9**, © The Granger Collection, New York; **2.10**, © Hirmer Fotoarchiv, Munich; **2.13**, © Vanni/Art Resource, NY; **2.14**, © Erich Lessing/Art Resource, NY; **2.15**, Courtesy The Metropolitan Museum of Art, Fletcher Fund, 1932. (32.11.1); **2.16**, © C. M. Dixon; **2.17**, © Hirmer Fotoarchiv, Munich; **2.18**, © C. M. Dixon; **2.19**, © Hirmer Fotoarchiv, Munich; **2.20**, © Hirmer Fotoarchiv, Munich. **Chapter 3 CO-3**, © Erich Lessing/Art Resource; **3.1**, Courtesy of the Arthur M. Sackler Museum, Harvard University Art Museums, Bequest of David M. Robinson. Photo by Michael Nedzweski, © President and Fellows of Harvard College, Harvard University; **3.2**, © Hirmer Fotoarchiv, Munich; **3.3**, © Hirmer Fotoarchiv, Munich; **3.4**, Courtesy Staatliche Museen, Berlin; **3.5**, © Hirmer Fotoarchiv, Munich; **3.6**, © Ara Guler/Magnum Photos, Inc.; **3.7**, © Erich Lessing/Art Resource, NY; **3.8**, © Ronald Sheridan/Ancient Art & Architecture Collection; **3.10**, © Kunsthistorisches Museum; **3.11**, © The British Museum; **3.12**, © The Granger Collection, New York; **3.13**, © C. M. Dixon; **3.14**, © Ronald Sheridan/Ancient Art & Architecture Collection; **3.15**, © Vanni/Art Resource, NY; **3.16**, © René Burri/Magnum Photos, Inc.; **3.17**, © Hirmer Fotoarchiv, Munich; **3.18**, © Hirmer Fotoarchiv, Munich; **3.19**, © Photo RMN/Hervé Lewandowski; **3.20**, © Scala/ Art Resource, NY; **3.21**, © Scala/Art Resource, NY; **3.22**, © Hirmer Fotoarchiv, Munich; **3.24**, © The British Museum; **3.25**, © Erich Lessing/Art Resource, NY; **3.26**, © Hirmer Fotoarchiv, Munich; **p. 84TL**, © R. Sheridan/Ancient Art & Architecture Collection; **p. 84TR**, © Corbis/Gianni Dagli Orti; **p. 84B**, © Dumbarton Oaks Research Library and Collections, Washington, DC; **p. 85T**, © Christie's Images, Ltd.; **p. 85B**, © Kyodo News International, Inc. **Chapter 4 CO-4**, Louvre, Paris, France/Peter Willi/ Bridgeman Art Library; **4.1**, Bibliothèque Nationale de France; **4.2**, © Bildarchiv Preussischer Kulturbesitz; **4.4**, © Photo RMN/Gérard Blot; **4.5**, Courtesy Yale University Art Gallery, Dura Europos Collection, Neg. #258; **4.6**, © Alinari/Art Resource, NY; **4.7**, Courtesy The Metropolitan Museum of Art, Rogers Fund, 1911. (11.90); **4.8**, © The British Museum; **4.9**, © C. M. Dixon; **4.10**, © Art Resource, NY; **4.11**, © Foto Marburg/Art Resource, NY; **4.12**, Pinacoteca Capitolina, Palazzo Conservatori, Rome, Italy/Index/© Bridgeman Art Library; **4.13**, Courtesy The Metropolitan Museum of Art, Rogers Fund, 1909. (09.39); **4.14**, © Erich Lessing/Art Resource, NY; **4.15**, Louvre, Paris, France/Peter Willi/Bridgeman Art Library; **4.16**, © Photo RMN/Hervé Lewandowski; **4.17**, © Nimatallah/Art Resource, NY; **4.18**, Courtesy Archivio Fotografico dei Musei Capitolini. Photo by Maria Teresa Natale; **4.19**, Vatican Museums and Galleries, Vatican City, Italy; © Index/Bridgeman Art Library. **Chapter 5 CO-5**, © Paul Chesley/Tony Stone Images; **5.1**, © Scala/Art Resource, NY; **5.2**, © Alinari/Art Resource, NY; **5.3**, © Scala/Art Resource, NY; **5.4**, © Alinari/Art Resource, NY; **5.5**, Leonard von Matt, Buochs, Switzerland; **5.6**, © Hirmer Fotoarchiv, Munich; **5.7**, © Fototeca Unione, Rome. American Academy in Rome; **5.8**, © Photo RMN-Jean/J. Schormans; **5.9**, © Ronald Sheridan/Ancient Art & Architecture Collection; **5.10**, © AKG London; **5.11**, © Scala/Art Resource, NY; **5.13**, © Giraudon/Art Resource, NY; **5.14**, © Scala/Art Resource, NY; **5.15**, © Paul Chesley/Tony Stone Images; **5.16**, © Steve Vidler/Tony Stone Images; **5.17**, Index/© Bridgeman Art Library; **5.18**, © Scala/Art Resource, NY; **5.19**, © Guido Rossi/The Image Bank; **5.20**, © Corbis/Bettmann; **5.21**, © Lionel Isy-Schwart/The Image Bank; **5.22**, © C. M. Dixon; **5.23**, Museum of Art, Rhode Island School of Design, Museum of Appropriation. Photograph by Del Bogart; **5.24**, © AKG London; **5.25**, © Nimatallah/Art Resource, NY; **5.26**, © Ronald Sheridan/Ancient Art & Architecture Collection; **5.27**, © Erich Lessing/Art Resource, NY; **5.28**, © Scala/ Art Resource, NY; **5.29**, © Scala/Art Resource, NY; **5.30**, © R. Sheridan/Ancient Art & Architecture Collection; **5.31**, © Erich Lessing/Art Resource, NY; **p. 142T**, © Boltin Picture Library; **p. 142B**, © Staatliche Museen zu Berlin/Preussischer Kulturbesitz Museum für Völkerkunde; **p. 143T**, © Dinodia Picture Agency; **p. 143M**, © Robert Harding Picture Library, London; **p. 143B**, © Barnaby's Picture Library. **Chapter 6 CO-6**, National Museum, Damascus, Syria/Topham Picturepoint/Bridgeman Art Library; **6.1**, © Israel Museum, Jerusalem; **6.2**, Courtesy of the Oriental Institute of the University of Chicago; **6.3**, © The Jewish Museum, NY/Art Resource, NY; **6.4**, © Zev Radovan, Jerusalem; **6.5**, © Richard T. Nowitz; **6.6**, National Museum, Damascus, Syria/Topham Picturepoint Bridgeman Art Library; **6.7**, © Israel Museum, Jerusalem; **6.9**, Courtesy of Nancy L. Lapp; **6.10**, © Zev Radovan, Jerusalem; **6.11**, © Zev Radovan, Jerusalem; **6.12**, © Carl Purcell/Words & Pictures; **6.13**, © Phototheque André Held; **6.14**, © Phototheque André Held; **6.15**, © Hirmer Fotoarchiv, Munich; **6.16**, © Scala/Art Resource, NY; **6.17**, © Erich Lessing/PhotoEdit; **6.18**, © Hirmer Fotoarchiv, Munich. **Chapter 7 CO-7**, © Hirmer Fotoarchiv, Munich; **7.1**, © Hirmer Fotoarchiv, Munich; **7.2**, © Erich Lessing/Art Resource, NY; **7.3**, © Vanni/Art Resource, NY; **7.4**, © C. M. Dixon; **7.5**, © Scala/Art Resource, NY; **7.6**, © Phototheque André Held; **7.8**, © Foto Marburg/Art Resource, NY; **7.9**, © Scala/Art Resource, NY; **7.11**, © AKG London; **7.12**, © Erich Lessing/Art Resource, NY; **7.13**, © Scala/Art Resource, NY; **7.14**, © Arch. Phot. Paris; **7.15**, Courtesy Ministero per i beni Culturali e Ambientali, Istituto Centrale per il Catalogo e la Documentazione; **7.16**, © C. M. Dixon; **7.17**, © Deutsches Archäologisches Institut; **7.18**, © Alinari/Art Resource, NY; **7.19**, © Biblioteca Apostolica Vaticana, Minature 15 (Fol. 106); **7.20**, © Scala/Art Resource, NY; **7.21**, © Phototheque André Held; **7.22**, © Hirmer Fotoarchiv, Munich. **Chapter 8 CO-8**, © George Holton/Photo Researchers, Inc.; **8.1**, © C. M. Dixon; **8.2**, © AKG London; **8.3**, © Bridgeman/Art Resource, NY; **8.4**, © Kurgan-Lisnet/Liaison Agency, Inc.; **8.5**, © Ian Berry/ Magnum Photos, Inc; **8.6**, © Scala/Art Resource, NY; **8.7**, © Scala/Art Resource, NY; **8.8**, © AKG London; **8.9**, © Colorphoto Hans Hinz; **8.10**, © Werner Foreman Archive/Art Resource, NY; **8.11**, Ampliaciones y Reproducciones MAS (Arxiu Mas), Barcelona; **8.12**, © The Granger Collection, New York; **8.13**, © George Holton/Photo Researchers, Inc.; **8.14**, © V&A Picture Library; **8.15**, Minbar from Kutubiyya Mosque, Marrakesh, Morocco. Islamic. Woodwork. 12th C., 1137–ca. 1145. H. 12 ft. 10 in.; W. 2 ft. 10-1/4 in.; D. 11 ft. 4-1/4 in. Three quarter view from the right. Photography by Bruce White. Photograph © 1998, The Metropolitan Museum of Art; **8.16**, © Ronald Sheridan/Ancient Art & Architecture Collection; **8.18**, © Mark Romanelli/The Image Bank; **8.19**, Reproduced by the kind permission of the Trustees of the Chester Beatty Library, Dublin; **8.20**, © Erich Lessing/Art Resource, NY; **8.22**, Bibliothèque Nationale de France; **8.23**, © Foto Marburg/Art Resource, NY; **8.24**, Bibliothèque Nationale de France; **8.25**, © Instituto Poligrafico e Zecca dello Stato; **8.26**, Bayerische Staatsbibliothek; **p. 216T**, © Tony Morrison/South American Pictures; **p. 216B**, © Frank Willet; **p. 217T**, © The British Museum; **p. 216M**, © D. Donne Bryant/Art Resource, NY; **p. 217B**, © Adam Woolfitt/Woodfin Camp and Associates. **Chapter 9 CO-9**, © Giraudon/Art Resource, NY; **9.1**, © Erich Lessing/Art Resource, NY; **9.2**, © Caisse Nationale des Monuments Historiques et des Sites; **9.3**, Bibliothèque Nationale de France; **9.4**, © Giraudon/Art Resource, NY, with special authorization of the City of Bayeux; **9.5**, © Alinari/Art Resource, NY; **9.6**, © The Granger Collection, New York; **9.7**, © Scala/Art Resource, NY; **9.8**, © Catherine Karnow/Woodfin Camp and Associates; **9.9**, © Giraudon/Art Resource, NY; **9.10**, © Scala/Art Resource, NY; **9.11**, © Jean Bernard; **9.12**, From *Drawings of Great Buildings* by W. Blaser and O. Hannaford. Birkhauser Verlag, Basel; **9.13**, © Anthony Scibilia/Art Resource, NY; **9.14**, © Photographie Bulloz; **9.15**, © Caisse Nationale des Monuments Historiques et des Sites; **9.16**, © Hirmer Fotoarchiv, Munich; **9.17**, Courtesy the Master and Fellows of Corpus Christi College, Cambridge. © Corpus Christi College, Cambridge; **9.19**, © Hirmer Fotoarchiv, Munich; **9.20**, From *Gardner's Art Through the Ages*, 6/e by Horst de la Croix and Richard G. Tansey, © 1975 by Harcourt Brace & Company. Reproduced by permission of the publisher; **9.21**, From *Drawings of Great Buildings* by W. Blaser and O. Hannaford. Birkhauser Verlag, Basel; **9.22**, © Hirmer Fotoarchiv, Munich; **9.23**, © Ronald Sheridan/Ancient Art & Architecture Collection; **9.24**, © Ronald Sheridan/Ancient Art & Architecture Collection; **9.25**, © Hirmer Fotoarchiv, Munich; **9.26**, © Hirmer Fotoarchiv, Munich; **9.27**, Jean Feuille/© C.N.M.H.S.; **9.28**, © Scala/Art Resource, NY; **9.29**, From *Drawings of Great Buildings* by W. Blaser and O. Hannaford. Birkhauser Verlag, Basel; **9.30**, © Hirmer Fotoarchiv, Munich; **9.31**, © Hirmer Fotoarchiv, Munich; **9.32**, Bibliothèque Nationale de France; **9.33**, Universitats Bibliothek, Munich; **p. 250TL**, © Frank Willet; **p. 250TR**, Courtesy Fundación Miguel Mujica Gallo, Museo Oro del Peru; **p. 250B**, © Werner Foreman Archive/Art Resource, NY; **p. 251T**, © Kyodo News International, Inc.; **p. 251M**, Private Collection/© Bridgeman Art Library; **p. 251B**, © Foto Wettstein & Kauf/Museum Rietberg, Zürich. **Chapter 10 CO-10**, © Photo RMN/J. G. Berizzi; **10.1**, Ampliaciones y Reproducciones MAS (Arxiu Mas), Barcelona; **10.2**, © Photo RMN; **10.3**, © Giraudon/Art Resource, NY; **10.4**, © Bibliothèque Royale Albert Ier, Bruxelles; **10.5**, © Scala/Art Resource, NY; **10.6**, Courtesy The Bancroft Library, University of California at Berkeley; **10.7**, © Foto Marburg/Art Resource, NY; **10.8**, © Scala/ Art Resource, NY; **10.9**, © Scala/Art Resource, NY; **10.10**, © Scala/Art Resource, NY; **10.11**, © G. Tortoli/Ancient Art & Architecture Collection; **10.12**, © Scala/Art Resource, NY; **10.13**, © Scala/ Art Resource, NY; **10.14**, © Art Resource, NY; **10.15**, © AKG London; **10.16**, © Bildarchiv Preussischer Kulturbesitz; **10.17**, © Scala/Art Resource, NY; **10.18**, © AKG London; **10.19**, © Alinari/Art Resource, NY; **10.20**, © Giraudon/Art Resource, NY; **10.21**, © Giraudon/Art Resource, NY; **10.22**, St. Bavo Cathedral, Ghent/© Giraudon/Art Resource, NY; **10.23**, © National Gallery, London; **10.24**, Photograph © Board of Trustees, National Gallery of Art, Washington, DC; **p. 286T**, © The British Museum; **p. 286M**, © N.J. Saunders/Art Resource, NY; **p. 286B**, Museo Nacional de Antropologia, Mexico City, Mexico; Sean Sprague/Mexicolore/© Bridgeman Art Library; **p. 287T**, © Mike Yamashita/Woodfin Camp and Associates; **p. 287B**, © Kim Newton/Woodfin Camp and Associates. **Chapter 11 CO-11**, © Scala/Art Resource, NY; **11.1**, © Erich Lessing/Art Resource, NY; **11.2**, © Scala/Art Resource, NY; **11.3**, © Erich Lessing/Art Resource, NY; **11.4**, © Scala/Art Resource, NY; **11.5**, © Scala/Art Resource, NY; **11.6**, © Scala/Art Resource, NY; **11.7**, From *Renaissance Architecture* by Peter Murray. © 1971 Electa International Publications, Drawing by Pepi Merisio; **11.8**, © Bill Chaitkin/Architectural Association, London; **11.9**, © Scala/Art Resource, NY; **11.10**, © Scala/Art Resource, NY; **11.11**, © Scala/Art Resource, NY; **11.12**, © Erich Lessing/Art Resource, NY; **11.13**, © Scala/Art Resource, NY; **11.14**, © Scala/Art Resource, NY; **11.15**, © Scala/Art Resource, NY; **11.16**, © Corbis/Karen Tweedy-Holmes; **11.17**, © AKG London; **11.18**, © Scala/Art Resource, NY; **11.19**, © Scala/Art Resource, NY; **11.20**, © Scala/Art Resource, NY; **11.21**, Galleria degli Uffizi Florence, Italy/© Bridgeman Art Library, London; **11.22**, © Erich Lessing/Art Resource, NY; **11.23**, © The Frick Collection, New York. **Chapter 12 CO-12**, © Artothek; **12.1**, © Erich Lessing/Art Resource, NY; **12.2**, © AKG London; **12.3**, © Hans Hinz/Artothek; **12.4**, © Elke Walford, Hamburg; **12.5**, © Scala/Art Resource, NY; **12.6**, © Artothek; **12.7**, © AKG London; **12.8**, Courtesy of the Vatican Museum. Photo by A. Bracchetti and P. Zigrossi; **12.9**, From *Italian Renaissance Painting* by James Beck © 1981. Reprinted by permission of HarperCollins Publishers, NY; **12.10**, © Scala/Art Resource, NY; **12.11**, Courtesy of the Vatican Museum. Photo by A. Bracchetti and P. Zigrossi; **12.12**, Courtesy of the Vatican Museum. Photo by A. Bracchetti and P. Zigrossi; **12.13**, © Erich Lessing/Art Resource, NY; **12.14**, © Erich Lessing/Art Resource, NY; **12.15**, © Scala/Art Resource, NY; **12.16**, © Superstock; **12.17**, Galleria degli Uffizi Florence, Italy/© Bridgeman Art Library, London; **12.18**, © Alinari/Art Resource, NY; **12.19**, Galleria dell'Accademia, Florence/ © Bridgeman Art Library, London; **12.20**, © Scala/Art Resource, NY; **12.21**, © SEF/Art Resource, NY; **12.22**, © Stephen Studd/Tony Stone Images; **12.23**, © Alinari/Art Resource, NY; **12.24**, From *Gardner's Art Through the Ages*, 6/e by Horst de la Croix and Richard G. Tansey, © 1975 by Harcourt Brace and Company. Reproduced by permission of the publisher; **12.25**, Courtesy of the Metropolitan Museum of Art, Gift of William Loring Andrews, 1888 (88.1 fol. 142b). **Chapter 13 CO-13**, © Blauel/Gnamm/ Artothek; **13.1**, © Erich Lessing/Art Resource, NY; **13.2**, Conjectural Reconstruction of the Globe Playhouse by C. Walter Hodges. From *Introducing Shakespeare*, by G. B. Harrison, 3/e © G. B. Harrison

1939, 1945, 1966; **13.3**, © Richard Kalina/Shakespeare's Globe; **13.4**, © Blauel/Gnamm/Artothek; **13.5**, Courtesy of the Fogg Art Museum, Harvard University Art Museums. Gift of William Gray from the collection of Francis Calley Gray; **13.6**, Musée d'Unterlinden, Colmar, France/© Giraudon/Bridgeman Art Library, London; **13.7**, Ampliaciones y Reproducciones MAS (Arxiu Mas), Barcelona; **13.8**, Photograph © 1984 The Detroit Institute of Arts, City of Detroit Purchase; **13.9**, © Hans Hinz/Artothek; **13.10**, Courtesy of the Metropolitan Museum of Art, Gift of Felix Warburg, 1920 (20.64.21); **13.11**, Print Collection, Miriam and Ira D. Wallach Division of Art, Prints and Photographs, The New York Public Library, Astor, Lennox and Tilden Foundations; **13.12**, © Bildarchiv Preussischer Kulturbesitz; **13.13**, Courtesy Musée Historique de la Réformation, Geneva; **13.14**, By courtesy of the National Portrait Gallery, London; **13.15**, Ampliaciones y Reproducciones MAS (Arxiu Mas), Barcelona; **13.16**, Toledo, S. Tome, Spain/Index/© Bridgeman Art Library, London; **13.17**, Courtesy of the Metropolitan Museum of Art, H. O. Havemeyer Collection, Bequest of Mrs. H. O. Havemeyer, 1929 (29.100.5); **13.18**, © linari/Art Resource, NY; **13.19**, Ampliaciones y Reproducciones MAS (Arxiu Mas), Barcelona; **13.20**, © Scala/Art Resource, NY; **p. 370T**, © President and Fellows Harvard College. Peabody Museum, Harvard University. Photograph by Hillel Burger, 2000; **p. 370B**, © The Granger Collection, New York; **p. 371TL**, The Nelson-Atkins Museum of Art, Kansas City, Missouri. Purchase: Nelson Trust; **p. 371TR**, © V&A Picture Library; **p. 371BL**, © Ronald Sheridan/Ancient Art & Architecture Collection; **p. 371BR**, © Dinodia Picture Agency. **Chapter 14 CO-14**, © Erich Lessing/Art Resource, NY; **14.1**, Reproduced by permission of the Trustees of The Wallace Collection, London; **14.2**, © Photographie Bulloz; **14.3**, From *Gardner's Art Through the Ages*, 6/e by Horst de la Croix and Richard G. Tansey, © 1975 by Harcourt Brace and Company. Reproduced by permission of the publisher; **14.4**, © Corbis/Bettmann; **14.5**, © Scala/Art Resource, NY; **14.6**, Santa Maria della Vittoria, Rome/© Bridgeman Art Library, London; **14.7**, © Scala/Art Resource, NY; **14.8**, Photograph © 1984 The Detroit Institute of Arts, Gift of Mr. Leslie H. Green; **14.9**, © Scala/Art Resource, NY; **14.10**, © Erich Lessing/Art Resource, NY; **14.11**, © Photo RMN—C. Jean/H. Lewandowski; **14.12**, © Photographie Bulloz; **14.13**, © Erich Lessing/Art Resource, NY; **14.14**, Louvre, Paris, France/Giraudon/© Bridgeman Art Library, London; **14.15**, © Joachim Blauel/Artothek; **14.16**, Courtesy Rijksmuseum Foundation, Amsterdam; **14.17**, Mauritshuis, The Hague/© Bridgeman Art Library, London; **14.18**, Louvre, Paris, France/Bridgeman Art Library, London; **14.19**, Gift of Mr. and Mrs. Robert Wood Bliss, © Board of Trustees, National Gallery of Art, Washington, DC. Photo by Lorene Emerson; **14.20**, © The National Gallery, London; **14.21**, © A. F. Kersting; **14.22**, Ampliaciones y Reproducciones MAS (Arxiu Mas), Barcelona; **p. 400T**, © Frank Willet; **p. 400B**, © Corbis/Charles & Josette Lenars; **p. 401T**, © V&A Picture Library; **p. 401M**, © Everton/The Image Works; **p. 401BL**, © K. Scholz/American Stock Photography; **p. 401BR**, © Vanni/Art Resource, NY. **Chapter 15 CO-15**, Courtesy Department of Library Services. American Museum of Natural History. Photo by Craig Chesek. Neg. #4825(2); **15.1**, Courtesy of the Bancroft Library, University of California at Berkeley; **15.2**, Courtesy Department of Library Services. American Museum of Natural History. Photo by Craig Chesek. Neg. #4825(2); **15.3**, The Huntington Library, San Marino, California; **15.4**, © The Granger Collection, New York; **15.5**, By courtesy of the National Portrait Gallery, London; **15.6**, © Erich Lessing/Art Resource, NY; **15.7**, © Erich Lessing/Art Resource, NY; **15.8**, Courtesy of the Bancroft Library, University of California at Berkeley; **15.9**, © Museum of the City of New York; **15.10**, © Photo RMN/Hugo Maertens; **15.11**, Bibliothèque Nationale de France. **Chapter 16 CO-16**, © The Frick Collection, New York; **16.1**, Photo: Nationalmuseum, Stockholm; **16.2**, From *A Diderot Pictorial Encyclopedia of Trades and Industry*, Dover Publications, © 1959, plate #34 (upper), New York; **16.3**, © Foto Marburg/Art Resource, NY; **16.4**, © Foto Marburg/Art Resource, NY; **16.5**, © Erich Lessing/Art Resource, NY; **16.6**, © AKG London; **16.7**, © Scala/Art Resource, NY; **16.8**, © Photo RMN/Gérard Blot; **16.9**, © The Frick Collection, New York; **16.10**, © Photographie Bulloz; **16.11**, © Erich Lessing/Art Resource, NY; **16.12**, © National Gallery, London; **16.13**, © Erich Lessing/Art Resource, NY; **16.14**, Courtesy The Metropolitan Museum of Art, Catherine Lorillard Wolfe Collection, Wolfe Fund, 1931 (31.45). Photograph © 1988 The Metropolitan Museum of Art; **16.15**, © English Heritage Photographic Library; **16.16**, © English Heritage Photographic Library; **16.17**, © Giraudon/Art Resource, NY; **16.18**, Bibliothèque Nationale de France; **p. 448TL**, © Angela Fisher/Carol Beckwith/Robert Estall Photo Library; **p. 448TR**, © Tony Morrison/South American Pictures; **p. 448B**, © Marion Morrison/South American Pictures; **p. 449T**, British Library, London, UK/© Bridgeman Art Library; **p. 449B**, © JTB Photo. **Chapter 17 CO-17**, © Giraudon/Art Resource, NY; **17.1**, City of Aberdeen Art Gallery and Museums Collections; **17.2**, © Phototheque des Musées de la Ville de Paris/Toumazet; **17.3**, © Giraudon/Art Resource, NY; **17.4**, Musée de l'Armée, Paris, France/Reunion des Musees Nationaux/© Bridgeman Art Library; **17.5**, © Giraudon/Art Resource, NY; **17.6**, Louvre, Paris, France/© The Bridgeman Art Library; **17.7**, Courtesy of the Metropolitan Museum of Art, Wolfe Fund, 1918, Catherine Lorillard Wolfe Collection. (19.77.2.). Photograph © 1987 The Metropolitan Museum of Art; **17.8**, © Robert C. Lautman Photography/Monticello; **17.9**, © 1995 Bob Leek/Washington Stock Photo; **17.10**, © Science & Society Picture Library; **17.11**, By courtesy of the National Portrait Gallery, London; **17.12**, © National Gallery, London; **17.13**, Yale Center for British Art, Paul Mellon Collection, USA/© Bridgeman Art Library; **17.14**, © Clore Collection, Tate Gallery, London/Art Resource, NY; **17.15**, © Clore Collection, Tate Gallery, London/Art Resource, NY; **17.16**, © Jörg P. Anders/Bildarchiv Preussischer Kulturbesitz; **17.17**, © Scala/Art Resource, NY; **17.18**, Courtesy The Museum of Fine Arts, Boston. Bequest of William P. Babcock. (B4165.43) Reproduced with permission. © 2000. The Museum of Fine Arts, Boston. Museo Nacional de Anthropologia, Mexico City, Mexico; **17.19**, © Erich Lessing/Art Resource, NY; **17.20**, © Erich Lessing/Art Resource, NY; **17.21**, © Giraudon/Art Resource, NY; **17.22**, © AKG London; **17.23**, © AKG London; **17.24**, © AKG London. **Chapter 18 CO-18**, © Scala/Art Resource, NY; **18.1**, © Giraudon/Art Resource, NY; **18.2**, © Ronald Sheridan/Ancient Art & Architecture Collection; **18.3**, Courtesy Museum of Fine Arts, Boston. Henry Lillie Pierce Fund. (99.22) Reproduced with permission. © 2000. Museum of Fine Arts, Boston. All rights reserved; **18.4**, Royal Holloway and Bedford New College, Surrey/© Bridgeman Art Library; **18.5**, © V&A Picture Library; **18.6**, © The Granger Collection, New York; **18.7**, Courtauld Institute Galleries, London; **18.8**, Louvre, Paris, France/Reunion des Musees Nationaux/© The Bridgeman Art Library; **18.9**, © Photo RMN/D. Arnaudet; **18.10**, Courtesy Musée Fabre; **18.11**, © Scala/Art Resource, NY; **18.12**, © The British Museum; **18.13**, Courtesy The Metropolitan Museum of Art, Bequest of Mrs. H. O. Havemeyer, 1929. The H. O. Havemeyer Collection. (29.100.129). Photograph © 1985 The Metropolitan Museum of Art; **18.14**, Courtesy Museum of Fine Arts, Boston. Gift of Quincy Adams Shaw through Quincy A. Shaw, Jr. and Mrs. Marian Shaw Haughton. (17.1485) Reproduced with permission. © 2000 Museum of Fine Arts, Boston. All rights reserved; **18.15**, © Erich Lessing/Art Resource, NY; **18.16**, Courtesy The Metropolitan Museum of Art, Gift of Cornelius Vanderbilt, 1887. (87.25). Photograph by Schecter Lee © 1986 The Metropolitan Museum of Art; **18.17**, © Photo RMN/J. G. Berizzi; **18.18**, Library of Congress; **p. 506TL**, © Musée de l'Homme; **p. 506TR**, Consejo Nacional para la Cultura y las Artes, Instituto Nacional de Bellas Artes, Museo Nacional de Arte, Mexico City. Photograph: Arturo Piera L.; **p. 506B**, © Visor; **p. 507TL**, © China Stock; **p. 507TR**, Christie's Images/© The Bridgeman Art Library; **p. 507B**, © Kyodo News International, Inc. **Chapter 19 CO-19**, Amsterdam, Van Gogh Museum (Vincent Van Gogh Foundation); **19.1**, Collection of Mr. and Mrs. Paul Mellon. Photograph © Board of Trustees, National Gallery of Art, Washington. © 2000 Artists Rights Society (ARS), New York/ADAGP, Paris; **19.2**, © Christie's London/Artothek; **19.3**, Carnegie Museum of Art, Pittsburgh; **19.4**, Eyre Crowe, *The Dinner Hour at Wigan*, © Manchester City Art Galleries; **19.5**, © The Granger Collection, New York; **19.6**, © Erich Lessing/Art Resource, NY; **19.7**, The Museum of Modern Art, New York. Acquired through the Lillie P. Bliss Bequest. Photograph © 2000 The Museum of Modern Art, New York; **19.8**, Courtesy of the Fogg Art Museum, Harvard University Art Museums, Bequest of Grenville L. Winthrop. © President and Fellows of Harvard College; **19.9**, Photo: J. Lathion, © Nasjonalgalleriet. © 2000 The Munch Museum/The Munch-Ellingsen Group/Artists Rights Society (ARS), New York; **19.10**, © Photo RMN; **19.11**, Carnegie Museum of Art, Pittsburgh, Acquired through the generosity of Mrs. Alan M. Scaife; **19.12**, © The Phillips Collection, Washington, DC; **19.13**, Collection of Mr. and Mrs. Paul Mellon. Photograph © Board of Trustees, National Gallery of Art, Washington; **19.14**, Mary Cassatt (American, 1844–1926) *The Bath*, 1891. Soft-ground etching with aquatint and drypoint on paper. 12-3/8 x 9-3/8". The National Museum of Women in the Arts. Gift of Wallace and Wilhelmina Holladay; **19.15**, Photograph © 2000 The Art Institute of Chicago, All Rights Reserved; **19.16**, Paul Cezanne, *Mont Sainte-Victorie*. 27-1/2 x 35-1/4". Philadelphia Museum of Art, The George W. Elkins Collection. Photo by Graydon Wood, 1995; **19.17**, Albright-Knox Art Gallery, Buffalo, NY. A. Conger Goodyear Collection, 1965; **19.18**, Amsterdam, Van Gogh Museum (Vincent Van Gogh Foundation); **19.19**, The Museum of Modern Art, New York. Acquired through the Lillie P. Bliss Bequest. Photograph © 2000 The Museum of Modern Art, New York; **19.20**, © 2000 Succession H. Matisse, Paris/Artists Rights Society (ARS), New York; **19.21**, The Museum of Modern Art, New York. Acquired through the Lillie P. Bliss Bequest. Photograph © 2000 The Museum of Modern Art, New York. © 2000 Estate of Pablo Picasso/Artists Rights Society (ARS), New York; **19.22**, The Museum of Modern Art, New York. Purchase. Photograph © 2000 The Museum of Modern Art, New York. © 2000 Estate of Pablo Picasso/Artists Rights Society (ARS), New York; **19.23**, Stedelijk Museum, Amsterdam. © 2000 Artists Rights Society (ARS), New York/ADAGP, Paris; **19.24**, Augustine Rodin. *Eve*. 67 x 18-1/2 x 23-1/4". The Rodin Museum, Philadelphia. Gift of Jules E. Mastbaum; **19.25**, © Wayne Andrews/Esto; **19.26**, © Chicago Historical Society. **Chapter 20 CO-20**, Private Collection, photo courtesy of Mary-Anne Martin/Fine Art, NY; **20.1**, © AKG London. © 2000 Estate of Pablo Picasso/Artists Rights Society (ARS), New York; **20.2**, © Imperial War Museum, London; **20.3**, Library of Congress; **20.4**, © AP/Wide World Photos; **20.5**, Margaret Bourke-White/Life Magazine, © Time, Inc.; **20.6**, © AP/Wide World Photos; **20.7**, Courtesy The Metropolitan Museum of Art, Bequest of Gertrude Stein, 1947 (47.106). Photograph © 1996 The Metropolitan Museum of Art. © 2000 Estate of Pablo Picasso/Artists Rights Society (ARS), New York; **20.8**, Jacob Lawrence. *In the North the African American had more educational opportunities*. Panel 58 from *The Migration Series*. (1940–41; text and titles revised by the artist, 1993). Tempera on gesso on compostion board, 12 x 18" (30.5 x 45.7 cm). The Museum of Modern Art, New York. Gift of Mrs. David M. Levy. Photograph © 2000 The Museum of Modern Art, New York; **20.9**, Thyssen-Bornemisza Foundation Collection, Madrid, Spain. © Estate of George Grosz/Licensed by VAGA, New York, NY; **20.10**, Yale University Art Gallery. © 2000 Artists Rights Society (ARS), New York/ADAGP, Paris; **20.11**, The Museum of Modern Art, New York. Photograph © 2000 The Museum of Modern Art; **20.12**, Piet Mondrian. *Broadway Boogie Woogie*. 1942–43. Oil on canvas, 50 x 50" (127 x 127 cm). The Museum of Modern Art, New York. Given anonymously. Photograph © 2000 The Museum of Modern Art, New York. © 2000 Beeldrecht, Amsterdam/Artists Rights Society (ARS), New York; **20.13**, Philadelphia Museum of Art. The A. E. Gallatin Collection. © 2000 Estate of Pablo Picasso/Artists Rights Society (ARS), New York; **20.14**, Georgia O'Keeffe, American, 1887–1986, *Cow's Skull with Calico Roses*, oil on canvas, 1932, 92.2 x 61.3 cm, Gift of Georgia O'Keeffe, 1947.712. Photograph © 2000 The Art Institute of Chicago, All Rights Reserved. © 2000 The Georgia O'Keeffe Foundation/Artists Rights Society (ARS), New York; **20.15**, Marcel Duchamp, *The Bride Stripped Bare by Her Bachelors, Even (The Large Glass)* Front View. 109-1/4 x 69-1/8". Philadelphia Museum of Art, Bequest of Katherine S. Dreier. © 2000 Artists Rights Society (ARS), New York/ADAGP, Paris/Estate of Marcel Duchamp; **20.16**, The Museum of Modern Art, New York. Given anonymously. Photograph © 2000 The Museum of Modern Art. © 2000 Foundation Gala-Salvador Dali/VEGAP, Madrid/Artists Rights Society (ARS), New York; **20.17**, © Artothek. © 2000 Artists Rights Society (ARS), New York/VG Bild-Kunst, Bonn; **20.18**, Private Collection, photo courtesy of Mary-Anne Martin/Fine Art, NY; **20.19**, The Baltimore Museum of Art, The Cone Collection, formed by Dr. Claribel Cone and Mrs. Etta Cone of Baltimore, Maryland. © 2000 Succession H. Matisse, Paris/Artists Rights Society (ARS), New York; **20.20**, Max Beckmann. *Departure*. (1932–33). Oil on canvas, triptych, center panel, 7' 3/4" x 45-3/8" (215.3 x 115.2 cm); side panels each 7' 3/4" x 39-1/4" (215.3 x 99.7 cm). The Museum of Modern Art, New York. Given anonymously (by exchange). Photograph © 2000 The Museum of Modern Art, New York. © 2000 Artists Rights Society (ARS), New York/VG Bild-Kunst, Bonn; **20.21**, © 2000 Artists Rights Society (ARS), NY/ADAGP, Paris/FLC/Anthony Scibilia/Art Resource, NY; **20.22**, © AKG London. © 2000 Estate of Pablo Picasso/Artists Rights Society (ARS), New York; **p. 572T**, Olowe of Ise, d. 1938, Africa, Nigeria, Ekiti, Ikere; Yoruba, Veranda post of Enthroned King (Opo Ogoga), wood, pigment, 1910/14, 152.5 x 31.7 x 40.6 cm, Major Acquistions Centennial Fund, 1984.550, right 3/4 view. Photograph by Bob Hashimoto. Photograph © 2000 The Art Institute of Chicago, All Rights Reserved; **p. 572B**, © Schalkwijk/Art Resource, NY; **p. 573TL**, Reproduced by permission of the Art Museum of the Chinese University of Hong Kong from the collection of the Art Museum; **p. 573TR**, © MOA Museum of Art, Atami; **p. 573B**, © Dinodia Picture Agency. **Chapter 21 CO-21**, Andy Warhol, American, 1930–1987, *Mao*, acrylic and silkscreen on canvas, 1973, 448.3 x 346.7 cm, Mr. and Mrs. Frank G. Logan Prize and Wilson L. Mead Fund. Photograph © 2000 The Art Institute of Chicago, All Rights Reserved. © 2000 Andy Warhol Foundation for the Visual Arts/Artists Rights Society (ARS), New York; **21.1**, © Robert Brenner/PhotoEdit; **21.2**, Andy Warhol, American, 1930–1987, *Mao*, acrylic and silkscreen on canvas, 1973, 448.3 x 346.7 cm, Mr. and Mrs. Frank G. Logan Prize and Wilson L. Mead Fund. Photograph © 2000 The Art Institute of Chicago, All Rights Reserved. © 2000 Andy Warhol Foundation for the Visual Arts/Artists Rights Society (ARS), New York; **21.3**, John Darnell/Life Magazine, © 1970 Time, Inc.; **21.4**, © Patrick Piel/Liaison Agency, Inc.; **21.5**, © AP/Wide World Photos; **21.6**, © Reuters/Mazlan Enjah/Archive Photos; **21.7**, Courtesy Carl Solway Gallery, Cincinnati, Ohio, photographer: Chris Gomien; **21.8**, © Judy Chicago, 1979/TTF Archives; **21.8 inset**, Sojourner Truth place setting, from *The Dinner Party*, © Judy Chicago, 1979, mixed media, 5' x 3'. Collection: The Dinner Party Trust. Photo © Donald Woodman; **21.9**, The Hirshhorn Museum and Sculpture Garden, Smithsonian Institution, Washington, DC. © Romare Bearden Foundation/Licensed by VAGA, New York, NY; **21.10**, Courtesy of Ronald Feldman Fine Arts, NY, Collection Evander D. Schley. Photo credit: D. James Dee; **21.11**, Reproduced by permission of The National Gallery of Australia, Canberra. © 2000 Pollock-Krasner Foundation/Artists Rights Society (ARS), NY; **21.12**, The Phillips Collection, Washington, DC. © 2000 Kate Rothko Prizel & Christopher Rothko/Artists Rights Society (ARS), New York; **21.13**, The Museum of Modern Art. Gift of Hymen N. Glickstein. Photograph © 2000 The Museum of Modern Art, New York; **21.14**, Courtesy Leo Castelli Gallery, New York. © Jasper Johns/Licensed by VAGA, New York, NY; **21.15**, Moderna Museet, KSK, Stockholm. © Untitled Press, Inc./Licensed by VAGA, New York, NY; **21.16**, © Tate Gallery, London/Art Resource, NY/© 2000 Andy Warhol Foundation for the Visual Arts/Artists Rights Society (ARS), New York.; **21.17**, Photo © Tate Gallery/Art Resource, NY/© Estate of David Smith/Licensed by VAGA, New York, NY; **21.18**, The Museum of Modern Art, New York. Gift of Mr. and Mrs. Ben Mildwoff. Photograph © The Museum of Modern Art, New York. © 2000 Estate of Louise Nevelson/Artists Rights Society (ARS), New York; **21.19**, Private Collection. © George Segal/Licensed by VAGA, New York, NY. Courtesy Sidney Janis Gallery, New York. Photograph © Geoffrey Clements; **21.20**, © Ezra Stoller/Esto; **21.21**, Courtesy Leonard and Eleanor Bellinson and The Donald Morris Gallery; **21.22**, Courtesy Marian Goodman Gallery, NY; **21.23**, © 1990 Sue Coe. Courtesy Galerie St. Etienne, New York; **21.24**, © Tate Gallery, London/Art Resource, NY/© 2000 Artists Rights Society (ARS), NY/DACS, London; **21.25**, Collection of Ann and Robert Freedman. Courtesy Knoedler & Company, New York. © 2000 Frank Stella/Artists Rights Society (ARS), New York; **21.26**, Courtesy ACA Galleries, NY/Munich; **21.27**, Courtesy of the artist and Luhring Augustine, New York; **21.28**, Ann Hamilton. *mantle* 1998. Installation View. Miami Art Museum, April 2–June 7, 1998. Photo by Thibault Jeanson. Courtesy Miami Art Museum; **21.29**, Courtesy Venturi, Scott Brown, and Associates. Photo © William Watkins; **21.30**, © Photri, Inc.; **21.31**, © Peter Mauss/Esto; **21.32**, Photo: Erika Ede/© Guggenheim Bilbao; **21.33**, © William Struhs; **21.34**, Courtesy of the artist and Metro Pictures; **p. 614T**, Photo © AKG London, © Fernando Botero, courtesy Marlborough Gallery, New York; **p. 614BL**, © Giraudon/Art Resource, NY; **p. 614BR**, © Tony Morrison/South American Pictures; **p. 615TL**, © Fukuoka Asian Art Museum; **p. 615TR**, Phillips, The International Fine Art Auctioneers/© Bridgeman Art Library; **p. 615B**, From *Japanese Art*, by Joan Stanlly Baker. © Thames & Hudson, 1984. Fig. 163.

INDEX

Page numbers in italics indicate pronunciation guides; page numbers in boldface indicate illustrations. For readers using the two-volume set of *The Western Humanities,* page numbers 1–344 (Chapters 1–12) refer to material in Volume I: *Beginnings through the Renaissance,* and page numbers 289–615 (Chapters 11–21) refer to material in Volume II: *The Renaissance to the Present.*

Aachen, 210, 211, **212**
Abbasid dynasty, 199
Abelard, Peter, *230–231*
Abraham, 146, 159
Abraham (Hrotswitha), 211
absolutism, 374–376, 414, 430, 440, 458
Abstract Expressionism, 593–594, **593**, **594**, **595**
  and music, 609
  sculpture, 597, **597**, **598**
abstract painting, 523, 528, 603, **604**. *See also specific styles and artists*
Académie de France, 437
a cappella music, 312, 342
Achilles, 35. *See also Iliad*
acropolis (Athens), **30**, 38, **39**, 59, 60
  Erechtheum, 73, 74–75, **74**
  See also Parthenon
Acts of the Apostles, 158–159
Adam, Robert, 439, **439**, **440**
Adamites, 354
Adams, John, 609
Adonai, 147
Aegean civilizations, 31–38
  Dark Ages, 36, 38
  map, **32**
  Minoan, 32–35, 37
  Mycenaean, 33, 35–37, **36**, **37**
  See also Greek Archaic Age; Greek Hellenic Age
Aegina, 48, **48**, 50, 52, **52**
Aeneid (Vergil), 106, 122, 184, **184**
Aeschylus, 40, 59, *63*, 82, 553
aesthete, 521
Afghanistan, 580
Africa, 88, 320, 429, 515, **515**, 579. *See also* European expansion; non-Western influences; windows on the world
African Americans
  Age of Anxiety, 577, 584, 585–586, **587**, 588, 591, 592
  Bourgeois Age, 494–495
  interwar period, 551, **552**
  music, 537
  See also specific people
Agamemnon (Aeschylus), 40, 63
Agasias of Ephesus, **105**
Age of Anxiety, 575–612
  map, **578**
  mass culture, 541, 548–549, 557, 605, **606**, 607, 611
  philosophy, 584–586
  political/economic development, 575–583, 611–612
  science, 586–588
  style characteristics, 583–584
  timeline, 582
  See also Late Modernism; Post-Modernism
"Age of Anxiety, The" (Auden), 583
Age of Reason, 423–446
  architecture, **428**, **431**, 435–436, **436**, 439–440, **439**, **440**
  legacy of, 446
  literature, 441–444
  map, **424**
  music, 444–446, **445**
  political/economic development, 423, 427–431
  political philosophy, 440–441
  sculpture, **442**
  timeline, 425
  See also Enlightenment; Neoclassical style; Rococo style
Age of the Masses/High Modernism. *See* interwar period
Agon (Stravinsky), 609
agora, 38
agrarian revolution, 3–4
agriculture. *See* political/economic development
Ahmose I (pharoah), *14*
Ahriman, 25
Ahuramazda, 25
Aïda (Verdi), 503
AIDS, 587
"Ain't I a Woman?" (Truth), 495
aisles, 180
Akhenaten (pharoah), *16*, 17, 21, **22**, 609
Akhnaten (Glass), 609
Akkadian empire, 5–6, 7, 10, 12, **12**, 146. *See also* Mesopotamia
A la recherche du temps perdu (Proust), 521
Alberti, Leone Battista, 298, **298**, 299, 300, 302–303
Albigensians, 228–229, 259
alchemy, 410
Alcuin of York, *210*
Alexander II (czar of Russia), 514
Alexander VII (pope), 380
Alexander the Great, 55, 60, **60**, 93, 116–117
  and Aristotle, 60, 70
  and Hellenistic philosophy, 95, **96**, 97
  and Hellenistic political systems, 87, 89, 90, 99
  and Judaism, 150
  and Persia, 25
  and sculpture, 80
Alexandria (Egypt), 88, 89, 90, **91**, 92, 140
Alexandrianism, 94, 121, 122
Alexiad (Comnena), 194, 208
Alexius Comnenus (Byzantine Emperor), 191, 194
Algeria, 579
Alhambra, 203–204, **205**
"alienation effect," 552
Allah, 198
Allegory of the Missionary Work of the Jesuits (Pozzo), 383–384, **385**
altars, 99, 100, **148**. *See also* architecture; religion
Amalienburg, **428**
Amarna revolution (Egypt), 16, 17, 21, **22**, 24
Ambrose, 175, **176**, 185, 186
ambulatory, 211, 237
Amen, 16, 21
Amenemhat (pharoah), *16*
American Exodus, An: A Record of Human Erosion (Lange), **544**
American Revolution, 124, 415, 429, 430, 441, 453–454, 479
American Telephone and Telegraph Headquarters (New York) (Johnson & Burgee), 607, **607**
Americas, 363
  American Revolution, 124, 415, 429, 430, 441, 453–454
  Baroque Age, 380, 416, **418**
  High Renaissance/early Mannerism, 320
  and Scientific Revolution, **402**, **405**
  See also European expansion; United States; windows on the world
Amiens Cathedral, **221**, 244, **244**, **245**, 246, **246**
Amos, 149
amphitheaters, 130–131, **131**
Anatomy Lesson of Dr. Tulp, The (Rembrandt), **410**
Anaxagoras, *68*
Anderson, Laurie, 610, **610**
Angelico, Fra, **288**, 307–308, **308**
Angles, 173, 205
Anglicanism, 360–361, 376
Anguissola, Sofonisba, *364*, **365**, 366
Animal Farm (Orwell), 551
Anna Karenina (Tolstoy), 494
Annales of Gilles Le Muisit, **259**
Annals (Tacitus), 123
Annunciation, The (Fra Angelico), **288**, 307–308, **308**
Annunciation, The (Ghiberti), 305, **305**
Antheil, George, *569*
Anthemius of Tralles, **191**, **195**
anthropology, 585
anthropomorphism, 8
Antigone (Sophocles), 63–64
Antigonus, 89
Antioch, 90, 186
Antiochus IV, *99*, 100, 150
Antiquities of Athens, The (Stuart & Revett), 437
anti-Semitism, 166, 546
Antoinette, Marie, 433, **434**, 435
Antony, 173
Anu, 8
Aphrodite, 42, 77, **77**
Aphrodite of Melos, 103, **105**
Apian, Peter, **404**
apocalypse, 149–150, 158, 160
Apocrypha, 154
Apollo, 42, 57, **114**
Apollo of Veii, **114**
Apology (Plato), 68
Appalachian Spring (Copland), 569
"Apparel of Women, The" (Tertullian), 162
apse, 180, 236
aqueducts, 131, **132**
Aquinas, Thomas. *See* Thomas Aquinas, Saint
arabesque, 201–202, **201**, 204, **205**
Aragon, 255
Ara Pacis, 133, **135**
arcade, 201
Archaic Age. *See* Greek Archaic Age
archaic smile, 50, **50**, **51**, 77
architecture
  Bourgeois Age, **483**, 496
  Byzantine Empire, **191**, 194–195, **194**, **195**, **196**, 201, 212
  Classical Baroque, 376, **377**, 387–388, **387**, **388**, 420, **431**
  and Counter-Reformation, 363, 380
  Early Gothic style, 240, **241**, 242, **242**
  Early Middle Ages, **207**, **210**, 211, **212**, 236
  Early Modernism, 523, 534–535, **535**, **536**
  Early Renaissance, 298, **298**, 299–303, **300**, **301**
  Egypt, 14, **15**, 16, 17–19, **18**
  Florid Baroque, 380, **380**, **381**, **382**
  Gothic innovations, 239–240, **239**, **240**, **241**
  Greek Archaic Age, 19, **30**, 38, **39**, 46–48, **47**, **48**
  Greek Hellenic Age, 70–75, **72**, **73**, **74**, 126
  Hellenistic Age, **91**, 93, 99–100, **99**, **100**
  High Gothic style, **218**, 242, 244–246, **244**, **245**, **246**
  High Renaissance/Early Mannerism, 339–342, **339**, **340**, **341**
  interwar period, 567, **567**
  Islamic world, **188**, **200**, 201–204, **201**, **202**, **204**, **205**
  Judaism, 155–157, **156**
  Late Gothic style, **258**, 265–267, **265**, **266**, **267**, 299
  Late Modernism, 599–600, **600**
  Mesopotamia, 12–13, **13**, 18, 126, 130
  Mycenaean, 35–36, **36**, **37**
  Neoclassical style, 439–440, **439**, **440**, **460**, 461, **461**, **462**
  Post-Modernism, **583**, 605–607, **606**, **607**, **608**
  Restrained Baroque, 393–394, **394**
  Rococo style, **428**, 435–436, **436**
  Romanesque style, 236–239, **236**, **237**
  See also Gothic style; Islamic architecture; late Roman architecture; pre-Christian Roman architecture
architrave, 46
Arch of Constantine, 179, **179**, 182, **183**
Arch of Titus, 129–130, **130**, 133, 136, **136**, 179
Arch of Trajan, **118**
Ardebil Carpet, **203**
A rebours (Huysmans), 521
Arena Chapel (Padua), 277, **278**
Ares, 42
Arianism, 173, 175
arias, 502
Aristarchus, 406
Aristophanes, *65*, 82
Aristotle, *70*, 262
  and Alexander the Great, 60, 70
  and Baroque Age, 395

Aristotle *(continued)*
and Early Middle Ages, 209
and High Middle Ages, 230, 231, 234
legacy of, 82
and Locke, 416
and Pre-Socratics, 67
and Renaissance, 296, 298, 332
and Scientific Revolution, 404–405, 409, 411
on tragedy, 62
Arius, *173*
Ark of the Covenant, 147, 148, 155
Armies of the Night, The (Mailer), 589
Armstrong, Louis, 569
Arnold, Matthew, 1
Arnolfini Wedding Portrait (van Eyck), 277, **281**, 282
Arouet, François-Marie. *See* Voltaire
Arrian, 124
art
Assyria, **25**
Egypt, 1, 19–25, **23**, 49
Greek Hellenic Age, 64, **66**
Mesopotamia, **9**, 11–12, **11**, 49, 50
Minoan, 32, **34**
Mycenaean, 36, **37**
Persia, 25, **26**
See also architecture; early Christian art; manuscript illumination; mosaics; painting; sculpture
Artemis, 42
art market, 389, 391, 433, **433**
Art Nouveau, **521**
Art of Love (Ovid), 122
art songs, 475, 503
asceticism. *See* monasticism
ashlars, 36, **36**
"Ash Wednesday" (Eliot), 551
Asia. *See* European expansion; non-Western influences; windows on the world
assemblage, 594, **596**
Assyria, 15, 25, **25**, 149
astrology, 98
astronomy, 406–409, **406**, 412, 418. *See also* science
ataraxia, 97
Aten, 16, 17, 21
Athanadoros, **86**, *106*, **106**
Athanasius, *173*
atheism, 411, 419, 551
Athena, 42, **57**
Athena Parthenos, **57**
Athens, 39, 42, 46, 59, 60, 100. *See also* acropolis; Greek Hellenic Age; Parthenon
athletics. *See* sports
atmospheric perspective, 299
atomic bombs, 548, 555, 583. *See also* nuclear weapons
Atomists, 67, 96
atonality, 537, 568, 608–609
Atonement, 159
atrium, 180
Attalos I, *101*
attic, 179
Auden, W. H., 583
Augsburg, Religious Peace of, 362–363, 378
Augustine, Saint, 175–177, 226, 227, 231
Augustus Caesar (Octavian) (Roman emperor), 89, 117, 170
and architecture, 129, 131
and art, 111, 126
and literature, 122
and sculpture, 133, 136
aulos, 66, 140
Austen, Jane, 458, 459
Austria
Age of Reason, 429, 430–431, **431**
Baroque Age, 374, 377
Bourgeois Age, 481, 483, 486
Early Modernism, 514, 518
interwar period, 544
revolution/reaction period, 456, 458
autarky, 95, 96, 97
authenticity, 554
Auxerre Cathedral, **229**
Auxerre Kore, 50, **51**
avant-garde, 518
Averroës (Ibn Rushd), *231*
Averroists, 231, 261
Avignonese popes, 257–258, 356
Awakening, The (Chopin), 520

Babel, Tower of, 12
Babylonia, 6, 7, 98, 146, 149, 151, 155. *See also* Mesopotamia
Bacchae, The (Euripides), 65
Bach, Johann Sebastian, 367, 397–398
Bacon, Roger, 262
Bacon, Francis, 410–411, 427, 490
Bactria, 89
bagpipe, 248
balance of power, 374, 377–379
baldacchino, 380–381, **382**
Baldwin, James, 588
ballades, 312
ballet, 537, 609
Ballet méchanique (Antheil), 569
balustrade, **339**, 340
Balzac, Honoré de, *493*
baptism, 226. *See also* baptisteries
baptisteries, 180, **182**, 236, 304–305, **305**
Bar at the Folies-Bergère, A (Manet), **491**
Barbizon school, 499, 523
bards, 43
Baroque Age, 373–398
Christianity, 375, 376, 377–378, 395, 419
and Counter-Reformation, 363, 379, 380
European expansion, 396, 416–417, **417**, **418**, 420
and Hellenistic Age, 106, 395
legacy of, 398
literature, 394–396, 417, 418–419
maps, **374**, **417**
music, 367, 396–398, **396**
political/economic development, 373, 374–379, 389, 413
political philosophy, 413–416, 420
style characteristics, 379
timeline, 376
See also Classical Baroque; Florid Baroque; Restrained Baroque; Scientific Revolution
barrel vault, 126, **127**
Barry, Charles, **483**, 496
Basil I (Byzantine emperor), 191
basilicas, 180, **180**, **181**
Bath, The (Cassatt), 527, **527**
Battleship Potemkin, The (Eisenstein), 568
Baudelaire, Charles, *498*
Bauhaus, 567, 599
Bayeux Tapestry, **225**
Bayle, Pierret, *418*–419, 426
Bay of Baiae, The, with Apollo and the Sibyl (Turner), 467, **467**
bays, 237
Bearden, Romare, **587**
Beardsley, Aubrey, **521**
Beat Generation, 589
Beatles, 611
Beaumarchais, Pierre, *446*
Beckett, Samuel, 590
Beckmann, Max, 563, **566**
Bede, 209–*210*
Beethoven, Ludwig van, *474*–*475*, **474**
beghards, 228
beguines, 228
Behn, Aphra, 396
Being and Nothingness (Sartre), 554
Being and Time (Heidegger), 554
bel canto, 397
Belgium, 485. *See also* Flemish style
Bellay, Jean-Baptiste, **455**
Bellini, Giovanni, 311–312, **312**, 333
Bellini, Jacopo, 311
Beloved (Morrison), 591
Benedict, Saint, 208
Benedictine order, 208, **210**, 225
Bentham, Jeremy, 426, 487
Berlin Academy of Science, 418
Berlin Wall, 577, **580**, 581
Berlioz, Hector, 475–*476*
Bernardino Campi Painting Sofonisba Anguissola (Anguissola), **365**
Bernard of Clairvaux, *227*
Bernini, Gianlorenzo, *380*–381, **380**, **381**, **382**, **383**
Berruguete, Pedro, **292**
Bible, Christian, 153, 154, 158, 160
and Hebrew Bible, 153, 154
higher criticism, 489–490
Late Middle Ages, 259
Vulgate, 175, 362
See also Christianity; manuscript illumination; *specific works of art*
Bible, Hebrew, 147, 148–149, **149**, **150**, 152–154
and early Christianity, 159, 160, 163, 165, **165**
and Egyptian culture, 16, 17
and Mesopotamian culture, 6, 10, 12
See also Judaism
Billy the Kid (Copland), 569
biology, 409–410, 522, 588. *See also* science
birth control pill, 587, 600
Birth of a Nation, The (Griffith), 567–568
Birth of Aphrodite, The, 77, **77**
Birth of Venus, The (Botticelli), 297, **297**, 310
Bismarck, Otto von, 482–483, 491, 512
Black Boy (Wright), 588
black consciousness movement, 584, 585–586, **587**
Black Death, **253**, **254**, 255, 259, 262–263, **263**, 291
Blair, Eric. *See* Orwell, George
Blair, Tony, 604
Blake, Peter, **602**, 603
Blaue Reiter school, 533–534
Bleak House (Dickens), 494
blind arcades, 240
Blinding of Samson, The (Rembrandt), 389–390, **389**
Bloomsbury Group, 550
Blue Poles (Pollock), **593**
blues, 537
Bluest Eye, The (Morrison), 591
Boccaccio, Giovanni, 262–263, 346
Boccioni, Umberto, **518**
Boethius, *209*, 230
Boffrand, Germain, *435*, **436**
Bohemia, 259
Bohr, Niels, 522, 523
Boilly, Louis-Leopold, **455**
Bonaparte, Louis-Napoleon. *See* Napoleon III
Bonaventure, Saint, *231*
Bonheur, Rosa, *499*–500, **501**
Boniface VIII (pope), 225, **226**
"Bonjour Monsieur Courbet" (Courbet), 496, **497**
Bonnard, Pierre, **510**
Book of Revelation, 160, 166
Book of the City of Ladies, The (de Pizan), 265
books. *See* literature; manuscript illumination
Borges, Jorgé Luis, *591*
Borghese Gladiator (Agasias), 103–104, **105**
Borgia, Cesare, 323
Borgia, Lucrezia, *292*
Bosch, Hieronymus, *353*–354, **353**
Bosnia, **583**
Bossuet, Bishop, *414*
botanical gardens, 19
Botticelli, Sandro, 294, 297, **297**, *308*–310, **310**, 335
Boucher, François, *433*, **434**
Bourbon dynasty, 375–376, 457–458. *See also specific kings*
Bourgeois Age, 479–504
architecture, **483**, 496
Christianity, 489–490, 494
legacy of, 504
literature, 491–495
maps, **480**, **484**
music, 502–503
Neoclassical painting, 495, **495**
philosophy, 487, 489
photography, 501–502, **502**
political/economic development, 479, 481–486, 488–489
Romantic painting, **484**, 495–496, **496**
science, 490, 491
sculpture, **481**
style characteristics, 490–491
timeline, 480
See also Realist painting
Bourke-White, Margaret, **547**
Boyle, Robert, 409–410, 412
Boy Struggling with a Goose, 101, **101**
Brady, Matthew, 502, **502**
Brahe, Tycho, 406, *407*, **407**, 412
Brahms, Johannes, 503
Bramante, Donato, 339–340, **339**, 380, 394
Brandenburg Concertos (Bach), 397–398
Brandenburg-Prussia. *See* Prussia
Braque, Georges, 532, *533*
Brecht, Bertolt, 551, *552*, 553
Brethren/Sisters of the Common Life, 259, 347
Bride Stripped Bare by Her Bachelors, Even, The (Duchamp), 560, **561**
Britain. *See* England
"Brit Pak" (Young British Artists), 604
Broadway, 549
Broadway Boogie Woogie (Mondrian), **558**
Brontë, Charlotte, 488, 492, 493
Brontë, Emily, 492–493
Bronze Age, 5, 7, 14, 32. *See also* Egypt; Mesopotamia
Brothers Karamazov, The (Dostoevsky), 494
Bruegel, Jan, **396**

Bruegel, Pieter the Elder, 353, *354*–356, **355**
Brunelleschi, Filippo, *298*, 299, 300, **300**, **301**, 303, 304, 307
Bruni, Leonardo, 295
Brutus, 133, **133**
Bruyas, Alfred, 496, **497**
bull-leaping, **34**, 35
Burckhardt, Jacob, 289
Burgee, John, **607**
Burgkmair, Hans, **342**
Burgundians, 173, 205
Burgundy, 306
Burial of Count Orgaz, The (El Greco), 363–364, **364**, 367
Bury Bible, **238**, 239
Byron, Lord, 462, 463–464, **464**, 471, 472
Byzantine Empire, 189–198, 209
  architecture, **191**, 194–195, **194**, **195**, **196**, 201, 212
  and Carolingian dynasty, 206, 207
  and Early Renaissance, 296, 306
  and High Middle Ages manuscript illumination, 239
  historical writing, 194
  law, 193–194
  legacy of, 215, 230
  map, **190**
  mosaics, **192**, 195, 197, **197**, **198**
  Orthodox Christianity, 190, 191, 193, **194**, 197–198, **198**
  political/economic development, 190–193, **192**, 292
  style characteristics, 193
  timeline, 192
  See also Eastern Roman Empire
Byzantium, 171. *See also* Byzantine Empire; Constantinople

Cage, John, 609
Cajun culture, 520
calculus, 409
calendars, 27, **139**, 157, 158, 271. *See also* mathematics
Callicrates, *73*, **73**, **74**
calligraphy, 202, **202**
Calvin, John, 357, 359–360, **360**, 361
Calvinism, 359–360, 375, 377
Cambrai, Treaty of (1529), 317
Camerata, 367
Camino de perfección (Teresa of Avila), 383
campanile, 266
Campi, Bernardino, 365
Camus, Albert, *588*
Candide (Voltaire), 442
canons
  Egyptian, 21, 23
  Jewish, 152, 160
Canterbury Tales, The (Chaucer), 264, **264**
canzones, 233
Canzoniere (Petrarch), 262
Capet, Hugh, 207, 223
capital (architecture), 47
Capital (Marx), 489
Caprichos (Goya), 468–469, **469**
Caravaggio, *381*–382, 383, **384**, 386, 590
Cardinal Guevara (El Greco), 364, **365**
Carmelite order, 383
Carneades, *96*
Carolingian dynasty, **190**, 206–207, 210, 212–213, 236
Carolingian miniscule, 210, **211**
Carolingian Renaissance, 210, 212–213
Carthage, 89, 116
Cassatt, Mary, **511**, 527, **527**
Castiglione, 321, *322*–*323*, **322**, 367
Cast Iron Bridge at Coalbrookdale, The (Rooker), **452**
castrati, 437
Catacomb of Callixtus, 163, **163**
catacombs, 163, **163**, 165, 184
Cateau-Cambrésis, Treaty of (1559), 318
Cathari. *See* Albigensians
cathedrals, 229, 230. *See also* architecture; *specific cathedrals*
cathedral schools, 230
Catherine of Aragon, 360
Catherine the Great (czar of Russia), 431
Catullus, *121*
cave paintings, 3, **3**
Cavour, Count Camillo Benso di, *483*
cella, 47
Celsus, 162
Celtic legends, 233
Centaurs, 79, **80**
Cereta, Laura, *295*, 296
Cervantes Saavedra, Miguel de, 366
Cézanne, Paul, *527*–*528*, **529**
Chairman Dances, The (Adams), 609
Chamber of the Velatio, **165**
chansons, 312, 342
chansons de geste, 232–234, 248
Chardin, Jean, 394
Chardin, Jean-Baptiste-Siméon, **424**
Charlemagne (Frankish king), 206–207, 210, 211, 316
  and High Middle Ages, 219, 220, 230, 232–233
Charles I (king of England), 376
Charles I (king of Spain). *See* Charles V
Charles II (king of England), 376, 378, 418
Charles IV (king of Spain), 468, **469**
Charles V (Holy Roman Emperor), 316, 317, 317–319, **319**, 320, **321**
  and Reformations, 319, 356, 360, 362
Charles VIII (king of France), 291, 294, 317
Charles Martel (Frankish king), 206
Charles the Bald, 212–213
Chartres Cathedral, **218**, **232**, **235**, 246–247
Chaucer, Geoffrey, 264, **265**
Chauvet caves, 3, **4**
Chekhov, Anton, *520*
chemistry, 409–410, 490, 522
chiaroscuro, 307, 311, 381, 382, **384**, **388**, 389
Chicago, Judy, **586**
Chicago School, 534–535, **535**
Children of Violence (Lessing), 589
China, 256, **418**, 515, 577, 579, 581. *See also* windows on the world
China Men (Kingston), 592
chivalric code, 220, 233
chivalric novel, 366
choir, 240, **240**, **241**, 242
Chomsky, Noam, *585*
Chopin, Frédéric, 492
Chopin, Kate, 520
choruses, 61
Chrétien de Troyes, *233*
Christian humanism, 345, 346–347, 361
Christianity
  Age of Anxiety, **587**, 589
  Age of Reason, 426, 430
  Baroque Age, 375, 376, 377–378, 395, 419
  Bourgeois Age, 489–490, 494
  Christian humanism, 345, 346–347, 361
  Early Middle Ages, 207–209, 210–211, **210**
  Early Renaissance, 294, 295, 296–298, 308, 309
  High Renaissance/Early Mannerism, 316, 317, 321, 325, 326, 351
  interwar period, 565
  and Islamic world, 198, 199, 200
  Late Middle Ages, 255, 257–258, 259–261
  and neo-Platonism, 124, 161, 162, 175
  Orthodox, 190, 191, 193, **194**, 197–198, **198**
  and Scientific Revolution, 408, 411, 412, 412–413, 486–487
  See also early Christianity; Gothic style; High Middle Ages Christianity; papacy; Reformations; Romanesque style; *specific works of art*
Christ Pantocrator, 198, **198**
Chronicle (Knighton), 260
chthonian deities, 41, 42, 63, 72, 98–99
Churchill, Winston, 547
Church of England, 360–361
Cicero, 120, 121–122, **122**, 295, 323, 347
Cimabue, *274*, **275**, 277
Cistercian order, 227
cities. *See* urban growth
Citizen Kane (Welles), 568
City of God, The (Augustine), 176–177
civilization, defined, 1
civil rights movement, 577
Civil War (United States), 485
Clarissa Harlowe (Richardson), 444
class divisions. *See* political/economic development
Classical Baroque, 379, 386–389, 391
  architecture, 376, **377**, 387–388, **387**, **388**, 420, **431**
  painting, 388–389, **388**
Classical culture, 60. *See also* Classicism; Greek Hellenic Age
Classical economics, 452–453
Classical music, 444–446, 474
Classicism, 61, 81, 82, 93–94. *See also* Byzantine Empire; Greek Hellenic Age; Hellenistic Age; Neoclassical style; Rome
clavier, 397
Cleisthenes, *40*
Clement VII (pope), **321**
Cleopatra, 89
clerestory windows, 180, 242
Clotilda, 206
Cloud Study (Constable), 465, **466**, 467
Clouet, Jean, **317**
Clovis (Frankish king), 205–206
Cluniac order, 225, 227, 236, 237
Coalbrookdale by Night (Louthebourg), **462**
Cocteau, Jean, *553*
Code of Hammurabi, 7, 10–11, **10**
Coe, Mandy, 602
Coe, Sue, **602**, 603
Coeur, Jacques, 258
cold war, 420, 575, 577–579, 593
Coleridge, Samuel Taylor, 463, 473
collage, 533, **587**
colonial independence, 579
colonialism. *See* European expansion
Color Purple, The (Walker), 591
Colosseum, 131, **131**
Columbus, Christopher, 292
comedy
  Baroque Age, 394
  Early Modernism, 521
  Greek Hellenic Age, 65, **66**
  Hellenistic Age, 94
  Rome, 94, 120
  See also drama
comedy of manners, 94, 521
Commentaries (Ghiberti), 305
Commentaries (Pius II), 294
Commodus, 117
Common Market. *See* European Economic Community
Commonwealth (England), 376
communes, 222
Communism, 545. *See also* Soviet Union
Communist Manifesto, The (Marx & Engels), 487, 489
Comnena, Anna, *194*, 208
Comnenus, Alexius (Byzantine Emperor), *191*, 194
Complexity and Contradiction in Architecture (Venturi), 605
computers, 587–588
Concerning the Spiritual in Art (Kandinsky), 533
concerto, 445
Concordat of Worms, 223
Concord Sonata (Ives), 569
condottieri, 291
confession, 227
Confessions (Augustine), 176
Confessions (Rousseau), 441
Congress of Vienna (1815), 457, 480, 481
Consolation of Philosophy (Boethius), 209
consorts, 342
Constable, John, 464–465, **466**, 467, 499
Constance, Council of (1414–18), 258, 259, 294
Constantine (Roman emperor), 175, **183**, 295
  and architecture, 179–180
  Arch of, 179, **179**, 182, **183**
  and Constantinople, 171, 172–173
  statue of, **172**, 181–182
Constantinople, 171, 172–173
  Byzantine Empire, 190, **191**, 193
  fall of, 190, 191, 255, 292, 296
  and Islamic world, 199
Constructivism, 557, 567, 594
contrapposto
  early Christianity, **164**
  Early Renaissance, 298, 305
  Greek Hellenic Age, 75, **75**, 77, 81, **81**
  Hellenistic Age, 103
  High Renaissance/Early Mannerism, **319**, **336**, 338
convents. *See* monasticism
Conversations on the Plurality of Worlds (Fontenelle), 418, 425
Copernicus, Nicolas, 406–407, **406**, 408, 412
Copland, Aaron, 569, **569**
Corcyra, 59
Cordoba, Great Mosque of, **201**
Corinth, 59
Corinthian style, 99–100, **99**, **150**, **156**
  High Renaissance/early Mannerism, 340, **340**
  pre-Christian Rome, 126
Corneille, Pierre, *395*

cornice, 47
Coronation of Napoleon and Josephine, The (David), 459, **459**, 461
Cosmographia (Apian), **404**
cosmology. *See* astronomy; natural philosophy; science
Cotton Bureau in New Orleans, The (Degas), **514**
Council at Jamnia, 160
Council of Constance (1414–18), 258, 259, 294
Council of Trent, 362, 363, 367, 379, 380, 394
Count Eckhart and Uta, **220**
Counter-Reformation, 346, 361–362, 379
  and architecture, 363, 380
  and literature, 234, 394
  and music, 363, 367
  and painting, 363
  and science, 407
Countess' Levée, The (Hogarth), 437, **437**
Couperin, François, *444*
Courbet, Gustave, **478**, *496–498*, **497**, 603
Courtier, The (Castiglione), 321, 322–323, 367
courtly love, 221, 233, 323
Court of the Lions (Alhambra), 204, **205**
covenant, 146, 154
Cow's Skull with Calico Roses (O'Keeffe), 560, **560**
Cranach, Lucas the Elder, **357**, **358**
Creation of Adam (Michelangelo), 327, **330**
Creole culture, 520
Crete. *See* Minoan civilization
Crick, Francis, 588
Crime and Punishment (Dostoevsky), 494
Cristofori, Bartolommeo, 444
Cromwell, Oliver, 376
cross vault, 126, **127**, 237, 239
Crowe, Eyre, **512**
cruciform design, 180, 236, **236**
Crusades, 191, 194, 208, 225, 233, 238, 239
Crystal Palace (England), 486, **486**, 488, 607
Cubism
  Early Modernism, 527, **532**, 533, 536
  interwar period, 550, 556, 557, 559, **559**, 567
Cubi XIX (Smith), 597, **597**
culture, defined, 1
cuneiform writing, 7–8, **8**
curia, 226
Curie, Marie Sklodowska, 522
Curie, Pierre, 522
Cuvilliés, François de, **428**
Cybele, 98, 119, 161
Cyclopedia (Chambers), 426
cylinder seals, **9**
Cynicism, 95, 96
Cyprian, 161
Cyrus, 149
Czechoslovakia, 259, 591

Dada, **553**, 560, **561**
Dafni, **198**
Daguerre, Louis-Jacques-Mandé, *501*
d'Alembert, Jean, 429
Dali, Salvador, *560*, **562**, 563
Dalton, John, 490
Dampier, William, 394
Dance of Death, **254**, 255
Dancer's Reward, The (Beardsley), **521**
Danse Macabre, **254**, 255
Dante Alighieri, *234*, 274, 395
Darius, **26**, *41*
Dark Ages (Greece), 36, 38
Darwin, Charles, 490, 491
Daumier, Honoré, *498–499*, **498**
David, 148
David (Donatello), **302**, 303, 337
David (Michelangelo), 303, **336**, 337–339
David (Verrocchio), **303**
David, Jacques-Louis
  Age of Reason, *437–439*, **438**, **450**
  revolution/reaction period, 456, 458, **458**, 459, 461, 471
David Copperfield (Dickens), 493
da Vinci, Leonardo, 306, 317, 326
  Early Renaissance, 310–311, **311**, 333
  The Last Supper, **314**, **324**, 325, 367
  Mona Lisa, 322, 325, **326**
Dead Sea Scrolls, 154, **154**
De Andrea, John, 603–604, **604**
Death of Klinghoffer, The (Adams), 609
Death of Marat (David), **450**, **458**, 459, 471
Death of Sardanapalus, The (Delacroix), 472, **473**
Death of Socrates, The (David), 439, **439**
De Beauvoir, Simone, *585*
Debussy, Claude, *536*
Decadence, 519, 520–521, **521**
Decameron, The (Boccaccio), 262–263, 346
Decius (Roman emperor), *161*
Declaration of Independence, 124, 453–454
Declaration of the Rights of Man and Citizen, The, 454
Decline and Fall of the Roman Empire (Gibbon), 187
deductive reasoning, 405
Deffand, Marie de Marquise du, *429*
Degas, Edgar, **514**
Degenerate Art exhibition (Germany), 562
Deinocrates, 91
Deir el Bahri, 18, 19, 21
Deism, 426
Delacroix, Eugène, *471–472*, **471**, **472**, **473**, 495–496, **496**, 531
de Lesseps, Ferdinand de, *486*
Delian League, 58–59
Delphi, 57, 71, **72**
Delphic Oracle, The (Michelangelo), **330**
Demeter, 42
de Mille, Agnes, 569
democracy
  Age of Anxiety, 581, 601
  Age of Reason, 440, 441
  American Revolution, 441, 454
  Bourgeois Age, 491
  Greece, 39, 40, 45, 57, 59, 65, 82
  interwar period, 545
  See also political/economic development
Democritus, *67*
demos, 40
Departure, The (Beckmann), 563, **566**
Departure from Cythera (Watteau), 432, **432**
Departure of the Volunteers, The (Rude), **481**
de Pizan, Christine, 264–265
Depression (1930s). *See* Great Depression
depth psychology, 584
De Rerum Natura (Lucretius), 121
de Roelas, Juan, **362**
Descartes, René, 410, *411–412*, **411**, 416
Descent of Man (Darwin), 490
de Staël, Madame, 462
de Stijl movement, 557, **558**
détente, 580–581
devotio moderna, 259
Diaghilev, Sergei, *537*
dialectics, 46
Diaspora, 149, 151, 161
Di Cambio, Anrolfo, **226**
Dichterliebe (Schumann), 503
Dickens, Charles, 493–494
Dickinson, Emily, 493
Diderot, Denis, 425, 426–427, **427**, 431
Digges, Thomas, **406**
Dinner Hour at Wigan, The (Crowe), **512**
Dinner Party, The (Chicago), **586**
Diocletian (Roman emperor), 117, *169*, 170–173, 181
  and architecture, 178–179, **178**, **179**
Diogenes, *95*, **96**
Dionysia, 42, 57, 61, 62, 94
Dionysus, 57
  in art, **43**, **58**
  and drama, 42, 57, 65
  Hellenistic Age, 98
di Pietro, Andrea (Palladio), 340–342, **341**, 461
diplomacy, 291, 375, 482, 491
Directory (France), 455–456
Discourse on Method (Descartes), 411
Discourses (Arrian), 124
Disney, Walt, 549
Dispute of a Man with His Soul, The, 17
Divine Comedy (Dante), 234, 395
divine right, 316, 414
Djoser (pharoah), *17*, 18
Doll's House, A (Ibsen), 520
domes
  Age of Reason, 440, **440**
  Baroque Age, 394
  Byzantine Empire, **191**, 194–195, **195**
  early Christianity, 180–181, **181**
  Early Renaissance, 299–300, **300**
  High Renaissance/Early Mannerism, 340, **340**
  Islamic world, **188**, 201, **202**, **204**
  Rome, 126, **127**, **128**
  See also architecture
Dominican order, 227, 261
Donatello, *298*, **302**, 303, **304**, 306, 337, 338
Donation of Constantine, 295
Donation of Pepin, 206
Donatism, 176
Don Juan (Byron), 464
Don Quixote (Cervantes), 366
Dorian mode, 66
Dorians, 36
Doric style, 47–48, **47**, **48**, 70, **72**, 73, **73**
  Jewish architecture, **156**
Doryphoros (Polykleitos), 77, **79**, 133
Dostoevsky, Feodor, *494*, 589
Douglass, Frederick, 494–495
drama
  Age of Anxiety, 588, 589–590
  Baroque Age, 394–395
  Early Middle Ages, 211
  Greek Archaic Age, 61
  Greek Hellenic Age, 40, 42, 57, 61–65, **62**, **64**, **66**, 82
  Hellenistic Age, 94, 120
  High Middle Ages, 227, 248
  interwar period, 551–553
  Late Mannerism, 366
  Northern Renaissance/Late Mannerism, 141, 348–350, **349**
  pre-Christian Rome, 94, 120, 211
  Rome, 94, 120, 123, 211, 394
Dream Play, The (Strindberg), 521
Dryden, John, 394
drypoint, 271
dualism, 25, 69, 124, 149, 160, 411–412
du Barry, Madame, 435
DuBois, W. E. B., 551
Duchamp, Marcel, *560*, **561**
Dumas, Alexandre, *503*
Duns Scotus, John, *261*
Dunstable, John, *312*
Dupin, Amandine-Aurore-Lucie. *See* Sand, George
Dura Europos synagogue, **144**, **152**
Dürer, Albrecht, **344**, *350–*351, **351**, **357**, 359
Dutch East India Company, 416–417
Dying Gaul, The, 101–102, **102**
Dying Slave (Michelangelo), **316**, 333

early Christian art, **178**
  catacombs, 163, **163**, 165, 184
  mosaics, **176**, 184–185, **185**, **186**
  painting, 163, **163**, 165, **165**
  style characteristics, 163, 165
  See also early Christian sculpture
early Christianity, 157–166
  controversies within, 173, 175
  and fall of Rome, 187
  Great Persecution, 172, 177
  and Hellenistic philosophies, 124, 161, 162, 163, 165, 175
  Late Roman architecture, 178, 179–181, **181**, **182**
  legacy of, 166
  literature, 162–163, 174–177
  map, **159**
  music, 186
  New Testament, 158–160
  and pre-Christian Rome, 157, 158, 160, 161–163, 169, 172, 173
  Roman toleration, 172, 173, 175, 178, 179, 182
  timeline, 158
  See also early Christian art; early Christian sculpture
early Christian sculpture
  late Rome, **170**, **178**, 182–184, **183**, **184**
  pre-Christian Rome, 163, **164**, 165, **165**
Early Dynastic Period (Egypt), 14
Early Gothic style, 240–243, **241**, **242**, **243**
Early Mannerism. *See* High Renaissance/Early Mannerism
early medieval West. *See* early Middle Ages
Early Middle Ages, 204–215
  architecture, **207**, **210**, 211, **212**, 236
  calendar, 157
  Christianity, 207–209, 210–211, **210**
  education, 208–209, 210, 230
  historical writing, 209–210
  law, 194
  legacy of, 215

literature, 208, 209–211
manuscript illumination, 211–213, **213**, **214**
map, **190**
medicine, 208–209
music, 207, 211
political/economic development, 205–207
timeline, 206
Early Modernism, 509–538
architecture, 523, 534–535, **535**, **536**
legacy of, 538
literature, 519–522
maps, **515**, **516**, **517**
music, 535–537
philosophy/psychology, 514, 518–519, 530, 537
political/economic development, 509–517
science, 510, 522–523
sculpture, **518**, 534, **534**
style characteristics, 517–518
timeline, 519
See also Early Modernist painting
Early Modernist painting
Art Nouveau, **521**
Cubism, 527, **532**, 533, 536
Expressionism, **508**, **522**, 529–530, **530**, **531**, 533, **533**
Fauvism, 530, **531**, 563
Impressionism, **511**, 523–527, **524–525**, **526**
Post-Impressionism, 527–530, **528**, **529**, **530**
primitivism, 528, **529**
Early Renaissance, 289–313
architecture, 298, **298**, 299–303, **300**, **301**
humanistic studies, 124, 166, 295
legacy of, 313
map, **291**
music, 312
philosophy, 296–298, 405
political/economic development, 290–294, **292**, **293**
science, 294, 311
sculpture, 298, 303–305, **303**, **304**, **305**
style characteristics, 294–295, 298–299
timeline, 293
See also Early Renaissance painting
Early Renaissance painting, **290**, **292**, **293**, 298–299, 306–312
Botticelli, 294, 297, **297**, 308–310, **310**, 335
da Vinci, 310–311, **311**, 333
Fra Angelico, **288**, 307–308, **308**
and Giotto, 271, 298–299
Masaccio, 299, 306–307, **306**, **307**
and neo-Platonism, 297, **297**, 309, 310
Piero della Francesco, 308, **309**
Early Republic (Rome), 116
Easter, 160
Eastern Roman Empire, 171, 172, 178, 185, **186**, 190. *See also* Byzantine Empire
Easter Rebellion (1916), 551
Eckhart, Meister, 228
Eclogues (Vergil), 122
economics. *See* political/economic development
Ecstasy of St. Teresa, The (Bernini), 381, **383**
Edict of Milan, 172, 175, 178, 179, 182
education
Age of Reason, 426
Baroque Age, 416
Early Middle Ages, 208–209, 210, 230
Early Modernism, 510, 512
Early Renaissance, 295
Greek Hellenic Age, 68
High Middle Ages, 227, 230–232
Roman influences, 141
sixteenth-century Europe, 347, 358–359
Education of Marie de' Medici, The (Rubens), 386, **387**
Egypt, 5, 13–25
architecture, 14, **15**, 16, 17–19, **18**
art, 1, 19–25, **23**, 49
Hellenistic Age, 88, 89, 90, **91**, 92, 98
and Judaism, 16, 17, 146–147
legacy of, 27
literature, 17, 19
map, **6**
and Mycenaean civilization, 32, 36
political/economic development, 5, 14–16
religion, 16–17, 19, 98, **98**, 119
under Rome, 117, 119
sculpture, 19–21, **20**, **21**, **22**, **24**, 25, 49
Suez Canal, 486, **486**
timeline, 14
writing systems, 2, 17, **17**
1848 revolutions, 481–482, 486, 487, 492, 496
Einhard, *210*
Einstein, Albert, 522, 523, 554
Einstein on the Beach (Glass), 609
Eisenstein, Sergei, *568*
El Djem Calendar, **139**
Eleanor of Aquitaine, 221, 227, 233
Elector Frederick the Wise (Dürer), **357**
Electra (Euripides), 63
Elementary Structures of Kinship, The (Lévi-Strauss), 585
Eleusis, 42
El Greco, 363–364, **364**, **365**, 367
Eliot, George, 494
Eliot, T. S., 551
Elizabeth I (queen of England), 348, **360**, 361
Ellesmere Manuscript, **264**
Ellington, Duke, 569
Empedocles, *67*
empiricism, 405, 416
Encomium Moriae (Erasmus), 347
Encyclopédie, 426–427, **427**, 429, **445**
Engels, Friedrich, 487, 489
England
Age of Anxiety, 576, 578, 579
Age of Reason, 427, 429, 430, 436–437, 439, 442–444
Baroque Age cultural trends, 391, 395–396, 418
Baroque Age political/economic development, 374, 376–377, 378, 379, 416–417
Bourgeois Age, 482, **483**, 485–486, 492–494, 496
Early Middle Ages, 208
Early Modernism, 510, 512, 515
Early Renaissance, 312
High Middle Ages, 223, **225**, 233
High Renaissance/Early Mannerism, 316
interwar period, 544–545, 546–547, 551
Late Middle Ages, 253, 255–256, 256–257, 259, 260
Late Roman Empire, 173
and Reformations, 360–361, 363
revolution/reaction period, 451, 452, 453, 456, 457, 458, 459, 463–464
sixteenth century, 348, 367
See also specific styles and artists
English Civil War, 376, 413, 414
English East India Company, 416–417
engraving, 271, **321**, 436
Enheduanna, 10
Enki, 8
Enlightenment, 423, 425–427, 429, 430
and Early Modernism, 518
and Hellenistic Age, 107
and music, 446
and revolution/reaction period, 457, 464
See also philosophes
Enlil, 8
entablature, 46–47
entasis, 48
Epic of Gilgamesh, The, 5, 7, 8–10, **9**
epic poetry
Baroque Age, 394, 395–396
Greek Archaic Age, 35, 36, 42, 43–44
Epictetus, *124*
epic theater, 552
Epicureanism, 96–97, 107, 123
Epicurus, *96–97*, **97**
Epidauros, **62**
Erasmus, Desiderius, 347, **347**, 351
Erechtheum, 73, 74–75, **74**
Eroica Symphony (Beethoven), 474–475
erotic themes. *See* sexuality
eschatology, 149
Essay Concerning Human Understanding, A (Locke), 416
Essay on Customs (Voltaire), 442
Essay on Man (Pope), 442–443
Essay on the Principle of Population (Malthus), 453
Essays (Montaigne), 348
Essenes, 154
ethics
Age of Anxiety, 588
early Christian, 159, 166
Greek Archaic Age, 44, 53
Greek Hellenic Age, 65, 70
Hellenistic Age, 97
Judaism, 146, 147, 166
and Reformations, 359–360
See also philosophy; religion
ethnic violence, 581, 583
Et in Arcadia Ego (Poussin), 388–389, **388**
Etruscans, 111, 113, **114**, 120, 126, 140
Eucharist, 226–227
Eumachia, **112**
Eumenes II, 91, 100
Eumenides (Aeschylus), 63
Euripides, 40, 59, 63, *64–65*, 82, 395
European Economic Community, 576–577
European expansion
Baroque Age, 396, 416–417, **417**, **418**, 420
Early Modernism, 510, 515–517, **515**, **516**
High Renaissance/Early Mannerism, 320
maps, **417**, **515**, **516**
European Union, 581
Eusebius, *177*
Euthyphro (Plato), 68
evangelists, 158
Evans, Mary Ann. *See* Eliot, George
Evans, Sir Arthur, 33
Eve (Rodin), 534, **535**
Everyman, 348
evolution, 490, 491
Exaltation of Inanna, The (Enheduanna), 10
Execution on the Third of May, The (Goya), 469, **470**, 579
Exekias, **43**, **44**
existentialism, 412, 474, 554, 583–585, 589
Exodus, 146–147
Expressionism
film, 568
literature, 519, 521–522, 551–553
music, 537
sculpture, 534
See also Expressionist painting
Expressionist painting
Early Modernism, **508**, **522**, 529–530, **530**, **531**, 533, **533**
interwar period, 563, **565**, **566**
and Post-Modernism, 603

fabliau, 264
Fall, The (Camus), 588
Family of Charles IV, The (Goya), 468, **469**
Fanon, Franz, *585*
fan vaulting, 266, **266**
fascism, 545–546, 563. *See also* Nazi Germany
Fate, 98
Faulkner, William, 550, 591
Faust (Goethe), 463, 464
Fauvism, 530, **531**, 563
Feast of Herod, The (Donatello), **302**, 303
Federico da Montefeltro and His Son Guidobaldo (Berruguete), **292**
Feltre, Vittorino da, *295*
Female on Eames Chair, Male on Swivel Stool (Pearlstein), **601**
Feminine Mystique, The (Friedan), 585
feminism
Age of Anxiety, 584, 585, **586**, 591, 603, 610
Early Modernism, 512, 520
See also women's status and roles
Ferdinand V (king of Spain), 316, 319
Fertile Crescent, 5. *See also* Mesopotamia
fêtes galantes, 431–432, **432**
feudalism
Byzantine Empire, 191
Early Middle Ages, 206
and fall of Rome, 173
feudal monarchies, 223–225
High Middle Ages, 219, 220–225
Islamic world, 199
Mycenaean civilization, 35
See also political/economic development
Fichte, Johann Gottlieb, *473*
Ficino, Marsilio, *296–297*
Fidelio (Beethoven), 475
fiefs, 220
Fielding, Henry, 444
film, 567–568
fin-de-siècle Vienna, 514, 518
First Intermediate Period (Egypt), 14, 17
First Jewish War, 130, 136, 150, 151, 157, 161
First Symphony (Beethoven), 474
First Temple (Jerusalem), 148, 155, 381

Fitzgerald, Ella, 569
Fitzgerald, F. Scott, 550
flagellants, 259, **259**
Flagellation, The (Piero della Francesca), 308, **309**
Flamboyant style, 265, **265**
Flanders, 255, 256, 259
Flaubert, Gustave, *493*, 494
Flemish style, 277, **279**, **280**, **281**, 282. *See also* Late Middle Ages
Florence
Baptistery, 304–305, **305**
Baroque Age, 377
Cathedral, 226, 266–267, **268**, 299, **300**
Early Renaissance, 292–294, **293**
High Renaissance/Early Mannerism, 317, 323, 337–338
Late Middle Ages, 255, 262
See also specific styles, artists, and buildings
Florid Baroque, 379–386
architecture, 380, **380**, **381**, **382**
painting, **372**, 381–386, **384**, **385**, **386**, 420
sculpture, 380–381, **383**
See also Baroque Age
Flowing Light of the Godhead, The (Mechthild of Magdeburg), 228
fluting, 48
flying buttresses, 239, 242, 244, **244**
Fontenelle, Bernard de, *418*, 425
forums, 129, **129**, 131, **132**
Fountains (Ravel), 536–537
4′33″ (Cage), 609
Four Books of Architecture, The (Palladio), 341–342
Fourier, Charles, *487*, 489, 497
Fourth Century style, 75, 80–81, **81**
Fourth Lateran Council (1215), 226
Fragonard, Jean-Honoré, **422**, *435*, **435**, 525, 527
France
Age of Anxiety, 576, 579
Age of Reason, 425–426, 428, 429–430, 439–440, 441–442
Baroque Age cultural trends, 386–389, 394–395, 397
Baroque Age political/economic development, 374, 375–376, 377, 378, 378–379, 416
Bourgeois Age, 481, 482, 483, 485, 486, 492, 493, 498–499
Early Middle Ages, 205–207, 220
Early Modernism, **510**, 512, 515, 520
Early Renaissance, 291, 294
High Middle Ages, 211, 220, 228–229, 233
High Renaissance/Early Mannerism, 316–318, 323–324
interwar period, 544–545, 553
July Revolution, 458, 471–472, **472**, 475, 481, 492
Late Middle Ages, 255, 256–257, 264–265
Napoleonic era, 456–457, 459
See also French Revolution; *specific styles and artists*
Franciscan Order, 227, 261
Francis Ferdinand, Archduke, 517
Francis I (king of France), 317, **317**
Francis of Assisi, Saint, 227, **228**
Francis Xavier, 362
Franco, Francisco, 546
Franco-Netherlandish school, 312
Franco-Prussian War (1870), 483, 512, 515
Frankenstein (Shelley), 464
Frankenthaler, Helen, *594*, **595**
Franklin, Benjamin, 426
Franks, 199, 205–207
Frederick Barbarossa (Holy Roman Emperor), 225, 227
Frederick II (Holy Roman Emperor), 225
Frederick II (the Great) (King of Prussia), 430
Frederick the Wise, 356, **357**, 358, 359
Freedom of the Press, The (Daumier), 498, **498**
French Academy, 376
French Academy of Science, 418, **419**
French Republic, 455
French Revolution, 430, 454–457
and Austria, 431
and Bourgeois Age, 479
and Locke, 415
and Neoclassical style, 440, 458, 459
and Romanticism, 462
and totalitarianism, 545
and women's status and roles, 426
fresco painting, 138, **138**, **324**, 325
Baroque Age, 383–384, **385**, 420
early Christian, 163, **163**, 165, **165**, 184
Early Renaissance, 298–299, 306–307, **306**, **307**, **314**
High Renaissance/Early Mannerism, **324**, 325, 327, **328–329**, **330**, **331**
Minoan, 32, **34**
Rococo style, 435, **436**
See also painting
Freud, Sigmund, 514, *518–519*, 537, 549, 553, 560
friars, 227
Friedan, Betty, 585
Friedrich, Caspar David, 467–468, **468**
Friends of God, 259
friezes, 32, 47, 79–80, **81**, 102–103, **103**, 165, **165**
Frith, W. P., **485**
fugue, 397
Futurists, **518**, 556, 569

Galen, 162, 409
Galileo Galilei, 406, 408, 412
Galla Placida, **168**, *185*, **186**
gallery, 242
Gandhi, Mohandas, 586, 609
García Márquez, Gabriel, *591*
Garden of Earthly Delights, The (Bosch), 353–354, **353**
gargoyles, 240
Garibaldi, Giuseppe, *483*
Gaskell, Elizabeth, 494
Gates of Hell, The (Rodin), 534
Gattamelata, 303–304, **304**
Gauguin, Paul, *527*, *528–529*, **529**, 530
Gauls, 89
Gehry, Frank O., 607, **608**
General Will, 441
genetics, 522, 588
Genoa, 255
genres, 17. *See also* literature
genre subjects, 101, **101**, 102, **103**
Gentileschi, Artemisia, *382–383*, **385**
geocentrism, 404–405
geology, 490
George Gordon, Lord Byron (Westall), **464**
George III (king of England), 430
George II (king of England), 430
George I (king of England), 430
Georgics (Vergil), 122
Géricault, Théodore, *469*, **470**, **471**, 472
Germany, 207, 319
Age of Anxiety, 576, 577, **580**, 581
Baroque Age, 377, 378
Bourgeois Age, 482–483, **484**, 486, 489–490
Early Middle Ages, 206
Early Modernism, 510, 512, **514**, 515, 518
High Middle Ages, 228, 248
interwar period, 542–544, 545, 546–547, 548, 554
northern humanism, 346
Romanticism, 462, 463, 467–468, 473–474
See also Holy Roman Empire; Northern Renaissance; Protestant order; Prussia
Germinal (Zola), 520
Gerowitz, Judy. *See* Chicago, Judy
Gersaint, François-Edmé, 432, **433**
Gheeraerts, Marcus the Younger, **360**
Ghent altarpiece (van Eyck), 277, **279**, **281**
Ghiberti, Lorenzo, *304–305*, **305**
Ghirlandaio, Domenico, **290**, 326
Giacometti, Alberto, **555**
Gibbon, Edward, 187, 425–426, 442, 443
Gilbert, Olive, 495
Gilgamesh, 5, 8–9, **9**
Ginsberg, Allen, 589
Giorgione, 311, 333, **334**
Giotto, 265, 294
architecture, *266–267*, **268**
painting, 271, 274, **276**, 277, **278**, 298–299
Girodet, Anne Louis, **455**
Giza, 17, 19–20
glasnost, 581
Glass, Philip, 609
Gleaners, The (Millet), 499, **500**
glissando, 609
global culture, 576, 581, 587, 611
Globe Playhouse, **349**
Glorious Revolution (1688) (England), 376, 430
Gloucester Cathedral, 266, **266**
gods. *See* religion
Goebbels, Joseph, 546
Goethe, Johann Wolfgang von, *463*, 464, 475, 554
Golden Milestone, 129
Golden Notebook, The (Lessing), 589
Golden Virgin of Amiens, **247**
goliards, 232
Good Shepherd, 163, **163**, **164**, 165, **168**, 185, **186**
Gorbachev, Mikhail, *580*–581
Gordon, George. *See* Byron, Lord
gospel, 537
Gospel Book of Otto III, 213, **214**
Gospel Book of St. Medard of Soissons, 212, **212**
Gospels, 158, 162
Go Tell It on the Mountain (Wright), 588
Gothic style, **229**, 235
Early Gothic architecture, 240, **241**, 242, **242**
Early Gothic sculpture, 242–243, **242**
High Gothic architecture, **218**, 242, 244–246, **244**, **245**, **246**
High Gothic sculpture, 246, **246**
innovations, 239–240, **239**, **240**, **241**
and Islamic architecture, 203
Late Gothic architecture, **258**, 265–267, **265**, **266**, **267**
Late Gothic sculpture, **226**, 267, **269**, 270–271, **270**, **272**
See also high Middle Ages
government. *See* political/economic development
Goya, Francisco, 468–469, **469**, **470**, 579
Goyton, J., **419**
Graham, Martha, 569
Granada, 203–204, **205**
gravitas, 111
Great Bridge to Rouen, The (Pissarro), **511**
Great Britain. *See* England
Great Depression (1930s), 544–545, 546
Great Exhibition of 1851 (England), 486, **486**
Great Fire of London, 378
Great Migration (United States), 551, **552**
Great Persecution, 172, 177
Great Schism, 258, 294, 312, 356
Great Sphinx, 20, **20**
Greece, 462, 471, **471**. *See also* Greek Archaic Age; Greek Hellenic Age; Mycenaean civilization
Greece Expiering on the Ruins of Missolonghi (Delacroix), 471, **471**
Greek Archaic Age, 38–53
architecture, 19, **30**, 38, **39**, 46–48, **47**, **48**
drama, 61
and early Christianity, **164**, 165
legacy of, 31, 53
literature, 35, 36, 42, 43–45, 53
map, **32**
and Minoan civilization, 35
philosophy, 45–46
political/economic development, 38–41
religion, 41–42, 43, 49, 53
sculpture, 49–52, **49**, **50**, **51**, 52, **52**, **164**, 165
sports, 40, 56
timeline, 40
vase painting, **43**, **44**
Greek cross, 194
Greek Hellenic Age, 40, 55–82
architecture, 70–75, **72**, **73**, **74**, 126
drama, 40, 42, 57, 61–65, **62**, **64**, **66**, 82
historical writing, 66–67
and Judaism, 155, **156**
legacy of, 82
map, **56**
music, 65–66, 140
philosophy, 67–70
political/economic development, 41, 55, 58–60
religion, 55, 57, 63, 68, 69, 71, 79, 81, 119
style characteristics, 60–61
timeline, 59
vase painting, **56**, **58**, **64**, **66**
See also Greek Hellenic Age sculpture
Greek Hellenic Age sculpture, **54**, **57**, 75–81, 170
Fourth Century style, 75, 80–81, **81**
and Greek Archaic Age, 52, **52**
High Classical style, **58**, 75, 77, **78**, 79–80, **81**
Severe style, **58**, 75, **75**, **76**, 77
sports in, **56**, **61**
Gregorian chant, 207, 211, 248, 367
Gregory of Tours, 209–210
Gregory VII (pope), 225
Gregory XI (pope), 258

Gregory the Great (pope), 207–208, 211, 227
Griffith, D. W., 567–568
groined vault. *See* cross vault
Gropius, Walter, *567*
Grosseteste, Robert, *261*–262
Grosz, George, **553**
Grotius, Hugh, *413*–414
Grünewald, Matthias, *352*, **352**
Guaranty Building (Buffalo), 534–535, **535**
Gudea, 12, **12**
Guernica (Picasso), **542**, 559
Guggenheim Museum (Bilbao), 607, **608**
Guido of Arezzo, *248*
Guild House (Philadelphia) (Venturi), 605, **606**, 607
guilds, 221–222
Gutenberg, Johan, 262
Guti tribes, 6

Hades, 42
Hadith, 200
Hadrian, 100
Hagesandros, **86**, *106*, **106**
Hagia Sophia, **191**, 194–195, **195**
Haiti, **455**
Hall of Mirrors (Versailles), 388, **388**, 428
Hals, Franz, 392, **411**
Hamilton, Ann, 605, **605**
Hamlet (Shakespeare), 350
Hamlet and Horatio in the Graveyard (Delacroix), 495–496, **496**
Hammurabi, *6*, 7, 10–11, **10**
Handbook (Arrian), 124
Handel, George Frideric, 367, 398
Hands Holding the Void (Giacometti), **555**
handwriting. *See* writing systems
Hannibal, 116
Hanoverian dynasty (England), 430
Hapsburg Empire, 317–319, 378, 430–431. *See also* Austria
Hapsburg-Valois rivalry, 317–319
Hardouin-Mansart, Jules, **377**, *387*, **388**
Hard Times (Dickens), 494
Harlem Renaissance, 551
Harold (king of England), 223, **225**
harpsichord, 444
Harvey, William, 409, 412
Hastings, Battle of, 223
Hathor, 15
Hatshepsut (pharoah), *16*, 18, 19, 21, **21**
Haydn, Franz Joseph, *445*, 474
Hay Wain, The (Constable), 465, **465**
Head of Brutus, 133, **133**
Hearing (Bruegel), **396**
Hebrews. *See* Bible, Hebrew; Judaism
Hegel, Georg Wilhelm Friedrich, 441, *473*–474, 487, 489
Hegira, 199
Heidegger, Martin, 553–*554*
Heine, Heinrich, 503
Heisenberg, Werner, *555*
heliocentrism, 405, 406–409
Hellenic Age. *See* Greek Hellenic Age
Hellenistic Age, 87–107
  architecture, **91**, 93, 99–100, **99**, **100**
  and early Christianity, 124, 161, 162, 163, 165, 175
  and Judaism, 90, 150–152, 155
  legacy of, 107, 141, 316, 395
  literature, 88, 94, 120
  map, **90**
  music, 140
  philosophy, 94–98, 107, 395
  political/economic development, 87, 89–92, 99
  and pre-Christian Rome, 89, 96, 117, 121
  religion, 70, 93, 95, **95**, 97, 98–99
  style characteristics, 93–94
  timeline, 89
  See also Hellenistic sculpture
Hellenistic sculpture, 81, **88**, **93**, **95**, **98**, 101–106
  African subjects, **88**
  female subjects, 103, **105**, 106
  genre subjects, 101, **101**, 102, **103**
  Pergamum school, 101–103, **102**, **104**
  Rhodes, **86**, 104, 106, **106**
Helots, 39–40
Hemingway, Ernest, 550
Henry III (king of England), 223
Henry II (king of England), 233
Henry IV (king of France), 375
Henry VIII (king of England), 357, 360–361
Henry VII (king of England), 257
Hephaestus, 42
Heptameron (Marguerite of Navarre), 346–347
Hera, 42, 47, 72
Heraclitus, *46*
Herakles, **52**
Hermes, 42
Hermes with the Infant Dionysus (Praxiteles), 81, **81**, 103
Hernani (Hugo), 492
Herodotus, *66*–*67*, 82
Herod the Great, 150, 155, 156, 157
Hestia, 42
Hetzendorf von Hohenberg, Johann Ferdinand, **431**
hieroglyphs, 17, **17**
High Classical style, **58**, 75, 77, **78**, 79–80, **81**
higher criticism, 489–490
High Gothic style, **221**, 244–247, **247**
  architecture, **218**, 242, 244–246, **244**, **245**, **246**
High Middle Ages, 219–249, 299
  education, 227, 230–232
  legacy of, 249
  literature, 227, 232–234, 248
  manuscript illumination, 227, **228**, 238–239, **238**, 247, **247**, **248**
  map, **222**
  music, 248
  political/economic development, **209**, 220–225, **221**, **222**, 239
  science, 405
  sculpture, **220**, **221**, **226**, **235**
  style characteristics, 229–230
  timeline, 224
  See also Gothic style; High Middle Ages Christianity; Romanesque style
High Middle Ages Christianity, 219, 225–229, 235
  and architecture, **218**, 235, 239, 240
  and education, 230–232
  and Holy Roman Empire, 223, 225
  lay piety, 227–229, 346
  and literature, 234
  monasticism, 227–229, 230, 232, 239
  Virgin Mary cult, **220**, 221, 230, 233, 242–243, **247**
  See also Gothic style
High Renaissance/Early Mannerism, 315–343, 379
  architecture, 339–342, **339**, **340**, **341**
  legacy of, 343
  literature, 321–324
  map, **318**
  music, 342, **342**
  political/economic development, 316–320, 323–324, 326
  style characteristics, 320–321
  timeline, 320
  See also High Renaissance/Early Mannerism painting; Michelangelo Buonarroti
High Renaissance/Early Mannerism painting, **317**, 324–335
  da Vinci, **314**, 322, **324**, 325, **326**, 367
  The Last Judgement, 327, **331**, 363
  Raphael, **322**, 327, 332–333, **332**, **333**
  Sistine Chapel ceiling, 294, 327, **328–329**, **330**, **331**, 363, 384, 534
  Titian, 311, **319**, 333–335, **334**, 386, 500
high tech style, **606**, 607
Hildegard of Bingen, 227, **228**, 229
Hindu world, 201
Hippolyte and Aricie (Rameau), 444
Hirohito (emperor of Japan), 545
Hiroshima bombing, 548, 583, 609
Historical and Critical Dictionary (Bayle), 419, 426
historical writing
  Age of Reason, 443
  Byzantine Empire, 194
  early Christianity, 177
  Early Middle Ages, 209–210
  Early Renaissance, 295
  Greek Hellenic Age, 66–67
  Islamic world, 200–201
  Judaism, 149, 151, 157
  Late Middle Ages, 265
  Rome, 123
Histories (Herodotus), 66–67
Histories (Tacitus), 123
Histories of Gargantua and Pantagruel, The (Rabelais), 346
History of Art (Winckelmann), 437
History of the Christian Church (Eusebius), 177
History of the Decline and Fall of the Roman Empire (Gibbon), 443
History of the English Church and People, A (Bede), 210
History of the Florentine People (Bruni), 295
History of the Franks (Gregory of Tours), 210
History of the Peloponnesian War (Thucydides), 67
History of Tom Jones, a Foundling, The (Fielding), 444
Hitler, Adolf, 545, 546. *See also* Nazi Germany
Hittites, 6, 15, 25, 32
HIV/AIDS, 587
Hobbes, Thomas, 414, 415, 420
Hockney, David, 603
Hodges, C. W., 349
Hodgkin, Howard, 603
Hogarth, William, 436–437, **437**
Hogarth Press, 550
Hohenstaufen dynasty, 223, 225
Holbein, Hans the Younger, **347**
Holiday, Billie, 569
Hollywood, 568
Holocaust, 547, 548, **548**, 578–579, 583, 593
Holy Roman Empire, 223, 225, 259, 316, 317–319, 546
Holy Trinity, The (Masaccio), 306–307, **306**
Homer, 34, 36, 42, 43–44, 53
  and early Christian church history, 177
  and Milton, 395
  sports in, 56
  and tragedy, 62
  and Vergil, 122
Homeric epithets, 44
Homo sapiens, 3
Horace, 122, 123, 140
Horse and Jockey (Artemision), 104, **105**
Horse Fair, The (Bonheur), 500, **501**
horses, 14
Horus, 15, 16
Hosea, 149
Hôtel de Soubise (Paris), 435, **436**
Houdon, Jean-Antoine, **442**
Houses of Parliament (England), **483**, 496
"How It Feels to Be Colored Me" (Hurston), 551
"Howl" (Ginsberg), 589
Hrotswitha, *211*
hubris, 41
Hughes, Langston, 551
Hugo, Victor, 492, 503
Huguenots, 375
Human Comedy, The (Balzac), 493
humanism
  and early Christianity, 162, 163, 166
  Early Renaissance, 124, 166, 295
  and Greek Hellenic Age, 82
  Hellenistic Age, 107
  High Renaissance/Early Mannerism, 124, 321
  Late Rome, 174
  and music, 367
  Northern, 345, 346–347, 361
humanitas, 321, 347
humanities, 53, 113, 321
Hume, David, 426
Hundred Years' War, 253, 255, 256–257, 263, 265
Hunefer Funerary Papyrus, 1, **23**
Hurston, Zora Neale, 551
Hus, Jan, 259
Hussites, 259, 356
Huysmans, Joris-Karl, *520*–521
hydraulic organ. *See* water organ
Hyksos, 14, 16, 146
hymns, 17, 175, 186
Hymn to Aten, 17
Hyrcanus, John, *155*

Ibn Rushd, 231
Ibn Tulun Mosque, 202, **204**
Ibsen, Henrik, 520
Ice Age, 3
Iconoclastic Controversy, 193, **193**, 197–198
Ictinus, 73, **73**
idealism, 46, 67, 69
  High Renaissance/Early Mannerism, 323, 325
  and Romanticism, 473–474, 492, 493
idée fixe, 476
ideograms, 7, **8**
Idylls (Theocritus), 92, 94
Iliad (Homer), 35, 36, 43–44, 56
illusionism, 383–384, **385**, 420
Imhotep, 18
Imitation of Christ, The (Kempis), 259
imperialism
  Rome, 116, 186
  See also European expansion

"impetus" theory, 405
Importance of Being Ernest, The (Wilde), 521
Impression: Sunrise (Monet), 523, **524**, 525
Impressionism, 523–527
  and Delacroix, 496
  music, 535–537
  painting, **511**, 523–527, **524–525**, **526**
  and Realist painting, 496, 500, 523
  sculpture, 534
  See also Early Modernism
impressionism (early Christian), 165, **165**, 182
Improvisation 33 for "Orient" (Kandinsky), **533**
Inanna, 10
India, 578
Indiana (Sand), 492
Indian Emperor, The (Dryden), 394
individualism, 94–95, 107, 474, 518
Indonesia, 578
inductive reasoning, 405
indulgences, 357
industrialism
  Bourgeois Age, 479, 485–486, **485**, 494
  Early Modernism, 510, **511**, 512, 514
  Late Middle Ages, 256
  revolution/reaction period, 427, 451–453, **452**, **462**
  and Romanticism, 462, **462**, 464
Industrial Revolution. *See* industrialism
Inés de la Cruz, Sor Juana, 394
infanticide, 88
Infernal Machine, The (Cocteau), 553
Ingres, Jean-Auguste-Dominique, **456**, **460**, *461*, 495, **495**
Innocent III (pope), 225, 226, 229, 257
Inquiry into the Nature and Causes of the Wealth of Nations, A (Smith), 427
Inquisition, 229, 259–260, 364, 408
installation art, 604–605, **605**
Institutes of the Christian Religion, The (Calvin), 359
Instruction of Amenemope, The, 19
interior design. *See* architecture
Interior of My Studio (Courbet), **478**, 496, **497**, 498
International style, 567, **567**, **576**
Internet, 582–583, 587–588, 611
Interpretation of Dreams, The (Freud), 519
interwar period, 541–570
  architecture, 567, **567**
  film, 567–568
  legacy of, 570
  literature, 549–553
  map, **543**
  music, 568–569
  philosophy, 553–554
  political/economic development, 542–549, 559
  science, 554–555
  sculpture, **555**
  style characteristics, 548–549
  timeline, 556
  See also interwar period painting
interwar period painting, 556–565, **566**
  Dada, **553**, 560, **561**
  De Stijl movement, 557, **558**
  Expressionism, 563, **565**, **566**
  Malevich, 528, 556–557, **557**
  O'Keeffe, 559–560, **560**
  Picasso, **542**, 557, 559, **559**, **569**
  Surrealism, **540**, **555**, 560, **562**, **564**
Intolerance (Griffith), 567–568
Ionia, 38, 41
Ionic style, 70, 74–75, **74**
Iphigenia in Aulis (Euripides), 63
Iphigenia in Taurus (Euripides), 63
Iran, 579
Ireland, 551
Isabella (queen of Spain), 316
Isaiah, 149, 159
Isenheim Altarpiece (Grünewald), 352, **352**
Ishtar, 10
Isidore of Miletus, **191**, **195**
Isis, 98, **98**, 119, **119**, 161
Islamic world, 189, 198–204, 256
  Age of Anxiety, 578
  architecture, **188**, **200**, 201–204, **201**, **202**, **204**, **205**
  and Aristotle, 70
  art, **202**, **203**, **205**
  and Carolingian dynasty, 206
  and High Middle Ages, 230, 231
  historical writing, 200–201
  and Iconoclastic Controversy, 193
  legacy of, 215
  map, **190**
  political/economic development, 198–199
  and Reformations, 363
  science, 201, 405
  sculpture, 204, **205**
  timeline, 199
  writing systems, 202, **202**
  See also crusades
Israel, 578–579
Israel, ancient, 146, 147–149
Italo-Alpine style, **212**
Italo-Byzantine style, 274
Italo-Roman style, 131
Italy
  Age of Reason, 430
  Baroque Age, 397
  Bourgeois Age, 482, 483, **484**, 486
  Early Middle Ages, 206
  Early Modernism, 514, 515
  Early Renaissance, 290–294
  High Middle Ages, 234
  High Renaissance/Early Mannerism, 317, 323–324
  interwar period, 545–546
  Late Mannerism, 366–367
  Late Middle Ages, 255, 256
  See also specific styles and artists
Ives, Charles, 569

Jackson, Michael, 611
Jacob's Ladder (Frankenthaler), **595**
Jacob's Room (Woolf), 549
Jacquerie, 255
James I (king of England), 376, 414
James II (king of England), 376
Jamnia, Council at, 160
Jane Eyre (Brontë), 493
Jansenism, 412
Japan
  Age of Anxiety, 576, 581
  Early Modernism, 515
  and Impressionism, 527
  interwar period, 545, 547, 548, 555, 583
  See also windows on the world
jazz, 537, 549, 551, 569
Jean-Baptiste Bellay (Girodet), **455**
Jeanneret, Charles-Edward. *See* Le Corbusier
Jefferson, Thomas, 126, **460**, 461, **461**
Jehan de Chelles, **243**
Jeremiah, 149
Jerome, Saint, 175, 177
Jerusalem, 148, **150**, 151, 155, 381
Jesuits, 361–362, 363
Jesus, 158, 160. *See also* Christianity
Jeux d'eau (Ravel), 536–537
Jewish Antiquities (Josephus), 157
Jewish War, The (Josephus), 151, 157
jihad, 199
Joan of Arc, Saint, 257
John, 158
John (king of England), 223
Johns, Jasper, 594, **596**
Johnson, Philip, **600**, 607, **607**
Joke, The (Kundera), 591
Joplin, Scott, 537
Joseph II (emperor of Austria), 430–431
Josephus, Flavius, 151, 157
Josquin des Prez, *312*, 342, 367, 396
Joyce, James, 549
Judah, 149, 151
Judaism, 145–157
  Age of Anxiety, 578–579
  architecture, 155–157, **156**
  and Aristotle, 70
  art, 154–155, **155**, **157**
  and early Christianity, 158–160
  and Egyptian culture, 16, 17, 146–147
  and Greek Hellenic Age fr, 155, **156**
  and Hellenistic Age, 90, 150–152, 155
  High Middle Ages, 231
  and Iconoclastic Controversy, 193
  and Islamic world, 198, 199, 200
  legacy of, 166
  literature, 148–149, **149**, 152–154, 157
  map, **146**
  music, 186
  and Orthodox Christianity, 193
  political/economic development, 145–152
  and pre-Christian Rome, 151, 155, 157, 161
  timelines, 146, 148
Judith and Her Maidservant with the Head of Holofernes (Gentileschi), 382–383, **385**
Julian (Roman emperor), 178
Julius Caesar (Roman emperor), 116–117
Julius II (pope), 327, 332, 333, 340
July Revolution (1830) (France), 458, 471–472, **472**, 475, 481, 492
Jung, Carl, 518, *519*, 593
Junius, Johannes, 413
Junius Bassus Sarcophagus, 184, **184**
jurisconsults, 124
Justinian (Byzantine emperor), 191, **192**, 193, 195
Justinian Code, 193–194
Jutes, 173
Juvenal, *123*

Kaaba, 198–199
Kafka, Franz, 521–522
Kahlo, Frida, **540**, *563*, **564**
Kairouan, Great Mosque of, **200**
Kaisersaal, 435–436, **436**
Kandinsky, Wassily, 528, *533*–534, **533**
Kant, Immanuel, *473*
Kashani, Maqsud, **203**
Keats, John, 464
Kempis, Thomas á, 259
Kent State, **579**
Kenwood House (London), 439, **440**
Kepler, Johannes, 307, 406, 408, 412
key, 445
keystone, 126
Khafre, 19, 20
Ibn Khaldun, *200*–201
Khamsah (Khosrow), **205**
Khosrow, Amir, **205**
Khrushchev, Nikita, 591
Khufu, 17
Al-Khwarizmi, *201*
Kiefer, Anselm, *600*, **601**, 603
King, Martin Luther, Jr., 493, 577, 585–586, 588
King Arthur story, 233
Kingston, Maxine Hong, 591–592
kithara, 140
Klee, Paul, 560, **562**, *563*
Kneller, Godfrey, **408**
Knight, Death, and the Devil (Dürer), 351, **351**
Knighton, Henry, 260
Knossos, 32, **33**, **34**
koine, 89
Komar, Vitaly, **590**
korai statues, 49, 50, **51**
Koran, 199, 200, 201, **202**. *See also* Islamic world
Korean War, 577
kouroi statues, 49–50, **49**, **50**, **164**
Kramer, Samuel, 5
Kritios, *75*, **75**, 77
Kundera, Milan, *591*
Kush (Nubia), 13
Kutubiyya Minbar, **203**
Kyd, Thomas, 348

Labors of the Months, **221**
Lacemaker, The (Vermeer), 391, **392**
Lady Chatterley's Lover (Lawrence), 550
laissez faire economics
  Age of Anxiety, 582
  Age of Reason, 427
  Bourgeois Age, 481
  Early Modernism, 512
  interwar period, 542
  revolution/reaction period, 452, 453
La Marseillaise. *See Departure of the Volunteers, The*
Lamentation (Giotto), 277, **278**
landscape
  High Renaissance/Early Mannerism, 311–312, **312**, 333, **334**
  Romanticism, 464–465, **465**, **466**, 467–468, **467**
Lange, Dorothea, **544**
Langland, William, 263–264
languages
  Age of Reason, 441
  Baroque Age, 379
  Byzantine Empire, 190
  and early Christianity, 160, 161, 162, 175, 186
  Early Middle Ages, 209
  Early Renaissance, 295
  Hellenistic Age, 89
  High Middle Ages, 230, 231, 232, 233, 248
  Islamic world, 198, 199
  and Judaism, 152
  Late Middle Ages, 259, 262, 264–265
  Rome, 120, 121–122, 141
Laocoön Group, **86**, 106, **106**, 316
Lares, 111, **113**
Large Glass, The (Duchamp), 560, **561**

Large Reclining Nude (Matisse), 563, **565**
Las Meninas (The Maids of Honor) (Velázquez), **372**, 386, **386**, 469
Last Judgement, The (Michelangelo), 327, **331**, 363
Last Judgement, The (Notre Dame), **242**
Last Pagan, The, **182**
Last Supper, The (da Vinci), **314**, **324**, 325, 367
Last Supper, The (Tintoretto), 366–367, **367**
Late Dynastic Period (Egypt), 14, 15
Late Gothic style, 265–271
  architecture, **258**, 265–267, **265**, **266**, **267**, 299
  sculpture, **226**, 267, **269**, 270–271, **270**, **272**
  See also Late Middle Ages; Late Middle Ages painting
Late Mannerism, 345, 363–367
  legacy of, 368
  literature, 366
  painting, 363–367, **364**, **365**, **367**
  style characteristics, 363
  See also sixteenth-century Europe
Late Middle Ages, 253–284
  Christianity, 255, 257–258, 259–261
  legacy of, 284
  literature, 122, 262–265
  map, **254**
  philosophy, 261
  plague, **253**, **254**, 255, 259, 262–263, **263**, 291
  political/economic development, **252**, 253–258, **256**, 263–264
  science, 256, 261–262, 405
  style characteristics, 265
  timeline, 257
  See also Late Gothic style; Late Middle Ages painting
Late Middle Ages painting, **259**, 271–282
  Flemish, 277, **279**, **280**, **281**, 282
  Italy, 271, **273**, 274, **275**, **276**, 277, **278**
  manuscript illumination, **254**, 271, **273**
  prints, 271, **274**
Late Modernism, 583–584, 593–600
  architecture, 599–600, **600**
  literature, 588–590
  music, 608–609
  painting, 593–596, **593**, **594**, **595**, **596**, **597**
  sculpture, 597–599, **597**, **598**, **599**
  See also Age of Anxiety
Late Republic (Rome), 116–117
Late Roman architecture, 178–181, **178**, **179**
  and Christianity, 178, 179–181, **181**, **182**
Late Roman sculpture, **172**, **175**, 181–184, **182**
  early Christian, **170**, **178**, 182–184, **183**, **184**
Late Rome, 169–187
  legacy of, 187
  literature, 174–177, 184, **184**
  manuscript illumination, 184, **184**
  map, **171**
  mosaics, 157, **157**, **168**, **176**, 184–185, **185**, **186**
  music, 186
  painting, 184, **184**
  political/economic development, 169–174, **172**, 186–187
  style characteristics, 177–178
  timeline, 170
  See also Late Roman architecture; Late Roman sculpture
Latin, 120, 121–122
  Baroque Age, 379
  early Christianity, 161, 162
  Early Middle Ages, 209
  Early Renaissance, 295
  High Middle Ages, 230, 231, 233
  Late Rome, 186
Latin America, 590–591
La Traviata (Verdi), 503
Laundresses Hanging Out the Wash (Morisot), **526**
La Valse (Ravel), 537
law
  Byzantine Empire, 193–194
  early Christianity, 161
  Early Middle Ages, 194
  High Middle Ages, 226, 232
  Islamic, 200
  Judaism, 147, 148–149
  Mesopotamia, 5, 7, 10–11
  Napoleonic Code, 456, 457, 492
  pre-Christian Rome, 124, 193–194
Law of War and Peace, The (Grotius), 414
Lawrence, D. H., 550, 560
Lawrence, Jacob, **552**
lay investiture, 223, 225
lays, 233
Lazarillo de Tormes, 366
League of Nations, 543
learning. *See* education
Leblanc, Madame Jacques Louis, **460**, *461*
Lebrun, Charles, **388**
Le Cid (Corneille), 395
Le Corbusier, *567*, **567**
Leibniz, Gottfried Wilhelm von, 409
leitmotifs, 503
Lenin, V. I., 545, 557
Le Nôtre, André, *387*, **387**
Leo III (pope), 193, 206–207, 212
Leo X (pope), 357
Leonardo da Vinci. *See* da Vinci, Leonardo
Les Demoiselles d'Avignon (Picasso), 530, **532**, 533
Les Misérables (Hugo), 492
Lespinasse, Julie, *429*
Lessing, Doris, 589
Letters on Morality (Seneca), 123
Le Vau, Louis, **377**, *387*
Leviathan (Hobbes), 414, **415**
Lévi-Strauss, Claude, *585*
lex talionis, 11
Leyster, Judith, 391, **392**
Libation Bearers (Aeschylus), 63, 64
liberalism, 414–415, 471
  Bourgeois Age, 481, 481–482, 487, 492
  Early Modernism, 512
  interwar period, 542
Liberty Leading the People (Delacroix), 471–472, **472**
librettos, 503
lieder, 475, 503
Life magazine, 547
Limbo, 234
Limbourg brothers, 271, **273**
Lincoln, Abraham, 485, 502, **502**
Linear A, 35
Linear B, 35
linguistics, 585
Lion Gate (Mycenae), 36, **36**
literature
  Age of Reason, 441–444
  Baroque Age, 394–396, 417, 418–419
  Bourgeois Age, 491–495
  early Christianity, 162–163, 174–177
  early Judaism, 148–149, **149**, 152–154, 157
  Early Middle Ages, 208, 209–211
  Early Modernism, 519–522
  Egypt, 17, 19
  Greek Archaic Age, 35, 36, 42, 43–45, 53
  Hellenistic Age, 88, 94, 120
  High Middle Ages, 227, 232–234, 248
  High Renaissance/Early Mannerism, 321–324
  interwar period, 549–553
  Late Mannerism, 366
  Late Middle Ages, 122, 262–265
  Late Modernism, 588–590
  Late Rome, 174–177, 184, **184**
  Mesopotamia, 8–10
  Neoclassical style, 442–443, 459
  Northern Renaissance, 141, 348–350, **349**
  Post-Modernism, 590–592
  pre-Christian Rome, 94, 111, 120–123
  Romanticism, 463–464, **464**, 491, 492–493
  and Scientific Revolution, 403, 417, 443–444
  sixteenth-century Europe, 321–324, 346–347, 366
  See also drama
lithography, 498, **498**
Little, Malcolm. *See* Malcolm X
liturgical drama, 248
liturgy, 160
Liudprand (bishop of Cremona), 209
local color, 520
Locke, John, 414–415, 420, 441, 454
loggias, 308
logical positivism, 553
logos, 97, 162
Lollards, 259, 260
Lombards, 206
Long Day's Journey into Night (O'Neill), 553
Lords John and Bernard Stuart (Van Dyck), 393, **393**
Louis IX, Saint (king of France), 247
Louis XIII (king of France), 395
Louis XIV (king of France), **375**
  and divine right, 374, 375–376, 414
  and drama, 395
  French Academy of Science, 418, **419**
  legacy of, 429, 431, 433
  and music, 397
  and Versailles, 376, 387, 388
  Wars of, 378–379, 413
Louis XV (king of France), 429, 431, 444
Louis XVI (king of France), 429, 430, 437, 454
Louis XVIII (king of France), 457
Louis Philippe (king of France), 458, 481
Louis the Pious (Frankish king), 212
Loutherbourg, Philip Jacques de, **462**
L'Ouverture, Toussaint, *455*
Lover Crowned, The (Fragonard), **422**, 435, **435**
Loyola, Ignatius, Saint, 361–362, **362**, 363, 385
Lucretius, *121*
Ludovisi Throne, 77, **77**
Luke, 158
Lully, Jean-Baptiste, *397*, 444
Luncheon of the Boating Party, The (Renoir), 525, **526**
lute, 248
Luther, Martin, 319, 347, 357–359, **357**, 361. *See also* Protestant order
Lutheranism, 319, 358, 361. *See also* Protestant order
Lydia, 162
Lydian mode, 66
Lyell, Charles, *490*
lyre, **11**, 44, 66, 140
Lyrical Ballads (Wordsworth), 463
lyric poetry, 44–45, 140
Lysimache, 39
Lysistrata (Aristophanes), 65
Lytton, Constance, 513

Maccabeans, 150–151, 155
Macedonia, 59–60, 89
Machiavelli, Niccolò, 321, *323*–*324*, 374
Machiavellianism, 324, 374
Madame Bovary (Flaubert), 493, 494
Madame Jacques Louis Leblance (Ingres), **460**, 461
Maderno, Carlo, *380*, **380**
Madonna, 611
Madonna and Child with Angels (Memling), 282, **283**
Madonna Enthroned (Cimabue), 274, **275**, 277
Madonna Enthroned (Giotto), **276**, 277
Madonna with the Long Neck (Parmigianino), 335, **335**
madrigals, 312, 367
maenads, 57
magic realism, 591
Magna Carta, 223
Magyars, 207
Maids of Honor, The (Las Meninas) (Velázquez), **372**, 386, **386**, 469
Mailer, Norman, 589
Maison Carrée, 126, **127**, 461
Malatesta, Sigismondo, 302
Malatesta Temple (Rimini), **298**, 300, 302–303
Malaysia, **583**
Malcolm X, 585
Malevich, Kasimir, 528, *556*–*557*, **557**
Malory, Thomas, 233
Malpighi, Marcello, *409*
Malthus, Thomas, 452, 453
Manao Tupapau—The Spirit of the Dead Watching (Gaugin), 528–529, **529**
Manet, Édouard, 299, **491**, 496, *500*, **501**, 527
Manichaeism, 229
Mannerism. *See* High Renaissance/Early Mannerism; Late Mannerism
manorialism, 206. *See also* feudalism
mantle (Hamilton), 605, **605**
manuscript illumination
  Early Middle Ages, 211–213, **213**, **214**
  High Middle Ages, 227, **228**, 238–239, **238**, 247, **247**, **248**
  Late Middle Ages, **254**, 271, **273**
  Late Rome, 184, **184**
Man with a Hat (Picasso), **532**, 533
Mao (Warhol), **574**, **579**
Mao Zedong, **574**, *577*, **579**
maps
  Aegean civilizations, **32**
  Age of Anxiety, **578**
  Age of Reason, **424**
  Baroque Age, **374**, **417**
  Bourgeois Age, **480**, **484**

maps *(continued)*
Byzantine Empire, **190**
early Christianity, **159**
Early Middle Ages, **190**
Early Modernism, **515**, **516**, **517**
Early Renaissance, **291**
Egypt, **6**
European expansion, **417**, **515**, **516**
Greek Archaic Age, **32**
Greek Hellenic Age, **56**
Hellenistic Age, **90**
High Middle Ages, **222**
High Renaissance/Early Mannerism, **318**
interwar period, **543**
Islamic world, **190**
Judaism, **146**
Late Middle Ages, **254**
Late Rome, **171**
Mesopotamia, **6**
revolution/reaction period, **457**
Roman successors, **178**
Rome, **110**, **171**
sixteenth-century Europe, **356**
Marat, Jean Paul, **450**, **458**, 459, 471
Marathon, Battle of, 41
March of the Legions, 133, 136, **136**
Marcus Aurelius (Roman emperor), 124, **125**, 136, **138**
Marcus (son of Cicero), 121
Marguerite of Angoulême (queen of Navarre), 346–347
Maria Theresa (empress of Austria), 430, 431
Marie Antoinette and Her Children (Vigée-Lebrun), 433, **434**, 435
Marie de France, 233
Marilyn Monroe (Warhol), **597**
Mark, 158, 160
Marlowe, Christopher, 348
Marriage à la Mode (Hogarth), 437, **437**
Marriage of Figaro, The (Mozart), 446
Martin V (pope), 258
Martin, Ricky, 611
Martyrdom of St. Matthew, The (Caravaggio), 382, **384**
Marx, Karl, 441, 474, 489, 545. *See also* Marxism
Marxism, 487, 489, 551, 554, 588. *See also* Marx, Karl
Mary II (queen of England), 376
Mary Magdalene, 162, 237
Masaccio, 299, *306*–*307*, **306**, **307**
Masada, **150**, 151, 155
mass culture, 541, 548–549, 557, 611
and architecture, 605, **606**, 607
See also interwar period
Masses, 312
materialism, 46, 67
Mathematical Principles of Natural Philosophy (Newton), 409
mathematics
Baroque Age, 394
Early Renaissance, 299, 300
Greek Archaic Age, 46, 48
Greek Hellenic Age, 71, 73
High Renaissance/Early Mannerism, 325, 340
Islamic world, 201
Late Middle Ages, 261–262
and Neoclassical style, 460
Rome, 113, 126
and Scientific Revolution, 405–406, 407, 408, 409, 411, 412, 419–420
See also calendars; science
Matisse, Henri, *530*, **531**, 550, 563, **565**
Matthew, 158
Maximilian I (Holy Roman Emperor), 319
Mazarin, Cardinal, 375
Mazzini, Giuseppe, *483*
Meat: Animals and Industry (Coe & Coe), 602
Mecca, 198, 199
Mechthild of Magdeburg, 228
medallions, 179
Medea (Euripides), 40
Medes, 25
Medici, Cosimo de', 293, 294, 296, 303, 307
Medici, Giovanni di Bicci de', *293*
Medici, Giuliano de', 294
Medici, Lorenzo de' (the Magnificent), 293–294, 326
Medici, Marie de' (queen of France), 386, **387**
Medici, Piero de', 293
Medici family, 293–294, 295, 296, 303, 307, 317, 324, 326
medicine
Age of Anxiety, 588
Bourgeois Age, 490
Early Middle Ages, 208–209
Early Modernism, 522
Islamic world, 201
Scientific Revolution, 409–410, **410**
Medieval Housebook, 271, **274**
medieval West. *See* Early Middle Ages; Late Middle Ages
Medina, 199
Meditations (Marcus Aurelius), 124
Meeting, The (Courbet), 496, **497**, 603
'Meeting, The,' or "Have a Nice Day, Mr. Hockney" (Blake), **602**, 603
Megiddo, 148
Melamid, Aleksander, **590**
Melos, 64
Melville, Herman, 610
memento mori, 306, 560, 605
Memling, Hans, 282, **283**
Memoirs of Usamah, The (Usamah), 208–209
Menander, *94*, 120
Mendel, Gregor Johann, 522
Mendeleev, Dmitri, *490*
Menes, *14*, 16
Menkure, 19, 20, 21
menorah, **147**
mercantilism, 427, 452
Merian, Maria Sibylla, **402**, **405**
Merici, Angela, 361
Merisi, Michelangelo. *See* Caravaggio
Merovingian dynasty, 206, 210
Mesolithic period, 3–4
Mesopotamia, 5–13
architecture, 12–13, **13**, 18, 126, 130
art, **9**, **10**, 11–12, **11**, **12**, 49, 50
law, 5, 7, 10–11
legacy of, 27
literature, 8–10
map, **6**
music, 11–12, **11**
political/economic development, 5, 6–7
religion, 8, 10, 16
timeline, 7
writing systems, 7–8, **8**
See also Judaism
Messiah, 150, 158, 160
Messiah (Handel), 398
Metamorphoses (Ovid), 123
Metamorphosis (Kafka), 521–522
Methodism, 426
metope, 47
Mexican Muralists, 563
Michelangelo Buonarroti, 305, *325*–*327*
David, 303, **336**, 337–339
"Dying Slave," **316**, 333
and Hellenistic Age, 106, 316
The Last Judgement, 327, **331**, 363
Pietàs, 335, **335**, 337, **338**, 339
Sistine Chapel ceiling, 294, 327, **328–329**, **330**, **331**, 363, 384, 534
St. Peter's basilica, 340, **340**, 394
Michelet, Jules, 471
Mickey Mouse, 549
microscope, 406, 409
Middle Ages. *See* Early Middle Ages; Late Middle Ages
Middle East, 578–579, 580
Middle Kingdom (Egypt), 14, 17
Middlemarch (Eliot), 494
Middle Republic (Rome), 116, 120
Mies van der Rohe, Ludwig, *599*–*600*, **600**, 607
Migration Series, No. 58 (Lawrence), **552**
Milesian school of philosophy, 46, 67
Militia Company of Captain Frans Banning, The. See Night Watch, The
Mill, John Stuart, 487
Millet, Jean-François, *499*, **499**, **500**
Milton, John, 379, 395–396, 420
minaret, 202
miniatures, 204, **205**
Minoan civilization, 32–35, **33**, **34**, 37
Minotaur, 34
minstrels, 233, 248
minuet, 445
Misanthrope, The (Molière), 395
Miser, The (Molière), 395
Mithraism, 98, 119, **120**, 161
Mnesicles, *74*–*75*, **74**
Modernism. *See* Early Modernism; interwar period; Late Modernism
Modern Man Followed by the Ghosts of His Meat (Coe), **602**, 603
modes, 66
Molière, 94, *395*
MOMA. *See* Museum of Modern Art
Mona Lisa (da Vinci), 322, 325, **326**
monasticism
Byzantine Empire, 193, **194**
Early Middle Ages, 205, 206, 207–209, 210–211, **210**
High Middle Ages, 227–229, 230, 232, 239
Late Middle Ages, 259
and northern humanism, 347
origins of, 173, 187
and Reformations, 356, 358, 361–362
Mondrian, Piet, *557*, **558**
Monet, Claude, 523, **524**, *525*, **525**
Mongols, 204, **205**
Monk by the Sea (Friedrich), 467–468, **468**
Monogram—Nationalism (Rauschenberg), 594, **596**
monotheism, 17, 147, 161. *See also* Christianity; Judaism
Monroe, Marilyn, **597**
Monsters of Grace (Glass), 609
montage, 568
Montagu, Lady Mary Wortley, 443
Montaigne, Michel de, *348*
Monte Cassino, 208
Montesquieu, 186, 425, *440*–441, 454
Monteverdi, Claudio, *397*
Monticello, **460**, 461
Mont Sainte-Victoire (Cézanne), 528, **529**
mood (music), 446
Moonlight sonata (Beethoven), 475
moralisme, 348
Moravian Brethren, 259
More, Thomas, 347
Morisot, Berthe, *525*, **526**, 527
Morning Toilette, The (Chardin), **424**
Morrison, Toni, 591, 592
mortar, 126
Le Morte d'Arthur (Malory), 233
mosaics
Byzantine Empire, **192**, 195, 197, **197**, **198**
Jewish, 155, **157**
Late Rome, 157, **157**, **168**, **176**, 184–185, **185**, **186**
pre-Christian Rome, **119**, 138, **139**, **140**
Moses, 6, 146–147
mosques, **200**, **201**, 202–203, **204**
motets, 248
Mother Courage (Brecht), 553
motion pictures. *See* film
Mount Athos, 193, **194**
Mount Vesuvius, 131
Mourning Becomes Electra (O'Neill), 553
movies. *See* film
Moyers, Bill, 592
Mozart, Wolfgang Amadeus, 445–446, 568
Mrs. Dalloway (Woolf), 549
Muhammad, 198–199, 200
Munch, Edvard, **522**
Muqaddima (Ibn Khaldun), 200–201
Muralists, 563
murals, 136, 563
muses, 41, 65, 106, **106**
Museum of Modern Art (MOMA), 593
music
Age of Reason, 444–446, **445**
Baroque Age, 367, 396–398, **396**
Bourgeois Age, 502–503
Classical style, 444–446, 474
early Christianity, 186
Early Middle Ages, 207, 211
Early Modernism, 535–537
Early Renaissance, 312
Greek Archaic Age, 46
Greek Hellenic Age, 65–66, 140
Hellenistic Age, 140
High Middle Ages, 248
High Renaissance/Early Mannerism, 342, **342**
interwar period, 568–569
Judaism, 186
Late Modernism, 608–609
Mesopotamia, 11–12, **11**
Post-Modernism, 609
Rococo style, 444
Romantic, 474–476, **474**, 502–503
Rome, 140, **140**, 186
sixteenth-century Europe, 363, 367
music dramas, 503. *See also* opera
Mussolini, Benito, *545*–*546*
Mycenaean civilization, 33, 35–37, **36**, **37**
My Faust (Stations) (Paik), **584**, 605
mystery cults, 42, 98–99, **98**, 161, 163
mystery plays, 248
mythology, 35

Nagasaki bombing, 548, 583
Naked and the Dead, The (Mailer), 589
Nana (Zola), 520
Nanna, 13
Napoleon III (emperor of France), 482, 483, 492, 500, 501

Napoleon Bonaparte, 456–457, **456**, **457**, 458, 459, **459**, 461
and Romanticism, 462, 466, 469, 470, 474
Napoleonic Code, 456, 457, 492
Narrative of the Life of Frederick Douglass (Douglass), 494–495
narthex, 238
Nash, Paul, **542**
Nash, Joseph, **486**
nationalism
Age of Anxiety, 581
Age of Reason, 441
Bourgeois Age, 481, 483, 496
Early Modernism, 512
High Middle Ages, 233
interwar period, 462, 544, 545
Late Middle Ages, 259, 263
and Romanticism, 462, 474
sixteenth-century Europe, 346
See also political/economic development
National Organization for Women (NOW), 585
National Socialism. *See* Nazi Germany
Native Son (Wright), 588
NATO. *See* North Atlantic Treaty Organization
Naturalism, 519, 520
natural law, 124, 414, 427
natural philosophy, 45–46, 67–70. *See also* philosophy; science
natural rights, 415, 454
Naumburg Cathedral, **220**
nave, 180, 237, **237**, **241**, 244, **245**, 380
Nazi Germany, 546–548, **546**, **548**
and art, 562, 563, 567, 568
and Great Depression, 545
and nationalism, 462, 546
and philosophy, 518, 554
Near Eastern civilizations
legacy of, 27, 41
successor kingdoms, 25–26
See also Egypt; Mesopotamia
Nefertiti, 21, **22**
Nefrusobk, 16
"Negro Speaks of Rivers, The" (Hughes), 551
Neoclassical style, 425, 437–440, 490
Age of Reason painting, 437–439, **438**
architecture, 439–440, **439**, **440**, **460**, 461, **461**, **462**
Bourgeois Age painting, 495, **495**
literature, 442–443, 459
revolution/reaction period painting, **450**, 458, **458**, 459–461, **459**, **460**
sculpture, **442**
See also Age of Reason; revolution/reaction period
Neoclassicism (Hellenistic Age), 103–104
Neoclassicism (music), 568
Neoclassicism (Post-Modern), 600, **602**, 603, 607, **608**
Neoexpressionism, 600, **601**, **602**, 603
Neolithic period, 4–5, 14
Neo-Platonism
and early Christianity, 161, 162, 175
Early Renaissance, 124, 296–298, **297**, 309, 310
High Renaissance/Early Mannerism, 124, 327, 328, 330
Late Rome, 183, **183**
and Scientific Revolution, 406, 407, 412
Neorealism, 600, **601**, 603–604, **604**
Nero, 124
Netherlands, 363
Age of Anxiety, 578
Age of Reason, 427, 430
Baroque Age, 378, 389–391, 416–417
Calvinism, 360
Late Middle Ages, 259
See also Flemish style
Neumann, Balthasar, *435*–436, **436**
Nevelson, Louise, 597, **598**
New Comedy, 94, 120
New Kingdom (Egypt), 14–15, 16
architecture, **18**, 19
art, 21, **21**, **22**, **23**, **24**, 25
literature, 17, 19
New Testament, 158–160
Newton, Isaac, 394, 406, 408–409, **408**, 410, 412, 420, 426
New Voyage Round the World, A (Dampier), 394
New World. *See* Americas
New York Kouros, 49, **49**
Nicene Creed, 173
Nicholas II (czar of Russia), 515
Nicholas V (pope), 294
Nicomachean Ethics (Aristotle), 70
Nietzsche, Friedrich, *518*, 531, 554
Night (Wiesel), 547
Night Watch, The (Rembrandt), 390–391, **390**
Nike of Samothrace, **93**
Nile River, 13. *See also* Egypt
1984 (Orwell), 551
nineteenth century. *See* Bourgeois Age; revolution/reaction period
Ninety-Five Theses (Luther), 357, 358
Nineveh, 25
Ninhursag, 8
Ninth Symphony (Beethoven), 475
Nitiqret, 16
Nixon, Richard M., 580
Nixon in China (Adams), 609
noble savage myth, 396
No Exit (Sartre), 588
Nominalism, 231, 261
No Name in the Street (Baldwin), 588
nonconformity, 463
non-Western influences
Age of Anxiety, 584
Baroque Age, 394, 396
Bourgeois Age, 494
Early Modernism, 53, 527, **527**, 528–529, **529**
Norisring (Stella), 603, **603**
Norman invasion of England, 223, **225**
North and South (Gaskell), 494
North Atlantic Free Trade Association (NAFTA), 582
North Atlantic Treaty Organization (NATO), 577
northern humanism, 345, 346–347, 361. *See also* sixteenth-century Europe
Northern Renaissance, 345, 348–356
legacy of, 368
literature, 141, 348–350, **349**
painting, 350–356, **351**, **352**, **353**, **355**
style characteristics, 348
Notes from Underground (Dostoevsky), 494
Not I (Beckett), 590
Notre Dame, 240–243, **241**, **242**, **243**
novel, 443–444. *See also* literature
NOW. *See* National Organization for Women
Nubia (Kush), 13, 14, 15
nuclear weapons, 575, 577, 600. *See also* atomic bombs
Nude (Grosz), **553**
Nude on a Sofa (Boucher), 433, **434**
numerology, 234
nunneries. *See* monasticism

Oath of the Horatii (David), 437, **438**, 439
Ochre and Red on Red (Rothko), **594**
Ockham's razor, 261
Octavian. *See* Augustus Caesar
oculus, **128**, 129
"Ode to Joy" (Beethoven), 475
Odoacer, *174*
Odo of Metz, **212**
Odyssey (Homer), 35, 36, 43–44
Oeconomicus (Xenophon), 71
Oedipus at Colonus (Sophocles), 64
Oedipus the King (Sophocles), 64
"official art," 491
O'Flaherty, Catherine. *See* Chopin, Kate
oil crisis, 580
O'Keeffe, Georgia, 559–560, **560**
Old Comedy, 65
Old Kingdom (Egypt), 14
architecture, 14, **15**, 16, 17, **18**, 19
art, 19–20, 23
literature, 17
Old Market Woman, 102, **103**
Old Testament, 152, 160. *See also* Bible, Hebrew
oligarchies, 38, 40
Oliver Twist (Dickens), 493
Olympia (Manet), 500, **501**
Olympian deities, 41, 42, 63, 102. *See also specific deities*
Olympieum, 99–100, **99**
One Day in the Life of Ivan Denisovich (Solzhenitsyn), 589
One Hundred Years of Solitude (García Márquez), 591
O'Neill, Eugene, 553
On Germany (de Staël), 462
On Liberty (Mill), 487
On the Duty of Civil Disobedience (Thoreau), 493
On the Motion of Mars (Kepler), 407
On the Origin of Species (Darwin), 490
OPEC. *See* Organization of Petroleum Exporting Countries
Open Window, Collioure (Matisse), 530, **531**
opera, 397, 444, 446, 502–503, 568, 609
Oppenheimer, Robert, *555*
Oration on the Dignity of Man (Pico), 298
oratorio, 398
orchestra, 61
Ordo Virtutatum (Hildegard of Bingen), 227
Oresme, Nicholas, *262*
Oresteia (Aeschylus), 63, 64, 553
Orfeo (Monteverdi), 397
organic architecture, 535
Organization of Petroleum Exporting Countries (OPEC), 580
organum, 248
Orientalism, 494
Origen, *162*, 163
Oroonoko (Behn), 396
Orpheus, 98, 163, **178**
Orthodox Christianity, 190, 191, 193, **194**, 197–198, **198**, 307. *See also* Byzantine Empire
Orwell, George, 551
Osiris and Isis (Kiefer), **601**
Ostrogoths, 205
Otto I (the Great) (German king), 207, 209, 223
Ottoman Empire, 191, 193, 292, 296, 363
Baroque Age, 377
fall of Constantinople, 190, 191, 255, 292, 296
Greek independence, 462, 471, **471**
High Renaissance/Early Mannerism, 319
and Islamic world, 199
Late Middle Ages, 255
Ovid, *122*–*123*
Owen, Robert, 487, 489

Pachomius, *173*
Paestum. *See* Poseidonia
Paik, Nam June, **584**, 605
painting
Classical Baroque, 388–389, **388**
early Christian, 163, **163**, 165, **165**
Egypt, 23–25, **23**, **24**
Florid Baroque, **372**, 381–386, **384**, **385**, **386**, 420
Late Mannerism, 363–367, **364**, **365**, **367**
Late Modernism, 593–596, **593**, **594**, **595**, **596**, **597**
Late Rome, 184, **184**
Minoan, 32, **34**
Northern Renaissance, 350–356, **351**, **352**, **353**, **355**
Post-Modernism, **590**, 600–603, **601**, **602**, **603**
pre-Christian Rome, 136, 138, **138**
prehistory, **4**
primitivist, 528, **529**
Rococo style, **422**, 431–435, **432**, **433**, **434**, **435**, 436–437, **436**, **437**
sixteenth-century Europe, **347**
See also art; Early Renaissance painting; Expressionist painting; fresco painting; High Renaissance/Early Mannerism painting; interwar period painting; Late Middle Ages painting; manuscript illumination; Neoclassical style; Realist painting; Restrained Baroque; Romantic painting
Pakistan, 578
Palace Chapel, 211, **212**
Palaeologus, Michael, *191*
paleoanthropology, 2
Paleolithic period, 2–3
Palestrina, Giovanni Pierluigi da, *367*
Palladio, *340*–342, **341**, 461
Palli *Cassone*, **293**
Pamela, or Virtue Rewarded (Richardson), 444
pantheism, 8
Pantheon (Paris), 440, **440**
Pantheon (Rome), **108**, 126, **128**, 129, 181
pantomimes, 140
papacy
Baroque Age, 379–380
Early Middle Ages, 206–207
Early Renaissance, 294
High Middle Ages, 223, 225, 226, **226**
High Renaissance/Early Mannerism, 317, 321
Late Middle Ages, 257–258
origins of, 158
and Reformations, 356, 357, 361, 362
See also Reformations; Roman Catholic Church

Parable of the Blind, The (Bruegel), 354, **355**, 356
Paradise Lost (Milton), 395–396, 420
Paris, **52**
Paris (France), Notre Dame, 240–243, **241**, **242**, **243**
Paris, Rue de Parme on Bastille Day (Bonnard), **510**
Parks, Rosa, 577
Parliament (England), 223, 257, 360, 361, 376–377, 430
  Houses of (building), **483**, 496
Parmenides, *67*
Parmigianino, *335*, **335**
Parthenon, 57, 73–74, **73**
  sculpture, **54**, **57**, 77, 79–80, **80**, **81**, 170
Parthia, 89
Pascal, Blaise, 410, *412*
Passover, 157, 160
Pasteur, Louis, *490*
pastoral, 94, 464–465, **465**
paterfamilias, 111, **112**
Pathétique sonata (Beethoven), 475
pathos, 391
Paul, 158–159, 160, 161, 162, 176, 226
Paul III (pope), 361, 406
Paul V (pope), 380
Paulina, 174
pavane, 537
Pavane pour une infante defunte (Ravel), 537
Pax Romana, 117, 118
Pazzi Chapel, 300, **301**
Peace of God, 220
Peace of Lodi (1454), 291, 317
Peace of the Church (Edict of Milan), 172, 175, 178, 179, 182
Pearlstein, Philip, 600, **601**
Peasants' Revolt (1381), 255–256, 264
Peasants' War (1523), 359
pediment, 46
Pelagianism, 176
Pelli, Cesar, **583**
Peloponnesian War, 59, 65, 68
penance, 226, 227
Penates, 111
pendentive, 194, **195**, 201
Penderecki, Krzystof, *609*
Penelope, 44
Penn, William, 416
Pensées (Pascal), 412
Pentateuch. *See* Torah
Pepin the Short (Frankish king), 206
Peplos Kore, 50, **51**
Pepys, Samuel, 378
perestroika, 581
Perfit Description of the Celestiall Orbes, A (Digges), **406**
performance art, 610, **610**, **611**
Pergamum, 89, 90, **91**, 100, **100**
  sculpture, 101–103, **102**, **104**
Pergolesi, 568
Pericles, *59*, **59**
peristyle, 179, **179**
Perpendicular style, 265–266, **266**
Perpetua, Vibia, 162–163
Persephone, 42
Persia, 25, **26**
  and Greek Archaic Age, 40–41, 46, 50
  and Greek Hellenic Age, 58–59, 60, 66
  Hellenistic Age, 89, 98
  and Islamic world, 201
  and Jews, 149
  Mongol period, 204, **205**
Persian Letters (Montesquieu), 441
Persistence of Memory, The (Dali), 560, **562**, 563
perspective, 274, 299, 306, **306**, 307, 308, 352, **352**
Peter, 158
Peter the Great (czar of Russia), 431
Peter the Hermit, 208
Petrarch, Francesco, *262*, 295, 322
Petronas Towers (Kuala Lumpur), **583**
Phaedo (Plato), 68
Pharisees, 160
Phèdre (Racine), 395, 444
Phidias, **57**, *77*, 79–80, **80**, **81**
Philip II (king of Spain), 319, 363, 364
Philip IV (king of France), 223
Philip of Macedon, 60
Philippines, 578
Philip the Bold (duke of Burgundy), 271
Philip the Good (duke of Burgundy), 277
philosophes, 425–426, 437, 439
  and architecture, 440
  and literature, 441–442, 443
  and political/economic development, 429, 430, 431
  and women's status, 426, 429
  See also Enlightenment
philosophy
  Age of Anxiety, 584–586
  Bourgeois Age, 487, 489
  and early Christianity, 162
  Early Modernism, 518–519, 537
  Early Renaissance, 296–298, 405
  Greek Archaic Age, 45–46
  Greek Hellenic Age, 67–70
  Hellenistic Age, 94–98, 107, 395
  interwar period, 553–554
  Late Middle Ages, 261
  pre-Christian Rome, 96, 121–122, 123–124
  and Romanticism, 473–474
  and Scientific Revolution, 107, 232, 261, 403, 406, 407, 410–412, 416
  See also Enlightenment; science
Phoenicians, 32, 152
phonograms, 7
photography, 299, 491, 501–502, **502**, **544**, **547**
Phrygian mode, 66
physics, 406–409, **406**, 412, 418
  Early Modernism, 522–523
  interwar period, 554–555
  See also science
Physiocrats, 427, 452
Piano, Renzo, **606**, 607
pianoforte, 444
picaresque novel, 366
Picasso, Pablo
  and Age of Anxiety, 593
  Early Modernism, 530, **532**, 533, **533**, **550**
  interwar period, **542**, 557, 559, **559**, **569**
Pico della Mirandola, *297–298*
pictograms, 7, **8**
Picture of Dorian Gray, The (Wilde), 521
Piero della Francesca, *308*, **309**
Pierrot lunaire (Schoenberg), 537
piers, 239
Pietà (1498–99) (Michelangelo), **335**, 337
Pietà (before 1555) (Michelangelo), **338**, 339
Pietà (Giotto), 277, **278**
pilasters, 300
pilgrimage churches, 236–237, 240
Pillars of the Faith, 200
Pindar, 60
Pisa Cathedral, **269**
Pisan Council (1409), 258
Pisano, Giovanni, 267, **267**, **269**, 270, **270**, 275
Pissarro, Camille, **511**
Pius II (pope), 294
plague, **253**, **254**, 255, 259, 262–263, **263**, 291
Planck, Max, 522–523, 554–555
Plato, 69–70
  and early Christian church history, 177
  and High Middle Ages, 231
  legacy of, 82
  on music, 66
  and Renaissance, 296, 297, 322, 323, 332–333
  on Sappho, 44
  and Socrates, 68, 69
  See also Neo-Platonism
Platonism, 69. *See also* Neo-Platonism
Plautus, *120*
Pleistocene epoch, 3
Plotinus, **183**
podium, 100
Poetics (Aristotle), 62, 64
poetry
  Age of Anxiety, 589
  Age of Reason, 442
  Baroque Age, 394, 395–396
  Greek Archaic Age, 35, 36, 42, 43–45
  High Middle Ages, 232–233, 234
  High Renaissance/Early Mannerism, 322
  interwar period, 551
  Mesopotamia, 10
  Romanticism, 464, 493
  Rome, 120–123
  See also literature
Pointillism, 527, **528**
Poland, 255, 256, 377, 580
polis, 38
Polish School, 609
political/economic development
  Age of Anxiety, 575–583, 611–612
  Age of Reason, 423, 427–431
  agrarian revolution, 3–4
  Baroque Age, 373, 374–379, 389, 413
  Bourgeois Age, 479, 481–486, 488–489
  Byzantine Empire, 190–193, **192**, 292
  Early Middle Ages, 205–207
  Early Modernism, 509–517
  Early Renaissance, 290–294, **292**, **293**
  Egypt, 5, 14–16
  Greek Archaic Age, 38–41
  Greek Hellenic Age, 41, 55, 58–60
  Hellenistic Age, 87, 89–92, 99
  High Middle Ages, **209**, 220–225, **221**, **222**, 239
  High Renaissance/early Mannerism, 316–320, 323–324, 326
  interwar period, 542–549, 559
  Islamic world, 198–199
  Judaism, 145–152
  Late Middle Ages, **252**, 253–258, **256**, 263–264
  Late Rome, 169–174, **172**, 186–187
  Mesopotamia, 5, 6–7
  Near Eastern successor kingdoms, 25
  pre-Archaic Aegean civilizations, 32, 35–36, 38
  pre-Christian Rome, 111, 113, 115–118, 123, 124, 131, 134
  revolution/reaction period, 451–458, **452**, **462**
  sixteenth-century Europe, 356–363, 359
  See also political philosophy
political philosophy
  Age of Reason, 440–441
  Baroque Age, 413–416, 420
  Bourgeois Age, 487, 489
  Greek Hellenic Age, 69–70
  and Romanticism, 474
  See also political/economic development
Politics (Aristotle), 70
Pollock, Jackson, 593, **593**, 609
Polydoros, **86**, *106*, **106**
Polykleitos, 77, **79**, 133
polyphony, 211, 248, 312, 367
polytheism, 8, 16, 41, 198
Pompadour, Madame de, 429
Pompeii, 131, **132**, 138, **138**, **140**
Pompidou Center (Paris) (Rogers & Piano), **606**, 607
Pont du Gard, 131, **132**
Pontifex Maximus, 129
Pop Art, 563, **574**, **579**, 594, **597**, 599, **599**, 603
Pope, Alexander, 409, 442–443
popular culture. *See* mass culture
population, 221, 255, 319, 452, 453
Poquelin, Jean Baptiste. *See* Molière
porticoes, 19
Portrait of Braque (Picasso). *See Man with a Hat*
Portrait of Don Carlos (Anguissola), **365**, 366
Portugal, 292, 363
Poseidon, 42, **54**, **78**
Poseidonia (Paestum), 47–48, **48**, **72**, 73
post-and-lintel construction, 12, 46, **156**
post-beam-triangle construction, 46, 126
Post-Impressionism, 527–530, **528**, **529**, **530**
Post-Modernism, 584, 600–607
  architecture, **583**, 605–607, **606**, **607**, **608**
  and Impressionism, 527
  installation art, 604–605, **605**
  literature, 590–592
  music, 609
  and Naturalism, 520
  painting, **590**, 600–603, **601**, **602**, **603**
  performance art, 610, **610**, **611**
  and political/economic development, 581, 583
  sculpture, **584**, 599, 603–604, **604**
  video art, **584**, 605
  See also Age of Anxiety
Pound, Ezra, 551
Poussin, Nicolas, *388*–389, **388**, 529
Pozzo, Andrea, *383*–384, **385**
praetor, 124
Praise of Folly, The (Erasmus), 347
Praxitelean curve, 81
Praxiteles, 81, **81**, 103, 164
pre-Christian Roman architecture, **110**, 117, 126–131
  amphitheaters, 130–131, **131**
  aqueducts, 131, **132**
  arch innovations, 126, **127**
  Colosseum, 131, **131**
  forums, 129, **129**, 131, **132**

and Hellenistic Age, 99
Maison Carrée, 126, **127**, 461
Pantheon, **108**, 126, **128**, 129, 181
and Pax Romana, 117, **118**
pre-Christian Roman sculpture, **111**, **115**, 131, 132–136
early Christian, 163, **164**, 165, **165**
Greek influence, **114**, 126
idealistic style, 133, **134**, **135**, 136, **136**, **137**
realistic style, 133, **134**
relief, 133, **135**, 136, **136**, **137**
and women's status and roles, **112**
pre-Christian Rome, 109–141
Christianity in, 157, 158, 160, 161–163, 169, 170, 172, 173
drama, 94, 120, 211, 394
and early Christianity, 157, 158, 160, 161–163, 169, 172, 173
Etruscan and Greek influences, 111, 113, **114**, 120, 121, 126, 140
First Jewish War, 130, 136, 150, 151, 157, 161
and Hellenistic Age, 89, 96, 117, 121
and Judaism, 151, 155, 157, 161
law, 124, 193–194
legacy of, 141
literature, 94, 111, 120–123
map, **110**
mosaics, **119**, 138, **139**, **140**
music, 140, **140**
painting, 136, 138, **138**
philosophy, 96, 121–122, 123–124
political/economic development, 111, 113, 115–118, 123, 124, 131, 134
religion, 98, 111, **113**, 118–120, **119**, **120**, 126
style characteristics, 117–118
timeline, 115
See also pre-Christian Roman architecture; pre-Christian Roman sculpture
predestination, 359
prehistory, 2–5, **4**, **5**
Prélude à l'après-midi d'un faune (Debussy), 536
Presentation of the Virgin in the Temple (Titian), 334–335, **334**
Presley, Elvis, 611
pre-Socratic philosophers, 67–68
Prevalence of Ritual, The: Baptism (Bearden), **587**
Pride and Prejudice (Austen), 459
Prima Porta statue of *Augustus*, 133, **134**, 135
Primavera (Botticelli), 309–310, **310**
primitivism, 528, **529**, 537, 551, 560
Prince, The (Machiavelli), 323–324
Principia (Newton), 409
Principles of Political Economy and Taxation (Ricardo), 453
Principles of Political Economy (Mill), 487
printing, 256, 262, 510, **511**
prints, 271, **274**
Priscilla, 162
problem play, 520
program music, 474, 476, 503, 536–537
prophets, 149
Propylaea, 73
Protagoras, 31, *68*
protected classes, 220–221
Protestant order, 321, 345–346, 357–361
Baroque Age, 379
and Holy Roman Empire, 319
and northern humanism, 347, 361
and Northern Renaissance/Late Mannerism, 350, 354
See also Christianity; Reformations; *specific styles*
Proust, Marcel, *521*
Provençal language, 233
Prussia
Age of Reason, 429, 430
Baroque Age, 374, 377, 378, 379
Bourgeois Age, 482–483
revolution/reaction period, 456, 458
See also Germany
Psalter of Saint Louis IX, 247, **247**
psyche, 68
psychoanalysis, 519
psychology, 412, 420, 494, 584
Early Modernism, 514, 518–519, 530, 537
Ptah, 16
Ptolemaic kingdom, 89, 90
Ptolemy, 405, 406, 408
Ptolemy I (king of Egypt), 89, 98
Ptoon Kouros, 49–50, **50**
Pugin, A. W. N., **483**, 496
Pulcinella (Stravinsky), 568
Punic Wars, 116, 119
purgatory, 227, 234
Puritanism, 360, 376, 395
purity, 535
putti genre, 185, **185**
pyramids, 14, **15**, 16, 17, **18**
Pyrrho, *96*
Pythagoras, *46*, 65–66, 67, 71, 163, 406

quadrivium, 141, 230
quantum theory, 522–523, 555
Quattro Libri dell' Architettura (Palladio), 341–342

Ra, 16
Rabbinic Judaism, 151
Rabelais, Françaís, *346*
Racine, Jean, *395*, 420, 444
radio, 549, 589
radiochemistry, 522
Raft of the Medusa, *The* (Géricault), 469, **470**, 471, 472
ragtime, 537
Railway Station, The (Frith), **485**
Rake's Progress, The (Stravinsky), 568
Rameau, Jean-Philippe, 444
Raphael, **322**, *327*, 332–333, **332**, **333**
rationalism, 231, 232, 261
Rauschenberg, Robert, 533, *594*, **596**
Ravel, Maurice, *536–537*
Ravenna, 171, 173, 178
architecture, 195, **196**, 211
mosaics, **168**, 185, **186**, **192**, **197**
Raynal, Abbé, *455*
Rayonnant style, 243
Reading "Le Figaro" (Cassatt), **511**
Realism (art), 491
literature, 444, 491–492, 493–495, 520, 588–589
See also Bourgeois Age; Realist painting
Realism (philosophy), 230–231, 261
Realist painting, 496–500
Baroque Age, 381, 382
Bonheur, 499–500, **501**
Courbet, **478**, 496–498, **497**, 603
Daumier, 498–499, **498**
and Impressionism, 496, 500, 523
Manet, 299, **491**, 496, 500, **501**, 527
Millet, 499, **499**, **500**
realpolitik, 482, 491
Reason, Age of. *See* Age of Reason
recitatives, 502
Reconstruction (United States), 485
Reformation Parliament (England), 360
Reformations, 345–346, 348, 356–363
and Holy Roman Empire, 319, 360, 362
legacy of, 368
reasons for, 356–357
timeline, 346
and warfare, 362–363, 373, 377–379
See also Christianity; Counter-Reformation; Late Mannerism; Northern Renaissance; Protestant order; sixteenth-century Europe
regalia, 21
Reichnau school, 213, **214**
Reign of Terror, 455
relativity theory, 523, 554
relief sculptures, 47
Assyria, **25**
early Christian, 165, **165**
Early Renaissance, **302**, 303, 304–305, **305**
Egypt, **22**
Greek Hellenic Age, **54**, **61**, **77**, 79–80, **80**, **81**
Hellenistic Age, **95**, **96**, **104**
High Middle Ages, **221**, **237**, **238**
Late Rome, 179, 182, 183–184, **183**, **184**
Persia, **26**
pre-Christian Rome, **120**, 133, **135**, 136, **136**, **137**
Sumer, **10**
See also art; sculpture
religion
Egypt, 16–17, 19, 98, **98**, 119
Greek Archaic Age, 41–42, 43, 49, 53
Greek Hellenic Age, 55, 57, 63, 68, 69, 71, 79, 81, 119
Hellenistic Age, 70, 93, 95, **95**, 97, 98–99
late Rome, 170–171, 172, 174, 178
Mesopotamia, 8, 10, 16
Minoan, **34**, 35
Mycenaean, 36
pre-Christian Rome, 98, 111, **113**, 118–120, **119**, **120**, 126
prehistory, 3
Zoroastrianism, 25, 98, 149, 160, 228–229
See also Christianity; ethics; Islam; Judaism
Religious Peace of Augsburg, 362–363, 378
reliquary, 237
Rembrandt van Rijn, 389–391, **389**, **390**, **391**, **410**, 420
Remembrance of Things Past (Proust), 521
Renaissance, 94
scholarly interpretations, 289–290
timelines, 290, 293, 320
See also Early Renaissance; High Renaissance/Early Mannerism
Renaissance man, 310
Renaissance space, 299, 306, **306**, 533
Renoir, Auguste, *525*, **526**
Republican Portrait of a Man, 133, **134**
Republic (Plato), 70
Requiem Canticles (Stravinsky), 609
Residenz (Würzburg), 435–436, **436**
Restoration (England), 376
Restrained Baroque, 379, 389–394
architecture, 393–394, **394**
Leyster, 391, **392**
Rembrandt, 389–391, **389**, **390**, **391**, **410**, 420
and Scientific Revolution, **402**, **405**
Van Dyck, 391, 393, **393**
Vermeer, 391, **392**
See also Baroque Age
revenge tragedy, 350
Revett, Nicholas, 437
Revolution of the Viaduct (Klee), **562**, 563
revolution/reaction period (1760–1830), 451–476
Industrial Revolution, 427, 431, 451–453, **452**
legacy of, 476
map, **457**
political/economic development, 451–458, **452**, **462**
timeline, 453
See also French Revolution; Neoclassical style; Romanticism; Romantic painting
Revolutions of the Heavenly Bodies (Copernicus), 406–407
Rhineland, 256, 259
Rhodes, **86**, 104, 106, **106**
ribbed vault, 239
Ricardo, David, 452, 453
Richardson, Samuel, 444
Richelieu, Cardinal, 375, 376
Rigoletto (Verdi), 503
Ring of the Nibelung, The (Wagner), 503
Rite of Spring, The (Stravinsky), 537
Rivera, Diego, 563
Roads to Freedom (Sartre), 588
Robert and Ethel Scull (Segal), 599, **599**
Robespierre, 545
rocaille, **428**, 435
rock and roll, 569
Rococo style, 425, 431–437
architecture, **428**, 435–436, **436**
English response, 436–437, **437**
music, 444
painting, **422**, 431–435, **432**, **433**, **434**, **435**, 436–437, **436**, **437**
See also Age of Reason
Rodeo (Copland), 569
Rodin, Auguste, *534*, **534**, 599
Roentgen, Wilhelm Conrad, *522*
Rogers, Richard, **606**, 607
Roman Catholic Church, 158, 159, 407
Age of Reason, 426, 430
and Aristotle, 70
and Bible, 154, 175
and Orthodox Church, 193
See also Christianity; Counter-Reformation; High Middle Ages Christianity; Inquisition; papacy
romances (High Middle Ages), 233
Romanesque style, 235, 236–239, 266
architecture, 236–239, **236**, **237**
manuscript illumination, 238–239, **238**
sculpture, **235**, 237–238, **237**, **238**
Romanticism, 458, 461–472
and Age of Reason, 441, 442, 461, 463, 464, 492
and Bourgeois Age, 479, 490
and idealism, 473–474, 492, 493
literature, 463–464, **464**, 491, 492–493
music, 474–475, 474–476, **474**, 502–503
and nationalism, 462
See also revolution/reaction period; Romantic painting

Romantic painting, **462**, 464–472, **464**
Bourgeois Age, **484**, 495–496, **496**
Delacroix, 471–472, **471**, **472**, **473**, 495–496, **496**, 531
England, 464–467, **465**, **466**, **467**
Géricault, 469, **470**, **471**, 472
Goya, 468–469, **469**, **470**, 579
and Impressionism, 523
sack of (1527), 317, 321, 360
Rome. *See* Italy; Late Rome; papacy; pre-Christian Rome; Roman mosaics; *specific styles, artists, and buildings*
Romulus Augustulus, 174
Rooker, Michael Angelo, **452**
Room of One's Own, A (Woolf), 550
Roosevelt, Franklin Delano, 545
Rosetta Stone, 2
rose window (Notre Dame), 240, **243**
Rothko, Mark, *594*, **594**
Rougon-Macquart series (Zola), 520
Rousseau, Jean-Jacques, 425, 426, 429, 440
and Romanticism, *441*, 461, 463, 464, 492
Royal Academy of Painting and Sculpture (France), 376, 432, 491, 495, 496, 499–500
Royal Society (England), 418
Rubens, Peter Paul, 384, 386, **387**, 391
Rude, François, **481**
Russia
Age of Reason, 428, 429, 430, 431
Baroque Age, 374
Bourgeois Age, 482, 494
and Byzantine Empire, 191
Early Modernism, 514–515, 520
interwar period, 545
revolution/reaction period, 458
See also Russian Republic; Soviet Union
Russian Republic, 581
Russo-Japanese War (1904–1905), 515

Sabin, Albert, 588
sack of Rome (1527), 317, 321, 360
sacraments, 226–227
"Sailing to Byzantium" (Yeats), 551
Sainte-Marie-Madeleine, Church of (Vézelay), **236**, 237–238, **237**, **238**
Saint-Simon, Comte de, *487*, 489
Sakkareh, 17, **18**
Salk, Jonas, 588
Salomé (Wilde), **521**
Salon. *See* Royal Academy of Painting and Sculpture
"Salon de la Princesse" (Boffrand), 435, **436**
Salon des Refusés, 500
salons, 429
Samarkand, **202**
sanctuaries, 71, **72**
Sand, George, 492
San Marco monastery (Florence), 307–308, **308**
Santa Croce Church (Florence), 300, **301**
Santa Maria del Carmine, Church of (Florence), 307, **307**
Santa Maria Novella, Church of (Florence), 306–307, **306**
Sant' Apollinare, 195, **196**
Sant' Ignazio, Church of (Rome), 383–384, **385**
Santo Domingo, 455
San Vitale, **192**, 195, **196**, 197, **197**, 211
Sappho, 39, *44–45*
sarcophagi, 163, 165, **165**, 182–184, **183**, **184**
Sargon, 6, 10
Sartre, Jean-Paul, *554*, 588
"Satchmo." *See* Armstrong, Louis
satire, 122, 123
Satyagraha (Glass), 609
satyr-plays, 62
Saul, 148
Savonarola, Fra, *294*
Savoye House (Le Corbusier), 567, **567**
Saxons, 173, 205, 206
scenographic style, 339
Schelling, Friedrich Wilhelm Joseph von, *473*
scherzo, 445
Schiller, Friedrich von, *475*
Schoenberg, Arnold, *537*, 568, 608
scholasticism, 230, 411
Schönbrunn Palace (Vienna), 430, **431**
School of Athens, The (Raphael), 332, **332**
Schopenhauer, Arthur, 563
Schubert, Franz, *475*, 503
Schumann, Robert, 503
science
Age of Anxiety, 586–588
Bourgeois Age, 490, 491
Early Modernism, 510, 522–523
Early Renaissance, 294, 311
High Middle Ages, 405
interwar period, 554–555
Islamic world, 201, 405
Late Middle Ages, 256, 261–262, 405
and Romanticism, 464, 466
See also natural philosophy; Scientific Revolution
Scientific Revolution, 373, **402**, 403–413
and art, **402**, **405**, 419–420
astronomy and physics, 406–409, **406**
chemistry, 409–410
contradictions of, 412–413
and earlier cosmology, 404–405, 409, 411
legacy of, 420
and literature, 403, 417, 443–444
medicine, 409–410, **410**
and philosophy, 107, 232, 261, 403, 406, 407, 410–412, 416
responses to, 417–420
and technology, 406
timeline, 404
See also Baroque Age
scientific societies, 418, **419**
Scivias (Hildegard of Bingen), 227, **228**, 229
Scotland, 360
Scream, The (Munch), **522**
scriptures, 152. *See also specific scriptures*
sculpture
Assyria, **25**
Bourgeois Age, **481**
early Christian, 163, **164**, 165, **165**, **170**
Early Gothic style, 240, **241**, 242, **242**
early Judaism, **155**
Early Modernism, **518**, 534, **534**
Early Renaissance, 298, 303–305, **303**, **304**, **305**
Egypt, 19–21, **20**, **21**, **22**, **24**, 25, 49
Florid Baroque, 380–381, **383**
Greek Archaic Age, 49–52, **49**, **50**, **51**, **52**, **164**, 165
High Gothic style, 246, **246**
High Middle Ages, **220**, **221**, **226**, **235**
interwar period, **555**
Islamic world, 204, **205**
Late Gothic style, **226**, 267, **269**, 270–271, **270**, **272**
Late Modernism, 597–599, **597**, **598**, **599**
Mesopotamia, 12, **12**
Mycenaean, 36, **37**
Neoclassical style, **442**
Persia, **26**
Post-Modernism, **584**, 599, 603–604, **604**
prehistory, 3, **5**
Romanesque style, **235**, 237–238, **237**, **238**
See also Greek Hellenic Age sculpture; Hellenistic sculpture; Late Roman sculpture; Michelangelo Buonarroti; pre-Christian Roman sculpture
Seagram Building (New York) (Mies van der Rohe & Johnson), 599–600, **600**
Sea Peoples, 15
Second Industrial Revolution, 510
Second Intermediate Period (Egypt), 14
Second Sex, The (de Beauvoir), 585
Second Stage, The (Friedan), 585
Second String Quartet (Schoenberg), 537
Second Temple (Jerusalem), **150**, 151, 157
Second Temple of Hera (Poseidonia), **72**, 73
Secretum (Petrarch), 262
Segal, George, 599, **599**
Segesta, 59
Seleucia, 90
Seleucid kingdom, 89, 98, 150
Seleucus, 89
Self-Portrait (Dürer), **344**
Self-Portrait (Leyster), 391, **392**
Self-Portrait (Rembrandt), 391, **391**
Self Portrait as the Allegory of Painting (Gentileschi), 382
Self-Portrait Dedicated to Dr. Eloesser (Kahlo), **540**, 564, **564**
Self-Portrait with a Gray Hat (van Gogh), **508**, 530, **530**
Selket, **24**, 25
Seneca, *123–124*
Senmut, 18, 19
Senusert I (pharoah), 17
Septimius Severus (Roman emperor), 163
Septuagint, 152, 154
Serapis, 98
Serbia, 517
serfdom, 221, 428
serial music, 568, 608–609
Seurat, Georges, *527*, **528**
Seven Years' War, 429, 430, 453
Severe style, **58**, 75, **75**, **76**, *77*
sexuality
Age of Anxiety, 587, 591, 600, 604
Age of Reason, 431, 433, **434**, 437
Baroque Age, 395
Bourgeois Age, 500
early Christianity, 159, 162
Early Modernism, 537
Hellenistic Age, 96
High Renaissance/Early Mannerism, 322, 323, 354
interwar period, 549, 550, 560, 563
and jazz, 537
Mesopotamia, 11
Neo-Platonism, 183
and northern humanism, 347
pre-Christian Rome, 122
revolution/reaction period (1760–1830), 453
See also women's status and roles
sfumato, 311, 325
shaft graves, 36, **37**
Shaker Loops (Adams), 609
Shakespeare, William, 94, 141, 348, **349**, 350, 475
Shamash, 10, 11
Shari'a, 200
Shelley, Mary Wollstonecraft, 464
Shelley, Percy Bysshe, 464
Sherman, Cindy, 610, **611**
Sicilian school of philosophy, 46, 67
Siena Cathedral, 266, **267**
Siglo de Oro, 366
Sign for Gersaint's Shop, The (Watteau), 432–433, **433**
signori, 291, 295
Silenus, **58**
Simon Chenard as a Sans-culotte (Boilly), **455**
simony, 225
Sistine Chapel, 294, 327, **328–329**, **330**, 384, 534
The Last Judgement, 327, **331**, 363
Sistine Madonna (Raphael), 333, **333**
sixteenth-century Europe
legacy of, 368
map, **356**
music, 363, 367
northern humanism, 345, 346–347, 361
painting, **347**
political/economic development, 356–363, 359
timeline, 346
See also High Renaissance/Early Mannerism; Late Mannerism; Northern Renaissance
Sixtus III (pope), 181
Sixtus IV (pope), 294, 327
skene, 61–62
Skepticism, 95–96, 411, 419
Sky Cathedral (Nevelson), 597, **598**
slave narrative, 494–495
slavery
Age of Reason, 429
Baroque Age, 420
Bourgeois Age, **484**, 485, 494–495
Greek Archaic Age, 39–40
Hellenistic Age, 88
High Middle Ages, 221
High Renaissance/Early Mannerism, 320
revolution/reaction period, 454, 455
Rome, 116, 162
Slave Ship, The (Turner), **484**
Sleep of Reason, The (Goya), 468–469, **469**
Sluter, Claus, 271, **272**
Smith, Adam, 426, 427, 452, 453
Smith, David, 597
Snowstorm: Hannibal and His Army Crossing the Alps (Turner), **466**, 467
social contract, 414, 415, 441
Social Contract, The (Rousseau), 441
socialism, 479, 482, 486, 487, 489, 512. *See also* Marxism; Soviet Union
Socialist Realism, 557
Society of Jesus. *See* Jesuits
Socrates, 65, 67, 68, 69, **69**, 71
Solidarity (Poland), 580
Solomon, 148–149
Solomon's Temple, 148, 155, 381

Solon, 40, 45
Solzhenitsyn, Alexander, *589*
sonata form, 444–445
Song of Roland, 232–233, **232**, 246–247
Song of Solomon, The (Morrison), 591
Songs and Stories from "Moby Dick" (Anderson), 610, **610**
"Sophisticated Lady" (Ellington), 569
Sophists, 67, 68
Sophocles, 59, *63–64*, 82, 553
Sorrows of Young Werther, The (Goethe), 463
Soufflot, Jacques Germain, *439–440*, **440**
Sound and the Fury, The (Faulkner), 550
Southern Christian Leadership Conference, 586
Soviet Union, 545, 551
  Age of Anxiety, 575, 577, 580–581, 589, **590**, 591
  art, 557
  World War II, 547, **547**, 548
  See also Russia
Sower, The (Millet), 499, **499**
space program, 587
Spain, 292, 363
  Age of Reason, 430
  Baroque Age, 378
  Early Middle Ages, 206
  High Renaissance/Early Mannerism, 316–318, 323–324
  interwar period, **542**, 545, 546
  Late Mannerism, 363–366
  Late Middle Ages, 256
  Romanticism, 468–469, **469**, **470**
Spanish Armada, 363
Spanish Civil War, **542**, 546, 559
Sparta, 39–40, 50, 58–59
Spearbearer. *See Doryphoros*
Sphinx (De Andrea), 603–604, **604**
sphinxes, 19–20, **20**
Spirit of the Laws, The (Montesquieu), 440–441
spirituals, 537, 551
sports, 40, 56, **56**, 60, **61**, **185**
Sta. Constanza, Church of, 180, **181**, 185, **185**
stained glass, **218**, **232**, 235, **235**, 240, 243, **243**, 246–247
Stalin, Joseph, 545, 577, **590**
Sta. Maria Maggiore basilica, 180, **181**
Stampa, Gaspara, 322
Starry Night, The (van Gogh), 530, **531**
State Capitol of Virginia, 461, **461**
St. Denis, Church of, 240, **240**
Stein, Gertrude, **550**
stele, 11
Stella, Frank, 603, **603**
St. Francis in Ecstasy (Bellini), 311–312, **312**, 333
St. Gall monastery, **210**
St. Maclou, Church of, **265**
St. Mark's Cathedral (Venice), **172**
St. Matthew Passion (Bach), 397
Stoicism, 97–98, 107, 123–124, 161, 162
  and Baroque Age, 395, 414
Stone Age culture, 2–4, **4**, **5**
Story of Sinuhe, 17
St. Pantaleon, Church of, **207**
St. Paul Bible, 212–213, **213**
St. Paul's Cathedral (London), 129, 394, **394**, 440
St. Peter's Basilica (Rome), 180, **180**, 340, **340**, 394
  Baroque Age, 380–381, **380**, **381**, **382**
  and Roman Pantheon, 129
Stradivari, Antonio, 444
Stravinsky, Igor, *537*, 550, 568, **569**, 608–609
stream-of-consciousness writing, 549–550
Strindberg, August, 521
Stroke (About March 3, 1953) (Komar & Melamid), **590**
structuralism, 584–585
Struhs, William, **610**
Stuart, James, 437
Stuart dynasty (England), 376
studia humanitatis, 295
Sturm und Drang, 463
style galant, 444
stylobate, 47
Sublime, 462, 464, **466**, 467
Such Sweet Thunder (Ellington), 569
Suetonius, 133, 210
Suez Canal, 486, **486**
Suger, *239*
Sula (Morrison), 591
Sullivan, Louis, 534–535, **535**
Sumer, 5, 6, 7, **8**, **9**, 10, **10**, **11**. *See also* Mesopotamia
Summa Theologica (Thomas Aquinas), 231–232
Sun Also Rises, The (Hemingway), 550
Sunday Afternoon on the Island of La Grande Jatte, A (Seurat), 527, **528**
Suprematism, 556–557, **557**
Suprematist Composition (Malevich), 557, **557**
Surrealism, **540**, **555**, 560, **562**, **564**
Sweden, 378, 430
symbolic realism, 178, **178**, 182
Symmachus, 182
Symphonie fantastique (Berlioz), 476
symphony, 445
Symphony of Psalms (Stravinsky), 568
synagogues, **144**, 151, **152**, 155
syncopation, 537
syncretism, 118
synoptic Gospels, 158
Syntactic Structures (Chomsky), 585
synthesizer, 609

tableau vivant, 282
tabula rasa, 416
Tacitus, *123*
Taine, Hippolyte, 488–489
Talbot, William Henry Fox, 501
Talmud, 151
Target with Plaster Casts (Johns), 594, **596**
Tarquin the Proud, 113
Tartuffe (Molière), 395
Tausret, 16
Taylor, Harriet, 487
technology. *See* science
telescope, 406
television, 587, 611
Tempest, The (Giorgione), 333, **334**
Tempietto (Rome) (Bramante), 339–340, **339**, 394
Tempio Malatestiano (Rimini), **298**, 300, 302–303
Temple of Aphaia (Aegina), 48, **48**, 50, 52, **52**
Temple of Athena Nike, 73, **74**
Temple of Hera (Poseidonia), 47–48, **48**
temples. *See* architecture
tempo, 445
Ten Commandments, 147
Terence, 120, 211
Teresa of Avila, Saint, 383
Tertullian, *162*, 163
terza rima, 234
tetrarchs, 171, **172**
textual criticism, 295
Thales, *46*, 67
theater. *See* drama
theater of the absurd, 589–590
Thebes, 59, 60
theocracy, 16
Theocritus, 92, *94*
Theodora (Byzantine Empress), 195, **197**
Theodosius I (the Great) (Roman emperor), *173*
theology, 159. *See also* Christianity; Reformations
Theosophists, 557
Theotokopoulous, Domenikos. *See* El Greco
Thermopylae, Battle of, 41
Thespis, 61
Third-Class Carriage, The (Daumier), 498–499, **498**
Third Symphony (*Eroica*) (Beethoven), 474–475
Third World, 578–579, 581, 585. *See also* windows on the world
Thirty-Nine Articles, 361
Thirty Years' War, 377–378, 397, 413
Thomas, Dylan, 589
Thomas Aquinas, Saint, 227, *231*–232, 234, 253, 261
Thomism, 231–232, 261
Thoreau, Henry David, 493, 586
Three Hebrews in the Fiery Furnace, **165**
Three Musicians, The (Picasso), 557, 559, **559**
Three-penny Opera, The (Weill), 552–553
Three Sisters, The (Chekhov), 520
Threnody for the Victims of Hiroshima (Penderecki), 609
Thucydides, *67*, 82, 194
Thutmose III (pharoah), *16*, 21
tibia, 140
Tiepolo, Giovanni Battista, *435*, **436**
Tigris-Euphrates valley, 5. *See also* Mesopotamia
timelines
  Age of Anxiety, 582
  Age of Reason, 425
  Baroque Age, 376
  Bourgeois Age, 480
  Byzantine Empire, 192
  early Christianity, 158
  Early Modernism, 519
  Egypt, 14
  Greek Archaic Age, 40
  Greek Hellenic Age, 59
  Hellenistic Age, 89
  interwar period, 556
  Islamic world, 199
  Judaism, 146, 148
  Mesopotamia, 7
  Middle Ages, 206, 224, 257
  Minoan and Mycenaean civilizations, 33
  Near Eastern successor kingdoms, 26
  prehistory, 3
  Renaissance, 290, 293, 320
  revolution/reaction period, 453
  Rome, 115, 170
  Scientific Revolution, 404
  sixteenth-century Europe, 346
  See also windows on the world
Timgad, **118**
Timur Lenk, Tomb of, **188**, **202**
Tintoretto, *366–367*, **367**
Titian, 311, **319**, *333–335*, **334**, 386, 500
Titus, 130, 151
Titus, Arch of, 129–130, **130**, 133, 136, **136**, 179
Tolstoy, Leo, *494*
Torah, 151, 153
Torso of Miletus, **76**, 77
Toscani, Giovanni, **293**
totalitarianism, 542, 545–546, **546**, 551
To the Lighthouse (Woolf), 549–550
Tours, Battle of, 206
traceries, 243, 246
Tractatus Logico-Philosophicus (Wittgenstein), 554
trade. *See* political/economic development
tragedy
  Baroque Age, 394, 395
  Greece, 57, 61–65, **62**
  Rome, 123, 394
  See also drama
Traini, Francesco, **263**
Trajan (Roman emperor), 129, 130
Trajan's column, 129, **130**, 133, 136, **137**
Transcendentalism, 493
transept, 180, 236
Travels in Persia (Chardin), 394
Trent, Council of, 362, 363, 367, 379, 380, 394
Très Riches Heures du Duc de Berry, 271, **273**
Trial, The (Kafka), 522
Tribute Money, The (Masaccio), 307, **307**
Trier, 180, **181**, 183
triglyph, 47
Triple Alliance, 515, 517
Triple Entente, 515, 517
triptych, 353–354, **353**
triumphal arches, 129–130, **130**
Triumph of Death (Traini), **263**
trivium, 141, 230
Trojan War, 36, 43, **44**, 64
Trojan Women, The (Euripides), 64
tropes, 248
Trotsky, Leon, 563
troubadors, 233
Troy, François de, **375**
Truth, Sojourner, 495
Turkish Bath, The (Ingres), 495, **495**
Turks. *See* Ottoman Empire
Turner, Joseph Mallord William, **446**, 464, 467, **467**, **484**
Tutankhamen (pharoah), 24, 25
Twelve Tables, 124
twelve-tone scale, 568
Two Treatises of Government (Locke), 414–415
Tyler, Wat, 260
tympanum, 238, **238**, **242**
tyrants (Greek Archaic Age), 38–39

Ugly One with the Jewels (Anderson), 610
ukiyo-e, *527*
Ulfilas, *173*
Ulysses (Joyce), 549
Unam sanctam, 225
Unbearable Lightness of Being, The (Kundera), 591
uncertainty principle, 555
Under Milk Wood (Thomas), 589
Unique Forms of Continuity in Space (Boccioni), **518**
United Nations, 576, **576**, 581

United States
American Revolution, 124, 415, 429, 430, 441, 453–454
Asian-Americans, 591–592
Bourgeois Age, 483, 485, 486, 493, 494–495
cold war, 420, 575, 577–579, 593
current dominance of, 549, 581, 582–583, 611
Early Modernism, 510, 512, 513–514, **514**, 515, 537
feminism, 585
film, 568
Great Depression, 544, **544**, 545
interwar period cultural trends, 550, 559–560, 569
revolution/reaction period, **460**, 461, **461**
World War II, 547, 548
See also African Americans; Americas
universities, 92, 231, 375
University of Padua, 409
University of Paris, 231, 405
Ur, 10, 12, **13**
uraeus, 21
urban growth
Early Modernism, 510, **511**
High Middle Ages, 221–223, **222**, 230
High Renaissance/early Mannerism, 319
Late Middle Ages, 255, 256, 263
See also political/economic development
Urban VIII (pope), 382
Urbino, 292
Ursulines, 361
Uruk, 10
Urukagina, 5
Usamah, 208–209
utilitarianism, 487
utopian socialism, 487, 489
Utrecht, Treaty of (1713), 379

Valerian (Roman emperor), 161
Valla, Lorenzo, 295
Valses nobles et sentimentales (Ravel), 537
Vandals, 173
van Dyck, Anthony, *391*, 393, **393**
van Eyck, Hubert, 277, **279**, **280**
van Eyck, Jan, *277*, **279**, **280**, **281**, 282
van Gogh, Vincent, **508**, *529*–530, **530**, **531**
vanishing point, 299, 303, 307–308
Variations for Orchestra (Schoenberg), 568
Vasari, Giorgio, 274, 337
vase painting
Greek Archaic Age, **43**, **44**
Greek Hellenic Age, **56**, **58**, **64**, **66**
vassals, 220
Vatican. *See* papacy
Vatican Library, 294
vaults, 126
Vega, Lope de, 366
Velázquez, Diego, **372**, 384, *386*, **386**, 469
Venice, 255, 256, 306, 317, 377, 389. *See also specific styles and artists*
Venturi, Robert, 605, **606**, 607
Venus de Milo, 103, **105**
Venus of Willendorf, 3, **5**
Verdi, Giuseppe, 502, *503*
Vergil, 106, *122*, 184, **184**, 234, 395
Vermeer, Jan, *391*, **392**, 459
vernacular (architecture), 605, **606**, 607
vernacular languages, 232, 233, 264–265, 348
Verona, **110**
Verrocchio, Andrea del, **303**
Versailles, 376, **377**, 387–388, **387**, **388**, 420, 428
Versailles, Treaty of (1919), 388, 543, 546
Vesalius, Andreas, *409*, 410
Vesta, 111
via antiqua, 261
via media, 231, 261
via moderna, 261
Via Sacra, 130
Victoria (queen of England), 482, 486, 490
video art, **584**, 605
Vien, Joseph-Marie, 437
Vienna, 514, 518
Vietnam War, 577, 577–578, **579**
Vigée-Lebrun, Elisabeth-Louise, *433*, **434**, 435
Vikings, 207
Villa Capra. *See* Villa Rotonda
Villa of the Mysteries (Pompeii), 138, **138**
Villa Rotonda (Palladio), 340–342, **341**, 461
Vindication of the Rights of Women, A (Wollstonecraft), 426
Viollet-le-Duc, 243
Virgin Mary cult, **220**, 221, 230, 233, 242–243, **247**
Virgin of the Rocks, The (da Vinci), 310–311, **311**, 325
virtuosos, 397, 417
Visigoths, 173, 205
Vision of Piers Plowman, The, 263–264
Vita Caroli (Einhard), 210
Voltaire, 425, 429, 440, 441–442, **442**
von Bora, Katherine, 358, **358**
Von Werner, Anton, **514**
voussoirs, 126
Vulgate, 175

Wagner, Richard, 502–*503*, 535, 537
Wailing Wall, 151, 157
Waiting for Godot (Beckett), 590
Walden (Thoreau), 493
Waldmüller, Ferdinand Georg, **474**
Walker, Alice, 591
Wanamaker, Sam, 349
War and Peace (Tolstoy), 494
warfare. *See* political/economic development
Warhol, Andy, **574**, **579**, 594, **597**
War of the Spanish Succession, 379
Warsaw Pact, 577
"Waste Land, The" (Eliot), 551
Watergate scandal, 580
Water Lilies (Monet), **524–525**
Waterloo, Battle of (1812), 457
water organ, 140
Watson, James, 588
Watt, James, 452
Watteau, Jean-Antoine, *431*–433, **432**, **433**, 435
Wealth of Nations (Smith), 453
We Are Making a New World (Nash), **542**
Weary Blues, The (Hughes), 551
weaving, **203**, **252**
Wedding Dance (Bruegel), 354, **355**
Weelkes, Thomas, *367*
Weill, Kurt, *552*–*553*
Weimar Republic, 544, 545
Weisskunig, Der (Burgkmair), **342**
Welles, Orson, 568
Well of Moses, The (Sluter), 271, **272**
Well-Tempered Clavier, The (Bach), 397
Wertherism, 463
Wesley, John, 426
Westall, Richard, **464**
Westphalia, Treaty of (1648), 377–378
Whiteread, Rachel, 604, **604**
Whitman, Walt, 493
Wieck, Clara, 503
Wiesel, Elie, 547
Wilde, Oscar, 521
Willaert, Adrian, *342*
Willendorf goddess figure, 3, **5**
William I (king of Prussia/Kaiser of Germany), 482, 512, **514**
William III (king of England), 376
William (the Conqueror) (king of England), 223, **225**
William of Champeaux, *230*–231
William of Ockham, 261
Williams, William Carlos, 591
Willits house (Wright), **536**
Wilson, Robert, 609
Wilson, Woodrow, 543
Winckelmann, Johann Joachim, 437
Windows on the World
Age of Anxiety, 614–615
Age of Reason, 448–449
Baroque Age, 400–401
Bourgeois Age, 506–507
Greek Hellenic Age, 84–85
High Middle Ages, 250–251
interwar period, 572–573
Late Middle Ages, 286–287
Late Roman period, 216–217
Near Eastern civilizations period, 28–29
pre-Christian Roman period, 142–143
sixteenth century, 370–371
wine production, **252**, **256**
"Winged Victory," **93**
wisdom literature, 19
witchcraft, 260, 413
Wittgenstein, Ludwig, *553*, 554
Wollstonecraft, Mary, 426, 464
Woman from Samos, The (Menander), 94
Woman Warrior, The: Memoirs of a Girlhood Among Ghosts (Kingston), 592
women's status and roles
Age of Anxiety, 584, 585, **586**, 591, 603, 610
Age of Reason, 426, 428–429
Baroque Age, 382–383, 391
Bourgeois Age, 486, 489, 492, 495, 501
early Christianity, 161–163
Early Middle Ages, 206, 208
Early Modernism, **511**, 512, **512**, 513, 520
Early Renaissance, 292, 294–295, 296
Egypt, 16, 20, 21
and French Revolution, 426
Greek Archaic Age, 39, 40, 44, 50
Greek Hellenic Age, 59
Hellenistic Age, 88, 96, 101, 106
High Middle Ages, 220–221, 222–223, 227, 228, 230, 233
High Renaissance/early Mannerism, 322, 323
Islamic world, 200
Judaism, 151–152
Late Middle Ages, 260, 264–265
Mesopotamia, 7, 11
prehistory, 2
and Reformations, 358, 359, 361
revolution/reaction period, 426, 454, 455, 456, 459
Rome, 111, **112**, 161, 171, 183
sixteenth-century Europe, 358, 359, 361, 366
woodcut prints, 271
Woolf, Virginia, 549–550
Woolf, Leonard, 550
word paintings, 367
Wordsworth, William, 442, 463, 464
World War I (1914–1918), 483, 517, **517**, 537, 542–544, 550
World War II (1939–1945), 543, 546–548, **547**, **548**, 555, 576, 583, 593
World Wide Web. *See* Internet
Worms, Concordat of, 223
Would-Be Gentleman, The (Molière), 395
Wren, Sir Christopher, 379, 393–394, **394**
Wretched of the Earth, The (Fanon), 585
Wright, Frank Lloyd, 535, **536**
Wright, Richard, 588
writing systems
Early Middle Ages, 210, **211**
Egypt, 2, 17, **17**
Etruscan, 113
Islamic world, 202, **202**
Judaism, 152
Late Middle Ages, 256, 262
Mesopotamia, 7–8, **8**
Minoan, 35
Wuthering Heights (Brontë), 492–493
Wycliffe, John, 259

Xenophon, 71
Xerxes, **26**, *41*
X rays, 522

Yahweh, 147, 160, 166
Yathrib. *See* Medina
Yeats, William Butler, 551
Yeltsin, Boris, 581
Young British Artists (YBA), 604
Yugoslavia, former, 583

Zarathustra. *See* Zoroastrianism
Zealots, 150, 151
Zen Buddhism, 609
Zeus, 35, 42, 43, **78**, **95**
ziggurats, 12–13, **13**, 18
Zimbabwe, 579, 589
Zola, Émile, *520*
zoos, 19
Zoroastrianism, *25*, 98, 149, 160, 228–229